PRODUCTION ECONOMICS

AN EMPIRICAL APPROACH

PRODUCTION ECONOMICS

AN EMPIRICAL APPROACH

Charles B. Moss
University of Florida, USA

World Scientific

NEW JERSEY • LONDON • SINGAPORE • BEIJING • SHANGHAI • HONG KONG • TAIPEI • CHENNAI • TOKYO

Published by

World Scientific Publishing Co. Pte. Ltd.
5 Toh Tuck Link, Singapore 596224
USA office: 27 Warren Street, Suite 401-402, Hackensack, NJ 07601
UK office: 57 Shelton Street, Covent Garden, London WC2H 9HE

Library of Congress Cataloging-in-Publication Data
Names: Moss, Charles B. (Charles Britt) author.
Title: Production economics : an empirical approach /
Charles B. Moss, University of Florida, USA.
Description: Hackensack, NJ : World Scientific, 2022. |
Includes bibliographical references and index.
Identifiers: LCCN 2021035838 | ISBN 9789811238864 (hardcover) |
ISBN 9789811241260 (ebook) | ISBN 9789811241277 (ebook other)
Subjects: LCSH: Production (Economic theory) | Economics--Mathematical models.
Classification: LCC HB241 .M677 2022 | DDC 338.5--dc23
LC record available at https://lccn.loc.gov/2021035838

British Library Cataloguing-in-Publication Data
A catalogue record for this book is available from the British Library.

For any available supplementary material, please visit
https://www.worldscientific.com/worldscibooks/10.1142/12332#t=suppl

Desk Editors: Balasubramanian Shanmugam/Lum Pui Yee

Typeset by Stallion Press
Email: enquiries@stallionpress.com

To my grand children — Claire, Aria, and Ben Tetzlaff

Preface

As I finish this book on production economics, I look back on 40 years as an agricultural economist. I began this journey in Stillwater, Oklahoma, in January of 1980. At that time, the Agricultural Economics Department at Oklahoma State University was known for farm management. I added to that training in my Master's studies at Oklahoma State University with a course in production economics that focused on the primal approach — the estimation and use of the production function. Moving to Purdue University in August of 1984, I took the standard microeconomics course. This course tended to spend a lot of time on the consumer model with a brief coverage of the producer's problem with the promise that the producer's problem is almost the same as the consumer problem. My formal training in production economics was then completed with a summer course (I think it was AgEcon 613) which included coverage of the dual (under Professor Hertel), risk (under Professor Sanders), and dynamics (under Professor Fletcher). This progression of classes (along with production in applications covered in a series of econometric classes) highlights the importance that the agricultural economics profession put on understanding the economic decisions made by producers. Producer decisions were important in part because farmers and agribusinesses were an integral part of the farm economy. Basically, the unstated truth was the colleges of agriculture were about farmers.

As I moved into the faculty ranks in the Food and Resource Economics Department at the University of Florida in 1987, the focus had changed somewhat. A large contingent in the Food and Resource Economics Department at the University of Florida were interested in applied marketing. I will admit that marketing had been an important part of the agricultural economics curriculum during my course work, but I did as little of it as possible. These two fields still bracketed the farm problem in my mind. The problem was to understand farmer's production decisions within the context of the demand for agricultural outputs.

As time has progressed into the "modern era," the field of agricultural economics has broadened. Resource and environmental economics now claims more of our students than production and demand put together. Even in the case of production economics, decisions of farmers in developing economies represent a large portion of the production economics published. The push into development economics has led to certain modifications such as Randomized Control Trials and the use of selection models. The point is that while resource and environmental economics and applications in developing economies often draw the classical models from production economics, they also contain new formulations that I have not integrated in this textbook.

One vexing question is always — why this book? To answer this question, I will recount some of the history of the Ph.D. program in the Food and Resource Economics at the University of Florida. Before the 1980s, there were two microeconomic courses in the department — a course in production economics and a course in demand theory. In the mid-1980s, the decision was made to discontinue these courses (or at least not to require them). Instead students would take the Microeconomic Theory course in the Economics Department. While the idea sounded good in theory, the faculty found that the students understood the theory (e.g., they could take the derivatives), but they could not apply the concepts to real-world data. As often the case in history of Ph.D. programs, the faculty voted to require students to take both Microeconomic Theory in the Economics Department as well as Production Economics and Demand Theory in the Food and Resource Economics Department. The argument was that agricultural economists should be able to use economic theory to address real-world problems. In this book, I focus on this concept — understand theory and know how to combine this theory with data to address real-world problems.

Many of the datasets used in this textbook along with some of the R Code and many of the answers to the exercises are available at http://www.charlesbmoss.com:8080/Book.Production.Economics/. I intend to add slides and other material that will be useful in teaching this course. There may even be a hidden directory with keys to the assignments.

Books are long journeys. On this journey, I have had several fellow travelers that I would like to thank. First, I would like to thank my fellow students from Purdue University, Jay Akridge, Allen Featherstone, Anne Marie Hillberg (Seitzinger), Scott Irwin, Warren Preston and Calum Turvey, who struggled with me to master these concepts so long ago. Second, I would like to thank Scott Shonkwiler, who mentored me when I was a freshly minted faculty member at the University of Florida. Next, I would like to remember Henri Theil. When I graduated from Purdue, I thought I was competent at econometrics. After about 10 years working with Henri, I understood econometrics. In addition, most of my work on the differential production formulation grew out of the time I spent with Hans. Finally, I would like to recognize several excellent students that I have worked with at the University of Florida: Mara Bampasidou, Femi Bolarinwa, Grigorios Livanis, Octavio Ramirez, Matthew Salois, Dong Hee Suh, and Amy Purvis-Thurow. While each student was exemplary, I would like to make special mention of Grigoris Livanis and Dong Hee Suh whose collaborative work on the differential supply function forms the core of Chapter 7. I would also like to thank my current students, Ting Cao and Dongso Lee, for putting up with me as I completed this draft. I would also like to thank my wife Susan — note that I did not make her read this book unlike the math/stat book.

Charles B. Moss
Gainesville, Florida
January 7, 2022

About the Author

Charles B. Moss received his Ph.D. in 1987, joining the University of Florida's Food and Resource Economics Department in September of 1987. His research has primarily focused on the areas of financial risk and stress in the farm sector. His research activities have produced over 180 research publications including six edited volumes, 31 book chapters, and 130 refereed journal articles. Charles had the privilege to serve as a McKethan-Matherly fellow in the Economics Department at the University of Florida from 1989 to 1994 working with the late Professor Henri Theil and is an affiliate member of the Center for Applied Optimization and the Center for Latin American Studies, both at the University of Florida. In 2006, Charles received the *Journal of Agricultural and Resource Economics's* Outstanding Journal Article award. In addition, he received the American Agricultural Economics Association's Quality of Research Discovery Award in 2007 and that associations Quality of Communication Award in 2013. In 2013, Charles was also recognized with the Southern Agricultural Economics Association's Lifetime Achievement Award. Charles has served as Co-Editor of the *Journal of Agricultural and Applied Economics* and on the editorial boards of the *American Journal of Agricultural Economics*, *Journal of Agricultural and Resource Economics*, and the *Journal of Agricultural and Applied Economics.*

Charles's teaching program includes graduate level courses in Agricultural Finance, Agricultural Risk Analysis and Decision-Making, Static and Dynamic Optimization, Optimal Control, Mathematical Programming, Production Economics, Statistics for Food and Resource Economics, and Econometric Methods II. He has served on 17 graduate student committees, including for students from Universidad Autonoma de Chapingo and Vanderbilt University in addition to the University of Florida. In addition to courses, Charles has authored four textbooks — *Risk, Uncertainty and the Agricultural Firm* (2010), *Agricultural Policy, Agribusiness, and Rent-Seeking Behaviour* (2010), *Agricultural Finance* (2013), and *Mathematical Statistics for Applied Econometrics* (2014).

Contents

List of Figures

List of Tables

Chapter 1

Basic Notions of Production Functions

1.1 Overview of the Production Function

At the turn of the 21st century, there are two dominant approaches to production economics: the primal approach and the dual approach. Each approach is founded on the same basic axioms of optimizing behavior and economic rationality. However, the primal approach is, in a way, the more basic approach to production. Specifically, the primal approach involves estimating the technological envelope (in this chapter referred to as the production function) and then deriving the optimizing behavior from this relationship. The dual approach assumes that producers are choosing the set of inputs and outputs which either minimize cost or maximize profit. It involves estimating the optimizing behavior directly based on input and output prices. Implicitly, the dual approach assumes that producers know the technological trade-offs they face (i.e., the trade-offs between inputs and outputs available to them). However, either approach implicitly assumes that there exists a production function or technology which embodies the minimum combination of inputs which can be used to produce any combination of outputs. This chapter presents some of the economist's basic notions about the production function.

The *production function* is a technical relationship depicting the technical transformation of inputs into outputs. The production function in and of itself is devoid of economic content. In the development of production functions, we are interested in certain characteristics that make it possible to construct economic models based on optimizing behavior.

> The production function (and indeed all representations of technology) is a purely technical relationship that is void of economic content. Since economists are usually interested in studying economic phenomena, the technical aspects of production are interesting to economists only insofar as they impinge upon the behavior of economic agents.... Because the economist has no inherent interest in the production function, if it is possible to portray and to predict economic behavior accurately without direct examination of the production function, so much the better. This principle, which sets the tone for much of the following discussion, underlies the intense interest that recent developments in duality have aroused (Chambers, 1988, p. 7).

The point of these two statements is that economists are not engineers and have no insights into why technologies take on any particular shape. We are only interested in those properties that make the production function consistent with optimizing behavior.

The development of the production function has a rather extended history. Humphrey (1997) traces the foundations of production function to Turgot who in 1767 depicted the production relationship in a table with positive first derivatives and negative second derivatives. Others working in the area include Malthus in 1798 and Ricardo in 1817. However, Johan Heinrch von Thunen serves as an important starting point of our discussion. Von Thunen hypothesized a series of declining marginal products, implying that production followed an exponential production function.

In more recent times, we trace the development of the production function to Philip Wicksteed (1894) who developed the concept of a production function to discuss the distribution of economic rents. Specifically, Wicksteed develops the production function within the general framework of rents to farmland:

$$P = \Psi\left(L, C\right) \tag{1.1}$$

where P is the economic value generated by agriculture, L is the amount of land used in production, and C is the combination of capital and labor. Without explicitly recognizing the property that we will develop as homogeneity of degree one, Wicksteed then rewrites the production function as

$$m\Pi = \Psi\left(m\Lambda, K\right) \tag{1.2}$$

where m is the number of acres, Π is the return per acre, Λ is one acre of land, and K (the Greek uppercase letter kappa) is the amount of capital labor used per acre. His basic contention was that when the marginal value of inputs equaled the marginal cost of that input

$$F'(c) = f_c(c) = w \tag{1.3}$$

the input market was in equilibrium — the entrepreneur's value of the last unit of each input was equal to the amount paid. Wicksteed then goes on to develop the profit (or rent for farmland) based on this allocation:

$$\int_0^{x^*} f_c(x)\,dx - x^* f_c(x^*) \tag{1.4}$$

where $f_c(x^*) = w$ by assumption.

Plea for Further Work on the Production Function

Forty-two years ago in 1927, Professor Charles W. Cobb and I read a paper before the American Economic Association which attempted to approximate the production function for American Manufacturing. We wished to test the theory of the diminishing increment of production (P) resulting from successive applications of the factors labor (L) and capital (C)

$$\frac{d\log P}{d\log L} \text{ and } \frac{d\log P}{d\log C}$$

(Senator Paul H. Douglas, 1969)

Philip Wicksteed — Why a Mathematical Production Function?

It may seem that little is to be gained by putting such truisms [Production Functions] into mathematical form. But I think it will be found otherwise on investigation. The law of value, too, resting as it does on the law of indifference and the phenomena of marginal utility, amounts to nothing in the world

(*Continued*)

(Continued)

by the assertion that the purchaser will not give more than he must for an article and will in no case give more for it than he thinks it is worth to him. This was of course well known to everyone and is constantly assumed in every economic treatise of whatsoever date; but nevertheless its exact expression in mathematical language has made an epoch and is making a revolution in economic sciences (Wicksteed, 1894, p. 11).

Building on these historical concepts, we start with a general concept of a production function as a map (possibly a topology) written as

$$f : R_n^+ \to R_m^+ \tag{1.5}$$

which states that the production function (f) is a function that maps n inputs into m outputs. By convention, we are only interested in positive input bundles that yield positive output bundles.[1] In this section, we focus on the production function as a continuous function as students have probably seen it in previous courses. In the following section, we develop the concept of the production function more rigorously.

1.1.1 *One Product, One-Variable Factor Relationship*

A commonly used form of the production function is the "closed-form" representation where the *total physical product* is depicted as a function of a vector of inputs

$$y = f(x) \tag{1.6}$$

where y denotes the scalar (single) output and x denote the vector (multiple) inputs. In most cases, we use closed-form representations of production functions (see the discussion of closed-form solutions in Appendix A). Focusing for a moment on the single output case,

[1] See the formulation in http://www.charlesbmoss.com:8080/Book.Production.Economics/Chapter-1/NonparametricMapping.pdf.

we could simplify the above representation to

$$y = f\left(x_1 \left| x_2\right.\right). \tag{1.7}$$

Here, we are interested in examining the relationship between x_1 and y given that all the other factors of production (here x_2) are held constant.

Using this relationship, we want to identify three primary relationships:

- *Total physical product*, which is the original production function.
- *Average physical product*, defined as the average output per unit of input

$$APP = \frac{y}{x} = \frac{f(x)}{x}. \tag{1.8}$$

- *Marginal physical product*, defined as the rate of change in total physical product at a specific input level

$$MPP = \frac{dTPP}{dx} = \frac{dy}{dx} = \frac{df(x)}{dx} = f'(x). \tag{1.9}$$

Given these notions of a production function, we can introduce the classical shape of the production function in Figure 1.1. This production function was taken from Moss and Schmitz (2006). This shape is referred to as a "sigmoid shaped" curve. The exact function form in this figure can be attributed to Zellner (1951). The mathematical form of the function is

$$f(x_1, x_2) = \frac{ax_1^3}{\exp\left[b\frac{x_1}{x_2}\right] - 1}. \tag{1.10}$$

Zellner's production function "... exhibits the Law of Variable Proportions and a proportionality relation between the size of the plant and the variable input..." (Zellner, 1951, p. 188), where the variable input is x_1 and x_2 is the plant input.[2] The average function in Figure 1.1 sets $x_2 = 1.0$, $a = 0.0005433$, and $b = 0.01794$. Figure 1.1

[2]It is interesting that it is Zellner's first major article in his interview with Peter Rossi (Rossi and Zellner, 1989).

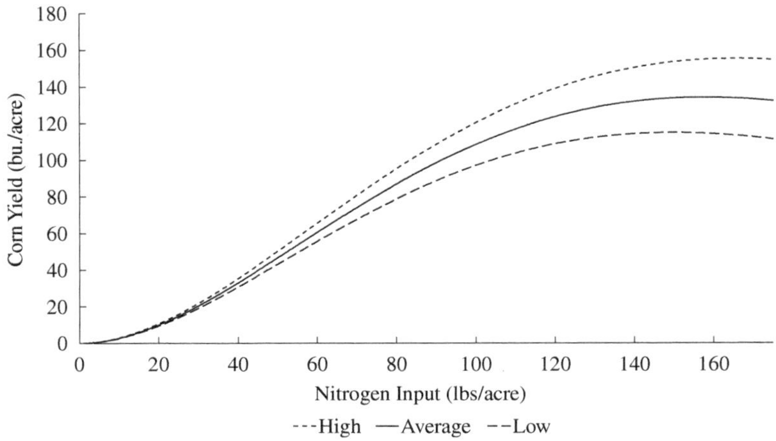

Fig. 1.1 Three Production Functions

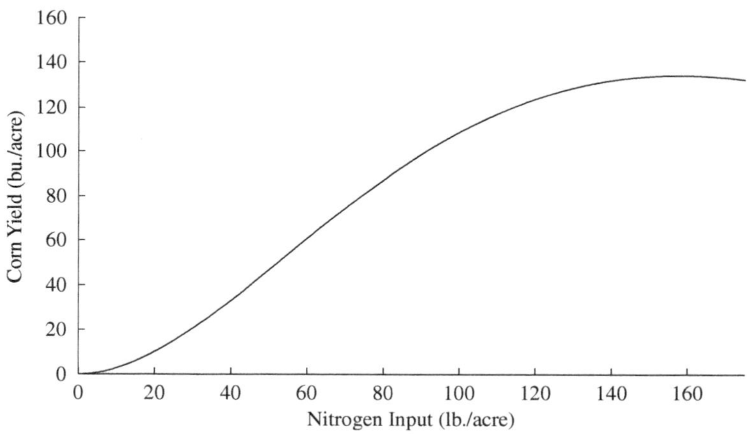

Fig. 1.2 Production Function for Average Yield

depicts the effect of a change in plant variable. In this case we hypothesize that plant variable is some input outside the control of the farmer (e.g., rainfall). If the rainfall is "high" (maybe optimal), the yield is high. Alternatively, if the rainfall is low (maybe a drought scenario), the crop yield is low. The average production function (i.e., the middle graph from Figure 1.1) is presented in Figure 1.2.

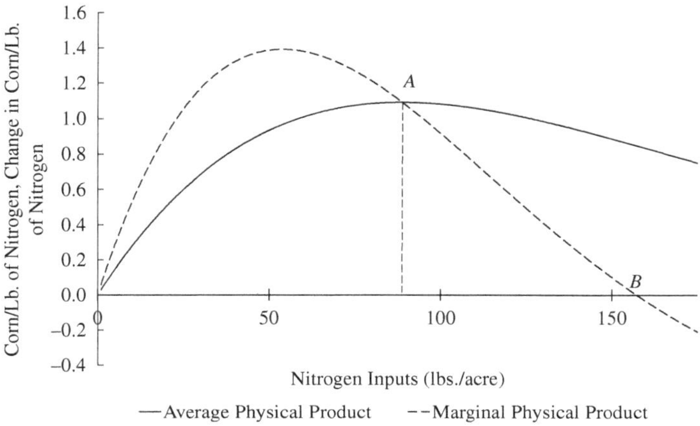

Fig. 1.3 Average and Marginal Physical Product Graphs

The marginal physical product and average physical product graphs for this average production function are presented in Figure 1.3.

Given the average physical product and marginal physical product relationships, we can define the stages of production. While the production function itself is devoid of economic content, we use the physical relationships to define the economically valuable production region. The stages of production are defined as follows:

- *Stage I*: This stage of the production function is defined as that region where the average physical product is increasing. In this region, the marginal physical product is greater than the average physical product. Also, in this region, each additional unit of input yields relatively more output on average.
- *Stage II*: This stage of the production process corresponds with the economically feasible region of production. Marginal physical product is positive and each additional unit of input produces less output on average.
- *Stage III*: This stage of production implies negative marginal returns on inputs.

These stages of production imply certain restrictions on the shape of the production function. The production function is a positively valued initially increasing function. Further, around the point of optimality, the production function is concave in variable inputs.

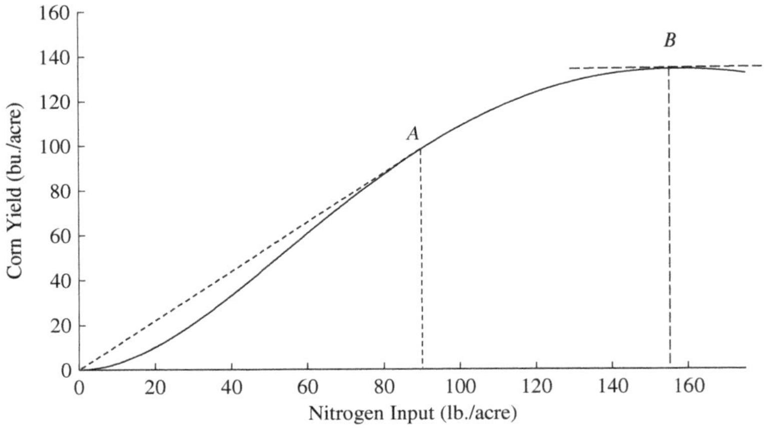

Fig. 1.4 Stages of Production on Total Physical Product Graph

The stages of production can also be defined using total physical product, as depicted in Figure 1.4. In this representation, the Stage I/Stage II boundary point is identified by the maximum slope of a ray originating from the origin that is tangent to the total physical product curve. This point defines the maximum of the average physical product relationship in output or total physical product space. Similarly, the Stage II/Stage III boundary is defined by the point where a horizontal line is tangent to the total physical product relationship. Again, this tangency defines the point where the marginal physical product relationship in Figure 1.3 is equal to zero.

1.1.2 *Elasticity of Production*

Elasticities are often used in economics to produce a unit-free indicator of the shape of a function. Most are familiar with the elasticity of consumer demand. Specifically, the elasticity of demand is defined as the percentage change in the quantity that consumers demand in response to a 1% change in the price of the output. We typically think of three regions of a linear demand curve based on this elasticity. If the demand curve has an elasticity of less than -1.0, it is elastic — the percentage change in the quantity demanded is greater than the percentage change in price. The second region is actually a point on the linear demand curve, that is, the point of unitary elasticity where the elasticity of demand is equal to -1.0. The final region is referred to as the inelastic portion of the demand curve. In this region the elasticity of demand is greater than -1.0 (and typically less than zero). The regions of the demand curve defined by these elasticities have implications. A monopolist only chooses to produce in the elastic region. Also, in this region, increasing the output increases total revenue. Necessities like food are typically characterized by an inelastic demand in developed economies. Different factor elasticities also have implications for production.

In defining the production function, we are interested in the *factor elasticity*. The factor elasticity is defined as

$$\eta = \frac{\%\Delta y}{\%\Delta x} = \frac{dy}{dx}\frac{x}{y} = \frac{MPP}{APP}. \tag{1.11}$$

A plot of the factor elasticity for the Zellner production function is depicted in Figure 1.5. There is a specific relationship between the average physical product and the marginal physical product when the average physical product is maximized:

$$MPP = \frac{dTPP}{dx} = \frac{d\,(xAPP)}{dx} = APP + x\frac{dAPP}{dx}. \tag{1.12}$$

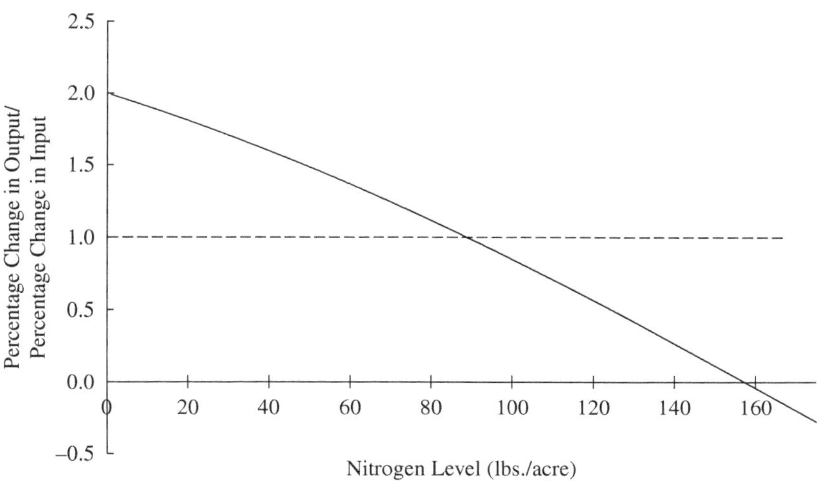

Fig. 1.5 Factor Elasticity for the Zellner Function

Thus, when average physical product is maximized,

$$\frac{d\,APP}{dx} = 0 \Rightarrow MPP = APP. \tag{1.13}$$

Following through on this relationship, we have

$$\begin{aligned} \frac{d\,APP}{dx} &> 0 \Rightarrow MPP > APP \Rightarrow \eta > 1 \\ \frac{d\,APP}{dx} &= 0 \Rightarrow MPP = APP \Rightarrow \eta = 1. \\ \frac{d\,APP}{dx} &< 0 \Rightarrow MPP < APP \Rightarrow \eta < 1 \end{aligned} \tag{1.14}$$

In addition, we know that $\eta = 0 \Leftrightarrow MPP = 0$ and total physical product is maximum, and if $\eta < 0 \Leftrightarrow MPP < 0$. Thus, if $\eta > 1$, then the production function is in Stage I, while if $0 < \eta < 1$, production is in Stage II. Finally, if $\eta < 0$, then the production function is in Stage III.

Again, the characteristics of the production function may place significant restrictions on the factor elasticities. For example, the factor elasticity for the Zellner production function in Figure 1.5 appears linear. To demonstrate the potential nonlinearity in the elasticity of production with respect to a single input, consider the second-order (quadratic) approximation of the Zellner production function around $x_1 = 150$ presented in Figure 1.6. The factor elasticity for this quadratic approximation is depicted in Figure 1.7.

1.1.3 *One Product, Two-Variable Factors*

Expanding the production relationship, we start by considering the case of two inputs producing one output. In the general functional mapping notation,

$$f : R_2^+ \to R_1^+. \tag{1.15}$$

The univariate production functions are simply "slices" out of the multivariate production functions. Figure 1.8 presents a three-dimensional depiction of the Zellner production function introduced in Equation (1.10). This function still has average physical products and marginal physical products, but they are conditioned on

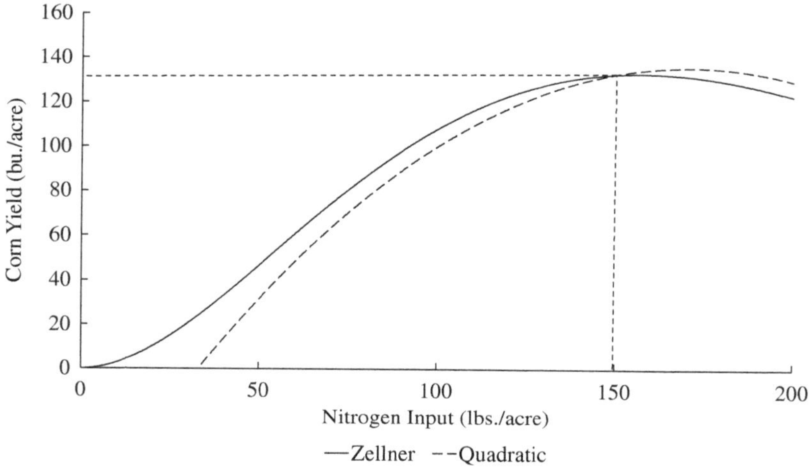

Fig. 1.6 Quadratic Approximation to the Zellner Production Function

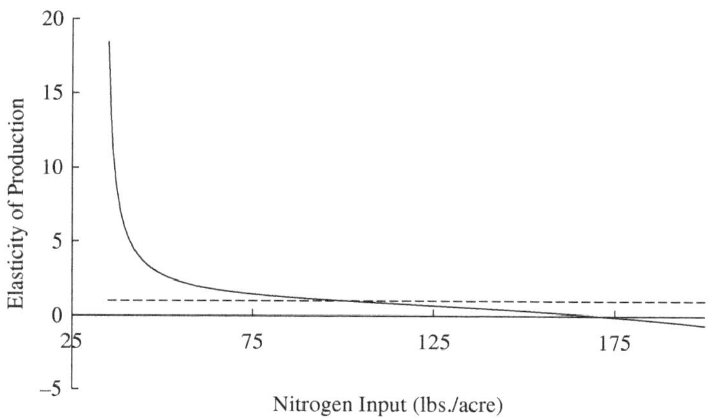

Fig. 1.7 Factor Elasticity for a Quadratic Production Function

the level of other inputs. For example, the average physical product relationships become

$$\begin{aligned} APP_1 &= \frac{y}{x_1} = \frac{f(x_1, x_2)}{x_1} \\ APP_2 &= \frac{y}{x_2} = \frac{f(x_1, x_2)}{x_2} \end{aligned} . \tag{1.16}$$

Similarly, the marginal physical products are defined by the partial derivatives of the production function

Schumpeter — History of Economic Analysis

Mathematically, the production function enters the theoretical set-up in order to yield demand functions for productive services, as a restriction upon the firms' behavior: these strive to maximize net profits *subject* to the possibilities listed in the production function. We might try to crowd into a single expression the whole of the technological facts that, for any purpose in hand, seem relevant to us. But even where this is possible, it is much more convenient to make a single relation basic — we shall of course choose one that has some primary economic significance, of this presently — and then to introduce other facts (hypotheses) that are to be taken into account as further restrictions that we regard as fundamental. The best way of making this clear is as follows. Suppose we have n services which define a 'production surface' in $(n+1)$ dimension hyperspace. In general, we shall find that firms cannot move about freely over the whole of this surface and that technological conditions permit choice only within the boundaries of certain regions (Schumpeter, 1994, p. 1030).

$$\begin{aligned} MPP_1 &= \frac{\partial y}{\partial x_1} = \frac{\partial f(x_1, x_2)}{\partial x_1} \\ MPP_2 &= \frac{\partial y}{\partial x_2} = \frac{\partial f(x_1, x_2)}{\partial x_2} \end{aligned}. \tag{1.17}$$

It is useful at this point to briefly consider the notion of the Taylor series expansion of an unknown function (a detailed discussion of Taylor series expansions is presented in Appendix B). First, we depart from the Zellner production function depicted in Figure 1.8 to a translog production function (a more general form of the Cobb–Douglas introduced in the following section) because of difficulties in the concavity of Zellner production function with respect to second input (x_2). Hence, we use the production function

$$
\begin{aligned}
f(x_1, x_2) = \exp \Big(&4.697 + 0.00159 \log(x_1) + 0.00891 \log(x_2) \\
&- 0.000343 \frac{\log(x_1)\log(x_1)}{2} - 0.0000768 \log(x_1)\log(x_2) \\
&- 0.0000436 \frac{\log(x_2)\log(x_2)}{2}\Big). \qquad (1.18)
\end{aligned}
$$

This output function is presented graphically in Figure 1.9.

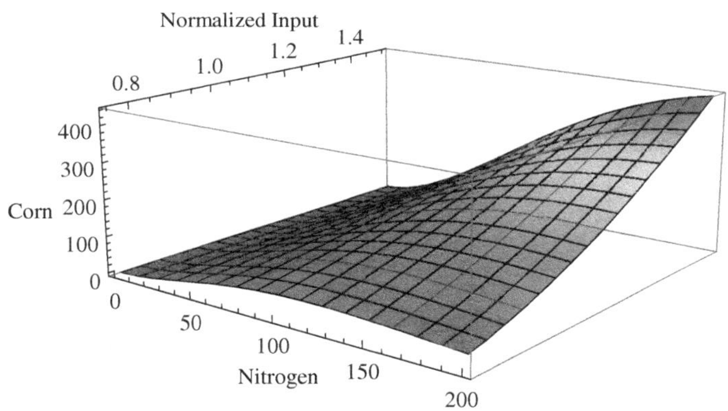

Fig. 1.8 Production of a Single Output with Two Inputs

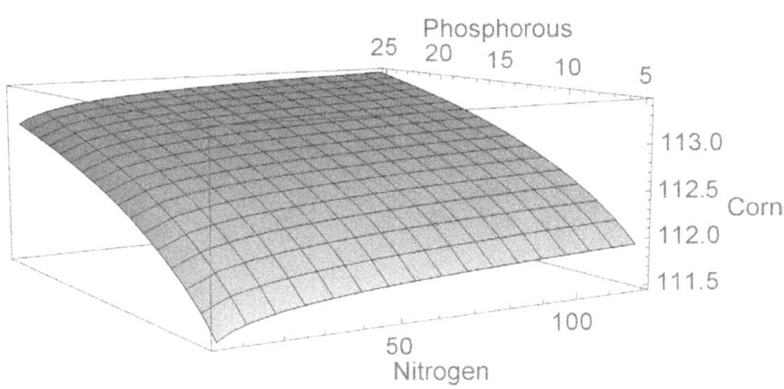

Fig. 1.9 Translog Production Function for Corn

Taking the second-order expansion of the production function yields

$$\tilde{f}\left(x_1,x_2\right) \approx f\left(x_1^0,x_2^0\right) + \begin{bmatrix} \dfrac{\partial f(x_1,x_2)}{\partial x_1} & \dfrac{\partial f(x_1,x_2)}{\partial x_2} \end{bmatrix} \begin{bmatrix} dx_1 \\ dx_2 \end{bmatrix}$$
$$+ \frac{1}{2}\begin{bmatrix} dx_1 & dx_2 \end{bmatrix} \begin{bmatrix} \dfrac{\partial^2 f(x_1,x_2)}{\partial x_1^2} & \dfrac{\partial^2 f(x_1,x_2)}{\partial x_1 \partial x_2} \\ \dfrac{\partial^2 f(x_1,x_2)}{\partial x_1 \partial x_2} & \dfrac{\partial^2 f(x_1,x_2)}{\partial x_2^2} \end{bmatrix} \begin{bmatrix} dx_1 \\ dx_2 \end{bmatrix}. \tag{1.19}$$

Using the translog production function in Equation (1.18)

$$\tilde{f}\left(x_1,x_2\right) = 112.93 + \begin{bmatrix} 0.001200 \\ 0.062636 \end{bmatrix}' \begin{bmatrix} x_1 - 100 \\ x_2 - 15 \end{bmatrix}$$
$$+ \frac{1}{2}\begin{bmatrix} x_1 - 100 \\ x_2 - 15 \end{bmatrix}' \begin{bmatrix} -0.00001276 & -0.000005114 \\ -0.000005114 & -0.004185 \end{bmatrix} \begin{bmatrix} x_1 - 100 \\ x_2 - 15 \end{bmatrix}. \tag{1.20}$$

Note that this function is rather linear (as depicted in Figure 1.10). The approximation is exact in the case of either a linear or quadratic production function. However, if we focus on a linear production

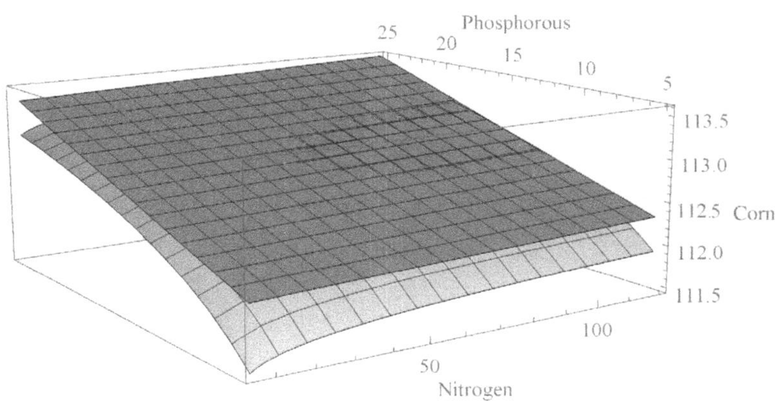

Fig. 1.10 Quadratic Approximation of the Translog Production Function for Corn

function, it is clear that

$$\begin{aligned} dy &= \frac{\partial f(x_1, x_2)}{\partial x_1} dx_1 + \frac{\partial f(x_1, x_2)}{\partial x_2} dx_2 \\ dy &= k_1 dx_1 + k_2 dx_2 \end{aligned} \tag{1.21}$$

where $k_1 = \partial f(x_1, x_2)/\partial x_1$ and $k_2 = \partial f(x_1, x_2)/\partial x_2$ are constants.

1.1.3.1 *Some typical multivariate production functions*

Numerous production functions have been used in theoretical and empirical studies. Each function comes with advantages and disadvantages. Here, we present six specifications of the production function which are frequently used in theoretical and empirical literate:

- **Linear Production Function:** The linear production function is simple, but does not yield optimum interior solutions (e.g., the solutions are typically corner solutions). This function is typically found in linear programming.

$$y = b_1 x_1 + b_2 x_2. \tag{1.22}$$

- **Quadratic Production Function:** The quadratic production function is simple and allows for optimal solutions. However, the function yields a global maximum which limits its applicability for some models such as computable general equilibrium. In addition, the constant second-order terms may have some unfortunate consequences for concavity.

$$\begin{aligned} y &= a_1 x_1 + a_2 x_2 + \frac{1}{2}\left(A_{11} x_1^2 + A_{12} x_1 x_2 + A_{22} x_2^2\right) \\ y &= \begin{bmatrix} a_1 \\ a_2 \end{bmatrix}' \begin{bmatrix} x_1 \\ x_2 \end{bmatrix} + \frac{1}{2} \begin{bmatrix} x_1 \\ x_2 \end{bmatrix}' \begin{bmatrix} A_{11} & A_{12} \\ A_{12} & A_{22} \end{bmatrix} \begin{bmatrix} x_1 \\ x_2 \end{bmatrix} \end{aligned} . \tag{1.23}$$

- **Cobb–Douglas Production Function:** The Cobb–Douglas function is relatively easy to be estimated (i.e., it is linear in logs). In addition, it allows for a simple derivation of optimal behavior. However, its structure yields an independence between inputs (known as separability).

$$y = A x_1^{b_1} x_2^{b_2}. \tag{1.24}$$

  The Cobb–Douglas function was proposed by Charles W. Cobb and Paul H. Douglas (1928).

- **Transcendental Production Function:** The transcendental function allows for more flexibility than the Cobb–Douglas function, but it is still separable limiting the ability to model substitutability or complementarity between inputs.

$$y = Ax_1^{a_1} e^{b_1 x_1} x_2^{a_2} e^{b_2 x_2}. \tag{1.25}$$

The Transcendental function was proposed by J.G. Hocking and Halter *et al.* (1957) as an extension of the Cobb–Douglas function. Mundlak (1964) proposes an extension of the transcendental production function for multiple outputs.

- **Translog Production Function:** The translog production function can be conceptualized as an alternative extension of the Cobb–Douglas form or as a logarithmic second-order expansion of an unknown production function

$$\begin{aligned} y &= \exp\left(a_0 + a_1 \ln(x_1) + a_2 \ln(x_2)\right. \\ &\quad + 1/2\left(A_{11} \ln(x_1)\ln(x_1) + 2A_{12}\ln(x_1)\ln(x_2)\right. \\ &\quad \left.\left. + A_{22}\ln(x_2)\ln(x_2)\right)\right) \\ \ln(y) &= a_0 + \begin{bmatrix} a_1 \\ a_2 \end{bmatrix}' \begin{bmatrix} \ln(x_1) \\ \ln(x_2) \end{bmatrix} \\ &\quad + \frac{1}{2}\begin{bmatrix} \ln(x_1) \\ \ln(x_2) \end{bmatrix}' \begin{bmatrix} A_{11} & A_{12} \\ A_{12} & A_{22} \end{bmatrix} \begin{bmatrix} \ln(x_1) \\ \ln(x_2) \end{bmatrix}. \end{aligned} \tag{1.26}$$

This function was originally proposed by Christensen *et al.* (1973).

- **Constant Elasticity of Substitution:** The constant elasticity function allows for a specific form of interaction between inputs. However, the function is limited in solvability and is fairly difficult to estimate.

$$y = A\left[bx_1^{-g} + (1-b)x_2^{-g}\right]^{-\frac{v}{g}}. \tag{1.27}$$

The CES production function was proposed by Arrow *et al.* (1961).

This list is by no means exhaustive, but covers most of the standard examples. The Cobb–Douglas function is a frequently used example for solving optimizing behavior on microeconomic homework and examinations. In fact, we will frequently use it as an example in this book.

1.1.3.2 *Isoquants*

Given the multivariate nature of the production function, it is possible to define the *isoquant* or the relationship that depicts the combinations of inputs that yield the same output. Starting from the basic production function,

$$y = f(x_1, x_2) \Rightarrow x_2 = f^*(x_1, y). \tag{1.28}$$

That is, we are interested in constructing a functional mapping of x_2 based on the level of x_1 and y. The isoquant is then defined as the levels of x_1 and x_2 that produce a specific quantity of y. We could solve for these surfaces by mathematically solving for the implicit function. For example, in the case of the Cobb–Douglas function as presented in Equation (1.24) where $A = 1$, $b_1 = \alpha$, and $b_2 = 1 - \alpha$, we can solve for x_2 in terms of x_1 and y as

$$y = x_1^{\alpha} x_2^{1-\alpha} \Rightarrow x_2^{1-\alpha} = \frac{y}{x_1^{\alpha}} \Rightarrow x_2 = \frac{y^{\frac{1}{1-\alpha}}}{x_1^{\frac{\alpha}{1-\alpha}}}. \tag{1.29}$$

The isoquants for the Cobb–Douglas production function are closed form — we can solve analytically for the level of x_2 based on y and x_1. Figure 1.11 depicts six isoquants for the Zellner production

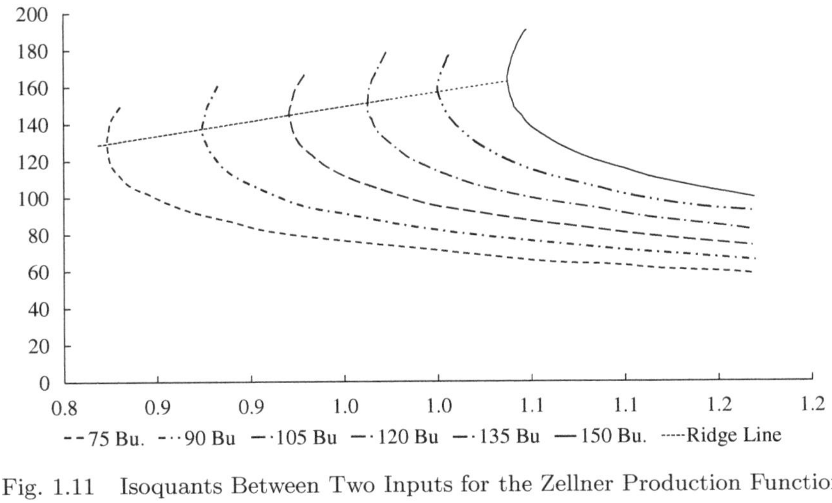

Fig. 1.11 Isoquants Between Two Inputs for the Zellner Production Function

function. These require numeric (e.g., instead of analytical solutions) developed later in this section.

The isoquants are useful in defining the *rate of technical substitution* which is the rate at which one input must be traded for the other input. Mathematically,

$$dy = f_1 dx_1 + f_2 dx_2 = 0 \Rightarrow \frac{dx_1}{dx_2} = -\frac{f_2}{f_1} \tag{1.30}$$

from the first-order Taylor series approximation in Equation (1.21). From the application to the translog production surface in Equation (1.20),

$$\begin{aligned} dy &= 0.001200 dx_1 + 0.062636 dx_2 = 0 \\ \Rightarrow \frac{dx_1}{dx_2} &= -\frac{0.062636}{0.001200} = -52.20 \end{aligned} \tag{1.31}$$

at the point $x_1 = 100$ and $x_2 = 15$.

Building on the slopes of isoquants, we define the *isoclines* and *ridgelines* (Figure 1.12). Each of these relationships comprises those points that have the same rate of technical substitution. The ridgelines are the isoclines where the rate of technical substitution is equal to zero or infinity. They represent the maximum physical output for

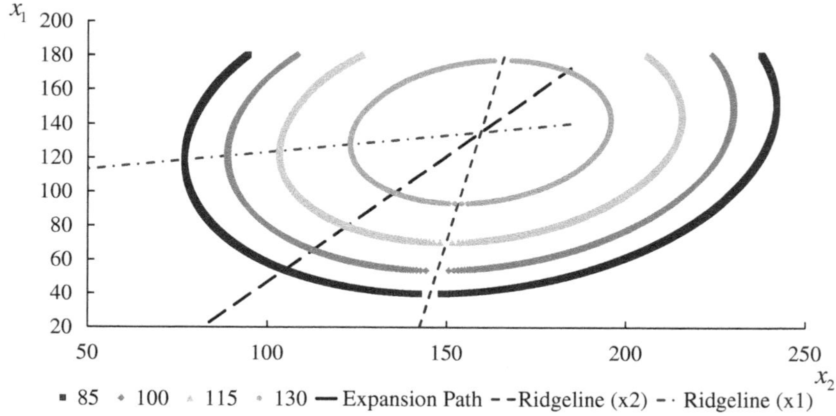

Fig. 1.12 Isoquants, Isoclines, and Ridgelines

one variable while holding the other variable constant. Factor independence: Two factors are independent if the marginal physical product of one factor is not a function of the marginal physical product of the other factor.

The simplest example of this is a quadratic production function with $A_{12} = A_{21} = 0$. In this case, the isoquants are circles (or ellipses):

$$y = a_1 x_1 + a_2 x_2 + \frac{1}{2}\left(A_{11} x_1^2 + A_{22} x_2^2\right) \Rightarrow \begin{cases} \dfrac{\partial y}{\partial x_1} = a_1 + A_{11} x_1 \\ \dfrac{\partial y}{\partial x_2} = a_2 + A_{22} x_2 \end{cases}. \tag{1.32}$$

- **Case I:**

$$\frac{\partial^2 y}{\partial x_1 \partial x_2} = \frac{\partial \left(\dfrac{\partial y}{\partial x_1}\right)}{\partial x_2} = f_{12} > 0 \tag{1.33}$$

then x_1 and x_2 are technically complementary.
- **Case II:** If $f_{12} = 0$, then x_1 and x_2 are technically independent.
- **Case III:** If $f_{12} < 0$, then x_1 and x_2 are technically competitive.

Because of the importance of the isoquant in the definition of the level set $(L(y))$ defined as

$$L(y) = [x : f(x) = y, x \text{ non-negative}] \tag{1.34}$$

in the development of the dual, we take some time to develop an empirical version of the isoquant.

Consider the transcendental production function

$$f(x_1, x_2) = 10.0 x_1^{0.45} x_2^{0.35} \exp(-0.00035 x_1 - 0.00025 x_2). \tag{1.35}$$

Our contention is that any closed-form solution of Equation (1.35) would be horrible to work with. Hence, we derive an empirical form of the isoquant using numerical methods. The first problem is how to construct an input combination that is on a particular isoquant. To do this, consider the scenario $f(x_1, 10) = 50$, or suppose that we want to derive the input level for x_1 that would yield 50 units of output given that x_2 is equal to 10. A simple approach to solve for this point is using the first-order Taylor series expansion

$$\begin{aligned} f(x_1, 10) &= f\left(x_1^0, 10\right) + \left.\frac{\partial f()}{\partial x_1}\right|_{x_1=x_1^0} \left(x_1 - x_1^0\right) \\ x_1 &= x_1^0 + \frac{f(x_1, 10) - f\left(x_1^0, 10\right)}{\left.\frac{\partial f()}{\partial x_1}\right|_{x_1=x_1^0}}. \end{aligned} \tag{1.36}$$

For the scenario where we are trying to solve for $f(x_1, 10) = 50$,

$$x_1 = x_1^0 + \frac{50 - f\left(x_1^0, 10\right)}{\left.\frac{\partial f()}{\partial x_1}\right|_{x_1=x_1^0}}. \tag{1.37}$$

Suppose we start at $x_1 = 10$, $f(10, 10) = 55.8977$ and $\partial f()/\partial x_1|_{x_1=10} = 2.4958$. Hence,

$$x_1 = 10 + \frac{50 - 55.8977}{2.4958} = 7.6397 \tag{1.38}$$

which implies that $f(7.6397, 10) = 49.5528$ which is close to 50, but not close enough. Setting $x_1^0 = 7.6397$ and using Equation (1.37) once more yields $x_1 = 7.7911$ where $f(7.7911, 10) = 50$.

This numeric procedure is useful because it can be used to justify the fact that (at least for this production function) a level set can be generated for any input. For example, consider the case where we want to generate a level set for 75 (i.e., $x \in L(75)$). Adjusting Equation (1.37) slightly,

$$x_1 = x_1^0 + \frac{75 - f\left(x_1^0, 10\right)}{\left.\frac{\partial f()}{\partial x_1}\right|_{x_1=x_1^0}}. \tag{1.39}$$

Starting again at $x_1 = 10$ yields the sequence

$$\begin{aligned} (x_1, x_2) = (10, 10) &\Rightarrow f(x_1, x_2) = 49.5528 \\ &\Rightarrow (17.6537, 10) \Rightarrow f(x_1, x_2) = 71.9957 \\ &\Rightarrow (19.3135, 10) \Rightarrow f(x_1, x_2) = 74.9231 \\ &\Rightarrow (19.3582, 10) \Rightarrow f(x_1, x_2) = 75.0000 \end{aligned} \tag{1.40}$$

Returning to the original question, given that $f(7.7911, 10) = 50$, how do we generate the rest of the isoquant. Going back to Equation (1.37), we solve for the next point, for example, where $x_2 = 15$ using $x_1 = 7.7911$ as a starting point

$$x_1 = x_1^0 + \frac{50 - f\left(x_1^0, 15\right)}{\left.\dfrac{\partial f()}{\partial x_1}\right|_{x_1 = x_1^0}} \tag{1.41}$$

which yields the sequence

$$\begin{aligned}(x_1, x_2) = (7.7911, 15) &\Rightarrow f(x_1, x_2) = 56.3941\\ \Rightarrow (5.8161, 15) &\Rightarrow f(x_1, x_2) = 49.4764\\ \Rightarrow (5.9535, 15) &\Rightarrow f(x_1, x_2) = 50.0000.\end{aligned} \tag{1.42}$$

Repeating this process yields a numeric solution for each isoquant. This procedure is typically referred to as the Gauss–Seidel procedure.

1.1.4 *Economic Consequences of the Production Function*

Given these general notions of the production function, how are these notions used in applied economics? There are several ways to model economic implications of the production function. As a first step, we consider the selection of inputs that maximize the revenue to the producer:

$$\begin{aligned}&\max_x pf(x_1, x_2, x_3)\\ &\text{s.t. } w_1x_1 + w_2x_3 + w_3x_3 \leq C^*\end{aligned} \tag{1.43}$$

where p is the output price, x_1, x_2, and x_3 are the levels for each input, $f(x_1, x_2, x_3)$ is the production function, w_1, w_2, and w_3 are the input prices, and C^* is the fixed cost level. We will simplify the formulation of Equation (1.43) in a couple of ways. First, we drop the price p. In a later section, we will expand the discussion to develop the revenue function, but for our present purposes, the solution that maximizes output also maximizes revenue. Second, we will substitute an equality for the inequality in the cost constraint. Again, we will expand the discussion to consider the implications of an inequality constraint later. Given these two formulations, the maximization problem in Equation (1.43) can be formulated as a Lagrangian

$$L = f(x_1, x_2, x_3) + \lambda (C^* - w_1 x_1 - w_2 x_2 - w_3 x_3) \tag{1.44}$$

In this formulation, we introduce λ which is the marginal effect of the constraint on the optimized value. To solve the system, we take the first derivatives

$$\begin{aligned} \frac{\partial L}{\partial x_1} &= \frac{\partial f(x_1, x_2, x_3)}{\partial x_1} - \lambda w_1 = 0 \\ \frac{\partial L}{\partial x_2} &= \frac{\partial f(x_1, x_2, x_3)}{\partial x_2} - \lambda w_2 = 0 \\ \frac{\partial L}{\partial x_3} &= \frac{\partial f(x_1, x_2, x_3)}{\partial x_3} - \lambda w_3 = 0 \\ C^* &- w_1 x_1 - w_2 x_2 - w_3 x_3 = 0 \end{aligned} \tag{1.45}$$

Often solving these Lagrangian conditions is as much as an art as a science.

Theory of Maximizing Behavior — Samuelson

The general method involved may be very simply stated. In cases where the equilibrium values of our variables can be regarded as the solutions of an extremum (maximum or minimum) problem, it is often possible regardless of the number of variables involved in determining unambiguously the qualitative behavior of our solution values with respect to changes of parameters (Samuelson, 1947, p. 21).

For simplicity, in this example, we will use a numerically fit Cobb–Douglas production function for corn production in Illinois in 1993:

$$y = f(x_1, x_2, x_3) = 50.000 x_1^{0.126} x_2^{0.034} x_3^{0.045} \tag{1.46}$$

where x_1 is the pounds of nitrogen per acre, x_2 is the pounds of phosphorous per acre, and x_3 is the pounds of potash per acre. Using the production function in Equation (1.46) and noting that

$\partial a_0 x_1^{a_1} x_2^{a_2} / \partial x_1 = a_1 \left(a_0 x_1^{a_1} x_2^{a_2} \right) / x_1 = a_1 y / x_1$, the results in Equation (1.46) become

$$
\begin{aligned}
\frac{\partial L}{\partial x_1} &= 0.126 \frac{y}{x_1} - 0.158\lambda = 0 \\
\frac{\partial L}{\partial x_2} &= 0.034 \frac{y}{x_2} - 0.141\lambda = 0 \\
\frac{\partial L}{\partial x_3} &= 0.045 \frac{y}{x_3} - 0.108\lambda = 0 \\
39.34 - 0.158x_1 - 0.141x_2 &- 0.108x_3 = 0
\end{aligned}
\tag{1.47}
$$

where 39.34 is the cost of inputs and outputs at the sample average. The Cobb–Douglas form is extremely tractable in that we can solve for both x_2 and x_3 in terms of x_1:

$$
\begin{aligned}
\frac{0.034 \dfrac{y}{x_2}}{0.126 \dfrac{y}{x_1}} &= \frac{\lambda 0.141}{\lambda 0.158} \Rightarrow x_1 = 3.307x_2 \\
\frac{0.045 \dfrac{y}{x_3}}{0.126 \dfrac{y}{x_1}} &= \frac{\lambda 0.108}{\lambda 0.158} \Rightarrow x_1 = 1.914x_3
\end{aligned}
\quad .
\tag{1.48}
$$

Substituting these results into the constraint

$$
\begin{aligned}
&39.34 - 0.158x_1 - 0.141 \times 0.302x_1 - 0.108 \times 0.522x_1 \\
&\quad = 0 \Rightarrow x_1 = 153.036.
\end{aligned}
\tag{1.49}
$$

It follows that $x_2 = 153.036 \times 0.302 = 46.274$ and $x_3 = 153.036 \times 0.522 = 79.959$. The overall level of production is 130.769 and the value of the Lagrange multiplier is 0.681.

Of course, the solution in Equations (1.48) and (1.49) are based on first-order conditions. To confirm that this is truly the maximum, we need to check the bordered Hessian. To explain the basic concept, we return to the general Lagrangian form in Equation (1.44). In deriving the set of first-order conditions, we implicitly took the total differential of Equation (1.49) with respect to our endogenous variables (i.e., those variables that we can control), yielding

$$
\begin{aligned}
dL = & \left(\frac{\partial f(x_1,x_2,x_3)}{\partial x_1} - \lambda w_1\right) dx_1 + \left(\frac{\partial f(x_1,x_2,x_3)}{\partial x_2} - \lambda w_2\right) dx_2 \\
& + \left(\frac{\partial f(x_1,x_2,x_3)}{\partial x_3} - \lambda w_3\right) dx_3 \\
& + (C^* - w_1 x_1 - w_2 x_2 - w_3 x_3)\, d\lambda.
\end{aligned} \tag{1.50}
$$

In general, the total differential in Equation (1.50) is zero if the individual partial derivatives in Equation (1.45) are zero. However, Equation (1.50) can be used to derive the second derivative of the constrained function. Taking the derivatives of Equation (1.50) with respect to each controllable input yields

$$
\begin{aligned}
d^2 L = & \left(\frac{\partial^2 f(x_1,x_2,x_3)}{\partial x_1 \partial x_1} dx_1 + \frac{\partial^2 f(x_1,x_2,x_3)}{\partial x_1 \partial x_2} dx_2 \right. \\
& \left. + \frac{\partial^2 f(x_1,x_2,x_3)}{\partial x_1 \partial x_3} dx_3 - w_1 d\lambda\right) dx_1 \\
& + \left(\frac{\partial^2 f(x_1,x_2,x_3)}{\partial x_2 \partial x_1} dx_1 + \frac{\partial^2 f(x_1,x_2,x_3)}{\partial x_2 \partial x_2} dx_2 \right. \\
& \left. + \frac{\partial^2 f(x_1,x_2,x_3)}{\partial x_2 \partial x_3} dx_3 - w_2 d\lambda\right) dx_2 \\
& + \left(\frac{\partial^2 f(x_1,x_2,x_3)}{\partial x_3 \partial x_1} dx_1 + \frac{\partial^2 f(x_1,x_2,x_3)}{\partial x_3 \partial x_2} dx_2 \right. \\
& \left. + \frac{\partial^2 f(x_1,x_2,x_3)}{\partial x_3 \partial x_3} dx_3 - w_3 d\lambda\right) dx_3 \\
& + (-w_1 dx_1 - w_2 dx_2 - w_3 dx_3)\, d\lambda.
\end{aligned} \tag{1.51}
$$

Rewriting Equation (1.51) in matrix form, simplifying $\partial f(x_1,x_2,x_3)/\partial x_i \partial x_j = f_{ij}$,

$$
\begin{bmatrix} d\lambda \\ dx_1 \\ dx_2 \\ dx_3 \end{bmatrix}' \begin{bmatrix} 0 & -w_1 & -w_2 & -w_3 \\ -w_1 & f_{11} & f_{12} & f_{13} \\ -w_2 & f_{21} & f_{22} & f_{23} \\ -w_3 & f_{31} & f_{32} & f_{33} \end{bmatrix} \begin{bmatrix} d\lambda \\ dx_1 \\ dx_2 \\ dx_3 \end{bmatrix}. \tag{1.52}
$$

Imposing symmetry, the maximization problem meets its second-order conditions if the matrix

$$\begin{bmatrix} 0 & -w_1 & -w_2 & -w_3 \\ -w_1 & f_{11} & f_{12} & f_{13} \\ -w_2 & f_{12} & f_{22} & f_{23} \\ -w_3 & f_{13} & f_{23} & f_{33} \end{bmatrix} \tag{1.53}$$

is negative semi-definite. For the Cobb–Douglass function in Equation (1.46), this matrix becomes

$$\begin{bmatrix} 0 & -0.158 & -0.141 & -0.108 \\ -0.158 & -0.000615 & 0.000079 & 0.000061 \\ -0.141 & 0.000079 & -0.002001 & 0.000054 \\ -0.108 & 0.000061 & 0.000054 & -0.000879 \end{bmatrix} \tag{1.54}$$

which is negative semi-definite.

We started with the problem of maximizing revenue because the function shares several characteristics with the consumer's problem. However, in production economics, we are typically more interested in selecting inputs to minimize the cost of production given a fixed output level

$$\begin{aligned} &\min_x w_1x_1 + w_2x_2 + w_3x_3 \\ &\text{s.t. } f(x_1, x_2, x_3) \geq y. \end{aligned} \tag{1.55}$$

Again, we abstract away from the inequality for the moment. The Lagrangian formulation then becomes

$$L = w_1x_1 + w_2x_2 + w_3x_3 + \mu\,(y - f(x_1, x_2, x_3)). \tag{1.56}$$

Resource Combination and Cost Minimization — Heady

The problem of resource substitution is one of the combining factors in a manner to minimize the cost of producing a given amount of product. It is one which faces the individual entrepreneur in maximizing his profit. It is also one which concerns a nation or an economic unit of any other magnitude. The economic product from given resources, measured in profit at the farm or in other terms at the national level, can be at a maximum only if each unit of commodity is produced with a minimum cost or resource outlay (Heady, 1952).

Following the same series of steps, we take the derivative of Equation (1.57) with respect to each input level

$$\begin{aligned}\frac{\partial L}{\partial x_1} &= w_1 - \mu\frac{\partial f(x)}{\partial x_1} = 0\\ \frac{\partial L}{\partial x_2} &= w_2 - \mu\frac{\partial f(x)}{\partial x_2} = 0\\ \frac{\partial L}{\partial x_3} &= w_3 - \mu\frac{\partial f(x)}{\partial x_3} = 0\\ \frac{\partial L}{\partial \lambda} &= y - f(x_1, x_2, x_3) = 0\end{aligned} \quad . \tag{1.57}$$

Note that the first-order conditions in Equation (1.57) are similar to the first-order conditions in Equation (1.47). In fact, if you replace $\mu = 1/\lambda$, the first three first-order conditions are identical. Essentially, in this formulation, μ is the marginal cost of an additional unit of output.

Next, consider taking the matrix of second derivatives for Equation (1.57) — focusing on the first first-order condition

$$d\,\frac{\partial L}{\partial x_1} = -\frac{\partial f(x)}{\partial x_1}d\,\mu - \mu\frac{\partial^2 f(x)}{\partial x_1 x_1}d\,x_1 - \mu\frac{\partial^2 f(x)}{\partial x_1 \partial x_2}d\,x_2 - \mu\frac{\partial^2 f(x)}{\partial x_1 \partial x_3}d\,x_3. \tag{1.58}$$

By extension, the second-order differential can be written as

$$\begin{bmatrix} d\,\mu \\ d\,x_1 \\ d\,x_2 \\ d\,x_3 \end{bmatrix}' \begin{bmatrix} 0 & -f_1 & -f_2 & -f_3 \\ -f_1 & -\mu f_{11} & -\mu f_{12} & -\mu f_{13} \\ -f_2 & -\mu f_{21} & -\mu f_{22} & -\mu f_{23} \\ -f_3 & -\mu f_{31} & -\mu f_{32} & -\mu f_{33} \end{bmatrix} \begin{bmatrix} d\,\mu \\ d\,x_1 \\ d\,x_2 \\ d\,x_3 \end{bmatrix}. \tag{1.59}$$

Following the explanation from Henderson and Quandt (1980), we substitute

$$w_1 = \mu\frac{\partial f(x)}{\partial x_1} \Rightarrow \frac{w_1}{\mu} = f_1 \tag{1.60}$$

into Equation (1.59) to yield

$$\begin{bmatrix} 0 & -\frac{w_1}{\mu} & -\frac{w_2}{\mu} & -\frac{w_3}{\mu} \\ -\frac{w_1}{\mu} & -\mu f_{11} & -\mu f_{12} & -\mu f_{13} \\ -\frac{w_2}{\mu} & -\mu f_{21} & -\mu f_{22} & -\mu f_{23} \\ -\frac{w_3}{\mu} & -\mu f_{31} & -\mu f_{32} & -\mu f_{33} \end{bmatrix}. \tag{1.61}$$

First, note that we started with a minimization problem. In the minimization formulation, we are interested in showing that the second-order conditions are positive. However, given that all the parameters in Equation (1.61) are negative, we will multiply through by a negative one and demonstrate that

$$\begin{bmatrix} 0 & \frac{w_1}{\mu} & \frac{w_2}{\mu} & \frac{w_3}{\mu} \\ \frac{w_1}{\mu} & \mu f_{11} & \mu f_{12} & \mu f_{13} \\ \frac{w_2}{\mu} & \mu f_{21} & \mu f_{22} & \mu f_{23} \\ \frac{w_3}{\mu} & \mu f_{31} & \mu f_{32} & \mu f_{33} \end{bmatrix} \tag{1.62}$$

is negative semi-definite. Next, we are interested in multiplying columns 2, 3, and 4 of Equation (1.63) by $1/\mu$ — mathematically, let us represent this process as

$$A = \begin{bmatrix} 1 & 0 & 0 & 0 \\ 0 & \frac{1}{\mu} & 0 & 0 \\ 0 & 0 & \frac{1}{\mu} & 0 \\ 0 & 0 & 0 & \frac{1}{\mu} \end{bmatrix}$$

$$B = \begin{bmatrix} 0 & \frac{w_1}{\mu} & \frac{w_2}{\mu} & \frac{w_3}{\mu} \\ \frac{w_1}{\mu} & \mu f_{11} & \mu f_{12} & \mu f_{13} \\ \frac{w_2}{\mu} & \mu f_{21} & \mu f_{22} & \mu f_{23} \\ \frac{w_3}{\mu} & \mu f_{31} & \mu f_{32} & \mu f_{33} \end{bmatrix}$$

$$AB = C$$

$$C = \begin{bmatrix} 0 & \frac{w_1}{\mu^2} & \frac{w_2}{\mu^2} & \frac{w_3}{\mu^2} \\ \frac{w_1}{\mu^2} & f_{11} & f_{12} & f_{13} \\ \frac{w_2}{\mu^2} & f_{21} & f_{22} & f_{23} \\ \frac{w_3}{\mu^2} & f_{31} & f_{32} & f_{33} \end{bmatrix}. \tag{1.63}$$

The basic concept that we want to exploit is that $|AB| = |A|\,|B|$. Hence, in Equation (1.63), $|A| = 1/\mu^3$ — we get the same result as dividing three columns of C by μ. Expanding the solution in Equation (1.63) slightly, we multiply the first column by μ

$$\begin{gathered} A = \begin{bmatrix} \mu & 0 & 0 & 0 \\ 0 & \frac{1}{\mu} & 0 & 0 \\ 0 & 0 & \frac{1}{\mu} & 0 \\ 0 & 0 & 0 & \frac{1}{\mu} \end{bmatrix} \\ C^* = \begin{bmatrix} 0 & \frac{w_1}{\mu^2} & \frac{w_2}{\mu^2} & \frac{w_3}{\mu^2} \\ \frac{w_1}{\mu^2} & f_{11} & f_{12} & f_{13} \\ w_2 & f_{21} & f_{22} & f_{23} \\ \frac{w_3}{\mu^2} & f_{31} & f_{32} & f_{33} \end{bmatrix}. \\ AB = C \end{gathered} \tag{1.64}$$

Taking the determinant of A in Equation (1.64) yields $|A| = 1/\mu^2$ (e.g., the determinant of a diagonal matrix is simply the product of the diagonal elements). Hence,

$$\begin{gathered} |A|\,|B| = |C^*| \Rightarrow \frac{1}{\mu^2}\,|B| = |C^*| \\ |B| = \mu^2\,|C^*| \end{gathered}. \tag{1.65}$$

Hence, if $|B|$ is negative semi-definite, then $|C|$ is negative semi-definite as long as $\mu \gg 0$ which is guaranteed by the solution. As a final piece of the puzzle, we multiply the first row and column by μ^2, which yields the matrix for testing the second-order conditions as

$$C^{**} = \begin{bmatrix} 0 & w_1 & w_2 & w_3 \\ w_1 & f_{11} & f_{12} & f_{13} \\ w_2 & f_{21} & f_{22} & f_{23} \\ w_3 & f_{31} & f_{32} & f_{33} \end{bmatrix} \tag{1.66}$$

which is identical to the second-order matrix presented in Equation (1.53). Allowing for the fact that we flipped the inequalities between the problems.

As a final wrinkle, let us return to the difference between inequality and equality constraints. Consider a slight reformulation of the cost minimization problem posited in Equation (1.55):

$$\begin{aligned} &\min_x w_1x_1 + w_2x_2 + w_3x_3 \\ &\text{s.t. } y \geq f(x_1, x_2, x_3),\ x_1, x_2, x_3 \geq 0. \end{aligned} \tag{1.67}$$

The formulation in Equation (1.67) complicates our solution by introducing the possibility of "corner solutions". For example, the optimal value of x_1 and x_2 may be greater than zero, but the optimal value of x_3 may be equal to zero. This problem in Equation (1.67) is usually solved using the Kuhn–Tucker conditions which are modified forms of the typical Lagrangian conditions

$$\begin{aligned} &\left(w_1 - \lambda\frac{\partial f(x)}{\partial x_1}\right)x_1 = 0 \Rightarrow \begin{cases} \dfrac{\partial \lambda f(x)}{\partial x_1} = w_1 \text{ if } x_1 \gg 0 \\ \lambda\dfrac{\partial f(x)}{\partial x_1} \geq w_1 \text{ if } x_1 = 0 \end{cases} \\ &\left(w_2 - \lambda\frac{\partial f(x)}{\partial x_2}\right)x_2 = 0 \Rightarrow \begin{cases} \lambda\dfrac{\partial f(x)}{\partial x_2} = w_2 \text{ if } x_2 \gg 0 \\ \lambda\dfrac{\partial f(x)}{\partial x_2} \geq w_2 \text{ if } x_2 = 0 \end{cases} . \\ &\left(w_3 - \lambda\frac{\partial f(x)}{\partial x_3}\right)x_3 = 0 \Rightarrow \begin{cases} \lambda\dfrac{\partial f(x)}{\partial x_3} = w_3 \text{ if } x_3 \gg 0 \\ \lambda\dfrac{\partial f(x)}{\partial x_3} \geq w_3 \text{ if } x_3 = 0 \end{cases} \end{aligned} \tag{1.68}$$

In addition, the condition involving the constraint changes slightly

$$(y - f(x_1, x_2, x_3))\,\lambda = 0 \Rightarrow \begin{cases} \lambda \gg 0 \text{ if } y = f(x_1, x_2, x_3) \\ \lambda = 0 \text{ if } y \gg f(x_1, x_2, x_3) \end{cases} . \tag{1.69}$$

One key point is that as long as the solution is strictly in the interior, the optimality conditions are the same as the basic Lagrangian.

Taking a slightly different approach, we could derive a cost function by minimizing the cost of the two inputs subject to some level of production based on the Cobb–Douglas production function

$$\begin{aligned} &\min_{x_1,x_2} w_1x_1 + w_2x_2 \\ &\text{s.t. } y = x_1^{\alpha}x_2^{\beta}. \end{aligned} \tag{1.70}$$

Forming the Lagrangian of this optimization problem, we have

$$\begin{aligned} L &= w_1x_1 + w_2x_2 + \lambda\left(y - x_1^{\alpha}x_2^{\beta}\right) \\ \frac{\partial L}{\partial x_1} &= w_1 - \lambda\alpha\frac{x_1^{\alpha}x_2^{\beta}}{x_1} = 0 \\ \frac{\partial L}{\partial x_2} &= w_2 - \lambda\beta\frac{x_1^{\alpha}x_2^{\beta}}{x_2} = 0 \\ \frac{\partial L}{\partial \lambda} &= y - x_1^{\alpha}x_2^{\beta} = 0 \end{aligned} \quad . \tag{1.71}$$

Taking the first two first-order conditions together, we have

$$\frac{(\partial L/\partial x_1)}{(\partial L/\partial x_2)} \Rightarrow \frac{w_1}{w_2} = \frac{\lambda\alpha\frac{x_1^{\alpha}x_2^{\beta}}{x_1}}{\lambda\beta\frac{x_1^{\alpha}x_2^{\beta}}{x_2}} = \frac{\alpha x_2}{\beta x_1} \Rightarrow x_1 = \frac{\alpha w_2}{\beta w_1}x_2. \tag{1.72}$$

Substituting this relationship into the final first-order condition of Equation (1.71) yields

$$\frac{\partial L}{\partial \lambda} \Rightarrow y - \left(\frac{\alpha w_2}{\beta w_1}x_2\right)^{\alpha} x_2^{\beta} = 0 \Rightarrow x_2^*\left(w_1, w_2, y\right) = y^{\frac{1}{\alpha+\beta}}\left(\frac{\beta w_1}{\alpha w_2}\right)^{\frac{\alpha}{\alpha+\beta}}. \tag{1.73}$$

By substituting this relationship back into the respective previous condition that solves x_1 as a function of x_2, we have

$$x_1^*\left(w_1, w_2, y\right) = y^{\frac{1}{\alpha+\beta}}\left(\frac{\alpha w_2}{\beta w_1}\right)^{\frac{\beta}{\alpha+\beta}}. \tag{1.74}$$

Equation (1.74) represents the demand curve for x_1 conditional on the desired output. Note that both of these functions are declining in their own price and increasing in the price of the other input.

In addition, both input demand functions are increasing in the level of output.

Substituting both of these optimal relationships (output conditional input demand curves) back into the cost function yields

$$C(w_1, w_2, y) = w_1 \left[y^{\frac{1}{\alpha+\beta}} \left(\frac{\alpha}{\beta} \frac{w_2}{w_1} \right)^{\frac{\beta}{\alpha+\beta}} \right] + w_2 \left[y^{\frac{1}{\alpha+\beta}} \left(\frac{\beta}{\alpha} \frac{w_1}{w_2} \right)^{\frac{\alpha}{\alpha+\beta}} \right]$$

$$C(w_1, w_2, y) = y^{\frac{1}{\alpha+\beta}} w_1^{\frac{\alpha}{\alpha+\beta}} w_2^{\frac{\beta}{\alpha+\beta}} \left[\left(\frac{\alpha}{\beta} \right)^{\frac{\beta}{\alpha+\beta}} + \left(\frac{\beta}{\alpha} \right)^{\frac{\alpha}{\alpha+\beta}} \right]. \quad (1.75)$$

Thus, in the end, we are left with a cost function that relates input prices and output levels to the cost of production based on the economic assumption of optimizing behavior. Following Chamber's (1988) critique, the recent trend in economics is to skip the primal approach and go directly to the dual by assuming that producers know the general shape of the production function and select inputs optimally. Thus, economists only need to estimate the economic behavior in the cost function. Following this approach, economists only need to know things about the production function that affect the feasibility and nature of this optimizing behavior. In addition, production economics is typically linked to Shephard's Lemma that guarantees that we can recover the optimal input demand curves from this optimizing behavior.

1.2 Definition of the Production Function

Following our previous discussion, we then define a production function as a mathematical mapping function in Equation (1.5). However, we will now write it in implicit functional form

$$F(z) = 0. \quad (1.76)$$

This notation is sometimes referred to as a *netput* notation where we do not differentiate inputs or outputs. In more traditional terms, we differentiate inputs and outputs, yielding

$$F(y, x) = 0. \quad (1.77)$$

Following the mapping notation, we typically exclude the possibility of negative outputs or inputs, but this is simply a convention. In addition, we typically exclude inputs that are not economically scarce, such as sunlight. Finally, I like to refer to the production function as an envelope, implying that the production function characterizes the maximum amount of output that can be obtained from any combination of inputs. As such, the production function is a frontier function, which is somewhat at odds with some of the implications of ordinary least squares. The concept of production functions as frontier functions allows for the analysis of technical inefficiency.

1.2.1 *Properties of the Production Function*

Chambers (1988, p. 9) presents a list of general properties of the production function:

(1) Monotonicity and Strict Monotonicity
   (a) If $x' \geq x$, then $f(x') \geq f(x)$ (monotonicity).
   (b) If $x' > x$, then $f(x') > f(x)$ (strict monotonicity).

(2) Quasi-Concavity and Concavity
   (a) $V(y) = \{x : f(x) \geq y\}$ is a convex set (quasiconcave).
   (b) $f(\theta x^0 + (1-\theta)x^*) \geq \theta f(x^0) + (1-\theta) f(x^*)$ for any $0 \leq \theta \leq 1$ (concave as depicted in Figure 1.13).

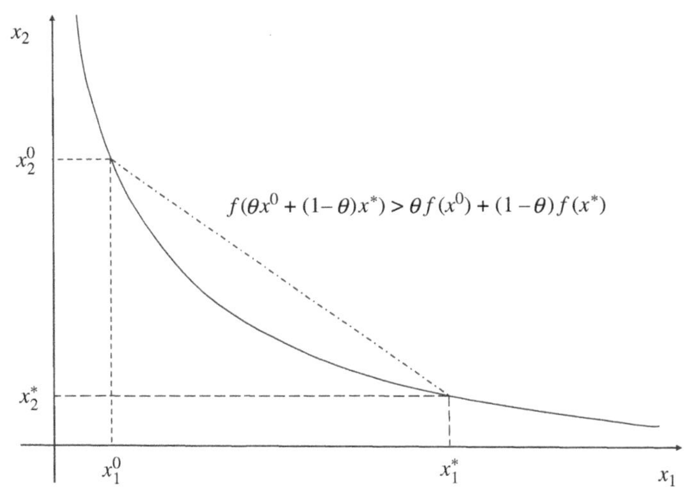

Fig. 1.13 Concavity

(3) Weakly essential and strictly essential inputs

(a) $f(0_n) = 0$, where 0_n is the null vector (weakly essential).

(b) $f(x_1, \ldots, x_{i-1}, 0, x_{i+1}, \ldots, x_n) = 0$ for all x_i (strictly essential).

(4) The set $V(y)$ is closed and non-empty for all $y > 0$.

(5) $f(x)$ is finite, non-negative, real-valued, and single-valued for all non-negative and finite x.

(6) Continuity

(a) $f(x)$ is everywhere continuous.

(b) $f(x)$ is everywhere twice continuously differentiable.

Properties (1a) and (1b) require the production function to be non-decreasing in inputs or that the marginal products be non-negative. In essence, these assumptions rule out Stage III of the production process or imply some kind of assumption of *free disposal.* One traditional assumption in this regard is that since it is irrational to operate in Stage III, no producer will choose to operate there. Thus, if we take a dual approach (as developed above), Stage III is irrelevant.

Properties (2a) and (2b) revolve around the notion of isoquants or as redeveloped here *input requirement sets* . The input requirement set is defined as that set of inputs required to produce at least a given level of outputs, *V*(*y*) (as depicted in Figure 1.14). Other notations used to note the same concept are the *level sets.* Strictly speaking, assumption (2a) implies that we observe a *diminishing rate*

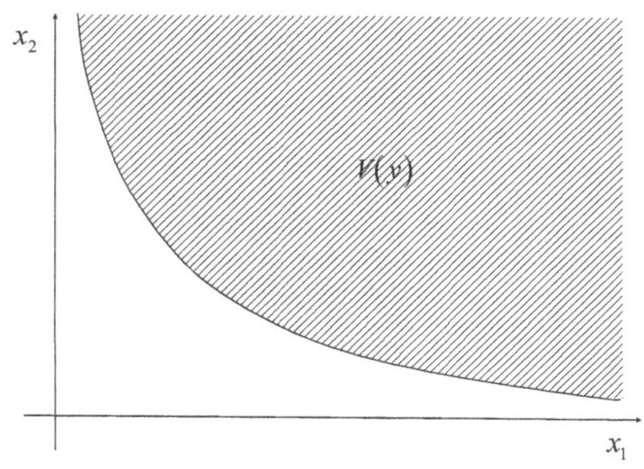

Fig. 1.14 Level Sets

of technical substitution, or that the isoquants are negatively sloping and convex with respect to the origin.

Assumption (2b) is both a stronger version of assumption (2a) and an extension. For example, if we choose both points to be on the same input requirement set, then Figure 1.13 depicts the level set. If we assume that the inputs are on two different input requirement sets, then

$$\begin{aligned} f\left(\theta x^0 + (1-\theta) x^*\right) &\geq \theta \left[f\left(x^0\right) - f\left(x^*\right)\right] + f\left(x^*\right) \\ f\left(\theta x^0 + (1-\theta) x^*\right) &\geq \theta \frac{\partial f\left(x^*\right)}{\partial x}\left(x^0 - x^*\right) + f\left(x^*\right) \end{aligned} . \quad (1.78)$$

Clearly, letting θ approach zero yields $f(x)$ approaching $f(x^*)$, however, because of the inequality, the left-hand side is less than the right-hand side. Therefore, the *marginal productivity* is non-increasing and, given a strict inequality, is decreasing. As noted by Chambers, this is an example of the law of diminishing marginal productivity that is actually assumed.

The notion of weakly and strictly essential inputs is apparent. The assumption of weakly essential inputs says that you cannot produce something out of nothing. Maybe a better way to put this is that if you can produce something without using any scarce resources, there is not an economic problem. The assumption of strictly essential inputs is that in order to produce a positive quantity of outputs, you must use a positive quantity of all resources. Different production functions have different assumptions on essential inputs. It is clear that the Cobb–Douglas form is an example of strictly essential resources.

The remaining assumptions are fairly technical assumptions for analysis. First, we assume that the *input requirement set* is closed and bounded. This implies that functional values for the input requirement set exist for all output levels (this is similar to the lexicographic preference structure from demand theory).

Also, it is important that the production function be finite (bounded) and real-valued (no imaginary solutions). The notion that the production function is a single-valued map simply implies that any combination of inputs implies one and only one level of output.

The continuity constraints are for mathematical nicety. The mathematical statement is $\lim_{x \leftarrow x^-} f(x) = \lim_{x \leftarrow x^+} f(x) = f(x)$. So, the function value is a smooth representation at that point.

1.2.2 *Law of Variable Proportions*

The assumption of continuous function levels, and first and second derivatives allows for a statement of the Law of Variable Proportions. The law of variable proportions is essentially a restatement of the law of diminishing marginal returns. The law of variable proportions states that if one input is successively increased at a constant rate with all other inputs held constant, the resulting additional product will first increase and then decrease. This discussion actually follows our discussion of the factor elasticity in Section 1.1.2:

$$\begin{aligned} \eta &= \frac{\%\Delta y}{\%\Delta x} = \frac{dy/y}{dx/x} = \frac{dy}{dx}\frac{x}{y} = \frac{MPP}{APP} \\ MPP &= \frac{dTPP}{dx} = \frac{dx\,APP}{dx} = APP + \frac{d\,APP}{dx} \end{aligned}. \tag{1.79}$$

Working the last expression backward, we derive

$$\frac{d\,APP}{dx} = \frac{1}{x}\left(MPP - APP\right) \tag{1.80}$$

or in multivariate and Chamber's notation

$$\frac{\partial\left(AP\right)_i}{\partial x_i} = \frac{1}{x_i}\left(\frac{\partial f}{\partial x_i} - \frac{y}{x_i}\right). \tag{1.81}$$

As an example, consider the transcendental production function

$$\begin{aligned} f\left[x_1, x_2, x_3\right) = \exp &(3.2616 + 0.0759 \ln\left(x_1\right) - 0.0481 \ln\left(x_2\right) \\ &- 0.2500 \ln\left(x_3\right) - 0.2243 \ln\left(x_1\right) \ln\left(x_1\right) \\ &+ 0.2385 \ln\left(x_1\right) \ln\left(x_2\right) + 0.2889 \ln\left(x_1\right) \ln\left(x_3\right) \\ &- 0.2381 \ln\left(x_2\right) \ln\left(x_2\right) + 0.2193 \ln\left(x_2\right) \ln\left(x_3\right) \\ &- 0.2146 \ln\left(x_3\right) \ln\left(x_3\right)]. \end{aligned} \tag{1.82}$$

Consider a slight reformulation of Equation (1.82) focusing on input x_1

$$f(x_1, x_2, x_3) = \exp[\alpha_0 + \alpha_1 \ln(x_1) + \alpha_2 \ln(x_1) \ln(x_1) + \alpha_3 \ln(x_1) \ln(x_2) + \alpha_4 \ln(x_1) \ln(x_3)] \times \exp[g(x_2, x_3)] \quad (1.83)$$

where $g(x_2, x_3)$ are the terms in Equation (1.82) that do not involve $\ln(x_1)$. Next, we can take the derivative of Equation (1.83) with respect to x_1 to yield

$$\frac{\partial f(x_1, x_2, x_3)}{\partial x_1} = \frac{\alpha_1 + 2\alpha_2 \ln(x_1) + \alpha_3 \ln(x_2) + \alpha_4 \ln(x_3)}{x_1} f(x_1, x_2, x_3) \quad (1.84)$$

Using the average of the sample $\bar{x}_1 = 124.50$, $\bar{x}_2 = 54.29$, and $\bar{x}_3 = 78.91$ (given that the estimation is based on the logarithms of the input levels, the use of geometric means appears appropriate), the marginal product of the production function for each input becomes

$$\nabla_x f(x_1, x_2, x_3) = \begin{bmatrix} \dfrac{\partial f(x_1, x_2, x_3)}{\partial x_1} \\ \dfrac{\partial f(x_1, x_2, x_3)}{\partial x_2} \\ \dfrac{\partial f(x_1, x_2, x_3)}{\partial x_3} \end{bmatrix} = \begin{bmatrix} 0.04278 \\ 0.12292 \\ 0.07757 \end{bmatrix}. \quad (1.85)$$

The vector of average products can be computed as

$$\begin{bmatrix} \dfrac{f(x_1, x_2, x_3)}{x_1} \\ \dfrac{f(x_1, x_2, x_3)}{x_2} \\ \dfrac{f(x_1, x_2, x_3)}{x_3} \end{bmatrix} = \begin{bmatrix} 0.33845 \\ 0.77616 \\ 0.53400 \end{bmatrix}. \quad (1.86)$$

Using the expression in Equation (1.81)

$$\begin{bmatrix} \dfrac{\partial (AP)_1}{\partial x_1} \\ \dfrac{\partial (AP)_2}{\partial x_2} \\ \dfrac{\partial (AP)_3}{\partial x_3} \end{bmatrix} = \begin{bmatrix} -0.00980 \\ -0.00403 \\ -0.00001 \end{bmatrix}. \quad (1.87)$$

Hence, the average product for each input is downward sloping around the geometric mean.

1.2.3 *Elasticity of Scale*

The law of variable proportions is related to how output changed as you increased one input. Next, we want to consider how output changes as you increase all inputs. In economic jargon, this is referred to as the elasticity of scale and is defined as

$$\epsilon = \left.\frac{\partial \ln\left[f(\lambda x)\right]}{\partial \ln[\lambda]}\right|_{\lambda=1} \tag{1.88}$$

> **Business Decisions and Scale — Black**
>
> Another phase of business which requires an understanding of economics is its organization. A business man is interested not only in the prices of what he buys and sells but also in organizing his business in such a way that he can turn out his product at the lowest possible cost, price of product being assumed. His costs will vary according to his volume of business, the relation between his volume of business and the size of his plant, the types of equipment and supplies used, the amount and kind of management employed, and a score of other things. These are all problems of utilization involving considerations of value and price (Black, 1962, p. 15).

This change implies the movement along a ray drawn from the origin, as depicted in Figure 1.15. The elasticity of scale takes on three important values:

- If the elasticity of scale is equal to 1, then the production surface can be characterized by constant returns to scale. Doubling *all* inputs doubles the output.
- If the elasticity of scale is greater than 1, then the production surface can be characterized by increasing returns to scale. Doubling *all* inputs more than doubles the output.
- Finally, if the elasticity of scale is less than 1, then the production surface can be characterized by decreasing returns to scale. Doubling *all* inputs does not double the output.

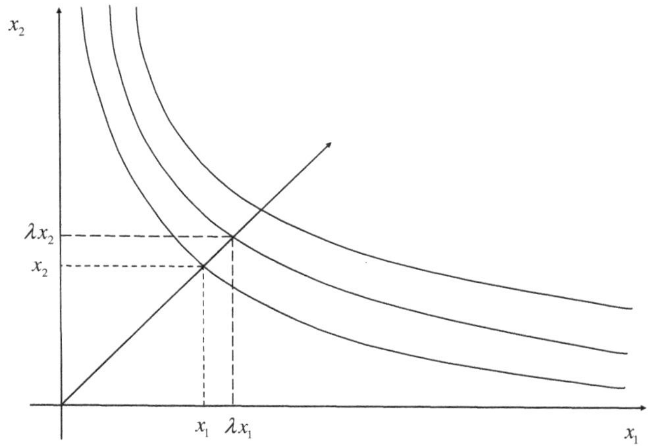

Fig. 1.15 Elasticity of Scale along a Ray from the Origin

Note the equivalence of this concept to the definition of homogeneity of degree k

$$\lambda^k f(x) = f(\lambda x). \tag{1.89}$$

For computational purposes,

$$\left.\frac{\partial \ln [f(\lambda x)]}{\partial \ln[\lambda]}\right|_{\lambda=1} = \sum_{i=1}^{n} \frac{\partial f}{\partial x_i}\frac{x_i}{y} = \sum_{i=1}^{n} \epsilon_i. \tag{1.90}$$

Returning to the production function in Equation (1.82) using the derivatives in Equation (1.85),

$$\begin{aligned}\left.\frac{\partial \ln [f(\lambda x)]}{\partial \ln[\lambda]}\right|_{\lambda=1} &= 0.04278\frac{124.50}{42.1381} + 0.12292\frac{54.29}{42.1381} + 0.07757\frac{78.91}{42.1381} \\ &= 0.12637 + 0.15836 + 0.14526 = 0.42999. \end{aligned} \tag{1.91}$$

So, the production function exhibits decreasing returns to scale at the geometric mean.

Building on these definitions, we next define the *ray average product* as

$$RAP = \frac{f(\lambda x)}{\lambda} \tag{1.92}$$

λ is a strictly positive scalar. In addition, we define the *ray marginal product*

$$RMP = \frac{\partial f(\lambda x)}{\partial \lambda} = \sum_{i=1}^{n} \frac{\partial f(\lambda x)}{\partial x_i} x_i. \tag{1.93}$$

To derive this result, substitute

$$\begin{aligned} \lambda x \rightarrow z(x) \Rightarrow \frac{\partial f(\lambda x)}{\partial \lambda} &= \frac{\partial f(z(x))}{\partial \lambda} \\ &= \frac{\partial f(z(x))}{\partial z(x)} \frac{\partial z(x)}{\partial \lambda} \\ &= \sum_{i=1}^{n} \frac{\partial f(\lambda x)}{\partial x_i} x_i. \end{aligned} \tag{1.94}$$

By extension of this result,

$$\frac{\partial^2 f(\lambda x)}{\partial \lambda^2} = \sum_{j=1}^{n} \sum_{i=1}^{n} \frac{\partial f(\lambda x)}{\partial x_i \partial x_j} x_i x_j. \tag{1.95}$$

In order to develop the concept behind these equations, we need to take a slice from the multivariate production function, as depicted in Figure 1.16. If we focus on the slice of the production function on the ray from the origin, the production function looks like a univariate production function. Differentiating the ray average product yields

$$\begin{aligned} \frac{\partial(RAP)}{\partial \lambda} = \frac{\partial f(\lambda x)/\lambda}{\partial \lambda} &= \frac{\partial f(\lambda x)}{\partial \lambda} \frac{1}{\lambda} + f(\lambda x) \frac{\partial(1/\lambda)}{\partial \lambda} \\ &= \frac{1}{\lambda} \left[\frac{\partial f(\lambda x)}{\partial \lambda} - \frac{f(\lambda x)}{\lambda} \right] \\ &= \frac{1}{\lambda} [RMP - RAP] \end{aligned} \tag{1.96}$$

which states that the ray average product is maximum when it is equal to the ray marginal product (RMP). Note that this relationship

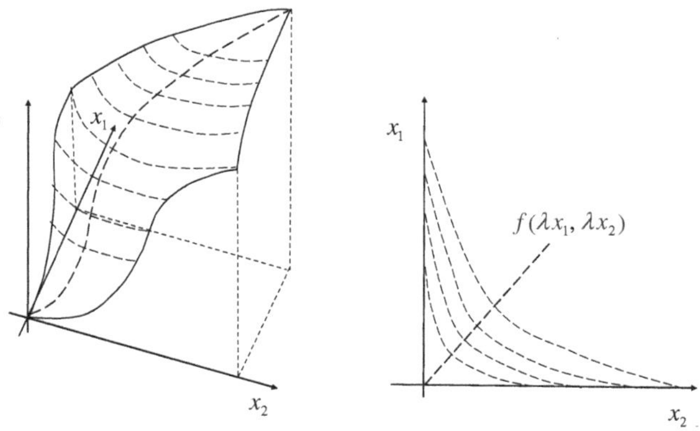

Fig. 1.16 Elasticity of Scale

is the same as the univariate relationship

$$\frac{d\,APP}{dx} = \frac{1}{x}\,(MPP - APP). \tag{1.97}$$

Applying these relationships to the Zellner production function from Equation (1.10),

$$f\,(\lambda x_1, \lambda x_2) = \frac{a\lambda^3 x_1^3}{\exp\left[b\dfrac{\lambda x_1}{\lambda x_2}\right] - 1} = \frac{a\lambda^3 x_1^3}{\exp\left[b\dfrac{x_1}{x_2}\right] - 1}. \tag{1.98}$$

Thus, x_2 does not affect the scale economies. The RMP is then

$$RMP = \frac{3a\lambda^2 x_1^3}{\exp\left[b\dfrac{x_1}{x_2}\right] - 1}. \tag{1.99}$$

The ray average product and ray marginal product are equivalent to the univariate production relationships presented in Figure 1.3. Recalling the general graph of the ray defining the ray average product and ray marginal product along the same ray from the origin yields the graphical representation in Figure 1.15. If $\epsilon = 1$ at point A, the production function exhibits constant returns to scale at x, since

$$\epsilon = \frac{\partial \ln\left[f(\lambda x)\right]}{\partial \ln(\lambda)} = \frac{\dfrac{\partial f(\lambda x)}{f(\lambda x)}}{\dfrac{\partial \lambda}{\lambda}} = \frac{\dfrac{\partial f(\lambda x)}{\partial \lambda}}{\dfrac{f(\lambda x)}{\lambda}} = \frac{RMP}{RAP} = 1. \tag{1.100}$$

If $\epsilon = 1$ is to the right of A, then the production function exhibits decreasing returns to scale at x since any ray from the origin to $f(\lambda x)$ for $\lambda > A$ will cut $f(\lambda x)$ from below. Thus, the *ray average product* is greater than the *ray marginal product.* If $\epsilon = 1$ to the left of A, $f(x)$ exhibits increasing returns to scale at x.

1.2.4 *Measures of Input Substitution*

Previously, we developed the idea of the rate of technical substitution defined as the movement along an isoquant. Now, we want to expand our discussion to discuss an *elasticity of substitution.* In general, we would like to define the elasticity of substitution as the percentage change in relative rate of input use. However, the exact nature of this elasticity is somewhat ambiguous.

There are three general elasticities of substitution. Hicks defined the first elasticity of substitution in 1963. The Hicksian or direct elasticity of substitution

$$\sigma_{ij}^{D} = \frac{d\left(\dfrac{x_i}{x_j}\right)\dfrac{\dfrac{f_j}{f_i}}{}}{d\left(\dfrac{f_j}{f_i}\right)\dfrac{x_i}{x_j}}. \tag{1.101}$$

To derive the elasticity of substitution, we follow Allen (1938, pp. 340–343). Allen's discussion of the elasticity of substitution follows his development of implicit differentiation. Specifically, he starts by assuming a production function which uses two inputs:

$$f(a, b) = x \tag{1.102}$$

where x is a constant. Next, we differentiate this production function to yield

$$\begin{gathered} f_a da + f_b db = 0 \\ f_a = \frac{\partial x}{\partial a}, \quad f_b = \frac{\partial x}{\partial b} \cdot \end{gathered} \tag{1.103}$$

Following our discussion elsewhere in this chapter, we can define the marginal rate of [technical] substitution as

$$\frac{d\,b}{d\,a} = -\frac{f_a}{f_b} \Rightarrow r = -\frac{d\,b}{d\,a} = \frac{f_a}{f_b} \tag{1.104}$$

so r is the rate at which you must add b to make up for a reduction in a to keep the level of output x unchanged. At this point, we recognize that r will not be constant if the production function is concave (or the input requirement set is convex). Recall the development of the isoquant (pp. 17–21).

Based on these definitions, Allen (1938, p. 341) defines the elasticity of substitution as

$$\sigma = \frac{\dfrac{a}{b} d\left(\dfrac{b}{a}\right)}{\dfrac{1}{r} d\,r}. \tag{1.105}$$

To understand this formulation, consider the relationship between the slope of the isoquant and the average ratio of inputs used depicted in Figure 1.17. Next, picture a change in this relationship as we decrease the amount of a used and increase the amount of b used such that the level of production remains unchanged in Figure 1.18.

To develop the consequences of this move mathematically, we start by examining the change from $\left(a^0, b^0\right)$ to (a', b') in Figure 1.18:

$$\begin{gathered} d\left(\frac{b}{a}\right) = \frac{a\,d\,b - b\,d\,a}{a^2} \\ d\,r = \frac{\partial r}{\partial b} d\,a + \frac{\partial r}{\partial b} d\,b \end{gathered} . \tag{1.106}$$

Next, by definition of the isoquant, we know that $d\,b = -f_a/f_b$ so that

$$d\,b = -\frac{f_a}{f_b} d\,a \Rightarrow d\left(\frac{b}{a}\right) = -\frac{ar + b}{a^2} d\,a. \tag{1.107}$$

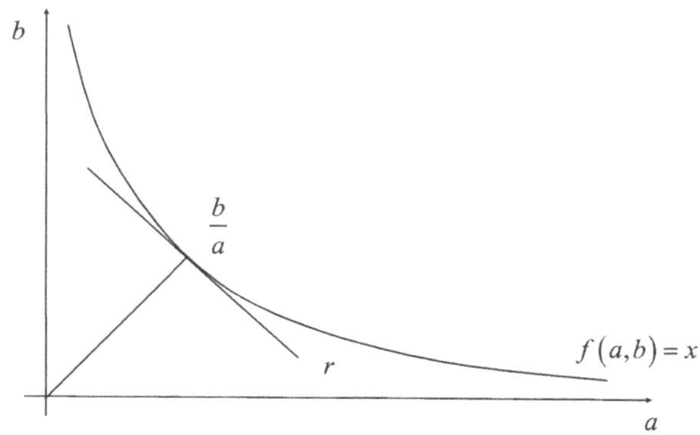

Fig. 1.17 Trade-off Between Inputs Along an Isoquant

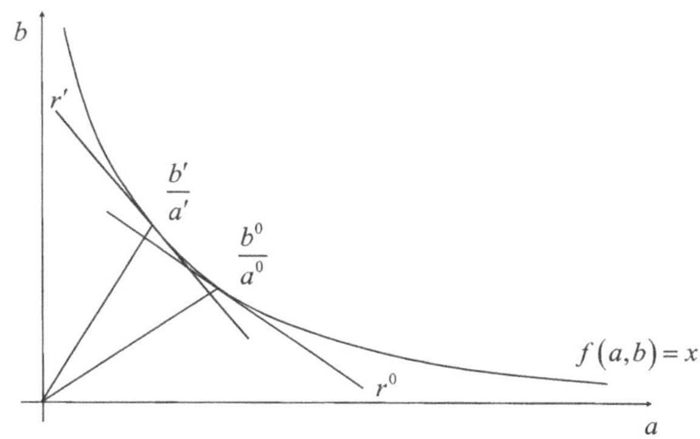

Fig. 1.18 Change in the Trade-off Between Inputs Along an Isoquant

Similarly, substituting this result into the $d\,r$ result,

$$\begin{aligned} d\,r &= \frac{\partial r}{\partial a} d\,a + \frac{\partial r}{\partial b}\left[-r d\,a\right] \\ &= \frac{\partial r}{\partial a} d\,a - r\frac{\partial r}{\partial b} d\,a \\ &= -\left(r\frac{\partial r}{\partial b} - \frac{\partial r}{\partial a}\right) d\,a. \end{aligned} \tag{1.108}$$

Combining Equations (1.106), (1.107), and (1.108) yields

$$\sigma = \frac{\dfrac{a}{b}\left[-\dfrac{ar+b}{a^2}\right]da}{\dfrac{1}{r}\left[-\left(r\dfrac{\partial r}{\partial b}-\dfrac{\partial r}{\partial a}\right)\right]da} = \frac{r}{ab}\frac{ar+b}{r\dfrac{\partial r}{\partial b}-\dfrac{\partial r}{\partial a}}. \tag{1.109}$$

Starting with $ar+b$, given $r = f_a/f_b$,

$$ar+b = a\frac{f_a}{f_b}+b = \frac{af_a+bf_b}{f_b}. \tag{1.110}$$

Substituting Equation (1.110) into (1.109) yields

$$\sigma = \frac{\dfrac{1}{f_b}[af_a+bf_b]}{ab\left[\dfrac{\partial r}{\partial b}-\dfrac{1}{r}\dfrac{\partial r}{\partial a}\right]}. \tag{1.111}$$

To finish the derivation, we work with the second term in the denominator of Equation (1.111)

$$\begin{aligned}\frac{\partial r}{\partial b}-\frac{1}{r}\frac{\partial r}{\partial a} &= \left[\frac{f_{ab}}{f_b}-\frac{f_af_{bb}}{f_b^2}\right]-\frac{f_b}{f_a}\left[\frac{f_{aa}}{f_b}-\frac{f_af_{ba}}{f_b^2}\right]\\ &= \frac{f_{ab}}{f_b}-\frac{f_af_{bb}}{f_b^2}-\frac{f_af_{aa}}{f_af_b}+\frac{f_af_bf_{ba}}{f_b^2}.\end{aligned} \tag{1.112}$$

Next, we want to substitute $f_{ab} = f_{ba}$ (i.e., Young's theorem) and factor out $1/f_b^2f_a$ from each term in Equation (1.112) to yield

$$\begin{aligned}\frac{\partial r}{\partial b}-\frac{1}{r}\frac{\partial r}{\partial a} &= \frac{1}{f_b^2f_a}\left[f_{ab}f_af_b-f_a^2f_{bb}-f_b^2f_{aa}+f_{ab}f_af_b\right]\\ &= \frac{1}{f_b^2f_a}\left[-f_a^2f_{bb}+2f_{ab}f_af_b-f_b^2f_{aa}\right].\end{aligned} \tag{1.113}$$

Substituting Equation (1.113) into Equation (1.111) yields

$$\sigma = \frac{f_a f_b \left(a f_a + b f_b\right)}{abT} \tag{1.114}$$

where

$$T = -\left(f_{aa} f_b^2 - 2 f_{ab} f_a f_b + f_{bb} f_a^2\right).$$

Note that T is a measure of the relative concavity of the production function.

Returning to the formulation in Equation (1.101), we compute the elasticity of substitution for the Cobb–Douglas production function:

$$f(x) = A x_1^{\alpha} x_2^{\beta} \Rightarrow \left\{ \begin{array}{l} \dfrac{\partial f(x_1, x_2)}{\partial x_1} = f_1 = \alpha \dfrac{A x_1^{\alpha} x_2^{\beta}}{x_1} \\ \dfrac{\partial f(x_1, x_2)}{\partial x_2} = f_2 = \beta \dfrac{A x_1^{\alpha} x_2^{\beta}}{x_2} \end{array} \right\} \Rightarrow \frac{f_1}{f_2} = \frac{\alpha x_2}{\beta x_1}. \tag{1.115}$$

Changing the variables in Equation (1.115), we start by letting

$$z(w) = \frac{f_1}{f_2} \text{ and } w = \frac{x_2}{x_1}. \tag{1.116}$$

Thus, the end result of Equation (1.115) substituting the result of Equation (1.116) yields

$$\frac{f_1}{f_2} = \frac{\alpha x_2}{\beta x_1} \Rightarrow z(w) = \frac{\alpha}{\beta} w. \tag{1.117}$$

Differentiating Equation (1.117) with respect to w yields

$$\frac{d\, z(w)}{dw} = \frac{\alpha}{\beta}. \tag{1.118}$$

Returning to the definition in Equation (1.101)

$$\frac{d\left(\dfrac{x_2}{x_1}\right)}{d\left(\dfrac{f_1}{f_2}\right)} = \frac{dw}{d\, z(w)} \Rightarrow \frac{1}{\dfrac{d\, z(w)}{dw}} = \frac{\beta}{\alpha}. \tag{1.119}$$

We conclude that

$$\sigma_{12}^{D} = \frac{\beta}{\alpha}\left(\frac{\dfrac{\alpha x_2}{\beta x_1}}{\dfrac{x_2}{x_1}}\right) = 1 \tag{1.120}$$

or the elasticity of substitution for the Cobb–Douglas is one by definition.

Allen partial elasticity of substitution is a generalization of the matrix expression above:

$$\sigma_{ij}^{D} = \frac{\sum_{i=1}^{n} x_i f_i}{x_i x_j}\frac{F_{ji}}{F}$$
$$F = \begin{vmatrix} 0 & f_1 & f_2 & \cdots & f_n \\ f_1 & f_{11} & f_{12} & \cdots & f_{1n} \\ f_2 & f_{12} & f_{22} & \cdots & f_{2n} \\ \vdots & \vdots & \vdots & \ddots & \vdots \\ f_n & f_{1n} & f_{2n} & \cdots & f_{nn} \end{vmatrix}. \tag{1.121}$$

Writing the bordered Hessian of the production surface,

$$F = \begin{vmatrix} 0 & f_1 & f_2 \\ f_1 & f_{11} & f_{12} \\ f_2 & f_{12} & f_{22} \end{vmatrix}. \tag{1.122}$$

This Hessian represents the changes in x_1 and x_2 such that y remains unchanged. Based on this transformation, the direct elasticity of substitution can be written as

$$\sigma_{12}^{D} = \frac{x_1 f_1 + x_2 f_2}{x_1 x_2}\frac{F_{12}}{F}$$
$$F_{12} = \begin{vmatrix} 0 & f_2 \\ f_1 & f_{12} \end{vmatrix} = -f_1 f_2$$
$$F = \begin{vmatrix} 0 & f_1 & f_2 \\ f_1 & f_{11} & f_{12} \\ f_2 & f_{12} & f_{22} \end{vmatrix} = -f_1\begin{vmatrix} f_1 & f_2 \\ f_{12} & f_{22} \end{vmatrix} + f_2\begin{vmatrix} f_1 & f_2 \\ f_{11} & f_{12} \end{vmatrix}$$

$$
\begin{aligned}
&= -f_1\left(f_1 f_{22} - f_2 f_{12}\right) + f_2\left(f_1 f_{12} - f_2 f_{11}\right) \\
&= -f_1^2 f_{22} + 2 f_1 f_2 f_{12} - f_2^2 f_{11}.
\end{aligned} \tag{1.123}
$$

Note that the result of Equation (1.123) is equivalent to the measure T in Equation (1.114).

In order to demonstrate the mechanics of this definition, we apply Equation (1.123) to the Cobb–Douglas production function. To simplify our derivations, we use a slight modification to the marginal products of this production function:

$$
\begin{aligned}
\frac{\partial f(x_1, x_2)}{\partial x_1} &= \alpha x_1^{\alpha-1} x_2^{\beta} = \frac{\alpha x_1^{\alpha} x_2^{\beta}}{x_1} = \alpha \frac{y}{x_1} \\
\frac{\partial f(x_1, x_2)}{\partial x_2} &= \beta x_1^{\alpha} x_2^{\beta-1} = \frac{\beta x_1^{\alpha} x_2^{\beta}}{x x_2} = \beta \frac{y}{x_2}
\end{aligned} \tag{1.124}
$$

since $x_1^{\alpha} x_2^{\beta} = y$. Extending the results in Equation (1.124) to the second derivatives, the F matrix can be computed as

$$
F = \begin{vmatrix}
0 & \alpha \dfrac{y}{x_1} & \beta \dfrac{y}{x_2} \\
\alpha \dfrac{y}{x_1} & \alpha(\alpha - 1)\dfrac{y^2}{x_1^2} & \alpha\beta \dfrac{y^2}{x_1 x_2} \\
\beta \dfrac{y}{x_2} & \alpha\beta \dfrac{y^2}{x_1 x_2} & \beta(\beta - 1)\dfrac{y^2}{x_2^2}
\end{vmatrix}. \tag{1.125}
$$

Using the results in (1.125) implies

$$
F_{12} = (-1)^{1+2} \begin{vmatrix}
0 & \beta \dfrac{y}{x_2} \\
\alpha \dfrac{y}{x_1} & \alpha\beta \dfrac{y^2}{x_1 x_2}
\end{vmatrix} = \frac{\alpha\beta y^2}{x_1 x_2}. \tag{1.126}
$$

Again, building on the results for $|F_{12}|$ in (1.126) yields

$$
\frac{F_{12}}{F} = \frac{\dfrac{\alpha\beta y^2}{x_1 x_2}}{\dfrac{\alpha\beta(\alpha+\beta) y^3}{x_1^2 x_2^2}} = \frac{x_1 x_2}{(\alpha+\beta) y}. \tag{1.127}
$$

Finally, integrating the results for Equation (1.127) with the specification of the elasticity of substitution in Equation (1.123) yields

$$\sigma_{12}^{D} = \frac{x_1 \dfrac{\alpha y}{x_1} + x_2 \dfrac{\beta y}{x_2}}{x_1 x_2} \frac{x_1 x_2}{(\alpha + \beta)\, y} = \frac{\alpha y + \beta y}{x_1 x_2} \frac{x_1 x_2}{(\alpha + \beta)\, y} = 1. \tag{1.128}$$

In order to more fully understand the elasticity of substitution formula, we start from the first- and second-order conditions from the constrained maximization problem. Specifically, assume that we want to determine the point that maximizes an objective function $f(x)$ subject to the constraint $g(x) = b$. Mathematically, the problem becomes

$$\begin{aligned} &\max_x f(x) \\ &\text{s.t. } g(x) = b. \end{aligned} \tag{1.129}$$

Transforming the problem into the Lagrange form yields

$$\max_{x,\lambda} L = f(x) - \lambda\,(b - g(x)) \tag{1.130}$$

where L is the value of the constrained optimum and λ is the Lagrange multiplier which depicts the derivative of the objective function with respect to the right-hand side of the constraint at the optimal point. The first-order necessary conditions for the optimum are then derived as

$$\nabla_{(\lambda,x)} L = \begin{bmatrix} b - g\,(x) \\ -\lambda \dfrac{\partial g\,(x)}{\partial x_1} + \dfrac{\partial f\,(x)}{\partial x_1} \\ \vdots \\ -\lambda \dfrac{\partial g\,(x)}{\partial x_n} + \dfrac{\partial f\,(x)}{\partial x_n} \end{bmatrix} = \begin{bmatrix} 0 \\ 0 \\ \vdots \\ 0 \end{bmatrix} \tag{1.131}$$

which are the standard first-order conditions. To determine the point that maximizes the objective function, we solve for the point that satisfies these $n+1$ first-order conditions simultaneously. Given that such a point exists, the next step is to verify that this stationary point is a maximum. Following the standard rules of calculus, this requires the bordered Hessian constructed from Equation (1.131) to be negative semi-definite. Thus, computing

$$\nabla^2_{(\lambda,x)(\lambda,x)}L = \begin{bmatrix} d\lambda \\ dx_1 \\ \vdots \\ dx_n \end{bmatrix}' \begin{bmatrix} 0 & \frac{\partial g(x)}{\partial x_1} & \cdots & \frac{\partial g(x)}{\partial x_n} \\ \frac{\partial g(x)}{\partial x_1} & -\lambda\frac{\partial^2 g(x)}{\partial x_1^2} + \frac{\partial^2 f(x)}{\partial x_1^2} & \cdots & -\lambda\frac{\partial^2 g(x)}{\partial x_1 \partial x_n} + \frac{\partial^2 f(x)}{\partial x_1 \partial x_n} \\ \vdots & \vdots & \ddots & \vdots \\ \frac{\partial g(x)}{\partial x_n} & -\lambda\frac{\partial^2 g(x)}{\partial x_n \partial x_1} + \frac{\partial^2 f(x)}{\partial x_n \partial x_1} & \cdots & -\lambda\frac{\partial^2 g(x)}{\partial x_n^2} + \frac{\partial^2 f(x)}{\partial x_n^2} \end{bmatrix} \times \begin{bmatrix} d\lambda \\ dx_1 \\ \vdots \\ dx_n \end{bmatrix} \leq 0 \tag{1.132}$$

for all $d\lambda, dx_1, \ldots, dx_2$.

Modifying Equation (1.132) slightly, we consider a different form of the Hessian matrix

$$\begin{bmatrix} dY \\ dx_1 \\ dx_2 \\ dx_3 \end{bmatrix}' \begin{bmatrix} 0 & f_1 & f_2 & f_3 \\ f_1 & f_{11} & f_{12} & f_{13} \\ f_2 & f_{21} & f_{22} & f_{23} \\ f_3 & f_{31} & f_{32} & f_{33} \end{bmatrix} \begin{bmatrix} dY \\ dx_1 \\ dx_2 \\ dx_3 \end{bmatrix}. \tag{1.133}$$

Working through this matrix multiplication yields

$$2\,dY \left(\sum_{i=1}^{3} f_i x_i \right) + \sum_{i=1}^{3} \sum_{j=1}^{3} f_{ij} dx_i dx_j. \tag{1.134}$$

This first part of the expression guarantees that dx_i/dx_j is constrained so that there is no change in output (or the movement is around an isoquant)

$$dY = f_1 dx_1 + f_2 dx_2 + f_3 dx_3 = 0. \tag{1.135}$$

The remainder is simply a concavity measure for the production function. Thus, we have a measure of the relative concavity subject to an isoquant constraint. To refine the measure, let us restrict our attention to a production function with three inputs:

$$\begin{bmatrix} dY \\ dx_1 \\ dx_2 \\ dx_3 \end{bmatrix}' \begin{bmatrix} 0 & f_1 & f_2 & f_3 \\ f_1 & f_{11} & f_{12} & f_{13} \\ f_2 & f_{21} & f_{22} & f_{23} \\ f_3 & f_{31} & f_{32} & f_{33} \end{bmatrix} \begin{bmatrix} dY \\ dx_1 \\ dx_2 \\ dx_3 \end{bmatrix} \leq 0. \tag{1.136}$$

Next, consider using the linear relationship in Equation (1.136) to solve for the value of a change in the value of x_2 (dx_2)

$$\begin{bmatrix} 0 & f_1 & f_2 & f_3 \\ f_1 & f_{11} & f_{12} & f_{13} \\ f_2 & f_{21} & f_{22} & f_{23} \\ f_3 & f_{31} & f_{32} & f_{33} \end{bmatrix} \begin{bmatrix} dY \\ dx_1 \\ dx_2 \\ dx_3 \end{bmatrix} = \begin{bmatrix} 0 \\ 0 \\ dx_2 \\ 0 \end{bmatrix}. \tag{1.137}$$

Thus, we want to solve for the change in the other variables based on a change in x_2 that keeps the output constant (e.g., such that the production constraint is met). Simplifying this expression slightly

$$\begin{bmatrix} 0 & f_1 & f_2 & f_3 \\ f_1 & f_{11} & f_{12} & f_{13} \\ f_2 & f_{21} & f_{22} & f_{23} \\ f_3 & f_{31} & f_{32} & f_{33} \end{bmatrix} \begin{bmatrix} \frac{dY}{dx_2} \\ \frac{dx_1}{dx_2} \\ \frac{dx_2}{dx_2} \\ \frac{dx_3}{dx_2} \end{bmatrix} = \begin{bmatrix} 0 \\ 0 \\ 1 \\ 0 \end{bmatrix}. \tag{1.138}$$

Hence, we can solve for the change in one input (say x_1) with respect to another (say x_2) such that the total physical product remains unchanged using Cramer's rule

$$\frac{dx_1}{dx_2} = \frac{\begin{vmatrix} 0 & 0 & f_2 & f_3 \\ f_1 & 0 & f_{12} & f_{13} \\ f_2 & 1 & f_{22} & f_{23} \\ f_3 & 0 & f_{32} & f_{33} \end{vmatrix}}{\begin{vmatrix} 0 & f_1 & f_2 & f_3 \\ f_1 & f_{11} & f_{12} & f_{13} \\ f_2 & f_{21} & f_{22} & f_{23} \\ f_3 & f_{31} & f_{32} & f_{33} \end{vmatrix}} = \frac{(-1)^{(1+2)} \begin{vmatrix} 0 & f_2 & f_3 \\ f_1 & f_{12} & f_{13} \\ f_3 & f_{32} & f_{33} \end{vmatrix}}{\begin{vmatrix} 0 & f_1 & f_2 & f_3 \\ f_1 & f_{11} & f_{12} & f_{13} \\ f_2 & f_{21} & f_{22} & f_{23} \\ f_3 & f_{31} & f_{32} & f_{33} \end{vmatrix}}. \tag{1.139}$$

Thus, the general form of Equation (1.121)

$$\sigma_{ij}^{D} = \frac{\sum_{i=1}^{n} x_i f_i}{x_i x_j} \left. \frac{dx_i}{dx_j} \right|_{dY=0} . \tag{1.140}$$

As an example, consider the Allen partial elasticities for the constant elasticity of substitution production function

$$f(x_1, x_2, x_3) = \left[0.6870 x_1^{-0.0526} + 0.0886 x_2^{-0.0526} + 0.1838 x_3^{-0.0526}\right]^{-19} . \tag{1.141}$$

Starting with the partial derivatives

$$\begin{aligned}
\frac{\partial f(x_1, x_2, x_3)}{\partial x_1} &= \frac{0.6866}{x_1^{1.0526}\left(\frac{0.1838}{x_3^{0.0526}} + \frac{0.0886}{x_2^{0.0526}} + \frac{0.6870}{x_1^{0.0526}}\right)^{20}} \\
\frac{\partial f(x_1, x_2, x_3)}{\partial x_2} &= \frac{0.08855}{x_2^{1.0526}\left(\frac{0.1838}{x_3^{0.0526}} + \frac{0.0886}{x_2^{0.0526}} + \frac{0.6870}{x_1^{0.0526}}\right)^{20}} . \\
\frac{\partial f(x_1, x_2, x_3)}{\partial x_3} &= \frac{0.18369}{x_3^{1.0526}\left(\frac{0.1838}{x_3^{0.0526}} + \frac{0.0886}{x_2^{0.0526}} + \frac{0.6870}{x_1^{0.0526}}\right)^{20}}
\end{aligned} \tag{1.142}$$

The second derivatives can then be derived as follows:

$$\begin{aligned}
\frac{\partial f^2(x_1, x_2, x_3)}{\partial x_1^2} &= \frac{0.4962}{x_1^{2.1052}\left(\frac{0.1838}{x_3^{0.0526}} + \frac{0.0886}{x_2^{0.0526}} + \frac{0.6870}{x_1^{0.0526}}\right)^{21}} \\
&\quad - \frac{0.7227}{x_1^{2.0526}\left(\frac{0.1838}{x_3^{0.0526}} + \frac{0.0886}{x_2^{0.0526}} + \frac{0.687}{x_1^{0.0526}}\right)^{20}} \\
\frac{\partial f^2(x_1, x_2, x_3)}{\partial x_1 \partial x_2} &= \frac{0.06399}{x_1^{1.0526} x_2^{1.0526}\left(\frac{0.1838}{x_3^{0.0526}} + \frac{0.0886}{x_2^{0.0526}} + \frac{0.687}{x_1^{0.0526}}\right)^{21}}
\end{aligned}$$

$$\frac{\partial f^2(x_1,x_2,x_3)}{\partial x_1 \partial x_3} = \frac{0.1328}{x_1^{1.0526} x_3^{1.0526}\left(\frac{0.1838}{x_3^{0.0526}}+\frac{0.0886}{x_2^{0.0526}}+\frac{0.687}{x_1^{0.0526}}\right)^{21}}$$

$$\frac{\partial f^2(x_1,x_2,x_3)}{\partial x_2^2} = \frac{0.008253}{x_2^{2.1052}\left(\frac{0.1838}{x_3^{0.0526}}+\frac{0.0886}{x_2^{0.0526}}+\frac{0.6870}{x_1^{0.0526}}\right)^{21}} - \frac{0.09320}{x_2^{2.0526}\left(\frac{0.1838}{x_3^{0.0526}}+\frac{0.0886}{x_2^{0.0526}}+\frac{0.687}{x_1^{0.0526}}\right)^{20}}.$$

$$\frac{\partial f^2(x_1,x_2,x_3)}{\partial x_2 \partial x_3} = \frac{0.01712}{x_2^{1.0526} x_3^{1.0526}\left(\frac{0.1838}{x_3^{0.0526}}+\frac{0.0886}{x_2^{0.0526}}+\frac{0.687}{x_1^{0.0526}}\right)^{21}}$$

$$\frac{\partial f^2(x_1,x_2,x_3)}{\partial x_3^2} = \frac{0.03552}{x_3^{2.1052}\left(\frac{0.1838}{x_3^{0.0526}}+\frac{0.0886}{x_2^{0.0526}}+\frac{0.687}{x_1^{0.0526}}\right)^{21}} - \frac{0.1934}{\left(x_3^{2.0526}\frac{0.1838}{x_3^{0.0526}}+\frac{0.0886}{x_2^{0.0526}}+\frac{0.687}{x_1^{0.0526}}\right)^{20}} \tag{1.143}$$

The numerical value of the determinant matrix in Equation (1.121) can be expressed as

$$F = \begin{bmatrix} 0 & 1.5714 & 0.2027 & 0.4204 \\ 1.5714 & -0.09406 & 0.03053 & 0.06334 \\ 0.2027 & 0.03053 & -0.03873 & 0.008169 \\ 0.4204 & 0.06334 & 0.008169 & -0.07156 \end{bmatrix} \tag{1.144}$$

assuming that $x_1 = 5$, $x_2 = 5$, and $x_3 = 5$.

First considering the elasticity of substitution between input 1 and input 2 yields a principle minor of

$$F_{12} = (-1)^{1+2} \begin{vmatrix} 0 & 1.5714 & 0.4204 \\ 0.2027 & 0.03053 & 0.008169 \\ 0.4204 & 0.06334 & -0.07156 \end{vmatrix} \tag{1.145}$$

yielding an empirical estimate of the elasticity of

$$\sigma_{12}^{D} = \frac{10.9722}{25}\frac{-0.02818}{-0.01302} = 0.9501. \tag{1.146}$$

The Hicksian elasticities of substitution have one interesting characteristic — they are symmetric. As a final extension, we consider the Morishima elasticities which are a general formulation of the Hicksian elasticities such that $\sigma_{ij} = \sigma_{ji}$ if and only if the production function exhibits constant-elasticity of substitution (Murota, 1977). As a starting point, consider a slight reformulation of Equation (1.101)

$$\sigma_{ij} = \frac{\partial \ln\left(\frac{x_j}{x_i}\right)}{\partial \ln\left(\mu_i^j\right)},\ \mu_i^j = \frac{f_k\left(x_1, x_2, x_3\right)}{f_i\left(x_1, x_2, x_3\right)}. \tag{1.147}$$

Note by the logarithmic differential form

$$\partial \ln\left(\frac{x_j}{x_i}\right) = \frac{1}{\frac{x_j}{x_i}}\partial\left(\frac{x_j}{x_i}\right) \tag{1.148}$$

and

$$\partial \ln\left(\mu_i^j\right) = \partial \ln\left(\frac{f_k}{f_i}\right) = \frac{1}{\frac{f_k}{f_i}}\partial\left(\frac{f_k}{f_i}\right) \tag{1.149}$$

which yields exactly Equation (1.101).

Taking the derivative in Equation (1.147) yields

$$\sigma_{ij} = \frac{\mu_i^j}{x_i}\frac{\partial x_i}{\partial \mu_i^j} - \frac{\mu_i^j}{x_j}\frac{\partial x_j}{\partial \mu_i^j} \tag{1.150}$$

since $\ln(x_j/x_i) = \ln(x_j)\ln(x_i)$. The key concept is that $\partial x_i/\partial \mu_i^j$ and $\partial x_j/\partial \mu_i^j$ can be computed in two ways. First, we can assume that y and x_k are fixed and that x_i, x_j, and μ_i^j are variable:

$$\begin{aligned} \left.\frac{\partial x_i}{\partial \mu_i^j}\right|_{y \text{ and } x_k \text{ constant}} &= f_i^2 f_j\left(-f_j^2 f_i i + 2 f_i f_j f_{ij} - f_1^2 f_{jj}\right) \\ \left.\frac{\partial x_j}{\partial \mu_i^j}\right|_{y \text{ and } x_k \text{ constant}} &= f_i^3\left(-f_j^2 f_{ii} + 2 f_i f_j f_{ij} - f_i^2 f_{jj}\right) \end{aligned}. \tag{1.151}$$

Second, we can assume that y and μ_i^k are fixed while the factors and other marginal rates of substitution are variable:

$$\begin{aligned} \left.\frac{\partial x_i}{\partial \mu_i^j}\right|_{y \text{ and } \mu_i^k \text{ constant}} &= \frac{f_i F_{ij}}{F} \\ \left.\frac{\partial x_j}{\partial \mu_i^j}\right|_{y \text{ and } \mu_i^k \text{ constant}} &= \frac{f_i F_{jj}}{F} \end{aligned} . \tag{1.152}$$

The first set of assumptions yields the standard Hicksian elasticity

$$\sigma_{ij}^D = \frac{f_i f_j \left(f_i f_j + f_i x_j\right)}{x_i x_j \left(-f_j^2 f_{ii} + 2 f_i f_j f_{ij} - f_i^2 f_{jj}\right)} \tag{1.153}$$

while the second yields the Morishima elasticity of substitution

$$\sigma_{ij}^M = \frac{f_j}{x_i} \frac{F_{ij}}{F} - \frac{f_j}{x_j} \frac{F_{jj}}{F}. \tag{1.154}$$

This generalization can be rewritten as a function of the Allen elasticities as

$$\sigma_{ij}^M = \frac{f_j x_j}{\sum_k f_k x_k} \left(\sigma_{ij} - \sigma_{jj}\right). \tag{1.155}$$

Another comparison of Hicksian and Morishima elasticities is provided by Blackorby and Russell (1981, 1989) within the context of cost functions.

1.3 Some Simple Production Mechanics

Up until this point, we have been primarily interested in the technical relationships implied by the production function (with the exception of Section 1.1.4 where we derived the cost function and the conditional demand function). However, returning to our original discussion, economists are not engineers. We are interested in the production function in that it allows us to say something about economic behavior. This section examines economic behavior based on the production function.

Wicksteed on Input Use

In a like manner [to consumption], if he contemplates taking on or discharging a workman, he will ask himself whether that workman will be worth his wage or not, i.e., whether he will increase the product, other factors remaining constant, at least to the extent of his wage; and he will take on more men as long as the last one earns at least as much as his wage, but no longer. The man, on his side, can insist on having as much as the marginal significance of his work, i.e., as much as the difference to the product the withdrawal of his work would make. Preserving a uniform notation, we may say that the market price of K is determined by the significance of an increment or decrement of K to the total communal product, which we will call P. Then, from the general point of view, any particular kind of labor, K, can insist on remuneration at the rate dP/dK per unit, and from the individual point of view (the price of labor being fixed at $w = dP/dK$), the individual entrepreneur will go on feeding his land, capital, etc., with that particular kind of labor, until in his particular concern, the relation is established: $dP/dK = w = dP/dK$ (Wicksteed, 1894, p. 12).

1.3.1 *Single Produce Primal Optimization*

1.3.1.1 *Profit maximization*

Starting with the Cobb–Douglas production function and maximizing profit with respect to input choice yields,

$$
\max\ \pi = p_Y x_1^{\alpha} x_2^{\beta} - w_1 x_1 - w_2 x_2
$$

$$
\left.\begin{aligned}
\frac{\partial \pi}{\partial x_1} &= p_Y \alpha \frac{Y}{x_1} - w_1 = 0 \\
\frac{\partial \pi}{\partial x_2} &= p_Y \beta \frac{Y}{x_2} - w_2 = 0
\end{aligned}\right\} \Rightarrow x_2 = \frac{w_1}{w_2}\frac{\beta}{\alpha} x_1 \tag{1.156}
$$

where p_Y is the output, w_1 is the input price for the first input, and w_2 is the price of the second input. Substituting this result back into the first-order condition yields

$$\begin{aligned} p_Y \alpha \left(x_1^{\alpha-1} x_2^{\beta} \right) &= w_1 \\ p_Y \alpha \left(x_1^{\alpha-1} \left[\frac{w_1}{w_2} \frac{\beta}{\alpha} x_1 \right]^{\beta} \right) &= w_1 \\ x_1^{\alpha+\beta-1} &= p_Y^{-1} \alpha^{\beta-1} \beta^{-\beta} w_2^{\beta} w_1^{1-\beta} \\ x_1 = p_Y^{-\frac{1}{\alpha+\beta-1}} \alpha^{\frac{\beta-1}{\alpha+\beta-1}} \beta^{-\frac{\beta}{\alpha+\beta-1}} & w_2^{\frac{\beta}{\alpha+\beta-1}} w_1^{\frac{1-\beta}{\alpha+\beta-1}} \end{aligned} \quad . \tag{1.157}$$

Production in the Economic Sense — Frisch

The fundamental question of the place of judgment in the analysis is encountered in every aspect of the theory of production, as soon as we proceed beyond the purely technical description of the production process. By production in the *economic* sense, we mean the attempt to create a product which is *more highly valued* than the original input elements. Examples of this come readily to mind.

When a farmer has to decide whether he is to produce grain or potatoes in his fields, he does so — assuming that he belongs to the great majority who are primarily concerned with economic gain — by comparing the prices of grain and potatoes with the costs involved in these two kinds of production. In other words, in his case, the basis of value judgment is simply provided by the market prices. Market prices provide the *evaluation coefficients* on which he bases himself, i.e., the coefficients he uses to reduce goods and services to a common denominator, so that they are capable of comparison. On this basis, there is a comparison which enables him to define the concept of *economic* production.

But agricultural production can also be evaluated in other ways. A nutrition expert, for example, will reckon in terms of calories and vitamins and other basic constituents of foodstuffs, and this yardstick is in no way less realistic than the price gauge (Frisch, 1965, pp. 8–9).

The second demand curve is then derived from the relationship between the two first-order conditions

$$\begin{aligned} x_2 &= \frac{w_1}{w_2}\frac{\beta}{\alpha}\left[p_Y^{-\frac{1}{\alpha+\beta-1}}\alpha^{\frac{\beta-1}{\alpha+\beta-1}}\beta^{-\frac{\beta}{\alpha+\beta-1}}w_2^{\frac{\beta}{\alpha+\beta-1}}w_1^{\frac{1-\beta}{\alpha+\beta-1}}\right] \\ x_2 &= p_Y^{-\frac{1}{\alpha+\beta-1}}\alpha^{-\frac{\alpha}{\alpha+\beta-1}}\beta^{\frac{\alpha-1}{\alpha+\beta-1}}w_2^{\frac{1-\alpha}{\alpha+\beta-1}}w_1^{\frac{\alpha}{\alpha+\beta-1}} \end{aligned}. \tag{1.158}$$

By convention

$$\begin{aligned} x_1^*(p_Y, w_1, w_2) &= p_Y^{\frac{1}{1-\alpha-\beta}}\left[\frac{\alpha}{w_1}\right]^{\frac{1-\beta}{1-\alpha-\beta}}\left[\frac{\beta}{w_2}\right]^{\frac{\beta}{1-\alpha-\beta}} \\ x_2^*(p_Y, w_1, w_2) &= p_Y^{\frac{1}{1-\alpha-\beta}}\left[\frac{\alpha}{w_1}\right]^{\frac{\alpha}{1-\alpha-\beta}}\left[\frac{\beta}{w_2}\right]^{\frac{1-\alpha}{1-\alpha-\beta}} \end{aligned}. \tag{1.159}$$

These factor demands are not conditioned on the level of output (e.g., the output response is part of the formulation as derived below).

Substituting the optimum levels of x_1 and x_2 into the production function can then derive the supply function. This yields production as a function of output and input prices:

$$\begin{aligned} Y^*(p_Y, w_1, w_2) &= \left[p_Y^{\frac{1}{1-\alpha-\beta}}\left(\frac{\alpha}{w_1}\right)^{\frac{1-\beta}{1-\alpha-\beta}}\left(\frac{\beta}{w_2}\right)^{\frac{\beta}{1-\alpha-\beta}}\right]^{\alpha} \\ &\quad\times\left[p_Y^{\frac{1}{1-\alpha-\beta}}\left(\frac{\alpha}{w_1}\right)^{\frac{\alpha}{1-\alpha-\beta}}\left(\frac{\beta}{w_2}\right)^{\frac{1-\alpha}{1-\alpha-\beta}}\right]^{\beta} \\ &= p_Y^{\frac{\alpha+\beta}{1-\alpha-\beta}}\left[\frac{\alpha}{w_1}\right]^{\frac{\alpha-\alpha\beta+\alpha\beta}{1-\alpha-\beta}}\left[\frac{\beta}{w_2}\right]^{\frac{\beta-\alpha\beta+\alpha\beta}{1-\alpha-\beta}} \\ &= p_Y^{\frac{\alpha+\beta}{1-\alpha-\beta}}\left[\frac{\alpha}{w_1}\right]^{\frac{\alpha}{1-\alpha-\beta}}\left[\frac{\beta}{w_2}\right]^{\frac{\beta}{1-\alpha-\beta}}. \end{aligned} \tag{1.160}$$

The dual profit function is simply the supply function and demand functions substituted into the original profit formulation

$$\begin{aligned}\pi^*(p_Y, w_1, w_2) = p_Y & \left[p_Y^{\frac{\alpha+\beta}{1-\alpha-\beta}} \left(\frac{\alpha}{w_1}\right)^{\frac{\alpha}{1-\alpha-\beta}} \left(\frac{\beta}{w_2}\right)^{\frac{\beta}{1-\alpha-\beta}}\right] \\ & - w_1 \left[p_Y^{\frac{1}{1-\alpha-\beta}} \left(\frac{\alpha}{w_1}\right)^{\frac{1-\beta}{1-\alpha-\beta}} \left(\frac{\beta}{w_2}\right)^{\frac{\beta}{1-\alpha-\beta}}\right]. \\ & - w_2 \left[p_Y^{\frac{1}{1-\alpha-\beta}} \left(\frac{\alpha}{w_1}\right)^{\frac{\alpha}{1-\alpha-\beta}} \left(\frac{\beta}{w_2}\right)^{\frac{1-\alpha}{1-\alpha-\beta}}\right]\end{aligned} \tag{1.161}$$

Most of the interesting dual results follow directly from Equation (1.161). The derivative of the profit function with respect to the output price yields the supply function while the derivative of the profit function with respect to an input price yields the input demand functions.

1.3.1.2 *Cost minimization*

The cost minimization derivation for the Cobb–Douglas production is presented in Section 1.1.4. However, the profit maximization relationship presented in Equation (1.161) can be derived from the cost function presented in Equation (1.75) by solving

$$\max \pi = p_Y Y - C(Y, w_1, w_2) \tag{1.162}$$

using the result from Equation (1.160)

$$Y^*(p_Y, w_1, w_2) \Rightarrow Y \text{ s.t. } p_Y - \frac{\partial C(Y, w_1, w_2)}{\partial Y} = 0. \tag{1.163}$$

Actually, the solution of $Y^*(.)$ will be the supply function above.

1.3.2 *Multiproduct Primal Functions*

We want to briefly discuss the theoretical application of the multiproduct primal function within the context of a planting problem. Specifically, assume that there exists a multivariate production function, $f(y, x)$, where y is a vector of (two) outputs and x is a vector of (two) inputs. The profit function for this formulation can be formulated as

$$\begin{gathered} \max \pi = p_1 y_1 + p_2 y_2 - w_1 x_1 - w_2 x_2 \\ \text{s.t. } f(y, x) = 0. \end{gathered} \tag{1.164}$$

Again, the Lagrangian for this formulation becomes

$$L = p_1 y_1 + p_2 y_2 - w_1 x_1 - w_2 x_2 - \lambda (f(y, x)) \tag{1.165}$$

which yields the first-order conditions

$$\begin{gathered} \frac{\partial L}{\partial y_1} = p_1 - \lambda \frac{\partial f(.)}{\partial y_1} \leq 0, \; \frac{\partial L}{\partial y_2} = p_2 - \lambda \frac{\partial f(.)}{\partial y_2} \\ \frac{\partial L}{\partial y_1} y_1 = 0, \; \frac{\partial L}{\partial y_2} y_2 = 0 \\ \frac{\partial L}{\partial x_1} = -w_1 - \lambda \frac{\partial f(.)}{\partial x_1} \leq 0, \; \frac{\partial f(.)}{\partial x_2} = -w_2 - \lambda \frac{\partial f(.)}{\partial x_2} \leq 0 \\ \frac{\partial L}{\partial x_1} x_1 = 0, \; \frac{\partial L}{\partial x_2} x_2 = 0 \end{gathered}. \tag{1.166}$$

Taken together, these conditions imply that the value of marginal product of each input equals the input price if positive quantities of each output are produced and positive quantities of inputs are used. These conditions admit three possible solutions. First, if only y_1 could be produced,

$$\begin{gathered} \frac{\partial L}{\partial y_1} = p_1 - \lambda \frac{\partial f(.)}{\partial y_1} = 0, \; y_1 > 0 \\ \frac{\partial L}{\partial y_2} = p_2 - \lambda \frac{\partial f(.)}{\partial y_2} < 0, \; y_2 = 0 \end{gathered}. \tag{1.167}$$

Second, if only y_2 could be produced,

$$\begin{gathered} \frac{\partial L}{\partial y_1} = p_1 - \lambda \frac{\partial f(.)}{\partial y_1} < 0, \; y_1 = 0 \\ \frac{\partial L}{\partial y_2} = p_2 - \lambda \frac{\partial f(.)}{\partial y_2} = 0, \; y_2 > 0 \end{gathered}. \tag{1.168}$$

Third, if both outputs could be produced,

$$\begin{aligned}\frac{\partial L}{\partial y_1} &= p_1 - \lambda\frac{\partial f(.)}{\partial y_1} = 0,\ y_1 > 0 \\ \frac{\partial L}{\partial y_2} &= p_2 - \lambda\frac{\partial f(.)}{\partial y_2} = 0,\ y_2 > 0\end{aligned}. \tag{1.169}$$

Joint Production — Frisch

Finally, we have the case of *joint* production and joint products. In this case, the technical process itself contains an element which makes it impossible (or very difficult) to produce one product without at the same time producing one or more other products. Gas, coke, and tar are in this sense joint products, and the same is true of wool and mutton. According to the value that the various products represent out of the total production value, we speak of main products, bi-products, and waste products. A change in the price situation may result in the bi-product or even the waste product being elevated to the status of main product.

The relative quantities of joint products produced are not always determined strictly on technical grounds, but are capable of being varied, at any rate, within certain limits. Thus, by changing over from one breed of sheep to another, one might get more wool and less meat, or vice versa. As a rule, any change of this kind will involve costs (measured in terms of prices or other value judgment coefficients), and the question of which relative quantity to aim at will therefore be one of profitability (Frisch, 1965, pp. 361–362).

If both goods are produced, the optimum ratio of production can be depicted:

$$\frac{p_1}{p_2} = \frac{\lambda\dfrac{\partial f(.)}{\partial y_1}}{\lambda\dfrac{\partial f(.)}{\partial y_2}} = \frac{\partial y_2}{\partial y_1}. \tag{1.170}$$

To make this clearer, we need some concept of what this multi-output production function would look like. One alternative would be to take a general expansion of the generic production function in Equation (1.77). For example, taking the second-order Taylor series expansion of Equation (1.77) yields

$$F(y,x) \approx \alpha_0 + \begin{bmatrix} \alpha_1 \\ \alpha_2 \\ \beta_1 \\ \beta_2 \\ \beta_3 \end{bmatrix}' \begin{bmatrix} y_1 \\ y_2 \\ x_1 \\ x_2 \\ x_2 \end{bmatrix} \qquad . \tag{1.171}$$
$$\frac{1}{2}\begin{bmatrix} y_1 \\ y_2 \\ x_1 \\ x_2 \\ x_2 \end{bmatrix}' \begin{bmatrix} A_{11} & A_{12} & \Gamma_{11} & \Gamma_{12} & \Gamma_{13} \\ A_{12} & A_{22} & \Gamma_{21} & \Gamma_{22} & \Gamma_{23} \\ \Gamma_{11} & \Gamma_{21} & B_{11} & B_{12} & B_{13} \\ \Gamma_{12} & \Gamma_{22} & B_{12} & B_{22} & B_{23} \\ \Gamma_{13} & \Gamma_{23} & B_{13} & B_{12} & B_{33} \end{bmatrix} \begin{bmatrix} y_1 \\ y_2 \\ x_1 \\ x_2 \\ x_2 \end{bmatrix} = 0$$

For identification purposes, we divide through by α_1, implicitly identifying the empirical model on y_1:

$$\tilde{\alpha}_0 + \begin{bmatrix} 1 \\ \tilde{\alpha}_2 \\ \tilde{\beta}_1 \\ \tilde{\beta}_2 \\ \tilde{\beta}_3 \end{bmatrix}' \begin{bmatrix} y_1 \\ y_2 \\ x_1 \\ x_2 \\ x_2 \end{bmatrix} \qquad . \tag{1.172}$$
$$\frac{1}{2}\begin{bmatrix} y_1 \\ y_2 \\ x_1 \\ x_2 \\ x_2 \end{bmatrix}' \begin{bmatrix} \tilde{A}_{11} & \tilde{A}_{12} & \tilde{\Gamma}_{11} & \tilde{\Gamma}_{12} & \tilde{\Gamma}_{13} \\ A_{12} & A_{22} & \tilde{\Gamma}_{21} & \tilde{\Gamma}_{22} & \tilde{\Gamma}_{23} \\ \tilde{\Gamma}_{11} & \tilde{\Gamma}_{21} & \tilde{B}_{11} & \tilde{B}_{12} & \tilde{B}_{13} \\ \tilde{\Gamma}_{12} & \tilde{\Gamma}_{22} & \tilde{B}_{12} & \tilde{B}_{22} & \tilde{B}_{23} \\ \tilde{\Gamma}_{13} & \tilde{\Gamma}_{23} & \tilde{B}_{13} & \tilde{B}_{12} & B_{33} \end{bmatrix} \begin{bmatrix} y_1 \\ y_2 \\ x_1 \\ x_2 \\ x_2 \end{bmatrix} = 0$$
$$\left[\tilde{\alpha} + y'\tilde{A} + x'\tilde{\Gamma}\right] y = \tilde{\beta}x + x'\tilde{B}x$$

Holding $\tilde{\Gamma}$ equal to zero for the moment, the matrix specification in Equation (1.172) becomes

$$\left[\tilde{\alpha} + y'\tilde{A}\right] y = \tilde{\beta}x + x'\tilde{B}x \tag{1.173}$$

which is a general form of an ellipse. For example, using the ERS productivity data (Ball *et al.*, 2016) for Florida, we estimate a simplified form of Equation (1.173) as

$$
\begin{aligned}
-1.4591 + \begin{bmatrix} 1.0 \\ -1.35277 \\ 1.08752 \end{bmatrix}' \begin{bmatrix} y_1 \\ y_2 \\ y_3 \end{bmatrix} \\
+ \begin{bmatrix} y_1 \\ y_2 \\ y_3 \end{bmatrix}' \begin{bmatrix} -0.08389 & 0.06502 & -0.05441 \\ 0.06502 & -0.09944 & 0.08408 \\ -0.05441 & 0.08408 & -0.07197 \end{bmatrix} \begin{bmatrix} y_1 \\ y_2 \\ y_3 \end{bmatrix} \\
+ \begin{bmatrix} -0.2762 \\ -0.1871 \\ -0.0300 \\ -0.2511 \end{bmatrix}' \begin{bmatrix} x_1 \\ x_2 \\ x_3 \\ x_4 \end{bmatrix} = 0
\end{aligned}
\tag{1.174}
$$

where y_1 is the level of crop output, y_2 is the level of livestock output, y_3 is the level of "farm-related product" output, x_1 is the level of capital, x_2 is the quantity of land, x_3 is the quantity of labor, and x_4 is the quantity of materials for the state of Florida for 1964–2006. This multioutput form presented in Figure 1.19 yields the standard production possibility frontier graph. The first production possibility frontier holds the level of inputs at the sample mean. The second frontier shifts outward as the input levels are increased by 25%.

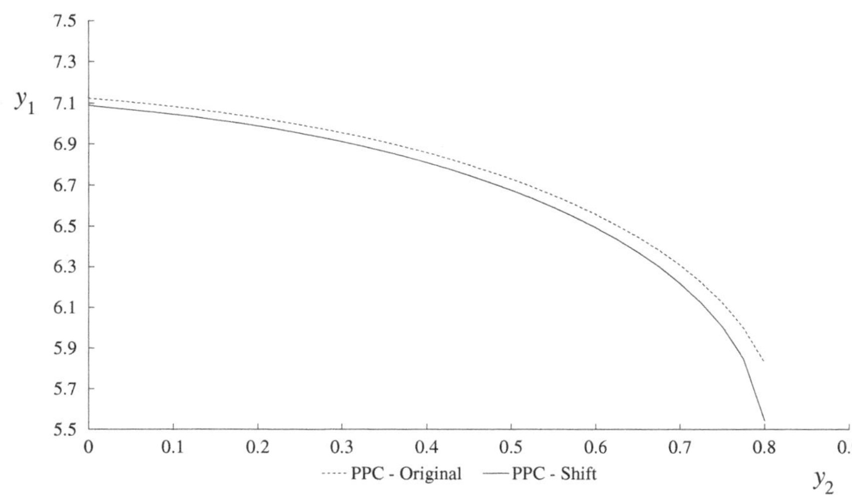

Fig. 1.19 Multi-output Production Function

The empirical results in Equation (1.174) and production possibilities curves presented in Figure 1.19 suggest that the empirical specification of the multioutput production function is at least feasible. However, the simple specification in Equation (1.172) raises many sticky issues. To develop these issues, let us start with the constant elasticity of transformation specification that can be traced (at least in part) to Powell and Gruen (1968)

$$\left(\delta_1 y_1^c + \delta_2 y_2^c\right)^{1/c} = g\left(x_1, x_2, x_3\right). \tag{1.175}$$

Note that Equation (1.175) trades outputs against one another using a constant elasticity of transformation form while allowing the inputs to enter in a general way. Another possibility is a Cobb–Douglas form

$$y_1 y_2^{\delta} = \alpha_0 x_1^{\alpha_1} x_2^{\alpha_2} x_3^{\alpha_3} \tag{1.176}$$

which can be characterized as a logarithmic–linear Taylor series expansion similar to the quadratic form in Equation (1.171) (attributed by Just, Zilberman, and Hochman to Lawrence Klein).

Just *et al.* (1983) object to the standard multioutput specifications. One of the basic justifications for the estimation of the multiproduct form is that farmers know how much input they purchase (i.e., total tons of nitrogen), but may not be able to recall how much input was used for each crop. Hence, following Florida ERS dataset,

$$x_1 = x_{11} + x_{12} + x_{13} \tag{1.177}$$

where x_1 is the total amount of capital used in Florida which is the sum of the capital used in the production of crops (x_{11}), the capital used to produce livestock (x_{12}), and capital used to produce farm-related outputs (x_{13}). Just, Zilberman, and Hochman demonstrate the absurdity of this specification by joining the specification in Equation (1.176) with the implications of Equation (1.177):

$$\begin{aligned} y_1 y_2^{\delta} = {} & \alpha_0 \left(x_{11} + x_{12} + x_{13}\right)^{\alpha_1} \left(x_{21} + x_{22} + x_{23}\right)^{\alpha_2} \\ & \times \left(x_{31} + x_{32} + x_{33}\right)^{\alpha_3}. \end{aligned} \tag{1.178}$$

To develop the difficulties with this specification, consider two different bundles of x_1 – $\{100, 0, 25\}$ and $\{75, 25, 25\}$ with the other input allocations remaining unchanged. By Equation (1.176), these bundles yield the same combination of outputs.

While Just, Zilberman, and Hochman raise difficulties with the original specifications, their model is based in part on this formulation. Specifically, building on the formulation in Equation (1.174), assume that we have four inputs and three outputs. In this model, we start by specifying the input sums and general form of the three outputs:

$$\begin{aligned} x_1 &= x_{11} + x_{21} + x_{31} \\ x_2 &= x_{12} + x_{22} + x_{32} \\ x_3 &= x_{13} + x_{23} + x_{33} \\ x_4 &= x_{14} + x_{24} + x_{34} \quad . \\ y_1 &= f_1\left(x_{11}, x_{12}, x_{13}, x_{14}\right) \\ y_2 &= f_2\left(x_{21}, x_{22}, x_{23}, x_{24}\right) \\ y_3 &= f_2\left(x_{31}, x_{32}, x_{33}, x_{34}\right) \end{aligned} \tag{1.179}$$

Using Equation (1.179) as a starting point, we can formulate the production functions $f_1(x)$ and $f_2(x)$ by rewriting x_{11} and x_{21} as functions of x_1:

$$\begin{aligned} &f_1\left(x_1 - (x_{21} + x_{31}), x_{12}, x_{13}, x_{14}\right) \\ &f_2\left(x_1 - (x_{11} + x_{31}), x_{22}, x_{23}, x_{24}\right) \end{aligned} . \tag{1.180}$$

Hence, the *marginal rate of transformation* (MRT) given x_1 can be derived by taking the derivatives of Equation (1.180) with respect to x_1

$$MRT_{y_1,y_2,x_1} = \frac{\dfrac{\partial f_1(x)}{\partial x_{11}}}{\dfrac{\partial f_2(x)}{\partial x_{21}}} = \frac{\dfrac{\partial f_1(x)}{\partial x_1}}{\dfrac{\partial f_2(x)}{\partial x_1}} = \frac{\partial y_1}{\partial y_2}. \tag{1.181}$$

Given that each of the production functions are Cobb–Douglas,

$$\begin{aligned} y_k &= x_{k1}^{\beta_{k1}} x_{k2}^{\beta_{k2}} x_{k3}^{\beta_{k3}} x_{k4}^{\beta_{k4}} \\ &\Rightarrow \frac{\partial y_k}{\partial x_{kj}} = \beta_{kj} \frac{y_k}{x_{kj}} \end{aligned} \tag{1.182}$$

the "joint Cobb–Douglas" in Equation (1.176).

Specifically, the formulation of the joint Cobb–Douglas in Equation (1.176) can be extended to three outputs and four inputs as

$$y_1 y_2^{\delta_2} y_3^{\delta_3} = \alpha_0 x_1^{\alpha_1} x_2^{\alpha_2} x_3^{\alpha_3} x_4^{\alpha_4} \tag{1.183}$$

where $\delta_1 = 1$ (implicitly to normalize on the first output). Note if $\beta_{1j} = \alpha_j$, $\beta_{2j} = \alpha_j/\delta_2$, and $\beta_{3j} = \alpha_j/\delta_3$, the individual Cobb–Douglas functions in Equation (1.182) imply the general joint form in Equation (1.183).

Building on these results, Just, Zilberman and Hochman propose estimating the multioutput relationship using a system of univariate production functions

$$y_{ikt} = \left(\prod_{j=1}^{J} x_{ijkt}^{\alpha_{jk}} \right) \exp\left(\beta_{kt} + \gamma_k m_i + \epsilon_{ikt}^{y}\right) \qquad (1.184)$$

where x_{ijkt} is the amount of input j farmer i used on output k at time t. The common factors of production (the ones that cannot be allocated to individual outputs) are then parametrized in the exponential term — m_i is a measure of the human capital of farmer i and β_{kt} is a constant that measures the impact of other factors (i.e., unallocatable inputs) on a crop/year combination.

1.4 Chapter Summary

- This chapter develops the traditional "primal approach" to addressing producer questions. This primal approach develops the economic question by understanding the technical relationship between inputs and outputs.
- The primary device used to model the technical relationship between inputs and outputs is the production function. As emphasized in the early part of the chapter, the production function is a technical relationship without economic content. Economic content is layered on an engineering relationship by the development of the characteristics of the production function necessary to support optimizing conditions.
- Given the properties of the production function developed in Section 1.2.1, we can derive relationships that define economic behavior including the conditional and unconditional derived demand for inputs and the supply of output.
- In addition to these economic relationships, this chapter also develops the concept of the elasticity of substitution — how one input replaces another in production. This formulation can be used to

address concepts such as the trade-off between equipment, labor and material inputs such as fertilizer.

1.5 Review Questions

1. What is the difference between the primal and dual approaches to production economics?
2. What is meant by the stages of production and how are these stages determined?
3. What is the relationship between Average Physical Product and Marginal Physical Product when the Average Physical Problem is at its maximum?
4. What is an isoquant and how is it related to the rate of technical substitution?
5. What are the various formulations for the elasticity of substitution? Why are they different?

1.6 Exercises

Table 1.1 presents the estimated parameters for two production functions based on the USDA's productivity data.[3] Columns 1 and 2 report the parameters for the translog cost function

$$\begin{aligned} f\left(x_1, x_2, x_3\right) = \exp\Bigg(& a_0 + a_1 \ln\left(x_1\right) + a_2 \ln\left(x_2\right) + a_3 \ln\left(x_3\right) \\ & + \frac{1}{2} A_{11} \ln\left(x_1\right) \ln\left(x_1\right) + A_{12} \ln\left(x_1\right) \ln\left(x_2\right) \\ & + A_{13} \ln\left(x_1\right) \ln\left(x_3\right) + \frac{1}{2} A_{22} \ln\left(x_2\right) \ln\left(x_2\right) \\ & + A_{23} \ln\left(x_2\right) \ln\left(x_3\right) + \frac{1}{2} A_{33} \ln\left(x_3\right) \ln\left(x_3\right) + \delta T \Bigg) \end{aligned} \tag{1.185}$$

[3]These data are provided in http://www.charlesbmoss.com:8080/Book.Production.Economics/Chapter-1/AggregateUSDA.csv.

Table 1.1 Numeric Estimates of Production Functions for Chapter 1

Translog		Mitscherlich–Baule		
Parameter	Estimate	Parameter	Least Squares	Maximum Likelihood
a_0	-3.22469^{***}	b_0	34.17697^{***}	44.15677^{***}
	(0.80866)[a]		(6.35547)	(0.00000)
a_1	0.28332	b_{11}	8.63210	-0.47312^{***}
	(1.15066)		(6.91990)	(0.02934)
a_2	0.73907	b_{12}	1.34350^{*}	0.12431^{***}
	(0.55999)		(0.81531)	(0.00974)
a_3	2.44893^{***}	b_{21}	-0.70703^{***}	-0.77195^{***}
	(0.80391)		(0.05806)	(0.02110)
A_{11}	−0.04676	b_{22}	0.26388^{***}	0.17606^{***}
	(0.33371)		(0.02191)	(0.00499)
A_{12}	0.04690	b_{31}	-0.25575^{***}	-0.04810^{***}
	(0.28322)		(0.04355)	(0.00470)
A_{13}	0.00014	b_{32}	0.02316^{**}	0.01316^{***}
	(0.43824)		(0.00986)	(0.00089)
A_{22}	−0.05728	δ	0.93304^{***}	1.74288^{***}
	(0.18827)		(0.04103)	(0.04811)
A_{23}	−0.17646			
	(0.27035)			
A_{33}	−0.58736			
	(0.37104)			
δ	1.26460^{***}			
	(0.07514)			

Notes: [a]Numbers in parenthesis denote standard errors.
***denotes statistical significance at the 0.01 level of confidence.
**denotes statistical significance at the 0.05 level of confidence.
*denotes statistical significance at the 0.10 level of confidence.

where x_1 is the capital level, x_2 is the level of labor employed, x_3 is the level of intermediate inputs, and T is a trend variable ($T = 0.5$ for our purposes). The second production function is a Mitscherlich–Baule

$$g(x_1, x_2, x_3) = b_0(1 - \exp(b_{11} - b_{12}x_1))(1 - \exp(b_{21} - b_{22}x_2)) \times (1 - \exp(b_{31} - b_{32}x_3))\exp(\delta T). \tag{1.186}$$

Table 1.2 Sample Statistics for Productivity Data

Variable	Min	1st Qu.	Median	Mean	3rd Qu.	Max
Output	14.060	18.880	26.410	26.770	35.090	41.970
Capital	9.362	9.644	11.557	10.955	11.932	12.673
Labor	6.618	8.146	10.539	12.782	15.490	29.128
Intermediate	10.120	14.520	18.300	17.740	21.270	24.080
Output Price	0.230	0.278	0.592	0.543	0.659	1.130
Capital Price	0.085	0.123	0.387	0.431	0.604	1.559
Labor Price	0.035	0.073	0.240	0.384	0.660	1.121
Intermediate Price	0.137	0.164	0.441	0.443	0.576	1.146

In addition, Table 1.2 presents the sample statistics for the productivity data (note that I divided the original quantity data by 10,000 to scale the estimation).

1. Use logarithmic differentiation to demonstrate that

$$h(x_1, x_2, x_3) = 3.1610 x_1^{0.2223} x_2^{0.1513} x_3^{0.4285} \tag{1.187}$$

   is the Cobb–Douglas approximation to the least squares estimates of for the Mitscherlich–Baule.
2. Demonstrate that the Mitscherlich–Baule is a valid production function at the point $x = \{9.3778, 7.1645, 17.5931\}$. Also demonstrate that this point maximizes profit.
3. Demonstrate that translog is a valid production function at the sample mean.
4. Compute the input levels that maximize profit given the sample average input and output prices.
5. Derive the conditional and unconditional input demand functions for Cobb–Douglas production function in Question 1.
6. Compute the Hicks–Allen input substitutions for Mitscherlich–Baule. Are these results similar to the input substitutions for the Cobb–Douglas production function? Why?
7. Derive the isoquant for the Cobb–Douglas form in Question 1 at the sample mean.
8. Derive the isoquant for the Mitscherlich–Baule production function at the sample mean using the numerical approach.

9. Take the second-order approximation of the translog production function around the sample mean to yield the quadratic production function. Compute the elasticity of substitution for the quadratic production function.
10. Prove that the expansion paths (i.e., the set of points that have the same rate of technical substitution) for the Cobb–Douglas production function are linear.

Chapter 2

Estimation of the Primal

Chapter 1 laid out the primal production function from a producer choice perspective. Specifically, it addressed questions, such as "What are the required properties that a production function must possess for optimizing behavior?" In this process, several stylized production functions such as the Cobb–Douglas, translog, and constant elasticity of substitution were proffered to demonstrate these key properties. Given the basic characteristics of the production function developed in Chapter 1, this chapter presents a variety of methodologies used to estimate the production functions for applied work. These methodologies are largely econometric in nature. Specifically, we are interested in using mathematical specifications of the production function based on economic theory along with data and statistical methods to estimate production functions that are useful for empirical economic research.

Statistics — Schumpeter

It stands to reason that for economics, statistics, that is, the statistical figure or series of figures, must be of vital importance. In practice, this has been recognized *at least* since the 16th and 17th centuries when a large part of the work of the Spanish *politicos*, for example, consisted in the collection and interpretation of statistical figures — not to mention the

(*Continued*)

(Continued)

English econometricians, who were called political arithmeticians, and their fellow workers in France, Germany, and Italy. We need statistics not only for explaining things but also in order to know precisely what there is to explain... It is impossible to understand statistical figures without understanding how they have been compiled. It is equally impossible to extract information from them or to understand the information that specialists extract from the rest of us without understanding the methods by which this is done — and the epistemological background of these methods. Thus, an adequate command of modern statistical methods is a necessary (but not a sufficient) condition for preventing the modern economist from producing nonsense, though very much more so in some fields than in others; our stake in these methods is too great for us to leave judgement on the virtues or shortcomings, say, of the variate-difference method to specialists even if they were unanimous about it (Schumpeter, 1994, pp. 113–114).

2.1 Imputing the Parameters of a Production Function from Sample Means

Before we delve into various econometric models to estimate the production function, let us consider a simple method for imputing the values of the Cobb–Douglas production function using sample statistics. Specifically, I would like to demonstrate how to use the means from the data to construct the Cobb–Douglas model presented in Equation (1.46). As a starting point, suppose that we have the geometric means for nitrogen, phosphorous, and potash at the United States Department of Agriculture's Cropping Practicing Survey of Agriculture (1995) for corn production in Illinois for 1993 (presented in Table 2.1). Recall the profit-maximization problem for the firm

Table 2.1 Corn Input, Yield and Price Data for Illinois (1993)

Variable	Mean	Price
Nitrogen	136.429	0.158
Phosphorous	63.276	0.141
Potash	81.715	0.108
Corn	130.093	3.814

$$\max_x pf(x_1, x_2, x_3) - w_1x_1 - w_2x_2 - w_3x_3. \tag{2.1}$$

We can use this to derive a set of four conditions with four unknowns based on the Cobb–Douglas production function

$$\begin{aligned} y &= a_0 x_1^{a_1} x_2^{a_2} x_3^{a_3} \\ a_1 \frac{y}{x_1} &= \frac{w_1}{p} \\ a_2 \frac{y}{x_2} &= \frac{w_2}{p} \\ a_3 \frac{y}{x_3} &= \frac{w_3}{p} \end{aligned} . \tag{2.2}$$

This system of equation is simple to solve. Specifically, the individual first-order conditions imply the solution of each of the exponential coefficients

$$\begin{aligned} a_1 &= \frac{w_1x_1}{py} = \frac{136.429 \times 0.158}{130.093 \times 3.814} = 0.043 \\ a_2 &= \frac{w_2x_2}{py} = \frac{63.276 \times 0.141}{130.093 \times 3.814} = 0.018 \\ a_3 &= \frac{w_3x_3}{py} = \frac{81.715 \times 0.108}{130.093 \times 3.814} = 0.018 \\ a_0 &= \frac{y}{x_1^{a_1} x_2^{a_2} x_3^{a_3}} = \frac{130.093}{136.429^{0.043} 63.276^{0.018} 81.715^{0.018}} = 90.283. \end{aligned} \tag{2.3}$$

Hence, we can solve for the coefficients of Cobb–Douglas that are "exactly identified" — we have four conditions and four unknowns.

Since the system in Equation (2.2) is exactly identified, we can impute its parameters directly. However, we could solve for the parameters by minimizing the sum of the implied errors squared:

$$S^2 = (y - a_0 x_1^{a_1} x_2^{a_2} x_3^{a_3})^2 + \left(a_1 \frac{y}{x_1} - \frac{w_1}{p}\right)^2 + \left(a_2 \frac{y}{x_2} - \frac{w_2}{p}\right)^2 + \left(a_3 \frac{y}{x_3} - \frac{w_3}{p}\right)^2. \tag{2.4}$$

Throughout the remainder of this book, R Code which implements estimators or other numerical techniques will be presented in the text. In this case the R Code that solves numerically for the coefficients using Equation (2.4) is as follows:

R Code — Impute the Values of a Cobb–Douglas Production Function

```
avgEst <- function(a) {
  err   <- matrix(0,4,1)
  yhat      <- a[1]*quant[1]^a[2]*quant[2]^a[3]*
  quant[3]^a[4]
  err[1,1] <- quant[4]-yhat
  err[2,1] <- a[2]*yhat/quant[1]-price[1]/price[4]
  err[3,1] <- a[3]*yhat/quant[2]-price[2]/price[4]
  err[4,1] <- a[4]*yhat/quant[3]-price[3]/price[4]
  return(t(err)%*%err)
}

a0 <- c(34.0,0.24,0.09,0.11)

res0 <- solnp(a0,avgEst,LB = c(0.01,0.01,0.01,0.01),
                              UB = c(50.0,0.75,0.75,
                                     0.75))
```

where quant[1], quant[2], and quant[3] are the average levels of nitrogen, phosphorous, and potash in pounds per acre, quant[4] is the average corn yield in bushels per acre, price[1], price[2], and price[3] represent the price in each nutrient in dollars per pound, and price[4] is the corn price in dollars per bushel. This minimization problem yields $a_0 = 50.0$, $a_1 = 0.126$, $a_2 = 0.034$, $a_3 = 0.045$.

The advantage to the numerical approach is that it allows the solution of slightly more complicated production functions. For example, consider the three input translog production function yields four conditions:

$$
\begin{aligned}
f\left(x_{1t}, x_{2t}, x_{3t}\right) = \exp & \left(a_0 + \begin{bmatrix} a_1 \\ a_2 \\ a_3 \end{bmatrix}' \begin{bmatrix} x_{1t} \\ x_{2t}, x_{3t} \end{bmatrix} \right. \\
& \left. + \frac{1}{2} \begin{bmatrix} x_{1t} \\ x_{2t} \\ x_{3t} \end{bmatrix}' \begin{bmatrix} A_{11} & A_{12} & A_{13} \\ A_{12} & A_{22} & A_{23} \\ A_{13} & A_{23} & A_{33} \end{bmatrix} \begin{bmatrix} x_{1t} \\ x_{2t} \\ x_{3t} \end{bmatrix} \right) \\
\left[a_1 + A_{11}x_{1t} + A_{12}x_{2t} + A_{13}x_{3t}\right] \frac{f()}{x_{1t}} &= \frac{w_{1t}}{p_t} \\
\left[a_2 + A_{12}x_{1t} + A_{22}x_{2t} + A_{23}x_{3t}\right] \frac{f()}{x_{2t}} &= \frac{w_{2t}}{p_t} \\
\left[a_3 + A_{13}x_{1t} + A_{23}x_{2t} + A_{33}x_{3t}\right] \frac{f()}{x_{3t}} &= \frac{w_{3t}}{p_t}.
\end{aligned}
\tag{2.5}
$$

In this case, we have four conditions per observation, but 10 parameters. We could solve for the parameters by minimizing the sum of squared error between these conditions for a set of parameters on three observations. For example, we could use the state averages for Illinois for 1993, 1994, and 1995. Note that this process may require side conditions to make the production function valid (e.g., positive first derivatives at each point and concavity).

2.2 Estimation Using Ordinary Least Squares

The most straightforward concept in the estimation of production function is the application of ordinary least squares. Taking the quadratic production function as a starting point

$$
\begin{aligned}
y = a_0 + a_1x_1 + a_2x_2 + a_3x_3 + A_{11}x_1^2 + A_{12}x_1x_2 + A_{13}x_1x_3 \\
+ A_{22}x_2^2 + A_{23}x_2x_3 + A_{33}x_3^2 + \epsilon.
\end{aligned}
\tag{2.6}
$$

Table 2.2 Population Statistics for Corn Production in Illinois

Statistics	Nitrogen	Phosphorous	Potash	Corn
Minimum	4.0	1.0	0.6	60.0
First Quartile	123.0	46.0	60.0	110.0
Median	159.0	69.0	100.0	143.0
Mean	151.1	72.4	99.0	137.5
Third Quartile	184.0	92.0	120.0	168.0
Maximum	578.0	644.0	361.00	247.7

Note that we have already applied symmetry on the quadratic. From an estimation perspective, since $x_1x_2 = x_2x_1$, any other approach would not work.

For most of the initial examples in this chapter, we will use corn production data from the United States Department of Agriculture's Cropping Practicing Survey of Agriculture (1995) for corn production in Illinois for 1993–1995.[1] Specifically, we use the data on nitrogen, phosphorous, and potash application per acre and the corn yield in bushels per acre. Because we know what to compare the results of the quadratic with both the Cobb–Douglas and the transcendental forms, we eliminate those observations with zero input and zero output levels. This leaves us with 1,212 observations on corn production. The population statistics for this data are presented in Table 2.2.[2]

We apply ordinary least squares to this specification to these data to yield the estimates for the quadratic production surface in Table 2.3. Implicitly, applying ordinary least squares could make several assumptions. First, if we have a small sample, it is typical to assume that the residual (ϵ) is normally distributed. Hence, we can use traditional t-ratios. Alternatively, we could assume that we have a large sample. In this situation, the normality of the estimated coefficients is guaranteed from the central limit theorem.

Do the estimates in Table 2.3 make sense from an economic point of view? What is wrong? First, the negative linear coefficient (α_2) on

[1]The data is available in a spreadsheet at http://www.charlesbmoss.com:8080/Book.Production.Economics/Chapter-2/IllinoisCorn.csv.

[2]The R Code for these estimations is available at http://www.charlesbmoss.com:8080/Book.Production.Economics/Chapter-2/IllinoisCorn.R.

Table 2.3 Estimates of the Quadratic Production Function

Parameter	Estimate
α_0 Constant	66.77819***
	(6.91443)[a]
α_1 Nitrogen	0.33013***
	(0.05215)
α_2 Phosphorous	−0.43900
	(0.10948)
α_3 Potash	0.51258***
	(0.08389)
A_{11} Nitrogen × Nitrogen	−0.00038
	(0.00277)
A_{12} Nitrogen × Phosphorous	0.00026
	(0.00066)
A_{13} Nitrogen × Potash	−0.00123**
	(0.00044)
A_{22} Phosphorous × Phosphorous	−0.00049
	(0.00074)
A_{23} Phosphorous × Potash	−0.00092
	(0.00064)
A_{33} Potash × Potash	−0.00190**
	(0.00067)

Notes: [a]Numbers in parenthesis denote standard errors.
***denotes statistical significance at the 0.01 level of confidence.
**denotes statistical significance at the 0.05 level of confidence.
*denotes statistical significance at the 0.10 level of confidence.

phosphorous indicates that output may not be positively monotonic in nitrogen. Another possible difficulty is the concavity of the production surface. At first glance, the results do not appear too bad. Specifically, the Hessian of the production function becomes

$$\nabla^2_{xx} f(x_1, x_2, x_3) = \begin{bmatrix} -0.00038 & 0.00026 & -0.00123 \\ 0.00026 & -0.00049 & -0.00092 \\ -0.00123 & -0.00092 & -0.00190 \end{bmatrix} \tag{2.7}$$

so that the diagonal elements are all negative. However, the eigenvalues of the matrix are $-0.0029, 0.0004, -0.0002$, so the matrix is not negative definite. The estimated relationship is not concave in inputs. The relevant question is then — does it matter if the results make economic sense? Basically, if the estimated results do not conform

Table 2.4 Estimates of the Cobb–Douglas Function

Parameter	Estimate
α_0 Constant	3.6254***
	(0.0971)[a]
α_1 Nitrogen	0.1109***
	(0.0183)
α_2 Phosphorous	0.0589*
	(0.0230)
α_3 Potash	0.1030**
	(0.01730)

Notes: [a]Numbers in parenthesis denote standard errors.
***denotes statistical significance at the 0.01 level of confidence.
**denotes statistical significance at the 0.05 level of confidence.
*denotes statistical significance at the 0.10 level of confidence.

with economic assumptions, we cannot use the estimates to estimate economic behavior.

Turning to the Cobb–Douglas form, we estimate

$$y = Ax_1^\alpha x_2^\beta x_3^\gamma \Rightarrow \ln(y) = \ln(A) + \alpha \ln(x_1) + \beta \ln(x_2) + \gamma \ln(x_3). \tag{2.8}$$

One alternative is then to run the regression

$$\ln(y) = \alpha_0 + \alpha_1 \ln(x_1) + \alpha_2 \ln(x_2) + \alpha_3 \ln(x_3) + \epsilon. \tag{2.9}$$

The results for this regression are presented in Table 2.4. What are some of the problems with this specification? First, the one problem is that there may be zero input levels. What is the production theoretic problem with zero input levels? Moss (2000) examines the implications of zero input levels for the Cobb–Douglas specification and the impact of these assumptions on the share of inputs chosen by the producer. In general, substituting a small number for the zero tends to do the least damage to the share of cost spent on each input. In our application, we have circumvented this problem by dropping the zeros. This is actually an assumption that imposes assumptions on the surface. Second, what is the assumption of the error term?

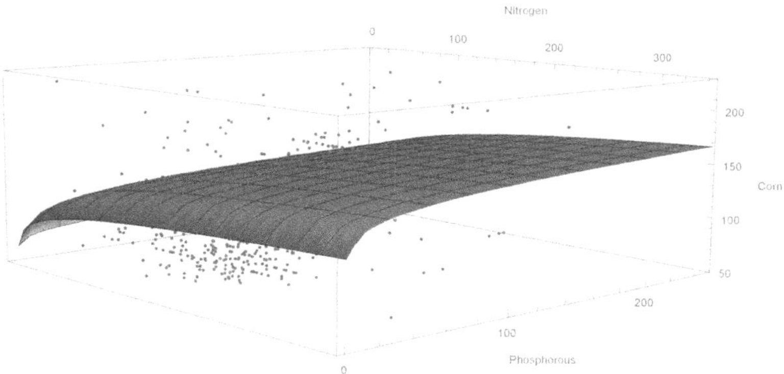

Fig. 2.1 Estimated Frontier Using the Cobb–Douglas Production Function

Implicitly, respecifying the production function as Equation (2.9) typically assumes that residuals in the output space (e.g., bushels of corn instead of the natural logarithm of the bushels of corn) are lognormally distributed. This assumption implies that the expected value of the yields becomes

$$\begin{aligned} &\mathrm{E}\left[f(x_1, x_2, x_3)\right] \\ &\quad = \exp\left[\left(\hat{\alpha}_0 + \hat{\alpha}_1 \ln\left[x_1\right] + \hat{\alpha}_2 \ln\left[x_2\right] + \hat{\alpha}_3 \ln\left[x_3\right]\right) + \frac{\hat{\sigma}^2}{2}\right]. \quad (2.10) \end{aligned}$$

Similarly, the variance becomes somewhat more complex.

Figure 2.1 presents the estimated frontier and projected points of production for the Illinois corn data using the Cobb–Douglas production specification.[3] Note that most of the errors do not appear to be symmetric around the estimated frontier. The lognormal distribution has a right skewness.

---

[3]While the original data are in a four-dimensional space — nitrogen, phosphorous, potash, and corn — we project the levels into a three-dimensional space:

$$f(x_1, x_2, \bar{x}_3) \approx y + \frac{\partial f\left(x_1, x_2, x_3\right)}{\partial x_3}\left(\bar{x}_3 - x_3\right) + \frac{1}{2}\frac{\partial^2 f\left(x_1, x_2, x_3\right)}{\partial x_3^2}\left(\bar{x}_3 - x_3\right)^2.$$

This allows us to plot the production function in a three-dimensional space correcting for differences in x_3.

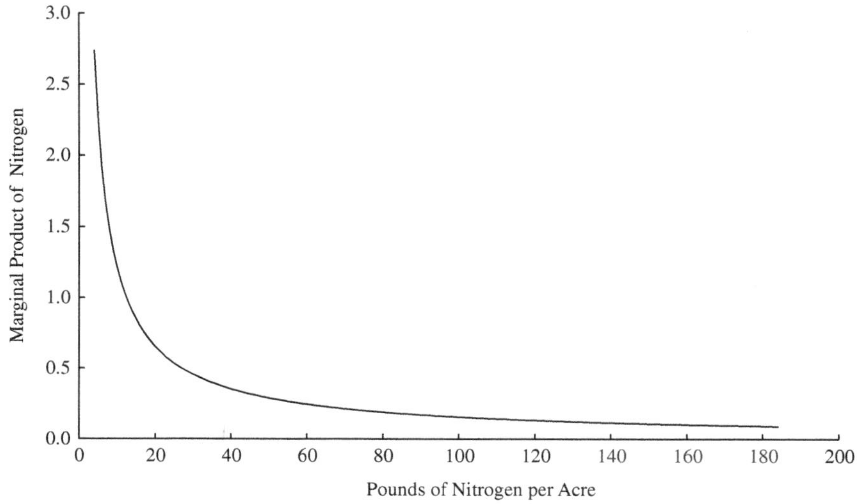

Fig. 2.2 Marginal Product of Nitrogen in Cobb–Douglas Form

Figure 2.2 presents the estimated marginal product of nitrogen for the Cobb–Douglas specification, while Figure 2.3 presents the marginal product of phosphorous. In general, the curves are downward sloping throughout the entire range of output levels. While not presented on these figures, the average physical product is also declining throughout the range. Mathematically,

$$MP - AP = \alpha \frac{A x_1^{\alpha} x_2^{\beta} x_3^{\gamma}}{x_1} - \frac{A x_1^{\alpha} x_2^{\beta} x_3^{\beta}}{x_1} = (\alpha - 1) \frac{y}{x_1}. \tag{2.11}$$

Thus, as long as $0 \leq \alpha \leq 1$, the average physical product is greater than the marginal physical product — the production system is in stage II. Note that the predicted value from the Cobb–Douglas function (142.74) is about 4% higher than the actual sample mean (even after adjusting for the expectation of the lognormal distribution).

Next, consider the estimation of the transcendental production function. The transcendental production function has many of the same problems as the Cobb–Douglas function. Specifically, the production function can be written as

$$y = A x_1^{a_1} e^{b_1 x_1} x_2^{a_2} e^{b_2 x_2} x_3^{a_3} e^{b_3 x_3}. \tag{2.12}$$

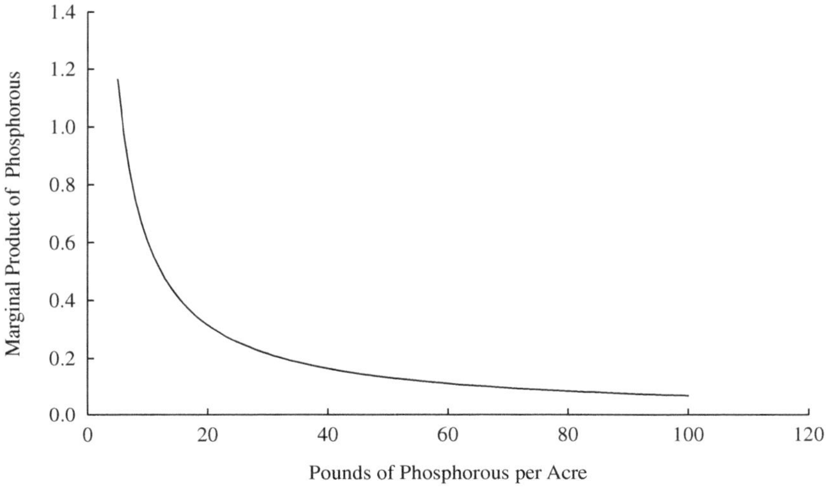

Fig. 2.3 Marginal Product of Phosphorous in Cobb–Douglas Form

Thus, it is estimated in a logarithmic form, like the Cobb–Douglas function:

$$\begin{aligned} \ln(y) &= a_0 + a_1 \ln(x_1) + b_1 x_1 + a_2 \ln(x_2) \\ &\quad + b_2 x_2 + a_3 \ln(x_3) + b_3 x_3 + \epsilon. \end{aligned} \tag{2.13}$$

Again, what are the assumptions about zeros or the distribution of error terms. The results for this specification are presented in Table 2.5. The results in Table 2.5 have several problems from an economic point of view. First, while the marginal product is positive at the sample mean for all inputs, the marginal product for nitrogen is increasing in the neighborhood around the sample mean, as presented in Figure 2.4.

2.3 Maximum Likelihood

As we discussed in our applications of ordinary least squares, the implicit error distribution for production economics is typically normality. Whether the recognition is explicit or not, the distribution of the residual typically depends on the econometric formulation and vice versa. For example, normality is typically required for the

Table 2.5 Estimates of the Transcendental Function

Parameter	Estimate
a_0 Constant	4.02330***
	(0.159129)[a]
a_1 Log of Nitrogen	0.006450
	(0.01565)
b_1 Nitrogen	0.001183***
	(0.00039)
a_2 Log of Phosphorous	0.08367**
	(0.03972)
b_2 Phosphorous	−0.00041
	(0.00055)
a_3 Log of Potash	0.05543*
	(0.03160)
b_3 Potash	0.000734*
	(0.00043)

Notes: [a]Numbers in parenthesis denote standard errors.
***denotes statistical significance at the 0.01 level of confidence.
**denotes statistical significance at the 0.05 level of confidence.
*denotes statistical significance at the 0.10 level of confidence.

researcher to use t-test. Ordinary least squares estimators are basically additive functions of random variables (see Moss, 2014, pp. 244–252). Since, summations of normal random variables are also normal, it follows that if we assume that the residuals are normally distributed, then the estimated parameters that are linear functions of those values are also normal. Alternatively, normality for least squares estimates can be based on the central limit theorem. In this approach, we state that least squares estimators are typically unbiased, and unbiased estimators are consistent. Thus, the central limit theorem can be used to conclude that ordinary least squares estimates are asymptotically normal as long as the variance is bounded and can be consistently estimated. Thus, arguing that our sample is large enough (e.g., 1,212 observations), our estimates of the quadratic production function are normally distributed regardless of the true distribution of the residuals.

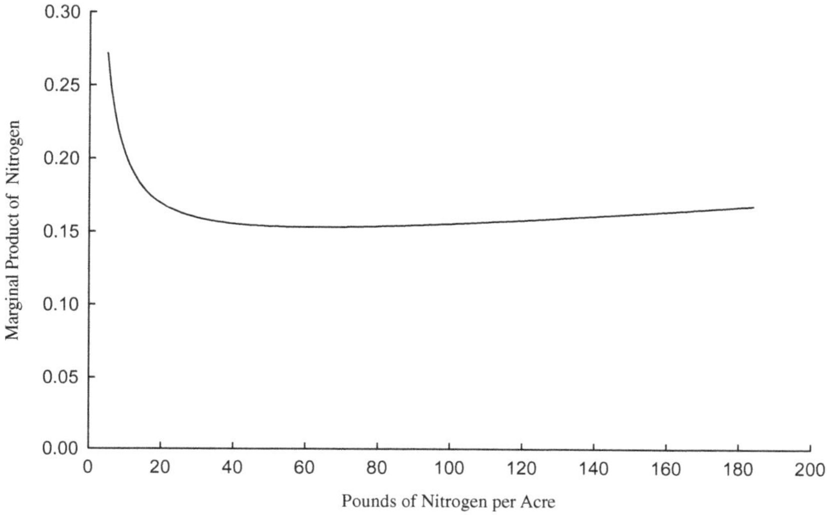

Fig. 2.4 Marginal Product of Nitrogen with Transcendental Form

Despite the robustness of least squares, however, we are sometimes interested in directly recognizing the fact that the residuals of the production function may be non-normal. One case is the possibility that producers may be technically inefficient. We will develop this formulation in the stochastic production function later in Section 2.6.1. At the present time, let us simply consider the explicit use of non-normality by developing the maximum likelihood estimator.

2.3.1 *Maximum Likelihood and Normality*

Despite our interest in the potential non-normality of the residuals, it is useful to start our discussion of maximum likelihood by assuming normality. Let us start by considering the logarithmic form of the Cobb–Douglas distribution in Equation (2.12). One way to estimate the parameters is to assume that

$$\epsilon_t = \ln(y_t) - \alpha_0 - \alpha_1 \ln(x_{1t}) - \alpha_2 \ln(x_{2t}) - \alpha_3 \ln(x_{3t}) \sim N\left(0, \sigma^2\right) \tag{2.14}$$

where $\sim$ denotes distributed (e.g., distributed normal with a zero mean and a variance of σ^2). Following Moss (2014, pp. 176–180), we express Equation (2.14) inside the normal distribution function

$$f\left(y_t, x_t\middle|\, \alpha, \sigma^2\right) = \frac{1}{\sqrt{2\pi\sigma^2}} \times \exp\left[-\frac{\left[\ln\left(y_t\right) - \alpha_0 - \alpha_1 \ln\left(x_{1t}\right) - \alpha_2 \ln\left(x_{2t}\right) - \alpha_3 \ln\left(x_{3t}\right)\right]^2}{2\sigma^2}\right]. \tag{2.15}$$

In most applications, we use Equation (2.15) to make the statement that the probability of drawing the combination of y_t and x_t given the parameters (α and σ^2) can be expressed as $f(y_t, x_t|\, \alpha, \sigma^2)$. However, another way to look at the expression is to say that the values of y_t and x_t are fixed and observed. Equation (2.15) then gives us the probability of the parameters α and σ^2. Thus, we rewrite $f(\alpha, \sigma^2|\, y_t, x_t)$.

Next, instead of a single value of y_t and x_t, we collect a sample $(y_t, x_t) \ni: t = 1, \ldots, T$. Assuming that the observations are independently and identically distributed, the likelihood of the sample can then be written as

$$L\left(\alpha, \sigma^2\middle|\, \{y\}\ {}_t^T, \{x\}\ {}_t^T\right) = \left(\frac{1}{\sqrt{2\pi\sigma^2}}\right)^T \exp\left[-\sum_{t=1}^{T} \frac{\left[\begin{array}{c}\ln\left(y_t\right) - \alpha_0 - \alpha_1 \ln\left(x_{1t}\right) \\ -\alpha_2 \ln\left(x_{2t}\right) - \alpha_3 \ln\left(x_{3t}\right)\end{array}\right]^2}{2\sigma^2}\right]. \tag{2.16}$$

Thus, Equation (2.16) represents the probability of drawing an observed sample given a set of random parameters. One approach to estimation is then to choose the values of the parameters that maximize the likelihood of drawing the observed sample (e.g., choose as your estimates the values that maximize Equation (2.16)). This is usually accomplished using numerical optimization techniques. The variance of the estimated parameters is then computed as the inverse of the negative of the expected Hessian function for Equation (2.16) (e.g., the Cramer–Rao lower bound).

As developed by Moss (2014, pp. 176–177), the parameter values that minimize the normal likelihood function for the linear model are identical to the least squares estimators. Essentially, least squares is the same as the maximum likelihood estimator under normality when the residuals are independently and identically distributed.

2.3.2 *Estimating the Gamma Distribution*

To demonstrate the use of maximum likelihood other than normality, consider the Gamma distribution

$$f\left(x|\,\alpha,\beta\right)=\frac{x^{\alpha-1}\exp\left(-\frac{x}{\beta}\right)}{\Gamma\left(\alpha\right)\beta^{\alpha}} \tag{2.17}$$

note that $\Gamma(\alpha)$ is function whose general form does not have a closed-form solution

$$\Gamma\left(\alpha\right)=\int_{0}^{\infty}x^{\alpha-1}\exp\left(-x\right)dx. \tag{2.18}$$

Following the general approach described above, the likelihood function for the parameters based on a sample of observed random variables becomes

$$L\left(\alpha,\beta|\left\{x_t\right\}\,_t^T\right)=\frac{1}{\left(\Gamma(\alpha)\beta^{\alpha}\right)^T}\prod_{t=1}^{T}x_t^{\alpha-1}\exp\left[-\frac{x_t}{\beta}\right]. \tag{2.19}$$

Taking the logarithm of Equation (2.19) yields

$$\begin{aligned}\ln\left(L\left(\alpha,\beta|\left\{x_t\right\}\,_t^T\right)\right)&=-T\ln\left(\Gamma\left(\alpha\right)\right)-T\alpha\ln\left(\beta\right)\\&\quad+\left(\alpha-1\right)\sum_{t=1}^{T}\ln(x_t)-\frac{1}{\beta}\sum_{t=1}^{T}x_t.\end{aligned} \tag{2.20}$$

Defining T_1 and T_2 as sufficient statistics

$$\begin{aligned}T_1&=\sum_{t=1}^{T}\ln(x_t)\\T_2&=\sum_{t=1}^{T}x_t\end{aligned} \tag{2.21}$$

the sample likelihood function becomes

$$\begin{aligned}\ln\left(L\left(\alpha,\beta|\left\{x_t\right\}\,_t^T\right)\right)&=-T\ln\left(\Gamma\left(\alpha\right)\right)-T\alpha\ln\left(\beta\right)\\&\quad+\left(\alpha-1\right)T_1-\frac{1}{\beta}T_2.\end{aligned} \tag{2.22}$$

Table 2.6 Cotton Production in Mississippi (1964–2010)

Year	Nitrogen	Phosphorous	Potash	Year	Nitrogen	Phosphorous	Potash
1964	77	50	50	1985	104	56	59
1965	104	58	55	1986	102	54	63
1966	98	54	55	1987	106	52	71
1967	98	56	57	1988	110	49	59
1968	91	52	53	1989	103	49	65
1969	93	56	57	1990	109	50	78
1970	96	60	61	1991	109	50	76
1971	93	55	63	1992	112	57	98
1972	92	64	65	1993	111	57	94
1973	90	64	65	1994	122	54	101
1974	103	64	64	1995	112	54	86
1975	92	59	66	1996	100	47	100
1976	90	53	54	1997	109	50	95
1977	98	57	57	1998	107	57	99
1978	92	54	59	1999	111	50	109
1979	87	61	63	2000	114	52	97
1980	92	50	55	2001	112	51	98
1981	91	45	59	2003	109	46	106
1982	94	54	65	2007	117	58	106
1983	98	50	63	2010	100	47	91
1984	103	57	68				

The likelihood function in Equation (2.22) is impossible to maximize analytically, primarily due to the definition of $\Gamma(\alpha)$. Hence, we solve for the parameters using a Newton–Raphson technique, as described in Appendix B.

In order to more fully develop this estimator, consider the data for cotton production in Mississippi for 1964–2010 presented in Table 2.6. As a first step, consider a Mitscherlich–Baule production function

$$f(x_1, x_2, x_3) = y_M \prod_{i=1}^{3} \left(1 - \exp\left(\alpha_i\left(\beta_i - x_i\right)\right)\right) \tag{2.23}$$

where x_i is the level of nitrogen applied to cotton in pounds per acre, x_2 is the level of phosphorous applied to cotton, x_3 is the level of potash applied, y_M is the maximum cotton yield in pounds per acre, and α_i and β_i are coefficients for each respective input. Modifying the

Mitscherlich–Baule production function in Equation (2.23) slightly, we can express the residuals as

$$\begin{aligned}\xi_t &= y_M b_1 \left(1 - \exp\left(b_2 - b_3 x_{1t}\right)\right)\left(1 - \exp\left(b_4 - b_5 x_{2t}\right)\right)\\ &\quad \times \left(1 - \exp\left(b_6 - b_7 x_{3t}\right)\right) - y_t. \end{aligned} \tag{2.24}$$

The log-likelihood function can then be defined as

$$\begin{aligned}\ln(L) &= -T\ln\left(\Gamma(\alpha)\right) - T\alpha\ln(\beta) + (\alpha - 1)\sum_{t=1}^{T}\xi_t\\ &\quad -\frac{1}{\beta}\sum_{t=1}^{T}\ln\left(\xi_t\right)\\ \xi_t &= y_M b_1 (1 - \exp\left(b_2 - b_3 x_{1t}\right))\left(1 - \exp\left(b_4 - b_5 x_{2t}\right)\right)\\ &\quad \times \left(1 - \exp\left(b_6 - b_7 x_{3t}\right)\right) - y_t. \end{aligned} \tag{2.25}$$

The first step in the estimation of Equation (2.25) is using nonlinear least squares (i.e., simply minimizing $\sum_{t=1}^{T}\xi_t^2$). These values can be used as starting values for the maximum likelihood problem. Table 2.7 presents nonlinear least squares and maximum likelihood estimates for the Mitscherlich–Baule production function for Mississippi cotton production.

2.3.3 *Transformations to Normality*

One alternative to the estimation of non-normal distribution functions, maximum likelihood techniques can be used with transformations to normality to estimate deviations from normality. Specifically, following Moss and Shonkwiler (1993), we could estimate the inverse hyperbolic sine transformation to transform a non-normal random variable ϵ_t into a normal random variable ν_t

$$\nu_t\left(\epsilon_t, \delta, \theta\right) = \frac{\ln\left(\theta\left(\epsilon_t - \mu\right) + \left[\left(\theta\left[\epsilon_t - \mu\right]\right)^2 + 1\right]^{1/2}\right)}{\theta} \sim N\left(\delta, \sigma^2\right) \tag{2.26}$$

where θ and δ are parameters of the transformation. Moss (2010, pp. 257–264) develops the moments of this formulation.

Table 2.7 Mitscherlich-Baule Production Function for Cotton in Mississippi

Parameter	Nonlinear Least Squares	Maximum Likelihood
b_1	1.1909	1.7496
	(2.2819)	(3.7355)
b_2	−1.3287	−1.9743***
	(157.0784)	(0.3040)
b_3	0.0043	−0.0021
	(4.4221)	(35.4411)
b_4	0.8611	−676.2045
	(636.6758)	(782.4292)
b_5	0.4360	905.9164**
	(276.6840)	(421.8859)
b_6	−0.1384	−0.3768
	(1.4415)	(0.2479)
b_7	0.0151	0.0130
	(0.0311)	(0.0634)
α		8.6520
		(5.9315)
β		41.7477
		(515.3909)

Notes: [a]Numbers in parenthesis denote standard errors.
***denotes statistical significance at the 0.01 level of confidence.
**denotes statistical significance at the 0.05 level of confidence.
*denotes statistical significance at the 0.10 level of confidence.

As a starting point, consider the probability density function for the transformed random variable

$$g\left(y_t\middle|\,\theta,\mu,\delta,\sigma^2\right) = \frac{1}{\sqrt{2\pi\sigma^2}} \times \exp\left(-\frac{1}{2\sigma^2}\left[\frac{\ln\left(\theta\left[y_t-\mu\right]+\left[\theta^2\left(y_t-\mu\right)^2+1\right]^{1/2}\right)}{\theta}-\delta\right]^2\right) \times\left(\theta^2\left[y_t-\mu\right]^2+1\right)^{-1/2} \tag{2.27}$$

where the last term in Equation (2.27) is the Jacobian of the transformation. Letting $\mathrm{E}\left[y-\mu\right]=0$, we can focus on ϵ_t and Equation (2.27) can be simplified to

$$g\left(\epsilon_t|\,\theta,\delta,\sigma^2\right)=\frac{1}{\sqrt{2\pi\sigma^2}}\times\exp\left(-\frac{1}{2\sigma^2}\left[\frac{\ln\left(\theta\epsilon_t+\left[\theta^2\epsilon_t^2+1\right]^{1/2}\right)}{\theta}-\delta\right]^2\right)\times\left(\theta^2\epsilon_t^2+1\right)^{-1/2}. \tag{2.28}$$

Given this simplification, Moss (2010) solves for the mean, variance, skewness, and kurtosis of the distribution. A couple of these results are worth noting. The transformation can produce both negative and positive skewness, but only positive kurtosis (leptokurtosis).

From a production vantage point, researchers may be interested in the skewness and kurtosis for several reasons. Moss and Shonkwiler (1993) were primarily interested in the impact of skewness and kurtosis on risk reduction concepts, such as crop insurance. However, as we will develop in Section 2.6.1, the skewness also has implications for measuring technical inefficiency — negative skewness implies that some of the producers may be technically inefficient.

To develop the concept a little further, we consider whether the residuals from the quadratic production function are skewed or kurtotic. To test for non-normality, we use the test proposed by Jarque and Bera (1987). Given that the mean of the residuals from the quadratic regression is zero by construction, the estimated second, third, and fourth central moments of the residuals can be defined as

$$\begin{aligned}\mu_2^*\left(\epsilon\right)&=\frac{1}{T}\sum_{t=1}^{T}\epsilon_t^2\\ \mu_3^*\left(\epsilon\right)&=\frac{1}{T}\sum_{t=1}^{T}\epsilon_t^3.\\ \mu_4^*\left(\epsilon\right)&=\frac{1}{T}\sum_{t=1}^{T}\epsilon_t^4\end{aligned} \tag{2.29}$$

Jarque and Bera's test for skewness is then

$$\alpha_3 = \frac{\mu_3^*(\epsilon)}{(\mu_2^*(\epsilon))^{3/2}} \Rightarrow \sqrt{T}\hat{\alpha}_3 \sim N(0,6). \tag{2.30}$$

For our data, $\sqrt{T}\hat{\alpha}_3 = -0.9723$ which is statistically significant at any conventional level of confidence. Next, the test for kurtosis is

$$\alpha_4 = \frac{\mu_4^*(\epsilon)}{(\mu_2^*(\epsilon))^{2}} \Rightarrow \sqrt{T}(\hat{\alpha}_4 - 3) \sim N(0,24). \tag{2.31}$$

For our data, $\sqrt{T}(\hat{\alpha}_4 - 3) = 1.8753$ which is statistically significant at any conventional level of confidence. The joint test for normality is

$$\frac{T}{6}\left(\hat{\alpha}_3^2\right) + \frac{T}{24}\left(\hat{\alpha}_4 - 3\right)^2 \sim \chi_2^2. \tag{2.32}$$

The estimated statistic is 7.9755 which is statistically significant at the 0.05 level.

Merging the inverse hyperbolic sine transformation with the quadratic production function in Equation (2.6), we have the likelihood function

$$\begin{aligned} L\left(\alpha,\theta,\delta,\sigma^2\middle| y,x\right) &= \left(2\pi\sigma^2\right)^{-\frac{T}{2}} \\ &\times \prod_{t=1}^{T}\exp\left(-\frac{1}{2\sigma^2}\left[\frac{\ln\left(\theta\epsilon\left(y_t,x_t,\alpha\right) + \left[\theta^2\epsilon\left(y_t,x_t,\alpha\right)^2+1\right]^{\frac{1}{2}}\right)}{\theta} - \delta\right]^2\right) \\ &\times\left(\theta^2\epsilon\left(y_t,x_t,\alpha\right)^2+1\right)^{-\frac{1}{2}} \end{aligned}$$

$$\begin{aligned} \epsilon\left(y_t,x_t,\alpha\right) = y_t &- \alpha_0 - \alpha_1 x_{1t} - \alpha_2 x_{2t} - \alpha_3 x_{3t} - A_{11}x_{1t}^2 \\ &- A_{12}x_{1t}x_{2t} - A_{13}x_{1t}x_{3t} - A_{22}x_{2t}^2 \\ &- A_{23}x_{2t}x_{3t} - A_{33}x_{3t}^2. \end{aligned} \tag{2.33}$$

Mathematically, we typically estimate the natural logarithm of Equation (2.33)

$$\ln\left(L\left(.\right)\right) \propto -\frac{T}{2}\ln\left(\sigma^{2}\right) - \sum_{t=1}^{T}\left[\frac{1}{2\sigma^{2}}\left(\frac{\ln\left(\theta\epsilon\left(y_{t},x_{t},\alpha\right)+\left[\theta^{2}\epsilon\left(y_{t},x_{t},\alpha\right)^{2}+1\right]^{\frac{1}{2}}\right)}{\theta}-\delta\right)^{2} - \frac{1}{2}\ln\left(\theta^{2}\epsilon\left(y_{t},x_{t},\alpha\right)^{2}+1\right)\right]. \tag{2.34}$$

Appendix B.2 describes the empirical implementation of the maximum likelihood based on Equation (2.34). The results from the estimation are presented in Table 2.8 to the data for Indiana corn production. Consistent with our expectations, the distribution is negatively skewed (e.g., $\delta \ll 0$). Identification of the inverse hyperbolic sine transformation is easier for Indiana than Illinois because the distribution has a kurtosis greater than 3.0 (e.g., the kurtosis for normality).

2.4 Simultaneity

The above discussion (and estimates) makes the experimental plot design assumption regarding the data. Specifically, we essentially assumed that the data are being generated from some sort of experimental design so that the errors are truly random. If the data are actually the result of farm-level decisions, the data are endogenous (e.g., input and output prices affect the choice of input and output levels — this choice could complicate the consistency of the estimates).

To develop the endogeneity problem, we start with a three-input Cobb–Douglas production function $y = Ax_1^{\alpha}x_2^{\beta}x_3^{\gamma}$. Next, following the presentation from Section 1.3.1, we assume that farmers choose

Table 2.8 Estimates of the Inverse Hyperbolic Sine Transformation

Parameter	Ordinary Least Squares	Maximum Likelihood
a_0 Constant	110.59270***	141.71780***
	(4.82415)[a]	(7.48807)
a_1 Nitrogen	0.00358	−0.08569*
	(0.05746)	(0.06330)
a_2 Phosphorous	0.14551**	0.20627***
	(0.06318)	(0.06278)
a_3 Potash	0.08361	0.05220
	(0.06561)	(0.06316)
A_{11} Nitrogen × Nitrogen	0.00002	0.00043
	(0.00042)	0.00054
A_{12} Nitrogen × Phosphorous	0.00007	0.00039
	(0.00038)	(0.00045)
A_{13} Nitrogen × Potash	0.00094***	0.00120***
	(0.00036)	(0.00035)
A_{22} Phosphorous × Phosphorous	−0.00048	−0.00118***
	(0.00045)	(0.00036)
A_{23} Phosphorous × Potash	−0.00109***	−0.00108***
	(0.00032)	(0.00027)
A_{33} Potash × Potash	−0.00042	−0.00039
	(0.00043)	(0.00040)
δ		−24.55829***
		(4.95898)
σ		30.14082***
		(1.19200)
θ		0.01805***
		(0.00205)

Notes: [a]Numbers in parenthesis denote standard errors.
***denotes statistical significance at the 0.01 level of confidence.
**denotes statistical significance at the 0.05 level of confidence.
*denotes statistical significance at the 0.10 level of confidence.

inputs to maximize profit defined as

$$\max_{x_1,x_2,x_3} \pi = p_y(Ax_1^{\alpha}x_2^{\beta}x_3^{\gamma}) - x_1w_1 - x_2w_2 - x_3w_3 \tag{2.35}$$

yielding the first-order condition in natural log space of

$$\ln(y) = -\ln(\alpha) - \ln(p_y) + \ln(x_1) + \ln(w_1). \tag{2.36}$$

Taking the natural logarithm of the production along with the result of Equation (2.35) and appending a residual term to each equation implies

$$\begin{aligned}\ln(y) &= \ln(A) + \alpha \ln(x_1) + \beta \ln(x_2) + \gamma \ln(x_3) + \epsilon_1 \\ \ln(y) &= -\ln(\alpha) - \ln(p_y) + \ln(x_1) + \ln(w_1) + \epsilon_2.\end{aligned} \tag{2.37}$$

Ignoring for a moment x_2 and x_3 (or simply setting $\beta = \gamma = 0$), we can solve for $\ln(x_1)$ by equating the two equations in Equation (2.37):

$$\ln(x_1) = \frac{\ln(\alpha) + \ln(p_y) - \ln(w_1)}{1-\alpha} + \frac{\epsilon_1 - \epsilon_2}{1-\alpha}. \tag{2.38}$$

Substituting the result of Equation (2.38) into the first equation of Equation (2.37) (holding $\beta = \gamma = 0$) yields

$$\ln(y) = \ln(A) - \alpha\left(\frac{\ln(\alpha) + \ln(p_y) - \ln(w_1)}{1-\alpha} + \frac{\epsilon_1 - \epsilon_2}{1-\alpha}\right) + \epsilon_1. \tag{2.39}$$

From Equation (2.39), it is apparent that $\ln(x_1)$ is correlated with the residual of the production equation $\ln(y)$ (the first equation in Equation (2.37)) and, hence, ordinary least squares estimation of the parameters of the production function are biased.

The effect of the endogeneity of input choice on the estimation of the Cobb–Douglas production function was first developed by Hoch (1958). Using the production function from Equation (2.8) implies

$$y = A\prod_{i=1}^{3} x_i^{a_i} \tag{2.40}$$

where $a_1 = \alpha$, $a_2 = \beta$, and $a_3 = \gamma$ from Equation (2.8).

Assuming profit maximization, an output price of p_y, and input prices of w_i, we have the profit maximization conditions

$$p_y \frac{\partial y}{\partial x_i} = p_y\left(a_i \frac{y}{x_i}\right) = w_i. \tag{2.41}$$

Dividing through by w_i

$$a_i\left(\frac{y p_y}{x_i w_i}\right) = a_i \frac{R}{E_i} = 1 \tag{2.42}$$

where R is the total value of output and E_i is the total expenditure on input i. Klein (1946) demonstrates that the best linear unbiased estimate of a_i is

$$\hat{a}_i = \prod_{t=1}^{T} \left(\frac{E_{it}}{R_t} \right)^{\frac{1}{T}}. \tag{2.43}$$

In this approach, the "average" firm is defined to be the optimal firm. Note the similarity between this approach and the method of imputing the coefficients for the Cobb–Douglas form in Section 2.1.1.

As an alternative,

$$p_y \left(a_i \frac{y}{x_i} \right) = R_i w_i \tag{2.44}$$

where R_i is a constant which is equal to one if the choices made under the Cobb–Douglas production function is consistent with profit maximization. Essentially multiply the right-hand side of Equation (2.41) by R_i. The assumption is that each individual firm may have a slightly different R_i, but on average we assume that the firms exhibit profit-maximizing behavior. Thus, the researcher is interested in testing whether profit-maximizing behavior holds across the sample as a whole.

Single equation estimates are biased when the equation is a member of a system of equations in the following way: the system is such that some of the "independent" variables, as well as the dependent variable, are functions of the disturbance in the given equation.

Two models of simultaneity are as follows:

- **Model 1:** Production disturbances do not affect the "independent" variables, that is, if inputs are fixed or predetermined as is the case for field trials for crops. In this case, the error term affects the output level, but not the input values. In this case, approaches such as ordinary least squares are appropriate.
- **Model 2:** Production disturbances transmitted affect the "independent variables". In this case, ordinary least squares produce biased estimates. Among the approaches that can be used to remove this bias are systems approaches such as indirect least squares (ILS) or two-stage least squares (2SLS). Another approach which can be used to produce unbiased estimates is generalized instrumental variable estimation (GIVE).

2.4.1 *Indirect Least Squares*

Starting with a simple two-factor Cobb–Douglas production function, we transform the general form of the production function into its log-linear form and append an error ϵ (as demonstrated in Equation (2.8)):

$$\begin{aligned} y &= Ax_1^{a_1}x_2^{a_2} \\ \ln(y) &= \ln(A) + a_1\ln(x_1) + a_2\ln(x_2) + \epsilon. \end{aligned} \tag{2.45}$$

Next, we derive the first-order conditions for input $i = 1, 2$ by

$$x_i = a_i\left(\frac{p_y}{w_i}y\right). \tag{2.46}$$

Taking the logarithm of Equation (2.46) and adding a residual term ν_i yield

$$\ln(x_i) = \ln(a_i) + \ln\left(\frac{p_y}{w_i}\right) + \ln(y) + \nu_i. \tag{2.47}$$

Substituting $\tilde{y} = \ln(y)$, $\tilde{x}_i = \ln(x_i)$, $\tilde{k}_i = \ln(a_i)$, and $\tilde{z}_i = \ln(p_y/w_i)$ into Equations (2.45) and (2.47) yields a system of three equations and three unknowns:

$$\begin{aligned} \tilde{y} &= \alpha_0 + \alpha_1\tilde{x}_1 + \alpha_2\tilde{x}_2 + \epsilon \\ \tilde{x}_1 &= \tilde{k}_1 + \tilde{z}_1 + \tilde{y} + \nu_1 \\ \tilde{x}_2 &= \tilde{k}_2 + \tilde{z}_2 + \tilde{y} + \nu_2 \end{aligned} \quad . \tag{2.48}$$

Substituting the second and third equations from Equation (2.48) into the first equation from Equation (2.48) yields

$$\tilde{y} = \alpha_0 + \alpha_1\left(\tilde{k}_1 + \tilde{z}_1 + \tilde{y} + \nu_1\right) + \alpha_2\left(\tilde{k}_2 + \tilde{z}_1 + \tilde{y} + \nu_2\right) + \epsilon. \tag{2.49}$$

Simplifying Equation (2.49) yields an expression of the quantity produced as a function of relative prices and constants

$$\begin{aligned} \tilde{y} =& \frac{\alpha_0 + \alpha_1\tilde{k}_1 + \alpha_2\tilde{k}_2}{1-\alpha_1-\alpha_2} + \frac{\alpha_1}{1-\alpha_1-\alpha_2}\tilde{k}_1 \\ &+ \frac{\alpha_2}{1-\alpha_1-\alpha_2}\tilde{k}_2 + \frac{\alpha_1\nu_1 + \alpha_2\nu_2 + \epsilon}{1-\alpha_1-\alpha_2}. \end{aligned} \tag{2.50}$$

Empirically, the researcher actually estimates the reduced form of this expression

$$\tilde{y} = \beta_0 + \beta_1 \tilde{k}_1 + \beta_2 \tilde{k}_2 + \epsilon^* \tag{2.51}$$

using ordinary least squares.

Comparing Equation (2.50) with Equation (2.51), we see that

$$\beta_0 = \frac{\alpha_0 + \alpha_1 \tilde{k}_1 + \alpha_2 \tilde{k}_2}{1 - \alpha_1 - \alpha_2}, \beta_1 = \frac{\alpha_1}{1 - \alpha_1 - \alpha_2}, \beta_2 = \frac{\alpha_2}{1 - \alpha_1 - \alpha_2}. \tag{2.52}$$

Hence, we have to use estimated values of β_0, β_1, and β_2 to derive the values of α_0, α_1, and α_2. To start with, we resolve the second and third results in Equation (2.52) for α_1 and α_2

$$\begin{aligned} (1 - \alpha_1 - \alpha_2)\, \beta_1 &= \alpha_1 \\ (1 - \alpha_1 - \alpha_2)\, \beta_2 &= \alpha_2 \end{aligned}. \tag{2.53}$$

Taking the ratio of the two results from Equation (2.53) yields

$$\frac{(1 - \alpha_1 - \alpha_2)\beta_1}{(1 - \alpha_1 - \alpha_2)\beta_2} = \frac{\alpha_1}{\alpha_2} \Rightarrow \alpha_2 = \frac{\beta_2}{\beta_1}\alpha_1. \tag{2.54}$$

Substituting this result into the third expression in Equation (2.53) yields

$$\begin{aligned} \beta_2 &= \frac{\dfrac{\beta_2 \alpha_1}{\beta_1}}{\dfrac{\beta_1 - \beta_1 \alpha_1 - \beta_2 \alpha_1}{\beta_1}} \\ &\Rightarrow \beta_2 \beta_1 - \beta_2 \beta_1 \alpha_1 - \beta_2 \beta_2 \alpha_1 = \beta_2 \alpha_1 \\ &\Rightarrow \beta_2 \beta_1 = \beta_2 \alpha_1 (1 + \beta_1 + \beta_2) \\ &\Rightarrow \alpha_1 = \frac{\beta_1}{1 + \beta_1 + \beta_2}. \end{aligned} \tag{2.55}$$

Using the result from Equation (2.55) with the results from Equation (2.54) yields

$$\alpha_2 = \frac{\beta_2}{1 + \beta_1 + \beta_2}. \tag{2.56}$$

Finally, substituting the estimates for α_1 and α_2 back into the first result from (2.52) yields

$$\alpha_0 = \beta_0(1 - \alpha_1 - \alpha_2) - \alpha_1 \ln(\alpha_1) - \alpha_2 \ln(\alpha_2). \tag{2.57}$$

To demonstrate this approach, consider the pseudo-data presented in Table 2.9. This data was generated by estimating the parameters of a Cobb–Douglas production function for data from the USDA's chemical use survey for 1994 for the state of Illinois. Given these parameter estimates, we then constructed the table by deriving the choice of each fertilizer that would maximize profit for the actual corn, nitrogen, phosphorous, and potash prices for the United States for 1964–2009.

Extending the above derivation to include three endogenous inputs yields three inverse mapping conditions:

$$\begin{aligned} \alpha_1 &= \frac{\beta_1}{1+\beta_1+\beta_2+\beta_3}, \quad \alpha_2 = \frac{\beta_2}{1+\beta_1+\beta_2+\beta_3}, \\ \alpha_3 &= \frac{\beta_3}{1+\beta_1+\beta_2+\beta_3}. \end{aligned} \tag{2.58}$$

Table 2.9 presents a pseudo-dataset generated from the ordinary least squares estimates of the corn production function using data for Illinois from the USDA's chemical use dataset for 1994 under conventional tillage ($\alpha_0 = 4.0400$, $\alpha_1 = 0.0537$, $\alpha_2 = 0.0190$, and $\alpha_3 = 0.1118$). Running the simple regression from Equation (2.9) yields the regression results presented in Table 2.10. Following our discussion, we next formulate the regression model for indirect least squares from Equation (2.47). The results for this regression are presented in Table 2.11. Using these results for βs, we derive the parameters of the production function of $\alpha_0 = 4.0117$, $\alpha_1 = 0.0392$, $\alpha_2 = 0.0178$, $\alpha_3 = 0.1676$, so the estimated values are fairly close to the values that were used to generate the dataset.

2.4.2 *Two-Stage Least Squares and Instrumental Variables*

The fact that indirect least squares allows for the estimation of only exactly identified systems does not appear particularly constraining

Table 2.9 Pseudo-Data Based on Corn Prices and a Cobb–Douglas Production Function

Output	Nitrogen	Phosphorous	Potash	Corn Price	Nitrogen Price	Phosphorous Price	Potash Price
176.04	268.06	100.97	841.54	1.15	0.0399	0.0405	0.0270
182.11	261.82	74.75	832.28	1.12	0.0394	0.0405	0.0268
182.27	295.42	125.47	922.72	1.23	0.0383	0.0405	0.0275
180.33	267.16	79.33	711.53	0.99	0.0371	0.0421	0.0268
187.03	314.15	80.97	856.00	1.05	0.0340	0.0392	0.0246
182.08	357.92	109.73	982.29	1.15	0.0309	0.0370	0.0239
193.31	463.31	129.57	1142.51	1.36	0.0300	0.0376	0.0255
170.74	304.22	86.83	666.81	1.01	0.0317	0.0383	0.0291
187.95	487.78	125.80	1129.70	1.56	0.0324	0.0390	0.0294
206.96	782.63	245.32	1910.56	2.51	0.0357	0.0438	0.0308
202.66	473.41	132.97	1659.99	3.03	0.0695	0.0750	0.0407
183.06	265.64	84.61	981.04	2.48	0.0930	0.1070	0.0510
176.87	291.84	89.04	877.02	2.10	0.0675	0.0790	0.0480
180.19	270.46	98.51	818.09	1.97	0.0705	0.0730	0.0479
186.80	332.27	66.24	937.67	2.23	0.0700	0.0755	0.0482
182.22	356.67	126.04	969.63	2.55	0.0690	0.0805	0.0535
187.03	386.37	80.49	956.69	3.16	0.0825	0.1235	0.0675
164.22	240.48	40.13	625.97	2.47	0.0925	0.1240	0.0760
176.39	242.83	54.30	569.54	2.41	0.0975	0.1150	0.0775
187.29	342.17	121.32	943.89	3.30	0.0925	0.1070	0.0715
170.11	222.90	74.28	685.18	2.60	0.0990	0.1145	0.0725
177.22	218.05	77.66	660.71	2.20	0.0960	0.1030	0.0640
165.72	125.34	54.46	491.49	1.53	0.0855	0.0950	0.0555
164.89	253.28	56.60	700.42	2.08	0.0785	0.0970	0.0575
182.78	286.06	95.24	675.64	2.65	0.0830	0.1110	0.0785
171.84	223.13	76.16	564.20	2.47	0.0945	0.1145	0.0815
167.97	228.90	92.35	569.75	2.31	0.0900	0.1005	0.0775
166.35	232.76	96.72	590.41	2.45	0.0920	0.1085	0.0780
157.85	209.96	71.43	522.87	2.09	0.0890	0.1030	0.0750
167.27	242.59	92.30	666.56	2.51	0.0930	0.0950	0.0730
170.73	219.41	52.31	567.65	2.25	0.0980	0.1060	0.0730
186.20	307.00	103.11	869.62	3.38	0.1115	0.1170	0.0775
165.03	211.26	78.28	685.19	2.78	0.1165	0.1290	0.0765
162.44	187.86	65.18	632.04	2.53	0.1135	0.1285	0.0760
162.41	177.06	49.95	477.33	2.11	0.0965	0.1265	0.0815
153.56	186.63	56.30	415.15	1.88	0.0905	0.1275	0.0840

(*Continued*)

Table 2.9 (*Continued*)

Output	Nitrogen	Phosphorous	Potash	Corn Price	Nitrogen Price	Phosphorous Price	Potash Price
154.79	154.38	37.29	405.15	1.90	0.0970	0.1165	0.0825
147.45	99.19	57.98	413.25	1.98	0.1300	0.1180	0.0850
163.71	223.99	46.91	552.03	2.41	0.0975	0.1105	0.0820
167.47	188.26	71.81	570.83	2.53	0.1215	0.1215	0.0825
158.56	107.92	56.08	382.02	1.99	0.1315	0.1330	0.0905
155.31	112.36	48.62	263.11	2.00	0.1460	0.1495	0.1225
156.37	141.33	55.94	398.94	3.17	0.1830	0.1620	0.1365
167.30	206.68	81.85	564.85	4.39	0.1910	0.2090	0.1400

Table 2.10 Estimates of the Cobb–Douglas for the Pseudo-Data

Parameter	Estimate
β_0	4.0360***
	(0.0519)[a]
β_1	0.0544
	(0.0463)
β_2	0.0125
	(0.0576)
β_3	0.1169***
	(0.0443)

Notes: [a]Numbers in parenthesis denote standard errors.
***denotes statistical significance at the 0.01 level of confidence.

for the estimation of Cobb–Douglas systems. However, more general methodologies have been developed to overcome the endogeneity problem. Two of the procedures that we will present here are two-stage least squares developed by Theil (1953) and the generalized instrumental variable estimator (GIVE) Bowden and Turkington (1984).

Starting by the two-stage least squares approach pioneered by Theil (1953), we estimate two sets of regression equations. The first estimates the endogenous variables as functions of exogenous (non-systematic or predetermined) variables. Then given that these

Table 2.11 Estimates of the Cobb–Douglas Function Using Indirect Least Squares

Parameter	Estimate
β_0	4.3692***
	(0.0519)[a]
β_1	0.0392
	(0.0463)
β_2	0.0178
	(0.0576)
β_3	0.1676***
	(0.0443)

Notes: [a]Numbers in parenthesis denote standard errors.
***denotes statistical significance at the 0.01 level of confidence.

estimates are the best linear unbiased estimates of the mean value of the endogenous variables, we estimate the systematic or structural specification of the endogenous variables as a function of both the unbiased estimates of the endogenous variables and the exogenous variables.

In the Cobb–Douglas specification, we return to Equation (2.37) and specify four equations:

$$\begin{aligned} \ln(y) &= \ln(A) + \alpha_1 \ln(x_1) + \alpha_2 \ln(x_2) + \alpha_3 \ln(x_3) + \epsilon_1 \\ \ln(x_1) &= \ln(\alpha_1) + \ln(y) + \ln(p_y) - \ln(w_1) + \epsilon_2 \\ \ln(x_2) &= \ln(\alpha_2) + \ln(y) + \ln(p_y) - \ln(w_2) + \epsilon_3 \\ \ln(x_3) &= \ln(\alpha_3) + \ln(y) + \ln(p_y) - \ln(w_3) + \epsilon_4 \end{aligned} \quad . \tag{2.59}$$

In this specification, we are interested in three endogenous variables: $\ln(x_1)$, $\ln(x_2)$, and $\ln(x_3)$. The first stage then posits each of these variables as functions of four exogenous variables: $\ln(p_y)$, $\ln(w_1)$, $\ln(w_2)$, and $\ln(w_3)$. Specifically, we estimate three equations:

$$\begin{aligned} \ln(x_1) &= \beta_{10} + \beta_{11} \ln(p_y) + \beta_{12} \ln(w_1) + \beta_{13} \ln(w_2) + \beta_{14} \ln(w_3) + \epsilon_2 \\ \ln(x_2) &= \beta_{20} + \beta_{21} \ln(p_y) + \beta_{22} \ln(w_1) + \beta_{23} \ln(w_2) + \beta_{24} \ln(w_3) + \epsilon_3 \\ \ln(x_3) &= \beta_{30} + \beta_{31} \ln(p_y) + \beta_{32} \ln(w_1) + \beta_{33} \ln(w_2) + \beta_{34} \ln(w_3) + \epsilon_4 \end{aligned} \tag{2.60}$$

Table 2.12 First Stage Estimates

Parameter	$\ln(x_1)$	$\ln(x_2)$	$\ln(x_3)$
Constant	1.2396	0.7844	2.2216
$\ln(p_y)$	1.2907	1.1779	1.2062
$\ln(w_1)$	−1.2160	0.1282	−0.1110
$\ln(w_2)$	0.0537	−1.3639	0.0358
$\ln(w_3)$	−0.1179	0.0979	−1.1374

Table 2.13 Second Stage Estimates of the Cobb–Douglas Production Function

Parameter	Estimate
α_0	4.0022***
	(0.0858)[a]
α_1	0.0209
	(0.0377)
α_2	0.0158
	(0.0413)
α_3	0.1481***
	(0.0394)

Notes: [a]Numbers in parenthesis denote standard errors.
***denotes statistical significance at the 0.01 level of confidence.

separately. For the sample dataset presented in Table 2.9, these first stage estimates are presented in Table 2.12. Next, given these estimates, we generate estimated values of $\ln(x_1)$, $\ln(x_2)$, and $\ln(x_3)$. Using these estimated values of the endogenous variables, we estimate the first equation of Equation (2.59). These estimates are presented in Table 2.13.

Note that the regressions in Equation (2.60) are overspecified (or contain more exogenous variables than endogenous variables). Specifically, the system of three endogenous variables have four independent variables. In a sense, the production system is "recursively" defined. Basically, the production function includes no variables other than the endogenous input levels. A couple of interesting points in this regard: First, the ratio between the output price and the input price in a given equation should approach -1. Mathematically, $\beta_{11}/\beta_{12} = -1$, in our estimates $1.2906/(-1.2161) = -1.0614$. This is the result of an overidentification condition involving profit maximization. Second, while there is a relationship between the two-stage least squares estimates, and the indirect least squares estimates, they are different.

The two-stage least squares estimator can be accomplished in a single step using the generalized instrumental variable estimator. Specifically, following the discussion of Bowden and Turkington (1984), we can define the instrumental variable estimator as the value of β that minimizes

$$(y - x\beta)P_z(y - x\beta) \tag{2.61}$$

where P_z is defined as a spanning space of the proposed instrumental variables

$$P_z = Z(Z'Z)^{-1}Z. \tag{2.62}$$

Instrumental variables are variables that are correlated with the dependent variable, but not the residual. In our Cobb–Douglas production example, the logarithm of output and input prices are correlated with $\ln(y)$, but not with the residual (see Equation (2.49)). Hence, the GIV estimator of β becomes

$$\beta = (x'P_zx)^{-1}(x'P_zy). \tag{2.63}$$

It can be verified that using a constant and the logarithms of output and input prices (as in the first stage regressions presented in Equation (2.60) yields the same estimated parameters as two-stage least squares.

2.5 Stochastic Production Functions

Up until this point, our development of the random characteristics of the production function was largely one of convenience. We started with a production function that we wanted to estimate, such as the Cobb–Douglas production function

$$f(x_1, x_2) = \alpha_0 x_1^{\alpha_1} x_2^{\alpha_2} \tag{2.64}$$

or the quadratic production function

$$g(x_1, x_2) = a_0 + a_1 x_1 + a_2 x_2 + A_{11} x_1^2 + 2A_{12} x_1 x_2 + A_{22} x_2^2. \quad (2.65)$$

In order to estimate each function, we multiplied or added a random term to each specification

$$\begin{aligned} f(x_1, x_2) &= \alpha_0 x_1^{\alpha_1} x_2^{\alpha_2} e^u \\ &\Rightarrow \ln(f(x_1, x_2)) = \alpha_0 + \alpha_1 \ln(x_1) + \alpha_2 \ln(x_2) + u \end{aligned} \quad (2.66)$$

or the quadratic production function

$$g(x_1, x_2) = a_0 + a_1 x_1 + a_2 x_2 + A_{11} x_1^2 + 2A_{12} x_1 x_2 + A_{22} x_2^2 + v. \quad (2.67)$$

In the case of the Cobb–Douglas function, we typically assume that $u \sim N(0, \sigma^2)$ so that the error in the randomness in the production function is multiplicatively lognormal (i.e., $\exp(u) \sim LN(1, \tilde{\sigma}^2)$). In the case of the quadratic, we implicitly assume that the randomness is additively normal. These assumptions may have dramatic consequences for the stochastic nature of the production function.

Just and Pope (1978) discuss three different specifications of the stochastic production function:

$$\begin{aligned} y = F_1(X) &= f(X)e^{\varepsilon}, & E(\varepsilon) &= 0 \\ y = F_2(X) &= f(X)\varepsilon, & E(\varepsilon) &= 1. \\ y = F_3(X) &= f(X) + \varepsilon, & E(\varepsilon) &= 0 \end{aligned} \quad (2.68)$$

Each of these specifications has "problematic" implications. For example, the Cobb–Douglas specification implies that all inputs increase the risk of production:

$$\begin{aligned} V[f(x_1, x_2)] &= E\left[(\alpha_0 x_1^{\alpha_1} x_2^{\alpha_2} e^{\varepsilon})^2\right] - [E(\alpha_0 x_1^{\alpha_1} x_2^{\alpha_2} e^{\varepsilon})]^2 \\ &\Rightarrow \frac{\partial V[f(x_1, x_2)]}{\partial x_1} > 0. \end{aligned} \quad (2.69)$$

Note that this expectation is complicated by the fact of the expectation of the exponential. Specifically, under lognormal distributions,

$$E[e^{\varepsilon}] = e^{\mu + \frac{1}{2}\sigma^2}. \quad (2.70)$$

Just and Pope propose eight propositions that "seem reasonable and, perhaps, necessary to reflect stochastic, technical input–output relationships":

- **Postulate 1:** Positive production expectations $E[y] > 0$.
- **Postulate 2:** Positive marginal product expectations $\partial E[y]/\partial X_i > 0$.
- **Postulate 3:** Diminishing marginal product expectations $\partial^2 E[y]/\partial X_i^2 < 0$.
- **Postulate 4:** A change in variance for random components in production should not necessarily imply a change in expected output when all production factors are held constant, $\partial E[y]/\partial V(\epsilon) = 0$ is possible.
- **Postulate 5:** Increasing, decreasing, or constant marginal risk should all be possibilities $\partial V(y)\ \partial X_i \Leftrightarrow 0$ where $V(y) = E[y - E[y]]^2$.
- **Postulate 6:** A change in risk should not necessarily lead to a change in factor use for a risk-neutral (profit-maximizing) producer, $\partial X_i^*\ \partial V(\epsilon) = 0$ is possible where X_i^* is the optimal input level.
- **Postulate 7:** The change in the variance of marginal product with respect to a factor change should not be constrained in sign *a priors* without regard to the nature of the input, $\partial V(\partial y/\partial X_i)\ \partial X_J \Leftrightarrow 0$ is possible.
- **Postulate 8:** Constant stochastic returns to scale should be possible, $F(\theta X) = \theta F(x)$ for a positive scalar θ.

The Cobb–Douglas, transcendental, and translog production functions are consistent with postulates 1, 2, 3, and 8. However, in the case of postulate 5,

$$\begin{aligned} E(y) = f(X)E(e^z), \quad V(y) = f^2(X)V(e^z), \\ \frac{\partial E(y)}{\partial X_i} = f_i E(e^z), \quad \frac{\partial V(y)}{\partial X_i} = 2ff_i V(e^z). \end{aligned} \tag{2.71}$$

The marginal effect of input use on risk must always be positive. Thus, no inputs can be risk-reducing. For postulate 4, under normality,

$$\frac{\partial E(y)}{\partial V(\epsilon)} = \frac{1}{2\sigma} f(X) e^{(\frac{\sigma}{2})}. \tag{2.72}$$

Thus, it is obvious that our standard specification of stochastic production functions is inadequate.

An alternative specification would be

$$\begin{aligned} y = F_4(X) &= f(x) + h(x)\epsilon \\ E(\epsilon) = 0,\ V(\epsilon) &= \sigma^2 \end{aligned} . \tag{2.73}$$

This would yield an econometric specification of

$$\begin{aligned} y_t &= f(Z_t, \alpha) + h(Z_t, \beta)\epsilon_t \\ E(\epsilon_t) = 0, E(\epsilon_t^2) &= 1, E(\epsilon_t \epsilon_s) = 0, t \neq s \\ \ln(f(Z_t, \alpha)] &= (\ln(Z_t))'\alpha = z_t'\alpha \\ \ln(h(Z_t, \beta)] &= (\ln(Z_t))'\beta = z_t'\beta \\ Z_t &= Z(X_t) \end{aligned} . \tag{2.74}$$

To develop a consistent estimator, rewrite the error term as

$$u_t = h(Z_t, \beta)\epsilon_t. \tag{2.75}$$

So, the production function can be rewritten as

$$y_t = f(Z_t, \alpha) + u_t\,,\ E(u_t) = 0 \tag{2.76}$$

where the disturbances are heteroscedastic. Under appropriate assumptions, a nonlinear least squares estimate of this expression yields consistent estimates of α. Thus, these estimates can be used to derive consistent estimates of u_t:

$$\hat{u}_t = y_t - f(Z_t, \hat{\alpha}). \tag{2.77}$$

Consistent estimates of β are obtained in the second stage by regressions on $\hat{u}_t$. Following the method suggested by Hildreth and Houck (1968),

$$\hat{u}_t^2 = h^2(Z_t, \beta). \tag{2.78}$$

For example, using the original Illinois corn data used to generate Table 2.9, we solve the nonlinear least squares problem

$$\min_{\alpha} \sum_{i=1}^{339} (y_i - \alpha_0 x_{i1}^{\alpha_1} x_{i2}^{\alpha_2} x_{i3}^{\alpha_3})^2. \tag{2.79}$$

This problem is solved using the Newton–Raphson technique and the ordinary least squares estimates of the logarithmic form of the Cobb–Douglas function as an initial point. With these assumptions,

Table 2.14 Nonlinear Estimates for Cobb–Douglas Production Function

Parameters	Ordinary Least Squares	Nonlinear Least Squares — Unweighted	Nonlinear Least Squares — Weighted
Constant	37.5345	40.9351***	38.2228***
	—	(3.0236)[a]	(2.5444)
Nitrogen	0.1109***	0.1159***	0.1209***
	(0.0183)	(0.0134)	(0.0135)
Phosphorous	0.0588**	0.0471***	0.0657***
	(0.0230)	(0.0145)	(0.0087)
Potash	0.1031***	0.0996***	0.0921***
	(0.0175)	(0.0121)	(0.0114)

Notes: [a]Numbers in parenthesis denote standard errors.
***denotes statistical significance at the 0.01 level of confidence.
**denotes statistical significance at the 0.05 level of confidence.

Table 2.15 Regression on Estimated Error Squared

Parameter	Estimate
Constant	1851.7854***
	(190.1111)[a]
Nitrogen	−0.3206
	(1.0912)
Phosphorous	−3.6680*
	(1.9423)
Potash	−0.7351
	(1.4441)

Notes: [a]Numbers in parenthesis denote standard errors.
***denotes statistical significance at the 0.01 level of confidence.
*denotes statistical significance at the 0.10 level of confidence.

the nonlinear least squares results are presented in column 3 of Table 2.14. Next, we generate the error squared for the nonlinear least squares estimate and fit the linear model for Equation (2.77). The estimated parameters for error squared estimation are presented in Table 2.15. The results suggest that the level of phosphorous is statistically significant in predicting the variance at the 0.10 level of confidence. Hence, we divide by square root of the estimated error squared and re-estimate the production function. These results are presented in column 4 of Table 2.14.

2.6 Panel Data Estimation

Returning to the original estimation problem in Equation (2.8), we would like to develop a slightly different approach to the problem. Assume that we want to fit a production function using data for N states over T production periods. At one level, we could assume that each state has a unique production function

$$\ln(y_{it}) = \alpha_i + \beta_{i1}\ln(x_{1,it}) + \beta_{it}\ln(x_{2,it}) + \beta_{i3}\ln(x_{3,it}) + \epsilon_{it}. \quad (2.80)$$

Alternatively, we could assume that the production function is unique for each year (which is a little less likely from an agronomic perspective), yielding a production function specification of

$$\ln(y_{it}) = \alpha_t + \beta_{t1}\ln(x_{1,it}) + \beta_{t2}\ln(x_{2,it}) + \beta_{t3}\ln(x_{3,it}) + \epsilon_{it}. \quad (2.81)$$

In either case, we are limited in the amount of information we can use at one time in the regression. Specifically, in Equation (2.80), we have N different regressions each with T observations, while in Equation (2.81) we have T different regressions each with N observations. The idea is that as long as the underlying production surfaces are equivalent, we could improve the fit by combining information across samples. However, to the degree that the underlying production surfaces are dissimilar, combining information across samples adds additional noise to the estimation and reduces the efficiency of the estimation. The concept of pooling individuals or time periods is typically known as panel data analysis.

As a starting point, we consider the specification where the underlying production technology is similar in the way that output responds to variable input, but assume that each state has a somewhat different constant. Mathematically, this estimation problem is specified as

$$\begin{aligned} \ln(y_{it}) &= \alpha_i + \beta_1\ln(x_{1,it}) + \beta_t\ln(x_{2,it}) + \beta_3\ln(x_{3,it}) + \epsilon_{it} \\ \Rightarrow \tilde{y}_{it} &= \alpha_i + \beta\tilde{x}_{it} + \epsilon_{it}, i = 1,\ldots,N, t = 1,\ldots,T. \end{aligned} \quad (2.82)$$

Thus, we have NT observations. This specification is implicitly pooled, the values of the coefficients are the same for each individual at every point in time. This specification can be expanded to allow for differences in the slope coefficients across firms

$$\tilde{y}_{it} = \alpha_i + \beta_i \tilde{x}_{it} + \epsilon_{it} \tag{2.83}$$

where β_i represent firm-specific slope parameters. Testing for the poolability (or whether the states are similar enough to improve our estimates) then amounts to testing whether $\beta_i = \beta$ for all i.

Based on these alternative models, we conceptualize a set of nested tests. First, we test for overall pooling (i.e., the production function has the same constant and slope parameters for every firm). If pooling is rejected for both sets of parameters, we hypothesize that the constants differ for each firm, while the slope coefficients are the same.

2.6.1 *Analysis of Covariance*

In order to provide a slightly more rigorous development of the panel model, we follow the formulation of Hsiao (1986). Specifically, we assume the general panel specification

$$y_{it} = \alpha^* + \beta' x_{it} + \gamma' z_{it} + u_{it}, i = 1, \ldots, N, t = 1, \ldots, T \tag{2.84}$$

where x_{it} and z_{it} are $k_1 \times 1$ and $k_2 \times 1$ vectors of exogenous variables, α^*, β and γ are estimated parameters, and u_{it} is an independently and identically distributed (iid) error term with mean 0 and variance σ_u^2 It is well known that ordinary least squares (OLS) regressions of y_{it} on x_{it} and z_{it} are best linear unbiased estimators (BLUE) of α^*, β, and γ. However, the results are corrupted if we do not observe z_{it}. Specifically, if x_{it} and z_{it} are correlated, then OLS estimates of the β are biased. However, if repeated observations of a group of individuals are available (i.e., panel or longitudinal data), they may allow us to get rid of the effect of z_{it}.

For example, if $z_{it} = z_i$ (or the unobserved variable is the same for each individual across time), the effect of the unobserved variables can be removed by first differencing the dependent and independent variables:

$$y_{it} - y_{i,t-1} = \beta' (x_{it} - x_{i,t-1}) + \gamma' (z_{it} - z_{i,t-1}) + (u_{it} - u_{i,t-1}) \tag{2.85}$$

since $z_{it} = z_{i,t-1} = z_i$, yielding

$$y_{it} - y_{i,t-1} = \beta'(x_{it} - x_{i,t-1}) + (u_{it} - u_{i,t-1})\, i = 1, \ldots, N, t = 2, \ldots, T. \quad (2.86)$$

Similarly, if $z_{it} = z_t$ (or the unobserved variables are the same for every individual at any point in time), we can derive a consistent estimator by subtracting the mean of the dependent and independent variables for each individual:

$$y_{it} - \bar{y}_i = \beta' (x_{it} - \bar{x}_i) + \gamma' (z_{it} - \bar{z}_i) + (u_{it} - \bar{u}_i). \quad (2.87)$$

Since $z_{it} = \bar{z}_i$,

$$\begin{aligned} y_{it} - \bar{y}_i &= \beta' (x_{it} - \bar{x}_i) + (u_{it} - \bar{u}_i) \\ \bar{y}_i &= \frac{1}{T}\sum_{t=1}^{T} y_{it} \\ \bar{x}_i &= \frac{1}{T}\sum_{t=1}^{T} x_{it} \\ \bar{u}_i &= \frac{1}{T}\sum_{t=1}^{T} u_{it} \end{aligned} \quad . \quad (2.88)$$

OLS estimators then provide unbiased and consistent estimates of β. Unfortunately, if we have a cross-sectional dataset (i.e., $T = 1$) or a single time series (i.e., $N = 1$), these transformations cannot be used.

In order to derive a little different form of the panel estimator, we start from the pooled estimates:

$$y_{it} = \alpha^* + \beta' x_{it} + \nu_{it}. \quad (2.89)$$

We envision two sets of restrictions or hypotheses:

- **Case I:** Heterogeneous intercepts ($\alpha_i^* \neq \alpha^*$) and a homogeneous slope ($\beta_i = \beta$)
- **Case II:** Heterogeneous slopes and intercepts ($\alpha_i^* \neq \alpha_i, \beta_i \neq \beta$)

$$y_{it} = \alpha_i^* + \beta_i' x_{it} + \nu_{it} \quad (2.90)$$

- **Case III:** Homogeneous slopes and heterogeneous slopes (not typically addressed)

$$y_{it} = \alpha^* + \beta_i' + \nu_{it}. \tag{2.91}$$

This leads to an empirical system with three hypotheses from the general model:

- H_1: Regression slope coefficients are identical and the intercepts are not.
- H_2: Regression intercepts are the same and the slope coefficients are not (again infrequently tested).
- H_3: Both slopes and intercepts are the same.

One way to estimate the panel effects is by systematically structuring the variance matrix. As a starting point, define the average value of the endogenous and exogenous variables within each individual across time:

$$\begin{aligned} \bar{y}_i &= \frac{1}{T}\sum_{t=1}^{T} y_{it} \\ \bar{x}_i &= \frac{1}{T}\sum_{t=1}^{T} x_{it} \end{aligned}. \tag{2.92}$$

The panel specification can then be estimated using a series of variance and covariance matrices for each individual

$$W_{XX} = \sum_{i=1}^{N} W_{XX,i} = \sum_{i=1}^{N}\left(\sum_{t=1}^{T}(x_{it} - \bar{x}_i)(x_{it} - \bar{x}_i)'\right) \tag{2.93}$$

$$W_{XY} = \sum_{i=1}^{N} W_{XY,i} = \sum_{i=1}^{N}\left(\sum_{t=1}^{T}(x_{it} - \bar{x}_i)(y_{it} - \bar{y}_i)\right). \tag{2.94}$$

The ordinary least squares estimator for the panel data with fixed effects (or constant differences in the intercepts) can then be defined starting with the estimated value of the common β vector

$$\hat{\beta} = W_{XX}^{-1} W_{XY}. \tag{2.95}$$

The individual intercepts are then estimated based on the pooled estimator for the slope coefficients and the individual means of the dependent and independent variables from Equation (2.92):

$$\hat{\alpha}_i = \bar{y}_i - \hat{\beta}\bar{x}_i, i = 1, \ldots, N. \tag{2.96}$$

Using the dataset Cotton-small.csv, we limit our attention to four states (Arkansas [1], Louisiana [2], Mississippi [3], and Texas [4]). The datasets for these states are complete in that we have an estimate of the amount of nitrogen, phosphorous, and potash used per acre along with the estimates for average cotton yield per acre. Computing each variance matrix (i.e., $W_{xx,\,i}$ and $W_{XY,\,i}$)

$$W_{XX,\,1} = \begin{bmatrix} 0.0314 & 0.0016 & 0.0283 \\ 0.0016 & 0.0091 & 0.0036 \\ 0.0283 & 0.0036 & 0.0355 \end{bmatrix}, W_{XY,\,1} = \begin{bmatrix} 0.0356 \\ -0.0011 \\ 0.0359 \end{bmatrix} \tag{2.97}$$

$$W_{XX,\,2} = \begin{bmatrix} 0.0330 & 0.0009 & 0.0195 \\ 0.0009 & 0.0135 & 0.0033 \\ 0.0195 & 0.0033 & 0.0345 \end{bmatrix}, W_{XY,\,2} = \begin{bmatrix} 0.0163 \\ -0.0066 \\ 0.0161 \end{bmatrix} \tag{2.98}$$

$$W_{XX,\,3} = \begin{bmatrix} 0.0091 & -0.0011 & 0.0173 \\ -0.0011 & 0.0074 & -0.0035 \\ 0.0173 & -0.0035 & 0.0566 \end{bmatrix}, W_{XY,\,3} = \begin{bmatrix} 0.0088 \\ -0.0058 \\ -0.0249 \end{bmatrix} \tag{2.99}$$

$$W_{XX,\,4} = \begin{bmatrix} 0.0343 & 0.0032 & 0.0191 \\ 0.0032 & 0.0089 & 0.0042 \\ 0.0191 & 0.0042 & 0.0323 \end{bmatrix}, W_{XY,\,4} = \begin{bmatrix} 0.0254 \\ -0.0021 \\ 0.0068 \end{bmatrix}. \tag{2.100}$$

Constructing W_{XX} and W_{XY} from Equations (2.93) and (2.94) yields

$$W_{XX} = \begin{bmatrix} 0.1078 & 0.0046 & 0.0841 \\ 0.0046 & 0.0388 & 0.0075 \\ 0.0841 & 0.0075 & 0.1589 \end{bmatrix}, W_{XY} = \begin{bmatrix} 0.0861 \\ -0.0155 \\ 0.0839 \end{bmatrix} \tag{2.101}$$

(i.e., $W_{XX} = \sum_{i=1}^{N} W_{XX,i}$ and $W_{XY} = \sum_{i=1}^{N} W_{XY,i}$). Using these matrices,

$$\hat{\beta} = \begin{bmatrix} 0.6670 \\ -0.5165 \\ 0.1979 \end{bmatrix}. \tag{2.102}$$

The results in Equation (2.102) assumes that slope coefficients are constrained to be the same, but the intercepts are different. Note that we can use the same matrices to compute the estimates under the assumption that both slopes and constants are different across states. Specifically,

$$\hat{\beta}_i = W_{XX,i}^{-1} W_{XY,i}. \tag{2.103}$$

Following Equation (2.96), the constant for each state could then be estimated as

$$\hat{\alpha}_i^* = \bar{y}_i - \hat{\beta}_i \bar{x}_i. \tag{2.104}$$

Finally, a regression where both the constants and the slope parameters are constrained to be the same can be estimated with a similar formulation:

$$\bar{x} = \frac{1}{NT}\sum_{i=1}^{N}\sum_{t=1}^{T} x_{it} \tag{2.105}$$

$$\bar{y} = \frac{1}{NT}\sum_{i=1}^{N}\sum_{t=1}^{T} y_{it} \tag{2.106}$$

$$T_{XX} = \sum_{i=1}^{N}\sum_{t=1}^{T}(x_{it} - \bar{x})(x_{it} - \bar{x})' \tag{2.107}$$

$$T_{XY} = \sum_{i=1}^{N}\sum_{t=1}^{T}(x_{it} - \bar{x})(y_{it} - \bar{y})' \tag{2.108}$$

$$\hat{\beta} = T_{XX}^{-1} T_{XY} \tag{2.109}$$

$$\hat{\alpha}^* = \bar{y} - \hat{\beta}\bar{x}. \tag{2.110}$$

Table 2.16 presents the estimated parameters for the individual and fixed effect regressions. The regressions presented in Equations (2.103) and (2.104) are referred to as the within-group estimators. The ith group residual sum of squared errors can be expressed

Table 2.16 Fixed Effect Regressions

Parameter	Fixed Effect	Pooled	Arkansas	Louisiana	Mississippi	Texas
Nitrogen	0.6670	1.0731	0.7263	0.3025	0.3156	0.9489
Phosphorous	−0.5165	0.4432	−0.4322	−0.5964	−0.5877	−0.4376
Potash	0.1979	−0.0043	0.4770	0.3519	0.3073	−0.2966
Constant(AR)	4.6187					
Constant(LA)	4.7065					
Constant(MS)	4.6429					
Constant(TX)	4.6490	0.0056				
Constant			2.9101	5.9802	6.0824	4.6369

as

$$RSS_i = W_{YY,i} - W'_{XY,i}W^{-1}_{XX,i}W_{XY,i} \tag{2.111}$$

$$W_{YY,i} = \sum_{t=1}^{T}(y_{it} - \bar{y}_i)^2. \tag{2.112}$$

The unrestricted (i.e., without holding either the intercepts or the slopes equal across individuals) residual sum of squares is then

$$S_1 = \sum_{i=1}^{N} RSS_i. \tag{2.113}$$

The residual sum of squares for the estimated model holding the slopes equal across individuals but allowing the intercepts to change across individuals is defined as

$$S_2 = W_{YY} - W'_{XY}W^{-1}_{XX}W_{XY} \tag{2.114}$$

$$W_{YY} = \sum_{i=1}^{N} W_{YY,i}. \tag{2.115}$$

Finally, the residual sum of squares for the estimated model holding both slopes and intercepts constant across each panel member can be defined as

$$S_3 = T_{YY} - T'_{XY}T^{-1}_{XX}T_{XY} \tag{2.116}$$

$$T_{YY} = \sum_{i=1}^{N}\sum_{t=1}^{T}(y_it - \bar{y})^2. \tag{2.117}$$

Hence, to test for pooling both the slope and intercept terms

$$H_3 : \alpha_1^* = \alpha_2^* = \ldots \alpha_N^*,\ \beta_1 = \beta_2 = \ldots \beta_N \tag{2.118}$$

$$F_3 = \frac{\dfrac{S_3 - S_1}{[(N-1)(K+1)]}}{\dfrac{S_1}{[NT - N(K+1)]}} \sim F((N-1)(K+1), NT - N(K+1)). \tag{2.119}$$

If this hypothesis is rejected, we then test for homogeneity of the slopes, but heterogeneity of the constants

$$H_1 : \beta_1 = \beta_2 = \dots \beta_N \tag{2.120}$$

$$F_1 = \frac{\dfrac{S_2 - S_1}{[(N-1)(K+1)]}}{\dfrac{S_1}{[NT - N(K+1)]}} \sim F((N-1)K, NT - N(K+1)). \tag{2.121}$$

2.6.1.1 *Dummy variable formulation*

The analysis of covariance can be accomplished using dummy variables. Specifically, we could reformulate the regression model as

$$Y = \begin{bmatrix} y_1 \\ y_2 \\ \vdots \\ y_N \end{bmatrix} + \alpha_1^* \begin{bmatrix} e \\ 0 \\ \vdots \\ 0 \end{bmatrix} + \alpha_2^* \begin{bmatrix} 0 \\ 1 \\ \vdots \\ 0 \end{bmatrix} + \cdots \alpha_N^* \begin{bmatrix} 0 \\ 0 \\ \vdots \\ 3 \end{bmatrix} + \begin{bmatrix} x_1 \\ x_2 \\ \vdots \\ x_N \end{bmatrix} \beta + \begin{bmatrix} u_1 \\ u_2 \\ \vdots \\ u_N \end{bmatrix} \tag{2.122}$$

where

$$y_i = \begin{bmatrix} y_{i1} \\ y_{i2} \\ \vdots \\ y_{i,T} \end{bmatrix}, \; x_i = \begin{bmatrix} x_{11,i} & x_{21,i} & \cdots & x_{K1,i} \\ x_{12,i} & x_{22,i} & \cdots & x_{K2,i} \\ \vdots & \vdots & \ddots & \vdots \\ x_{1T,i} & x_{2T,i} & \cdots & x_{KT,i} \end{bmatrix} \tag{2.123}$$

and $e' \in M_{1\times T}$, $e' = [1, 1, \dots, 1]$, $u_i' \in M_{1\times T}$, $u_i' = [u_{i1}, u_{i2}, \dots, u_{iN}]$, $E[u_i] = 0$, $E[u_i u_i'] = \sigma^2 I_T$, and $E[u_i u_j'] = 0$, $i \neq j$.

2.6.1.2 *Sweep matrices*

A slight reformulation of the covariance specification involves the sweep matrix which removes the mean of either the individual component or time components of the model. As an example, consider a scenario where we want to estimate a panel specification with N individuals over 4 years. The sweep matrix which would remove the individual effects is written as

$$Q_T = I_T - \frac{1}{T}ee' \tag{2.124}$$

where e is a $T \times 1$ vector of ones. If $T = 4$,

$$Q_4 = \begin{bmatrix} 1\,0\,0\,0 \\ 0\,1\,0\,0 \\ 0\,0\,1\,0 \\ 0\,0\,0\,1 \end{bmatrix} - \frac{1}{4}\begin{bmatrix} 1\,1\,1\,1 \\ 1\,1\,1\,1 \\ 1\,1\,1\,1 \\ 1\,1\,1\,1 \end{bmatrix} \tag{2.125}$$

$$Q_4 = \begin{bmatrix} 1-\frac{1}{4} & -\frac{1}{4} & -\frac{1}{4} & -\frac{1}{4} \\ -\frac{1}{4} & 1-\frac{1}{4} & -\frac{1}{4} & -\frac{1}{4} \\ -\frac{1}{4} & -\frac{1}{4} & 1-\frac{1}{4} & -\frac{1}{4} \\ -\frac{1}{4} & -\frac{1}{4} & -\frac{1}{4} & 1-\frac{1}{4} \end{bmatrix}. \tag{2.126}$$

Suppose that we observe three individuals over these 4 years, multiplying the sweep matrix by each individual observation,

$$\tilde{e} = \begin{bmatrix} 1-\frac{1}{4} & -\frac{1}{4} & -\frac{1}{4} & -\frac{1}{4} \\ -\frac{1}{4} & 1-\frac{1}{4} & -\frac{1}{4} & -\frac{1}{4} \\ -\frac{1}{4} & -\frac{1}{4} & 1-\frac{1}{4} & -\frac{1}{4} \\ -\frac{1}{4} & -\frac{1}{4} & -\frac{1}{4} & 1-\frac{1}{4} \end{bmatrix} \times \begin{bmatrix} y_{11}-\alpha_1-x_{11}\beta & y_{12}-\alpha_2-x_{12}\beta & y_{13}-\alpha_3-x_{13}\beta \\ y_{21}-\alpha_1-x_{21}\beta & y_{22}-\alpha_2-x_{22}\beta & y_{23}-\alpha_3-x_{23}\beta \\ y_{31}-\alpha_1-x_{31}\beta & y_{32}-\alpha_2-x_{32}\beta & y_{33}-\alpha_3-x_{33}\beta \\ y_{41}-\alpha_1-x_{41}\beta & y_{42}-\alpha_2-x_{42}\beta & y_{43}-\alpha_3-x_{43}\beta \end{bmatrix}. \tag{2.127}$$

Taking the first row and first column of the matrix multiplication in Equation (2.127),

$$\tilde{e}_{1,1} = [y_1 1 - \alpha_1 - x_{11}\beta] - \frac{1}{4}\left[\sum_{i=1}^{4} y_{i1} - \alpha_1 - \left(\sum_{i=1}^{4} x_{i1}\right)\beta\right] \tag{2.128}$$

$$\tilde{e}_{1,1} = (y_{11} - \bar{y}_1) - (x_{11} - \bar{x}_1)\,\beta \tag{2.129}$$

which is similar to the expression in Equation (2.86). Thus, the sweep matrix removes the fixed effects from the linear regression model. Rewriting Equation (2.126), as a regression equation

$$Q_T y = Q_T x \beta + Q_T e. \tag{2.130}$$

Given that Q_T is an idempotent matrix, the least squares estimator for β then becomes

$$\hat{\beta} = \left(x' Q_T x\right)^{-1} \left(x' Q_T y\right). \tag{2.131}$$

If the y vector and x matrices are stacked,

$$\tilde{y} = \begin{bmatrix} y_1 \\ y_2 \\ \vdots \\ y_N \end{bmatrix}, \; \tilde{x} = \begin{bmatrix} x_{11} & x_{12} & \cdots & x_{1K} \\ x_{21} & x_{22} & \cdots & x_{2K} \\ \vdots & \vdots & \ddots & \vdots \\ x_{N1} & x_{N2} & \cdots & x_{NK} \end{bmatrix} \tag{2.132}$$

where y_1 is a vector containing T observations on the first individual in the panel and x_{1k} is the vector containing T observations on the first individual for the kth independent variable. The panel regression can then be expressed as

$$\hat{\beta} = \left[\tilde{x}' \left(I_N \otimes Q_T\right) \tilde{x}\right]^{-1} \left[\tilde{x}' \left(I_N \otimes Q_T\right) \tilde{y}\right] \tag{2.133}$$

which will yield identical estimates to the covariance estimates presented above.

2.6.2 *Random Effects Models*

Regression analysis typically assumes that a large number of factors affect the value of the dependent variable, while some of the variables are measured directly in the model, the remaining variables can be summarized by a random distribution:

$$\begin{aligned} y_{it} &= \alpha + \beta x_{it} + \gamma z_{it} + \epsilon_{it} \\ y_{it} &= \left(\alpha + \gamma E\left[z_{it}\right]\right) + \beta x_{it} + \left(\epsilon_{it} + \left[z_{it} - E\left[z_{it}\right]\right]\right). \end{aligned} \tag{2.134}$$

When "numerous observations" on individuals are observed over time, it is assumed that some of the omitted variables represent factors peculiar to individual and time periods. Going back to the panel specification,

$$\begin{aligned} y_{it} &= \alpha^* + \beta' x_{it} + v_{it} \\ v_{it} &= \alpha_i + \lambda_t + u_{it} \end{aligned}. \tag{2.135}$$

In this formulation, α^* is a random variable. Specifically, the random variable is the sum of three components: the first component is drawn for each individual $\alpha_i \sim N(E[\alpha_i], \sigma_\alpha^2)$; the second component is drawn for each time period $\lambda_t \sim N(E[\lambda], \sigma_\lambda^2)$; the third component is the random noise which is orthogonal to either the individual or time effect.

In order to identify each of the random components, we assume that the expected value of each individual and time component along with the orthogonal error are all zero. In addition, we assume that each effect is independent. Mathematically,

$$E[\alpha_i] = E[\lambda_t] = E[u_{it}] = E[\alpha_i \lambda_t] = E[\alpha_i u_{it}] = E[\lambda_t u_{it}] = 0. \tag{2.136}$$

In addition, we assume that the random components are independent across individuals and time periods

$$E[\alpha_i \alpha_j] = \begin{cases} \sigma_\alpha^2 \text{ if } i = j \\ 0 \text{ if } i \neq j \end{cases} \tag{2.137}$$

$$E[\lambda_t \lambda_s] = \begin{cases} \sigma_\lambda^2 \text{ if } t = s \\ 0 \text{ if } t \neq s \end{cases}. \tag{2.138}$$

$$E[u_{it} u_{js}] = \begin{cases} \sigma_u^2 \text{ if } i = j, t = s \\ 0 \text{ otherwise} \end{cases} \tag{2.139}$$

Finally, we assume that these random variables are uncorrelated with the independent variables

$$E[\alpha_i x_{it}'] = E[\lambda_t x_{it}'] = E[u_{it} x_{it}'] = 0. \tag{2.140}$$

The variance of y_{it} on x_{it} based on the assumption above is

$$\sigma_y^2 = \sigma_\alpha^2 + \sigma_\lambda^2 + \sigma_u^2. \tag{2.141}$$

Thus, this kind of model is typically referred to as a variance component (or error component) model. Letting

$$\tilde{X}_i = (e, X_i) \tag{2.142}$$

$$\delta = (\mu, \beta') \tag{2.143}$$

$$v_i' = (v_{i1}, \ldots, v_{iT}) \tag{2.144}$$

$$v_{it} = \alpha_i + u_{it} \tag{2.145}$$

the panel estimation model can be written in vector form as

$$y_i = \tilde{X}_i \delta + v_i \; i = 1, \ldots, N. \tag{2.146}$$

The variance of the residual becomes

$$E\left[v_i v_i'\right] = \sigma_u^2 I_T + \sigma_\alpha^2 ee' = V \tag{2.147}$$

$$V^{-1} = \frac{1}{\sigma_u^2}\left[I_T - \frac{\sigma_\alpha^2}{\sigma_u^2 + T\sigma_\alpha^2}\right]. \tag{2.148}$$

Following the regression estimator developed in Equation (2.133) (i.e., using the sweep matrix)

$$Q_T y_i = Q_T e\mu + Q_T X_i \beta + Q_T e\alpha_i + Q_T u_i \tag{2.149}$$

$$Q_T y_i = Q_T X_i \beta + Q_T u_i. \tag{2.150}$$

Whether α_i is fixed or random, the covariance estimator is unbiased. However, if α_i is random, the covariance estimator is not the best linear unbiased estimator (BLUE). Instead, a BLUE estimator can be derived using generalized least squares (GLS). Since both u_{it} and u_is contain α_i, they are correlated.

$$\delta = (\mu, \beta') \tag{2.151}$$

$$\left[\sum_{i=1}^{N} \tilde{X}_i' V^{-1} \tilde{X}_i\right] \hat{\delta}_{GLS} = \left[\sum_{i=1}^{N} \tilde{X}_i' V^{-1} y_i\right] \tag{2.152}$$

$$\begin{aligned} V^{-1} &= \frac{1}{\sigma_u^2}\left[\left(I_T - \frac{1}{T}ee'\right) + \psi \frac{1}{T}ee'\right] \\ &= \frac{1}{\sigma_u^2}\left[Q_T + \psi \frac{1}{T}ee'\right] \end{aligned} \tag{2.153}$$

$$\psi = \frac{\sigma_u^2}{\sigma_u^2 + T\sigma_\alpha^2}. \tag{2.154}$$

A procedure for estimation

$$\left[W_{\tilde{X}\tilde{X}} + \psi B_{\tilde{X}\tilde{X}}\right] \begin{bmatrix} \hat{\mu} \\ \hat{\beta} \end{bmatrix}_{GLS} = \left[W_{\tilde{X}y} + \psi B_{\tilde{X}y}\right] \tag{2.155}$$

$$T_{\tilde{X}\tilde{X}} = \sum_{i=1}^{N} \tilde{X}_i' ee' \tilde{X}_i \tag{2.156}$$

$$T_{\tilde{X}y} = \sum_{i=1}^{N} \tilde{X}_i' y_i \tag{2.157}$$

$$B_{\tilde{X}\tilde{X}} = \frac{1}{T} \sum_{i=1}^{N} \left(\tilde{X}_i' ee' \tilde{X}_i\right) \tag{2.158}$$

$$B_{\tilde{X}y} = \frac{1}{T} \sum_{i=1}^{N} \left(\tilde{X}_i' ee' y_i\right) \tag{2.159}$$

$$W_{\tilde{X}\tilde{X}} = T_{\tilde{X}\tilde{X}} - B_{\tilde{X}\tilde{X}} \tag{2.160}$$

$$W_{\tilde{X}y} = T_{\tilde{X}y} - B_{\tilde{X}y}. \tag{2.161}$$

This looks bad, but think about

$$\begin{aligned} \left(X'QX\right)\beta &= \left(X'Qy\right) \\ X'\left(I_T - \frac{1}{T}ee'\right)X &= X'\left(I_T - \frac{1}{T}ee'\right)y \\ X'X - \frac{1}{T}X'ee'X &= X'y - \frac{1}{T}X'ee'y. \end{aligned} \tag{2.162}$$

Relating this solution to the above covariance matrices,

$$\begin{aligned} T_{\tilde{X}\tilde{X}} &\Rightarrow X'X \\ B_{\tilde{X}\tilde{X}} &\Rightarrow \frac{1}{T}X'ee'X \\ W_{\tilde{X}y} &\Rightarrow X'y \\ B_{\tilde{X}y} &\Rightarrow \frac{1}{T}X'ee'y \end{aligned}. \tag{2.163}$$

Hence, substituting from Equation (2.142) into Equation (2.156) yields

$$\begin{bmatrix} \psi NT & \psi T \sum_{i=1}^{N} \bar{x}_i' \\ \psi T \sum_{i=1}^{N} \bar{x}_i & \sum_{i=1}^{N} X_i' Q X_i + \psi T \sum_{i=1}^{N} \bar{x}_i \bar{x}_i' \end{bmatrix} \begin{bmatrix} \hat{\mu} \\ \hat{\beta} \end{bmatrix}_{GLS}$$

$$= \begin{bmatrix} \psi NT \bar{y} \\ \sum_{i=1}^{N} X_i' Q y_i + \psi T \sum_{i=1}^{N} \bar{x}_i \bar{y}_i \end{bmatrix}. \tag{2.164}$$

Using the inverse of a partitioned matrix

$$\begin{aligned} \hat{\beta}_{GLS} &= \left[\frac{1}{T} \sum_{i=1}^{N} X_i' Q X_i + \psi \sum_{i=1}^{N} (\bar{x}_i - \bar{x})(\bar{x}_i - \bar{x})' \right]^{-1} \\ &\quad \times \left[\frac{1}{T} \sum_{i=1}^{N} X_i' Q y_i + \psi \sum_{i=1}^{N} (\bar{x}_i - \bar{x})(\bar{y}_i - \bar{y}) \right] \qquad (2.165) \\ &= \Delta \hat{\beta}_b + (I_K - \Delta) \hat{\beta}_{CV} \\ \hat{\mu}_{GLS} &= \bar{y} - \hat{\beta}_{GLS} \bar{x} \end{aligned}$$

where

$$\begin{aligned} \Delta &= \psi T \left[\sum_{i=1}^{N} X_i' Q X_i + \psi T \sum_{i=1}^{N} (\bar{x}_i - \bar{x})(\bar{x}_i - \bar{x})' \right]^{-1} \\ &\quad \times \left[\sum_{i=1}^{N} (\bar{x}_i - \bar{x})(\bar{x}_i - \bar{x})' \right] \qquad (2.166) \\ \hat{\beta}_b &= \left[\sum_{i=1}^{N} (\bar{x}_i - \bar{x})(\bar{x}_i - \bar{x})' \right]^{-1} \left[\sum_{i=1}^{N} (\bar{x}_i - \bar{x})(\bar{y}_i - \bar{y}) \right] \end{aligned}$$

where β_b is the between estimator. The variance of the estimator can be written as

$$V(\hat{\beta}_{GLS}) = \sigma_u^2 \left[\sum_{i=1}^{N} X_i' Q X_i + T\psi \sum_{i=1}^{N} (\bar{x}_i - \bar{x})(\bar{x}_i - \bar{x})' \right]^{-1}. \tag{2.167}$$

Given that we do not know ψ *a priori*, we estimate

$$\hat{\sigma}_u^2 = \frac{\sum_{i=1}^{N}\sum_{t=1}^{T}\left[(y_{it}-\bar{y}_i)-\hat{\beta}'_{CV}(x_{it}-\bar{x}_i)\right]^2}{N(T-1)-K}$$
$$\hat{\sigma}_\alpha^2 = \frac{\sum_{i=1}^{N}\left(\bar{y}_i-\bar{\mu}-\bar{\beta}\bar{x}_i\right)^2}{N-(K+1)} - \frac{1}{T}\hat{\sigma}_u^2 \quad . \tag{2.168}$$

Thus, the random effects model can be estimated by first estimating the "within" estimator individual by individual and then using those estimates to estimate $\hat{\sigma}_u^2$ by Equation (2.168). Then using the average values of the endogenous and exogenous variables $\hat{\sigma}_\alpha^2$ can be estimated using the residual from the regression on individual averages. This allows for the estimation of ψ using Equation (2.154).

2.7 Other Considerations and Specifications

2.7.1 *Stochastic Error Functions*

To introduce the composed error term, we will begin with a cursory discussion of technical efficiency which we develop more fully after the dual. We start with the standard production function

$$y_i = f(x_i, \beta). \tag{2.169}$$

We begin by acknowledging that firms may not produce on the efficient frontier

$$y_i = f(x_i, \beta)TE_i. \tag{2.170}$$

If we assume that $TE_i = 1$ (e.g., where $TE_i = 1$ denoting a technically efficient producer), the firm is efficient — its output is on the production function. However, in general,

$$TE_i = \frac{y_i}{f(x_i, \beta)} \tag{2.171}$$

where $TE_i \leq 1$. In the general case, we acknowledge the possibility that $y_i \leq f(x_i, \beta)$ or that the producer may be producing less output than is technically feasible from the inputs employed.

The specification in Equation (2.171) assumes that all the errors between the firm's output and the frontier relate to technical inefficiency. However, this assumption seems a little severe. Other factors beyond the control of the decision maker may cause decreases or even increases in production. Hence, this model is augmented with the possibility that random shocks may affect output that do not represent inefficiency

$$y_i = f(x_i, \beta) \times \exp(v_i) \times TE_i \tag{2.172}$$

where v_i represents randomness beyond the control of the decision maker (i.e., hurricanes).

Building on the model of technical inefficiency alone, we could estimate the production function using a one-sided error specification alone. Mathematical Programming (Goal Programming): First, we could solve two nonlinear programming problems. We could minimize the sum of the residuals such that we constrain the residuals to be positive:

$$\begin{aligned} &\min_{\beta_j, j=1,\ldots,K} \sum_{i=1}^{N} u_i \\ \text{s.t. } u_i &= \beta_0 + \sum_{i=1}^{N} \beta_k \ln(x_{ik}) - \ln(y_i) \\ u_i &\geq 0\,,\; i = 1, \ldots, N \end{aligned} \tag{2.173}$$

which approximates the distribution function for the exponential distribution with a log-likelihood function

$$\ln(L) = N \ln(\lambda) - \lambda \sum_{i=1}^{N} |u_i|\,. \tag{2.174}$$

Applying the specification in Equation (2.173) to the Illinois corn data for 1993 with the modification, we minimize the average residual, yielding the results in Table 2.17.

Table 2.17 Estimated Cobb–Douglas Coefficients Base on One-Sided Errors

	Illinois Corn Data			Pseudo-Data		
Parameter	Absolute Value	Exponential Likelihood	Half Normal	Absolute Value	Exponential Likelihood	Half Normal
β_0	5.0626	5.5121	5.5121	0.0000	4.6971	1.0148
		(5.6255)	(2.0714)		(7.1571)	(5.4771)
β_1	0.0000	0.0000	0.0000	0.9961	0.0000	0.3721***
		(4.9253)	(1.9105)		(4.0448)	(0.0311)
β_2	0.0000	0.0000	0.0000	0.0000	0.0000	0.2304***
		(0.8980)	(0.5982)		(2.2869)	(0.0086)
β_3	0.0000	0.0000	0.0000	0.0000	0.0000	0.1350***
		(0.8959)	(0.9742)		(0.9739)	(0.0088)
λ		1.5531			2,500.0***	
		(0.8932)			(1.9505)	
σ^2			0.5401			0.0015
			(0.6757)			(0.0079)

Notes: [a]Numbers in parenthesis denote standard errors.
***denotes statistical significance at the 0.01 level of confidence.

The second specification minimizes the sum of square residuals such that the residual is constrained to be positive:

$$\begin{aligned}
&\min_{\beta_j, j=1,\ldots,K} \sum_{i=1}^{N} u_i^2 \\
&\text{s.t. } u_i = \beta_0 + \sum_{k=1}^{K} \beta_k \ln(x_{ik}) - \ln(y_i) \\
&u_i \geq 0, \quad i = 1, \ldots, N
\end{aligned} \tag{2.175}$$

which approximates the half-normal distribution

$$\ln(L) = C - \frac{1}{2}\ln\left(\sigma_u^2\right) - \frac{1}{2\sigma_u^2}\sum_i u_i^2. \tag{2.176}$$

The results for the maximization problem in Equation (2.176) are presented in Table 2.17.

In general, the solutions for the Illinois corn data in 1993 exhibit a solution similar to a "corner solution". In the solution, we have constrained the values of β_1, β_2, and β_3 to be greater than or equal to zero. Implicitly, these constraints appear to be binding, resulting in a single non-zero parameter $\beta_0 \approx \ln(\max(y)) = \ln(247.67) = 5.512$.

In order to better present the stochastic frontier model, consider the dataset "OneSidedPseudo.csv". This data is generated from the production function

$$y = f(x_1, x_2, x_3, x_4) = 2.5x_1^{0.35}x_2^{0.25}x_3^{0.15}x_4^{0.20} + \nu \tag{2.177}$$

where $\nu \sim \Gamma(1.35, 0.75)$. The data assumes that x_1, x_2, and x_3 are approximately optimal,[4] but the value of x_4 is assumed to be exogenous (e.g., beyond the control of the decision maker). Intuitively, x_4 in this formulation is a random component of production that cannot be modeled as a source of economic inefficiency. Table 2.17 finds

[4]The optimal levels of each input are adjusted by a random noise: $\tilde{x}_1 = x_1^* + \zeta_1$, $\tilde{x}_2 = x_2^* + \zeta_2$, and $\tilde{x}_3 = x_3^* + \zeta_3$ where x_1^*, x_2^*, and x_3^* are optimal levels of each input given input and output prices. The level of production is then

$$y = f(\tilde{x}_1, \tilde{x}_2, \tilde{x}_3, x_4) + \nu$$

a similar "corner solution" for the absolute value and exponential distribution formulations. The corner solution for the exponential formulation is additionally suspect given the extreme estimate of λ. However, it is interesting how close the estimates for the half-normal specification are to the assumed values in Equation (2.177).

2.7.1.1 *Corrected ordinary least squares*

Each of the preceding estimators are inherently nonlinear. Hence, we consider a complex of modifications to ordinary least squares that can be used to account for the one-sided error specification. The first we consider is *Corrected Ordinary Least Squares* (as presented in Kumbhakar and Lovell (2000, pp. 70–71) and Greene (2008)). In this approach, we first estimate the production function using ordinary least squares; then, we adjust the estimated frontier by adding a sufficient constant to the estimated intercept to make all the error terms negative:

$$\hat{\beta}_0^* = \hat{\beta}_0 + \max_i \{\hat{u}_i\}. \tag{2.178}$$

The estimated residuals are then

$$\hat{u}_i^* = \hat{u}_i - \max_i \{\hat{u}_i\}. \tag{2.179}$$

This procedure simply shifts the production function estimated with OLS upward, no information on the inefficiency is used in the estimation of the slope coefficients. This approach was first suggested by Winsten (1957) in his discussion of Farrell (1957).

The results for ordinary least squares and the residual correction for both Illinois and the pseudo-data are presented in Table 2.18. Figure 2.5 presents the frontier, projected output, and errors for the logarithm of corn. Note in Figure 2.5 the frontier function is uniformly above the observed output. This implies that the residual (e.g., the frontier minus the observed level of production) is always positive, which is confirmed in the figure. Figure 2.6 presents the same relationships for the pseudo-data. Again, the frontier production is uniformly above the observed data and the residual is always positive.

Table 2.18 Corrected Ordinary Least Squares

Parameter	Illinois Corn	Pseudo-Data
β_0	3.6253***	0.9799***
	(0.0971)[a]	(0.0189)
β_1	0.1109***	0.3536***
	(0.0183)	(0.0106)
β_2	0.0588**	0.2442***
	(0.0230)	(0.0099)
β_3	0.1031***	0.1391***
	(0.0175)	(0.0112)
max (u_i)	1.0767	0.0449

Notes: [a]Numbers in parenthesis denote standard errors.
***denotes statistical significance at the 0.01 level of confidence.
**denotes statistical significance at the 0.05 level of confidence.

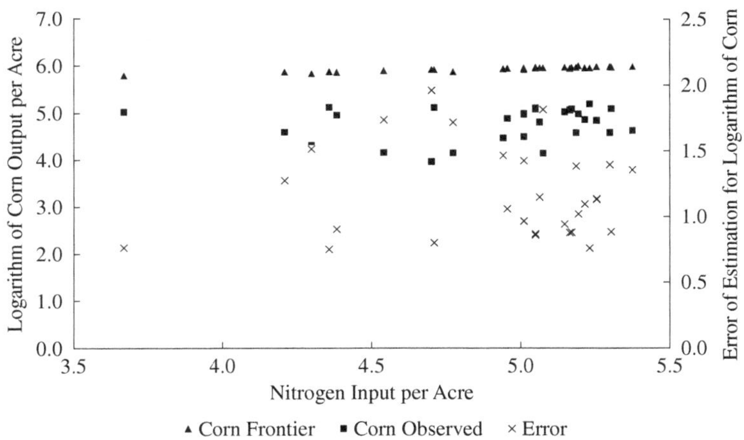

Fig. 2.5 Corrected Least Squares Frontier for Corn in Illinois

2.7.1.2 *Modified ordinary least squares*

A related two-step estimation procedure is used to again estimate the constant and slope parameters using ordinary least squares and then to fit a secondary distribution function (i.e., the half-normal,

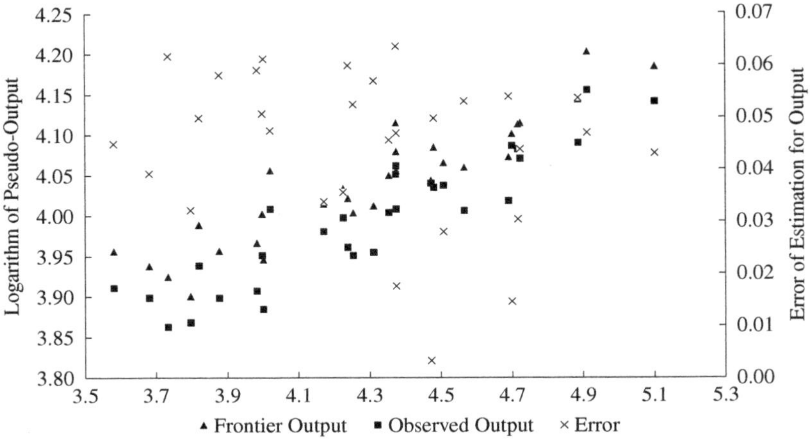

Fig. 2.6 Corrected Least Squares Frontier for Pseudo-Data

gamma, or exponential) to the residuals (Kumbhakar and Lovell, 2000, pp. 71–72 and Greene, 2008, pp. 106–107). The expected value of the residuals for this second distribution is then used to adjust the constant of the regression and the residuals:

$$\begin{aligned}\hat{\beta}_0^{**} &= \hat{\beta}_0 + E\left(\hat{u}_i\right) \\ \hat{u}_i^{**} &= \hat{u}_i - E\left(\hat{u}_i\right)\end{aligned}. \tag{2.180}$$

In addition to the constant shift in the production function addressed above, this specification does not necessarily guarantee that all the residuals will be negative. This approach was introduced by Afriat (1972).

Adding both technical variation and stochastic effects to the production model, we get

$$\ln\left(y_i\right) = \beta_0 + \sum_{k=1}^{K} \beta_k x_{ik} + v_i - u_i. \tag{2.181}$$

The overall error term of the regression is referred to as the composed error:

$$\begin{aligned}\ln\left(y_i\right) &= \beta_0 + \sum_{k=1}^{K} \beta_k \ln\left(x_{ik}\right) + \varepsilon_i \\ \varepsilon_i &= v_i - u_i\end{aligned}. \tag{2.182}$$

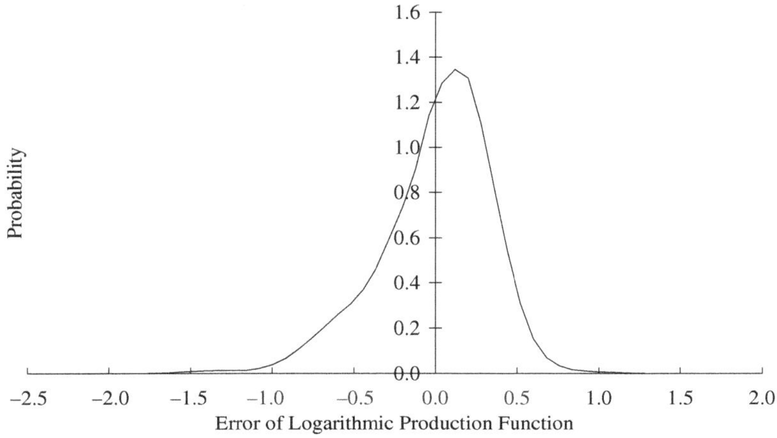

Fig. 2.7 Probability Density for Residuals from Illinois Corn Regression

Assuming that the components of the random error term are independent, OLS provides consistent estimates of the slope coefficients, but not of the constant. Further, OLS does not provide estimates of producer-specific technical inefficiency. However, OLS does provide a test for the possible presence of technical inefficiency in the data. Specifically, if technical inefficiency is present, then $u_i < 0$ so that the distribution is negatively skewed. Various tests for significant skewness are available, such as the Jarque and Bera (1987) test discussed in Section 2.3.3.

Turning to our examples, Figure 2.7 presents the probability density function for the logarithmic form of the Cobb–Douglas production function (e.g., the residuals for regression results in Illinois corn column of Table 2.18).[5] This figure suggests that the residuals are negatively skewed. The Jarque–Bera statistic for skewness is −0.918 which leads to a rejection of no skewness at any conventional level of significance. Following the modified ordinary least squares approach, we define the corrected error structure

$$\hat{u}_i = \delta + \max_i u_i - u_i \tag{2.183}$$

[5]The probability density functions used here are created using an *Averaged Shifted Histogram* approach described in Scott (1992, pp. 113–124).

Table 2.19 Gamma Distribution for Residuals from Illinois Corn Data

Parameter	Estimate
α	2.423***
	(0.031)[a]
β	0.448***
	(0.010)[a]

Notes: [a]Numbers in parenthesis denote standard errors.
***Denotes statistical significance at the 0.01 level of confidence.

where δ is a small constant to facilitate the gamma specification. Next, we estimate the α and β parameters for the Gamma distribution using the specification in Equations (2.19)–(2.22). This specification yields the estimates presented in Table 2.19. Note that these results tend to support the stochastic frontier specification.

2.7.1.3 *Maximum likelihood estimation*

We start by constructing a likelihood function based on the multiplication of the normal distribution and a half-normal distribution proposed by Aigner *et al.* (1977). To develop the maximum likelihood estimator of the stochastic frontier model, we will follow the derivation of Kumbhakar and Lovell (2000, pp. 72–77). We begin by specifying a general form of the stochastic production function

$$\tilde{y} = \tilde{x}\beta + u - v. \tag{2.184}$$

The required assumption is that the two random variables are uncorrelated. Let $v_i \sim N(0, \sigma_v^2)$ (or v_i is normally distributed) and $u_i \sim N^*(0, \sigma_u^2)$ be a half-normal distribution. The distribution for a zero-mean normal distribution can be written as

$$f(v) = \frac{1}{\sqrt{2\pi}\sigma_v} \exp\left(-\frac{v^2}{2\sigma_v^2}\right). \tag{2.185}$$

The half-normal distribution can then be written as

$$g(u) = \frac{2}{\sqrt{2\pi}\sigma_v} \exp\left(-\frac{u^2}{2\sigma_u^2}\right). \tag{2.186}$$

Assuming independence, the joint distribution function can be written as

$$f(u,v) = f(v)g(u) = \frac{2}{2\pi\sigma_u\sigma_v}\exp\left(-\frac{u^2}{2\sigma_u^2} - \frac{v^2}{2\sigma_v^2}\right). \tag{2.187}$$

Since $\epsilon = v - u$, or by definition of the composed error term,

$$f(u,\varepsilon) = \frac{2}{2\pi\sigma_u\sigma_v}\exp\left(-\frac{u^2}{2\sigma_u^2} - \frac{(\varepsilon+u)^2}{2\sigma_v^2}\right). \tag{2.188}$$

Next, we want to integrate out the one-sided error term u

$$f(\epsilon) = \int_0^\infty f(u,\epsilon)du. \tag{2.189}$$

To develop this integral, we start with two distribution functions for w and z (i.e., abstracting away from the specific problem in Equation (2.188) for the moment). Assume that w is distributed distribution

$$f(w) = \frac{1}{\sqrt{2\pi}}\exp\left(-\frac{w^2}{2}\right),\ w = \frac{W-\mu_W}{\sigma_W} \tag{2.190}$$

and z is distributed half-normal

$$g(z) = \begin{cases} \dfrac{f(z/\sigma)}{\sigma\left[1-\Phi(-a/\sigma)\right]},\ z \geq -a \\ 0,\ z < -a \end{cases},\quad z = \frac{Z-\mu_z}{\sigma_Z}. \tag{2.191}$$

To demonstrate that $g(z)$ is the half-normal distribution, let $a = 0$

$$g(z) = \frac{f(z/\sigma)}{\sigma[1-\Phi(0)]} = \frac{f(z/\sigma)}{\sigma\left[1-\dfrac{1}{2}\right]} = \frac{2f(z/\sigma)}{\sigma} \tag{2.192}$$

which after adjusting for $1/\sigma$ is exactly the distribution in Equation (2.185). Therefore, at $a = 0$ and letting $\sigma = \sigma_Z/\sigma_W$, Equation (2.192) becomes

$$g(z) = \frac{2}{\sqrt{2\pi}\sigma_W \dfrac{\sigma_Z}{\sigma_W}} \exp\left[-\frac{z^2}{2\left(\dfrac{\sigma_Z}{\sigma_W}\sigma_W\right)^2}\right] = \frac{2}{\sqrt{2\pi}\sigma_Z} \exp\left[-\frac{z^2}{2\sigma_Z^2}\right]. \tag{2.193}$$

Integrating the product of distribution function Equation (2.190) for all possible w and Equation (2.192) up to point $t \leq a$, we have

$$Q(t) = \int_{-\infty}^{t} \int_{-\infty}^{\infty} g(z - w) f(w) dw dz. \tag{2.194}$$

Substituting the result from Equation (2.192) into Equation (2.194) yields

$$Q(t) = \frac{1}{[1 - \Phi(-a/\sigma)]} \int_{-\infty}^{t} \int_{-\infty}^{z+a} f\left(\frac{z - w}{\sigma}\right) f(w) dw dz \tag{2.195}$$

with the change in the bounds of the second integral from the definition of the one-sided error term (i.e., see Equation (2.191)). Next, reversing the order of the integrals and integrating with respect to z yields

$$Q(t) = \frac{1}{[1 - \Phi(-a/\sigma)]} \int_{-\infty}^{t+a} \left[\Phi\left(\frac{t - x}{\sigma}\right) - \Phi\left(\frac{-a}{\sigma}\right)\right] f(x) dx. \tag{2.196}$$

Again, if $a = 0$ and using the result from Equation (2.192),

$$Q(t) = \frac{1}{[1 - \Phi(0)]} \int_{-\infty}^{t} \left[\Phi\left(\frac{t - x}{\sigma}\right) - \Phi(0)\right] f(x) dx \tag{2.197}$$

$$Q(t) = 2 \int_{-\infty}^{t} \frac{1}{2} \left[2\Phi\left(\frac{t - x}{\sigma}\right) - 1\right] f(x) dx. \tag{2.198}$$

Thus, using the result from Equation (2.198),

$$f(\epsilon) = \int_0^\infty f(u, \epsilon) du \tag{2.199}$$

$$f(\epsilon) = \frac{2}{\sqrt{2\pi}\sigma}\left[1 - \Phi\left(\frac{\epsilon\lambda}{\sigma}\right)\right]\exp\left[-\frac{\epsilon^2}{2\sigma^2}\right] \tag{2.200}$$

$$f(\epsilon) = \frac{2}{\sigma}\phi\left(\frac{\epsilon}{\sigma}\right)\Phi\left(-\frac{\varepsilon\lambda}{\sigma}\right) \tag{2.201}$$

where

$$\sigma = \sqrt{\sigma_u^2 + \sigma_v^2} \tag{2.202}$$

$$\lambda = \frac{\sigma_u}{\sigma_v}. \tag{2.203}$$

Note that as $\lambda \to 0$, either $\sigma_v^2 \to \infty$ or $\sigma_u^2 \to 0$ or the symmetric error dominates the one-sided component. Alternatively, as $\lambda \to \infty$, either $\sigma_u^2 \to \infty$ or $\sigma_v^2 \to 0$ or the one-sided component dominates the symmetric error.

The parameters of the model can be estimated by maximizing

$$\ln(L) \propto N\ln(\sigma) + \sum_{i=1}^N \ln\left(\Phi\left(-\frac{\epsilon_i\lambda}{\sigma}\right)\right) - \frac{1}{2\sigma^2}\sum_{i=1}^N \epsilon_i^2 \tag{2.204}$$

where

$$\lambda = \frac{\sigma_u}{\sigma_v} \Rightarrow \sigma_u = \lambda\sigma_v \tag{2.205}$$

$$\sigma_u^2 = \lambda^2\sigma_v^2 \tag{2.206}$$

$$\sigma^2 = \lambda^2\sigma_v^2 + \sigma_v^2 \Rightarrow \sigma^2 = \sigma_v^2\left(\lambda^2 + 1\right) \tag{2.207}$$

$$\sigma_v^2 = \frac{\sigma^2}{\lambda^2 + 1} \tag{2.208}$$

$$\sigma_u^2 = \sigma^2 - \sigma_v^2. \tag{2.209}$$

To demonstrate the application, we fit the Cobb–Douglas half-normal specification for the stochastic frontier model to the 1993 Illinois corn data. Using R, we maximize the function

Table 2.20 Stochastic Frontier Estimations for Corn Production in Illinois

Parameter	Ordinary Least Squares	Stochastic Frontier Model
β_0	3.6253***	3.6248***
	(0.0971)[a]	(0.3125)
β_1	0.1109***	0.1109***
	(0.0183)	(0.0183)
β_2	0.0588**	0.0588***
	(0.0230)	(0.0225)
β_3	0.1031***	0.1031***
	(0.0175)	(0.0170)
$\max(u_i)$	1.0767	
σ		0.3272***
		(0.0069)
λ		0.0018
		(1.1298)

Notes: [a]Numbers in parenthesis denote standard errors.
***denotes statistical significance at the 0.01 level of confidence.
**denotes statistical significance at the 0.05 level of confidence.

R Code — Half-Normal Likelihood Function

```
hlfnorm <- function(a){
  err  <- (a[1]+a[2]*dta$Lnit+a[3]*dta$Lpho+a[4]*
                  dta$Lpot) - dta$Lcorn
  like <- -nrow(dta)*log(a[5])+sum(log(pnorm(-err*a[6]/
                  a[5]))) - sum(err^2)/(2*a[5]^2)
  return(-like)
}
```

using Rsolnp (Ghalanos and Theussl, 2015). The estimated parameters are presented in Table 2.20 along with the estimates of the simple linear model. Note that there is very little difference in the two specifications. The reason for the similarity is that the one-sided component is very small (e.g., the estimated value for λ is small and statistically insignificant).

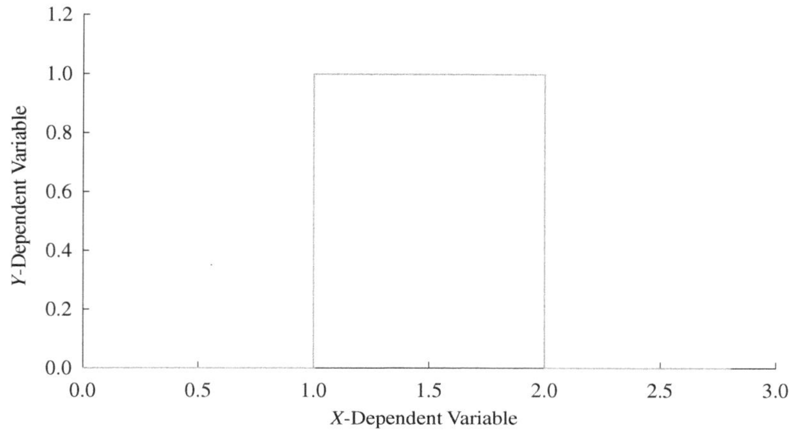

Fig. 2.8 Box-Response Function

2.7.2 *Non-parametric Functions*

It is clear from our discussions on production functions that the choice of production function may have significant implications for the economic results from the model. The Cobb–Douglas function has linear expansion paths that has implications for the input demand functions. While the Cobb–Douglas function has no stage III, the quadratic production function is practically guaranteed a stage III. Thus, one approach is used to generate non-parametric functional forms. These non-parametric functional forms are intended to allow for the maximum flexibility in the input–output map. However, the flexibility is purchased at a cost. It may be hard to apply economic decisions to the non-parametric forms.

2.7.2.1 *Fourier expansions*

A Fourier transformation is a flexible functional form that allows the researcher to approximate very complex functions. To demonstrate the Fourier transformation, consider box-response function depicted in Figure 2.8. Obviously, it will be difficult to fit this form with a "smooth" function. However, as a starting point, we could consider a simple quadratic function

$$y = f(x) = \beta_0 + \beta_1 x + \beta_2 x^2. \qquad (2.210)$$

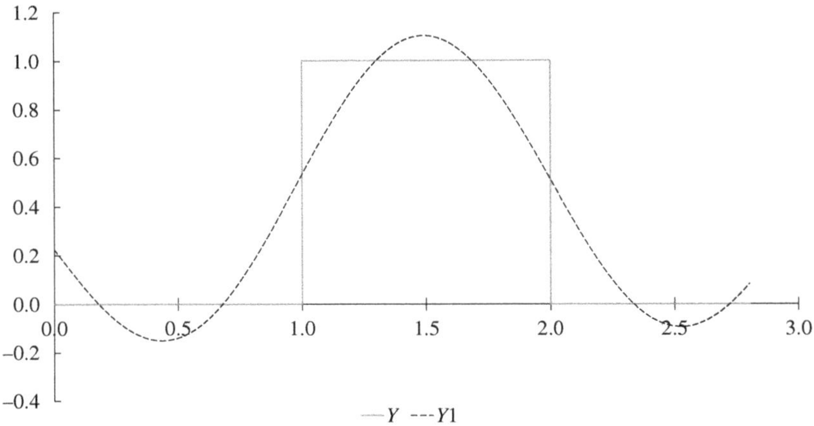

Fig. 2.9 Box-Response and First-Order Fourier Function

This function will not work very well. However, consider adding a sinusoid term

$$y_1 = \beta_0 + \beta_1 x + \beta_2 x^2 + B_1 \cos(\omega x) + B_2 \sin(\omega x) \tag{2.211}$$

where ω_1 is period of the function. In this case, the period is π, since the function passes through a complete cycle from $x = 0$ to $x = 2 - \omega = 2\pi/(2-0) = \pi$. The results for Equation (2.211) are presented in Figure 2.9. In general, this curve does little better than a simple quadratic term because the two trigonometric functions have much the same shape over the range modeled. However, consider an expansion of Equation (2.211):

$$y_n = \beta_0 + \beta_1 x + \beta_2 x^2 + \sum_{k=1}^{K} [B_{1k} \cos(k\omega x) + B_{2k} \sin(k\omega x)]. \tag{2.212}$$

Hence, setting $K = 1$ yields Equation (2.211) and setting $K = 2$ yields

$$\begin{aligned} y_2 = \beta_0 + \beta_1 x + \beta_2 x^2 + [B_{11} \cos(\omega x) + B_{21} \sin(\omega x)] \\ + [B_{12} \cos(2\omega x) + B_{22} \sin(2\omega x)]. \end{aligned} \tag{2.213}$$

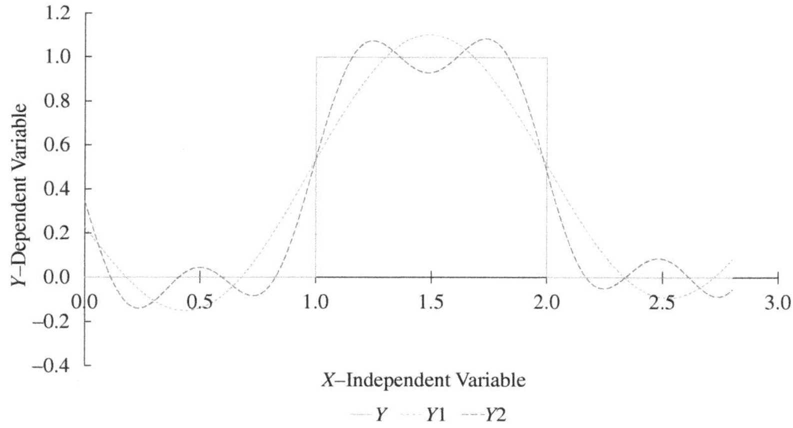

Fig. 2.10 Box-Response with First- and Second-Order Fourier Functions

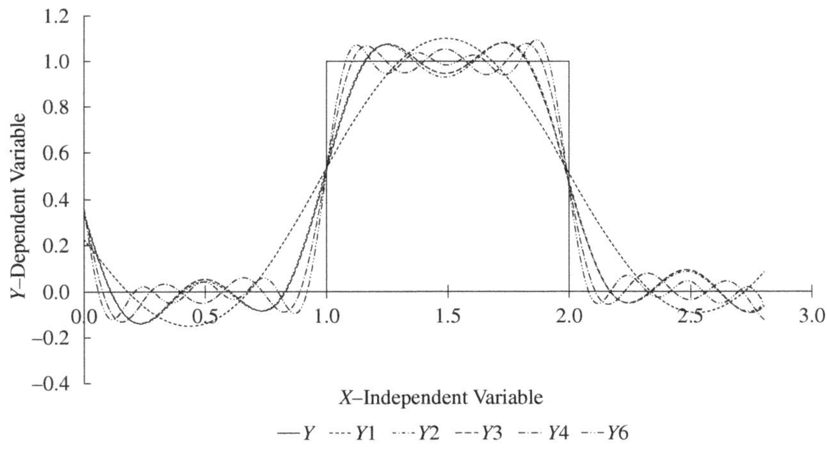

Fig. 2.11 Box-Response with Sixth-Order Fourier Function

Figure 2.10 presents the results for $K = 2$ (e.g., Equation (2.213)). As the number of Fourier terms increases, the approximation does a better job. As depicted in Figure 2.11, as $K = 6$, the error of approximation approaches zero.

The next step is to expand the Fourier approximation to the multivariate case. To develop a "simple" form of the multivariate Fourier approximation, consider a three-variable case (e.g., the Illinois corn data for 1993). The first step is to define multi-indexes

$$\lambda_1 = \begin{bmatrix} 1 \\ 0 \\ 0 \end{bmatrix}, \; \lambda_2 = \begin{bmatrix} 0 \\ 1 \\ 0 \end{bmatrix}, \; \lambda_3 \begin{bmatrix} 0 \\ 0 \\ 1 \end{bmatrix}. \tag{2.214}$$

The construction of the multi-indexes implies significant complexities. However, we note that the above multi-indexes are of "first order." Specifically,

$$\sum_{k=1}^{3} |\lambda_{ik}| = 1 \, \forall \, i. \tag{2.215}$$

We can define a sequence of "second-order" multi-indexes such as

$$\lambda_1 = \begin{bmatrix} 2 \\ 0 \\ 0 \end{bmatrix}, \; \lambda_2 = \begin{bmatrix} 1 \\ 1 \\ 0 \end{bmatrix}, \; \lambda_3 = \begin{bmatrix} 1 \\ 0 \\ 1 \end{bmatrix}, \; \lambda_4 = \begin{bmatrix} 0 \\ 1 \\ 1 \end{bmatrix}, \ldots . \tag{2.216}$$

Note that applying Equation (2.215) yields the definition of the second-order multi-index.

Bringing the concept of ω from our preceding discussion, consider the functional form

$$\begin{aligned} f(x) = \beta_0 &+ \begin{bmatrix} \beta_1 \\ \beta_2 \\ \beta_3 \end{bmatrix}' \begin{bmatrix} x_1 \\ x_2 \\ x_3 \end{bmatrix} + \frac{1}{2} \begin{bmatrix} x_1 \\ x_2 \\ x_3 \end{bmatrix}' \begin{bmatrix} B_{11} & B_{12} & B_{13} \\ B_{21} & B_{22} & B_{23} \\ B_{31} & B_{32} & B_{33} \end{bmatrix} \begin{bmatrix} x_1 \\ x_2 \\ x_3 \end{bmatrix} \\ &+ \beta_{11} \cos \left(\omega \lambda_1' \begin{bmatrix} x_1 \\ x_2 \\ x_3 \end{bmatrix} \right) + \gamma_{11} \sin \left(\omega \lambda_1' \begin{bmatrix} x_1 \\ x_2 \\ x_3 \end{bmatrix} \right) \\ &+ \beta_{12} \cos \left(\omega \lambda_2' \begin{bmatrix} x_1 \\ x_2 \\ x_3 \end{bmatrix} \right) + \gamma_{12} \sin \left(\omega \lambda_2' \begin{bmatrix} x_1 \\ x_2 \\ x_3 \end{bmatrix} \right) \\ &+ \beta_{13} \cos \left(\omega \lambda_3' \begin{bmatrix} x_1 \\ x_2 \\ x_3 \end{bmatrix} \right) + \gamma_{13} \sin \left(\omega \lambda_3' \begin{bmatrix} x_1 \\ x_2 \\ x_3 \end{bmatrix} \right). \end{aligned} \tag{2.217}$$

Note that the "first-order" multi-indexes in Equation (2.214) pick out each individual variable. Collecting the terms in Equation (2.217), we can increase the flexibility of the multivariate Fourier. First, we can focus on different periodicities

$$f(x) = \beta_0 + \begin{bmatrix} \beta_1 \\ \beta_2 \\ \beta_3 \end{bmatrix}' \begin{bmatrix} x_1 \\ x_2 \\ x_3 \end{bmatrix} + \frac{1}{2} \begin{bmatrix} x_1 \\ x_2 \\ x_3 \end{bmatrix}' \begin{bmatrix} B_{11} & B_{12} & B_{13} \\ B_{21} & B_{22} & B_{23} \\ B_{31} & B_{32} & B_{33} \end{bmatrix} \begin{bmatrix} x_1 \\ x_2 \\ x_3 \end{bmatrix} + \sum_{k=1}^{K} \sum_{l=1}^{L} \left[\beta_{kl} \cos \left(k\omega\lambda_l' \begin{bmatrix} x_1 \\ x_2 \\ x_3 \end{bmatrix} \right) + \gamma_{kl} \sin \left(k\omega\lambda_l' \begin{bmatrix} x_1 \\ x_2 \\ x_3 \end{bmatrix} \right) \right]. \tag{2.218}$$

Second, we can envision additional multi-index orders. Adding all the concepts together, we have the ultimate form of the Fourier approximation

$$\begin{aligned} f(x) &= \beta_0 + \beta' x + \frac{1}{2} x' B x \\ &\quad + \sum_{k=1}^{K} \left[\beta_{0k} + \sum_{l=1}^{L} \left(\beta_{jl} \cos \left(k\lambda_l' x \right) + \gamma_{jl} \sin \left(k\lambda_l' x \right) \right) \right] \\ B &= -\sum_{k=1}^{K} \beta_{0k} \lambda_k \lambda_k'. \end{aligned} \tag{2.219}$$

To demonstrate the Fourier approximation, we fit the production function in levels for 1993 corn production in Illinois. As a starting point, let us consider the three "first-order" multi-indexes given in Equation (2.214), which yield the specification in Equation (2.217). The first step is to layout the periodicity specification. As a starting point, consider the quantiles of the inputs presented in Table 2.21. The basic concept is that our first sinusoid should cycle within the range of the observed values of the input. Starting with nitrogen, we recognize that the data includes a small number of observations with no nitrogen input. For this application, we let

$$\omega = \frac{2 \times \pi}{200.00} = 0.03142 \tag{2.220}$$

or we define the initial period between zero and the 90 percentile of nitrogen use. However, we recognize that we could have set the period to

$$\tilde{\omega} = \frac{2 \times \pi}{200.00 - 77.48} = 0.05128 \tag{2.221}$$

Table 2.21 Distribution of Inputs for 1993 Illinois Corn Data

Percentile	Nitrogen	Phosphorous	Potash
10	77.48	32.50	33.00
25	122.96	46.00	60.00
50	159.00	69.00	100.00
75	184.00	92.00	120.00
90	200.00	104.00	150.00

to define the period between the 10 and 90 percentile. Next, note that we need to define a comparable period for phosphorous and potash. However, it is more convenient to transform these variables to have the same period as nitrogen. Specifically, we define two constants:

$$\begin{aligned}\tau_2 &= \frac{200.00}{104.00} = 1.9231\\ \tau_3 &= \frac{200.00}{150.00} = 1.3333\end{aligned}. \tag{2.222}$$

Thus, we redefine $x_2^* = \tau_2 x_2$ and $x_3^* = \tau_3 x_3$. The resulting specification becomes

$$\begin{aligned}f(x) = \beta_0 &+ \begin{bmatrix}\beta_1\\ \beta_2\\ \beta_3\end{bmatrix}' \begin{bmatrix}x_1\\ x_2^*\\ x_3^*\end{bmatrix} + \frac{1}{2}\begin{bmatrix}x_1\\ x_2^*\\ x_3^*\end{bmatrix}' \begin{bmatrix}B_{11} & B_{12} & B_{13}\\ B_{21} & B_{22} & B_{23}\\ B_{31} & B_{32} & B_{33}\end{bmatrix}\begin{bmatrix}x_1\\ x_2^*\\ x_3^*\end{bmatrix}\\
&+ \beta_{11}\cos\left(\omega\lambda_1'\begin{bmatrix}x_1\\ x_2^*\\ x_3^*\end{bmatrix}\right) + \gamma_{11}\sin\left(\omega\lambda_1'\begin{bmatrix}x_1\\ x_2^*\\ x_3^*\end{bmatrix}\right)\\
&+ \beta_{12}\cos\left(\omega\lambda_2'\begin{bmatrix}x_1\\ x_2^*\\ x_3^*\end{bmatrix}\right) + \gamma_{12}\sin\left(\omega\lambda_2'\begin{bmatrix}x_1\\ x_2^*\\ x_3^*\end{bmatrix}\right)\\
&+ \beta_{13}\cos\left(\omega\lambda_3'\begin{bmatrix}x_1\\ x_2^*\\ x_3^*\end{bmatrix}\right) + \gamma_{13}\sin\left(\omega\lambda_3'\begin{bmatrix}x_1\\ x_2^*\\ x_3^*\end{bmatrix}\right).\end{aligned} \tag{2.223}$$

This transformation really does not change the estimation itself, but it requires some caution in interpreting the results.

The results for the Fourier approximation in Equation (2.223) are presented in the first columns of Table 2.22. The difference between the simple quadratic specification on the Fourier specification in

Table 2.22 Fourier Results for 1993 Illinois Corn Data

First-order		Second-order				Interaction			
Par.	Est.	Par.	Est.	Par.	Est.	Par.	Est.	Par.	Est.
b_0	79.42225***	b_0	81.89650***	g_{21}	−5.80528***	b_0	81.90305***	g_{21}	−5.81789***
	(7.02313)[a]		(6.20315)		(1.03613)		(7.23138)		(1.15090)
b_1	0.24746***	b_1	0.20990***	b_{22}	1.94767	b_1	0.20991***	b_{22}	1.92585**
	(0.06063)		(0.06041)		(1.38635)		(0.07009)		(0.94434)
b_2	−0.02558	b_2	−0.03191	g_{22}	−1.13659	b_2	−0.03187	g_{22}	−1.14484
	(0.05674)		(0.05475)		(1.18544)		(0.05680)		(0.73369)
b_3	0.36204***	b_3	0.37244***	b_{23}	2.64319***	b_3	0.37207***	b_{23}	2.62701***
	(0.06529)		(0.07014)		(1.00766)		(0.07145)		(0.75469)
B_{11}	−0.00026	B_{11}	−0.00015	g_{23}	0.72131	B_{11}	−0.00015	g_{23}	0.70672
	(0.00026)		(0.00028)		(0.63188)		(0.00029)		(0.86856)
B_{12}	−0.00013	B_{12}	0.00002			B_{12}	0.00002	b_{24} – [λ_4]	3.20360***
	(0.00033)		(0.00032)				(0.00033)		(0.82485)
B_{13}	−0.00077**	B_{13}	−0.00082***			B_{13}	−0.00082**	g_{24} – [λ_4]	−0.60586
	(0.00031)		(0.00031)				(0.00032)		(0.66256)
B_{22}	0.00006	B_{22}	0.00001			B_{22}	0.00001	b_{25} – [λ_5]	2.79860***
	(0.00019)		(0.00019)				(0.00020)		(0.93819)
B_{23}	0.00035	B_{23}	0.00028			B_{23}	0.00028	g_{25} – [λ_5]	1.23761*
	(0.00024)		(0.00024)				(0.00024)		(0.72754)
B_{33}	−0.00109***	B_{33}	−0.00103***			B_{33}	−0.00103***	b_{26} – [λ_6]	0.46678
	(0.00040)		(0.00040)				(0.00040)		(0.79266)
b_{11}	13.48437***	b_{11}	11.36022***			b_{11}	1.42500*	g_{26} – [λ_6]	0.76187

(*Continued*)

Table 2.22 (*Continued*)

First-order		Second-order				Interaction			
Par.	Est.	Par.	Est.	Par.	Est.	Par.	Est.	Par.	Est.
	(1.53546)		(1.35077)				(0.86332)		(0.89819)
g_{11}	−0.96505	g_{11}	−1.08681			g_{11}	−1.50211	b_{27} – [λ_7]	1.06899
	(1.41047)		(1.35205)				(1.09248)		(1.07101)
b_{12}	2.48408	b_{12}	2.62472**			b_{12}	0.51841	g_{27} – [λ_7]	0.35042
	(1.54484)		(1.19165)				(0.79678)		(1.12225)
g_{12}	−1.65999	g_{12}	−2.22988*			g_{12}	−0.25298	b_{28} – [λ_8]	2.84041***
	(1.85682)		(1.34790)				(1.15154)		(0.91725)
b_{13}	−1.80260	b_{13}	−1.43866			b_{13}	−2.3890**	g_{28} – [λ_8]	−0.56300
	(1.58630)		(1.12423)				(1.10756)		(1.07740)
g_{13}	3.78274**	g_{13}	3.72105**			g_{13}	−0.62191	b_{29} – [λ_9]	−0.49967
	(1.78593)		(1.50994)				(0.94094)		(0.64264)
		b_{21}	1.04494			b_{21}	1.04522	g_{29} – [λ_9]	−1.76145*
			(0.92791)				(1.02412)		(1.04365)

Notes: [a]Numbers in parenthesis denote standard errors.
***denotes statistical significance at the 0.01 level of confidence.
**denotes statistical significance at the 0.05 level of confidence.
*denotes statistical significance at the 0.10 level of confidence.

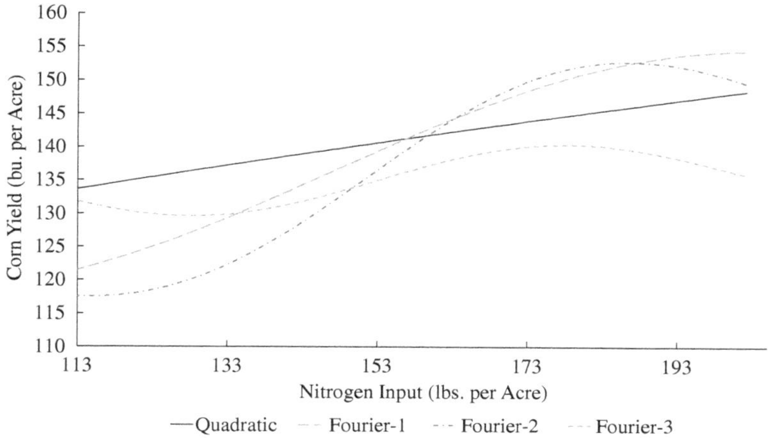

Fig. 2.12 Fourier Estimates of Illinois Corn Data

Equation (2.223) is depicted graphically in Figure 2.12 as Fourier-1. The most interesting implication Fourier-1 is that the concavity increases. As a second step, we add the simple "second-order" terms (e.g., adding the $2 \times \omega$ terms):

$$
\begin{aligned}
f(x) = \beta_0 &+ \begin{bmatrix} \beta_1 \\ \beta_2 \\ \beta_3 \end{bmatrix}' \begin{bmatrix} x_1 \\ x_2^* \\ x_3^* \end{bmatrix} + \frac{1}{2} \begin{bmatrix} x_1 \\ x_2^* \\ x_3^* \end{bmatrix}' \begin{bmatrix} B_{11} & B_{12} & B_{13} \\ B_{21} & B_{22} & B_{23} \\ B_{31} & B_{32} & B_{33} \end{bmatrix} \begin{bmatrix} x_1 \\ x_2^* \\ x_3^* \end{bmatrix} \\
&+ \beta_{11} \cos\left(\omega \lambda_1' \begin{bmatrix} x_1 \\ x_2^* \\ x_3^* \end{bmatrix}\right) + \gamma_{11} \sin\left(\omega \lambda_1' \begin{bmatrix} x_1 \\ x_2^* \\ x_3^* \end{bmatrix}\right) \\
&+ \beta_{12} \cos\left(\omega \lambda_2' \begin{bmatrix} x_1 \\ x_2^* \\ x_3^* \end{bmatrix}\right) + \gamma_{12} \sin\left(\omega \lambda_2' \begin{bmatrix} x_1 \\ x_2^* \\ x_3^* \end{bmatrix}\right) \\
&+ \beta_{13} \cos\left(\omega \lambda_3' \begin{bmatrix} x_1 \\ x_2^* \\ x_3^* \end{bmatrix}\right) + \gamma_{13} \sin\left(\omega \lambda_3' \begin{bmatrix} x_1 \\ x_2^* \\ x_3^* \end{bmatrix}\right) \\
&+ \beta_{21} \cos\left(2\omega \lambda_1' \begin{bmatrix} x_1 \\ x_2^* \\ x_3^* \end{bmatrix}\right) + \gamma_{21} \sin\left(2\omega \lambda_1' \begin{bmatrix} x_1 \\ x_2^* \\ x_3^* \end{bmatrix}\right) \\
&+ \beta_{22} \cos\left(2\omega \lambda_2' \begin{bmatrix} x_1 \\ x_2^* \\ x_3^* \end{bmatrix}\right) + \gamma_{22} \sin\left(2\omega \lambda_2' \begin{bmatrix} x_1 \\ x_2^* \\ x_3^* \end{bmatrix}\right) \\
&+ \beta_{23} \cos\left(2\omega \lambda_3' \begin{bmatrix} x_1 \\ x_2^* \\ x_3^* \end{bmatrix}\right) + \gamma_{23} \sin\left(2\omega \lambda_3' \begin{bmatrix} x_1 \\ x_2^* \\ x_3^* \end{bmatrix}\right).
\end{aligned} \tag{2.224}
$$

These results for this specification are presented in the second set of columns in Table 2.22. Turning to Figure 2.12, this specification is depicted as Fourier-2. Note that this specification is more concave than Fourier-1, but appears to pick up a stage I (e.g., the output function between 113 and 133 appears to be increasing at an increasing rate).

As a final extension, we consider defining the interaction terms in "second-order" multi-index case. First, note that the first three multi-indexes for $\sum_{k=1}^{K}|\lambda_k| = 2$ have already been included:

$$\omega\begin{bmatrix}2\\0\\0\end{bmatrix} = 2\omega\begin{bmatrix}1\\0\\0\end{bmatrix},\ \omega\begin{bmatrix}0\\2\\0\end{bmatrix} = 2\omega\begin{bmatrix}1\\0\\0\end{bmatrix},\ \omega\begin{bmatrix}0\\0\\2\end{bmatrix} = 2\omega\begin{bmatrix}0\\0\\1\end{bmatrix}. \quad (2.225)$$

Hence, the "second-order" terms we need to add are the interactions:

$$\lambda_4 = \begin{bmatrix}1\\1\\0\end{bmatrix},\ \lambda_5 = \begin{bmatrix}1\\0\\1\end{bmatrix},\ \lambda_6 = \begin{bmatrix}0\\1\\1\end{bmatrix},$$
$$\lambda_7 = \begin{bmatrix}1\\-1\\0\end{bmatrix},\ \lambda_8 = \begin{bmatrix}1\\0\\-1\end{bmatrix},\ \lambda_9 = \begin{bmatrix}0\\1\\-1\end{bmatrix}. \quad (2.226)$$

These estimates are given in the third set of columns of Table 2.22 and graphically depicted as Fourier-3 in Figure 2.12. This addition appears to go the wrong way. Specifically, the production function flattens out and the cyclical nature appears to be larger. One of the additional dimensions of flexibility in this last modification (e.g., including the interactions) is an increase in the flexibility of interactions between the input terms. Both dimensions are apparent in the nitrogen–potash interactions depicted in Figure 2.13.

2.7.2.2 *Non-parametric regressions*

The final method for depicting a production function that we want to consider is commonly referred to as a non-parametric regression or, more specifically, a kernel-based non-parametric regression. In general, this technique is primarily attributed to Hardle (1990).

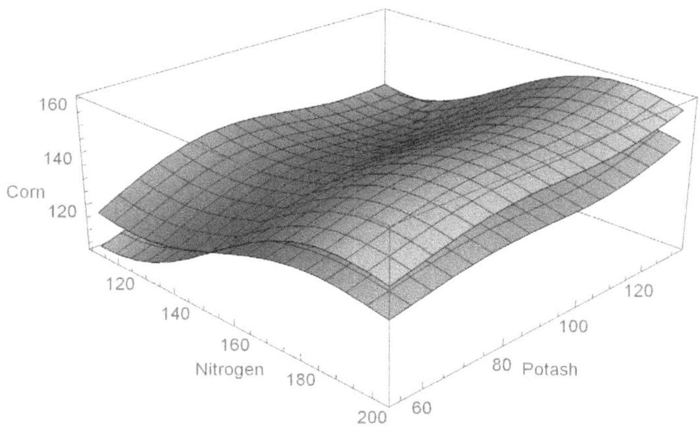

Fig. 2.13 Comparison of Interaction Terms in Fourier Function for Illinois Corn

There are several forms of the non-parametric regression, but for our purposes, we are interested in the kernel-based approach which is basically a moving average of the response variable where the weights of the moving average are functions of the independent variables.

As a starting point, consider a simple production function where the amount of corn produced is equal to a function of the amount of nitrogen applied. The basic kernel estimator models the level of corn produced as a weighted average of the other levels of corn produced:

$$y(x_0) = \int_{-\infty}^{\infty} y(x_1)k(x_0, x_1, \delta)d\,x_1 \tag{2.227}$$

where $k\,(x_0, x_1, \delta)$ is a weighting function known as a kernel density function, x_0 is the point or level of nitrogen for which we want to approximate or predict corn production, x_0 is some other level of nitrogen in the neighborhood around x_1 at which we know the level of corn production, and δ is a parameter of the kernel called the bandwidth that predicts "closeness" to the point of estimation or approximation. The kernel is defined such that

$$\begin{gathered}\int_{-\infty}^{\infty} k\,(x_0, x_1, \delta) = 1 \\ k\,(x_0, x_1, \delta) \geq 0\,\forall\, x_0, x_1.\end{gathered} \tag{2.228}$$

There are several functions that meet the general condition in Equation (2.228), but one that is particularly useful is the Epanechnikov

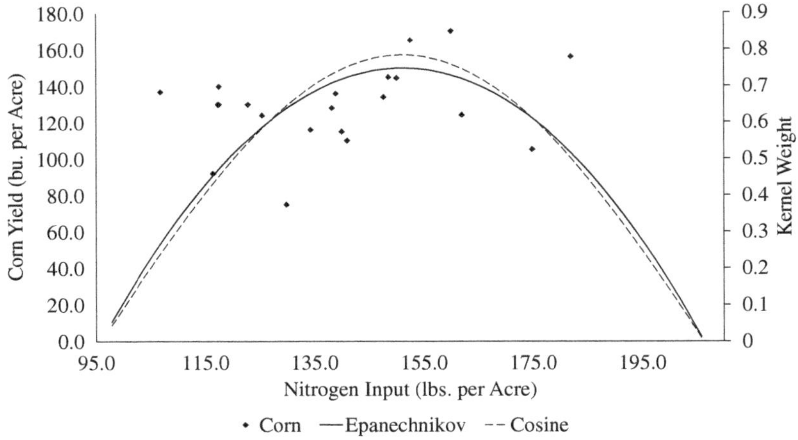

Fig. 2.14 Kernel Functions for Corn Yields as a function of Nitrogen

kernel:

$$k(u) = \frac{3}{4}\left(1 - u^2\right) I(|u|)$$
$$u = \frac{x_1 - x_0}{\delta} \tag{2.229}$$

where $I(|u|)$ is an indicator function that is one if $|u| \leq 1$ and 0 otherwise. A similar kernel is the Cosine kernel:

$$k(u) = \frac{\pi}{4}\cos\left(\frac{\pi}{2}u\right) I(u). \tag{2.230}$$

Figure 2.14 presents the value for each kernel centered around the point $N = 151.101$ for a subsample of the Illinois 1995 corn data. The first 25 observations for this data are presented in Table 2.23. The second and fourth columns of Table 2.22 provide the continuous values of each kernel. To implement the non-parametric estimator, we need to transform the kernel to a discrete function. Specifically, we compute the discrete weight for each kernel in columns 5 and 6 as

$$w_{ni}(x) = \frac{k(x_i, x_n, \delta)}{\hat{f}_n}$$
$$\hat{f}_n = \sum_{i=1}^{N} k(x_i, x_n, \delta) \tag{2.231}$$

Table 2.23 Kernel Density for Selected Illinois Corn Data

Data		Continuous Function		Discrete Function	
Nitrogen	Corn	Epanechnikov	Cosine	Epanechnikov	Cosine
138.2	128.0	0.7091	0.7331	0.04092	0.04164
138.2	128.0	0.7091	0.7331	0.04092	0.04164
125.4	124.0	0.5876	0.5847	0.03391	0.03321
117.5	130.0	0.4724	0.4532	0.02726	0.02574
117.5	140.0	0.4724	0.4532	0.02726	0.02574
129.9	75.0	0.6395	0.6469	0.03690	0.03674
129.9	75.0	0.6395	0.6469	0.03690	0.03674
106.8	137.0	0.2674	0.2402	0.01543	0.01364
106.8	137.0	0.2674	0.2402	0.01543	0.01364
152.6	165.0	0.7495	0.7847	0.04325	0.04457
182.0	156.0	0.5155	0.5015	0.02975	0.02848
174.9	105.0	0.6113	0.6129	0.03528	0.03481
134.3	116.0	0.6806	0.6974	0.03928	0.03961
160.0	170.0	0.7305	0.7604	0.04216	0.04319
162.0	124.0	0.7208	0.7480	0.04160	0.04249
138.9	136.0	0.7134	0.7386	0.04117	0.04195
117.3	130.0	0.4694	0.4499	0.02709	0.02555
116.4	92.0	0.4539	0.4329	0.02619	0.02459
116.4	92.0	0.4539	0.4329	0.02619	0.02459
141.0	110.0	0.7249	0.7532	0.04183	0.04278
141.0	110.0	0.7249	0.7532	0.04183	0.04278
148.5	145.0	0.7483	0.7833	0.04318	0.04449
148.5	145.0	0.7483	0.7833	0.04318	0.04449
140.0	115.0	0.7197	0.7466	0.04153	0.04241

where x_n is the point of approximation. The estimated value of y at point x_n is then

$$\hat{y}(x_n) = \sum_{i=1}^{N} w_{ni}(x) y_i. \tag{2.232}$$

The estimated value of y given that $N = 151.101$ under the Epanechnikov kernel is 127.0361, while the estimated value under the cosine kernel is 127.2303. Extending to all y_i between 65 pounds of nitrogen per acre to 227 pounds of nitrogen per acre yields the production function estimates presented in Figure 2.15. In Figure 2.15,

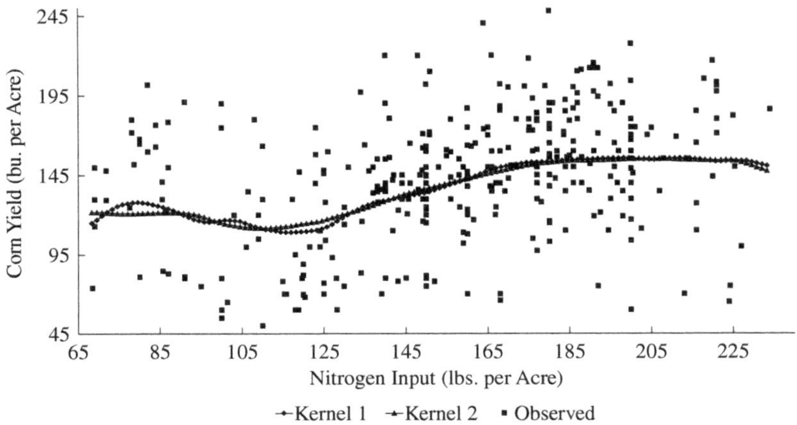

Fig. 2.15 Non-parametric Production function for Nitrogen

Kernel 1 is an Epanechnikov kernel with a bandwidth of 15, while Kernel 2 expands the bandwidth to 25. In general, the estimated function becomes more smooth as the bandwidth increases. Intuitively, the bandwidth becomes very large, the non-parametric function becomes a constant at the average yield.

In addition to estimating the production function, the non-parametric regression allows the researcher to estimate of a non-parametric representation of the derivative of the production function. Specifically, we can take the derivative of the production function with respect to x_i at point $\hat{y}_i$ by taking the derivative of the kernel:

$$\frac{\partial \hat{y}_i}{\partial x_i} = \sum_{n=1}^{N} \frac{y_n}{f_n} \left[1 - \frac{k\left(x_i, x_{ni}, \delta\right)}{f_n} \right] \frac{\partial k\left(x_i, x_{ni}, \delta\right)}{\partial x_i} \tag{2.233}$$

that is taking the derivative of Equation (2.231) with respect to x_i holding the y_{ni} constant. The estimated derivatives for the two kernels presented in Figure 2.15 are presented in Figure 2.16.

Expanding past the univariate non-parametric specification, we consider the two-variable case, assume that we have a single output y, but now we have two inputs $x = (x_1\ x_2)$. In this case, we can write a multivariate form of the non-parametric regression:

$$\hat{y}(x^0) = \int_{-\infty}^{\infty} \int_{-\infty}^{\infty} y(x) f(x^0, x, \delta) d x_1 d x_2. \tag{2.234}$$

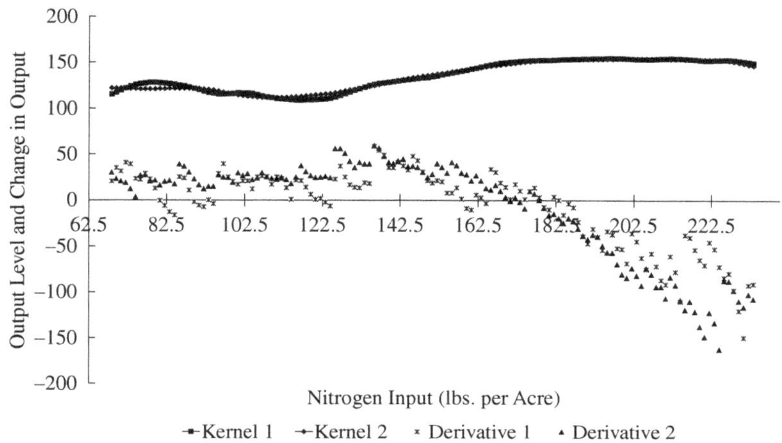

Fig. 2.16 Non-parametric Derivatives for the Production Functions for Nitrogen

In this case, $\hat{y}(x^0)$ is the estimated function value conditioned on the level of inputs x^0. The value $y(x)$ is the observed output level at observed input level x. $f(x^0, x, \delta)$ is a kernel function which weights the observations based on a distance from the point of approximation. Several multivariate kernels exist, but for our purposes, we will use the Gaussian kernel. As the first step, let us assume that our Gaussian kernel is "independent":

$$k\left(x^0, x, \delta\right) = \frac{1}{\sqrt{2\pi}}\delta^{-1} \exp\left[-\frac{\left(x_1 - x_1^0\right)^2}{2\delta} - \frac{\left(x_2 - x_2^0\right)^2}{2\delta}\right]. \tag{2.235}$$

The multivariate form raises several normalization questions. One way to normalize the Gaussian kernel is to use the matrix formulation

$$k\left(x^0, x, \delta\right) = \frac{1}{\sqrt{2\pi}}\left|\delta A\right|^{-1/2} \exp\left[-\frac{1}{2}\left(x - x^0\right)'\left(\delta A\right)^{-1}\left(x - x^0\right)\right] \tag{2.236}$$

where A is a diagonal variance matrix (e.g., the variance matrix with the covariance terms held to zero). Again, following Equation (2.229), we transform the continuous kernel into a discrete kernel and then define the estimated value at point x^0 following Equation (2.230). The plot for the multivariate normal form of the Illinois corn data with $\delta = 0.75$ is presented in Figure 2.17.

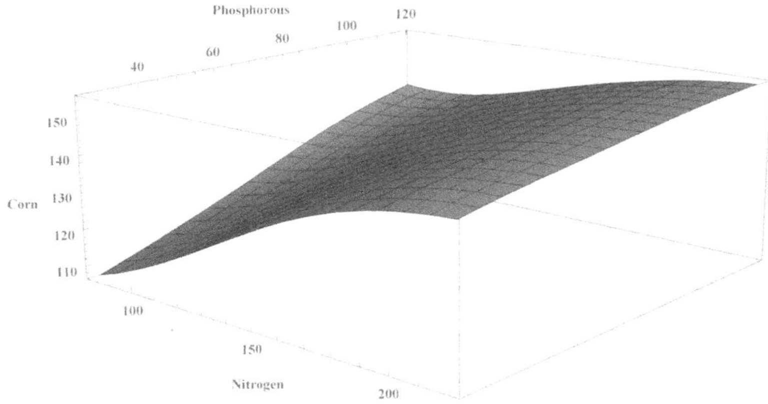

Fig. 2.17 Non-parametric Nitrogen–Phosphorous Production Surface for Illinois Corn

2.8 Chapter Summary

- One of the defining characteristics of agricultural economics has been its empirical nature. The discipline builds on economic theory to answer questions posed by the changing nature of agriculture and agricultural policy.
- Given this empirical focus, this textbook explicitly develops the estimation of production functions using a variety of econometric specifications.
- As a starting point, we consider the application of ordinary least squares to linearized models including the logarithm of the Cobb–Douglas and the quadratic production function.
- An important point of consideration is the question — where does our data come from? Most simple ordinary least squares applications implicitly assume that data is the result of "field trials". However, most of our meaningful datasets (i.e., dataset-based real-world questions) are the result of observed economic behavior. Hence, this chapter develops the concept of endogeneity and estimation approaches, such as indirect least squares, two-stage least squares, and the generalized instrumental variable estimator that directly address this endogeneity.
- Another consequence of real data is the complexity of production function residual. This complexity includes the panel data specifications where we attempt to pool data across individuals.

Empirical approaches to address this complication include fixed and random effects estimators. Other difficulties include the effect of technical inefficiency. This complexity leads to the stochastic production function specification.
- Finally, we confront the fact that our traditional specifications are not flexible enough to fit real-world data. The chapter develops two potential responses. The first is the Fourier expansion which is typically referred to as a semi-flexible function form. The second is the non-parametric estimator of the production function.

2.9 Review Questions

1. The common approach is to start with a simple model of production and then to add complications as it becomes obvious that the econometric results are not consistent with economic axioms (e.g., an iterative Occam's razor approach). Suppose that you have estimated a quadratic production function using ordinary least squares, what properties are necessary for the estimates to be consistent with economic behavior? How would you examine the results to make sure that the estimates have these properties?
2. Ordinary least squares is typically the starting point for econometric estimation. What properties of ordinary least squares make it desirable?
3. What are the implications of our implicit assumption that the production function data are the result of field trials? If the data used in your analysis are from observed behavior, how does the estimation change?
4. What are the advantages and potential cost to a panel dataset?
5. Why do we anticipate the residuals in real-world data to be negatively skewed? What is the first test we typically want to run to verify the significance of this skewness? What estimator explicitly addresses the effect of skewness?

2.10 Exercises

For questions 1–6, we use the dataset PsuedoDraw.csv. This dataset is constructed by simulating the results of the aggregate translog production function in Table 1.1.

1. Estimate the quadratic production function using ordinary least squares. Do the results conform to the required characteristics for the production function?
2. Are the residuals of the quadratic production function normally distributed? If not, what does this imply for the production function?
3. Estimate the translog production function using ordinary least squares. Are the estimated parameters consistent with the characteristics required for profit maximization? [Note: The translog production function should be concave in inputs — not the transformed (logarithmic) function].
4. Estimate the stochastic production function using the Cobb–Douglas specification.
5. Estimate the translog production function incorporating simultaneity.
6. Estimate the Cobb–Douglas form to estimate the Just and Pope production function. Is there evidence that any input is risk increasing?
7. Use the dataset PsuedoPanelData.csv to estimate fixed and random effects Cobb–Douglas production functions.

Chapter 3

Empirical Examples of the Primal

At times, nomenclature — what we call things — adds confusion instead of understanding. For most of my career, I have attached the label *microeconomics* to the study of individual decisions and the implications of those decisions. Intuitively, the economics of small units within the economy (i.e., the micro) contrasts with the analysis of the overall or larger economy — macroeconomics. In this juxtaposition, I have included production economics in microeconomics. Specifically, I have been interested in what production has to say about individual firm or household decisions. However, in retrospective, this taxonomy may not serve the student of economics or agricultural economics well. The production function in general and the Cobb–Douglas function in particular have found its way into several macroeconomic analyses. In fact, the original article which introduced the Cobb–Douglas form to the general economics profession deals with wages in a very macroeconomic way:

> The progressive refinement during the recent years in the measurement of the volume of production in manufacturing suggests the possibility of attempting (1) to measure the changes in the amount of labor and capital that have been used to turn out this volume of goods, and (2) to determine what relationships existed between the three factors of labor, capital, and product (Cobb and Douglas, 1928, p. 139).

Several concepts within this quotation are worth noting. First, a large part of quantitative work in economics during the early part of the

20th century involved estimating the overall scale of the economy. Determination of whether the economy was growing or not required some measures of economic activity and inputs. A large portion of Cobb and Douglas's article details how they created their data series from different sources of information and filled in the gaps. Second, given the Herculean task of assembling data, the next question was the estimation of the productivity of labor and capital.

> If the relative supply from year to year of labor and capital were thus even approximately ascertained, a number of further problems would inevitably present themselves for solution of which the following are typical.
>
> (1) Can we estimate, within limits, whether this increase in production was purely fortuitous, whether it was primarily caused by technique, and the degree, if any, to which it responded to changes in the quantity of labor and capital?
>
> (2) May it be possible to determine, again within limits, the *relative* influence upon production of labor compared with capital?
>
> (3) As the proportions of labor to capital changed from year to year, may it be possible to deduce the relative amount added to the total physical product by each unit of labor and capital and what is more important still by the *final* units of labor and capital in these respective years (Cobb and Douglas, 1928, p. 139).

Point (1) in this quote lays out the general problem — why has output been increasing? Has it been increasing because the overall level of labor and capital in the economy has been increasing, because there has been technical change (i.e., improvements in our techniques), or have we simply been lucky over the last decade or so? Following this general problem statement, Cobb and Douglas lay out an additional set of related problems — if output is increasing because we have more labor and capital, will this rate of return (primarily to labor) continue to increase or will the economy experience diminishing marginal productivity? Diminishing marginal productivity for labor may imply a stagnation or decline in real wages. Alternatively, the continued investment in capital could stabilize or even increase real wages. Douglas continued this work in his book, *The Theory of Wages* (Douglas, 1934).

3.1 The Problem with Data

Chapter 2 provides an overview of several different econometric techniques for the estimation of the production function, but it leaves certain important questions unanswered other than a discussion of endogeneity. Before we review a selection of the examples of the primal approach, we pause to examine several data issues that appear throughout the empirical literature.

As a starting point, consider two different aggregation assumptions implicitly raised by Cobb and Douglas (1928). At one level, they assume aggregation across individuals and across inputs. As stated above, microeconomics typically involves individual decisions — either firms or consumers. However, Cobb and Douglas analyze the relationship between labor, capital, and output across firms. Hence, one of the first aggregation questions is whether conditions necessary for the production function are also valid at the aggregate or macroeconomic level. Another question which Cobb and Douglas do address in their article is the aggregation of different types of capital into a single capital variable. For example, how does one aggregate machinery, structures, land, and operating capital to form a single measure of capital?

To add a little more structure to our discussion, consider a simple mathematical formulation for each question. As a starting point, suppose that we have three firms that use three inputs:

$$\begin{aligned}
y_1 &= f_1\left(x_{11}, x_{21}, x_{31}\right) = A_1 x_{11}^{\alpha_{11}} x_{21}^{\alpha_{21}} x_{31}^{\alpha_{31}} \\
y_2 &= f_2\left(x_{12}, x_{22}, x_{32}\right) = A_2 x_{12}^{\alpha_{12}} x_{22}^{\alpha_{22}} x_{32}^{\alpha_{32}} \\
y_3 &= f_3\left(x_{13}, x_{23}, x_{33}\right) = A_3 x_{13}^{\alpha_{13}} x_{23}^{\alpha_{23}} x_{33}^{\alpha_{33}} \\
y_T &= f_T\left(x_{1T}, x_{2T}, x_{3T}\right) = A_T x_{1T}^{\tilde{\alpha}_1} x_{2T}^{\tilde{\alpha}_2} x_{3T}^{\tilde{\alpha}_3} \\
y_T &= \sum_{i=1}^{3} y_i\,,\; x_{1T} = \sum_{i=1}^{3} x_{1i}\,,\; x_{2T} = \sum_{i=1}^{3} x_{2i}\,,\; x_{3T} = \sum_{i=1}^{3} x_{3i}. \quad (3.1)
\end{aligned}$$

Note that certain parts of Equation (3.1) hold with equality. Specifically, the sum of the quantities produced by each firm is y_T and the sum of the inputs used by each firm is x_{jT} (for $j = 1, 2, 3$). The question is whether the aggregate production function resembles the individual decisions.

The second aggregation issue can be developed based on the Cobb–Douglas formulation. Specifically, assume that we have two types of labor: owner/operator (x_1) and hourly harvest labor (x_2). In addition, assume that we have three types of capital: land (x_3), machinery (x_4) and structures (x_5). The basic Cobb–Douglas function can be expressed as

$$y = A x_1^{\alpha_1} x_2^{\alpha_2} x_3^{\alpha_3} x_4^{\alpha_4} x_5^{\alpha_5}$$
$$y = \tilde{A}\left(x_1 + x_2\right)^{\tilde{\alpha}_1}\left(x_3 + x_4 + x_5\right)^{\tilde{\alpha}_2}. \qquad (3.2)$$

Again, the question is — when is the second expression in Equation (3.2) an adequate representation of the underlying technology? To further confuse the issue, the dependent variable is also an aggregate. Specifically, many early studies use the total value of production as the measure of output:

$$\tilde{y}_O = \sum_{k=1}^{K} p_i y_i \Rightarrow \tilde{y}_O = \tilde{A}\left(x_1 + x_2\right)^{\tilde{\alpha}_1}\left(x_3 + x_4 + x_5\right)^{\tilde{\alpha}_2}. \qquad (3.3)$$

In the end, we are left to consider whether the estimated relationship in Equation (3.3) has any resemblance to a real-world economic problem of interest.

3.1.1 *Aggregation Across Firms*

As a starting point, we consider the problem of aggregation as defined by Theil:

> The relations postulated by the economic theory of individual households (the *microtheory*) will be called *microrelations* or *microequations*. These variables of these equations are the *microvariables*; the parameters (constants) specifying these relations are the *microparameters*. Aggregation implies that microvariables are replaced by *aggregates* or *macrovariables*, which are certain functions of the microvariables. The *macrotheory* postulates that the macrovariables are connected by *macrorelations* or *macroequations*, which are in turn specified by a number of *macroparameters* (Theil, 1954a, p. 2).

Following the description in Equation (3.1), we have a theory based on individual behavior — microtheory in Theil's parlance.

These decisions are based on microvariables. However, for some reason, we are interested in constructing a macromodel. In the original empirical approach of Cobb–Douglas, we want to know how wages and employment (e.g., macrovariables) are affected by changes in capital or the labor force. How do we typically do this? As described by Theil:

> The usual way of constructing aggregates and macrotheories is of a very simple nature. Aggregates are averages, index numbers, or national totals and macrotheories are derived from microtheories by means of analogy considerations. E.g. if microtheory tells us that a firm's demand for labor depends on the quantity produced, the macrotheory is usually given in the form: total demand for labor depends upon a production index (Theil, 1954a, p. 6).

Backing up a little, we substitute Theil's formulation for the aggregation in Equation (3.1). Specifically, we adopt the simple linear model:

Linear Aggregation of Economic Relations — Theil

A serious gap exists between the greater part of rigorous economic theory and the pragmatic way in which economic systems are empirically analysed. Axiomatically founded theories refer mostly to individuals, for instance, the consumer or the entrepreneur. Empirical descriptions of economic actions in large communities, on the other hand, are nearly always extremely global: they are confined to the behaviour of groups of individuals. The necessity of such a procedure can scarcely be questioned: How could one handle the tremendous mass of relations governing the actions of millions of individuals? But the introduction of relations pretending to describe the reactions of groups of individuals instead of a single individual raises questions of fundamental importance, which are not very well understood: What are the connections between the functional relationships postulated by the economic theories of individual households and the relationships for groups of individuals postulated by the empirical researcher (Theil, 1954a, p. 1).

$$y_i(t) = \alpha_i + \sum_{l=1}^{L} \beta_{li} x_{li}(t) + u_i(t) \tag{3.4}$$

where $i = 1, \ldots, N$ are individuals, $l = 1, \ldots, L$ are different independent variables, and $t = 1, \ldots, T$ are time periods. From our current perspective, we could visualize x_{li} as the logarithm of the lth input, so the overall specification is the traditional Cobb–Douglas. However, we could also let some of $x_{li} = x_{mi} \times x_{ni}$ so the overall specification could be a quadratic or translog. Given the formulation in Equation (3.4), we could form the aggregate outputs and inputs:

$$y(t) = \sum_{i=1}^{N} y_i(t)$$

$$x_l(t) = \sum_{i=1}^{N} x_{li}(t). \tag{3.5}$$

Taking Equations (3.4) and (3.5) yields the macrorelation defined on macrovariables:

$$y(t) = \alpha + \sum_{l=1}^{L} \beta_l x_l(t) + u(t). \tag{3.6}$$

This sequence raises two questions: (1) What is the relationship between α_i and α, and β_{li} and β_l? (2) Which relationship are we really interested in?

Noting that Equation (3.5) is one of an infinite number of possible weights, Theil generalizes the aggregation process:

$$\tilde{y}(t) = \sum_{i=1}^{N} s_i y_i(t)$$

$$\tilde{x}_l(t) = \sum_{i=1}^{N} r_{li} x_{li}(t) \tag{3.7}$$

where s_i and r_{li} are fixed weights. Building on these weights, (3.6) can be rewritten as

$$s_i y_i(t) = s_i \alpha_i + \sum_{l=1}^{L} \frac{s_i \beta_{li}}{r_{li}} [r_{li} x_{li}(t)] + s_i u_i(t)$$

$$\Rightarrow \tilde{y}(t) = \tilde{a} + \sum_{l=1}^{L} \tilde{\beta}_l \tilde{x}_l(t) + \tilde{u}(t) \tag{3.8}$$

which yields a *fixed weight aggregation.* Note that input levels in Equation (3.8) are double weighted. Implicitly,

$$\tilde{\beta}_l = \sum_{i=1}^{N} \frac{s_i \beta_{li}}{r_{li}} \tag{3.9}$$

is weighted by the overall weight on the firm s_i and the relative weight of the input for the firm r_{li}. For example, suppose that we want to weight by firm size, so $s_1 = 0.05$ or firm 1 accounts for 5% of the total output. Next, assume that input 1 accounts for 0.15 or 15% of firm 1's overall inputs (i.e., the average input cost for input 1 divided by the average total input cost). In this case, the total weight on β_{li} (e.g., the coefficient for input 1 on firm 1's output) would be 1/3. Note that the input level is then weighted by r_{li}. Implicitly, the share weight for the firm's input use cancels out: $s_i\beta_{li}/r_{li} \times r_{li}x_{li}(t) = s_i\beta_{li}x_{li}(t)$.

To make the discussion a little more concrete, let us examine the first 10 industries of Jorgenson's KLEM (Capital [K], Labor [L], Energy [E], and Materials [M]) data. To make the discussion a little more interesting, we have split materials up into materials from agriculture (qma) and materials not from agriculture (qmo). We want to consider the effect of how the regressions differ based on individual industrial regressions versus an "aggregate" regression. Further, we consider a straightforward aggregation by adding the data and a weighted aggregation following Equation (3.8). Table 3.1 presents the Cobb–Douglas results for each industry and the two methods of aggregation. This aggregation is not very viable; however, it will provide an interesting starting point to demonstrate the implications of aggregation.

Table 3.1 Aggregation Results for First 10 KLEM Industries

Industry	Constant	Capital	Labor	Energy	Materials	
					Agricultural	Non-Agricultural
Agriculture	−7.0041***	1.6217***	0.4363***	−1.1331	0.3887	1.2081***
	(0.7944)[a]	(0.3016)	(0.1291)	(0.1875)	(0.2628)	(0.2829)
Metal Mining	2.1704***	0.2574***	0.2794***	−0.5496***	0.4291*	0.4895**
	(0.8093)	(0.0836)	(0.0440)	(0.1237)	(0.2286)	(0.1937)
Coal Mining	1.9760***	0.1352	−0.372***	0.5783**	−0.2974**	0.2041
	(0.3316)	(0.1949)	(0.0973)	(0.2785)	(0.1369)	(0.2001)
Crude Oil	2.8176***	0.1500	0.2502***	0.0196	−0.1860**	0.0786
	(0.4521)	(0.1240)	(0.0690)	(0.0438)	(0.0786)	(0.1021)
Non-Metalic Mining	1.3364***	−0.0066	0.2081***	0.3231	−0.0146**	0.5910
	(0.1440)	(0.1070)	(0.0682)	(0.0676)	(0.0546)	(0.0583)
Construction	3.2616***	−0.1337***	0.1015	0.1286***	0.1162**	0.4284
	(0.2537)	(0.0406)	(0.0905)	(0.0382)	(0.0590)	(0.0898)
Food and Kindred Prod.	0.7740***	0.4019***	0.0295	−0.0921***	0.4556***	0.2875***
	(0.2316)	(0.0698)	(0.0573)	(0.0195)	(0.0721)	(0.0777)
Tobacco	3.6833***	0.104*	0.3531***	0.3107***	0.2049***	−0.5616***
	(0.3459)	(0.0566)	(0.0598)	(0.1004)	(0.0652)	(0.0765)

Textiles	1.6681***	0.5458***	−0.3477***	0.0749	0.6915***	0.1377
	(0.2778)	(0.0589)	(0.0784)	(0.0832)	(0.1083)	(0.1259)
Apparel	1.2800***	0.3365***	0.3340***	−0.0085	0.2963***	0.1530***
	(0.1184)	(0.0188)	(0.0456)	(0.0292)	(0.0304)	(0.0340)
Aggregations						
Unweighted	24.5780***	−0.0907	0.0088	0.1810	0.0847	0.5762***
	(4.5642)	(0.1336)	(0.1252)	(0.1271)	(0.2128)	(0.2095)
Simple Avg.	1.1963	0.3413	0.1272	−0.0348	0.2084	0.3016
Weighted	3.5820***	0.0424	−0.0567	−0.0252	0.1130***	0.1880***
	(0.1980)	(0.0323)	(0.0360)	(0.0894)	(0.0423)	(0.0291)
Weighted Avg.	0.6458	0.0754	0.0356	−0.0033	0.0959	0.1419
Fixed Effect		0.0068	1.7229***	2.3030***	1.0437***	0.5868***
		(0.1368)	(0.0803)	(0.1568)	(0.0413)	(0.0641)

Notes: [a]Numbers in parenthesis denote standard errors.
***,**,*Denote statistical significance at the 0.01, 0.05, 0.10 levels of confidence, respectively.

While the aggregation does not make sense, it is obviously quite poor. The question is — why? To explain why, Theil suggests a series of regressions:

$$x_{li}(t) = A_{li} + B_{1,li}x_1(t) + B_{2,li}x_2(t) + B_{3,li}x_3(t) + B_{4,li}x_4(t) + B_{5,li}x_5(t) + \nu_{li}(t) \quad (3.10)$$

such that the level of each input for each individual is explained by the aggregated input levels. To be a little more explicit, consider the application of Equation (3.10) to capital and labor (e.g., $l = 1, 2$) for agriculture (e.g., $i = 1$):

$$\begin{aligned} x_{11}(t) &= A_{11} + B_{1,11}x_1(t) + B_{2,11}x_2(t) + B_{3,11}x_3(t) + B_{4,11}x_4(t) \\ &\quad + B_{5,11}x_5(t) + \nu_{11}(t) \\ x_{21}(t) &= A_{21} + B_{1,21}x_1(t) + B_{2,21}x_2(t) + B_{3,21}x_3(t) + B_{4,21}x_4(t) \\ &\quad + B_{5,21}x_5(t) + \nu_{21}(t). \end{aligned} \quad (3.11)$$

Following Equation (3.11), A_{11} and A_{12} are the constants in the levels of capital and labor for agriculture, $B_{1,11}$ and $B_{1,21}$ are the "effects" of the aggregate capital level on capital and labor used in agriculture. The results of these regressions are presented in Table 3.2. Based on the formulation in Equation (3.10), Theil proposes a theorem for the relationship between the individual regression coefficients and the regression coefficients for the aggregated data.

Theorem 3.1 (First Part). *The macroparameters α and β_l of Equation (3.8) are determined by the following regulations:*

$$\alpha = \sum_{i=1}^{N} \alpha_i + \sum_{l=1}^{L}\sum_{i=1}^{N} A_{li}\beta_{li} \quad (3.12)$$

$$\beta_l = \sum_{\tilde{l}}^{L}\sum_{i=1}^{N} B_{l,\tilde{l}i}\beta_{\tilde{l}i} \quad (3.13)$$

(Theil's Theorem 1 (Theil, 1954a, p. 13)).

Table 3.2 Relationship Between Individual and Aggregate Regression Variables

Independent					Materials	
Variable	Constant	Capital	Labor	Energy	Agricultural	Non-Agricultural
Agriculture						
Capital	3.4453****	0.0642***	−0.0088	−0.0027	−0.0215*	−0.0214*
	(0.2743)[a]	(0.0080)	(0.0075)	(0.0076)	(0.0128)	(0.0126)
Labor	4.8178***	−0.0465**	0.0051	−0.0178	0.1792***	−0.0444
	(0.7379)	(0.0216)	(0.0202)	(0.0205)	(0.0344)	(0.0339)
Energy	0.6240	0.0515***	−0.0058	0.0394*	−0.1376***	0.0518
	(0.8152)	(0.0239)	(0.0224)	(0.0227)	(0.0380)	(0.0374)
Agricultural Materials	2.5732***	0.0734***	0.0255	−0.0532***	−0.0759**	0.0244
	(0.6770)	(0.0198)	(0.0186)	(0.0188)	(0.0316)	(0.0311)
Non-Agricultural Materials	1.4374**	0.0334*	0.0208	−0.0179	−0.1619***	0.1117***
	(0.6397)	(0.0187)	(0.0176)	(0.0178)	(0.0298)	(0.0294)
Metal Mining						
Capital	−2.1091***	0.1733***	0.0428***	−0.0204	−0.0004	−0.0780***
	(0.4802)	(0.0141)	(0.0132)	(0.0134)	(0.0224)	(0.0220)
Labor	−8.1599***	−0.0218	0.3319***	−0.1425*	−0.3895***	0.2002
	(2.7438)	(0.0803)	(0.0753)	(0.0764)	(0.1279)	(0.1260)
Energy	−1.6693	−0.1959***	−0.0558	0.1373***	−0.1803***	0.2958***
	(1.5270)	(0.0447)	(0.0419)	(0.0425)	(0.0712)	(0.0701)
Agricultural Materials	−3.9280**	−0.3264***	−0.1065**	0.1010**	−0.0526	0.4039***
	(1.7346)	(0.0508)	(0.0476)	(0.0483)	(0.0809)	(0.0796)
Non-Agricultural Materials	−1.0243	−0.2637***	−0.0786*	0.0535	−0.1125	0.4057***
	(1.6319)	(0.0478)	(0.0448)	(0.0454)	(0.0761)	(0.0749)

(*Continued*)

Table 3.2 (*Continued*)

Independent Variable	Constant	Capital	Labor	Energy	Materials: Agricultural	Materials: Non-Agricultural
Coal Mining						
Capital	−1.4257*	0.1953***	0.0447	−0.0100	0.0419	−0.1108***
	(0.8160)	(0.0239)	(0.0224)	(0.0227)	(0.0380)	(0.0375)
Labor	−3.0739***	0.0810***	0.1886***	0.0482*	−0.0048	−0.0925*
	(1.0530)	(0.0308)	(0.0289)	(0.0293)	(0.0491)	(0.0483)
Energy	−6.2580***	0.1327**	0.1248**	0.0207	0.0938	−0.0288
	(2.1267)	(0.0623)	(0.0584)	(0.0592)	(0.0991)	(0.0976)
Agricultural Materials	−10.454***5	0.0975	0.1718**	−0.0491	0.1974	−0.0213
	(2.8725)	(0.0841)	(0.0788)	(0.0800)	(0.1339)	(0.1319)
Non-Agricultural Materials	−5.9252***	0.1662***	0.0893*	−0.0405	0.0052	0.0420
	(1.8095)	(0.0530)	(0.0496)	(0.0504)	(0.0843)	(0.0831)
Crude Oil						
Capital	1.0223	0.0797**	−0.0051	−0.0113	0.0694	0.0137
	(1.3574)	(0.0397)	(0.0372)	(0.0378)	(0.0633)	(0.0623)
Labor	0.2690	0.2865***	0.1679***	−0.0977*	−0.0676	−0.2504***
	(1.9154)	(0.0561)	(0.0526)	(0.0533)	(0.0893)	(0.0879)
Energy	4.2288**	0.0086	0.0771	0.1498***	0.0356	−0.1703**
	(1.9133)	(0.0560)	(0.0525)	(0.0533)	(0.0892)	(0.0878)
Agricultural Materials	−8.2081***	0.3065***	0.1166	−0.2182***	0.1478	−0.1755*
	(2.9045)	(0.0850)	(0.0797)	(0.0809)	(0.1354)	(0.1333)
Non-Agricultural Materials	−6.7840**	0.3091***	0.1760**	−0.2239***	0.0516	−0.0279
	(2.8020)	(0.0820)	(0.0769)	(0.0780)	(0.1306)	(0.1286)

Non-Metalic Mining						
Capital	-0.8495^{*}	0.1385^{***}	-0.0110	0.0083	-0.0582^{**}	-0.0054
	(0.5083)[a]	(0.0149)	(0.0139)	(0.0142)	(0.0237)	(0.0233)
Labor	-1.4516^{*}	-0.0595^{***}	0.0776^{***}	0.0039	-0.0036	0.0730^{**}
	(0.7551)	(0.0221)	(0.0207)	(0.0210)	(0.0352)	(0.0347)
Energy	0.2511	0.0391	-0.0188	0.0908^{***}	-0.0589^{*}	-0.0148
	(0.7062)	(0.0207)	(0.0194)	(0.0197)	(0.0329)	(0.0324)
Agricultural Materials	3.8847^{***}	-0.1784^{***}	-0.0771^{**}	0.0094	0.1854^{***}	-0.0737
	(1.3721)	(0.0402)	(0.0376)	(0.0382)	(0.0640)	(0.0630)
Non-Agricultural Materials	1.8309	-0.0280	-0.0815^{**}	-0.0263	-0.0240	0.1086^{*}
	(1.4242)	(0.0417)	(0.0391)	(0.0397)	(0.0664)	(0.0654)
Construction						
Capital	3.3998^{***}	0.1517^{***}	-0.0648^{***}	-0.0298^{*}	-0.0844	-0.0129
	(1.2424)[a]	(0.0364)	(0.0341)	(0.0346)	(0.0579)	(0.0570)
Labor	4.7445^{***}	-0.0141	-0.0273	-0.0045	0.0464	0.0491
	(0.7072)	(0.0207)	(0.0194)	(0.0197)	(0.0330)	(0.0325)
Energy	4.5777^{***}	-0.0168	-0.1191^{***}	0.0975^{**}	0.0727	-0.0021
	(1.4730)	(0.0431)	(0.0404)	(0.0410)	(0.0687)	(0.0676)
Agricultural Materials	4.8251^{***}	-0.0055	-0.1311^{***}	0.0768^{***}	0.0500^{*}	0.0567^{*}
	(0.6311)	(0.0185)	(0.0173)	(0.0176)	(0.0294)	(0.0290)
Non-Agricultural Materials	5.4495^{***}	0.0000	-0.0971^{***}	0.0138	-0.0055	0.1010^{**}
	(0.9432)	(0.0276)	(0.0259)	(0.0263)	(0.0440)	(0.0433)

(*Continued*)

Table 3.2 (*Continued*)

Independent					Materials	
Variable	Constant	Capital	Labor	Energy	Agricultural	Non-Agricultural
Food and Kindred Products						
Capital	1.6449***	0.0526***	−0.0179	−0.0086	0.0104	0.0482**
	(0.4620)	(0.0135)	(0.0127)	(0.0129)	(0.0215)	(0.0212)
Labor	3.1926***	−0.0286*	−0.0097	0.0064	−0.0474*	0.0834***
	(0.5802)	(0.0170)	(0.0159)	(0.0162)	(0.0270)	(0.0266)
Energy	0.5634*	0.0441***	−0.0124	0.0650***	−0.0671***	0.0216
	(0.3269)	(0.0096)	(0.0090)	(0.0091)	(0.0152)	(0.0150)
Agricultural Materials	3.2459***	0.0541***	0.0060	−0.0229**	0.0302*	0.0105
	(0.3902)	(0.0114)	(0.0107)	(0.0109)	(0.0182)	(0.0179)
Non-Agricultural Materials	2.8056***	−0.0066	−0.0206	0.0092	−0.0640***	0.1030***
	(0.4931)	(0.0144)	(0.0135)	(0.0137)	(0.0230)	(0.0226)
Tobacco Manufacturing						
Capital	−2.2335**	0.0736***	0.0329	0.0073	0.0545	0.0284
	(0.9333)	(0.0273)	(0.0256)	(0.0260)	(0.0435)	(0.0428)
Labor	−3.6127***	−0.0795*	0.1156***	0.0200	0.1107*	0.0731
	(1.3942)	(0.0408)	(0.0383)	(0.0388)	(0.0650)	(0.0640)
Energy	−2.5429**	−0.0238	−0.0175	0.0405	0.0647	0.0179
	(1.2257)	(0.0359)	(0.0336)	(0.0341)	(0.0571)	(0.0563)
Agricultural Materials	5.3862**	0.0611	−0.0774	−0.0325	0.2299**	−0.1662*
	(2.1615)	(0.0633)	(0.0593)	(0.0602)	(0.1008)	(0.0992)
Non-Agricultural Materials	−1.4301	−0.0522*	−0.0054	−0.0286	0.1158***	0.1177***
	(0.9543)	(0.0279)	(0.0262)	(0.0266)	(0.0445)	(0.0438)

Textiles						
Capital	0.0097	0.0203	−0.0150	0.0398**	−0.0128	0.0471
	(0.6452)	(0.0189)	(0.0177)	(0.0180)	(0.0301)	(0.0296)
Labor	1.9346***	−0.0589***	0.0531***	0.0827***	0.0332	−0.0103
	(0.6890)	(0.0202)	(0.0189)	(0.0192)	(0.0321)	(0.0316)
Energy	0.5088	−0.0103	0.0006	0.1545***	0.0245	−0.0448*
	(0.5858)	(0.0172)	(0.0161)	(0.0163)	(0.0273)	(0.0269)
Agricultural Materials	1.4894	−0.0344	0.0232	0.0651**	0.0608	0.0103
	(0.9639)	(0.0282)	(0.0264)	(0.0268)	(0.0449)	(0.0443)
Non-Agricultural Materials	2.6767***	−0.0658***	−0.0207	0.1339***	0.0139	0.0405
	(0.7882)	(0.0231)	(0.0216)	(0.0219)	(0.0367)	(0.0362)
Apparel						
Capital	−2.9041***	0.0507***	0.0023	0.0272	0.0011	0.0911***
	(0.6293)	(0.0184)	(0.0173)	(0.0175)	(0.0293)	(0.0289)
Labor	1.3397	−0.0587**	0.0973***	0.1013***	0.1436***	−0.0811**
	(0.9001)	(0.0264)	(0.0247)	(0.0251)	(0.0420)	(0.0413)
Energy	−0.2835	−0.0291	0.0268	0.2046***	0.1526**	−0.1264**
	(1.2827)	(0.0376)	(0.0352)	(0.0357)	(0.0598)	(0.0589)
Agricultural Materials	1.1860	−0.0479	0.0490	0.1236***	0.2270***	−0.0689
	(1.5447)	(0.0452)	(0.0424)	(0.0430)	(0.0720)	(0.0709)
Non-Agricultural Materials	0.9635	−0.0923**	0.0177	0.1268***	0.1813***	−0.0023
	(1.2809)	(0.0375)	(0.0351)	(0.0357)	(0.0597)	(0.0588)

Notes: [a]Numbers in parenthesis denote standard errors.
***,**,*Denote statistical significance at the 0.01, 0.05, 0.10 levels of confidence, respectively.

To examine this results, we rewrite Equation (3.12) as

$$\alpha = \sum_{i=1}^{N} \left[\alpha_i + \sum_{l=1}^{N} A_{li}\beta_{li} \right]. \tag{3.14}$$

Applying this relationship to the KLEM data yields

$$\begin{aligned} &(-7.0041 + 1.6217 \times 3.4453 + 0.4363 \times 4.8118 - 1.1331 \times 0.6240 \\ &\quad + 0.3887 \times 2.5732 + 1.2081 \times 1.4374) \\ &\quad + (2.1704 - 0.2574 \times 2.1091 - 0.2795 \times 8.1599 + 0.5496 \times 1.6694 \\ &\quad - 0.4291 \times 3.9280 - 0.48954 \times 1.0243) + \cdots \\ &\quad (1.2800 - 0.3365 \times 2.9041 + 0.3340 \times 1.3397 - 0.3339 \times 0.2836 \\ &\quad - 0.0085 \times 1.1860 + 0.1530 \times 0.9635) = 25.7781 \end{aligned} \tag{3.15}$$

which is close to the value given in Table 3.1 (probably off by a rounding error). So, what does this mean? Theil draws three conclusions:

(i) Both α and β_l depend on the microvalues $x_{li}(t)$ because the coefficients A_{li} and $B_{l,\tilde{l}i}$ are dependent on these values.
(ii) The macroparameter α depends not only on the "*corresponding microparameters*" α_i but also on the other *non-corresponding microparameters* β_{li}.
(iii) The macroparameters β_l do not depend on the microparameters α_i, but they do depend on all the parameters $\beta_{\tilde{l}i}$ (Theil, 1954a, pp. 13–14).

To develop the scenario where the aggregated microparameters and the macroparameters are the same, Theil presents the second part of his Theorem 1.

Theorem 3.2 (Second Part). *The sum of the "weights" A_{li} over all i is, for each l, equal to zero. The sum of the "weights" $B_{l,\tilde{l}i}$ over all i is equal to unity if $\tilde{l} = l$ and equal to zero if $\tilde{l} = l$ (Theil's Theorem 1 (Theil, 1954a, p. 15)).*

Mathematically from the KLEM results

$$\sum_{i=1}^{N} A_{1i} = 3.4453 - 2.1091 \cdots - 2.9041 = 0 \tag{3.16}$$

and

$$\sum_{i=1}^{N} B_{1,1i} = 0.0642 + 0.1733 \;\cdots + 0.507 = 1$$

$$\sum_{i=1}^{N} B_{1,2i} = -0.0465 - 0.0218 \;\cdots - 0.0587 = 0. \tag{3.17}$$

Next, if we assume that β_{li} is the same for every individual, then using Equations (3.16) and (3.17),

$$\sum_{i=1}^{N} A_{1i}\beta_{1i} = \beta_{1i}\sum_{i=1}^{N} A_{1i} = 0$$

$$\sum_{i=1}^{N} B_{1,1i}\beta_{1i} = \beta_{1i}\sum_{i=1}^{N} B_{1,1i} = \beta_{1i}$$

$$\sum_{i=1}^{N} B_{1,2i}\beta_{1i} = \beta_{1i}\sum_{i=1}^{N} B_{1,2i} = 0 \tag{3.18}$$

or the estimates would converge to their true values. However, let us assume that not all the β_{li} are the same. Instead, let us introduce an "average" $\beta_{li} \rightarrow \bar{\beta}_l$. The weighted difference between the observed β_{li} and the average $\bar{\beta}_l$ can then be written as

$$\sum_{i=1}^{N} A_{li}\left(\beta_{li} - \bar{\beta}_l\right) \tag{3.19}$$

which is a correlation coefficient. The result in Equation (3.19) leads Theil to conclude as follows:

> Hence, if (and only if) the parameters β_{li} and the weights A_{li} are uncorrelated, the macroparameter α will not depend on the β_{li}. In the same way it can be proved that

> β_l does not depend on the non-corresponding microparameters $\beta_{\tilde{l}i}$ $(\tilde{l} \neq l)$, if and only if the series
>
> $$\begin{matrix} B_{l,\tilde{l}1} & B_{l,\tilde{l}2} & \cdots & B_{l,\tilde{l}N} \\ \beta_{\tilde{l}1} & \beta_{\tilde{l}2} & \cdots & \beta_{\tilde{l}N} \end{matrix} \tag{3.20}$$
>
> are uncorrelated (Theil, 1954a, p. 16).

Expanding the basic results in terms of covariances, the covariance between the β_{li} coefficients can be written as

$$\begin{aligned} C_{0l} &= \frac{1}{N}\sum_{i=1}^{N} A_{li}\beta_{li} \\ C_{l\tilde{l}} &= \frac{1}{N}\sum_{i=1}^{N}\left[B_{l,\tilde{l}i} - \frac{1}{N}\sum_{j=1}^{N} B_{l,\tilde{l}j}\right]\beta_{\tilde{l}i}. \end{aligned} \tag{3.21}$$

The results for Equations (3.12) and (3.13) can then be rewritten as

$$\begin{aligned} \alpha &= \sum_{i=1}^{N} + N\sum_{l=1}^{L} C_{0l} \\ \beta_l &= \bar{\beta}_l + N\sum_{\tilde{l}=1}^{L} C_{l\tilde{l}}\ ,\ l = 1, \ldots, L. \end{aligned} \tag{3.22}$$

Theil then states the following:

> Hence the macrointercept is equal to the sum of the microintercepts and the macroslope is equal to the average of the corresponding microslopes, both apart from certain covariance corrections (Theil, 1954a, p. 16).

What do these results for aggregation mean for the estimation of production functions? First, we know that aggregating production data (both inputs and outputs) may yield results that are different from the individual-level production function. We can do some things to minimize the impact of this distortion. I want to briefly discuss two possibilities: scaling the data and choosing the variables for aggregation. From a scaling perspective, we know that if $\beta_{li} = \beta_{lj}$, there is no bias (see Equation (3.18)). Hence, we could guarantee this result by the appropriate scale of $x_{li}(t)$

$$\begin{aligned} \tilde{x}_{li}(t) &= r_{li} x_{li}(t) \\ \tilde{\beta}_{lj} &= \frac{\beta_{li}}{r_{li}}. \end{aligned} \tag{3.23}$$

Another way of minimizing the aggregation effect involves choosing the firm-level aggregation better. We will discuss the use of aggregated inputs at the individual or firm level more in the following section, but it will be sufficient at this point to point out that many of our empirical variables are aggregates of more detailed inputs. Livestock feed may be the sum of a function of corn, protein supplements, and roughage (e.g., hay). Several mechanisms exist for aggregating these variables, but one of the most widely used (especially in early literature) is to sum the values of each input:

$$x_{1i}(t) = w_c(t)\, x_{ci}(t)\,(t) + w_p(t)\, x_{pi}(t) + w_h(t)\, x_{ht}(t) \tag{3.24}$$

where $x_{1i}(t)$ is the "aggregated" feed input used by firm i, $w_c(t)$ is the cost of corn, $x_{ci}(t)$ is the quantity of corn used, $w_p(t)$ is the price of protein supplement, $x_{pi}(t)$ is the quantity of protein supplement used, $w_h(t)$ is the price of hay, and $x_{hi}(t)$ is the quantity of hay used by individual i at time t. The following section examines how the selection of this aggregation affects the firm level, our model of firm decisions and the econometric estimation of parameters at the individual level. However, from an aggregation perspective, the effect of aggregation would be minimized if

$$x_{li}(t) = A_{li} + B_{l,li} x_l(t) \tag{3.25}$$

or when the individual data for input l (e.g., in Equation (3.10)) is "mostly explained" by the aggregated value of that input. Under this scenario, the confounding effect $(\sum_{\tilde{l} \neq l} B_{l,\tilde{l}i} \beta_{\tilde{l}})$ becomes zero. The relationship is exact if $A_{li} = 0$ and $B_{l,li} = 1/N$. Hence, the better the separability, the better the aggregation.

The second major point about aggregating the data involves the type of research question asked. In our discussion of the primal, we are interested in decisions made by farm firms. Hence, to the degree that the level of aggregation across firms changes the first-order conditions for the production function, it reduces the appropriateness of the result for policy and other economic analysis. Specifically, the aggregated production function may not represent actual decisions made by any individual in the sample.

3.1.2 *Aggregation of Inputs*

So, what are we really worried about when aggregating inputs along the lines of Equation (3.3)? Leontief (1947a,b) provides an overall description of the problem (see the following box on **A Theory of Internal Relationships**). As a first step, we want to establish conditions where we can divide the set of inputs into groups in such a way that the economic decisions remain unchanged. For example, suppose that we have a production function with four inputs $f(x_1, x_2, x_3, x_4)$. One concept is that we could separate this function into two additive pieces:

$$f(x_1, x_2, x_3, x_4) = f_1(x_1, x_2) + f_2(x_1, x_2). \tag{3.26}$$

A Theory of Internal Relationships — Leontief

Breaking down an intricate quantitative system with many variables into several simpler relationships — each involving fewer variables — is a standard analytical procedure. Let us consider, for example, the process of steel production. The final output depends here on a very great number of different inputs. If one goes back far enough, these will comprise the quantities of various kinds of labor, machinery, explosives, and other auxiliary materials used in extraction of coal; they will also include a not less heterogeneous collection of cost factors of the iron-mining industry. To be complete, this list

(*Continued*)

(Continued)

should contain as well a long array of tools, labor skills, and materials used directly in the operation and maintenance of blast furnaces and open-hearth units.

... The overall relationships between the set of the independent variables $x_1, x_2, \ldots, x_8$ and the dependent variable, y, can be conveniently thought of as a combination of many separate, intermediate relationships involving not only these original but also some additional intermediate variables. Let, for example, x_1, x_2, x_3 represent those of the eight factors which are actually used in the production of coal and x_4, x_5, x_6, x_7 represent those which constitute the cost elements of the iron-mining industry. Let, furthermore, z_1 stand for the amount of coal and z_2 the quantity of ore going into the production of steel and x_8 be the amount of labor used in servicing the blast furnaces. On the basis of appropriate technical information, one can establish three intermediate production functions:

$$z_1 = {}_1f\left(x_1, x_2, x_3\right) \tag{I.2}$$

$$z_2 = {}_2f\left(x_4, x_5, x_6, x_7\right) \tag{I.3}$$

$$y = {}_0f\left(z_1, z_2, x_8\right) \ldots \tag{I.4}$$

Given these three partial relationships, the overall production function can be reconstructed by substituting of ${}_1f\left(x_1, x_2, x_3\right)$ and ${}_2f\left(x_4, x_5, x_6, x_7\right)$ for z_1 and z_2 back into I.4. Indeed, the consistency that necessarily must exist between the three intermediate and the one overall relationship can be stated in the form of the following identity:

$$\begin{aligned} &F\left(x_1, x_2, \ldots, x_8\right) \\ &\quad = {}_0f\left[{}_1f\left(x_1, x_2, x_3\right), {}_2f\left(x_4, x_5, x_6, x_7\right), x_8\right] \end{aligned} \tag{I.5}$$

(Leontief, 1947a, pp. 361–362).

From an economic perspective, we would like the optimizing choice to remain unchanged. For example, suppose that we started with the profit maximization problem

$$\begin{aligned}
& pf(x_1,x_2,x_3,x_4) - w_1x_1 - w_2x_2 - w_3x_3 - w_4x_4 \\
& \quad = p\left[f_1(x_1,x_2) + f_2(x_3,x_4)\right] - w_1x_1 - w_2x_2 - w_3x_3 - w_4x_4 \\
& \quad \Rightarrow \begin{cases}
\dfrac{\partial f(x_1,x_2,x_3,x_4)}{\partial x_1} = \dfrac{\partial f_1(x_1,x_2)}{x_1} \\
\dfrac{\partial f(x_1,x_2,x_3,x_4)}{\partial x_2} = \dfrac{\partial f_1(x_1,x_2)}{\partial x_2} \\
\dfrac{\partial f(x_1,x_2,x_3,x_4)}{\partial x_3} = \dfrac{\partial f_2(x_3,x_4)}{\partial x_3} \\
\dfrac{\partial f(x_1,x_2,x_3,x_4)}{\partial x_4} = \dfrac{\partial f_2(x_3,x_4)}{\partial x_4}
\end{cases}.
\end{aligned} \tag{3.27}$$

One alternative to meet the conditions in Equation (3.27) is a "block diagonal" quadratic function

$$\begin{aligned}
f(x_1,x_2,x_3,x_4) = \alpha_0 &+ \begin{bmatrix}\alpha_1\\ \alpha_2\\ \alpha_3\\ \alpha_4\end{bmatrix}' \begin{bmatrix}x_1\\ x_2\\ x_3\\ x_4\end{bmatrix} \\
&+ \frac{1}{2}\begin{bmatrix}x_1\\ x_2\\ x_3\\ x_4\end{bmatrix}' \begin{bmatrix}A_{11} & A_{12} & 0 & 0\\ A_{12} & A_{22} & 0 & 0\\ 0 & 0 & A_{33} & A_{34}\\ 0 & 0 & A_{34} & A_{44}\end{bmatrix} \begin{bmatrix}x_1\\ x_2\\ x_3\\ x_4\end{bmatrix}.
\end{aligned} \tag{3.28}$$

However, it is interesting that the Cobb–Douglas form also meets the separation concept:

$$\begin{aligned}
f(x_1,x_2,x_3,x_4) &= x_1^{\alpha_1}x_2^{\alpha_2}x_3^{\alpha_3}x_4^{\alpha_4} \\
&\Rightarrow f_1(x_1,x_2)\,f_2(x_3,x_4) = \left(x_1^{\alpha_1}x_2^{\alpha_2}\right)\left(x_3^{\alpha_3}x_4^{\alpha_4}\right).
\end{aligned} \tag{3.29}$$

To establish the equivalence,

$$\left.\begin{aligned}\frac{\partial f\left(x_1,x_2,x_3,x_4\right)}{\partial x_1}&=\alpha_1\frac{y}{x_1}\\\frac{\partial f\left(x_1,x_2,x_3,x_4\right)}{\partial x_2}&=\alpha_2\frac{y}{x_2}\\\frac{\partial f\left(x_1,x_2,x_3,x_4\right)}{\partial x_3}&=\alpha_3\frac{y}{x_3}\\\frac{\partial f\left(x_1,x_2,x_3,x_4\right)}{\partial x_4}&=\alpha_4\frac{y}{x_4}\end{aligned}\right\}$$
$$\Rightarrow\left\{\begin{aligned}\frac{\partial f_1\left(x_1,x_2\right)f_2\left(x_3,x_4\right)}{\partial x_1}&=\frac{\partial f_1\left(x_1,x_2\right)}{\partial x_1}f_2\left(x_3,x_4\right)=\alpha_1\frac{y}{x_1}\\\frac{\partial f_1\left(x_1,x_2\right)f_2\left(x_3,x_4\right)}{\partial x_2}&=\frac{\partial f_1\left(x_1,x_2\right)}{\partial x_2}f_2\left(x_3,x_4\right)=\alpha_2\frac{y}{x_2}\\\frac{\partial f_1\left(x_1,x_2\right)f_2\left(x_3,x_4\right)}{\partial x_3}&=\frac{\partial f_2\left(x_3,x_4\right)}{\partial x_3}f_1\left(x_1,x_2\right)=\alpha_3\frac{y}{x_3}\\\frac{\partial f_1\left(x_1,x_2\right)f_2\left(x_3,x_4\right)}{\partial x_4}&=\frac{\partial f_2\left(x_3,x_4\right)}{\partial x_4}f_1\left(x_1,x_2\right)=\alpha_4\frac{y}{x_4}\end{aligned}\right. . \tag{3.30}$$

This grouping concept has its uses, but takes the concept a little too far. To examine the usefulness of the structure, assume that x_3 and x_4 are uncontrollable and unobserved inputs. Under these assumptions, we could substitute $\epsilon = f_2\left(x_1, x_2\right)$ in both cases, yielding

$$\begin{aligned}f\left(x_1,x_2,\epsilon\right)&=f_1\left(x_1,x_2\right)+\epsilon\quad\text{or}\\f\left(x_1,x_2,\epsilon\right)&=f_1\left(x_1,x_2\right)\epsilon\end{aligned}\tag{3.31}$$

so that the unobserved and uncontrollable terms add noise, but do not introduce a bias (i.e., in the quadratic function (Equation (3.28)), the lack of interaction terms such as x_1x_3 means that the level of x_3 does not affect the estimation of A_{11}).

Building the degree of complexity, let us first consider the slight reformulation of Equation (3.26).

$$f\left(x_1,x_2,x_3,x_4\right)=\tilde{f}\left(f_1\left(x_1,x_2\right),\quad f_2\left(x_1,x_2\right)\right). \tag{3.32}$$

Note that Equation (3.32) simply generalizes Equation (3.26). The question of aggregating several inputs into a composite input (i.e., different types of labor into a single labor variable) follows directly from Equation (3.32):

$$f(x_1, x_2, x_3, x_4) \Leftrightarrow \tilde{f}(z_1, z_2)$$
$$z_1 = x_1 + x_2, \quad z_2 = x_3 + x_4. \tag{3.33}$$

As a final modification to Equation (3.32), consider a scenario where we observe the levels of some inputs, but aggregate other inputs into an index (i.e., we aggregate liquid propane, gasoline, and diesel into a fuel input):

$$f(x_1, x_2, x_3, x_4) = \tilde{f}(x_1, x_2, \quad z(x_3, x_4)). \tag{3.34}$$

The question is then — how does this aggregation affect our empirical specification?

For simplicity, consider the quadratic specification for Equation (3.34):

$$\tilde{f}(x_1, x_2, z(x_3, x_4)) = \alpha_0 + \begin{bmatrix} \alpha_1 \\ \alpha_2 \\ \alpha_3 \end{bmatrix}' \begin{bmatrix} x_1 \\ x_2 \\ z \end{bmatrix}$$
$$+ \frac{1}{2} \begin{bmatrix} x_1 \\ x_2 \\ z \end{bmatrix}' \begin{bmatrix} A_{11} & A_{12} & A_{13} \\ A_{12} & A_{22} & A_{23} \\ A_{13} & A_{23} & A_{33} \end{bmatrix} \begin{bmatrix} x_1 \\ x_2 \\ z \end{bmatrix}$$
$$z(x_3, x_4) = \beta_0 + \begin{bmatrix} \beta_1 \\ \beta_2 \end{bmatrix}' \begin{bmatrix} x_3 \\ x_4 \end{bmatrix} + \frac{1}{2} \begin{bmatrix} x_3 \\ x_4 \end{bmatrix}' \begin{bmatrix} B_{11} & B_{12} \\ B_{12} & B_{22} \end{bmatrix} \begin{bmatrix} x_3 \\ x_4 \end{bmatrix}. \tag{3.35}$$

While it is somewhat messy, substituting the second equation in Equation (3.35) into the first will produce the unrestricted quadratic function. The basic problem is that we want to determine the values of the second equation in Equation (3.35) "outside" of the current estimation. For example, if we simply want to combine two types of labor, $\beta_0 = 0$, $\beta_1 = 1$, $\beta_2 = 1$ and $B_{ij} = 0$ for all i and j.

The Nobel Laureate Wassily Leontief (1906–1999) was one of the first to rigorously examine the implications of these questions in the guise of separability Leontief (1947b). As a starting point, Leontief divides the set of variables into two groups as in Equation (3.34):

$$y = f(X) = \psi\left(\phi(S), S'\right) \Leftrightarrow \psi\left(\phi\left(x_3, x_4\right), x_1, x_2\right) \tag{3.36}$$

so that $\phi(S)$ is a function of a set of inputs $S = \{x_3, x_4\}$ and S' is the complementary set of inputs (e.g., $S' = \{x_1, x_2\}$). The key factor that we are really interested in is the notion that the trade-off between x_3 and x_4 is not affected by a variable in the other group, say x_1. Mathematically, Leontief defines ${}_{ij}R$ to be the marginal rate of technical substitution between inputs:

$${}_{ij}R = \frac{\dfrac{\partial f(X)}{\partial x_i}}{\dfrac{\partial f(X)}{\partial x_j}} = \frac{f_i}{f_j}. \tag{3.37}$$

Leontief then states that the necessary and sufficient conditions for ${}_{ij}R$ to be independent of x_k is for the derivative of Equation (3.37) to be zero:

$${}_{ij}R_k = \frac{f_{ik}f_j - f_{jk}f_i}{\left(f_j\right)^2} = 0. \tag{3.38}$$

Backing up a little bit, we are interested in the scenario where the choice between x_3 and x_4 is not affected by x_1. Economically, the choice between x_3 and x_4 using Leontief's notation becomes

$$\frac{f_3}{f_4} = \frac{w_3}{w_4} \tag{3.39}$$

where w_3 and w_4 are the input prices for x_3 and x_4, respectively. This trade-off is unaffected by x_1 if

$${}_{34}R_1 = \frac{f_{31}f_4 - f_{41}f_3}{\left(f_4\right)^2} = 0. \tag{3.40}$$

Hence, let us assume that x_3 is the level of liquid propane gas and x_4 is the amount of diesel used by the farmer. These conditions tell us the conditions where the decision regarding the choice between liquid propane gas and diesel is unaffected by the choice of another input, say nitrogen fertilizer. Also, note that if ${}_{34}R_1 = 0$, then ${}_{43}R_1 = 0$ by Young's theorem.

Extending the basic result in Equation (3.38), Leontief notes that

$$ {}_{il}R_k f_l f_i = {}_{il}R_k f_l f_i - {}_{ij}R_k \left(f_i\right)^2 . \tag{3.41}$$

The simplest way to verify Equation (3.41) is using a "method of undetermined coefficients" approach. Specifically, let us start with the formulation

$$ {}_{il}R_k f_l f_i = {}_{il}R_k f_l f_i - K. \tag{3.42}$$

If we can demonstrate that $K = {}_{ij}R_k \left(f_i\right)^2$, then we have confirmed Equation (3.41). Hence, starting with Equation (3.42), we get

$$\begin{aligned} \frac{f_{jk} f_l^2 f_i - f_{lk} f_j f_i f_l}{f_l^2} &= \frac{f_{ik} f_l^2 f_j - f_{lk} f_j f_i f_l}{f_l^2} - K \\ \Rightarrow K &= f_{jk} f_i - f_{ik} f_j. \end{aligned} \tag{3.43}$$

Multiplying K in Equation (3.43) by f_j^2/f_j^2 yields the result ${}_{ij}R_k \left(f_i\right)^2$. Hence, if ${}_{il}R$ and ${}_{ij}R$ are independent of x_k, then ${}_{jl}R$ is also independent of x_k. In addition, Leontief states that

$$ {}_{ik}R_j - {}_{jk}R_i = {}_{ij}R_k \left(\frac{f_i}{f_k}\right)^2 \tag{3.44}$$

which implies that if ${}_{ik}R$ is independent of x_i and ${}_{jk}R$ is independent of x_i, then ${}_{ij}R$ is independent of x_k.[1]

The above results support Leontief's Theorem I.

[1]To fully understand Leontief's (1947b) derivations, let us comfirm the conjecture in Equation (3.44). As a starting point, let us define ${}_{ik}R_j$ from scratch:

$$\begin{aligned} {}_{ik}R &= \frac{f_i}{f_k} \Rightarrow {}_{ik}R_j = \frac{d}{dx_j}\frac{f_i}{f_k} \\ \Rightarrow {}_{ik}R_j &= \frac{f_{ij}}{f_k} - \frac{f_{kj} f_i}{f_k^2} = \frac{f_{ij} f_k - f_{kj} f_i}{f_k^2}. \end{aligned}$$

By the steps,

$$ {}_{jk}R_i = \frac{f_{jk} f_k - f_{ki} f_j}{f_k^2}.$$

Therefore,

$$\begin{aligned} {}_{ik}R_j - {}_{jk}R_i &= \frac{f_{ij} f_k - f_{kj} f_i}{f_k^2} - \frac{f_{ji} f_k - f_{ki} f_j}{f_k^2} \\ &= \frac{f_{ki} f_j - f_{kj} f_i}{f_k^2} \end{aligned}$$

Theorem 3.3. *A subset S is locally functionally separable from X in $f(X)$ if and only if the following set of equations is satisfied: ${}_{S_iS_j}R_{S'} = 0$. The first two subscripts to R refer to any two identical or different elements in the subset S, while the last subscript indicates any element of the subset S' which is complementary to S in X (Leontief, 1947b, p. 344).*

The point of the proof is then — given the formulation in Equation (3.36) — if x_i and x_j are both elements of S,

$$ {}_{ij}R = \frac{f_i}{f_j} = \frac{\phi_i(S)}{\phi_j(S)}. \tag{3.45} $$

Hence, given that x_k is an element of S', ${}_{ij}R_k = 0$ and the functional form is locally separable.

Based on these results, Leontief offers the lemma.

Lemma 3.1. *Given A, B, C, three mutually exclusive subsets of the set X and G the rest of X, if each of the sets A, B, C is locally functionally separable from X in $f(X)$, these subsets can also be separated simultaneously from X in $f(X)$ (Leontief, 1947b, p. 345).*

Lemma 3.1 yields the generalization the result:

$$ f(X) = \Phi(\alpha(A), \beta(B), \gamma(C), G). \tag{3.46} $$

In terms of the description of the production of steel in Box, **A Theory of Internal Relationships**, we have conditions for the production function:

$$ \begin{aligned} &F(x_1, x_2, x_3, x_4, x_5, x_6, x_7, x_8) \\ &\quad = f(f_1(x_1, x_2, x_3), f_2(x_4, x_5, x_6, x_7), x_8) \end{aligned} \tag{3.47} $$

as described by Leontief (1947a).

To frame this aggregation problem within Leontief's results, consider Jorgenson's KLEM data. The data contain several

---

applying Young's theorem so that $f_{ij} = f_{ji}$. Finally, we are going to factor the f_k^2 out of the denominator and multiply by the form of one — f_i^2/f_i^2

$$ \frac{f_{ki}f_j - f_{kj}f_i}{f_k^2}\frac{f_i^2}{f_i^2} = \frac{f_{ki}f_j - f_{kj}f_i}{f_i^2}\frac{f_i^2}{f_k^2} = {}_{ij}R_k\left(\frac{f_i}{f_k}\right)^2. $$

different representations. In Section 3.1.1, we used a variant of the data that decomposes materials into materials from an agricultural origin and non-agricultural materials. Mathematically, the empirical model estimated for our discussion of aggregation across individuals was

$$y = \alpha_0 x_K^{\alpha_1} x_L^{\alpha_2} x_E^{\alpha_3} x_A^{\alpha_4} x_O^{\alpha_5} \tag{3.48}$$

where y is the logarithm of output, x_K is the logarithm of the capital input, x_L is the logarithm of labor, x_E is the logarithm of energy, x_A is the logarithm of agricultural materials, and x_O is the logarithm of non-agricultural materials (e.g., other materials). This decomposition is intended on estimating the derived demand for agricultural outputs from other industries (i.e., the derived demand for agricultural outputs for the food and kindred product industry in the KLEM data). However, for most uses, the two types of inputs are aggregated into a single material input using a Tornqvist–Theil index. Specifically, following the general approach in Equation (3.24), we could envision aggregating the two materials into a total value variable

$$X_M = w_A X_A + w_O X_O \tag{3.49}$$

where X_M is the value of materials used in production, w_A is the price of agricultural materials, X_A is the quantity of agricultural materials used, w_O is the price of other materials, and X_O is the quantity of non-agricultural materials used. However, this approach typically raises difficulties because the quantity measure is confused by changes in prices. Hence, instead of using the simple value index, we compute the Tornqvist–Theil measure of change in quantity between periods:

$$\begin{aligned} T(t) &= \frac{w_A(t) X_A(t)}{w_A(t) X_A(t) + w_O(t) X_O(t)} \frac{d \log (X_A(t))}{dt} \\ &\quad + \frac{w_O(t) X_O(t)}{w_A(t) X_A(t) + w_O(t) X_O(t)} \frac{d \log (X_O(t))}{dt} \\ \Rightarrow T(t) &= \left[\frac{1}{2}(s_A(t) + s_A(t-1))\right][x_A(t) - x_A(t-1)] \\ &\quad + \left[\frac{1}{2}(s_O(t) + s_O(t-1))\right][x_O(t) - x_O(t-1)] \end{aligned} \tag{3.50}$$

where $s_A(t)$ and $s_O(t)$ are the share of expenditures on agricultural and non-agricultural materials, respectively. $T(t)$ is the growth in the total quantity from time $t-1$ to t. To flush out this process, consider the KLEM data in Table 3.3. The first step is to compute the expenditure shares for each input, for example, for 1990,

$$s_A\,(1990) = \frac{186{,}346 \times 0.9123}{186{,}346 \times 0.9123 + 94{,}230 \times 0.8816} = 0.6742$$

$$s_O\,(1990) = \frac{94{,}230 \times 0.8816}{186{,}347 \times 0.9123 + 94{,}230 \times 0.8816} = 0.3258. \quad (3.51)$$

Next, we compute the aggregated change index for the change in quantity:

$$T\,(1991) = \frac{1}{2}\,(0.6675 + 0.6742)\log\left(\frac{187{,}257}{186{,}346}\right) + \frac{1}{2}\,(0.3325 + 0.3528)\log\left(\frac{94368}{94230}\right) = 0.0038. \quad (3.52)$$

Note that we substitute $\log\,(x_2/x_1) = \log\,(x_2) - \log\,(x_1)$.

A minor point of complication involves the "base year" for the aggregation. Most aggregated indexes have a starting point or a base year. In the case of KLEM, that base year is 1996; hence, all the prices in 1996 are one. The base quantity is then set as the total value of the input or output in that base year. In Table 3.3, the total value of agricultural materials in 1996 is \$200,599 while the total value of non-agricultural materials is \$102,075 (assuming that both prices are 1.0). Hence, the aggregated quantity for materials in 1996 is taken to be 200,599 + 102,075 = 302,674. To compute the quantity of the aggregated materials in 1995, we can "walk back" this aggregated quantity using the Tornqvist–Theil index:

$$X_M\,(1995) = \frac{302{,}674}{\exp\,(-0.0033)} = 303{,}687. \quad (3.53)$$

To compute the value of materials in 1997, we "walk forward" the quantity using the index:

$$X_M\,(1997) = 302{,}674 \times \exp\,(0.0206) = 308{,}959. \quad (3.54)$$

To allow comparisons of the computations with the KLEM data, we present the aggregated values of materials presented in the KLEM dataset and the aggregation of the material prices in Table 3.3.

Table 3.3 Aggregating Materials Inputs from KLEM Using Tornqvist–Theil Index.

	Agricultural Materials		Non-Agricultural Materials		Shares		Quantities				
							Weighted Change		Change	Total	KLEM
Year	Quantity	Price	Quantity	Price	Agricultural	Non-Agricultural	Agricultural	Non-Agricultural	Quantity	Materials	Value
1990	186,346	0.9224	94,230	0.8816	0.6742	0.3258				280,548	280,548
1991	187,257	0.9123	94,368	0.9018	0.6675	0.3325	0.0033	0.0005	0.0038	281,603	281,604
1992	199,797	0.9041	96,003	0.9156	0.6727	0.3273	0.0434	0.0057	0.0491	295,775	295,777
1993	201,256	0.9451	94,933	0.9335	0.6822	0.3178	0.0049	−0.0036	0.0013	296,164	296,166
1994	200,535	0.9271	98,655	0.9545	0.6638	0.3362	−0.0024	0.0126	0.0102	299,189	299,190
1995	204,945	0.9691	98,776	0.9872	0.6707	0.3293	0.0145	0.0004	0.0149	303,687	303,688
1996	200,599	1.0000	102,075	1.0000	0.6628	0.3372	−0.0143	0.0109	−0.0033	302,674	302,674
1997	208,559	1.0098	100,408	1.0137	0.6742	0.3258	0.0260	−0.0055	0.0206	308,959	308,960
1998	217,769	0.9763	107,446	1.0270	0.6583	0.3417	0.0288	0.0226	0.0514	325,255	325,255
1999	212,372	0.9822	106,629	1.0375	0.6534	0.3466	−0.0165	−0.0026	−0.0191	319,106	319,106
2000	212,790	0.9977	105,406	1.0566	0.6559	0.3441	0.0013	−0.0040	−0.0027	318,247	318,247
							Prices				
							Weighted Change		Change	Total	KLEM
							Agricultural	Non-Agricultural	Quantity	Materials	Value
1990										0.9088	0.9088
1991							0.0000	0.9088	0.0000	0.9088	0.9088
1992							−0.0010	0.9079	−0.0010	0.9079	0.9079
1993							0.0363	0.9414	0.0363	0.9414	0.9414
1994							−0.0056	0.9362	−0.0056	0.9362	0.9362
1995							0.0407	0.9751	0.0407	0.9751	0.9751
1996							0.0252	1.0000	0.0252	1.0000	1.0000
1997							0.0111	1.0111	0.0111	1.0111	1.0111
1998							−0.0182	0.9929	−0.0182	0.9929	0.9929
1999							0.0075	1.0003	0.0075	1.0003	1.0003
2000							0.0165	1.0170	0.0165	1.0170	1.0170

As a starting point, we note that the Cobb–Douglas is separable using Leontief's results. Specifically, focusing on the separability of the trade-off between capital and labor given materials from agriculture from Equation (3.48), we note

$$
{}_{KL}R = \frac{\alpha_1 \dfrac{y}{x_K}}{\alpha_2 \dfrac{y}{x_L}} = \frac{\alpha_1 x_L}{\alpha_2 x_K}. \tag{3.55}
$$

Obviously, $\partial\left(\alpha_1 x_L/\alpha_2 x_K\right)/\partial x_A = 0$, but let us strictly apply Leontief's result from Equation (3.38):

$$
\begin{aligned}
{}_{KL}R_A &= \frac{\dfrac{\alpha_1\alpha_4 y}{x_K x_A}\dfrac{\alpha_2 y}{x_L} - \dfrac{\alpha_2\alpha_4}{x_L x_A}\dfrac{\alpha_1 y}{x_K}}{\left[\dfrac{\alpha_4 y}{x_A}\right]^2} \\
&= \frac{\alpha_1 y}{x_K}\frac{\alpha_2 y}{x_L} - \frac{\alpha_2 y}{x_L}\frac{\alpha_1 y}{x_K} = 0.
\end{aligned} \tag{3.56}
$$

Hence, the Cobb–Douglas function form itself is separable. What does this mean for estimation? Consider two alternative specifications for the Food and Kindred product component of KLEM. The first specification divides material inputs into agricultural and nonagricultural inputs following Equation (3.48), while the second combines the material inputs into a single material input using the Tornqvist–Theil approach. The specification for the second model is then

$$
y = \tilde{\alpha}_0 x_K^{\tilde{\alpha}_1} x_L^{\tilde{\alpha}_2} x_E^{\tilde{\alpha}_3} x_M^{\tilde{\alpha}_4}. \tag{3.57}
$$

The results for each specification are presented in Table 3.4. These results suggest that the two specifications are different. There are minor changes in the coefficients of capital and energy, but estimate for labor when materials are aggregated is three times larger than the disaggregated specification. In this case, the difficulty lies not in the function form which is separable, but in the data itself.

Table 3.4 Separability for Materials Input in Food and Kindred Product Regression

Input	Disaggregated Materials	Aggregated Materials
Constant	0.7740*** (0.2316)[a]	0.3887 (0.2859)
Capital	0.4019*** (0.0698)	0.4351*** (0.0658)
Labor	0.0295 (0.0573)	0.0919 (0.0403)
Energy	−0.0921*** (0.0195)	−0.0813*** (0.0187)
Materials — Agricultural	0.4556*** (0.0721)	
Materials — Non-Agricultural	0.2875*** (0.0777)	
Materials — Total		0.6487*** (0.1002)

Notes: [a]Numbers in parenthesis denote standard errors.
***Denotes statistical significance at the 0.01 level of confidence.

To develop the issue with this aggregation, we return to Theil (1954). Theil rearranges the aggregation model as

$$\begin{aligned} y(t) &= \alpha + \sum_{l=1}^{L} \sum_{h=1}^{H} \beta_{lh} x_{lh}(t) + u(t) \\ x_l(t) &= \sum_{k=1}^{H} r_{lk} x_{lk}(t) \\ &\Rightarrow y(t) = \alpha + \sum_{l=1}^{L} \tilde{\beta}_l x_l(t) + \tilde{u}(t). \end{aligned} \tag{3.58}$$

In terms of our current aggregation,

$$\begin{aligned} y(t) = \alpha_0 &+ \beta_1 \log(x_K(t)) + \beta_2 \log(x_L(t)) + \beta_3 \log(x_E(t)) \\ &+ \beta_4 \log(r_{44} x_A(t) + r_{45} x_O(t)). \end{aligned} \tag{3.59}$$

Hence, aggregating over independent variables shares several attributes with the aggregation over individuals. Theil demonstrates the behavior of the *macroparameters* (i.e., the β_l for the aggregated inputs) in the theorem.

Theorem 3.4. *The macroparameters α and β_l of Equation (3.58) are given by the following relations:*

$$\alpha = \sum_{i=1}^{N} \alpha_i + \sum_{l=1}^{L} \sum_{h=1}^{H_l} A_{lh} \sum_{i=1}^{N} \beta_{lh,i}; \tag{3.60}$$

$$\beta_l = \sum_{\tilde{l}=1}^{L} \sum_{h=1}^{H_{\tilde{l}}} B_{l,\tilde{l}h} \sum_{i=1}^{N} \beta_{\tilde{l}h,i}\ , l = 1, \ldots, L. \tag{3.61}$$

The sum of the "weights" A_{lh} over all h $(h = 1, \ldots, H_l)$ is, for each l, equal to zero. The sum of the "weights" $B_{l,\tilde{l}h}$ over all h $\left(h = 1, \ldots, H_{\tilde{l}}\right)$ is equal to unity if $\tilde{l} = l$ and to zero if $\tilde{l} \neq l$ (Theorem 2 (Theil, 1954a, p. 30)).

Hence, aggregating the two material variables introduces additional covariance between the aggregated material variable and other inputs in the specification (e.g., labor). In this case, aggregating the two material variables likely introduces a bias in the other parameter estimates. While the functional form may be separable, the data indicate that the underlying production function is not separable. Aggregating the two materials yields a specification bias.

Backing up our discussion to Equations (3.37) and (3.38), we note that this expression shares several features with the Hicks–Allen elasticity of substitution from Equation (1.101):

$$\sigma_{ij}^{D} = \frac{d\left(\dfrac{x_i}{x_j}\right)\dfrac{\dfrac{f_j}{f_i}}{}}{d\left(\dfrac{f_i}{f_j}\right)\dfrac{x_i}{x_j}}. \tag{1.101}$$

Berndt and Christensen (1973) exploit this relationship to derive more general conditions for separability. Beginning with basic concepts of separability, they start with

$$f_i = \frac{\partial F}{\partial X_i} i = 1, \ldots, n$$

$$f_{ij} = \frac{\partial^2 F}{\partial X_i \partial X_j} i, j = 1, \ldots, n. \tag{3.62}$$

They state that the production function is weakly separable with respect to some partition R if the marginal rate of substitution between two inputs X_i and X_j from a subset N_s, $s = 1, \ldots, r$ is independent of the quantities outside N_s

$$\frac{\partial}{\partial X_k}\left(\frac{f_i}{f_j}\right) = 0, \forall i, j \in N_s \quad \text{and} \quad k \notin N_s. \tag{3.63}$$

Berdnt and Christensen then define $F(X)$ as strongly separable with respect to a partition R if the marginal rate of substitution between the two inputs in N_s and N_t does not depend on the quantities of inputs outside these two groups:

$$\frac{\partial}{\partial X_k}\left(\frac{f_i}{f_j}\right) = 0, \forall i \in N_s\,, j \in N_t\,, k \notin N_s \cup N_t. \tag{3.64}$$

The linkage between the Allen elasticity of substitution (AES) and separability is developed in Theorem 3.5.

Theorem 3.5. *Weak separability of $F(X)$ with respect to the partition R at any point in the input space is necessary and sufficient for all proper AES σ_{ik}, σ_{jk} $(i, j \in N_s, k \notin N_s)$ to be equal at that point (Theorem 3, (Berndt and Christensen, 1973, p. 406)).*

Starting with our definition of the Allen elasticity of substitution (AES) in Equation (1.121)

$$\sigma_{ij}^D = \frac{\sum_{i=1}^n x_i f_i}{x_i x_j} \frac{F_{ji}}{F}. \tag{1.109}$$

To demonstrate the result, we need a result from Section 5.3 (Equation (5.58))

$$\frac{dx_i}{dw_j} = \frac{1}{\lambda} \frac{|F_{ij}|}{|F|} \Rightarrow \frac{|F_{ij}|}{|F|} = \lambda \frac{dx_i}{dw_j}. \tag{5.58}$$

Substituting this result into the definition of AES,

$$\sigma_{ik} = \frac{\sum_{h=1}^{n} w_h X_h}{X_i X_k} \frac{\partial X_i}{\partial w_k}. \tag{3.65}$$

Borrowing another result from duality,

$$X_i = \frac{\partial C(y, w)}{\partial w_i} = H(y) \frac{\partial G(w)}{\partial w_i} = H(y) G_i. \tag{3.66}$$

Therefore, we get for each input i and j

$$\frac{\partial X_i}{\partial w_k} = H(y) \frac{\partial G_i}{w_k} = H(y) G_{ik} \quad \text{and} \quad \frac{\partial X_j}{\partial w_k} = H(y) G_{jk}. \tag{3.67}$$

Working through the implications, first let us tackle

$$\sum_{h=1}^{n} w_h X_h = C(y, w) = H(y) G(w) \tag{3.68}$$

by definition of the cost function. Substituting for each of the pieces

$$\sigma_{ik} = \frac{H(y) G(w)}{H(y) G_i \times H(y) G_k} H(y) G_{ik} = \frac{G G_{ik}}{G_i G_k}. \tag{3.69}$$

Completing the proof from Equation (3.69), if $\sigma_{ik} - \sigma_{jk} = 0$,

$$\begin{aligned} \frac{G G_{ik}}{G_i G_k} - \frac{G G_{jk}}{G_j G_k} &= 0 \\ \frac{G_j G G_{ik} - G_i G G_{jk}}{G_i G_k G_j} &= 0 \\ G_j G_{ik} - G_i G_{jk} &= 0 \end{aligned} \tag{3.70}$$

which implies separability (i.e., $F_j F_{ik} - F_i F_{jk} = 0$ — the numerator in Equation (3.38)). This proof is actually in dual cost space (i.e., we have implicitly used the AES measure for the cost function — see Section 5.3); however, the notion is that given that the AES results hold, separability exists. Further, the notion that two inputs i and j are weakly separable with respect to input k if they have the same elasticity of substitution with input k at the point of estimation is an extension of Leontief's original result.

Based on the results of Berndt and Christensen (1973), we turn to the derivation of separation conditions for specific function forms as developed by Blackorby, Primont, and Russell (Blackorby *et al.*, 1977). As a starting point, Blackorby, Primont, and Russell use the general concept of a functional mapping

$$F : \Omega^n \to R \tag{3.71}$$

so that n inputs are mapped into a single output through function F. Within this context, their definition of separability is

$$\frac{\partial}{\partial x_k}\left(\frac{\partial F\left(x\right)/\partial x_i}{\partial F\left(x\right)/\partial x_j}\right) = 0. \tag{3.72}$$

Next, they specify a "general quadratic flexible form"

$$F\left(X\right) = \sum_{iinI} \alpha_i f_i\left(x_i\right) + \sum_{i\in I}\sum_{j\in I} \beta_{ij} f_i\left(x_i\right) f_j\left(x_j\right) \ni: \beta_{ij} = \beta_{ji}. \tag{3.73}$$

Separability Restrictions on Flexible Function Forms — Blackorby, Primont, and Russell

Until recently, econometric research on the estimation of supply and/or demand systems generated by profit or utility maximization has employed highly structured objective functions (e.g., the Cobb–Douglas and CES functions and affine transformations of them). These specifications maintain restrictive separability assumptions. The development of operational nonlinear estimation programs has made it possible to estimate less structured functional forms. The result has been a proliferation in the use of the so-called flexible functional forms.

Basically, the class of flexible functional forms is defined by the property that these forms can provide a second-order approximation to an arbitrary twice differentiable function. This property of flexible forms has considerably enhanced the capabilities for testing structural hypotheses with fewer maintained hypotheses than were heretofore necessary. This expanded potential for hypothesis testing has in turn reinforced the nexus between theoretical and empirical research (Blackorby *et al.*, 1977, p. 195).

For example, if we were interested in a standard quadratic, $f_i(x_i) = x_i$; however, when we evaluate the translog, $f_i(x_i) = \ln(x_i)$.

Using the general functional form in Equation (3.73) with the definition of separability in Equation (3.72), the input relationship $\{i, j\}$ from input k if and only if

$$\alpha_j \beta_{ik} - \alpha_i \beta_{jk} + 2 \sum_{l=1}^{n} (\beta_{jl}\beta_{ik} - \beta_{il}\beta_{jk}) f_l(x_l) \equiv 0. \tag{3.74}$$

Hence, the function is separable if and only if

$$\alpha_j \beta_{ik} - \alpha_i \beta_{jk} = 0 \tag{3.75}$$

and

$$\beta_{jl}\beta_{ik} - \beta_{il}\beta_{jk} \, \forall l \in I. \tag{3.76}$$

This leads to the special "additive separability case":

$$\beta_{ik} = \beta_{jk} = 0. \tag{3.77}$$

This result leads to Blackorby, Primont and Russell's Theorem 1.

Theorem 3.6. *The pair $\{i, j\}$ is separable form the kth variable $j \neq k \neq i$ if and only if Equation (3.77) holds or $\{i, j\}$ is separable for all variables in $I - \{i, j\}$ (Blackorby et al., 1977, p. 198).*

Note the consistency of these results with the original formulation of the simple quadratic presented in Equation (3.28).

Returning to the KLEM data, we could investigate the separability, the level of labor used in the food and kindred product sector and the choice between agricultural materials (X_A) and non-agricultural materials (X_O) within the translog formulation by estimating

$$y = \alpha_0 + \begin{bmatrix} \alpha_K \\ \alpha_L \\ \alpha_E \\ \alpha_A \\ \alpha_O \end{bmatrix}' \begin{bmatrix} x_K \\ x_L \\ x_E \\ x_A \\ x_O \end{bmatrix}$$

$$+ \begin{bmatrix} x_K \\ x_L \\ x_E \\ x_A \\ x_O \end{bmatrix}' \begin{bmatrix} A_{KK} & A_{KL} & A_{KE} & A_{KA} & A_{KO} \\ A_{KL} & A_{LL} & A_{LE} & A_{LA} & A_{LO} \\ A_{KE} & A_{LE} & A_{EE} & A_{EA} & A_{EO} \\ A_{KA} & A_{LA} & A_{EA} & A_{AA} & A_{AO} \\ A_{KO} & A_{LO} & A_{EO} & A_{AO} & A_{OO} \end{bmatrix} \begin{bmatrix} x_K \\ x_L \\ x_E \\ x_A \\ x_O \end{bmatrix} \tag{3.78}$$

where $x_i = \ln(X_i)$. Testing for separability between labor and the choice of materials would then involve the test $A_{LA} = A_{LO} = 0$.

In addition to the simple three-variable scenario described in Equation (3.77), Blackorby, Primont and Russell develop a more complex test of separability where groups of variables are additively separable (Blackorby *et al.*, 1977, p. 198). However, the simple scenario is sufficient for our purposes here.

Again, to wrap up our discussion of separability, we may be interested in separability for a specific production relationship. For example, in the KLEM data, we may be interested in whether the trade-off between agricultural materials and non-agricultural materials is affected by the level of capital or labor in the production of food and kindred products. However, separability also has something to say about our aggregation of inputs in empirical specifications. In advanced applications such as the measurement of productivity which we will discuss in Chapter 6, aggregating different types of hired labor (e.g., machinery operators and harvest crews) may have impacts on the measurement of the productivity of other inputs (e.g., capital). In the empirical examples of production function applications in the remainder of this chapter, various aggregations are used (i.e., different types of equipment are aggregated into a single capital variable). It is important to realize that these aggregations may affect other parameters (i.e., the Cobb–Douglas parameter for labor).

3.1.3 *The Capital Question*

At first glance, capital may appear to be a rather simple input. For example, suppose that the production process for some crop such as cotton involved a single capital input, a tractor, along with two variable inputs, labor and fertilizer. In a standard Cobb–Douglas world, employing a single tractor would imply

$$\begin{aligned}\pi &= p_y\left(\alpha_0 x_T^{\alpha_1} x_L^{\alpha_2} x_F^{\alpha_3}\right) - w_T x_T - w_L x_L - W_F x_F\\ \left.\frac{\partial \pi}{\partial x_T}\right|_{x_T \to 1} &= p_y \alpha_1 y - w_1 = 0\\ w_1 &= \alpha_1 p_y y.\end{aligned} \tag{3.79}$$

Hence, if you have a single tractor, the price of that tractor should be equal to its Cobb–Douglas parameter times revenue. We will use an extension of this result known as Euler's theorem to decompose profit into payments to factors later in this chapter. However, for our current purposes, we take the discussion of this result in two directions: what is w_1 (the price of the tractor) and what is $\alpha_1 p_y y \neq w_1$ (more or less than one tractor is optimal).

To start our discussion, let us begin by realizing that some agricultural equipment is quite expensive. As of January 2017, a 2013 Caterpillar Challenger MT845C is listed for sale at \$286,500. This tractor is rated at 331.68 drawbar horsepower. Two such tractors would probably be sufficient for five sections (5,120 acres) of delta land in Arkansas producing cotton, corn, and soybeans. One approach would be to allocate the cost of this tractor over the cultivated acres resulting in \$55.96/acre. However, this would be inaccurate. Unlike variable inputs (e.g., fertilizer or labor hours hired), the Cat Challenger's complete value will not be used up in this production period. The question is then — how much of this tractor's value will be used in the current period? One approach is to examine the change in market value. In 2013, the MT845C sold for \$397,457. Thus, we could compute the average rate of value loss as

$$\tau = \frac{\ln(285{,}500) - \ln(397{,}457)}{3} = -0.1091. \tag{3.80}$$

Using this relationship, the Cat at the end of 2017 will be \$256,883, or \$29,687 loss in value. Thus, we expect that the value of tractor used up in this production year, \$29,687 $\rightarrow V\left(1 - \exp\left(\tau\right)\right) = V \times 0.1034$, where $V = 286{,}500$ or the value of the asset at the beginning of the year.

In addition to this direct loss in value, we also want to account for the "opportunity cost" of owning the Cat Challenger. Typically, this is measured as the value of the asset at the beginning of the period r. Let us assume that the opportunity cost of capital is 7.5% ($\kappa = \ln(1.075) = 0.0723$) — the opportunity cost of owning the tractor is \$21,488 (e.g., $286{,}500 \times 0.075$).

The total ownership cost of the tractor could then be written as

$$\begin{aligned} r^* V &= \left[\left(1 - \exp\left(\tau\right)\right) + \exp\left(\kappa\right)\right] V \\ &= \left[0.1034 + 0.075\right] V = 0.1784V \end{aligned} \tag{3.81}$$

What Do We Economize? — Black

To economize is to get along with a little of something to make a given amount go a long way... [i]t does not tell us what is economical. We shall presently discover that in the last analysis it is always human effort in one form or another that is economized. We economize in the use of land, it is true; but this is merely to make labor go as far as possible. A little labor may be used on a large tract of land or a large amount on a little land. If we are wasteful in the use of land, we must use more labor. Labor and land are therefore in a sense substitutes for each other. We also economize in the use of machinery and buildings and supplies; but these are in large part simply stored-up labor. Being wasteful in the use of a building is being wasteful of all the labor that went into the erecting of it and into the sawing of the lumber for it, the felling of trees, the hauling of the logs, and the mining and smelting of the iron that went into its doors and hinges, as well as of the land that went into the trees and iron. When we economize natural resources, and the various forms of commodities derived from man and nature together, we are in the last analysis only economizing the human effort which they represent in one way or another (Black, 1962, p. 4).

or \$51,104 in 2017 or \$9.98 per acre. This represents the use value of the tractor. Intuitively, we could use the value V in the production function coupled with one of the two prices (e.g., depending on whether the choice problem was formulated at the firm level or on a per acre basis).

The next question involves the "integer nature" of most capital investments. Specifically, the farmer can typically decide whether to own one tractor or two tractors. Going back to the first-order condition from Equation (3.79),

$$\frac{\partial \pi}{\partial x_T} = p_y \alpha_1 \frac{y}{x_T} - w_1 = 0. \tag{3.82}$$

Again, let us consider corn production in southeastern Arkansas (Mississippi Delta area). Assuming a corn price of \$3.83/bushel, a yield of 150 bushel per acre and $\alpha_1 = 0.075$ yields a marginal value product for a single tractor of \$11.25 per acre (e.g., $x_T = 1$). Note that this value is higher than the marginal cost of the Cat Challenger of \$9.98 per acre. Hence, following our basic axioms, the farmer would attempt to expand production (and probably the land he farms) to increase profit. However, note that is it is not worth going all the way to two tractors because the marginal value of two tractors per acre is \$5.63. What should the farmer do? One alternative is to hire a neighbor's tractor for about 1/8 of the annual period. The point is that capital investments are not smooth, but integer in nature. Disaggregation may appear to "fix" the problem (i.e., computing everything on a per acre basis may hide the problem), but the error may affect the estimated value of the production function.

Real Capital — Bawerk

It is not my intention to do as Senior did and try to make Saving a third factor in production along with Nature and Labor. It does not stand beside these factors, but behind them. It does not share with them in the work of production in such a way that any part of the same is due to it solely and particularly; it only ensures that the productive powers, nature and labor, which in any case must do the whole work of production, are directed straight to this and no other goal — the production of capital and not of consumption goods. In a word, it has its place, not among the means of production, but among the motives of production — the motives which decide the direction of production (Bawerk, 2007, II.VI.6).

A further complication occurs because a complement of machinery is typically required for any business. In the case of southeastern Arkansas, farmers will have more than on tractor, a cotton stripper, a combine, a sprayer, and several different field implements drawn by the tractor, including a planter. As in our preceding discussion, we could envision aggregating these different pieces of machinery into a single capital variable. Further, we could compute the price for each piece of equipment following Equation (3.81) and then aggregating these prices into a single price of equipment. However, we must recognize that the choice of a specific machinery complement may introduce the same separability problems discussed above.

Capital Theory — Hayek

The term "capital" is a convenient description of the aggregate of non-permanent resources and one difficult to dispense with entirely. Its use is, however, as we have observed before, beset with dangers. Not the least serious of these, and one to which the majority of economists have succumbed at one time or another, is the temptation to regard the stock of "capital" as a quasi-homogeneous, quantitatively determined magnitude which can, like the supply of any other factor of production, be treated as a datum of economic analysis. One of the main conclusions of the whole preceding discussion is that the supply of capital cannot be treated as a single quantity in this sense. Nevertheless, in view of the established position this idea occupies in economic theory, it seems advisable to examine it further (von Hayek, 2009, p. 294).

To this point, our discussion of capital has been "data-centered" — we have defined capital by example. Tractors, trucks, buildings, and backhoes are capital. The definition is implicit in the common features. Physical capital is an item whose value extends over one time period (typically a year) that provides a service flow. Note that this definition includes several consumption items — homes, cars, refrigerators. These capital items are sometimes important in household production models, such as those proposed by Becker (1965). Note that some objects are not physical, but provide a service flow such as a license or a patent — do we recognize these items as capital?

Given this data-centered approach, it is easy to define the value of capital — capital is the sum of "market values" of these items. However, the economic profession can raise difficulties with many topics that appear clear cut to the rest of the world. First, as hinted to in the Boxes, **What Do We Economize**, **Real Capital**, and **Capital Theory**, some have suggested that capital is not "an independent factor of production." Capital is forgone consumption from labor (and possibly the resource flow from natural resources). Hence, the level of capital is at least in part determined by economic decisions at the current point in time. Consider a small and stylized general equilibrium model:

$$\begin{aligned} D_1(y, p_1, p_2, p_3) - S_1(p_1, p_2, p_3, x_{11}, x_{21}, x_{31}) &\le \zeta_1 \\ D_2(y, p_1, p_2, p_3) - S_2(p_1, p_2, p_3, x_{12}, x_{22}, x_{32}) &\le \zeta_2 \\ D_3(y, p_1, p_2, p_3) - S_3(p_1, p_2, p_3, x_{13}, x_{23}, x_{33}) &\le \zeta_3 \\ x_{11} + x_{12} + x_{13} &\le x_{1T} \\ x_{21} + x_{22} + x_{23} &\le x_{2T} \\ x_{31} + x_{32} + x_{33} &\le x_{3T} \\ y = w_1 x_{1T} + w_2 x_{2T} + w_3 x_{3T} & \end{aligned} \tag{3.83}$$

where $D_1()$ is the demand for consumption goods, $D_2()$ is the demand for production goods that will be consumed in the current production period, $D_3()$ is the demand for capital goods, y is the aggregate income which is the result of factor payments to households (i.e., the sum of a wage or factor price w_i times the amount of the good used in production x_{iT}), p_i is the price of each output and ζ_i is the excess demand for each product. For simplicity, assume that x_{1T} is the labor, x_{2T} is the flow from natural resources, and x_{3T} is the capital. Under this formulation, we hypothesize that some vector of prices $\tilde{P} = \{p_1, p_2, p_3, w_1, w_2, w_3\}$ that reduces the level of excess demand to zero for each commodity. In this world, the price and level of capital along with the level of one-period production goods could be determined. However, note that some production goods carry-over

$$x_{31} + x_{32} + x_{33} \le x_{3T} + \delta x_{3T,t-1} \tag{3.84}$$

where δ is the one minus the rate of decay. This dynamic in the capital equation fostered the capital debate:

> We are concerned, in this paper, with capital as a factor of production, that is capital in the sense in which it consists of a mass of buildings, machinery, roads, ditches, stocks of goods, &c. We are not at the moment interested in drawing the line between capital goods and land, or between producer's and consumer's capital. We are concerned rather with the problems of measurement which arise after the decision has been made as to what concrete items are to be included in the enumeration.
>
> In particular, we are concerned with the difficulty that arises out of the fact that the use of capital goods is spread out through time while the measure that we are looking for is a value at a moment of time (Robinson, 1959, p. 157).

Robinson's objection involves the fact that the value of capital is unique to a given equilibrium. In a different equilibrium, the value of capital itself changes. This critique suggests that work with an aggregate Cobb–Douglas cost function makes little sense: $y = f(k[y], l)$. Most of this debate has occurred in the macroeconomics arena, particularly in the area of economic growth. However, the critique may have merit for aggregate production.

3.1.3.1 *Multiple quasi-fixed assets*

Departing from renewable capital, we turn to the valuation of farmland. Again, we have several options to incorporate farmland into our production analysis. One approach is simply to estimate crop production on a "per acre" basis. A second alternative is to incorporate a physical measure of farmland into the production function (i.e., number of acres or hectares cultivated). A final alternative is to use the value of farmland (much like our variable for machinery above) into the production function (i.e., dollars of farmland). The last approach has the advantage of providing a mechanism for accounting for different values of farmland (e.g., more productive farmland has a higher value and implicit cost of service flow). The value approach is used to measure changes in productivity in Chapter 6.

The valuation of farmland for agricultural purposes has been a constant topic of research in agricultural economics. Farmland in the United States accounted for 70%–80% of all agricultural assets between 1960 and 1999. Hence, fluctuations in farmland values has significant implications for farmer wealth and solvency. Despite the significance of farmland to the health of the farm sector, efforts to explain changes in farmland values have not been widely successful, especially in the short run. Schmitz (1995) found that the present value formulation holds in the long run; however, the correlation of residuals in the short run implies the existence of short-run profits from speculation which is inconsistent with efficient pricing of assets. The existence of short-run disequilibria is consistent with the findings of Chavas and Thomas (1999) and Lence and Miller (1999) who conclude that transaction costs limit the adjustment of farmland prices. Finally, a constant question in the estimation of the value of farmland is the measurement of returns. In the standard pricing model, the value of farmland is equal to the discounted expected returns. Historically, we have used observed residual returns to measure expected returns (Featherstone and Baker (1987) and Moss (1997)); however, Alston (1986) used cash rents.

Mishra *et al.* (2004) propose a different approach to farmland valuation based on Ricardian rents (adjusted for other input fixities). Historically, most studies have modeled farmland values as the source of Ricardian rents — they have ignored the contribution of other fixed factor in agricultural production. While farmland may be the most fixed factor of production, other fixed factors exist. Most agricultural machinery has limited value outside the sector. In addition, farm labor and management may be fixed into agriculture in the short run. Mishra, Moss, and Erickson demonstrate that other quasi-fixed factors such as machinery, labor and management affect the measurement of residual rents. Their results show that, in the presence of multiple quasi-fixed factors, the rate of return to farmland is generally understated by residual measurement.

3.1.3.2 *Basic imputed value problem*

Two measures are typically used to value the returns on farmland: cash rents and imputed returns. The basic question under both approaches is. "What is the value of land in production?" Cash rents assume that buyers and sellers observe the value of land in a perfectly operating market. However, the cash rent approach leaves the greater question unanswered — it does not address how the renter determines the value of farmland. The concept of imputed cash returns follows from the Ricardian notion of cash rents as that amount left over after all other factors of production have been paid. Imputed measures the rate of return to farmland as the revenue less all variable costs minus an appropriate return for other factors, such as labor, management, and capital. It is at this point that the traditional definition raises some difficulties: "What is the appropriate price for labor and capital?" We turn to the basic profit maximization problem to answer this question:

$$\max_{x_1,x_2,x_3,x_4} p\,f(x_1,x_2,x_3,x_4) - w_1x_1 - w_2x_2$$
$$\text{s.t. } x_3 = x_3^0,\ x_4 = x_4^0 \tag{3.85}$$

where p is the output price, $f\,()$ is the production function, w_1 and w_2 are the input prices, x_1 and x_2 are the variable inputs and x_3

and x_4 are the quasi-fixed inputs. Rewriting Equation (3.85) in a Lagrange form,

$$\begin{aligned} L = p\,f(x_1, x_2, x_3, x_4) - w_1 x_1 - w_2 x_2 \\ + \lambda_3 \left(x_3^0 - x_3\right) + \lambda_4 \left(x_4^0 - x_4\right) \end{aligned} \tag{3.86}$$

where λ_3 is the marginal value of x_3, x_3^0 is the fixed value of input 3, λ_4 is the marginal value of x_4, and x_4^0 is the fixed value of this input. Differentiating with respect to variable input values implies

$$\begin{aligned} d\,L = \left[p\frac{\partial f}{\partial x_1} - w_1\right] d\,x_1 + \left[p\frac{\partial f}{\partial x_2} - w_2\right] d\,x_2 \\ + \left[p\frac{\partial f}{\partial x_3} - \lambda_3\right] d\,x_3 + \left[p\frac{\partial f}{\partial x_4} - \lambda_4\right] d\,x_4. \end{aligned} \tag{3.87}$$

The first two terms in Equation (3.87) imply that the marginal value product of the variable inputs equal their respective price. However, the second terms in Equation (3.87) imply that the marginal value product of the quasi-fixed inputs set the value of λ_3 and λ_4. Dividing Equation (3.87) by $d\,x_3$ yields

$$\begin{aligned} \frac{dL}{d\,x_3} = \left[p\frac{\partial f}{\partial x_1} - w_1\right] \frac{d\,x_1}{d\,x_3} + \left[p\frac{\partial f}{\partial x_2} - w_2\right] \frac{d\,x_2}{d\,x_3} \\ + p\frac{\partial f}{\partial x_3} - \lambda_3 + \left[p\frac{\partial f}{\partial x_4} - \lambda_4\right] \frac{d\,x_4}{d\,x_3} = 0. \end{aligned} \tag{3.88}$$

From left to right (if the current solution is optimum with respect to the two variable inputs), the first two terms on the right-hand side of the equation are zero (e.g., the marginal value product of each of the variable inputs equals the price of the respective input). Again, the optimality condition implies that the shadow value for each input (e.g., λ_3 and λ_4) are determined by their respective marginal value product.

Next, we explicitly solve for the shadow value of x_3, assuming that the variable inputs are paid their marginal values, we have

$$\lambda_3 = p\frac{\partial f}{\partial x_3} + \left[p\frac{\partial f}{\partial x_4} - \lambda_4\right] \frac{dx_4}{dx_3}. \tag{3.89}$$

Hence, Equation (3.89) indicates that the shadow value of x_3 is correctly imputed if either the return to x_4 is set equal to its shadow value or the production function is separable in the inputs. Substituting the market value of x_4 (w_4) for the shadow value yields

$$\lambda_3 = p\frac{\partial f}{\partial x_3} + (\lambda_4 - w_4)\frac{dx_4}{dx_3}. \tag{3.90}$$

This result is obtained by adding and subtracting $w_4 dx_4/dx_3$ to Equation (3.89), yielding

$$\lambda_3 = p\frac{\partial f}{\partial x_3} + \left(p\frac{\partial f}{\partial x_4} - \lambda_4 + w_4 - w_4\right)\frac{dx_4}{dx_3} \tag{3.91}$$

$$\lambda_3 = p\frac{\partial f}{\partial x_3} + \left(p\frac{\partial f}{\partial x_4} - w_4\right)\frac{dx_4}{dx_3} + (w_4 - \lambda_4)\frac{dx_4}{dx_3}. \tag{3.92}$$

Based on these results, the marginal value of input 3 is overstated if $\lambda_4 > w_4$ and the two inputs are compliments. Alternatively, the shadow value of input 3 is understated if $\lambda_4 < w_4$ and the two inputs are compliments.

Hence, the imputed rate of return is appropriate if inputs are correctly classified as variable versus quasi-fixed. If a quasi-fixed input is treated as variable by using a market price in place of a shadow value, then the imputed value of the input in question is misstated. These results also suggest that a dual specification is required to truly allocate the return to fixed factors when more than one fixed factor exists in the production function.

3.1.3.3 *Empirical model*

While we are interested in the effect of asset valuation on the specification of the primal production function, empirical models of quasi-fixed variables have most recently relied on a dual profit function which will be further developed in Chapters 4 and 5. For our purposes here, we assume a multivariate form of Equation (3.85), we could then derive a profit function such that the optimal level of profit is a function of output prices, input prices and the level of quasi-fixed variables. A flexible quadratic form of the dual profit function could then be specified as

$$\pi(p,w,z) = \alpha_0 + \alpha g(p) + \frac{1}{2} g(p)' A g(p) + \beta g(w) + \frac{1}{2} g(w)' B g(w) + g(p)' \Gamma g(w) + g(z)\phi + g(z)' \Phi g(z) + g(p)' \Psi_1 g(z) + g(w)' \Psi_2 g(p) \quad (3.93)$$

where $\pi(.)$ is the profit, α, A, β, B, Γ, ϕ, Φ, Ψ_1, and Ψ_2 are estimated parameters, $g(.)$ is a general functional mapping that allows for either the quadratic, translog, or generalized Leonteif,[2] p is the vector of output prices, w is the vector of input prices, and z is the vector of quasi-fixed variables. Using Sheppard; lemma as described in Chapters 4, the general profit specification in Equation (3.92) yields a system of output supply and input demand equations which, together with the profit function, can then be estimated using either seemingly unrelated regression or maximum likelihood.

The derivative of the profit function with respect to each quasi-fixed input coupled with the estimated parameters yields the estimated shadow value for each quasi-fixed input. The dual value of the quasi-fixed inputs are linear assuming a normalized quadratic profit function

$$\lambda_i = \varphi_i + \Phi_{\bullet i} z + \Psi_{1,\bullet i} p + \Psi_{2,\bullet i} w \quad (3.94)$$

where $\Phi_{.i}$ denotes the ith row of the Φ matrix, $\Psi_{1,\dots,i}$ denotes the ith row of the Ψ_1 matrix and $\Psi_{2,\dots,i}$ denotes the ith row of the Ψ_2 matrix. The test for the effect of multiple quasi-fixed variables would then be a Wald test for

$$\lambda_i = r_i \, \forall \, i = 1, \dots, k \quad (3.95)$$

where r_i is the observed market price for the ith quasi-fixed variable. Single variable examples of this procedure in the agricultural economics literature include Chambers and Vasavada (1983) and Taylor and Kalaitzandonakes (1990).

[2]Specifically,

$$g(p,\sigma) = \frac{p^\sigma}{\sigma}.$$

Hence, if $\sigma \to 1$, the function is a quadratic, if $\sigma \to 1/2$ the function is a generalized Leontief and if $\sigma \to 0$, the function is a translog.

Mishra *et al.* (2004) use a different but related approach to valuing the quasi-fixed inputs. Specifically, starting with the profit function in Equation (3.85), they define the excess profit (e.g., the profit above variable operating cost) as a function of the level of quasi-fixed variables:

$$p'y - w'x = \kappa_0 + \kappa_1 \text{Land} + \kappa_2 \text{Labor} + \kappa_3 \text{Intermediate} \qquad (3.96)$$

where p is the output price, y is the level of outputs, w is the price of variable inputs, x is the level of variable inputs, Land is the acres in agriculture, Labor is the labor hours used, and Intermediate is the quantity of intermediate capital. This specification examines whether residual profit is a function of land, labor, and capital. If each quasi-fixed input is in market equilibrium, then the estimated regression coefficient will equal the market price for each input. Focusing on the labor input (κ_2) will equal the wage rate if labor is in equilibrium. If the coefficient is less than the wage rate, labor is trapped in agriculture. If the estimated coefficient is greater than the wage rate, then some barrier of entry exists for labor. Focusing on the point of their analysis, if labor or intermediate capital is significantly different from its market value, the residual approach systematically misstates the rate of return to farmland.

Comparing the formulations in Equations (3.92) and (3.96), Equation (3.96) imposes a strong form of homotheticity on the production process. The model in Equation (3.96) does not allow for the shadow value of each input to change as the price of outputs or other quasi-fixed factors change. Implicitly, changes in relative output prices or input prices are assumed not to affect the values of each quasi-fixed input. Some support for this restriction can be found in Capalbo and Denny (1986). Mishra, Moss, and Erickson estimate the model specified in Equation (3.96) using a fixed effect model. Hence, the simple linear form of the model is parsimonious and will allow for the use of greater statistical information.

3.1.3.4 *Data*

Data for their analysis are from four different (1996, 1997, 1998, 1999) Agricultural Resource Management Studies (ARMS). The ARMS is a collaborative effort among the USDA, Economic Research Service (ERS) and the National Agricultural Statistics Service (NASS) to annually collect and summarize information on farm resource use and finances. Unfortunately, since different farms are sampled each year, we do not have a longitudinal dataset. The survey collects data to measure the financial condition (farm income, expenses, assets, and debts) and operating characteristics of farm businesses, and the cost of producing agricultural commodities. In addition, the survey also collects information on time spent working on the farm by the operator, spouses, and other unpaid family members, value of machinery and equipment on the farms, and total acres operated.

The dependent variable in Mishra, Moss and Erickson measures the gross income to the farming operation. The three independent variables in the model are the value of intermediate capital which is composed of three categories of capital goods: (1) automobiles; (2) farm tractors; (3) farm equipment and agricultural machinery excluding tractors, the land operated by the farm including owned, rented, and leased, and farm labor which measures the number of hours worked on the farm, as reported by the farm operator. The fixed effect model is estimated for the aggregate level (U.S.) for 4 years. Additional estimates are reported for the Heartland region of the United States for the same years. In addition, they estimate the shadow values for the quasi-fixed variables for different farm sizes (e.g., retirement and low resource farms are found to have lower shadow values of labor while very large farms have much higher values of labor) within the Heartland region.

3.1.3.5 *Estimates for continental United States*

The estimated shadow value of farmland across the 48 contiguous United States are presented in Table 3.5. These results vary between \$154.08/acre in 1996 without a constant to \$89.59/acre in 1999 without a constant. The constant appears to have little effect on the results of each regression. However, the results indicate a general decline in farmland values between 1996 and 1999. This decline is consistent with the general decline in agricultural profitability observed over the same time period.

The results for labor show more relative disparity between estimates with and without intercepts. The estimated shadow values without intercepts are much lower (ranging from \$1.65/hour in 1998 to \$5.73/hour in 1996 without an intercept to \$10.81/hour in 1998 to

Table 3.5 Estimates of the Marginal Value of Labor, Land and Intermediate Capital

Year	Intercept	Labor	Land	Intermediate Capital
48 Contiguous states, 1996–1999				
1999	−21,026.00	10.82*	89.81***	0.9797***
1999		1.98	89.59***	0.9812***
1998	−22,997.00	10.81**	103.24***	0.4195***
1998		1.65	101.67***	0.4191***
1997	−20,277.00	12.57**	127.52***	0.7000***
1997		4.61	129.83***	0.7036***
1996	−25,576.01	16.08***	154.08***	0.6061***
1996		5.73*	149.18***	0.6233***
Heartland Region, 1996–1999				
1999	7084.16	0.54	89.034***	0.1089***
1999		3.78*	108.52***	0.1187***
1998	714.86	6.11**	109.42***	0.1774***
1998		6.57**	110.04***	0.1777***
1997	1393.45	4.86***	111.13***	0.2317***
1997		5.67***	112.36***	0.2345***
1996	−20,556.00	13.80***	111.47***	0.6500***
1996		5.02***	106.16***	0.6589***

Notes: ***,**,*Denote statistical significance at the 0.01, 0.05, 0.10 levels of confidence respectively.

$16.08/hour in 1996 with an intercept). The disparity in estimates can be traced to the basic assumption in Equation (3.96). Assuming a constant allows the average values of other excluded quasi-fixed variables to be removed while assuming no intercept allocates all returns above variable costs to these three quasi-fixed factors.

The exact interpretation of the regression coefficients for intermediate capital presented in Table 3.5 are somewhat ambiguous. Intuitively, the coefficients yield the annual return to an additional dollar of intermediate capital which ranges from $0.42/dollar of intermediate capital in 1998 to $0.98/dollar of intermediate capital in 1999. It is tempting to interpret this result as an interest rate. However, if intermediate capital has a finite life, some of the return is required to offset depreciation. Alternative reasons for the coefficient value may include adjustments for relative risk.

3.1.3.6 *Estimated shadow values based on Heartland*

One potential factor contributing to the variability of the shadow values presented in Table 3.5 is the variation across agricultural resources and crops within the contiguous United States. In an attempt to remove this variability, we next estimated Equation (3.96) using data from the Heartland region as defined by the USDA. These results are also presented in the second part of Table 3.5. These results are consistent with the aggregate estimates. Table 3.6 presents the results for the same specification using the USDA's farm typology.

The annual estimates of shadow values in the second part of Table 3.5 show less variability than the results presented in the first part of Table 3.5, but some divergence remains. Specifically, while the shadow value of operator labor with and without intercepts are more similar in 1997 and 1998, the estimated value of operator labor is much higher ($13.80/hour) in 1996 without an intercept and much

Table 3.6 Estimates of the Marginal Value of Labor, Land and Intermediate Capital by Farm Typology

Typology	Intercept	Labor	Land	Intermediate Capital
Limited Resource Farms	−0.88	11.24***	54.31*	0.0576
		11.24***	54.31*	0.0577
Retirement Farms	8,366.39*	2.13	59.26***	0.0373
		6.64*	70.78***	0.0555
Residential Farms	8,511.47*	9.09***	39.14***	0.2181***
		11.65***	42.53***	0.2327***
Farming Occupation (Lower-Sales)	92,420***	9.17***	42.88***	0.0923***
		32.98***	66.6***	0.1356***
Farming Occupation (Higher-Sales)	262 719***	7.46	65.06***	0.0938
		70.48***	97.51***	0.1534**
Large Farms	116 002***	6.55**	69.46***	0.0530
		31.55***	101.41***	0.12017***
Very Large Farms	191 630***	19.29**	68.82***	0.0179
		63.18***	104.78***	0.0933*

Notes: ***,**,*Denote statistical significance at the 0.01, 0.05, 0.10 levels of confidence respectively.

lower (\$0.54/hour) in 1999 with an intercept. The estimates are much better behaved with respect to capital, however. The marginal value of capital is below 25% except for 1996. Thus, restricting the analysis to the Heartland region produces more consistent estimators for the shadow values of quasi-fixed factors. Further, the most questionable results occur in 1996, a period of significant agricultural prosperity resulting in high shadow values for all quasi-fixed assets.

The estimated shadow values presented in Table 3.6 explain the variations in shadow values with variations in farm resources. Specifically, the shadow value of labor is fairly consistent for Limited Resource Farms, Retirement Farms, and Residential Farms. In each case, the value of farmer labor is less than \$12/hour. As would be expected, the value of operator labor for Retirement Farms is the lowest at \$2.13/hour with an intercept and \$6.64/hour without an intercept, and the shadow value of labor being around \$11/hour for both Limited Resource and Residential Farms. The shadow value of labor for farms whose operators declare farming as their primary occupation shows more variability. Without an intercept, the estimate of the shadow value of labor is around \$8.00/hour while shadow value of labor without an intercept rises to \$70.48/hour for Farmer Occupation-High Sales farms. The divergence between these results may be attributed to the possibility of excluded quasi-fixed variables. Specifically, the \$70.48/hour may include a return to management, risk, etc.

The remaining shadow values follow similar predictable patterns. The value of farmland increases with the overall size of the farm. This result is consistent with increasing returns to scale in agriculture. Similarly, the value of intermediate capital is highest for Residential Farms and Lowest for Very Large Farms. This comparison implies that as the farm size expands, the equipment compliment becomes more efficient, consistent with increasing returns to scale. The results on farmland and intermediate capital may be linked to the type of agriculture practiced in the Heartland region.

3.1.3.7 *Test for quasi-fixity*

Given that the shadow values of the quasi-fixed factors of production are relatively close to our expectations, we turn to a formal test of whether the shadow value of land and labor equals their respective market price. If one of the factor markets exhibit quasi-fixity, then the hypothesis that the shadow value equals the market value will be rejected. Given the ARMS data, we were able to test this hypothesis for both farmland and labor across both the United States and the Heartland for 1998 and 1999, but we were only able to test for quasi-fixity in farmland for the Heartland region in 1996 and 1997.

The hypothesis that the shadow value equals the market price for labor was rejected for the Continental United States in the 1996 sample and for the Heartland region in every year. Thus, the statistical results suggest that operator labor is quasi-fixed in production, or that the market price does not represent the true value of labor at the farm level. Similarly, the hypothesis that the shadow value of farmland equals the cash rent on farmland is rejected for each region and year. Thus, we conclude that farmland is quasi-fixed.

3.1.3.8 *Implications*

Mishra, Moss, and Erickson develop a theoretical model that demonstrated the linkage between multiple quasi-fixed factors and the imputed return to farmland. This formulation shows that the imputation procedure implicitly assumes that all other quasi-fixed factors are paid their market price. Further, if any of the other quasi-fixed factors (labor, intermediate capital, etc.) do not earn their market price (are fixed in production), then the imputed returns misrepresent the return to farmland. Based on this theoretical formulation, they then developed an empirical model of the shadow values of the labor, land, and intermediate capital. The empirical results of this formulation demonstrate that farmer labor is quasi-fixed in 1996–1999 in the Heartland region of the United States and in 1996 in the Continental United States as a whole. Similarly, the results indicate that farmland values deviate from cash rental rates in all time periods and regions (both Heartland and the Continental United States).

Their empirical results have several implications for the farmland market in the United States. The results directly imply that the shadow value of farmland differs from its observed cash rental value. The exact reasons for this deviation are not apparent in the results, but the empirical estimates of the shadow value for farmland in 1999 supports the notion that the value of farmland is an increasing function of the size of the farm, or that significant economies of scale exist in agriculture. While this conjecture is not new, their results suggest that the interaction between farm size and investment in intermediate capital may hold significant insight into the phenomenon.

Given that the cash rental rates may misstate the shadow value of farmland, the results support the use of imputed returns to farmland in the analysis of farmland values. However, the empirical results also suggest caveats to this procedure. Specifically, the rejection of market conditions for farmer labor implies that the use of wages in imputing returns to farmland is inappropriate. Over the time period analyzed by this study, the shadow value of operator labor has been persistently below the market price of labor. Thus, using the wage rate in imputing biases the return to farmland downward. This downward bias may contribute to some of the anomalies reported in the farmland pricing literature.

Pure versus Applied Economics — Black

Like other sciences, economics has its pure and its applied aspects. The pure science of economics attempts to account for economic phenomena, just as physics and chemistry try to account for natural phenomena. A great storm center sweeps across the continent traveling southeastwardly at first and then northeastwardly, accompanied by a falling barometer, rising temperatures, heavy rainfall, and a succession of wind changes. Why do such storm centers develop? Why do they usually develop in the Northwest? Why do they characteristically follow a certain course? These are all questions which a natural science tries to answer, and in answering which, it sets up a body of principles or statements of causes and effects. Similarly, at irregular intervals, usually between 7 and 10 years, business depressions descend upon us, manifesting themselves first in the centers of industry and trade, but presently permeating to the remotest villages, accompanied by falling prices, unemployment, reduced volume of trade, "frozen credits," business failures, etc. Economic science tries to explore these phenomenan, and in doing so, it set up a body of principles or statements of causes and effects.

(*Continued*)

(Continued)

The body of principles, so far as discovered, which explains the foregoing and similar economic phenomena in terms of cause and effect, is the *pure science of economics.*

The applied economic sciences attempt to make use of these principles in administering economic enterprises in directing economic activity. To know why storm centers behave as they do is of no immediate value to us unless it will provide us with a way of controlling them or preparing for their coming. To explain the phenomena of business cycles is of no immediate value to us unless it helps us to cope with them to better advantage. There will always be those who will study economics as a pure science, who will be content merely to explain the causes of things, and give no heed as to whether or not their findings ever prove of any value to humanity. Such men render a very high service. It has been demonstrated many times that most of our great discoveries are made by such workers. But without workers of another sort, the applied scientists, to follow up their discoveries and apply them and demonstrate their value, their work would all go for naught (Black, 1962, pp. 11–12).

3.2 Production Functions in Agriculture

Over time, agriculture has provided the basis for the estimation of numerous production functions. Several factors contribute to the popularity of agricultural production functions. First, and perhaps most important, is the fact that the agricultural production data exist. From field trials to farm record keeping systems, the U.S. Land Grant University system has generated data. Additional data are generated through surveys conducted by the Economic Research Service and National Agricultural Statistical Service of the United States Department of Agriculture. Further, in contrast to data from manufacturing firms, farms have been providing this data (either knowingly or unknowingly) to researchers. More recently concerns have been raised about confidentiality, but even data from the Agricultural

Resource Management Survey are available to researchers fairly readily given certain protocols are followed. Another facet of this availability is that farmer data is not subject to "trade secrets" that may be inherent in other industries. Specifically, Intel may not wish Advanced Micro Devices (AMD) to have access to its cost of production data for microprocessors. Second, most agricultural production processes are relatively homogeneous. Farms in Arkansas, Illinois, Indiana, Iowa, Missouri, Ohio, and Mississippi all produce roughly the same quality of corn and soybeans. Further, we can probably assume that the response of corn yield to an additional unit nitrogen fertilizer is roughly the same in each state; however, this hypothesis is testable. Finally, agriculture has presented a problem set of public interest amenable to the estimation of production functions. The evolution of agricultural policies with the onset of Great Depression raised several production questions.

The 20th century saw several significant shifts in agricultural policy. Among these shifts was the establishment of acreage allotments in the Agricultural Adjustment Act of 1953 (see the box from Halcrow). The basic concept of operating the agricultural program under an acreage allotment in depicted in Figure 3.1. In Figure 3.1, $\tilde{S}$ is the supply curve for one of the program crops covered under the acreage allotment system. The imposition of allotments makes the effective supply curve more inelastic because farmers are no longer

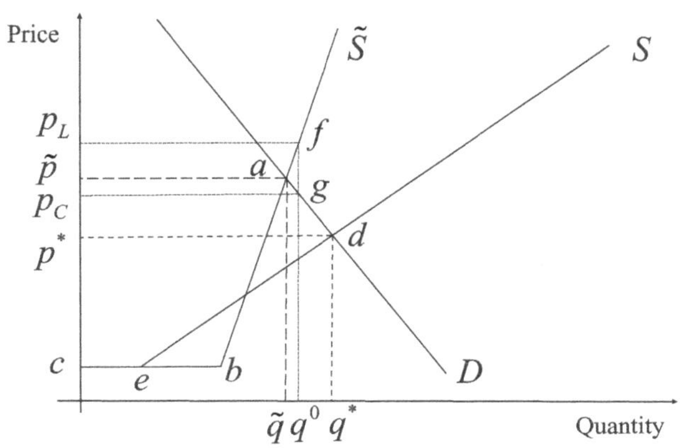

Fig. 3.1 Effect of Acreage Allotments

free to increase the acreage of the program crop by shifting land from less profitable crops. The supply curve is still upward sloping because farmers may still increase other inputs (primarily fertilizer).

The net result of imposing these allotments is to increase the price for program crops from p^* to $\tilde{p}$ while reducing the quantity of crop produced from q^* to $\tilde{q}$. The effect of allotments on producer surplus is $\tilde{p}abc - p^*bec$. In addition to the allotment system, the original act provided for loan rates (or price floors) depicted as p_L in Figure 3.1.

> But production adjustment, which aimed at the raising and stabilizing of price through control of output and marketing, remains as one of the most controversial features of agricultural policy. Every major agricultural act that has been passed in recent years [i.e., before 1953] continues provisions for production adjustment (Halcrow, 1953, pp. 286–287).

Following the firm's problem, the original production problem before the introduction of allotments was

$$\max_{x_1,x_2,A_C} p_C f_C(x_{11},x_{12}) A_C + p_O f_O(x_{21},x_{22})(A_T - A_C) - w_1(x_{11}+x_{21}) - w_2(x_{12}+x_{22}) \tag{3.97}$$

where $f_C(x_{11},x_{12})$ is the production function for a "program crop" such as cotton, $f_O(x_{21},x_{22})$ is the production function for a non-program crop such as hay, x_{i1} and x_{i2} are the amounts of variable inputs used on each crop, p_C is the price for the program crop, p_O is the price for the non-program crop, A_C is the acreage devoted to the program crop, and A_T is the total acres available to the farmer. In our analysis of the effects of quotas, we begin by assuming that p_C and p_O are determined by market forces. It is possible that Equation (3.84) results in a "corner solution" where the farmer decides to produce only the program crop. Given the imposition of quotas, we add the constraint:

$$A_C \leq A_C^* \tag{3.98}$$

Acreage Allotments under the Agricultural Adjustment Act of 1933

Production adjustment programs emphasizing acreage allotments and sometimes employing market quotes and marketing agreements have been one of the most prominent and widely publicized features of United States agricultural policy since the passage of the Agricultural Adjustment Act of 1933. From the passage of this act to World War II (from 1933 to 1941), nationwide programs of acreage allotments were developed under the Agricultural Adjustment Administration (AAA) and applied to six basic commodities, wheat, cotton, corn, tobacco, rice and peanuts (Halcrow, 1953, p. 287).

however, we also increase the price of the program crop — $p_C^* \gg p_C$. What are the impacts on production? Following the classical economist reaction, it depends. First, we note the increased price of our results in more variable input being used per acre ($x_{11}^* \geq x_{11}$ and $x_{12}^* \geq x_{12}$). Hence, the production per acre increases. It is conceivable that a large enough allotment will be given to a particular producer that his production of the program crop will actually increase. However, this is unlikely. In either case, the difference between production per before and after allotments assigned is typically referred to as slippage — the slope of $\tilde{S}$ in Figure 3.1 is not perfectly vertical. The second effect is in the non-program crop. The supply of this crop increases over the non-allotment scenario. Hence, our standard conjecture is that the price of this crop will decline.

Other policy issues inherent in agricultural policy include the effect of Research & Development expenditures through the Land Grant University System, the United States Department of Agriculture and the CGIAR (Consulting Group for International Agricultural Research) and the effect of environmental consequences of agricultural production.

Iowa State University provided some of the first econometric estimates of the production functions. The first estimation by Gerhard Tintner (1907–1983) examines the relationship between the acres of farmland (measured in acres), labor (measured in total number of labor months), the value of farm improvements, liquid assets held by the farm (including livestock supplies and seed), working capital (mostly machinery and breeding livestock), and expenditures on operating expenses on the total value of agricultural output produced (Tintner (1944)). Tintner is particularly interested in whether the estimated Cobb–Douglas coefficients make sense and whether different types of agriculture (i.e., crop versus livestock) exhibit increasing, constant, or decreasing returns to scale.

Development of Allotments

The most essential and probably difficult feature of the allotment plans is the determination of the allotment rights to individual producers.

Size of Total Allotment: According to the transferable rights plan, the allotment is to be equal to the total consumption by domestic mills using wheat, less wheat equivalent of wheat flour and other wheat products both exported and imported.

Individual Allotments:

A. Have the Division of Crops and Livestock Estimates determine wheat "quotas" for each state, county, and township, using the following as a basis: (a) reports in its files and in files of cooperating state agencies; (b) federal census data for 1910, 1920, and 1925, including township summaries, which can be worked up by the Census Bureau at small cost; (c) state census data where available. Yields are even more important than acreages. It is assumed that the yields of the three census periods combined with the data in the files of the crop-reporting service will furnish the basis for yield estimates that will be sufficiently close to the truth.

B. Have an Allotment Commission in each wheat-growing state which will be responsible for the individual allotments.

This Commission will have for its first task collecting for every wheat grower in the state of the information as to his acreage, yield and production of wheat that is needed for determining his fair and proper allotment. This information

(*Continued*)

(*Continued*)

is as follows: (a) acreage of wheat planted and harvested on his farm in each of the past 5 years (3 years will do if necessary, but five or more are desirable); (b) yield for the same years; (c) sales for the same years.

The state Allotment Commission will then determine according to some method, which is as mechanical as possible, the allotments for each farm, publish these in local newspapers, and make adjustments where complaints furnish evidence that a mistake has been made (Black, 1929).

In a similar article based on fewer farms, Tintner and Brownlee (1944) estimate the coefficients for the same Cobb–Douglas specification presented in Table 3.7. In their discussion, they note that the three negative coefficients in the results are inconsistent with the production function (i.e., these results imply that output [farm revenues] decreases as input use increases). However, since none of the negative coefficients are statistically significant at any conventional confidence level, we could conclude that these inputs do not affect farm production. In addition, they conclude that all the firms with the exception of crop-producing firms exhibit decreasing returns to scale. However, taking the standard deviations for the coefficients into account, it is likely we would fail to reject the hypothesis that the sum of the elasticities equals one (e.g., constant returns to scale) farm type with the possible exception of dairy. Tintner and Brownlee conclude that land is worth more for crop production. Finally, the authors conclude that labor has its lowest value in dairy production which would appear somewhat inconsistent given the labor intensity of milk production in 1939.

Role of Econometric Models

Econometric models and their statistical representation of the real world serve three functions in the study of policy:

- Econometric models and the underlying economic theory indicate significant interrelationships among economic variables in the real world. Such knowledge is necessary in

(*Continued*)

(Continued)

understanding the way the economy actually functions. In this context, econometric models add to our theoretical insights about the economy.

- Econometric models are of assistance in determining or verifying the reasons why a particular situation differs from the optimum.
- Econometric models indicate the probable effects of alternative means or programs. This is the essentially predictive role of econometric models, and as such models are developed, this may represent their most significant contribution to the study of policy.

We may indicate at this point what econometric models do not contribute to the study of policy:

(a) Econometric models do not help in the choice of ends or statement of optimum conditions.
(b) Econometric models do not aid in evaluating the special characteristics of the acting agent.
(c) Econometric models do not reflect the influence of normative conditions in determining the choice among alternative means.

Johnson (1948b).

Another significant figure in the estimation of production functions at Iowa State University was Earl O. Heady (1916–1987). Heady (1946) provide the estimates of the Cobb–Douglas production function for average farmers (as opposed to the better farms sampled by Tintner and Brownlee) using a random sample of Iowa farms (Heady, 1946, p. 991). In justifying the use of a random sample, Heady states, "[t]he results are of interest in themselves since they indicate returns under more representative conditions (Heady, 1946, p. 989)." Heady's results are presented in Table 3.8. Similar to the findings of Tintner and Brownlee, most of the estimated production functions exhibit decreasing returns to scale. However, a formal test of constant returns to scale is not presented.

Table 3.7 Cobb–Douglas Regression Results of Tintner and Brownlee

Type	Land (Acres)	Labor (Months)	Liquid Improvements (Dollars)	Working Assets (Dollars)	Cash Assets (Dollars)	Expenses (Dollars)	Sum
Total	0.3434*	0.2364*	0.0431	0.1729*	0.0795	0.1118*	0.9871
Hogs	0.2229*	0.2272**	0.0387	0.2568*	0.0617	0.1393*	0.9466
Beef Feeder	0.3983*	0.2995**	0.0753	0.2380*	−0.0551	0.0396*	0.9956
Dairy	0.2728***	0.0099	0.0097	0.2314	0.0923	0.2657**	0.8818
Crops	0.5114*	0.3825**	0.0595	−0.1036	0.0880	0.1266***	1.0644
General	0.4742**	−0.1909	0.0082**	0.3101	0.1437	0.2166***	0.9619

Notes: ***,**,*Denote statistical significance at the 0.01, 0.05, 0.10 levels of confidence respectively.

Table 3.8 Cobb–Douglas Regression Results from Heady

Region/Group	Land	Labor	Equipment	Livestock and Feed	Miscellaneous Operating	Total
Northeast Dairy	0.2081*	−0.0449	0.0871**	0.6136**	0.0223**	0.8862
Cash Gain	0.3425*	0.1131	0.0757**	0.4115**	0.0174**	0.9502
Western Meat	0.1037**	0.0107	0.0888	0.5511**	0.0310**	0.7853
Southern Pasture	0.1624*	−0.0508	0.1325	0.4944**	0.0438**	0.7823
Eastern Meat	0.1918*	0.2364	0.0952	0.4263*	0.0245**	0.9742
Crop	0.2412*	−0.0748	0.0761**	0.5294	0.0166**	0.9381
Hog	0.0691*	0.0209	0.0965	0.7449**	0.0343**	0.9657
Dual Purposes and Dairy	0.1029	0.0074	0.0636	0.6294**	0.0178**	0.8211
General	0.1737**	0.1192	0.1586*	0.4555**	0.0302**	0.9372
Special	0.2970**	−0.0070	0.1097**	0.3512**	0.0379**	0.7888
"Large"	0.2814**	0.0001	0.1126**	0.5378**	0.0286**	0.9605
"Small"	0.2131**	0.0482	0.0843**	0.4271**	0.0324**	0.8051
All farms	0.2316**	0.0282	0.0844**	0.4767**	0.0317**	0.8526

Notes: **,*Denote statistical significance at the 0.01, 0.05 levels of confidence respectively.

Use of Production Functions — Heady and Dillon

The production function is a concept in physical and biological science. However, it was largely developed and, until recently, used mainly by economists. Historically, refinements in concepts relating to production functions grew out of economics probably because of the following reasons:

(1) The nature of production functions is important in economic development and in determining the extent to which national products can be increased from given resource stocks.
(2) The magnitude of production coefficients serves as the base for determining optimal patterns of international or interregional trade.
(3) The concept is basic to certain theories in the functional distribution of income. The conditions under

(*Continued*)

(*Continued*)

which a total output can be imputed to the factors from which it is produced with the product just exhausted depend on the nature of the production function.

(4) The production function provides half or one of two general categories of the data needed in determining or specifying the use of resources and the pattern of outputs which maximize firm profits.

(5) The algebraic nature of supply functions rests, in large part, upon the nature of the production function (Heady and Dillon, 1961, p. 1).

Heady suggests that management is not formally incorporated into the production function, but conjectures that the effect of management may be inferred by the difference in parameters across the firm size. Specifically, Heady suggests that larger farms are typically considered to be better managed. Comparing the results in Table 3.8, the coefficient for Land, Equipment, and Livestock and Feed are larger for large farms than for small farms. Hence, the fact that large farms produce more output than small farms may be due to a combination of the facts that large farms have more land and equipment, and the statistical conjecture that they make better use of these resources. Of course, formal statistical tests are needed to support the conjecture that large farms have higher marginal products for these inputs.

While most of the literature we have reviewed focuses on crops or aggregate inputs, a significant quantity of production literature examines the production of livestock. Paris *et al.* (1970) examine the production function for milk using feeding trials from the Animal Husbandry Experiment Station in Rome. Historically, dairy production is one of the most policy-involved production areas. In the United States, milk was marketed under a two-price plan. The first tier was fluid milk sold for consumption and the second tier was processed milk products, such as butter and ice cream. Under this policy regime, the quantity of milk required to generate a specific weighted price would be set by policy (e.g., where the price of fluid milk could be increased relatively more than processed milk products by reducing the quantity sold). Similar milk programs have existed in Europe. Hence, the production function had policy consequences.

The amount of milk produced and feed fed for each cow was recorded over a 23-week period. The quantity of whole milk produced (H) was estimated as a function of hay H and concentrates C fed, a time trend T, the body weight of the cow P, a "Ratio effect" and a "Level Effect":

$$\begin{aligned} Y_{ikt} &= \alpha_0 + \alpha_1 H_{ikt} + \alpha_2 H_{ikt}^2 + \alpha_3 C_{ikt} + \alpha_4 C_{ikt}^2 + \alpha_4 T_{ikt} + \alpha_5 T_{ikt}^2 \\ &\quad + \alpha_7 H_{ikt} C_{ikt} + \alpha_8 H_{ikt} T_{ikt} + \alpha_9 C_{ikt} T_{ikt} + \alpha_{10} P_{ik,t-1} \\ &\quad + \alpha_{11} P_{ikt,t-1}^2 + \alpha_{12} E_{ikt} + \alpha_{13} E_{ikt}^2 + \alpha_{14} T_{ikt} P_{ik,t-1} \\ &\quad + \text{Ratio Effects} + \text{Level Effects} \qquad (3.99) \end{aligned}$$

where the ratio effect is determined by the fat converted to milk and the level effect is the "individual effect" in our fixed effect model expressed as a dummy. To examine whether the estimates are acceptable, Paris *et al.* (1970) compare the results with those of Heady *et al.* (1964).

Distribution — Black

Distribution deals with wages, rent, interest, and profits, which are merely names for the prices paid for the different elements used in production. It is therefore merely a further development of Value and Price. The price-making process determines the relative values placed upon different commodities and services, and hence also upon all the things that are used in the production of these commodities and services. Wages therefore result from price-making processes, and likewise rent, interest and profits. The major interest in economics in the past 100 years has been in Distribution. The public has been greatly concerned with the division of the income of society between labor, land and capital, and between the different economic classes. The labor movement and the growth of socialism have greatly stimulated interest in this problem. Obviously, if the condition of mankind is to be greatly improved, some means must be found for increasing still further the per capita production (Black, 1962, p. 21).

Wolfson (1958) applies a Cobb–Douglas function to compare regional differences in the share of profits going to labor across agricultural regions in the United States. Several researchers have used production functions — in particular, the Cobb–Douglas function — to analyze changes in the share of profit going to each resource. Specifically, Euler's Theorem was used in the debate regarding the distribution of returns across factors of production. Clark (1923) and Wicksteed (1933) used the Euler Theorem result to infer that distribution of factor returns generated by the market was optimal.

Euler's Theorem is a relationship between the partial derivatives of a function and its homogeneity:

$$t^{k-1} f(x) = \sum_{i=1}^{N} \frac{\partial f(tx)}{\partial x_i} x_i \tag{3.100}$$

$$t f(x) = \sum_{i=1}^{n} \frac{\partial f(tx)}{\partial x_i} x_i. \tag{3.101}$$

Taking the limit of Equation (3.101) as $t \to 1$ and multiplying each side by the output price yields

$$p f(x) = \sum_{i=1}^{n} p \frac{\partial f(x)}{\partial x_i} x_i. \tag{3.102}$$

Finally, using the profit maximization condition, the value of the marginal product

$$p f(x) = \sum_{i=1}^{n} r_i x_i. \tag{3.103}$$

If we let inputs 1 to $n-1$ be variable inputs and input n represent the land input, the appropriate factor payment for farmland can be derived by subtracting the payments to other factors from gross returns:

$$r_n x_n = p \frac{\partial f(x)}{\partial x_n} x_n \Rightarrow p y - \sum_{i=1}^{n-1} r_i x_i. \tag{3.104}$$

Hence, assuming homogeneity, each factor is paid its marginal product.

The use of the Cobb–Douglas function to estimate this allocation of rents is apparent. Following the general approach of Hoch (1958), we start with the cost minimization model:

$$\begin{aligned} &\min_{x_1, x_2} w_1 x_1 + w_2 x_2 \\ &\text{s.t. } \alpha_0 x_1^{\alpha_1} x_2^{\alpha_2} = y. \end{aligned} \tag{3.105}$$

Forming the Lagrange and taking the first-order conditions yields

$$\begin{aligned} \frac{w_1 x_1}{\lambda y} &= \alpha_1 \\ \frac{w_2 x_2}{\lambda y} &= \alpha_2 \end{aligned} \tag{3.106}$$

where λ is the Lagrange multiplier representing the marginal cost of production (e.g., the change in cost with respect to a change in y). Replacing λ with the price of the output yields the results in Equation (2.42). Early papers that take this approach include Johnson (1948a) and Ruttan and Stout (1960).

Table 3.9 presents Wolfson's estimated Cobb–Douglas parameters. Given these estimated parameters, Wolfson computes the correlation between the value of labor in agriculture implied by the Cobb–Douglas specification and the observed wages in counties. In general, he concludes as follows:

Table 3.9 Wolfson's Results for Agricultural Production

	Function		
Input	Cotton	Corn-hog	Wheat
Land	0.28892	0.34962	0.23154
Labor	0.44639	0.037410	0.40637
Machinery and Draft Animals	0.12685	0.16558	0.30459
Other Livestock	—	0.09450	0.04513
Feeder Cattle	—	0.01122	0.01271
All Livestock	0.03323		
Total	0.89539	0.99502	1.00034

> Turning now to an appraisal of the substantive results of this study, it seems quite clear that for the year 1939 there was a strong interregional relationship between agricultural wage rates and the marginal value productivity of labor, and that the intra-regional relationship was weaker but of respectable proportions. These wage differentials are, moreover, related to differences in the age, sex, racial and educational composition of the agricultural labor force and to differences in local consumer price levels. It is true that the degree of variance reduction associated with differences in the input mix appear to be greater than those associated with differences in labor force composition. Nevertheless, neither an accurate comparison nor an addition of these two sources of wage variance could have been made without introducing some important standardization procedures into the method for estimating labor inputs in the production functions. It can be said, however, that both types of factors must be considered as major sources of wage variance (Wolfson, 1958, p. 255).

Hence, differences in the agricultural wage rate and the productivity of agricultural labor tends to be correlated across regions, but within a region, there is more "noise." Hence, other factors are important.

3.3 Univariate Fitting of the Zellner Function — Valuation of Precision Agriculture

The advent of precision farming technologies has resurrected the issue of the primal production function by raising the question: How should I vary my inputs across a given field? This question can only be answered by specification of the primal. For example, Isik and Khanna (2002) use a linear-response plateau response function to estimate the value of precision agriculture, while Roberts *et al.* (2000) and Anselin *et al.* (2004) use a quadratic specification of the production function to model the effect of nitrogen.

Moss and Schmitz (2006) develop a semi-parametric estimation of the traditional Zellner (1951) production function for a single input. The single input is consistent with the present state of the art for precision agriculture. Precision agriculture typically refers to a large array of information technologies aimed at improving the efficiency of agricultural production. The specific precision technology at issue in this paper is the use of variable rate application of fertilizer.

The current technological standard is to apply varying rates of a single input based on ancillary samples of soil conditions, yield maps from last year's harvest, etc. Under typical assumptions, the amount of fertilizer can be varied to constantly equate the value of marginal product of the fertilizer with the output price consistent with agronomic differences in the soil's productivity (see Anselin *et al.* (2004) for more details on variable rate application of fertilizer). The difficulty with the estimation of this variable rate is the calculation of the effect of the single fertilizer input. Specifically, multiple fertilizers such as nitrogen, phosphorous, and potash affect crop yields. Thus, the marginal impact of one fertilizer is dependent on the levels of the other nutrients. The previous studies on precision agriculture have largely neglected this interaction between nutrients. Roberts *et al.* (2000) simply assume coefficients for the quadratic production function. Isik and Khanna (2002) rely on published agronomic coefficients. Anselin, Bongiovanni, and Lowenberg-DeBoer estimate a quadratic production response function for nitrogen ignoring other nutrients but consider the effect of other agronomic factors and spatial correlation. This section develops a semi-parametric estimator that removes the effect of the other fertilizers by using a non-parameteric kernel (Hardle, 1990). The marginal effect of nitrogen on yields is then estimated using a Zellner production function. The Zellner specification has the classic sigmoid three stage shape that provides more flexibility than either a quadratic, Cobb–Douglas, or the linear-response plateau specifications.

3.3.1 *Estimation*

The semi-parametric specification assumes that

$$f\left(x_1, x_2, x_3\right) = f_1\left(x_1\right) + f_2\left(x_2, x_3\right) \tag{3.107}$$

where $f_1(x_1)$ is the parametric form that the researcher is interested in and $f_2(x_2, x_3)$ is a semi-parametric or non-parameteric component that must be eliminated to produce an unbiased representation of $f_1(x_1)$. Moss and Schmitz (2006) assume that $f_1(x_1)$ is the Zellner production function:

$$f_1\left(x_1\right) = \frac{a x_1^3}{Exp\left[b\, x_1\right] - 1} \tag{3.108}$$

where x_1 is the level of nitrogen applied. This represents a slight modification from Zellner's original two-variable specification:

$$\varphi(v_1, v_2) = \frac{a\,v_1^3}{Exp\left[b\frac{v_1}{v_2}\right] - 1}. \tag{3.109}$$

Here, we implicitly set the scale variable v_2 to 1.

The second part of Equation (3.107) is a non-parametric estimate of the effect of phosphorous and potash. Mathematically, for a given observed level of production, y_i, the non-parametric estimate becomes

$$y_i = f(x_{2i}, x_{3i}) = \sum_{j=1}^{N} k\left(x_{2j}, x_{3j}, x_{2i}, x_{3i}, \delta\right) y_j \tag{3.110}$$

where $k(.)$ is a Gaussian kernel, x_{2i} and x_{3i} are the respective changes in phosphorous and potash for production point i, x_{2j}, x_{3j}, and y_j are the observed levels of phosphorous, potash, and yield at point j in the sample, and δ is the bandwidth of the kernel (see Section 2.7.2). This non-parametric estimator follows Hardle's 1990 definition of a non-parametric regression estimator. The bivariate Gaussian kernel is similar to the multivariate normal distribution function:

$$\begin{aligned} &k(x_{2i}, x_{3i}, x_{2j}, x_{3j}, \delta) \\ &= \frac{1}{\sqrt{2\pi}}\left|\delta A\right|^{-1} \times \exp\left[-\frac{1}{2\delta}\left(x_{2i} - x_{2j}\; x_{3i} - x_{3j}\right) A^{-1} \begin{pmatrix} x_{2i} - x_{2j} \\ x_{3i} - x_{3j} \end{pmatrix}\right] \end{aligned} \tag{3.111}$$

where A represents some positive definite symmetric matrix. In this study, we will set A to be the observed covariance between phosphorous and potash. The non-parametric regression is then a weighted average response across observations.

Merging Equations (3.107), (3.108) and (3.109), the estimated model then becomes

$$y_i = \sum_{j=1}^{N} k\left(x_{2i}, x_{3i}, x_{2j}, x_{3j}, \delta\right) y_j + \frac{a\,x_{1i}^3}{\exp\left[b\,x_{1i}\right] - 1} + \epsilon_i. \tag{3.112}$$

Given that δ is selected independent of a and b in Equation (3.110), this expression can be rewritten as

$$y_i - \sum_{j=1}^{N} k\left(x_{2i}, x_{3i}, x_{2j}, x_{3j}, \delta\right) y_j = \frac{a\, x_{1i}^3}{\exp\left[b\, x_{1i}\right] - 1} + \epsilon_i \tag{3.113}$$

and estimated using nonlinear least squares. Such a specification would result in a response function for nitrogen holding the level of phosphorous and potash at zero level.

A second alternative would be to use the non-parametric results to center the level of phosphorous and potash to their simple means. Mathematically, this is accomplished by adding the kernel at mean level of phosphorous and potash explicitly to the left-hand side of Equation (3.113) and implicitly to the right-hand side of the same equation:

$$y_i - \left[\sum_{j=1}^{N} k\left(x_{2i}, x_{3i}, x_{2j}, x_{3j}, \delta\right) y_j - \sum_{j=1}^{N} k\left(\bar{x}_2, \bar{x}_3, x_{2j}, x_{3j}, \delta\right) y_j\right]$$

$$= \frac{a\, x_{1i}^3}{\exp\left[b\, x_{1i}\right] - 1} + \epsilon_i. \tag{3.114}$$

Again, the coefficients a and b can be estimated using nonlinear least squares.

Finally, the specification in Equation (3.114) implicitly assumes that the level of nitrogen has no effect on the marginal productivity of either phosphorous or potash. To allow for such an effect, we next expand the kernel to include a non-parametric effect of nitrogen to yield

$$y_i - \left[\sum_{j=1}^{N} k\left(x_{1i}, x_{2i}, x_{3i}, x_{1j}, x_{2j}, x_{3j}, \delta\right) y_i \right.$$

$$\left. - \sum_{j=1}^{N} k\left(x_{1i}, \bar{x}_2, \bar{x}_3, x_{1j}, x_{2j}, x_{3j}, \delta\right) y_j\right] = \frac{a\, x_{1i}^3}{\exp\left[b\, x_{1i}\right] - 1} + \epsilon_i \tag{3.115}$$

where δ is exogenously determined, and a and b are estimated using nonlinear least squares.

3.3.2 *Empirical application*

The optimal application of a single fertilizer assuming a Zellner production function can then be estimated by applying the statistical model of corn production in Equation (3.115). Observed levels of nitrogen, phosphorous, and potash along with the associated yield at the farm level were obtained from the 1995 farming practices survey (USDA, 1996). The bandwidth, δ, was set to the bandwidth that minimized the root mean square error of the original sample. The resulting estimates are presented in Table 3.10.

In order to examine the reasonableness of the results presented in Table 3.10, we examine the parameters of the Zellner production function implied by optimizing behavior. Specifically, by assuming that farmers choose the level of nitrogen that maximizes profit, we can solve for the levels of parameters a and b that produce a production function that (1) runs through the average levels of nitrogen and corn yield and (2) equates the marginal value product of the input to the price of the input. Using the Zellner production function as the first equation and differentiating the production function with

Table 3.10 Semi-Parametric Estimates of the Zellner Production Function

State	Observations	Bandwidth	a	b
Illinois	142	0.4674	0.0005433	0.01794**
			(0.0008681)[a]	(0.009046)
Indiana	82	0.4017	0.001029	0.02162
			(0.002217)	(0.01419)
Iowa	282	3.1033	0.0008637	0.02093
			(0.001828)	(0.01458)
Michigan	42	6.1303	0.0006728	0.01918**
			(0.001019)	(0.009507)
Minnesota	102	13.3870	0.001214	0.02356*
			(0.002207)	(0.01359)
Ohio	56	1.6869	0.0004016	0.01597*
			(0.0007015)	(0.008978)

Notes: [a]Numbers in parenthesis denote standard errors.
**,*Denote statistical significance at the 0.05, 0.10 levels of confidence respectively.

Table 3.11 Zellner Production Function Implied by Optimizing Behavior

State	Average Nitrogen Use	Average Corn Yield	Price of Nitrogen	Price of Corn	a	b
Illinois	152.22	119.31	218	3.09	0.0005083	0.01820
Indiana	129.57	119.75	218	3.33	0.0008331	0.02146
Iowa	119.35	122.19	218	2.96	0.001086	0.02330
Michigan	141.93	115.19	218	2.97	0.0006024	0.01951
Minnesota	121.88	123.51	206	2.79	0.001031	0.02281
Ohio	169.25	127.61	218	3.15	0.0003932	0.01636

respect to nitrogen to derive the second equation yields

$$\begin{bmatrix} \dfrac{a\,x_1^3}{\exp(b\,x_1)-1} \\ \dfrac{3\,a\,x_1^2}{\exp(b\,x_2)-1} - \dfrac{a\,b\,\exp(b\,x_2)\,x_1^3}{[\exp(b\,x_2)-1]^2} \end{bmatrix} = \begin{bmatrix} y \\ \frac{p_1}{p_y} \end{bmatrix} \tag{3.116}$$

where x_1 and y are the average nitrogen applied and corn yield, respectively, and p_1 and p_y are the prices of nitrogen and corn, respectively. This system can be solved using Gauss–Seidel to yield estimates of parameters a and b. The parameters implied by the optimizing behavior of the firm are presented in Table 3.11. The largest discrepancies between the two estimates occur in the estimates of a. The profit-maximizing estimate of a for Iowa is 25% lower than the semi-parametric estimate, while the profit-maximizing estimate for Indiana and Minnesota are 19% and 15% higher, respectively. The estimates of the b parameters are much closer with the estimate from profit maximization being 11% lower in Iowa.

Table 3.12 compares the implied optimizing behavior under the estimated parameters against the observed sample behavior. In all cases except Iowa, the applied levels of nitrogen are quite close to the observed levels of nitrogen. However, the observed yield tends to be 10% lower on average than the predicted optimum. The result is a higher projected level of profit under the estimated parameters.

Given the observed versus predicted nature of the comparison in Table 3.12, there are several factors that may explain the differences in yields and profits. First, under traditional assumptions, the production function is concave in the area around the

Table 3.12 Changes in Optimizing Behavior

State	Observed		Profit-Maximizing		Percentage Difference		Observed	Predicted	Percentage
	Nitrogen	Yield	Nitrogen	Yield	Nitrogen	Yield	Profit	Profit	Difference
Illinois	152.22	119.31	154.56	133.71	−1.5	−12.1	348.50	396.30	−13.7
Indiana	129.57	119.75	128.95	144.71	0.5	−20.8	384.64	467.83	−21.6
Iowa	119.35	122.19	132.80	133.86	−11.3	−9.6	348.67	381.76	−9.5
Michigan	141.93	115.19	144.76	135.50	−2.0	−17.6	326.64	386.65	−18.4
Minnesota	121.88	123.51	118.15	131.92	3.1	−6.8	332.04	355.90	−7.2
Ohio	169.25	127.61	173.59	140.10	−2.6	−9.8	383.52	422.40	−10.1

profit-maximizing point. Thus, the lower yield may be a simple result of the concavity of the production function. A second, but related, possibility involves risk aversion. Sandmo (1971) demonstrated that risk-averse producers apply less variable inputs than risk-neutral producers. Thus, a parameterization of the production function that assumes profit maximization may bias the estimated production function downward.

3.3.3 *Application to precision agriculture*

In the late 1990s, precision agriculture grew in popularity in the United States. Several equipment companies are currently producing equipment such as combines, fertilizer spreaders, and sprayers to either provide input or respond to global positioning systems. The notion is that instead of treating fields as 100 acre units, new technologies can increase productivity by dividing the field into 30 foot by 30 foot units. Fertilizer and pesticide applications can then be tailored to these small tracts.

The whole philosophy of precision agriculture would appear sound. Specifically, the use of information to equate the marginal cost and revenue for each productive unit would appear to increase economic efficiency. However, as is typically the case, the information is not costless. The new measuring devices for combines may cost several thousand dollars per machine. In addition, the farmer faces a substantial commitment in time and must acquire additional human capital. Thus, some study of the marginal costs and potential returns to this technology would appear appropriate.

To analyze the potential payoff from precision agriculture, this section applies a standard primal approach. Specifically, we assume that each field is actually a combination of two fields with different primal production functions. The gain to precision agriculture is then the profit from identifying each tract of land. This gain must be compared against the cost of the new equipment. To simplify the study, we assume a single fertilizer input.

3.3.3.1 *Analysis based on the hyperbolic tangent production function*

Most production functions have at least one drawback. The traditional Cobb–Douglas function possesses a constant concavity ruling

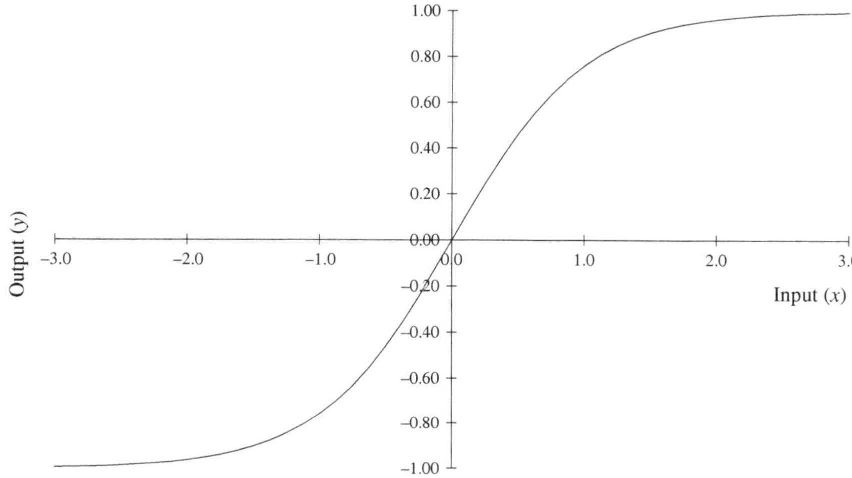

Fig. 3.2 Hyperbolic Tangent Function

out increasing yields at an increasing rate. However, the hyperbolic tangent production function also has a problem in that it does not possess a stage III.

Graphically, the hyperbolic tangent function in its original form is presented in Figure 3.2. Thus, we must modify it to make a legitimate production function. In this study, we define corn production as

$$f\left(x, \alpha_0, \alpha_1, \alpha_{\max}\right) = \frac{\alpha_{\max}}{2}\left[1 + \tanh\left(\alpha_0 + \alpha_1 x\right)\right] \tag{3.117}$$

where x represents the level of fertilizer applied while the parameters α_0, α_1, and $\alpha_{\max}$ allow us to control the shape of the function. The α_0 and α_1 parameters allow us to change the location of the inflection point and the relative steepness of the production function at every point while $\alpha_{\max}$ sets the maximum yield. Letting $\alpha_0 = -1.25$, $\alpha_1 = 0.05$, and $\alpha_{\max} = 150$ yields the stylistic production function in Figure 3.3.

Given this basic production function, we have several possibilities for varying production within the same field. For example, the soil may be of the same type, but past production practices may have changed the carryover level of nitrogen in the soil. In this case, it would be possible to envision several parallel production surfaces, as depicted in Figure 3.4. This figure depicts the difference between

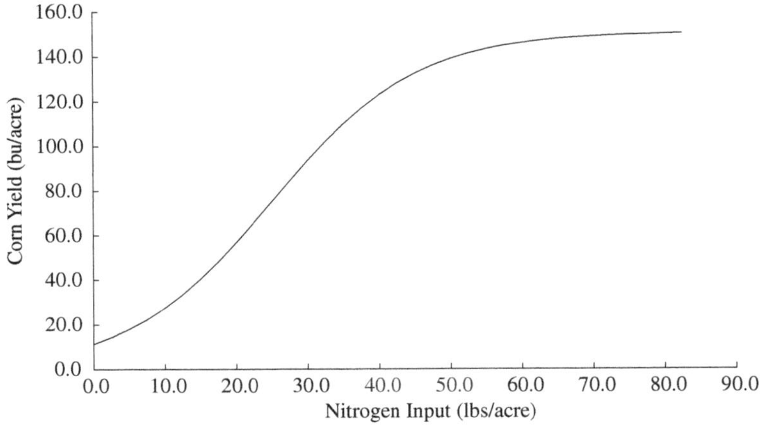

Fig. 3.3 Stylized Production Function

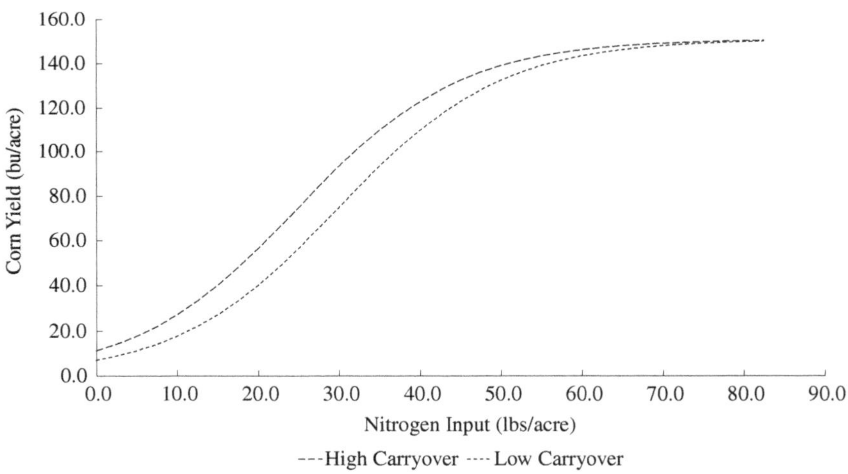

Fig. 3.4 Comparing Relative Nitrogen Carryover

$\alpha_0 = -1.25$ and $\alpha_0 = -1.50$. The production function with $\alpha_0 = -1.50$ would represent those pieces of ground with a higher nitrogen carryover.

An alternative is the case where the soil types are fundamentally different. For example, a field may have sand and sandy loam. In this scenario, the productive capacity of the land as well as the relative

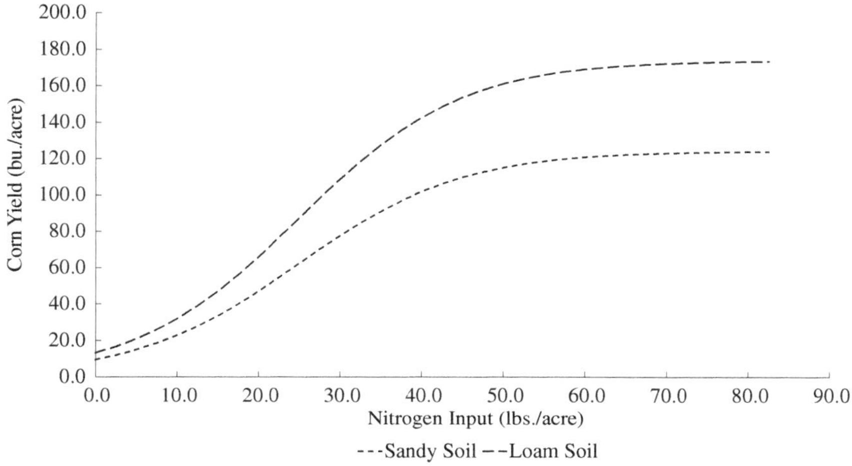

Fig. 3.5 Comparing Soil Quality Differences

nitrogen carryover may be altered, as depicted in Figure 3.5. In this scenario, we have changed from $\alpha_0 = -1.25$ to $\alpha_0 = -1.50$ and set $\alpha_{\max}$ to 125 for the poor soil and 175 for the good soil. Intuitively, this keeps the same average maximum yield at 150 bushels per acre.

Given these production relationships, we turn to the question: What is precision agriculture worth? We will accomplish this analysis in stages. The concept of a technology which separates a large field into several subfields automatically raises the question of accuracy. The first analysis will assume that the new technology separates the fields perfectly. Afterwards, we will build on those results by allowing for slippage so that the high carryover subfield is treated as a low carryover subfield. This scenario may be visualized as either an inaccuracy of the technology or the limit of the unit of measure (i.e., 30 foot by 30 foot instead of 10 foot by 10 foot).

3.3.3.2 *Perfect separation*

As a first step, we begin with the assumption that both the precision technology and the associated measurement are perfect. Assuming that δ is the percent of the land of the higher carryover type, the perfectly separated optimum is derived from the profit maximization problem:

$$\max_{x_1,x_2} \pi(\delta) = 3.00\left[\delta f(x_1, -1.25, 0.05, 150) + (1-\delta) f(x_2, -1.50, 0.05, 150)\right] - 0.50\left(\delta x_1 + (1-\delta)x_2\right) \tag{3.118}$$

where we have assumed that the corn price is \$3.00/bushel with a fertilizer price of \$0.50/pound. The numeric optimum for this optimization problem indicates that $x_1^* = 69.77$ pounds of fertilizer while $x_2^* = 74.77$ pounds. The profit per acre for this allocation is \$408.81.

The profit without separation can be derived from the maximization problem:

$$\max_{x} \pi(\delta) = 3.00\left[\delta f(x, -1.25, 0.05, 150) + (1-\delta) f(x, -1.50, 0.05, 150)\right] - 0.50x \tag{3.119}$$

where x is the level of fertilizer applied to both the high and low carryover parcels. The optimum level of fertilizer without separation can be derived as 72.57 pounds per acre. As we would expect, this level of fertilizer is about half way between the separated levels. The optimal level of profit without separation is \$408.66/acre. Thus, the net return to precision agriculture would be \$0.15/acre or, assuming that the farmer farms two sections, \$193.63/year. The amortized value of this gain over 10 years at a discount rate of 8% is \$1299.28.

In order to generalize the results, we consider a single expression for the benefit of precision agriculture derived from Equations (3.118) and (3.119)

$$\begin{aligned} B(\delta) = {} & \delta\left[\max_{x_1} pf(x_1, \alpha_0, \alpha_1, \alpha_{\max}) - wx_1\right] \\ & + (1-\delta)\left[\max_{x_2} pf\left(x_2, \alpha_0', \alpha_1, \alpha_{\max}\right) - wx_2\right] \\ & - \left[\max_{x_T} p\big(\delta f(x_T, \alpha_0, \alpha_1, \alpha_{\max}) \right. \\ & \left. + (1-\delta) f\left(x_T, \alpha_0', \alpha_1, \alpha_{\max}\right)\big) - wx_T\right] \end{aligned} \tag{3.120}$$

where α_0 and α_0' could be -1.25 and -1.50, respectively. The formulation in Equation (3.120) makes use of the implicit separability of optimization problem in Equation (3.118). Specifically, note that in Equation (3.118), the first-order conditions for x_1 is independent of the first-order conditions for x_2.

In order to develop the trade-off, consider the two "perfect information" solutions in Equation (3.120):

$$\begin{aligned}
&\max_x pf\left(x,\alpha_0,\alpha_1,\alpha_{\max}\right) - wx \\
&\Rightarrow \frac{p\alpha_{\max}\alpha_1}{2}\frac{1}{\cosh^2\left(\alpha_0+\alpha_1\right)} - w = 0 \\
&\Rightarrow \frac{1}{\cosh^2\left(\alpha_0+\alpha_1 x\right)} = \frac{2w}{p\alpha_{\max}\alpha_1} \\
&\cosh\left(\alpha_0+\alpha_1 x\right) = \sqrt{\frac{p\alpha_{\max}\alpha_1}{2w}}.
\end{aligned} \tag{3.121}$$

Solving the hyperbolic form[3] yields

$$\alpha_0+\alpha_1 x = \ln\left[\sqrt{\frac{p\alpha_{\max}\alpha_1}{2w}} \pm \sqrt{-1+\frac{p\alpha_{\max}\alpha_1}{2w}}\right]$$

$$x = \frac{\ln\left[\sqrt{\frac{p\alpha_{\max}\alpha_1}{2w}} \pm \sqrt{-1+\frac{p\alpha_{\max}\alpha_1}{2w}}\right] - \alpha_0}{\alpha_1} \tag{3.122}$$

which yields consistent results to the numerical solutions discussed above.

[3]Rewriting the result of Equation (3.121) slightly, $\cosh\left(h\left(x\right)\right) = k$ where $h\left(x\right)=\alpha_0+\alpha_1 x$ and $k=\sqrt{p\alpha_{\max}\alpha_1/2w}$, the $\cosh\left(\right)$ can be rewritten as

$$\begin{aligned}
\exp\left(h\left(x\right)\right)+\exp\left(-h\left(x\right)\right) &= 2k \\
\exp\left(2h\left(x\right)\right)+1 &= 2k\exp\left(h\left(x\right)\right) \\
\exp\left(2h\left(x\right)\right)-2k\exp\left(h\left(x\right)\right)+1 &= 0.
\end{aligned}$$

Note that this is actually a square. Rewriting the expression to complete the square yields

$$\begin{aligned}
\exp\left(h\left(x\right)\right)-2k+k^2 &= -1+k^2 \\
\left(\exp\left(h\left(x\right)\right)-k\right)^2 &= -1+k^2 \\
\exp\left(h\left(x\right)\right)-k &= \sqrt{-1+k^2} \\
h\left(x\right) &= \ln(k\pm\sqrt{-1+k^2}).
\end{aligned}$$

To derive the optimal behavior without precision agriculture, consider a slight reformulation of the profit function in third part of Equation (3.120):

$$\max_{x}\left[p\left(\delta f\left(x,\alpha_0,\alpha_1,\alpha_{\max},x\right)+\left(1-\delta\right)f\left(x,\alpha_0',\alpha_1,\alpha_{\max}\right)\right)-wx\right]. \tag{3.123}$$

Unfortunately, Equation (3.123) does not yield a tractable first-order condition. Hence, our discussion proceeds by solving the scenarios without precision numerically.

To estimate the value of precision agriculture, we start by assuming that $\alpha_0 = -1.350$, $\alpha_1 = 0.05$, and $\alpha_{\max} = 150$. Given this initial solution, we develop a symmetric change in α_0:

$$\alpha_0' = \alpha_0 + \frac{k}{2} \quad \text{and} \quad \tilde{\alpha}_0 = \alpha_0 - \frac{k}{2}. \tag{3.124}$$

In addition, we assume that $p = 3.00$ and $w = 0.50$. Table 3.13 presents the results of this formulation. In general, these results indicate that the gains to precision agriculture are increasing as difference between the production functions (k) increases and as the implied variance in the carryover increases. To develop the latter point, we could envision α_0 as a random variable that takes on two values following Equation (3.124). Implicitly, we have let $\alpha_0 \sim \text{Bernoulli}\left(\delta\right)$. Given that the optimal level of fertilizer is determined by the farmer maximizing the expected value of profit (in the undifferentiated case), the yield function also becomes a random variable conditional on this decision:

$$\begin{aligned} y' &= f\left(x_T^*,\alpha_0',\alpha_1,\alpha_{\max}\right)\\ \tilde{y} &= f\left(x_T^*,\tilde{\alpha}_0,\alpha_1,\alpha_{\max}\right). \end{aligned} \tag{3.125}$$

The average yield becomes $\delta y' + \left(1-\delta\right)\tilde{y}$. To relate the variance of output to the Bernoulli distribution, we transform the output variable into a variable z:

$$u = \frac{y-\tilde{y}}{y'-\tilde{y}}. \tag{3.126}$$

Hence, if $y = y'$ (e.g., $\alpha_0 = \alpha_0'$), then $u = 1$; however, if $y = \tilde{y}$ (e.g., $\alpha_0 = \tilde{\alpha}_0$), then $u = 0$. The random variable u has the classical

Table 3.13 Value of Precision Agriculture for Carry-over Scenario

k	x_1^*	$\pi(x_1)$	x_2^*	x_T^*	$\pi(x_T^*)$	$B(\delta, \kappa)$	
$\delta = 0.25$							
0.025	71.52	409.18	72.02	408.93	71.90	408.99	0.0011
0.050	71.27	409.31	72.27	408.81	72.03	408.93	0.0045
0.075	71.02	409.43	72.52	408.68	72.17	408.86	0.0101
0.100	70.77	409.56	72.77	408.56	72.31	408.79	0.0177
0.125	70.52	409.68	73.02	408.43	72.45	408.72	0.0275
0.150	70.27	409.81	73.27	408.31	72.60	408.64	0.0392
0.175	70.02	409.93	73.52	408.18	72.75	408.57	0.0530
0.200	69.77	410.06	73.77	408.06	72.91	408.49	0.0686
0.225	69.52	410.18	74.02	407.93	73.07	408.41	0.0860
0.250	69.27	410.31	74.27	407.81	73.23	408.33	0.1052
$\delta = 0.50$							
0.025	71.52	409.18	72.02	408.93	71.78	409.06	0.0015
0.050	71.27	409.31	72.27	408.81	71.78	409.05	0.0061
0.075	71.02	409.43	72.52	408.68	71.80	409.04	0.0137
0.100	70.77	409.56	72.77	408.56	71.82	409.03	0.0244
0.125	70.52	409.68	73.02	408.43	71.85	409.02	0.0381
0.150	70.27	409.81	73.27	408.31	71.88	409.00	0.0548
0.175	70.02	409.93	73.52	408.18	71.92	408.98	0.0745
0.200	69.77	410.06	73.77	408.06	71.96	408.96	0.0971
0.225	69.52	410.18	74.02	407.93	72.01	408.93	0.1228
0.250	69.27	410.31	74.27	407.81	72.07	408.91	0.1513
$\delta = 0.75$							
0.025	71.52	409.18	72.02	408.93	71.65	409.12	0.0012
0.050	71.27	409.31	72.27	408.81	71.53	409.18	0.0047
0.075	71.02	409.43	72.52	408.68	71.42	409.23	0.0106
0.100	70.77	409.56	72.77	408.56	71.31	409.29	0.0189
0.125	70.52	409.68	73.02	408.43	71.21	409.34	0.0298
0.150	70.27	409.81	73.27	408.31	71.11	409.39	0.0432
0.175	70.02	409.93	73.52	408.18	71.01	409.44	0.0592
0.200	69.77	410.06	73.77	408.06	70.92	409.48	0.0778
0.225	69.52	410.18	74.02	407.93	70.84	409.52	0.0991
0.250	69.27	410.31	74.27	407.81	70.76	409.56	0.1232

Bernoulli [0,1] structure with probability δ for $u = 1$. With this structure, we can define the "inverse map" for output

$$v = u\left(y' - \tilde{y}\right) + \tilde{y}. \tag{3.127}$$

The expected value of yield can then be derived as

$$\begin{aligned} \mathrm{E}\left[u\right] &= \mathrm{E}\left[u\left(y' - \tilde{y}\right) + \tilde{y}\right] \\ &= \delta y' + \left(1 - \delta\right)\tilde{y} \end{aligned} \tag{3.128}$$

and the variance of yields can be derived as

$$\begin{aligned} \mathrm{V}\left[v\right] &= \mathrm{E}\left[v^2\right] + \mathrm{E}\left[v\right]^2 \\ \mathrm{E}\left[v^2\right] &= \mathrm{E}\left[u^2\left(y' - \tilde{y}\right)^2 + u\left(y' - \tilde{y}\right)\tilde{y} + \tilde{y}^2\right] \\ &= \mathrm{E}\left[u^2\right] + \delta\left(y' - \tilde{y}\right)\tilde{y} + \tilde{y}^2 \\ E\left[u\right]^2 &= \left(\delta\left(y' - \tilde{y}\right) + \tilde{y}^2\right)^2 \\ &= \delta^2\left(y' - \tilde{y}\right)^2 + \delta\left(y' - \tilde{y}\right) + \tilde{y}^2 \\ &\Rightarrow \mathrm{V}\left[v\right] = \left(\mathrm{E}\left[v^2\right] - \delta^2\right)\left(y' - \tilde{y}\right)^2 \\ &= \delta\left(1 - \delta\right)\left(y' - \tilde{y}\right)^2 \end{aligned} \tag{3.129}$$

with the last equality following the results of the standard Bernoulli distribution.[4]

In general, the results indicate that gains to precision agriculture increase as the variance in yields increase. Figure 3.6 presents the results from Table 3.13 graphically. Note for each value of k, the value of precision agriculture peaks at $\delta = 0.5$. Intuitively, the value of precision agriculture increases as the variance of land quality increases. In addition, the variance of land quality increases with an increase in k or with an increase in δ up until the point where $\delta = 0.5$ (e.g., the value $\delta = 0.5$ maximizes the Bernoulli variance).

To complete our "perfect separation" scenario, we compute the gains to precision agriculture under the assumption that the

[4]First, we take

$$\begin{aligned} \mathrm{E}\left[v^2\right] &= \mathrm{E}\left[\delta 1^2 + \left(1 - \delta\right)0^2\right] = \delta \\ &\Rightarrow \mathrm{E}\left[v^2\right] - \delta^2 = \delta - \delta^2 = \delta\left(1 - \delta\right). \end{aligned}$$

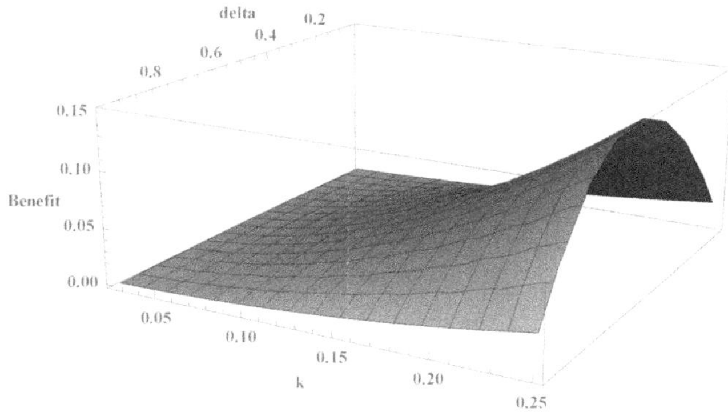

Fig. 3.6 Benefit of Precision Agriculture

Table 3.14 Value of Precision Agriculture with Different Soil Qualities

δ	x_T^*	$\pi(x_T^*)$	$B(\delta)$
0.050	74.52	403.93	0.0451
0.125	74.13	398.50	0.1067
0.250	73.43	389.47	0.1915
0.375	72.69	380.46	0.2514
0.500	71.90	371.49	0.2825
0.625	71.03	362.54	0.2800
0.750	70.09	353.64	0.2377
0.875	69.05	344.78	0.1479
0.950	68.38	339.49	0.0669

quality of land differs (e.g., sandy soil/loam soil scenario depicted in Figure 3.5: $\alpha_0' = -1.25$, $\tilde{\alpha}_0 = -1.50$, $\alpha_{\max}' = 125$, and $\tilde{\alpha}_{\max} = 150$). Table 3.14 presents the value of precision agriculture under this scenario. Again, the value of precision agriculture is an increasing function of the variability in soil types.

3.3.3.3 *Imperfect separation*

The above scenarios assume that precision agriculture is capable of perfectly separating between the various soil types or that there is no slippage. This assumption would appear unreasonable on two accounts. First, even reducing the field into 30 foot by 30 foot units may imply some variation within those 900 square foot grids. In this way, the implied cost of slippage indicates potential gains to greater efficiency in precision agriculture technologies. Second, typical applications of precision agriculture require numeric filtering to smooth out the input from field equipment. This second source of imperfection could be likened to a direct cost of statistical inaccuracy or measurement error. Specifically, let us assume that some piece of machinery generates a signal S (here, we assume that this signal takes on two possible values S_A or S_B). Based on this signal, the farmer concludes that the land under the fertilizer spreader is type A (high carryover) L_A or type B (low carryover) L_B. However, we need to allow for the possibility that the signal is imperfect:

$$S_A \rightarrow \begin{cases} P_{AA} \\ P_{AB} \end{cases}, \quad S_B \rightarrow \begin{cases} P_{BA} \\ P_{BB} \end{cases} \tag{3.130}$$

where P_{AA} is the probability that the land is type A when the signal indicates that it is type A, P_{AB} is the probability that the land is type B when the signal indicated that it was type A, P_{BA} is the probability of type A when the signal indicated that it should be type B, and P_{BB} is the probability that the signal was correct when it stated that the land was type B. The question is then — how does this imperfection affect the value of precision agriculture?

As a starting point, let us assume that s_A is the probability that the signal S_A will occur and S_B is the probability that S_B will occur. First, we impose an "adding-up" condition on the probabilities:

$$\begin{aligned} s_A P_{AA} + s_B P_{BA} &= \delta \\ s_A P_{AB} + s_B P_{BB} &= 1 - \delta \end{aligned} \tag{3.131}$$

which simply states that the signal probabilities must sum to the overall probabilities of type A and B land. Next, let us develop a way to guarantee that the overall matrix sums to one. As a starting point, let us assume that the probability that the land will be type A given S_A is γ_1. Similarly, let us assume that the probability that land is actually type B when the signal states that it is type B is γ_2. Given these two assumptions, we can rewrite Equation (3.131) in matrix form as

$$\begin{bmatrix} \gamma_1 & 1 - \gamma_2 \\ 1 - \gamma_1 & \gamma_2 \end{bmatrix} \begin{bmatrix} s_1 \\ s_2 \end{bmatrix} = \begin{bmatrix} \delta \\ 1 - \delta \end{bmatrix}. \tag{3.132}$$

In order to validate this probability structure, we carry out the matrix multiplication:

$$
\begin{aligned}
s_1\gamma_1 + s_2(1-\gamma_2) &= \delta \\
s_1(1-\gamma_1) + s_2\gamma_2 &= 1-\delta.
\end{aligned} \tag{3.133}
$$

Substituting the first equation in Equation (3.133) into the second equation yields

$$
\begin{aligned}
s_1(1-\gamma_1) + s_2\gamma_2 &= 1-(s_1\gamma_1 + s_2(1-\gamma_2)) \\
s_1 - s_1\gamma_1 + s_2\gamma_2 + s_1\gamma_1 + s_2 - s_2\gamma_2 &= 1 \\
&\Rightarrow s_1 + s_2 = 1.
\end{aligned} \tag{3.134}
$$

Hence, the probabilities sum to one if the probabilities of the signal sum to one.

For our purposes, we want to consider the reverse of the original signal problem. Specifically, we want to assume γ_1, γ_2, and δ and then infer what s_1 and s_2 must be to be consistent. To do this, we solve the matrix expression in Equation (3.132)

$$
\begin{bmatrix} s_1 \\ s_2 \end{bmatrix} = \begin{bmatrix} \gamma_1 & 1-\gamma_2 \\ 1-\gamma_1 & \gamma_2 \end{bmatrix}^{-1} \begin{bmatrix} \delta \\ 1-\delta \end{bmatrix}. \tag{3.135}
$$

A trivial result of Equation (3.135) is that if $\gamma_1 = 1$, and $\gamma_2 = 1$, then the probability of signal is exactly the probability land type — the problem degenerates to the certainty case. As an example of the process, consider the scenario where $\gamma_1 = 0.85$, $\gamma_2 = 0.95$ and $\delta = 0.50$, the probability of the prior $s_1^* = 0.5625$ and $s_2^* = 0.4375$ (where * denotes the fact that we have solved the system for consistent probabilities).

Using this structure, the probability matrix for each outcome is

$$
\tilde{P} = \begin{bmatrix} s_1^*\gamma_1 & s_2^*(1-\gamma_2) \\ s_1^*(1-\gamma_1) & s_2^*\gamma_2 \end{bmatrix}. \tag{3.136}
$$

The decision problem facing the producer (e.g., the maximizing expected profit given signals from precision agriculture) becomes

$$\max_{x_1,x_2} \pi\left(\delta,\gamma_1,\gamma_2\right) = p\left[\tilde{P}_{AA}f\left(x_1,-1.30,0.05,150\right)\right.$$
$$+\tilde{P}_{AB}f\left(x_1,-1.40,0.05,150\right)\tilde{P}_{BA}f\left(x_2,-1.30,0.05,150\right)$$
$$\left.+\tilde{P}_{BB}f\left(x_2,-1.40,0.05,150\right)\right] - w\left(s_1x_1+s_2x_2\right) \qquad (3.137)$$

assuming that $\alpha_0 = -1.30$ for type A land and $\alpha_0 = -1.40$ for type B land. Breaking down this expression a little bit, we can separate Equation (3.137) into the first part of the farmer's problem:

$$p\left[\tilde{P}_{AA}f\left(x_1,-1.30,0.05,150\right)+\tilde{P}_{AB}f\left(x_1,-1.40,0.05,150\right)\right] - ws_1x_1 \qquad (3.138)$$

which models the concept that the producer received a signal of S_1 and chooses the amount of fertilizer that maximizes profit given this signal. Specifically, dividing Equation (3.138) by s_1 yields

$$p[\gamma_1 f(x_1,-1.30,0.05,150)+(1-\gamma_1)f(x_1,-1.40,0.05,150)] - wx_1. \qquad (3.139)$$

The same development can be derived for the second part of farmer's problem:

$$p\left[\tilde{P}_{BA}f\left(x_2,-1.30,0.05,150\right)\right.$$
$$\left.+\tilde{P}_{BB}f\left(x_2,-1.40,0.05,150\right)\right] - ws_2x_s$$
$$\Rightarrow p\left[\left(1-\gamma_2\right)f\left(x_1,-1.30,0.05,150\right)\right.$$
$$\left.+\gamma_2 f\left(x_1,-1.40,0.05,150\right)\right] - wx_2. \qquad (3.140)$$

Note that formulation in Equation (3.137) includes the case where the precision technology is perfect: $\pi(\delta,1,1)$. The overall gain to precision agriculture can now be computed:

$$B(\delta, \gamma_1, \gamma_2) = \pi(\delta, \gamma_1, \gamma_2) - \tilde{\pi}(\delta)$$

$$\begin{aligned}\text{where } \tilde{\pi}(\delta) = \max_{x_T} p\,[\delta f(x_T, -1.30, 0.05, 150) \\ + (1-\delta) f(x_T, -1.40, 0.05, 150)] - w x_T \qquad (3.141)\end{aligned}$$

or $\tilde{\pi}(\delta)$ is the profit without precision agriculture. In addition to the value of precision agriculture, this formulation also allows for decomposition of gain into the loss of imprecision of the signal $\pi(\delta, 1, 1) - \pi(\delta, \gamma_1, \gamma_2)$ and the overall gain from precision agriculture. We will denote the relative loss due to impression as

$$R(\delta, \gamma_1, \gamma_2) = \frac{\pi(\delta, 1, 1) - \pi(\delta, \gamma_1, \gamma_2)}{\pi(\delta, 1, 1) - \tilde{\pi}(\delta)}. \qquad (3.142)$$

Table 3.15 presents the value of precision agriculture and the relative loss of value due to signal imperfection for $\delta = 0.50$ and $\delta = 0.45$. In general, the results indicate that the value of precision agriculture declines as the imperfection in the signal increases. If at either γ_1 or γ_2 equal to 0.50, the value of precision agriculture falls to zero. The general form of the loss in value to precision agriculture is presented in Figure 3.7. Note that the surface in Figure 3.7 is not linear (e.g., it is not a plane). As presented in Figure 3.8, there is nonlinear trade-off between γ_1 and γ_2.

3.3.3.4 *Using the Zellner and Cobb–Douglas specifications*

Moss and Schmitz (2001) extend the foregoing analysis by using the Zellner production function estimated by Moss and Schmitz (2006). As a starting point, they consider a scenario where a field is divided into S sub-section

$$F(V) = \sum_{i=1}^{S} f_i(v_i) \qquad (3.143)$$

where V is the overall field which contains $1 \times S$ input vectors for each sub-plot and $f_i(v_i)$ represents the production function for each sub-plot. In this application, we assume that S is a vector of different

Table 3.15 Gains to Precision Agriculture under Imperfect Signals

Probabilities		$\delta = 0.50$					$\delta = 0.45$				
γ_1	γ_2	x_1	x_2	$\pi(\delta, \gamma_1, \gamma 2)$	$B(\delta, \gamma_1, \gamma_2)$	$R(\delta, \gamma_1, \gamma_2)$	x_1	x_2	$\pi(\delta, \gamma_1, \gamma 2)$	$B(\delta, \gamma_1, \gamma_2)$	$R(\delta, \gamma_1, \gamma_2)$
0.9900	0.5125	69.34	72.13	408.91	0.0043	0.0281	70.04	72.72	408.94	0.0330	0.2183
0.9875	0.9000	69.35	73.87	409.03	0.1207	0.7978	80.00	72.13	408.92	0.1376	0.9329
0.9875	0.7750	69.35	73.34	408.99	0.0860	0.5682	69.35	73.87	408.90	0.1146	0.7774
0.9875	0.6500	69.35	72.78	408.95	0.0486	0.3216	69.35	73.34	408.86	0.0763	0.5177
0.9875	0.5250	69.35	72.19	408.91	0.0084	0.0557	69.35	72.78	408.82	0.0352	0.2387
0.9750	0.9125	69.43	73.92	409.03	0.1203	0.7951	80.00	72.19	408.87	0.0896	0.6075
0.9750	0.7875	69.43	73.39	408.99	0.0868	0.5740	69.43	73.92	408.90	0.1150	0.7800
0.9750	0.6625	69.43	72.84	408.96	0.0509	0.3365	69.43	73.39	408.86	0.0780	0.5293
0.9750	0.5375	69.43	72.25	408.92	0.0122	0.0807	69.43	72.84	408.82	0.0383	0.2601
0.9625	0.9250	69.51	73.97	409.03	0.1197	0.7911					
0.9625	0.8000	69.51	73.45	408.99	0.0875	0.5783	69.51	73.97	408.90	0.1152	0.7813
0.9625	0.6750	69.51	72.89	408.96	0.0529	0.3499	69.51	73.45	408.86	0.0795	0.5394
0.9625	0.5500	69.51	72.31	408.92	0.0157	0.1039	69.51	72.89	408.83	0.0412	0.2797
0.9500	0.9375	69.59	74.02	409.02	0.1189	0.7860	79.93	72.31	408.78	0.0000	0.0000
0.9500	0.8125	69.59	73.50	408.99	0.0879	0.5813	69.59	74.02	408.90	0.1152	0.7814
0.9500	0.6875	69.59	72.95	408.96	0.0547	0.3617	69.59	73.50	408.87	0.0808	0.5481
0.9500	0.5625	69.59	72.37	408.92	0.0189	0.1252	69.59	72.95	408.83	0.0439	0.2977
0.9375	0.9500	69.66	74.07	409.02	0.1180	0.7797	69.59	72.37	408.79	0.0041	0.0281
0.9375	0.8250	69.66	73.55	408.99	0.0882	0.5830	69.66	74.07	408.90	0.1150	0.7801
0.9375	0.7000	69.66	73.01	408.96	0.0563	0.3720	69.66	73.55	408.87	0.0819	0.5552
0.9375	0.5750	69.66	72.43	408.93	0.0219	0.1449	69.66	73.01	408.83	0.0463	0.3140

0.9250	0.9625	69.74	74.12	409.02	0.1168	0.7723	69.66	72.43	408.79	0.0080	0.0543
0.9250	0.8375	69.74	73.61	408.99	0.0882	0.5834	69.74	74.12	408.90	0.1147	0.7776
0.9250	0.7125	69.74	73.06	408.96	0.0576	0.3808	69.74	73.61	408.87	0.0827	0.5610
0.9250	0.5875	69.74	72.49	408.93	0.0246	0.1628	69.74	73.06	408.83	0.0485	0.3287
0.9125	0.9750	69.82	74.17	409.02	0.1155	0.7637	69.74	72.49	408.80	0.0116	0.0788
0.9125	0.8500	69.82	73.66	408.99	0.0881	0.5824	69.82	74.17	408.90	0.1141	0.7739
0.9125	0.7250	69.82	73.12	408.96	0.0587	0.3881	69.82	73.66	408.87	0.0834	0.5654
0.9125	0.6000	69.82	72.55	408.93	0.0271	0.1790	69.82	73.12	408.84	0.0504	0.3418
0.9000	0.9875	69.89	74.22	409.02	0.1141	0.7541	69.82	72.55	408.80	0.0149	0.1014
0.9000	0.8625	69.89	73.71	408.99	0.0878	0.5802	69.89	74.22	408.90	0.1134	0.7690
0.9000	0.7375	69.89	73.17	408.97	0.0596	0.3940	69.89	73.71	408.87	0.0838	0.5684
0.9000	0.6125	69.89	72.61	408.94	0.0293	0.1937	69.89	73.17	408.84	0.0521	0.3534
0.8875	0.9900	69.97	74.23	409.02	0.1105	0.7304	69.89	72.61	408.80	0.0180	0.1223
0.8875	0.8750	69.97	73.76	408.99	0.0873	0.5768	69.97	74.23	408.89	0.1103	0.7481
0.8875	0.7500	69.97	73.23	408.97	0.0603	0.3985	69.97	73.76	408.87	0.0841	0.5701
0.8875	0.6250	69.97	72.66	408.94	0.0313	0.2067	69.97	73.23	408.84	0.0536	0.3635
0.8875	0.5000	79.97	72.07	408.91	0.0000	0.0000	69.97	72.66	408.81	0.0209	0.1415
0.8750	0.8875	70.04	73.82	408.99	0.0866	0.5723	80.00	72.07	409.01	0.2211	1.4998
0.8750	0.7625	70.04	73.28	408.97	0.0608	0.4016	70.04	73.82	408.87	0.0841	0.5706

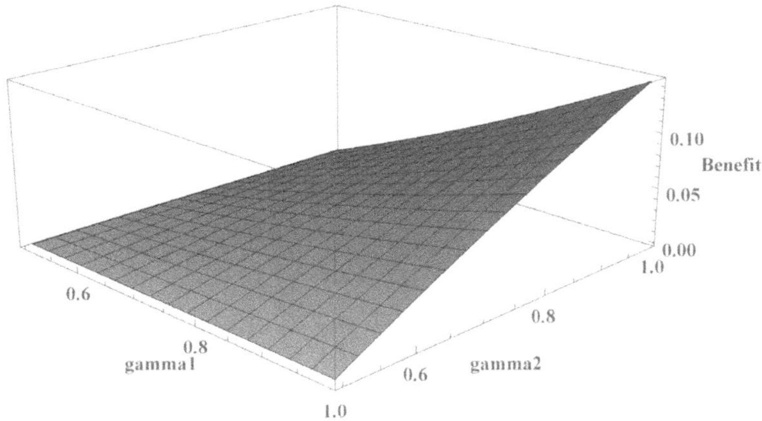

Fig. 3.7 Benefit of Precision Agriculture including Imprecision in Signal

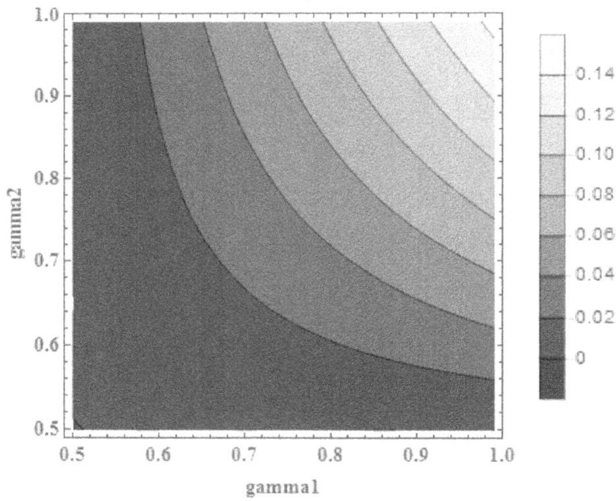

Fig. 3.8 Benefit of Precision Agriculture Including Imprecision in Signal, Trade-off Between γ_1 and γ_2

fertilizer levels. In general, the optimal value of vector S is determined by

$$\max_{v_s, s=1,\ldots,S} p \sum_{s=1}^{S} f_i\left(v_i\right) - w_v \sum_{i=1}^{S} v_i. \tag{3.144}$$

We are interested in two possible conditions. Under the first scenario, we set all the fertilizer levels to be the same $v_i = \bar{v}$ for all i. In this case, Equation (3.117) becomes

$$\max_{\bar{v}} \bar{B} = p\sum_{s=1}^{S} f_s\left(\bar{v}\right) - w\left(S\bar{v}\right) \Rightarrow p\sum_{s=1}^{S} \left.\frac{\partial f_s\left(v_s\right)}{\partial v_s}\right|_{v_s\to\bar{v}} - wS = 0$$

$$\Rightarrow p\frac{\displaystyle\sum_{s=1}^{S} \left.\frac{\partial f_s\left(v_s\right)}{\partial v_s}\right|_{v_s\to\bar{v}}}{S} - w = 0 \tag{3.145}$$

so that the average marginal product of fertilizer is equal to the price of fertilizer. Under the second condition, we solve for the optimal level of fertilizer for each sub-plot (e.g., we directly maximize Equation (3.145)), yielding

$$p\frac{\partial f_i\left(v_i\right)}{\partial v_i} = w_v \,\forall v_s \Rightarrow \tilde{B} = p\sum_{s=1}^{S} f_i\left(\tilde{v}_i\right) - w_v\sum_{s=1}^{S} \tilde{v}_s. \tag{3.146}$$

Combine the estimates of production function for corn from Moss and Schmitz (2006) presented in Table 3.16 and the cost of precision agriculture presented in Table 3.17. The amortized annual costs range from \$5.71–\$7.69 per acre. These estimates imply that, under 1995 nitrogen and corn prices and assuming an average coefficient of dispersion of 0.2, the use of precision technology for application of nitrogen would not have been profitable in the mid-western states in 1995. From Table 3.16, the average value of precision technology ranges from \$2.14/acre in Minnesota to \$2.78/acre in Indiana. Hence, they find that the improved returns are much lower than the estimated associated costs.

Moss and Schmitz extend their analysis to consider the possible effect of an alternative production function form. Specifically, they propose using the Cobb–Douglas function

$$f\left(x_1, x_2, x_3\right) = x_1^{\alpha} x_2^{\beta} x_3^{\gamma} \tag{3.147}$$

where x_1 is nitrogen in pounds per acre, x_2 is phosphorous, x_3 is potassium, and α, β, and γ are estimated parameters. They further

Table 3.16 Changes in Optimizing Behavior

State	Observed		Profit-Maximizing		Percentage Difference		Observed	Predicted	Percentage
	Nitrogen	Yield	Nitrogen	Yield	Nitrogen	Yield	Profit	Profit	Difference
Illinois	152.22	119.31	154.56	133.71	−1.5	−12.1	348.50	396.30	−13.7
Indiana	129.57	119.75	128.95	144.71	0.5	−20.8	384.64	467.83	−21.6
Iowa	119.35	122.19	132.80	133.86	−11.3	−9.6	348.67	381.76	−9.5
Michigan	141.93	115.19	144.76	135.50	−2.0	−17.6	326.64	386.65	−18.4
Minnesota	121.88	123.51	118.15	131.92	3.1	−6.8	332.04	355.90	−7.2
Ohio	169.25	127.61	173.59	140.10	−2.6	−9.8	383.52	422.40	−10.1

Table 3.17 Marginal Cost of Variable Rate Nitrogen Application[a]

Additional Cost	Amount per Acre	Cost Amortized over 5 Years[b]
Grid Sampling	\$3.00–\$10.00	\$0.79–\$2.64
Soil Assay	\$3.00	\$0.79
Computer Mapping	\$0.50–\$1.00	\$0.13–\$0.26
Variable Rate Application	\$4.00	\$4.00
Annual Cost of VRT		\$5.71–\$7.69

Notes: [a]The estimated cost of precision agriculture was obtained from Nyle Wollenhaupt at Ag-Chem Equipment Company.
[b]The annual cost for grid sampling, soil assay, and computer mapping assume a 5-year use of a single map and a 0.10 interest rate.

simplify the analysis by assuming that the level of phosphorous and potassium are held constant, so that

$$f(x_1) = Ax_1^{\alpha}. \tag{3.148}$$

Moss and Schmitz then solved for the parameters A and α, which approximate the Zellner function at the optimizing level of nitrogen. As with the Zellner production function, we then construct two production functions:

$$\begin{aligned} f_1(x_1) &= A\left(1-\frac{\mu}{2}\right)x_1^{\alpha\left(1-\frac{\mu}{2}\right)} \\ f_2(x_2) &= A\left(1+\frac{\mu}{2}\right)x_2^{\alpha\left(1+\frac{\mu}{2}\right)} \end{aligned} \tag{3.149}$$

where μ is selected to yield a coefficient of variation for yields of 20%. The parameters are estimated simultaneously and it is again assumed that the field can be divided into sub-plots of equal size.

The values of the parameters A and α for the Cobb–Douglas approximation are provided in Table 3.18. Also included in Table 3.18 are the μ required to generate a coefficient of variation in yields of 0.2, the optimal levels of nitrogen for each land type, the gross benefit of variable-rate fertilizer application, and the value of precision agriculture. A comparison of these results with those provided in Table 3.18, indicates that precision agriculture would be even less profitable if the underlying production functions were more closely

Table 3.18 Value of Precision Agriculture Under Cobb–Douglas Specification

State	A	α	μ	N_1	N_2	Gross Benefit	Value
Illinois	109.69	0.0408	0.33312	103.232	223.474	403.358	1.186
Indiana	126.57	0.0292	0.35145	85.313	186.612	474.956	1.024
Iowa	112.84	0.0365	0.34064	88.303	192.053	388.189	1.034
Michigan	112.36	0.0392	0.33603	96.476	209.239	393.406	1.117
Minnesota	113.55	0.0331	0.34666	78.321	170.970	361.589	0.879
Ohio	113.18	0.0429	0.32899	116.117	250.668	430.153	1.320

Table 3.19 Effect of Variance in Crop Yield on Value of Precision Agriculture

	Coefficients of Variation				
State	0.08	0.15	0.20	0.25	0.29
Illinois	0.39	1.38	2.44	3.80	5.08
Indiana	0.45	1.57	2.78	4.32	5.77
Iowa	0.38	1.31	2.32	3.61	4.83
Michigan	0.38	1.34	2.37	3.69	4.93
Minnesota	0.35	1.21	2.14	3.33	4.45
Ohio	0.42	1.48	2.62	4.07	5.45

approximated under the Cobb–Douglas specification. On average, the value of precision agriculture for the Cobb–Douglas specification is 45% of the value under the original Zellner function. The smaller value of precision agriculture can be attributed to the relative flatness of the Cobb–Douglas function and lack of a stage III.

In addition to examining the implications of alternative functional forms, Moss and Schmitz also examine the effect of accuracy of precision technology on the gains from precision agriculture (e.g., the effect of an imprecise technology developed above). They find that any type of inaccuracies inherent in the technology would simply reduce the estimates of the value of precision farming provided in Tables 3.16–3.19.

3.4 Chapter Summary

- Data remains to be one of the most vexing dimensions in applied economic analysis. One of the most significant dimensions of this confusion involves the level of estimation — farm level versus sector level.
- Datasets are replete with implicit assumptions. For example, some datasets such as the KLEM (Jorgenson's Capital(K), Labor(L), Energy(E), and Materials(M)) dataset is often used to model decisions within a sector — we may use the data for the Food and Kindred product component to estimate a derived demand for agricultural output. However, such implicit aggregation may introduce significant errors.
- This chapter reviews Theil (1954) formulation for determining whether the aggregation of data is important.
- Theil's formulation also provides an introduction into the question of separability. We demonstrate how the question of separability can actually be formulated within elasticity of substitution framework.
- An important concept that can be best estimated through the primal is the notion of slippage. Slippage refers to the shifting of inputs from unrestricted crops to restricted crops. Early agricultural programs were based on allotments that regulated the amount of farmland that could be devoted to a crop whose price was supported by a loan rate. While the law regulated land, it did not regulate labor or fertilizer. As a result, farmers increased the amount of inputs per acre used for regulated crops and decreased the inputs used on non-regulated crops. This reallocation resulted in increased production of the program crops relative to governments expectations. In the 1980s, a similar reallocation occurred as inputs were shifted from "set-aside" acres (mandatory production reductions).

3.5 Review Questions

1. What is the relationship between aggregated input levels and individual input levels when aggregation across individuals is valid?

2. Suppose that you have a quadratic production function with four inputs. How would you impose separability on the quadratic formulation?
3. What is the effect of multiple quasi-fixed variables on the valuation of each input?

3.6 Exercises

1. Suppose that the data in PsuedoPanelData.csv[5] represent a sample of individuals that will be aggregated into a single production function using a Cobb–Douglas production function. (a) Combine the data into a single observation for each year assuming equal weights and estimate the aggregate model. (b) Following Theil, estimate the relationship between the aggregated input and the individual production. Compute the correlation coefficients between the aggregate parameters and the individual parameters. (c) Do the results support aggregation?
2. Using the data AggregateUSDA.csv,[6] estimate the elasticity of substitution matrix for the quadratic specification where output is a function of capital, own labor, hired labor, and intermediate inputs. What do the estimates imply about the separability of the labor variable?
3. The AggregateUSDA.csv data include a decomposition of capital into general capital and farmland. Estimate two Cobb–Douglas specifications. In the first, estimate output as a function of non-land capital, land, labor, and intermediate assets. In the second specification, divide each observation by the quantity of farmland and estimate a production function per acre. If we assume that the quantity of farmland is fixed at its 2017 value, are the optimal levels of input different?
4. Estimate the shadow value of farmland using the formulation in Equation (3.96).

[5]This data is available at http://www.charlesbmoss.com:8080/Book.Production.economics/Chapter-3/PsuedoPanelData.csv.

[6]This data is available at http://www.charlesbmoss.com:8080/Book.Production.Economics/Chapter-1/AggregateUSDA.cv.

5. Using the AggregateUSDA.csv data with the translog specification output as a function of capital, labor, and intermediate inputs, compute the change in consumer and producer surplus for a price floor 15% above the market equilibrium. Suppose that the price floor increases the amount of land used in the production of land by 5% — how does this "slippage" effect change the distribution of consumer and producer surplus?
6. Use the semi-parametric Zellner production function to estimate the marginal physical product of own labor in the Aggregate-USDA.csv dataset (use the kernel specification to remove the effect of capital, hired labor, and intermediate inputs).

Chapter 4

Cost and Profit Functions

In the preceding chapters, we first developed the production function as a technological envelope, demonstrating how inputs can be mapped into outputs. Next, we showed how these functions could be used to derive input demand, cost, and profit functions based on these functions and optimizing behavior. In this development, we stated that economists had little to say about the characteristics of the production function. We were only interested in these functions in the constraints that they imposed on optimizing behavior. Thus, the insight added by the "dual" approach is the fact that we could simply work with the resulting optimizing behavior. In some cases, this optimizing behavior can then be used to infer facts about the technology underlying it. According to Gorman (1976): "Duality is about the choice of the independent variables in terms of which one defines a theory." Similarly, Chambers (1988, p. 49) states: "The essence of the dual approach is that technology (or in the case of the consumer problem, preferences) constrains the optimizing behavior of individuals. One should therefore be able to use an accurate representation of optimizing behavior to study the technology."

4.1 Definition of the Cost Function

The cost function is defined as

$$c(w, y) = \min_{x \geq 0} \left[w'x : x \in V(y) \right] \tag{4.1}$$

where $c(.)$ is the cost function, w is the vector of input prices, y is the vector of output levels, and $V(y)$ is the level set of outputs, or the combinations of inputs and outputs that are technologically feasible. Literally, the cost function is the minimum cost of producing a specified set of outputs. This definition depends on the production set $V(y)$. For example, this production set could be defined as the Cobb–Douglas production function. Intuitively, a technology constrains the optimizing behavior of economic agents. For example, we will impose the restriction that at least some input is used to produce any non-zero level of output. The goal is to place as few restrictions on the behavior of economic agents as possible to allow for the derivation of a fairly general behavioral response.

Not to lose sight of the goal, we are interested in being able to specify the cost function based on input prices and output prices:

$$c(w,y) = \alpha_0 + \alpha' w + {}^1\!/_2 w' A w + \beta' y + {}^1\!/_2 y' B y + w' \Gamma y \tag{4.2}$$

which is the standard form of the quadratic cost function that we use in empirical research. We are interested in developing the properties under which this function represents optimizing behavior. In addition, we will demonstrate Shephard's lemma which states that

$$\frac{\partial c(w,y)}{\partial w_i} = x_i^*(w,y) = \alpha_i + A_{*i} w + \Gamma_{i*} y \tag{4.3}$$

or that the derivative of the cost function with respect to the input price yields the demand equation for each input.

4.2 Properties of the Cost Function

The general properties of the cost function which make it consistent with optimizing behavior are as follows:

1. $c(w,y) > 0$ for $w > 0$ and $y > 0$ (non-negativity).
2. If $w' \geq w$, then $c(w',y) \geq c(w,y)$ (non-decreasing in w).
3. The cost function is concave and continuous in w.
4. $c(tw,y) = tc(w,y), t > 0$ (the cost function is positively linear homogeneous).
5. If $y \geq y'$, then $c(w,y) \geq c(w,y')$ (non-decreasing in y).
6. $c(w,0) = 0$ (no fixed costs).

In general, if the cost function is differentiable in w, then there exists a vector of costs minimizing the demand functions for each input formed from the gradient of the cost function with respect to w.

In order to develop these properties, we begin with the basic notion that technology set is closed and non-empty. Thus, $V(y)$ implies $x' \in V(y)$. Thus, the cost-minimizing set of inputs x^* is defined by the optimization problem:

$$\min_{x \geq 0} \{ w'x^* : w'(x^* - x) \leq 0 ; x \in V(y)\}. \tag{4.4}$$

The optimization problem is presented graphically in Figure 4.1. Breaking Figure 4.1 down, first in a two-input world,

$$w'x = w_1x_1 + w_2x_2. \tag{4.5}$$

However, we can use the term $w'(x^* - x)$ in Equation (4.4) to define the area below this constraint, or

$$w_1x_1 + w_2x_2 \leq w_1x_1^* + w_2x_2^* \tag{4.6}$$

for some index point $x^* = \{x_1^*, x_2^*\}$. Intuitively, this specification of the budget space yields a "half-space," as depicted in Figure 4.2. The budget line divides the space into two parts: those points that cost less than the index point x^* and those points that cost more than the index point. The upper half-space will become important — it represents the feasible set of expenditures to produce

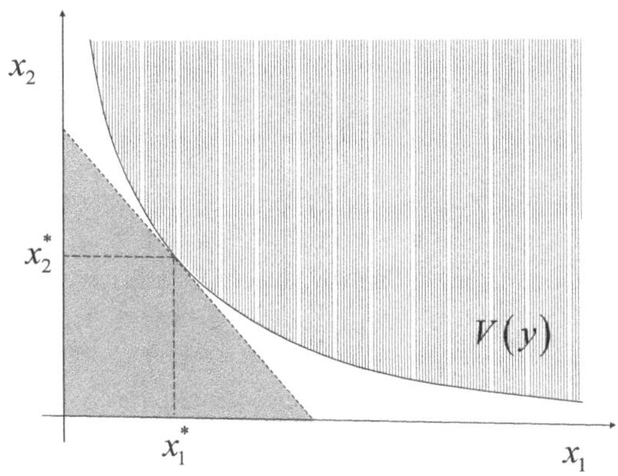

Fig. 4.1 Minimizing Cost with a Level Set

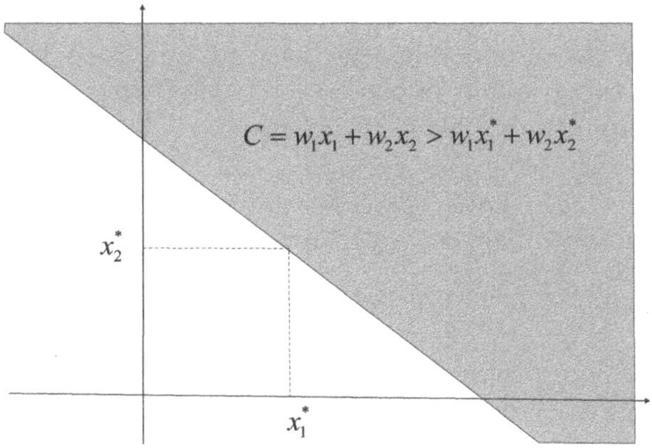

Fig. 4.2 Budget Constraint as a Half-Space

output $y \Leftrightarrow x \in V(y)$. However, at this point, we are interested in the lower half-space for minimization purposes.

4.2.1 *Positive Cost of Production*

Given the definition of the cost function in Equation (4.4), the conjecture that $C(x, y) \gg 0$ if you have positive prices and positive outputs would appear to follow. However, the implications of the Properties of the Production Function [1.2.1] lends itself to the development of certain concepts that will be useful in the construction of the dual. Recalling our development of the properties of the production function, we developed the concepts of strictly essential inputs and weakly essential inputs. If input x_i is strictly essential,

$$f(x_1, x_2, \ldots, x_i = 0, \ldots, x_n) = 0. \tag{4.7}$$

In this case, the input requirement set cannot intersect with axis for input i. If all the inputs are strictly essential, then the level sets do not intersect the input axes, as depicted in Figure 4.3. For example, all the inputs of the Cobb–Douglas production function are strictly essential.

An alternative technology is when at least one input is not strictly essential, as depicted in Figure 4.4. In this case, x_2 is not strictly essential, positive production can occur when the input is not used (i.e., at point $\tilde{x}_2$). The conjecture is then that at least one input must

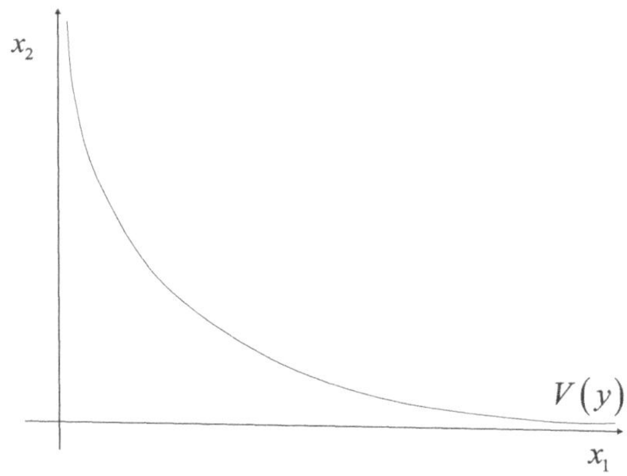

Fig. 4.3 Level Sets for Strictly Essential Inputs

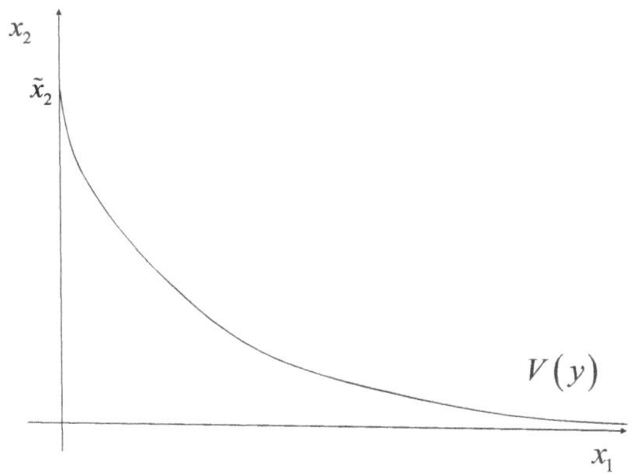

Fig. 4.4 Weakly Essential Input

be strictly essential — it is impossible to produce outputs without inputs. Basically, this assumption implies that the origin in the two-input case, $x_1 = 0$ and $x_2 = 0$, is not an element of a level set $\{x_1 = 0, x_2 = 0\} \notin V(y)$ for any $y \gg 0$.

4.2.2 *Higher Input Prices Imply Higher Cost*

Again, the second property is that an increase in input prices indicate that the new cost is at least the value of the cost before change would appear obvious. However, rigorously developing this result will be useful in developing the concavity of cost function. Suppose that we start with a vector of prices for two inputs $w = \left(w_1\, w_2\right)'$. Next, assume that we increase the price of the first input by τ_1 (i.e., $\tilde{w} = \left(w_1 + \tau_1\, w_2\right)'$). Graphically, the cost line has rotated inward from C to $\tilde{C}$, as depicted in Figure 4.5. Note that the budget set after the increase in price does not include any of the level set. In order to make the original output level feasible, the cost is increased from $\tilde{C}$ to $\hat{C}$.

Consider a slight reformulation of Figure 4.5 depicted in Figure 4.6. To demonstrate that the shift increases price, we are interested in the spending at the new point of production (i.e., $\hat{x}$ in Figure 4.6). This proof is a classical "triangular inequality":

$$(w - \tilde{w})'\,(x^* - \hat{x}) \leq 0 \tag{4.8}$$

$(C - \hat{C} \leq 0)$. Carrying the multiplication through

$$(w - \tilde{w})'\,(x^* - \hat{x}) = \left(w'x^* - w'\hat{x}\right) + \left(\tilde{w}'\hat{x} - \tilde{w}'x^*\right) \leq 0. \tag{4.9}$$

The result in Equation (4.9) is due to the fact that $w'x^* - w'\hat{x} \leq 0$ because x^* minimizes the cost for w and $\tilde{w}'\hat{x} - \tilde{w}'x^* \leq 0$ because x^* minimizes the cost at $\tilde{w}$.

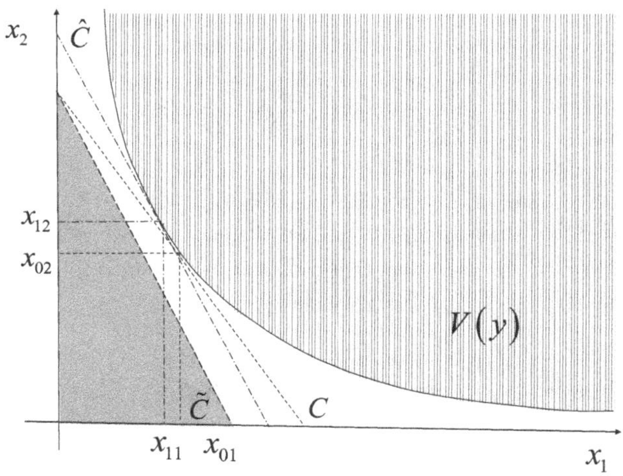

Fig. 4.5 Increase in Input Price

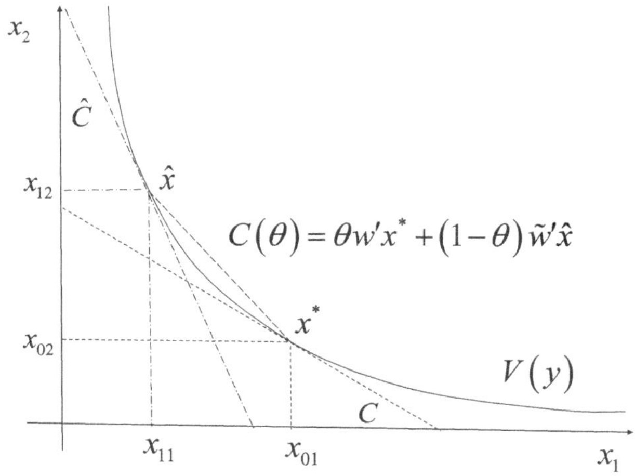

Fig. 4.6 Concavity of the Level Set

4.2.3 *Concavity of the Cost Function*

The concavity of the cost function then follows the strict inequality portion of the preceding analysis. Figure 4.6 depicts the linear combination of the optimizing behavior at the two price vectors:

$$\begin{aligned} c(\theta) &= \theta c(w, y) + (1-\theta)\, c(\tilde{w}, y) \\ &= \theta w' x^* + (1-\theta)\, \tilde{w}' \hat{x}. \end{aligned} \tag{4.10}$$

This average cost is more than the cost-minimizing point defined at the average price $\bar{w} = \theta w + (1-\theta)\,\tilde{w}$. Defining this choice as

$$\breve{x} = \min_{x \geq 0} \left\{ \bar{w}' x : \bar{w}'(x - x_0) \leq 0\,;\, x \in V(y) \right\}. \tag{4.11}$$

The result in Equation (4.11) implies that $\bar{w}'\breve{x} \leq \bar{w}'x^*$ and $\bar{w}'\breve{x} \leq \bar{w}'\hat{x}$. Therefore,

$$\bar{w}'\breve{x} \leq \theta \bar{w}' x^* + (1-\theta)\, \bar{w}'\tilde{x}. \tag{4.12}$$

Taking a slightly different approach, the conjecture that the cost function is continuous and concave in w is depicted in Figure 4.7. Note that A, B, and C lie on a straight line that is tangent to the cost function at B. Movement from B to C would assume that the input bundle optimal at B is also optimal at C. If, however, there are

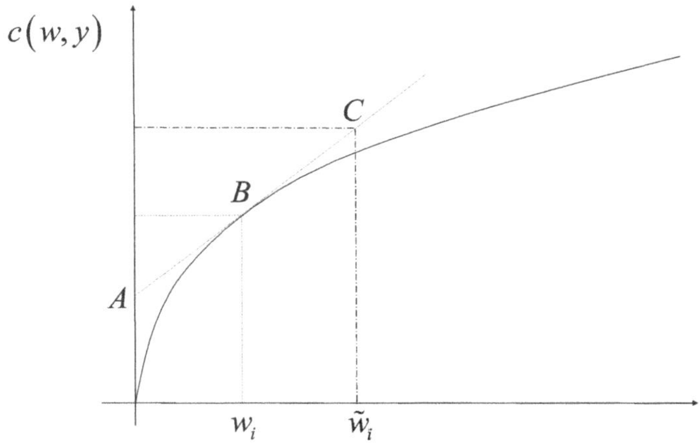

Fig. 4.7 Concavity in Input Price Space

opportunities to substitute one input for another, such opportunities will be used if they produce a lower cost. The general concept of this proof is similar to the preceding development on the level set. First, consider the points on the price line between w and $\tilde{w}$:

$$\hat{w} = \theta w + (1 - \theta)\,\tilde{w}. \tag{4.13}$$

To prove concavity, we want to show that

$$c\,(\hat{w}, y) \geq \theta c\,(w, y) + (1 - \theta)\,c\,(\tilde{w}, y). \tag{4.14}$$

Following the previous approach, we define the following:

$$x = \min_{x \geq 0} \left\{\, w'x : w'\,(x - x_0) \leq 0\,;\, x \in V\,(y)\right\}$$

$$\tilde{x} = \min_{x \geq 0} \left\{\, \tilde{w}'x : \tilde{w}'\,(x - x_0) \leq 0\,;\, x \in V\,(y)\right\}.$$

$$\hat{x} = \min_{x \geq 0} \left\{\, \hat{w}'x : \bar{w}'\,(x - x_0) \leq 0\,;\, x \in V\,(y)\right\} \tag{4.15}$$

The inequality in Equation (4.14) then follows since

$$w'x \leq w'\hat{x} \text{ and } \tilde{w}'\tilde{x} \leq \tilde{w}'\hat{x} \tag{4.16}$$

by the optimizing behavior at each end of the arc. More completely,

$$c\,(\hat{w}, y) = \hat{w}'\hat{x} = \left[\theta w + (1 - \theta)\tilde{w}\right]'\hat{x} = \theta w'\hat{x} + (1 - \theta)\tilde{w}'\hat{x}. \tag{4.17}$$

Hence,

$$\left.\begin{array}{l} w'\hat{x} \geq c\,(w,y) = w'x \\ \tilde{w}'\hat{x} \geq c\,(\tilde{w},y) = \tilde{w}'\tilde{x} \end{array}\right\} \Rightarrow \theta w'\hat{x} + (1-\theta)\tilde{w}'\hat{x} \geq \theta c(w`y) + (1-\theta)c(\tilde{w},y). \tag{4.18}$$

4.2.4 *Linear Homogeneity*

Linear homogeneity is actually an artifact of the linear cost (and profit) function. Specifically, starting with the definition of the cost function,

$$c\,(t \times w, y) = \min_{x \geq 0} \left\{ (t \times w)'\,x : x \in V\,(y) \right\}. \tag{4.19}$$

In simple terms, irrespective of the selection of x,

$$c = t \times w_1 x_1 + t \times w_2 x_2 + \cdots t \times w_n x_n = t(w_1 x_1 + w_2 x_2 + \cdots w_n x_n). \tag{4.20}$$

Therefore,

$$\begin{aligned} c\,(t \times w, y) &= t \times \min_{x \geq 0} \left\{ \; w'x : x \in V\,(y) \right\} \\ c\,(t \times w, y) &= t \times c\,(w, y). \end{aligned} \tag{4.21}$$

Therefore, the cost function is linear homogeneous or homogeneous of degree one. Doubling all the input prices doubles the optimum cost.

4.2.5 *Shephard's Lemma*

In general, Shephard's lemma holds that

$$\nabla_w c(w,y) = \begin{bmatrix} \dfrac{\partial c(w,y)}{\partial w_1} \\ \dfrac{\partial c(w,y)}{\partial w_2} \\ \vdots \\ \dfrac{\partial c(w,y)}{\partial w_n} \end{bmatrix} = \begin{bmatrix} x_1^*(w,y) \\ x_2^*(w,y) \\ \vdots \\ x_n^*(w,y) \end{bmatrix}. \tag{4.22}$$

This proof is an application of the envelope theorem. First, assume that we want to maximize some general function

$$f(x_1, x_2, \ldots, x_n, \alpha) \tag{4.23}$$

where we maximize $f(x, \alpha)$ by choosing x, but assume that α is fixed. To do this, we form the first-order conditions conditional on α

$$\begin{aligned} f_i(x_1, x_2, \ldots, x_n, \alpha) = 0 \Rightarrow x_i = x_i^*(\alpha) \\ y(x_1^*(\alpha), x_2^*(\alpha), \ldots, x_n^*(\alpha), \alpha) = \phi(\alpha). \end{aligned} \tag{4.24}$$

The question is then: How does the solution change with respect to a change in α? To see this, we differentiate the optimum objective function value with respect to α to obtain

$$\frac{\partial y^*(.)}{\partial \alpha} = \frac{\partial \phi(\alpha)}{\partial \alpha} = \sum_{i=1}^{n} \frac{\partial f(.)}{\partial x_i} \frac{\partial x_i^*(\alpha)}{\partial \alpha} + \frac{\partial f(.)}{\partial \alpha}. \tag{4.25}$$

Given $\dfrac{\partial f(.)}{\partial x_i} = 0 \ \forall \ i$ this result implies that

$$\frac{\partial y^*(.)}{\partial \alpha} = \frac{\partial f(.)}{\partial \alpha}. \tag{4.26}$$

Turning to the case of the constrained optimum,

$$\begin{aligned} &\max_{x_1, \cdots, x_n} f(x_1, x_2, \ldots, x_n, \alpha) \\ &\text{s.t. } g(x_1, x_2, \ldots, x_n, \alpha) = 0. \end{aligned} \tag{4.27}$$

Forming the Lagrangian,

$$L = f + \lambda g \Rightarrow \left\{ \begin{array}{c} \dfrac{\partial L}{\partial x_i} = f_i + \lambda g_i = 0 \\ \dfrac{\partial L}{\partial \lambda} = g = 0 \end{array} \right\} \Rightarrow \left\{ \begin{array}{l} x_i = x_i^*(\alpha) \\ \lambda = \lambda^*(\alpha) \end{array} \right. . \tag{4.28}$$

Substituting this back into the objective function in Equation (4.27),

$$f(x_1^*(\alpha), x_2^*(\alpha), \ldots, x_n^*(\alpha), \alpha) = y^*(x_1^*(\alpha), x_2^*(\alpha), \ldots, x_n^*(\alpha), \alpha) \tag{4.29}$$

since $g(x_1^*(\alpha), x_2^*(\alpha), \ldots, x_n^*(\alpha), \alpha) = 0$ by definition of the optimum (i.e., the constraint).

Again, differentiating the optimum with respect to α, we get

$$\frac{\partial y^*(.)}{\partial \alpha} = \sum_{i=1}^{n} \frac{\partial f(.)}{\partial x_i} \frac{\partial x_i^*(\alpha)}{\partial \alpha} + \frac{\partial f(.)}{\partial \alpha} \tag{4.30}$$

but $\partial f(.)/\partial x_i \neq 0 \Leftrightarrow \partial f(.)/\partial x_i = \lambda \partial g(.)/\partial x_i$, or the changes are subject to the constraint. Thus, to work this out, we also have to differentiate the constraint with respect to α:

$$\frac{\partial g(.)}{\partial \alpha} = \sum_{i=1}^{n} \frac{\partial g(.)}{\partial x_i} \frac{\partial x_i^*(\alpha)}{\partial \alpha} + \frac{\partial g(.)}{\partial \alpha}. \tag{4.31}$$

Thus, putting the two halves together (including the constraint) yields

$$\begin{aligned} \frac{\partial y^*(.)}{\partial \alpha} &= \sum_{i=1}^{n} \frac{\partial f(.)}{\partial x_i} \frac{\partial x_i^*(\alpha)}{\partial \alpha} \frac{\partial f(.)}{\partial \alpha} + \lambda \left(\sum_{i=1}^{n} \frac{\partial g(.)}{\partial x_i} \frac{\partial x_i^*(\alpha)}{\partial \alpha} + \frac{\partial g(.)}{\partial \alpha} \right) \\ \frac{\partial y^*(.)}{\partial \alpha} &= \sum_{i=1}^{n} \left(\frac{\partial f(.)}{\partial x_i} + \lambda \frac{\partial g(.)}{\partial x_i} \right) \frac{\partial x_i^*(\alpha)}{\partial \alpha} + \left(\frac{\partial f(.)}{\partial \alpha} + \lambda \frac{\partial g(.)}{\partial \alpha} \right) \end{aligned}. \tag{4.32}$$

Thus, imposing the optimality result $(\partial f(.)/\partial x_i - \lambda \partial g(.)/\partial x_i = 0 \forall i)$,

$$\frac{\partial y^*(.)}{\partial \alpha} = \frac{\partial f(.)}{\partial \alpha} + \lambda \frac{\partial g(.)}{\partial \alpha}. \tag{4.33}$$

Applying this formulation of the envelope theorem to the cost function, first we define the cost function as

$$\begin{aligned} c(w, y) = \min_{x_1, x_2} w_1 x_1 + w_2 x_2 \\ \text{s.t.} f(x_1, x_2) = y. \end{aligned} \tag{4.34}$$

Formulating the Lagrangian,

$$L = w_1 x_1 + w_2 x_2 + \lambda \left(y_0 - f(x_1, x_2) \right) \Rightarrow \frac{\partial c^*(w, y)}{\partial w_1} = \frac{\partial L^*}{\partial w_1} = x_1^*(w, y). \tag{4.35}$$

More explicitly,

$$\frac{\partial c^*(w, y)}{\partial w_1} = x_1^* + w_1 \frac{\partial x_1^*}{\partial w_1} + w_2 \frac{\partial x_2^*}{\partial w_1}. \tag{4.36}$$

By the first-order conditions from Equation (4.35), $w_1 - \lambda\partial f(x_1, x_2)/\partial x_1 = 0$ or $w_1 = \lambda\partial f(x_1, x_2)/\partial x_1$, and $w_2 - \lambda\partial f(x_1, x_2)/\partial x_2 = 0$ or $w_2 = \lambda\partial f(x_1, x_2)/\partial x_2$. Hence, substituting these results into Equation (4.36) yields

$$\frac{\partial c^*(w, y)}{\partial w_1} = x_1^* + \lambda^* \left(\frac{\partial f}{\partial x_1}\frac{\partial x_1^*}{\partial w_1} + \frac{\partial f}{\partial x_2}\frac{\partial x_2^*}{\partial w_1}\right). \tag{4.37}$$

However, differentiating the constraint of the minimization problem, we see

$$y_0 = f(x_1^*, x_2^*) \Rightarrow \frac{\partial y_0}{\partial w_1} = \frac{\partial f(.)}{\partial x_1}\frac{\partial x_1^*}{\partial w_1} + \frac{\partial f(.)}{\partial x_2}\frac{\partial x_2^*}{\partial w_2} = 0. \tag{4.38}$$

Thus, substituting the result from Equation (4.38) into Equation (4.37) yields

$$\frac{\partial c^*(w, y)}{\partial w_1} = x_1^*. \tag{4.39}$$

4.3 Comparative Statics

The most common results of the comparative statics with respect to input prices involve the intuition about derived demand functions. From the primal approach, we expect the demand functions for each input to be downward sloping with respect to input prices. Starting from the cost function,

$$\frac{\partial^2 c(w, y)}{\partial w_i \partial w_j} = \frac{\partial x_i^*(w, y)}{\partial w_j} \tag{4.40}$$

by Shephard's lemma.[1] We know that if $i = j$, then by the concavity of the cost function in input prices,

$$\frac{\partial^2 c(w, y)}{\partial w_i \partial w_i} = \frac{\partial x_i^*(w, y)}{\partial w_i} \leq 0. \tag{4.41}$$

[1]More explicitly,

$$\frac{\partial^2 c\,(w, y)}{\partial w_i \partial w_j} = \frac{\partial}{\partial w_j}\frac{\partial c\,(w, y)}{\partial w_i} = \frac{\partial}{\partial w_j} x^*\,(w, y).$$

In addition, we know that by Young's theorem, the Hessian matrix for the cost function is symmetric:

$$\frac{\partial^2 c(w,y)}{\partial w_i \partial w_j} = \frac{\partial^2 c(w,y)}{\partial w_j \partial w_i}. \tag{4.42}$$

The Hessian matrix for the cost function is also singular.

Euler's theorem is based on the definition of homogeneity:

$$f(tx) = t^r f(x). \tag{4.43}$$

Differentiating both sides with respect to t and applying the chain rule yields

$$\sum_{i=1}^{N} \frac{\partial f(tx)}{\partial (tx)} \frac{\partial t x_i}{\partial t} = \sum_{i=1}^{N} \frac{\partial f(tx)}{\partial (tx)} x_i = r t^{r-1} f(x). \tag{4.44}$$

Letting $t = 1$ then yields

$$\sum_{i=1}^{N} \frac{\partial f(x)}{\partial x_i} x_i = r f(x). \tag{4.45}$$

Coupling this result with the observation that if a function is homogeneous of degree r, then its derivative is homogeneous of degree $r - 1$. We know that the input demand functions are homogeneous of degree zero in prices. Thus,

$$\sum_{j=1}^{N} \frac{\partial x_i^*(w,y)}{\partial w_j} w_j = \sum_{j=1}^{N} \frac{\partial^2 c(w,y)}{\partial w_i \partial w_j} w_j = 0. \tag{4.46}$$

Multiplying this expression by $x_i^*(w,y)$ yields

$$\sum_{i=1}^{N} \frac{\partial x_i^*(w,y)}{\partial w_j} \frac{w_j}{x_i^*(w,y)} = \sum_{i=1}^{N} \epsilon_{ij} = 0. \tag{4.47}$$

Given that we know $\epsilon_{ii} < 0$, this result imposes restrictions on the cross-price elasticities.

Briefly, let us prove the homogeneity of the marginal cost function. It is a useful demonstration of the use of Shephard's lemma. Starting with the marginal cost, differentiate with respect to each price:

$$\frac{\partial c(w,y)}{\partial y} \Rightarrow \sum_{i=1}^{N} \frac{\partial^2 c(w,y)}{\partial w_i \partial y} = \frac{\partial}{\partial y} \sum_{i=1}^{N} \frac{\partial c(w,y)}{\partial w_i} w_i$$

$$\frac{\partial}{\partial y} \sum_{i=1}^{N} \frac{\partial c(w,y)}{\partial w_i} w_i = \frac{\partial}{\partial y} \sum_{i=1}^{N} x_i^*(w,y) w_i. \tag{4.48}$$

Working from the definition of the cost function,

$$c(w,y) = \sum_{i=1}^{N} x_i^*(w,y) w_i \Rightarrow \frac{\partial c(w,y)}{\partial y} = \sum_{i=1}^{N} \left(\frac{\partial}{\partial y} x_i^*(w,y) \right) w_i$$

$$\sum_{i=1}^{N} \left(\frac{\partial}{\partial y} x_i^*(w,y) \right) w_i = \sum_{i=1}^{N} \left(\frac{\partial}{\partial y} \frac{\partial c(w,y)}{\partial w_i} \right) w_i = \sum_{i=1}^{N} \frac{\partial c(w,y)}{\partial y \partial w_i} w_i. \tag{4.49}$$

Therefore, the marginal cost function is homogeneous of degree one.

Next, we develop the comparative statics with respect to output levels. Following from the restrictions on the cross-price elasticities above, the comparative statics with respect to output levels imply that not all inputs can be inferior or regressive. An inferior input is an input whose use declines as production increases while the use of a normal input increases as production increases. Like the cross-price results above, we start with the sum of the differences of individual demand functions with respect to the level of output

$$\sum_{i=1}^{N} \frac{\partial x_i^*(w,y)}{\partial y} w_i = \sum_{i=1}^{N} \frac{\partial^2 c(w,y)}{\partial w_i \partial y} w_i = \frac{\partial c(w,y)}{\partial y}. \tag{4.50}$$

In order to develop the effect of output on total cost, we start with the original Lagrangian from the primal problem (the general form of Equation (4.28))

$$L = w \times x + \lambda \left[y - f(x) \right] \Rightarrow \left\{ \begin{array}{c} L_x = w - \lambda \nabla_x f(x) = 0 \\ L_\lambda = y - f(x) = 0 \end{array} \right. . \tag{4.51}$$

Solving for the output using the first-order condition of the Lagrange multiplier and differentiating the solution yields

$$y = f(x) \Rightarrow dy = \sum_{i=1}^{N} \frac{\partial f(x)}{\partial x_i} dx_i. \tag{4.52}$$

From the first set of first-order conditions in Equation (4.51), we see that

$$\frac{\partial f(x)}{\partial x_i} = \frac{w_i}{\lambda}. \tag{4.53}$$

Therefore, by Equations (4.52) and (4.53),

$$dy = \sum_{i=1}^{N} \frac{w_i}{\lambda} dx_i \Rightarrow \lambda dy = \sum_{i=1}^{N} w_i dx_i. \tag{4.54}$$

Dividing each side of the last equality in Equation (4.54) by dy yields

$$\lambda = \sum_{i=1}^{N} w_i \frac{dx_i}{dy} \tag{4.55}$$

which proves the definition of λ is consistent with the envelope theory. Therefore,

$$\lambda^*(w, y) = \sum_{i=1}^{N} w_i \frac{dx_i^*(w, y)}{dy}. \tag{4.56}$$

Given this optimum λ, we can then sum over the initial first-order conditions:

$$\sum_{i=1}^{N} w_i x_i = \lambda(w, y) \sum_{i=1}^{N} \frac{\partial f\left[x^*(w, y)\right]}{\partial x_i} x_i(w, y). \tag{4.57}$$

Chambers (1988) defines

$$n(y, w) = \frac{\left[\dfrac{\partial c(w, y)}{\partial y}\right] y}{c(w, y)} = \frac{\partial \ln\left[c(w, y)\right]}{\partial \ln\left[y\right]} \tag{4.58}$$

as the cost flexibility (the ratio between the marginal and average costs). Remember the elasticity of scale in the production function

$$\varepsilon = \left.\frac{\partial \ln\left[f\left(\lambda x\right)\right]}{\partial \ln\left[\lambda\right]}\right|_{\lambda=1} = \sum_{i=1}^{N} \frac{\partial f\left(.\right)}{\partial x_i}\frac{\partial x_i}{\partial y} = \sum_{i=1}^{N} \varepsilon_i \tag{4.59}$$

which is the ratio between the marginal physical and average physical products. We understood that this measured the overall response of production to inputs levels along a ray from the origin. What is developed here is not quite the same, but is actually the elasticity of size. It answers the question: Do I build one large plant or several small ones? Defining $y^* = y/m$,

$$c\left(w, y\right) = c\left(w, my^*\right) = m^{\varsigma(m,y^*,w)}c\left(w, y^*\right) \tag{4.60}$$

$\varsigma(m, y^*, w)$ is related to the homogeneity of the cost function in terms of scale. Take

$$\lim_{m\to 1} \varsigma\left(m, y^*, w\right) = n\left(y^*, w\right). \tag{4.61}$$

1. If $n(y^*, w) > 1$, then $\varepsilon(y, x(w, y)) < 1$, there are no efficiencies to centralization (no diseconomies of scale).
2. If $n(y^*, w) < 1$, then $\varepsilon(y, x(w, y)) > 1$, there are efficiencies to centralization (economies of scale).

Figure 4.8 depicts the geometric interpretation of cost flexibility. Just like the MPP–APP comparisons, we can envision the ratio between marginal cost and average cost. It is clear that

$$n\left(y, w\right) = 1 \Rightarrow \frac{\dfrac{\partial c\left(w, y\right)}{\partial y}}{\dfrac{c\left(w, y\right)}{y}} = 1 \Rightarrow \frac{\partial c\left(w, y\right)}{\partial y} = \frac{c\left(w, y\right)}{y}. \tag{4.62}$$

Also, it is apparent that average cost equals marginal cost at the minimum of the average cost curve:

$$\frac{\left[\dfrac{\partial c(w, y)}{y}\right]}{\partial y} = \frac{\partial c(w, y)}{\partial y}\frac{1}{y} - \frac{c(w, y)}{y}\frac{1}{y}$$

$$\frac{\left[\dfrac{\partial c(w, y)}{y}\right]}{\partial y} = \left[\frac{\partial c(w, y)}{\partial y} - \frac{c(w, y)}{y}\right]\frac{1}{y} = 0. \tag{4.63}$$

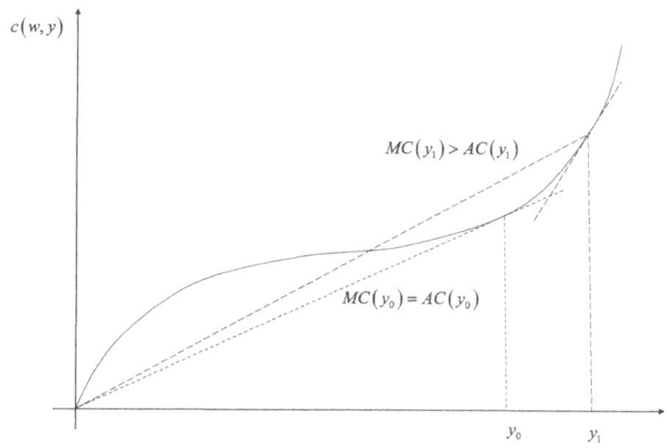

Fig. 4.8 Concavity in Input Price Space

4.4 The Duality Between Cost and Production Functions

In our discussion of the primal, we demonstrated how the production function placed restrictions on economic behavior. The question posed in duality is whether the optimizing behavior can be used to recover or reconstruct the properties of the production function. In this section, we look at three proofs of duality: one following Diewert (1971), one which follows Shephard (1970), and one that follows Lau (1976). Following Diewert's discussion:

> It is well known that, given fixed factor prices, and an n factor production function satisfying certain regularity conditions, we may derive a (minimum total) cost function under the assumption of minimizing behavior. What is not so well known is that, given a cost function satisfying certain regularity conditions, we may use this cost function to define a production function which in turn may be used to derive our original cost function. This duality property between cost and production functions was first proved by Shepard (1953). (Diewert, 1971, p. 483)

> There are at least three ways of describing the technology of a single output, n inputs firm: (i) by means of a production function, (ii) in terms of the firm's production possibility sets (see Debreu 1959, chap. 3), and (iii) by means of the firm's cost function (if the firm purchases the services of factors at fixed prices). (Diewert, 1971, p. 483)

The last point — that a production technology can be represented in three ways: using a production function, level sets, or a cost function — lays out the point to be proved in the dual. Specifically, in Chapter 1, we demonstrated how the Cobb–Douglas production function could be used to derive a cost function. The real question is: What properties or the characteristics are necessary for the production function to define a "valid" cost function, that is, a cost function that is consistent with optimizing behavior?

The "proofs" of duality then involve two steps. First, we must define each function (e.g., the production function, level set, and cost function) and develop the properties that make each function consistent with economic behavior. Second, we must show that the couplet (i.e., the definition of a representative technology and its properties) imply the other couplets. For example, a production function implies level sets exist. Finally, we need to document that these linkages between couplets are bidirectional (i.e., a production function implies levels sets and level sets imply that a production function exists). In Diewert's proof,

$$\begin{aligned} F(x) &\Rightarrow L(y) \Rightarrow c(w,y) \\ F(x) &\Leftarrow L(y) \Leftarrow c(w,y) \end{aligned} \tag{4.64}$$

where $F(x)$ is the production function which depicts the transformation of inputs into outputs ($y = F(x)$), $L(y)$ is the level set defined as those sets of inputs x that can be used to produce at least y (i.e., $x \in L(y)$), and $c(w,y)$ is the minimum cost that can be used to produce output y given prices w.

4.4.1 *Diewert's Proof*

Each of the three proofs that we examine uses slightly different sets of syntax to describe the production sets. Diewert's proof starts by defining the production function. Next, he defines the level set and demonstrates how the level set can be used to derive the production function. Finally, Diewert introduces the notion of the cost function.

4.4.1.1 *Conditions on the Production Function*

Diewert's development of the production function starts by stating conditions for the production function, which are similar to those developed in Section 1.2.1. Diewert's conditions on the production function $f(.)$ are as follows:

1. f is a real-valued function of n real variables for every $x \geq 0$. f is finite if x is finite.
2. $f(0) = 0$, and f is a non-decreasing function in x.
3. $f(x^n)$ tends to plus infinity for at least one non-negative sequence of vectors (x^n).
4. f is continuous from above or f is a right-continuous function.
5. f is quasi-concave over Ω.

The second condition follows the monotonicity conditions ([1] in the list in Section 1.2.1) while the fifth condition follows from the conditions on concavity (i.e., [2] in the list Section 1.2.1). Examining the remaining points — the third assumption basically says that the level of production can be increased to infinity (is unbounded) for same sequence of inputs. The fourth assumption states that the production function is continuous from above — if there are discrete jumps in the production process, the production point belongs to the right interval (i.e., $f(x) = z \Rightarrow x \in [x_0, \infty)$).

Definition 4.1. A set X is convex if for every x_1 and x_2 that belongs to X and for every λ, $0 \leq \lambda \leq 1$, we have $\lambda x_1 + (1 - \lambda)x_2$ belongs to X.

(Recall Figure 4.6.)

Definition 4.2. A real-valued function f defined over a convex set X is concave if for every x_1 and x_2 belonging to X and $0 \leq \lambda \leq 1$, we have

$$f[\lambda x_1 + (1 - \lambda)x_2] \geq \lambda f(x_1) + (1 - \lambda)f(x_2) \tag{4.65}$$

(Recall Figure 4.7.)

Definition 4.3. A real-valued function f defined over a set X is quasi-concave if, for every real number y, the set $L(y) = [x : f(x) = y, x \text{ belongs to } X]$ is a convex set.

Lemma 4.1. *A real-valued concave function defined over a convex set X is also quasi-concave. The proof is almost by definition. If x_1*

and x_2 both belong to a level set $L(y)$, then

$$\begin{aligned} f[\lambda x_1 + (1-\lambda)x_2] &\geq \lambda f(x_1) + (1-\lambda) f(x_2) \\ &\geq \lambda y + (1-\lambda) y \text{ by definition of } x_1, x_2 \in L(y) \\ &= y. \end{aligned} \tag{4.66}$$

Definition 4.4. The production possibility sets (or upper contour sets) are defined for every output level $y = 0$ by $L(y) = [x : f(x) = y, x \text{ non-negative}]$.

4.4.1.2 *Conditions on Production Possibility Sets $L(y)$*

1. $L(0) = \Omega$ for every $y > 0$, $L(y)$ is a non-empty closed set which does not contain the origin.
2. For every $y = 0$, $L(y)$ is a convex set.
3. If $x' = x$ (componentwise), where x belongs to $L(y)$, then x' also belongs to $L(y)$.
4. If $y_1 = y_2$, then $L(y_1)$ is a subset of $L(y_2)$.
5. For every x belonging to Ω, there exists a y such that x does not belong to $L(y)$.
6. Graph L is a closed set where graph $L = [x : f(x) = y$, x belongs to $L(y)]$, $x = 0$, $y = 0$.

Theorem 4.1. *The conditions on the production function imply that the conditions on the production possibility sets $L(y)$.*

Definition 4.5. Given a family of production possibility sets $L(y)$ satisfying the conditions for the production possibility sets above, define the following function on x:

$$f(x) = \max_{x \geq 0} [\mu : x \text{ belongs to } L(\mu)]. \tag{4.67}$$

This definition actually goes backward. Assume that we can define the production possibility set $L(y)$, then we can define a function $f(x)$ as the maximum output that can be produced from any bundle of inputs as the highest production possibility set that can be obtained from that set of inputs. The conditions on the production possibility set, $L(y)$, guarantee that function, f, obeys the conditions defined for the production function above.

Conjecture 4.1 (Condition a). *f is a real-valued function for very $x = 0$, $f(x)$ is finite if x is finite.*

The general idea is to show that the notion of a production set (the level set $V(y)$ or $L(y)$) implies a production set that is finite if x is finite. To show that $f(x)$ is finite, we have to demonstrate that under the definition of $L(y)$, there must exist an x' such that $x' > x$ which implies a higher production possibility set

$$f(x') = \max_{\mu \geq 0} \left[\mu : x \text{ belongs to } L\left(y'\right)\right] \ni: y' > y. \tag{4.68}$$

Looking back, we see that for every x belonging to Ω, there exists a y' such that x does not belong to $L(y')$. Thus, for any x, there exists a set $L(y')$ for $y' \geq 0$ such that x does not belong to that set. Thus, x implies an $f(x)$ that is bounded (or an $f(x')$ exists such that $f(x') > f(x)$.

Conjecture 4.2 (Condition b). *$f(0) = 0$ and f is non-decreasing in x.*

The first section is based on the notion that $L(0) = \Omega$ and for every $y > 0$, $L(y)$ is a non-empty set. The second part (non-decreasing) is based on the fact that if $y_1 = y_2$, then $L(y_1) \subset L(y_2)$. By definition, if $x_1 \in L(y_2)$ but $x_1 \notin L(y_1)$, then $x_2 \in L(y_1)$ and $x_2 \in L(y_2)$ is such that $x_2 > x_1$.

Conjecture 4.3 (Condition c). *$f(x^N)$ tends to plus infinity for at least one sequence of $x^N > 0$.*

For simplicity, let $y = N$. Thus, if we let $N \to \infty$, $y \to \infty$. Based on this, we see that

$$f(x^N) = \max\left[\mu : x^N \text{ belongs to } N\left(\mu\right) : \mu \to y, y \to \infty\right] \tag{4.69}$$

which guarantees that for some sequence, the output value goes to infinity.

Conjecture 4.4 (Condition d). *f is continuous from above, or f is a right-continuous function.*

Intuitively, if $L(y)$ is a closed function, then as you approach the production possibilities frontier from above, the production possibility set includes the production possibility frontier itself:

$$\begin{aligned} L^*(y) &= [x : f(x) \geq y, x \text{ non-negative}] \\ &= [x : \max \mu \geq y, x \text{ belongs to } L(\mu)] \text{ by definition of } f(x) \\ &= [x : x \text{ belongs to } L(\mu); \mu \geq y] \\ &= [x : x \text{ belongs to } L(y)] \text{ using the result from the} \\ &\quad \text{properties of } L(y) \\ &= L(y) \text{ is a closed set.} \end{aligned} \tag{4.70}$$

Conjecture 4.5 (Condition e). *f is a quasi-concave function.*

The simplest way to develop the concept of quasi-concavity is to choose two sets of input contained in a given level set (e.g., $x_1,\ x_2 \in L(y)$). By definition of the concave level set, a linear combination of the two points is also contained in the level set — $x = \lambda x_1 + (1 - \lambda) x_2$ is also contained in the level set. Thus, $f(x) \geq \min(f(x_1), f(x_2))$ which defines quasi-concavity. Basically, the same development is contained in Definition 4.2.

4.4.1.3 *Properties of the Cost Function*

Definition 4.6. Given a family of production possibility sets $L(y)$ satisfying the conditions for production possibility sets, then for any strictly positive price vector, we may define the producers cost function $C(y; p)$ by

$$C(y;p) = \min_x [p'x : x \text{ belongs to } L(y)]. \tag{4.71}$$

Based on this definition of the cost function, we can define five properties of this cost function:

1. $C(y; p)$ is a positive real-valued function defined and finite for all finite $y > 0$ and strictly positive price vector.
2. $C(y; p)$ is a non-decreasing left-continuous function in y and tends to plus infinity as y tends to infinity for every strictly positive price vector.

3. $C(y;p)$ is a non-decreasing function in p.
4. $C(y;p)$ is (positive) linear homogeneous in p for every strictly positive price vector.
5. $C(y;p)$ is a concave function in p for every $y > 0$.

Intuitively, we have demonstrated that a production function $f(x)$ implies a set of level sets $L(y)$. In addition, the level set implies the existence of the production function (so the construction is reversible). Next, we define a cost function $C(p;y)$ based on the level set $L(y)$. Again, reversing the logic, we demonstrate that the cost function implies a level set $M(y)$. Further, this level set implied by the cost function is the same as the level set which defines the cost function in the first place $M(y) = L(y)$. Hence, we start by defining a level set based on the cost function.

Definition 4.7. Define the family of sets $M(y)$, for $y \geq 0$, by

$$M(0) = \Omega = (x : x \geq 0)$$

$$y > 0, M(y) = \left[x : p'x \geq C(y;p) \text{ for every } p \gg 0, x \geq 0\right]. \quad (4.72)$$

Theorem 4.2. *Given a cost function satisfying the properties of the cost function discussed above, then the family of sets $M(y)$ generated by the cost function by means of the definition in E satisfy the conditions for a production possibility set.*

Conjecture 4.6 (Condition a). *$L(0) = \Omega$ for every $y > 0$. $L(y)$ is a non-empty, closed set which does not contain the origin.*

First, by definition, $M(0) = \Omega$. The trick is then to show that $M(y)$ is a non-empty set that does not contain the origin. First to demonstrate that $M(y)$ is closed, Diewert uses the linear homogeneity of the cost function:

$$\begin{aligned} M(y) &= [x : p'x \geq C(y;p) \text{ for every } p \gg 0, x \geq 0] \\ &\Rightarrow \left[x : p'x \geq C(y;p) \text{ for } p \gg 0 \ni: \textstyle\sum_{i=1}^{N} p_1 = 1, x \geq 0\right]. \end{aligned} \quad (4.73)$$

Given that the cost function is homogeneous in prices, the price vector is invariant to normalization. Thus, we can normalize it so that the sum of all prices is equal to one. For any set of prices strictly greater than zero, $[x : p'x = C(y;p), x = 0]$ is closed. Given that any price vector can be so normalized, every possible price vector is closed.

Given that the intersection of a family of closed sets is closed, $M(y)$ is closed. Given any y, we know that for any arbitrary price vector, we can normalize the price vector so that its sum is one without changing the cost function due to linear homogeneity. Thus, we know that each price vector (set of price ratios) yields a closed subset. Next, the intersection of all such subsets that yields the same level of input, y, is then defined as $M(y)$ or the set of all price ratios that can be used to generate a given output set.

Finally, $M(y)$ cannot be empty. If $M(y)$ were empty, then for any positive price vector, we could normalize the output vector (set x to be a vector of ones, then $x^N = N1$). Then there must exist a set of strictly positive prices p_N such that

$$p'_N x^N = N p'_N 1 = N < C(y; p_N) \tag{4.74}$$

but then $C(y;p)$ is unbounded for the price sequence (p_N) in violation of the property of the cost function.

Conjecture 4.7 (Condition b). *For every $y \geq 0$, $L(y)$ is a convex set.*

By extension of the above discussion, it is possible to show that the set is not only closed but also convex by Minkowski's theorem, as depicted in Figure 4.9.

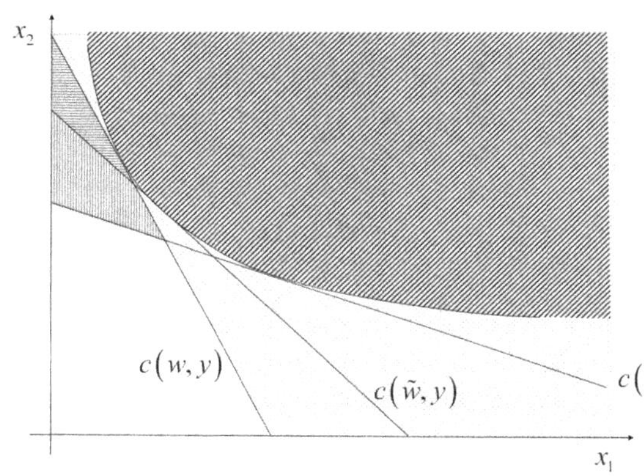

Fig. 4.9 Minokowski's Theorem — Intersection of Half-Spaces

Theorem 4.3 (Minkowski's Theorem). *A closed, convex set is the intersection of half-spaces that support it:*

$$X = \bigcap_{\lambda \in \Lambda} H_{\lambda}^{*}. \tag{4.75}$$

The half-space $H(m, k)$ is defined as

$$H\,(m,k) = \{x : m \cdot x \leq k\}. \tag{4.76}$$

Thus, based on the definition of a cost function, we have

$$N\,(w,y) = \{x : w \cdot x \leq c\,(w,y)\}. \tag{4.77}$$

This definition actually recovers the original production set:

$$V^{*}\,(y) = \{x : w \cdot x \geq c\,(w,y)\,\forall w > 0\}. \tag{4.78}$$

If $V^{*}(y) = V(y)$, the original technology can be recovered.

Conjecture 4.8 (Condition c). *If $x' \geq x$ (componentwise), where x belongs to $L(y)$, then x' also belongs to $L(y)$.*

This demonstration is rather straightforward. For a given price vector, if $x' \geq x$, then $p'x' \geq p'x \geq C(y;p)$. Since the cost function is non-decreasing in y, then if x belongs to $M(y)$.

Conjecture 4.9 (Condition d). *If $y_1 \geq y_2$, then $L(y_1) \subset L(y_2)$.*

Again, this is actually a slight restatement of the preceding condition. Specifically, in the step above, we showed that any increase in input usage implied an increase in cost. By using this property of the cost function that increased output levels imply increased cost, the next conclusion follows directly:

$$y_1 \geq y_2 \Rightarrow C(y_1;p) \geq C(y_2;p). \tag{4.79}$$

Thus, by definition of the family of sets,

$$\begin{aligned} M(y_1) &= [x : p'x \geq C(y_1;p) \text{ for every } p \gg 0, x \geq 0] \\ \subset M(y_2) &= [x : p'x \geq C(y_2;p) \text{ for every } p \gg 0, x \geq 0]. \end{aligned} \tag{4.80}$$

Conjecture 4.10 (Condition e). *For every x belonging to Ω, there exists a y such that x does not belong to $L(y)$.*

This condition is demonstrated by the fact that for any x and price vector p strictly greater than zero, a y can be used to define a cost function $C(y;p)$ such that

$$p'x < C(y;p) \tag{4.81}$$

since the cost function is defined for all y as y tends to infinity.

Conjecture 4.11 (Condition f). *Graph L is a closed set.*

The proof of this property relies on the left-continuous nature of the cost function. Note that we have been interested in the right-continuous properties of the input requirement sets. These requirements have resulted from the definition of $L(y)$ as that set of xs that generate at least y $[x : f(x) \geq y]$. Further $f(x)$ is defined as a right-continuous function. In these ways, the cost function is a minimization function. Thus, we are interested in the cost function being a left-continuous function. In each case, the continuity is required for the optimum to exist.

4.4.1.4 *Duality*

Taken together, the foregoing proofs prove the duality of the cost function. Specifically, the properties of the production function imply the existence of the production possibility sets (or input requirement sets). The properties of the input requirement sets imply the existence of a cost function. Going the other way, the properties of the cost function imply the existence of the production possibility set which implies the existence of the production function. Symbolically,

$$\begin{aligned} f(x) &\Rightarrow \exists\, L(y) \Rightarrow \exists\, C(p;y) \\ C(p;y) &\Rightarrow \exists\, M(y)\ \{L(y)\}\ \Rightarrow \exists\, f(x). \end{aligned} \tag{4.82}$$

4.4.1.5 *Shephard's Lemma*

Given this development, Diewert then proves Shephard's lemma:

$$\frac{\partial C(p;y)}{\partial p_i} = x_i(p;y). \tag{4.83}$$

Starting with the definition of the cost function, Diewert then hypothesizes a change in the price vector Δp where one price is changed. The cost function is then redefined as

$$\begin{aligned} C(y;p+\Delta p) &= \min_x \left[(p+\Delta p)'\, x : x \text{ belongs to } M(y)\right] \\ C(y;p+\Delta p) &= (p+\Delta p)'\, x^* \\ C(y;p+\Delta p) &= (p+\Delta p)'\, (\bar{x}+\Delta x) \end{aligned} \tag{4.84}$$

if we assume that x^* is the optimum choice of x at the new price vector, we have $x^* = \bar{x} + \Delta x$. Given the definition of the optimal input use, we have

$$\begin{aligned} C(p+\Delta p;y) \le (p+\Delta p)'\bar{x} &= p'\bar{x} + \Delta p'\bar{x} \\ &= p'\bar{x} + \Delta p'\bar{x} \\ &= C(p+\Delta p;y) + \Delta p_i \bar{x}_i. \end{aligned} \tag{4.85}$$

Given that $\Delta p_i > 0$,

$$\bar{x}_i \le \frac{C(p+\Delta p;y) - C(p;y)}{\Delta p_i} \tag{4.86}$$

which completes the proof.

4.4.2 *Shephard's Proof*

As a starting point of the discussion of the distance function, Shephard defines the space of possible inputs over the non-negative domain D. Then the space of all possible input bundles is segmented into a sequence of regions:

1. the origin 0;
2. interior points of D: $D_1 = \{x|x > 0\}$;
3. the boundary points of D excluding the origin

$$D_2 = \left\{ x|x \ge 0, \prod_{i=1}^{n} x_i = 0 \right\}. \tag{4.87}$$

D_2 is further divided into two regions:

a. $D_2' = \{x|x \in D_2, (\lambda x) \in L_\Phi(u) \text{ for some } u > 0, \lambda > 0\}$
b. $D_2'' = \{x|x \in D_2, (\lambda x) \notin L_\Phi(u) \text{ for some } u > 0, \lambda > 0\}$

The last segmentation separates D_2 (e.g., the axis points where either $x_1 = 0$ or $x_2 = 0$) into those points that are on a level set ($L_\Phi(u)$) and those points that are not on a level set. Looking at the definition if $x \in D_2 \Rightarrow x \geq 0, \prod_{i=1}^{N} x_i = 0$ at least one of x_i must be equal to 0. Thus, λx such that $\lambda \in (0, \infty)$ represents all possible xs such that x_i is equal to zero. We have segregated this set of points on the boundary into those points that are vertical and horizontal asymptotes of the production surface (i.e., the production function exhibits weak or strong necessity) (D_2') and those points where the isoquant intersects the axis (D_2''). The set D_2 is the union of both of these sets $D_2 = D_2' \cup D_2''$.

Each of these regions define a different distance measure. For example, consider the four points in Figure 4.10. Point x is an element of D_2 — it involves a zero level of input for x_1. However, the isoquant crosses the axes so production of u is possible with $x_1 = 0$ – $x \in D_2'$. Thus, we can define a distance measure λ for x defined as

$$\lambda = \min_{\lambda} \{\lambda : \lambda x \in L_\Phi(u)\} \tag{4.88}$$

that is the distance along the ray from the origin that is exactly on the level set. Points x' and x'' are in D_1 (i.e., all inputs being used at a positive level). However, we note that the level set $L_\Phi(u)$ does not cross the x_1 axis. Intuitively, x_2 is strictly essential for production. For our purposes, a distance function does not exist for the level set of output u — graphically, there is no λ for point $\tilde{x}$.

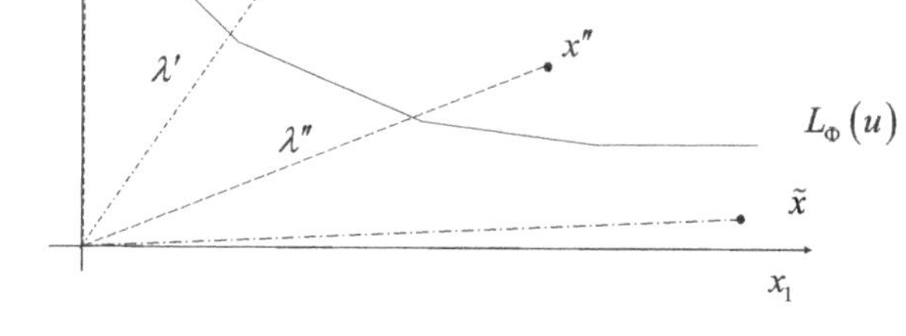

Fig. 4.10 Different Sets and Distances

The possible set of inputs D is defined as the union of all of these disjoint sets:

$$D = 0 \cup D_1 \cup D_2' \cup D_2''. \tag{4.89}$$

The distance function $\Psi(u, x)$ is then defined on D for the production possibility sets $L_\Phi(u)$, $u \in [0, \infty)$ as

$$\Psi(u, x) = \begin{cases} \dfrac{\|x\|}{\|\xi\|} & \text{for } x \in D_1 \cup D_2',\ u > 0 \\ 0 & \text{for } x \in 0 \cup D_2'',\ u > 0 \\ +\infty & \text{for } x \in D,\ u = 0 \end{cases} \tag{4.90}$$

where $\xi = \lambda_0 x$ and $\lambda_0 = \min\{\lambda : \lambda x \in L_\Phi(u)\}$ (i.e., Equation (4.88)). Breaking this definition down by parts, $\Psi(u, x)$ is a function of the output level u and an input vector x. $L_\Phi(u)$ is the level set of inputs that produce at least output u. λ_0 is the minimum length along that ray that will generate an output on that level set $\lambda_0 x \in L_\Phi(u)$ (see Figure 4.11).

The first scenario in Equation (4.90) includes two possibilities: (1) All inputs are being used at a positive level. This scenario depicts $x \in D_1$, then the input bundle produces u — an interior point in input–input space. (2) One of the inputs is not strictly necessary — $x \in D_2'$, or the input bundle is on one of the axes (i.e., $x_i = 0$ for some i).

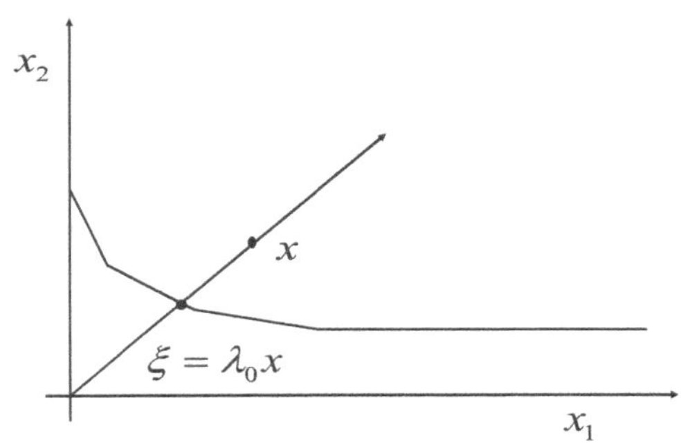

Fig. 4.11 Definition of the Distance Function

If the input bundle is associated with a valid output level, the distance function is defined as

$$\Psi\left(u,x\right)=\frac{\|x\|}{\|\xi\|}=\frac{\|x\|}{\|\lambda_0 x\|}. \tag{4.91}$$

Define the norm of a vector as

$$\|x\|=\sqrt{\sum_{i=1}^{n} x_i^2}. \tag{4.92}$$

Thus,

$$\Psi\left(u,x\right)=\frac{\|x\|}{\lambda_0\|x\|}=\frac{1}{\lambda_0}. \tag{4.93}$$

Graphically, the distance function is depicted in Figure 4.11. If the original input vector does not yield a valid level set, then $x \in 0 \cup D_2''$, $u > 0$, the value of the distance function is set to 0. Otherwise, $x \in D$, $u = 0$, the vector of inputs at the origin, the distance function is defined as $+\infty$.

In order to make the concept a little more concrete, consider the combinations of inputs and output generated from the transcendental production function introduced in Chapter 1:

$$f\left(x_1,x_2\right)=10x_1^{0.45}x_2^{0.35}\exp\left(-0.00035x_1-0.00025x_2\right)+\zeta \tag{4.94}$$

where ζ is a random variable which is distributed gamma. These data are presented in Table 4.1. Following Equation (4.88), we first define the set of xs such that the inputs yield at least 75 units of outputs:

$$\lambda_i=\min_{\lambda}\left\{\ \lambda:\lambda x\in L_\Phi\left(75\right)\right\}. \tag{4.95}$$

These observations are presented in Table 4.2 and graphically in Figure 4.12. Redefining Equation 4.95 for $L_\Phi\left(50\right)$ yields the distance results in Table 4.3.

Proposition 4.1 (Shephard's Proposition 14). *For any* $u \in [0,\infty)$,

$$L_\phi(u)=\{x|\Psi(u,x)\geq 1, x\in D\}. \tag{4.96}$$

So, the level set is defined as those input vectors x *that have a distance function value of* $\Psi\left(u,x\right)\geq 1$.

Table 4.1 Transcendental Data for Distance Computations

Obs.	x_1	x_2	Y	Obs.	x_1	x_2	Y
1	11.3426	9.4051	58.0610	26	3.3595	15.3676	38.9609
2	7.4441	9.5654	48.3455	27	13.0065	13.4051	68.5679
3	10.4883	5.1226	46.7750	28	5.3026	12.1365	44.5783
4	14.9439	8.0956	62.7818	29	9.3094	11.0515	55.7732
5	6.3922	15.3987	52.0170	30	5.4409	5.4613	35.5486
6	20.6834	15.3682	87.7413	31	5.4508	22.2421	53.9904
7	22.3023	11.9712	84.2381	32	9.9694	27.5997	75.3635
8	17.8273	12.3209	76.9367	33	6.5881	8.2770	43.8433
9	1.5203	12.0995	25.4184	34	9.3015	12.8227	58.2690
10	31.3959	5.4331	77.4007	35	11.9501	7.2292	54.9469
11	16.5561	17.7613	82.9715	36	7.3886	11.9547	51.4867
12	15.4640	7.9875	63.4893	37	10.2449	25.4174	74.4648
13	2.9278	15.7444	36.8916	38	7.5652	6.6255	43.6481
14	16.9118	20.3992	87.2536	39	5.9434	13.6374	48.5680
15	18.3845	10.6692	74.7291	40	7.4419	8.3519	46.4253
16	15.2791	33.5970	96.5524	41	19.4514	30.5316	104.5156
17	13.0784	14.4328	70.2588	42	12.7003	10.7296	63.5033
18	7.2867	38.0237	71.9314	43	25.4271	16.3276	97.8640
19	14.4622	13.2441	71.6269	44	7.0346	14.1833	52.9884
20	9.7641	21.3298	69.2198	45	15.2300	7.8365	62.7026
21	13.4874	8.7700	61.4279	46	17.5625	7.7100	66.4774
22	12.7641	18.4941	74.7924	47	29.6362	23.6347	116.7654
23	6.0977	20.4496	55.3839	48	10.1112	9.3295	55.0262
24	7.7591	4.1530	38.3968	49	21.6557	7.4715	72.2650
25	17.5761	14.5697	80.3519	50	4.1077	9.0759	36.4650

Table 4.2 Distance Results for L_Φ (75)

Obs.	λ_i	x_1	x_2	Y	$\lambda_i x_1$	$\lambda_i x_2$
6	0.8089	20.6834	15.3682	84.9376	16.7317	12.4320
7	0.8547	22.3023	11.9712	83.7973	19.0624	10.2321
8	0.9662	17.8273	12.3209	75.9443	17.2242	11.9041
10	0.9582	31.3959	5.4331	77.0900	30.0835	5.2060
11	0.8725	16.5561	17.7613	80.5716	14.4448	15.4964
14	0.8151	16.9118	20.3992	85.7311	13.7841	16.6266
16	0.7103	15.2791	33.5970	94.6269	10.8523	23.8630
25	0.9111	17.5761	14.5697	78.9353	16.0142	13.2749
32	0.9935	9.9694	27.5997	74.1136	9.9045	27.4199
41	0.6380	19.4514	30.5316	102.7232	12.4098	19.4788
43	0.6977	25.4271	16.3276	95.8856	17.7395	11.3912
47	0.5488	29.6362	23.6347	116.2799	16.2641	12.9706

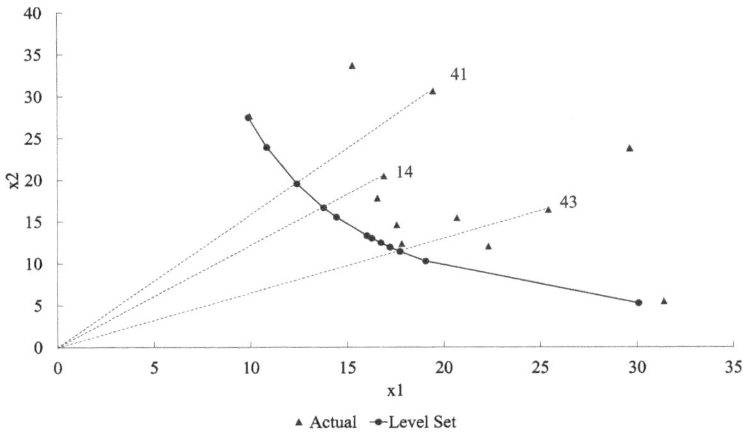

Fig. 4.12 Empirical Distance Function

If $x \in L_\Phi(u)$ for $u > 0$, $\xi \leq x$ — the input combination lies inside the level set — thus, $\|x\|/\|\xi\| \geq 1$. However, if $x \notin L_\Phi(u)$, $x < \xi$, the input point is below the level set and $\|x\|/\|\xi\| < 1$.

Proposition 4.2 (Shephard's Proposition 15). *For any $u \in (0, +\infty)$, the isoquant of a production set $L_\Phi(u)$ consists of those input vectors $x \geq 0$ such that $\Psi(u, x) = 1$.*

So, the distance function can be used to define the isoquant or the efficient set of inputs $E(u) = \{x|\Psi(u, x) = 1\}$. The isoquant is defined as the minimum combination of inputs that can be used to produce output u along any ray from the origin.

Proposition 4.3 (Shephard's Proposition 17).
$\Phi(x) = \max\{u|\Psi(u, x) \geq 1\}$, $x \in D$.

Thus, the distance function defines the production function.

4.4.2.1 *Shephard's Cost Function*

Following the distance function framework developed above, the cost function can be defined as

$$Q\,(u, w) = \min_x \left\{\, w'x|x \in L_\Phi(u)\right\} \;\; w \in D,\; u \in [0, \infty) \qquad (4.97)$$

Table 4.3 Distance Results for L_{Φ} (50)

Obs.	λ_i	x_1	x_2	Y	$\lambda_i x_1$	$\lambda_i x_2$
1	0.8181	11.3426	9.4051	55.6952	9.2789	7.6939
4	0.7363	14.9439	8.0956	58.7185	11.0037	5.9611
5	0.9482	6.3922	15.3987	50.7805	6.0614	14.6016
6	0.4688	20.6834	15.3682	84.9376	9.6954	7.2039
7	0.4952	22.3023	11.9712	83.7973	11.0444	5.9283
8	0.5599	17.8273	12.3209	75.9443	9.9806	6.8979
10	0.5543	31.3959	5.4331	77.0900	17.4042	3.0118
11	0.5056	16.5561	17.7613	80.5716	8.3705	8.9798
12	0.7253	15.4640	7.9875	57.8604	11.2160	5.7933
14	0.4723	16.9118	20.3992	85.7311	7.9874	9.6345
15	0.5822	18.3845	10.6692	72.2380	10.7043	6.2121
16	0.4114	15.2791	33.5970	94.6269	6.2857	13.8216
17	0.6328	13.0784	14.4328	68.5428	8.2764	9.1335
18	0.6119	7.2867	38.0237	70.2205	4.4588	23.2674
19	0.6166	14.4622	13.2441	69.9857	8.9173	8.1662
20	0.6454	9.7641	21.3298	67.2582	6.3021	13.7671
21	0.7583	13.4874	8.7700	59.5357	10.2275	6.6502
22	0.5816	12.7641	18.4941	74.2838	7.4234	10.7559
23	0.8715	6.0977	20.4496	52.8470	5.3139	17.8208
25	0.5280	17.5761	14.5697	78.9353	9.2799	7.6926
27	0.6540	13.0065	13.4051	67.5153	8.5057	8.7663
29	0.8635	9.3094	11.0515	54.8527	8.0384	9.5427
31	0.9018	5.4508	22.2421	51.5993	4.9156	20.0581
32	0.5753	9.9694	27.5997	74.1136	5.7349	15.8767
34	0.8141	9.3015	12.8227	56.3753	7.5724	10.4391
35	0.8810	11.9501	7.2292	54.5012	10.5275	6.3687
36	0.9614	7.3886	11.9547	48.9723	7.1035	11.4934
37	0.5847	10.2449	25.4174	70.8938	5.9907	14.8628
41	0.3696	19.4514	30.5316	102.7232	7.1900	11.2857
42	0.7252	12.7003	10.7296	60.9900	9.2097	7.7806
43	0.4043	25.4271	16.3276	95.8856	10.2789	6.6005
44	0.9250	7.0346	14.1833	50.5191	6.5067	13.1191
45	0.7376	15.2300	7.8365	61.7837	11.2332	5.7800
46	0.6817	17.5625	7.7100	65.8518	11.9718	5.2557
47	0.3180	29.6362	23.6347	116.2799	9.4247	7.5161
48	0.8793	10.1112	9.3295	53.5056	8.8905	8.2032
49	0.6090	21.6557	7.4715	70.4754	13.1873	4.5498

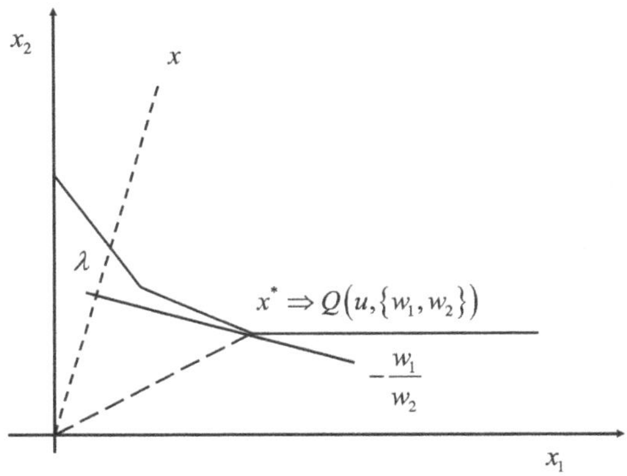

Fig. 4.13 Cost Minimization Subject to the Distance Function

graphically — the point of minimization is depicted in Figure 4.13. In Figure 4.13, we start from a point x which is an element of the level set $L_\Phi(u)$. This point/level set combination implies a distance λ. In addition, given a price vector $\{w_1, w_2\}$, there is a cost-minimizing point x^* in the level set $L_\Phi(u)$. This cost-minimizing point implies a cost $x_1^* w_1 + x_2^* w_2 = Q(u, \{w_1, w_2\})$. Hence, we can define the level set as that set of points that cost at least $Q(u, \{w_1, w_2\})$

$$L_\Phi(u) = \{x | w'x \geq Q(u, w)\} \quad \forall w \neq 0. \tag{4.98}$$

Put slightly differently, the cost structure can then be defined for the set of all possible input prices in a similar way as the level sets of inputs are defined in output space.

Shephard defines the cost structure as

$$\Lambda_Q(u) = \{w | Q(u, w) \geq 1, w \geq 0\} \tag{4.99}$$

(Shephard, 1970, pp. 96–97). To develop this concept, we note that $Q(u, w)$ can be defined as a distance function. Specifically, suppose we start with a particular result from Equation (4.97) (i.e., $Q(u, w) = \min_x \{w'x \,|x \in L_\Phi(u)\}$). Given this solution, we could normalize the vector of prices $w^* = w/Q(w, u)$ so that $Q(w^*, u) = 1$. Further, given that cost function is homogeneous of degree one

$$L_\Phi(u) = \{w'x \geq Q(u, w)\} = \{w^{*\prime}x \geq Q(u, w^*)\}. \tag{4.100}$$

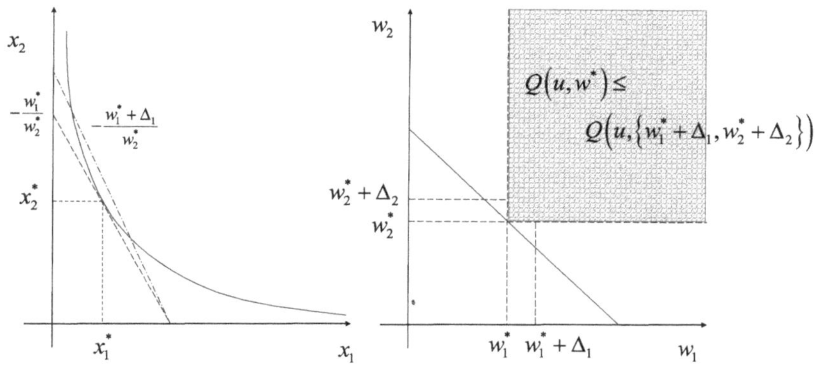

Fig. 4.14 Equivalence Between Input Choice and Input Price Space

Thus, we use this distance function concept of for the cost structure to define the concave relationship for input prices in Equation (4.99).

To develop this concept a little further, consider the cost-minimizing solution x^* defined from Equation (4.98). As depicted in Figure 4.14, this point (i.e., $x^* = \{x_1^*, x_2^*\}$) is associated with a point $w = \{w_1^*, w_2^*\}$ in the right panel. Focusing on the combinations of prices in this right panel, note that if we construct a set of prices $\tilde{w} = \{w_1^* + \Delta_1, w_2^* + \Delta_2\}$ where $\Delta_1, \Delta_2 \geq 0$ then $Q(u, \tilde{w}) \geq Q(u, w^*)$. Thus, this level of cost (i.e., $Q(u, \tilde{w})$) is large enough to produce u for any of these price combinations. Further, this set is strongly convex.

Next, we want to extend the points in $\Lambda_Q(u)$ to include some of the diagonal elements. Figure 4.15 considers a change in price such that $\Delta_2 \geq 0$ and $\Delta_1 \leq 0$. In this case, the quantity of x_1 increases while the quantity of x_2 declines. To demonstrate the existence of these points, we return to the production function defined in (4.94) (restricting the random component to zero). Table 4.4 presents the alternative prices that solve for $Q(w, u) \approx 7.4600$ such that $u = 50$. To develop this table, we use the implications of Shephard's lemma:

$$\begin{aligned} d\,c(w,u) &= x_1(w,u)\,d\,w_1 + x_2(w,u)\,d\,w_2 = 0 \\ &\Rightarrow \frac{d\,w_2}{d\,w_1} = -\frac{x_1(w,u)}{x_2(w,u)} \end{aligned} \tag{4.101}$$

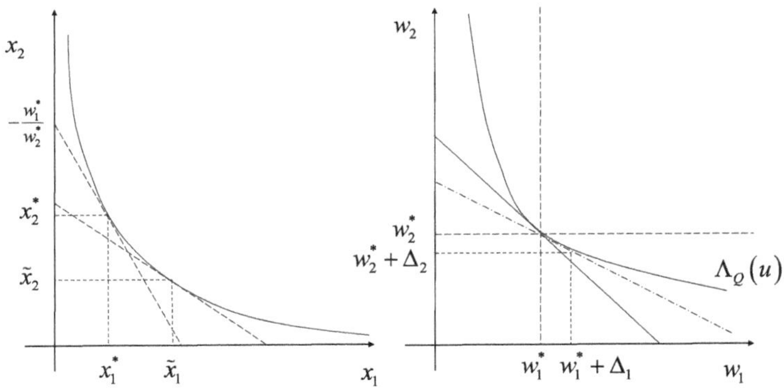

Fig. 4.15 Equivalence Between Input Choice and Input Price Space — Changes in Relative Prices

Table 4.4 Iso-Cost Function ($\Lambda_Q(u)$) for Transcendental Production Function

Obs.	Cost	w_1	w_2	w_2/w_1	x_1	x_2
1	7.4482	0.3250	0.8644	2.6598	12.8498	3.7852
2	7.4493	0.3350	0.8319	2.4833	12.4702	3.9329
3	7.4506	0.3475	0.7942	2.2854	12.0262	4.1193
4	7.4517	0.3600	0.7594	2.1094	11.6128	4.3076
5	7.4528	0.3725	0.7272	1.9522	11.2269	4.4977
6	7.4539	0.3850	0.6974	1.8114	10.8659	4.6897
7	7.4548	0.3975	0.6696	1.6846	10.5274	4.8835
8	7.4557	0.4100	0.6438	1.5702	10.2095	5.0790
9	7.4566	0.4225	0.6197	1.4667	9.9102	5.2762
10	7.4574	0.4350	0.5971	1.3727	9.6280	5.4751
11	7.4581	0.4475	0.5760	1.2870	9.3614	5.6756
12	7.4588	0.4600	0.5561	1.2089	9.1093	5.8778
13	7.4595	0.4725	0.5374	1.1374	8.8704	6.0815
14	7.4602	0.4850	0.5198	1.0718	8.6438	6.2868
15	7.4608	0.4975	0.5032	1.0115	8.4284	6.4936
16	7.4603	0.5125	0.4843	0.9450	8.1826	6.7451
17	7.4598	0.5250	0.4695	0.8942	7.9882	6.9565
18	7.4592	0.5375	0.4554	0.8473	7.8029	7.1694
19	7.4587	0.5500	0.4421	0.8038	7.6260	7.3837
20	7.4582	0.5625	0.4295	0.7635	7.4570	7.5995
21	7.4578	0.5750	0.4174	0.7260	7.2954	7.8166
22	7.4573	0.5875	0.4060	0.6911	7.1406	8.0351
23	7.4569	0.6000	0.3951	0.6585	6.9923	8.2550
24	7.4565	0.6125	0.3847	0.6281	6.8500	8.4762
25	7.4561	0.6250	0.3748	0.5997	6.7134	8.6988

holding the changes in x_1 and x_2 to the level set.[2] Thus, for a small change in input prices, if $dw_2/dw_1 \ll x_1(w,u)/x_2(w,u)$, then $c(\{w_1+dw_1, w_2+dw_2\}, u) \gg c(\{w_1, w_2\} u)$. The left panel in Figure 4.16 depicts the level set in input space ($L_\Phi(u)$) for Table 4.4 while the right panel in Figure 4.16 depicts the set of input price combinations with at least the cost $Q(u,w)$. Hence, the convexity in price relationship ($\Lambda_Q(u)$) is implied by the convexity of the level set ($Ł_\Phi(u)$) by cost minimization.

In order to fully develop the duality between quantity space ($L_\Phi(u)$) and price space ($\Lambda_Q(u)$), consider the relationship depicted in Figure 4.17. Starting with the input quantity panel (i.e., the left panel) of Figure 4.17, for a given vector of x^0 and level set $L_\Phi(u)$, we can define a distance λ such that $\lambda x \in L_\Phi(u)$. Next, we work somewhat "backwards" — assuming that a given cost value is feasible (i.e., $w^{0\prime}x^0$ is sufficient to produce our initial level of output (i.e., $w^{0\prime}x^0 \geq Q(u,w^0)$), we can define the distance θ^0. Here, w^0 performs the same function as w^* does in Equation (4.100) — it normalizes the original cost to one. Hence, all the other points on the iso-cost frontier in Figure 4.17 normalize to one.

---

[2]Starting with a total differentiation of the cost function,

$$dc(w,u) = \left[x_1 + w_1\frac{\partial x_1}{\partial w_1} + w_2\frac{\partial x_2}{\partial w_1}\right]dw_1 + \left[x_2 + w_1\frac{\partial x_1}{\partial w_2} + \frac{\partial x_2}{\partial w_2}\right]dw_2$$
$$+ w_1 dx_1 + w_2 dx_2 + \frac{\partial c(w,u)}{\partial u}du.$$

Next, following our discussion of Shephard's lemma, we substitute $w_1 = \lambda\partial f/\partial x_1$ and $w_2 = \lambda\partial f/\partial x_2$ into this result, yielding

$$x_1 + \lambda\left(\frac{\partial f(x_1,x_2)}{\partial x_1}\frac{\partial x_1}{w_1} + \frac{\partial f(x_1,x_2)}{\partial x_2}\frac{\partial x_2}{\partial w_1}\right) = x_1$$
$$x_2 + \lambda\left(\frac{\partial f(x_1,x_2)}{\partial x_1}\frac{\partial x_1}{w_2} + \frac{\partial f(x_1,x_2)}{\partial x_2}\frac{\partial x_2}{\partial w_2}\right) = x_2.$$

Holding $du = 0$, we have

$$dc(w,u) = x_1 dw_1 + x_2 dw_2 + dx_1 w_1 + dx_2 w_2 = 0.$$

In most of the previous analysis, we have held the prices constant (i.e., $dw_1 = dw_2 = 0$). This allowed us to focus on the level set (e.g., the changes in x_1 and x_2 that kept production feasible). In this case, we want to derive the changes in input prices, dw_1 and dw_2, which maintains feasibility and holds cost constant.

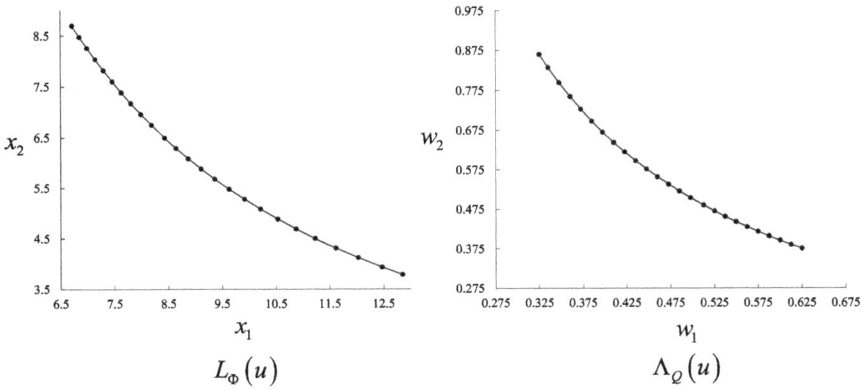

Fig. 4.16 Empirical Level Set for Inputs Quantities and Input Prices

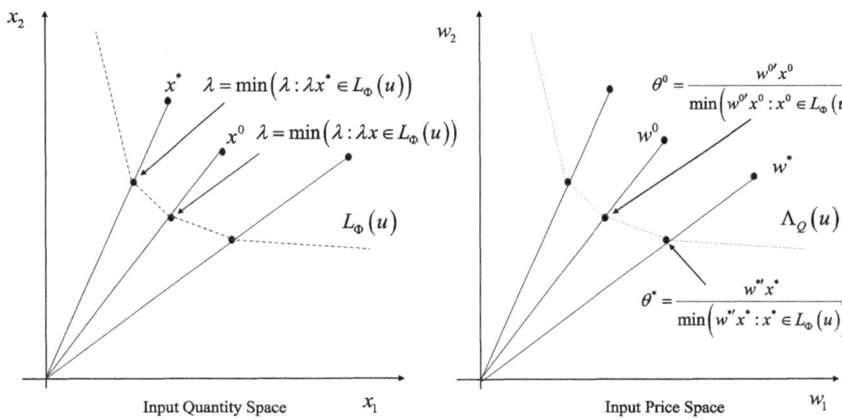

Fig. 4.17 Relationship Between Distance Functions in Input Quantity and Input Price Space

The claim of Shephard's duality is then

$$Q(u, w) = \min_x \left\{ w'x | \Psi(u, x) \geq 1 \right\}, \quad u \geq 0, \quad w \geq 0 \qquad (4.102)$$

$$\Psi(u, x) = \inf_w \left\{ w'x | Q(u, w) \geq 1 \right\}, \quad u \geq 0, \quad x \geq 0. \qquad (4.103)$$

Taking each equation in turn, Equation (4.103) defines the level set in cost space using the distance function (i.e., $\Psi(u, x) \Rightarrow Q(u, w)$).

Equation (4.103) then depicts how the cost set can be used to define the distance function. Specifically, constraining the cost function to be at least a fixed level ($w'x$ for some base input combination x), we can map out the set of points that minimize the distance to the origin for that set. Relating the concepts to Figure 4.16, each point in input quantity space ($L_\Phi(u)$) is defined by the distance function $\Psi(u,x)$ is associated with a point in price space ($\Lambda_Q(w)$) defined by distance function $Q(u,w)$ (based on a normalized price vector) in price space. The concavity of $L_\Phi(u)$ space supports the concavity of $\Lambda_Q(u)$ space.

4.5 Profit Functions

4.5.1 *Primal Approach to the Profit Function*

Taking as a starting point, the Cobb–Douglas form, we could formulate the profit function as

$$\max_x \pi = p_y x_1^\alpha x_2^\beta - w_1 x_1 - w_2 x_2$$

$$\left.\begin{aligned} \frac{\partial \pi}{\partial x_1} &= p_y \alpha \frac{y}{x_1} - w_1 = 0 \\ \frac{\partial \pi}{\partial x_2} &= p_y \beta \frac{y}{x_2} - w_2 = 0 \end{aligned}\right\} \Rightarrow \frac{\alpha x_2}{\beta x_1} = \frac{w_1}{w_2} \Rightarrow x_2 = \frac{\beta}{\alpha}\frac{w_1}{w_2} x_1. \tag{4.104}$$

Substituting this result back into the first-order conditions,

$$\begin{aligned} p_y \alpha x_1^{\alpha-1}\left(\frac{\beta}{\alpha}\frac{w_1}{w_2}x_1\right)^\beta &= w_1 \\ \Rightarrow x_1^{\alpha+\beta-1} &= \frac{1}{p_y}\left(\frac{w_2}{\beta}\right)^\beta\left(\frac{w_1}{\alpha}\right)^{1-\beta} \\ \Rightarrow x_1 &= p_y^{\frac{1}{1-\alpha-\beta}}\left(\frac{w_2}{\beta}\right)^{\frac{\beta}{1-\alpha-\beta}}\left(\frac{w_1}{\alpha}\right)^{\frac{1-\beta}{1-\alpha-\beta}} \\ \Rightarrow x_2 &= p_y^{\frac{1}{1-\alpha-\beta}}\left(\frac{w_2}{\beta}\right)^{\frac{1-\alpha}{1-\beta-\alpha}}\left(\frac{w_1}{\alpha}\right)^{\frac{\alpha}{1-\alpha-\beta}}. \end{aligned} \tag{4.105}$$

4.5.2 *Starting with the Cost Function*

If we use the Cobb–Douglas cost function,

$$\max_{y} \pi = p_y y - C(w, y)$$

$$\pi = p_y y - w_1 y^{\frac{1}{\alpha+\beta}} \left[\frac{w_2 \alpha}{w_1 \beta}\right]^{\frac{\beta}{\alpha+\beta}} - w_2 y^{\frac{1}{\alpha+\beta}} \left[\frac{w_1 \beta}{w_2 \alpha}\right]^{\frac{\alpha}{\alpha+\beta}}$$

$$\frac{\partial \pi}{\partial y} = p_y - \frac{1}{\alpha+\beta} y^{\frac{1-\alpha-\beta}{\alpha+\beta}} \left[w_1 \left(\frac{w_2 \alpha}{w_1 \beta}\right)^{\frac{\beta}{\alpha+\beta}} + w_2 \left(\frac{w_1 \beta}{w_2 \alpha}\right)^{\frac{\alpha}{\alpha+\beta}}\right] = 0$$

$$y = [(\alpha+\beta) p_y]^{\frac{\alpha+\beta}{1-\alpha=\beta}} \left[w_1 \left(\frac{w_2 \alpha}{w_1 \beta}\right)^{\frac{\beta}{\alpha+\beta}} + w_2 \left(\frac{w_1 \beta}{w_2 \alpha}\right)^{\frac{\alpha}{\alpha+\beta}}\right]^{\frac{\alpha+\beta}{\alpha+\beta-1}}. \tag{4.106}$$

4.5.3 *Properties of the Profit Function*

However, like our discussion regarding the cost function, we can bypass the primal form and derive the economic concepts of the dual profit function.

4.5.3.1 *Properties of the Profit Function*

- $\pi(p, w) \geq 0$,
- If $\tilde{p} \geq p$, then $\pi(\tilde{p}, w) \geq \pi(p, w)$ — Profit is non-decreasing in p,
- If $\tilde{w} \geq w$, then $\pi(p, \tilde{w}) \leq \pi(p, w)$ — Profit is non-increasing in w,
- $\pi(p, w)$ is convex and continuous in (p, w),
- $\pi(tp, tw) = t\pi(p, w), t > 0$ — Profit is positive linear homogenous.

Property 1 basically states that a producer faced with losing money from production will simply choose not to produce. Specifically, letting $x = 0$ implies $y = 0$, and in the absence of fixed cost, $\pi(p, w) = 0$.

Property 2 is based on the fact that we could at least produce the same bundle of outputs:

$$\pi(\tilde{p}, w) \geq \tilde{p}y - c(w, y) \geq py - c(w, y) = \pi(p, w). \tag{4.107}$$

The first inequality can be argued based on the concavity of the cost function:

$$\pi(\tilde{p}, w) = \max_{y} \tilde{p} - c(w, y)$$
$$\pi(\tilde{p}, w) = [py - c(w, y)] + [p - \nabla_y c(w, y)](\tilde{p} - p)$$
$$- \frac{1}{2}(\tilde{p} - p)\nabla^2_{xx} c(w, y)(\tilde{p} - p) \geq 0. \quad (4.108)$$

Property 3 follows a proof similar to Property 2

$$\pi(p, w) = py - c(w, y) \leq py - c(\tilde{w}, y) \leq \pi(p, \tilde{w}). \quad (4.109)$$

Similarly, the last inequality can be demonstrated by the concavity of the cost function.

Property 4 can actually be seen in our discussion of Property 2. Starting with the development of the property that profit is non-decreasing in output prices,

$$\pi(\tilde{p}, w) = [py - c(w, y)] + [p - \nabla_y c(w, y)](\tilde{p} - p)$$
$$\frac{1}{2}(\tilde{p} - p)\nabla^2_{yy} c(w, y)(\tilde{p} - p) \geq 0 \ni: p - \nabla_y c(w, y) = 0 \text{ for a max}$$
$$\Rightarrow \pi(\hat{p}, w) - [py - c(w, y)] - \frac{1}{2}(\hat{p} - p)\nabla^2_{yy} c(w, y)(\hat{p} - p)$$
$$\Rightarrow \nabla^2_{pp}\pi(p, w) = -\nabla^2_{yy} c(w, y). \quad (4.110)$$

4.5.4 *Netput Vector*

Expanding the discussion to the concept of a netput vector, let us rewrite the profit function as

$$\pi(p, w) = \pi(z) \ni: z = \begin{bmatrix} p \\ w \end{bmatrix}$$
$$\pi(p, w) = \alpha_0 + \alpha' p + \frac{1}{2}p' A p + \beta' w + \frac{1}{2}w' B w + p' \Gamma w$$
$$\pi(z) = \alpha_0 + \begin{bmatrix} \alpha \\ \beta \end{bmatrix}' z + \frac{1}{2}z' \begin{bmatrix} A & \Gamma \\ \Gamma' & B \end{bmatrix} z. \quad (4.111)$$

Thus, the Hessian matrix is

$$\pi_{zz}^2(p,w) = \begin{bmatrix} A & \Gamma \\ \Gamma' & B \end{bmatrix} \Rightarrow \begin{cases} \nabla_{pp}^2 \pi(p,w) = A \\ \nabla_{ww}^2 \pi(p,w) = B. \\ \nabla_{wp}^2 \pi(p,w) = \Gamma \end{cases} \tag{4.112}$$

4.5.5 *Hotelling's Lemma*

The above discussion leads into a discussion of Hotelling's lemma (a profit function counterpart to Shephard's lemma). This proof is an envelope proof similar to the first proof we established for Shephard's lemma:

$$\begin{aligned} &\pi(p,\tilde{w}) \geq p\tilde{y} - c(\tilde{w},\tilde{y}) \\ &\quad \Rightarrow L^*(p,\tilde{w},\tilde{y}) = \pi(p,\tilde{w}) - p\tilde{y} + c(\tilde{w},\tilde{y}) \\ &\quad \Rightarrow \nabla_p L^*(p,\tilde{w},\tilde{y}) = \nabla_p \pi(\tilde{p},\tilde{w}) - \tilde{y} = 0 \\ &\quad \Rightarrow y(y,w) = \nabla_p \pi(p,w) = \frac{\partial \pi(p,w)}{\partial p} \\ &\quad \Rightarrow \nabla_w L^*(p,\tilde{w},\tilde{y}) = \nabla_w \pi(\tilde{p},\tilde{w}) + \nabla_w c(\tilde{w},\tilde{y}) = 0 \\ &\quad \Rightarrow x(p,w) = \nabla_w c(w,y) = -\nabla_w \pi(p,w). \end{aligned} \tag{4.113}$$

Recall the simple proof of the Slutsky decomposition from demand theory:

$$\begin{aligned} x(p,y) &= x(p,e(p,U)) \\ &\Rightarrow \frac{dx(p,y)}{dp} = \frac{\partial x(p,e(p,U))}{\partial p} + \frac{\partial x(p,e(p,U))}{\partial e(p,U)} \frac{\partial e(p,U)}{\partial p} \\ &\Rightarrow \frac{dx(p,y)}{dp} = \frac{\partial(p,y)}{\partial p} + \frac{x(p,y)}{\partial y} x^H(p,U). \end{aligned} \tag{4.114}$$

The same effect occurs in the input demand equations:

$$\begin{aligned} x(p,w) &= x(w,y(p,w)) \\ \frac{\partial x(p,w)}{\partial w} &= \frac{\partial x(w,y)}{\partial w} + \frac{\partial x(w,y)}{\partial y} \frac{\partial y(p,w)}{\partial w}. \end{aligned} \tag{4.115}$$

Relying on the Hotelling's lemma results, we can then see the following:

$$\frac{\partial y(p,w)}{\partial p} = \frac{\frac{\partial \pi(p,w)}{\partial p}}{\partial p} = \frac{\partial^2 \pi(p,w)}{\partial p^2} \geq 0$$
$$\frac{\partial x_I(p,w)}{\partial w_i} = -\frac{\frac{\partial \pi(p,w)}{\partial w_i}}{\partial w_i} = -\frac{\partial^2 \pi(p,w)}{\partial w_i^2} \leq 0$$
$$\frac{x_i(p,w)}{\partial w_j} = \frac{\partial x_j(p,w)}{\partial w_i} = -\frac{\partial^2 \pi(p,w)}{\partial w_i \partial w_j}$$
$$\frac{\partial y(p,w)}{\partial w_i} = -\frac{\partial x_i(p,w)}{\partial y} = \frac{\partial^2 \pi(p,w)}{\partial w_i \partial p}. \tag{4.116}$$

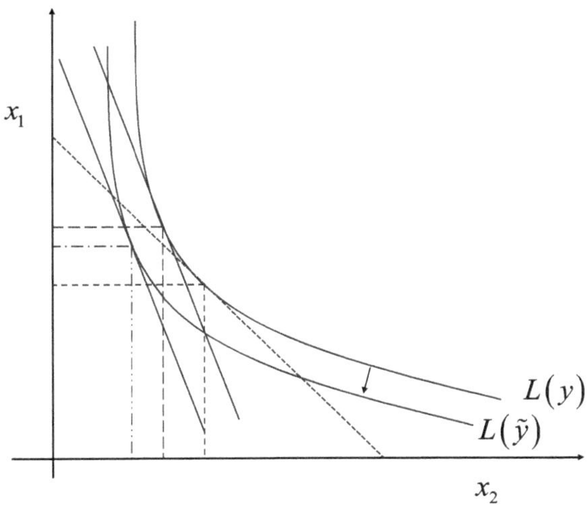

Like the Slutsky results,

$$x(p,w) = x(p, y(p,w))$$
$$\Rightarrow \frac{\partial x(p,w)}{\partial p} = \frac{\partial x(p, y(p,w))}{\partial y(p,w)} \frac{\partial y(p,w)}{\partial p}$$
$$\ni: \frac{\partial x(p,w)}{\partial p} = -\frac{\partial y(p,w)}{\partial w}$$

$$\Rightarrow -\frac{\partial y(p,w)}{\partial w} = \frac{\partial x(p,y(p,w))}{\partial y(p,w)}\frac{\partial y(p,w)}{\partial p}$$

$$\Rightarrow -\frac{\partial x(p,y)}{\partial y} = \frac{\dfrac{\partial y(p,w)}{\partial w}}{\dfrac{\partial y(p,w)}{\partial p}} \tag{4.117}$$

$$\begin{aligned} x_i(p,w) &= x_i(w,y(p,w)) \\ \frac{\partial x_i(p,w)}{\partial w_j} &= \frac{\partial x_i(w,y^*)}{\partial w_j} - \frac{\partial x_i(w,y^*)}{\partial y}\frac{\partial x_j(p,w)}{\partial p} \\ &= \frac{\partial x_i(w,y^*)}{\partial w_j} + \frac{\left(\dfrac{\partial y(p,w)}{\partial w_i}\right)\left(\dfrac{\partial x_j(p,w)}{\partial p}\right)}{\dfrac{\partial y(p,w)}{\partial p}} \\ &= \frac{\partial x_i(w,y^*)}{\partial w_j} - \frac{\left(\dfrac{\partial x_i(p,w)}{\partial p}\right)\left(\dfrac{\partial x_j(p,w)}{\partial p}\right)}{\dfrac{\partial y(p,w)}{\partial p}}. \end{aligned} \tag{4.118}$$

4.5.6 *Le Chatelier–Samuelson Principle*

With the last equation sufficient to demonstrate the Le Chatelier–Samuelson principle,

$$\frac{\partial x_i(p,w)}{\partial w_i} \leq \frac{\partial x_i(w,y^*)}{\partial w_i}. \tag{4.119}$$

4.5.7 *Dual Profit Function*

In our previous discussion of the dual, we showed that a cost function obeying the standard properties implied the existence of a production function that obeyed the properties we set out for a production technology. The profit function dual is similar to the cost function. Specifically, we want to show that the properties of the profit function imply the existence of a cost function with the properties outlined earlier:

- $c^*(w,y) \geq 0$, $w > 0$, $y > 0$,
- If $\tilde{w} \geq w$, the $c^*(\tilde{w},y) \geq c^*(w,y)$,

- $c^*(w, y)$ is concave and continuous in w,
- $c^*(tw, ty) = tc^*(w, y)$, $t > 0$,
- If $\tilde{y} \geq y$, then $c^*(w, \tilde{y}) \geq c^*(w, y)$,
- $c^*(w, 0) = 0$,
- $c^*(w, y)$ is convex and continuous in y.

To demonstrate these characteristics, we use the inverse of the relationship that has been useful above:

$$\pi(p, w) = py - c(w, y) \Rightarrow c(w, y) = py - \pi(p, w). \tag{4.120}$$

4.6 Chapter Summary

- The basic concept of duality in the cost and profit functions is that we can model optimizing behavior using several sets of variables:
  - In Chapter 1, we described how optimizing behavior can be modeled using a primal production function — the relationship between inputs and outputs.
  - In Chapter 4, we demonstrate how we can construct a model of that same optimizing behavior using decisions based on input prices and output levels.
  - In Chapter 4, we focus on the mathematical linkages between each specification.
- The basic concept of duality is that if a cost function that obeys certain properties exists, then a level set obeying the properties for optimization exists. Further, if a level set exists consistent with the properties for optimization, then a production function exists with similar properties.
- To emphasize the point a little further, we can estimate any point along the continuum. We estimate a flexible form of a cost function. If the estimated parameters imply that the cost function is greater than zero everywhere, increasing and concave in input prices, linear homogeneous, and increasing in output levels (along with the other properties, the cost function depicts economic behavior (e.g., cost minimization)).
- Given a valid cost function, a production function exists, which obeys the properties for economic behavior. We are typically not interested in recovering this function. The cost function gives us the representation of technology that we are interested in.

4.7 Review Questions

1. Prove Shephard's lemma using the envelope theorem.
2. What do we actually mean by Duality?
3. Sketch out Diewert's dual proof. What points do we need to establish?
4. What is a distance function? How does the distance function for the level set map out the production function?
5. What is the defining envelope for cost function in Shephard's proof?

4.8 Exercises

1. Derive the cost function for the Cobb–Douglas approximation from Equation (1.187).
2. Take the second-order expansion of the cost function from Question 1. Use the second-order expansion to derive the demand for capital.
3. Are the slopes of the derived demand for capital in Questions 1 and 2 similar?

Chapter 5

Estimating Dual Relationships

5.1 Flexible Functional Forms

The crux of the dual approach is to estimate a manifestation of behavior that economists know something about. Instead of estimating production functions that are purely physical forms that economists have little expertise in developing, we estimate the cost function that represents cost-minimizing behavior. We would then be able to determine whether the properties of these cost functions are consistent with our hypotheses about technology. However, it is often the direct implications of the cost-minimizing behavior that we are interested in: (1) How will farmers react to changes in agricultural prices through commodity programs?

$$\frac{\partial C(w;y)}{\partial y} = p + \Delta p. \tag{5.1}$$

Or what is the impact of a change in input prices (say in an increase in fuel prices) on agricultural output?

$$\frac{\partial C(w + \Delta w;y)}{\partial y} = p. \tag{5.2}$$

Thus, the dual cost function results are usually sufficient for most questions facing agricultural economists.

Given that we are interested in estimating the cost function directly, the next question involves how to specify the cost function? One approach to the estimation of cost functions would then be to hypothesize a primal production function and derive the theoretically consistent specification for the cost function based on this primal. For example, if we started with a Cobb–Douglas production function, we could specify a cost system consistent with that assumption; however, this approach would appear too restrictive. Specifically, we have shown that given that the cost function obeys certain properties, a valid technology exists, which would justify it. Instead, economists have typically turned to flexible functional forms that allow for a wide variety of technologies.

5.1.1 *Generalized Second-Order Taylor Series Expansion*

A basic approach to the specification of a cost function is to assume that an unspecified function exists and then derive a closed-form approximation of the function. One typical approach from optimization theory involves the Taylor series expansion:

$$f(x) = f(x_0) + \frac{\partial f(x)}{\partial x}|_{x=x_0}(x - x_0) + \frac{1}{2}\frac{\partial^2 f(x)}{\partial x^2}|_{x=x_0}(x - x_0)^2 + \cdots$$

$$f(x) = f(x_0) + \sum_{i=1}^{\infty} \frac{1}{i!}\frac{\partial^i f(x)}{\partial x^i}|_{x=x_0}(x - x_0)^i . \tag{5.3}$$

By theorem, the infinite series can be truncated to

$$f(x) = f(x_0) + \frac{\partial f(x)}{\partial x}|_{x=x_0}(x - x_0) + \frac{1}{2}\frac{\partial^2 f(x)}{\partial x^2}|_{x=x_0}(x - x_0)^2 + \frac{1}{6}\frac{\partial^3 f(x)}{\partial x^3}|_{x=x_0}(x - x^*)^3 \text{ for some } x^* \in [x, x_0]. \tag{5.4}$$

The real problem is that we don't know the value of x^*. As a result, we approximate this term with a residual, yielding

$$f(x) = f(x_0) + \frac{\partial f(x)}{\partial x}|_{x=x_0}(x - x_0) + \frac{1}{2}\frac{\partial^2 f(x)}{\partial x^2}|_{x=x_0}(x - x_0)^2 + \epsilon(x - x_0). \tag{5.5}$$

Given this approach, we can conjecture the relative size of the approximation error based on the relative size of the third derivative of the cost function.

Extending this result to vector space, we have

$$f(x) = f(x_0) + \nabla_x f(x_0)(x - x_0) + \frac{1}{2}(x - x_0)' \nabla^2_{xx} f(x_0)(x - x_0) + \epsilon(x - x_0). \quad (5.6)$$

Using the general form of the Taylor series expansion in Equation (5.6), we can express the flexible form of the cost function based on input prices w and output levels y as

$$c(w, y) \doteq C(w, y) = \alpha_0 + \begin{bmatrix} \alpha \\ \beta \end{bmatrix}' \begin{bmatrix} w \\ y \end{bmatrix} + \frac{1}{2} \begin{bmatrix} w \\ y \end{bmatrix}' \begin{bmatrix} A & \Gamma \\ \Gamma' & B \end{bmatrix} \begin{bmatrix} w \\ y \end{bmatrix} \quad (5.7)$$

where $c(w, y)$ is the true cost function, $C(w, y)$ is the flexible approximation to the true cost function, $\alpha = \nabla_w c(w, y)$, $\beta = \nabla_y c(w, y)$, $A = \nabla_{ww} c(w, y)$, $\Gamma = \nabla_{wy} c(w, y)$, and $B = \nabla_{yy} c(w, y)$. The system is typically written as

$$C(w, y) = \alpha_0 + \alpha' w + \frac{1}{2} w' A w + \beta' y + \frac{1}{2} y' B y + w' \Gamma y + \epsilon. \quad (5.8)$$

This form is typically referred to as the quadratic cost function. It is a second-order Taylor series expansion to an unknown cost function. Following the general concept (and ignoring for the moment the error of approximation), Shephard's lemma can be applied to this cost specification:

$$\frac{\partial C(w, y)}{\partial w_i} = x_i^*(w, y) = \alpha_i + A_{i\cdot} w + \Gamma'_{\cdot i} y. \quad (5.9)$$

This general concept gives a system of equations that can be simultaneously estimated (taking the four-input, two-output example):

$$\begin{aligned} C(w, y) &= \alpha_0 + \alpha' w + \frac{1}{2} w' A w + \beta' y \frac{1}{2} y' B y + w' \Gamma y \\ x_1 &= \alpha_1 + A_{11} w_1 + A_{12} w_2 + A_{13} w_3 + A_{14} w_4 + \Gamma_{11} y_1 + \Gamma_{12} y_2 \\ x_2 &= \alpha_2 + A_{12} w_1 + A_{22} w_2 + A_{23} w_3 + A_{24} w_4 + \Gamma_{21} y_1 + \Gamma_{22} y_2 \\ x_3 &= \alpha_3 + A_{13} w_1 + A_{23} w_2 + A_{33} w_3 + A_{34} w_4 + \Gamma_{31} y_1 + \Gamma_{32} y_2. \end{aligned} \quad (5.10)$$

Why have we imposed symmetry? By Young's theorem, $\partial^2 f(x,y)/\partial x\partial y = \partial^2 f(x,y)\,\partial y\partial x$ — so $A_{ij} = A_{ji}$ for any continuous function. Why are we only estimating three demand curves? From the dual function, we know that system "sums up."

One generalization of the Taylor series approach involves a transformation of variables. Specifically, if we assume

$$g(x) = \frac{x^\lambda}{\lambda} \tag{5.11}$$

the cost function can be expressed as

$$\begin{aligned} g\left[C(w,y),\lambda\right] &= \alpha_0 + \alpha' g\left[w,\lambda\right] + \frac{1}{2} g\left[w,\lambda\right]' A g\left[w,\lambda\right] + \beta' g\left[y,\lambda\right] \\ &\quad + \frac{1}{2} g\left[y,\lambda\right]' B g\left[y,\lambda\right] + g\left[w,\lambda\right]' \Gamma g\left[y,\lambda\right] + \epsilon. \end{aligned} \tag{5.12}$$

This transformation complicates Shephard's lemma slightly. Starting with the derivative of the cost function,

$$\begin{aligned} \frac{\partial\left(\dfrac{C(w,y)^\lambda}{\lambda}\right)}{\partial w_i} &= C(w,y)^{\lambda-1}\frac{\partial C(y,w)}{\partial w_i} \\ \Rightarrow \frac{\partial\left(\dfrac{C(w,y)^\lambda}{\lambda}\right)}{\partial w_i} &= C(w,y)^{\lambda-1}x_i \end{aligned} \tag{5.13}$$

(i.e., by Shephard's lemma). Turning to the right-hand side of Equation (5.12),

$$\frac{\partial\left[\dfrac{w^\lambda}{\lambda}\right]}{\partial w} = w^{\lambda-1}. \tag{5.14}$$

Putting the result in Equation (5.13) with the result from Equation (5.14) yields

$$\frac{\partial\left(\dfrac{C(w,y)^\lambda}{\lambda}\right)}{\partial\left(\dfrac{w^\lambda}{\lambda}\right)} = \frac{\partial C(w,y)}{\partial w}\frac{1}{\dfrac{\partial\left(\dfrac{w^\lambda}{\lambda}\right)}{\partial w}} = \left[\frac{C(w,y)}{w}\right]^{\lambda-1}x. \tag{5.15}$$

Letting $\lambda \rightarrow 0$,

$$\lim_{\lambda \rightarrow 0} \frac{w_i^{\lambda}}{\lambda} = \ln\left(w_i\right)$$

$$\lim_{\lambda \rightarrow 0} \left[\frac{C\left(w, y\right)}{w_i}\right]^{\lambda - 1} x_i = \frac{w_i x_i}{C\left(w, y\right)} = f_i \tag{5.16}$$

where f_i is the share of cost spent on input i.

The results of Equation (5.16) leads to the translog cost specification:

$$\begin{aligned}
\ln\left(C\right) &= \alpha_0 + \alpha' \ln\left(w\right) + \frac{1}{2} \ln\left(w\right)' A \ln\left(w\right) + \beta' \ln\left(y\right) \\
&\quad + \frac{1}{2} \ln\left(y\right)' B \ln\left(y\right) + \ln\left(w\right) \Gamma \ln\left(y\right) \\
f_1 &= \alpha_1 + A_{11} \ln\left(w_1\right) + A_{12} \ln\left(w_2\right) + A_{13} \ln\left(w_3\right) \\
&\quad + \Gamma_{11} \ln\left(y_1\right) + \Gamma_{12} \ln\left(y_2\right) \\
f_2 &= \alpha_2 + A_{12} \ln\left(w_1\right) + A_{22} \ln\left(w_2\right) + A_{23} \ln\left(w_3\right) \\
&\quad + \Gamma_{21} \ln\left(y_1\right) + \Gamma_{22} \ln\left(y_2\right) \\
f_3 &= \alpha_3 + A_{13} \ln\left(w_1\right) + A_{23} \ln\left(w_2\right) + A_{33} \ln\left(w_3\right) \\
&\quad + \Gamma_{31} \ln\left(y_1\right) + \Gamma_{32} \ln\left(y_2\right).
\end{aligned} \tag{5.17}$$

While $\lambda = 0$ yields the translog cost specification, $\lambda = 1$ yields the quadratic, and $\lambda = 1/2$ yields the Leontief.

5.1.2 *Fourier Expansion*

A slightly more general expansion is the Fourier expansion which approximates the derivatives of a function. This formulation follows the semi-parametric form of the production function developed in Section 2.7.2. First, consider the univariate form of the Fourier expansion:

$$f\left(x\right) = \alpha_0 \sum_{i=1}^{N} \left[\alpha_i \sin\left(\frac{2\pi x}{\lambda_i}\right) + \beta_i \cos\left(\frac{2\pi x}{\lambda_i}\right)\right] \tag{5.18}$$

where λ_i is a periodicity. Extending this representation to a multivariate form,

$$f(z) = \alpha_0 + b'z + \frac{1}{2}z'Cz$$
$$+ \sum_{\alpha=1}^{A} \left(u_{0\alpha} + 2\sum_{j=1}^{J} \left[u_{j\alpha} \cos\left(j\lambda k'_\alpha z\right) - v_{j\alpha} \sin\left(j\lambda k'_\alpha z\right) \right] \right)$$
$$C = -\lambda^2 \sum_{\alpha=1}^{A} u_{0\alpha} k_\alpha k'_\alpha \tag{5.19}$$

where λ is the periodicity and k_α is referred to as an elementary multi-index:

$$\left\{ k : |k|^* = \sum_{i=1}^{N} |k_i| \leq K \right\} \tag{5.20}$$

(see Chalfant and Gallant (1985)).

In our example, let

$$z = \begin{bmatrix} w_1 \\ w_2 \\ w_3 \\ y_1 \\ y_2 \end{bmatrix}. \tag{5.21}$$

For $K = 1$, we have

$$k_1 = \begin{bmatrix} 1 \\ 0 \\ 0 \\ 0 \\ 0 \\ 0 \end{bmatrix}; \; k_2 = \begin{bmatrix} 0 \\ 1 \\ 0 \\ 0 \\ 0 \\ 0 \end{bmatrix}; \; \cdots k_6 = \begin{bmatrix} 0 \\ 0 \\ 0 \\ 0 \\ 0 \\ 1 \end{bmatrix}. \tag{5.22}$$

If $K = 2$, in addition to the vectors in $K = 1$, we have

$$k_7 = \begin{bmatrix} 2 \\ 0 \\ 0 \\ 0 \\ 0 \\ 0 \end{bmatrix}; \; k_8 = \begin{bmatrix} 1 \\ 1 \\ 0 \\ 0 \\ 0 \\ 0 \end{bmatrix}; \; k_9 = \begin{bmatrix} 1 \\ 0 \\ 2 \\ 0 \\ 0 \\ 0 \end{bmatrix}; \; \cdots k_{12} = \begin{bmatrix} 1 \\ 0 \\ 0 \\ 0 \\ 0 \\ 1 \end{bmatrix};$$

$$k_{13} = \begin{bmatrix} 0 \\ 2 \\ 0 \\ 0 \\ 0 \\ 0 \end{bmatrix};\ k_{14} = \begin{bmatrix} 0 \\ 1 \\ 1 \\ 0 \\ 0 \\ 0 \end{bmatrix} \dots \tag{5.23}$$

This representation minimizes the Sobolev norm, which says it does a better job approximating the derivatives of the function. In fact, it represents up to kth derivative of the function.

Note that if the cost function is specified as a multivariate Fourier expansion, the system of demand equations can be defined by Shephard's lemma.

5.2 Estimation of Cost Systems

5.2.1 *Choice of Estimators*

Regardless of the function form, cost functions are typically estimated as systems of equations using seemingly unrelated regression, iterated seemingly unrelated regression, or maximum likelihood. I prefer maximum likelihood based on a concentrated likelihood function. The likelihood function for a system of equations can be specified as

$$\epsilon_t(\theta) = \begin{bmatrix} C_t - C(w_t, y_t) \\ x_{1t} - x_1(w_t, y_t) \\ \vdots \\ x_{n-1,t} - x_{n-1}(w_t, y_t) \end{bmatrix}$$

$$L \propto -\frac{T}{2}\ln|\Omega| - \frac{1}{2}\sum_{t=1}^{T}\epsilon_t(\theta)'\,\Omega^{-1}\epsilon_t(\theta). \tag{5.24}$$

For any level of θ, the maximum likelihood estimate of Ω is

$$\hat{\Omega}_{ML}(\theta) = \frac{1}{T}\sum_{t=1}^{T}\epsilon_t(\theta)\,\epsilon_t(\theta)'. \tag{5.25}$$

Therefore, the concentrated likelihood function involves substituting the result in Equation (5.25) into Equation (5.24), yielding

$$L \propto -\frac{T}{2} \ln \left| \hat{\Omega}_{ML}(\theta) \right|. \tag{5.26}$$

5.2.2 *Limits to Flexible Functional Forms*

The limitations of Flexible Functional Forms, particularly with respect to the limitations imposed by the Taylor series expansion varieties can be demonstrated in several ways. Chambers demonstrates the limitations of the functional forms based on limitations in imposing separability. These arguments are similar to arguments related to imposing separability on various demand systems (i.e., the AIDS models).

I prefer to demonstrate the limitations to Flexible Function Forms by resorting to the basic notions behind the Taylor Series expansion on which it is based. Specifically, focusing on the residual term from Equation (5.4),

$$\epsilon(x) = \frac{1}{6} \left. \frac{\partial^3 f(x)}{\partial \partial x^3} \right|_{x=x_0} (x - x^*)^3 \tag{5.27}$$

for some $x^* \in [x, x_0]$. As long as the third derivative of the function is non-zero at the point of approximation, we know that the Flexible Functional Form has a "specification" or "approximation" error. Further, if we bring this concept together with our typical notions of sampling theory, this approximation error may confound the estimation of parameters.

Finally, there is a problem with the estimation of a functional form and the point of approximation. Implicitly, we estimate the quadratic cost function, we parameterize the system based on approximations from the arithmetic average. Similarly, if the translog is used, the approximation is from the sample's geometric average. This raises problems from two perspectives. First, the sample average may not adequately represent a relevant production point. Second, this point of approximation plays into outlier problems.

5.2.3 *Aggregation Issues*

Again, issues of aggregation can be addressed at several different levels. One level of aggregation involves the use of a single cost function to depict decisions of numerous farmers. Again, one assumption is that farmers all face similar production functions. If there were heterogeneity in production functions, it would be difficult to argue that a single cost function could be used to approximate all the behaviors of all producers. A more alarming conclusion, however, can be drawn by assuming that all farmers face the same production function, but possess heterogeneous unobserved inputs such as human capital. This difficulty is similar to the aggregation of inputs to be discussed in the following.

An extension to the heterogeneity issue can be found if we parameterize an aggregate cost function. Capalbo and Denny (1986) examine the impact of changes in technology on U.S. agricultural production using a cost function approach:

$$C(w, y) = \alpha_0 + \alpha' w + \frac{1}{2} w' A w + \beta' y + \frac{1}{2} y' B y + w' \Gamma y + \theta t. \quad (5.28)$$

In this formulation, θ can be used to estimate the impact of changes in technology through time (e.g., assuming that the rate of technical change is constant). However, to estimate this model, we must assume that there exists an aggregate cost function. In other words, we could assume that agriculture in the United States is controlled by a single entity that minimizes cost. Alternatively, we could assume that the minimizing behavior of each individual is the same as an aggregate minimization.

A key element in the estimation of cost functions is parsimony. In general, the number of parameters in a quadratic system is

$$\frac{(n+m+1)(n+m)}{2} + (n+m) \quad (5.29)$$

where n is the number of inputs and m is the number of outputs. For accounting purposes in farm-level datasets and for degrees of freedom difficulties when aggregate data is used, we often aggregate inputs and/or outputs. We may aggregate diesel, gasoline, and L.P. gas into a single fuel category. Adding to this, we may aggregate fertilizer with fuel to form an agricultural chemical component. In each of these cases, we make fixed factor assumptions between the aggregated inputs.

Given that these aggregation issues exist, what can be done? One alternative would be to give up on applied work altogether. Another alternative is to use the best data possible, but take a more Bayesian approach — when do the results look right?

5.2.4 *Imposing Restrictions*

Given the development of the cost function, we are particularly interested in imposing three general conditions on the estimated parameters: homogeneity, symmetry, and concavity.

Homogeneity: The cost function is homogeneous of degree one in prices and the demand functions are homogeneous of degree zero in prices. The homogeneity restrictions are typically given by

$$\sum_{i=1}^{n} \alpha_i = 1$$
$$\sum_{j=1}^{n} A_{ij} = 0 \tag{5.30}$$

within the quadratic form, the second result is clear — A_{ij} the matrix of second derivatives which must be singular. One way to visualize these restrictions are through the demand function for each variable:

$$c\left(w,y\right) = \sum_{i=1}^{N} w_i x_i^*\left(w,y\right) \tag{5.31}$$

that is, substitute the input demand functions into the definition of cost. Following the quadratic flexible form,

$$\begin{aligned}\sum_{i=1}^{N} w_i x_i^*\left(w,y\right) &= \sum_{i=1}^{N} w_i\left[\alpha_i + A_{\cdot i}W + \Gamma_k' y\right]\\ &= \sum_{i=1}^{N} w_i\alpha_i + \sum_{i=1}^{N} w_i A_{\cdot i} w + \sum_{i=1}^{N} w_i \Gamma_k' y\\ &\Rightarrow w'Aw = 0 \text{ and } w'\Gamma y = 0\\ \sum_{i=1}^{N} w_i\alpha_i &= C\left(w,y\right) \Rightarrow \sum_{i=1}^{N} \frac{w_i\alpha_i}{C\left(w,y\right)} = 1.\end{aligned} \tag{5.32}$$

Given these restrictions, the next question is: How do we impose homogeneity? One way to impose homogeneity is to manually divide each input price by the last input price and drop a term into the constant:

$$w_i^* = \frac{w_i}{w_N} \tag{5.33}$$

which results in the normalized quadratic specification. In the translog approximation, this leads to the well-known subtraction of the Nth price:

$$ln\left(w_i^*\right) = \ln\left(w_i\right) - \ln\left(w_N\right) \Leftarrow \ln\left(\frac{w_i}{w_N}\right). \tag{5.34}$$

Symmetry: Symmetry is a standard linear restriction (i.e., $A_{ij} = A_{ji}$).

Concavity: As we have discussed, concavity is a result of optimizing behavior. If the cost function is not concave, then taking linear combination in price space could further reduce cost. Thus, a non-concave cost function is inconsistent with economic theory. There are two problems: imposing concavity and rejecting concavity.

I have used three approaches to impose concavity. First, in Featherstone and Moss (1994), I imposed concavity using Lau's decomposition. The simple way to describe this technique is to start with a simple linear model such that

$$x_{1t} = \alpha_0 + A_{11}w_{1t} + \Gamma_{11}y_{1t} + \epsilon_t \tag{5.35}$$

where Equation (5.35) is a single input demand equation. Under normal assumptions, we would anticipate that $A_{11} \ll 0$ or that the derived demand curve should be downward sloping in input price. However, suppose that our results indicated that $A_{11} \gg 0$. One approach to imposing negativity would be to estimate the nonlinear model:

$$x_{1t} = \alpha_0 - \sqrt{\tilde{A}_{11}}\sqrt{\tilde{A}_{11}}w_{1t} + \Gamma_{11}y_{1t} + \epsilon_t \tag{5.36}$$

so that $A_{11} \equiv -\sqrt{\tilde{A}_{11}}\sqrt{\tilde{A}_{11}} \leq 0$. Extending this approach to matrix space, the Lau decomposition is based on

$$w'Aw = x'P'Px = (Px)'(Px) \geq 0. \tag{5.37}$$

Thus, we hypothesize that A can be decomposed into two matrices whose product is positive semi-definite:

$$P = \begin{bmatrix} a_{11} & a_{12} & a_{13} \\ 0 & a_{22} & a_{23} \\ 0 & 0 & a_{33} \end{bmatrix}$$

$$P'P = \begin{bmatrix} a_{11} & 0 & 0 \\ a_{12} & a_{22} & 0 \\ a_{13} & a_{23} & a_{33} \end{bmatrix} \begin{bmatrix} a_{11} & a_{12} & a_{13} \\ 0 & a_{22} & a_{23} \\ 0 & 0 & a_{33} \end{bmatrix}$$

$$= \begin{bmatrix} a_{11}a_{11} & a_{11}a_{12} & a_{11}a_{13} \\ a_{11}a_{12} & a_{12}a_{12} + a_{22}a_{22} & a_{12}a_{13} + a_{22}a_{23} \\ a_{11}a_{13} & a_{12}a_{13} + a_{22}a_{23} & a_{13}a_{13} + a_{23}a_{23} + a_{33}a_{33} \end{bmatrix}. \tag{5.38}$$

The quadratic input price term in the cost function can then be estimated as

$$-\begin{bmatrix} w_1 \\ w_2 \\ w_3 \end{bmatrix}' \begin{bmatrix} a_{11}a_{11} & a_{11}a_{12} & a_{11}a_{13} \\ a_{11}a_{12} & a_{12}a_{12} + a_{22}a_{22} & a_{12}a_{13} + a_{22}a_{23} \\ a_{11}a_{13} & a_{12}a_{13} + a_{22}a_{23} & a_{13}a_{13} + a_{23}a_{23} + a_{33}a_{33} \end{bmatrix} \begin{bmatrix} w_1 \\ w_2 \\ w_3 \end{bmatrix}. \tag{5.39}$$

A second approach used by Talpaz *et al.* (1989) uses the fact that a positive definite symmetric matrix has all positive eigenvalues and a negative definite symmetric matrix has all negative eigenvalues. Thus, we could simply constrain

$$\max[\lambda_i] \leq 0 \ni: \lambda = \text{eigen}(A). \tag{5.40}$$

The final approach to imposing concavity implies a resampling of parameters (e.g., a pseudo-Bayesian technique) using a procedure developed by Terrell (1998). To demonstrate the approach, consider a simple (one equation) formulation of a similar problem. Again, suppose we have a quadratic cost function:

$$C_t = \alpha_0 + \alpha_1 w_{1t} + \alpha_2 w_{2t} + \alpha_3 w_{1t} w_{1t} + \alpha_4 w_{1t} w_{2t} + \alpha_5 w_{2t} w_{2t} + \epsilon_t \tag{5.41}$$

where C_t is the observed cost, w_{1t} and w_{2t} are the input prices and αs are the estimated parameters. Given that we want the derived demand curve to be downward sloping in input prices, we would like to impose

$$\frac{\partial C}{\partial w_1} = \hat{\alpha}_1 + 2\hat{\alpha}_3 \bar{w}_1 + \hat{\alpha}_4 \bar{w}_2 \leq 0 \tag{5.42}$$

where $\hat{\alpha}$s denote the estimated parameters and $\bar{w}_i$ denotes the sample average. Suppose that we estimate the regression and our results are not consistent with Equation (5.42). One alternative would be to resample our results to construct estimates that conform to the desired result. Specifically, using the estimated residuals from Equation (5.41), we construct a bootstrapped sample:

$$\begin{aligned} \tilde{C}_t &= \hat{C}_t + \hat{\epsilon}_s \quad s \in \{\, 1, 2, \ldots, T\} \\ \hat{C}_t &= \hat{\alpha}_0 + \hat{\alpha}_1 w_{1t} + \hat{\alpha}_2 w_{2t} + \hat{\alpha}_3 w_{1t} w_{1t} + \hat{\alpha}_4 w_{1t} w_{2t} + \hat{\alpha}_5 w_{2t} w_{2t} \end{aligned} \tag{5.43}$$

that is, ϵ_s is a randomly drawn error from the sample. Given the new sample of dependent variables, we re-estimate the parameters again (i.e., using ordinary least squares or some other consistent estimator), yielding $\tilde{\alpha}_s$. We then test to see whether the resampled results are consistent with the inequality constraint:

$$\begin{aligned} \frac{\partial C}{\partial w_1} &= \tilde{\alpha}_{1s} + 2\tilde{\alpha}_{3s} \bar{w}_1 + \tilde{\alpha}_{4s} \bar{w}_2 = K_s \\ I_s &= \begin{cases} 1 \text{ if } K_s \leq 0 \\ 0 \text{ otherwise} \end{cases} \end{aligned} \tag{5.44}$$

where I_s is a dummy variable indicating whether the results are consistent with the constraint. The estimated parameters are the average values of the resampled parameters that are consistent with the constraint:

$$\bar{\alpha}_s = \frac{1}{\sum_{s=1}^{S} I_s} \sum_{s=1}^{S} I_s \tilde{\alpha}_s. \tag{5.45}$$

Intuitively, the average of parameters that meet the condition also meets the condition. The resampled data can also be used to estimate the variance of $\bar{\alpha}_s$:

$$V(\bar{\alpha}_s) = \frac{1}{\sum_{s=1}^{S} I_s} \sum_{s=1}^{S} I_s (\alpha_s - \bar{\alpha}_s)(\alpha_s - \bar{\alpha}_s)'. \tag{5.46}$$

The same general approach can be used to impose concavity on flexible dual functions. Specifically, starting with the estimated cost system implied by Equation (5.28) assuming three inputs and two outputs,

$$\begin{aligned}
C_t &= \alpha_0 + \begin{bmatrix}\alpha_1\\ \alpha_2\end{bmatrix}' \begin{bmatrix}w_{1t}^*\\ w_{2t}^*\end{bmatrix} + \frac{1}{2}\begin{bmatrix}w_{1t}^*\\ w_{2t}^*\end{bmatrix}' \begin{bmatrix}A_{11} & A_{12}\\ A_{12} & A_{22}\end{bmatrix}\begin{bmatrix}w_{1t}^*\\ w_{2t}^*\end{bmatrix}\\
&\quad + \begin{bmatrix}\beta_1\\ \beta_2\end{bmatrix}' \begin{bmatrix}y_{1t}\\ y_{2t}\end{bmatrix} + \frac{1}{2}\begin{bmatrix}y_{1t}\\ y_{2t}\end{bmatrix}' \begin{bmatrix}B_{11} & B_{12}\\ B_{12} & B_{22}\end{bmatrix}\begin{bmatrix}y_{1t}\\ y_{2t}\end{bmatrix}\\
&\quad + \begin{bmatrix}w_{1t}^*\\ w_{2t}^*\end{bmatrix}' \begin{bmatrix}\Gamma_{11} & \Gamma_{12}\\ \Gamma_{21} & \Gamma_{22}\end{bmatrix}\begin{bmatrix}y_{1t}\\ y_{2t}\end{bmatrix} + \epsilon_{1t}\\
x_{1t} &= \alpha_1 + A_{11}w_{1t}^* + A_{12}w_{2t}^* + \Gamma_{11}y_{1t} + \Gamma_{21}y_{2t} + \epsilon_{2t}\\
x_{2t} &= \alpha_2 + A_{12}w_{1t}^* + A_{22}w_{2t}^* + \Gamma_{12}y_{1t} + \Gamma_{22}y_{2t} + \epsilon_{3t}\\
w_{it}^* &= \frac{w_{it}}{w_{3t}}
\end{aligned} \tag{5.47}$$

where the formulation in Equation (5.47) imposes homogeneity and symmetry. Assume that we have estimated the system of equations in Equation (5.47), the next step would be to test whether the system was concave in input prices and convex in output levels. To do this, we would compute the eigenvalues of $\hat{A}$ and $\hat{B}$ where these matrices are defined as

$$\hat{A} = \begin{bmatrix} \hat{A}_{11} & \hat{A}_{12} \\ \hat{A}_{12} & \hat{A}_{22} \end{bmatrix} \text{ and } \hat{B} = \begin{bmatrix} \hat{B}_{11} & \hat{B}_{12} \\ B_{12} & B_{22} \end{bmatrix}. \tag{5.48}$$

Note that both matrices are symmetric; hence, all the eigenvalues are real. To be consistent with theory,

$$\begin{aligned} &\max(\lambda_A) \leq 0 \ni: \lambda_A = \text{eigen}\left(\hat{A}\right) \\ &\min(\lambda_B) \geq 0 \ni: \lambda_B = \text{eigen}\left(\hat{B}\right). \end{aligned} \tag{5.49}$$

If one or both conditions in Equation (5.49) fail, we can resample the estimation. Following the procedure outlined in the univariate case, we use the estimated parameters and residuals (now a residual vector) to generate a new set of estimates $\tilde{A}_s$ and/or $\tilde{B}_s$. We then average the resampled values using a modifying Equation (5.44) to be $I_s = 1$ if the estimated matrices are concave or convex.

So, which technique is better for imposing concavity? Mathematically, the first two techniques (e.g., Lau's decomposition and constraining the eigenvalues) are the same. However, numerically, Lau's decomposition may be difficult for large matrices and selecting a starting value is problematic. The derivative of the likelihood function with respect to a_{ij} parameters is zero if $a_{ij} = 0$. In addition, constraining the eigenvalue is feasible but numerically complex. In either case, the solution typically imposes an additional flat space in the solution (e.g., the Hessian of the estimated matrix will probably be zero). However, we may be suspect of the resampling procedure implied in Terrell's method, especially when the sample size is relatively small. So, none of the techniques is perfect. Because of the additional flat space, I have tended toward the resampling approach.

5.3 Elasticities of Substitution

Returning to the general formulation in Section 1.2.4, we are interested in using the empirical dual cost function to estimate the elasticity of substitution between inputs. Specifically, let us return to the basic cost minimization problem:

$$L = w'x + \lambda (y - f(x)) \Rightarrow \begin{cases} \dfrac{\partial L}{\partial x_1} = w_1 - \lambda \dfrac{\partial f}{x_1} = 0 \\ \qquad \vdots \\ \dfrac{\partial L}{\partial x_n} = w_n - \lambda \dfrac{\partial f}{\partial x_n} = 0 \\ \quad y - f(x) = 0 \end{cases}. \tag{5.50}$$

Differentiating the first-order conditions then yields

$$\begin{aligned} d\,w_1 - \lambda \left(\frac{\partial^2 f}{\partial x_1 \partial x_1} d\,x_1 + \cdots \frac{\partial^2 f}{\partial x_1 \partial x_n} \right) - \frac{\partial f}{\partial x_1} d\,\lambda = 0 \\ \cdots \\ d\,w_n - \lambda \left(\frac{\partial^2 f}{\partial x_n \partial x_1} d\,x_1 + \cdots \frac{\partial^2 f}{\partial x_n \partial x_n} \right) - \frac{\partial f}{\partial x_n} d\,\lambda = 0 \\ d\,y - \frac{\partial f}{\partial x_1} d\,x_1 + \cdots \frac{\partial f}{\partial x_n} d\,x_n = 0. \end{aligned} \tag{5.51}$$

As in Section 1.2.4, we can write the system of equations in Equation (5.51) in the form $F d\,x = d\,w$ — specifically,

$$\begin{bmatrix} 0 & -\dfrac{\partial f}{\partial x_1} & -\dfrac{\partial f}{\partial x_2} & \cdots & -\dfrac{\partial f}{\partial x_n} \\ -\dfrac{\partial f}{\partial x_1} & -\lambda \dfrac{\partial^2 f}{\partial x_1 \partial x_1} & -\lambda \dfrac{\partial^2 f}{\partial x_1 \partial x_2} & \cdots & -\lambda \dfrac{\partial^2 f}{\partial x_1 \partial x_n} \\ -\dfrac{\partial f}{\partial x_2} & -\lambda \dfrac{\partial^2 f}{\partial x_1 \partial x_2} & -\lambda \dfrac{\partial^2 f}{\partial x_2 \partial x_2} & \cdots & -\lambda \dfrac{\partial^2 f}{\partial x_2 \partial x_n} \\ \vdots & \vdots & \vdots & \ddots & \vdots \\ -\dfrac{\partial f}{\partial x_n} & -\lambda \dfrac{\partial^2 f}{\partial x_n \partial x_1} & -\lambda \dfrac{\partial^2 f}{\partial x_n \partial x_2} & \cdots & -\lambda \dfrac{\partial^2 f}{\partial x_n \partial x_n} \end{bmatrix} \begin{bmatrix} d\,\lambda \\ d\,x_1 \\ d\,x_2 \\ \vdots \\ d\,x_n \end{bmatrix} = \begin{bmatrix} -d\,y \\ -d\,w_1 \\ -d\,w_2 \\ \vdots \\ -d\,w_n \end{bmatrix}. \tag{5.52}$$

Multiplying each row by a form of $(-\lambda)/(-\lambda)$ yields the "Hamermesh" form:

$$\begin{bmatrix} 0 & \frac{\partial f}{\partial x_1} & \frac{\partial f}{\partial x_2} & \cdots & \frac{\partial f}{\partial x_n} \\ \frac{\partial f}{\partial x_1} & \frac{\partial^2 f}{\partial x_1 \partial x_1} & \frac{\partial^2 f}{\partial x_1 \partial x_2} & \cdots & \frac{\partial^2 f}{\partial x_1 \partial x_n} \\ \frac{\partial f}{\partial x_2} & \frac{\partial^2 f}{\partial x_1 \partial x_2} & \frac{\partial^2 f}{\partial x_2 \partial x_2} & \cdots & \frac{\partial^2 f}{\partial x_2 \partial x_n} \\ \vdots & \vdots & \vdots & \ddots & \vdots \\ \frac{\partial f}{\partial x_n} & \frac{\partial^2 f}{\partial x_n \partial x_1} & \frac{\partial^2 f}{\partial x_n \partial x_2} & \cdots & \frac{\partial^2 f}{\partial x_n \partial x_n} \end{bmatrix} \begin{bmatrix} \frac{d\lambda}{\lambda} \\ d\,x_1 \\ d\,x_2 \\ \vdots \\ d\,x_n \end{bmatrix} = \begin{bmatrix} d\,y \\ \frac{d\,w_1}{\lambda} \\ \frac{d\,w_2}{\lambda} \\ \vdots \\ \frac{d\,w_n}{\lambda} \end{bmatrix}. \tag{5.53}$$

Next, we focus on a specific change — the response of each input demand to a change in w_1. These values can be derived using Cramer's rule. Specifically, setting all the changes except for $d\,w_1$ equal to zero,

$$\begin{bmatrix} 0 & \frac{\partial f}{\partial x_1} & \frac{\partial f}{\partial x_2} & \cdots & \frac{\partial f}{\partial x_n} \\ \frac{\partial f}{\partial x_1} & \frac{\partial^2 f}{\partial x_1 \partial x_1} & \frac{\partial^2 f}{\partial x_1 \partial x_2} & \cdots & \frac{\partial^2 f}{\partial x_1 \partial x_n} \\ \frac{\partial f}{\partial x_2} & \frac{\partial^2 f}{\partial x_1 \partial x_2} & \frac{\partial^2 f}{\partial x_2 \partial x_2} & \cdots & \frac{\partial^2 f}{\partial x_2 \partial x_n} \\ \vdots & \vdots & \vdots & \ddots & \vdots \\ \frac{\partial f}{\partial x_n} & \frac{\partial^2 f}{\partial x_n \partial x_1} & \frac{\partial^2 f}{\partial x_n \partial x_2} & \cdots & \frac{\partial^2 f}{\partial x_n \partial x_n} \end{bmatrix} \begin{bmatrix} \frac{d\lambda}{\lambda} \\ d\,x_1 \\ d\,x_2 \\ \vdots \\ d\,x_n \end{bmatrix} = \begin{bmatrix} 0 \\ \frac{d\,w_1}{\lambda} \\ 0 \\ \vdots \\ 0 \end{bmatrix}. \tag{5.54}$$

Next, divide each side by $d\,w_1$, yielding

$$\begin{bmatrix} 0 & \frac{\partial f}{\partial x_1} & \frac{\partial f}{\partial x_2} & \cdots & \frac{\partial f}{\partial x_n} \\ \frac{\partial f}{\partial x_1} & \frac{\partial^2 f}{\partial x_1 \partial x_1} & \frac{\partial^2 f}{\partial x_1 \partial x_2} & \cdots & \frac{\partial^2 f}{\partial x_1 \partial x_n} \\ \frac{\partial f}{\partial x_2} & \frac{\partial^2 f}{\partial x_1 \partial x_2} & \frac{\partial^2 f}{\partial x_2 \partial x_2} & \cdots & \frac{\partial^2 f}{\partial x_2 \partial x_n} \\ \vdots & \vdots & \vdots & \ddots & \vdots \\ \frac{\partial f}{\partial x_n} & \frac{\partial^2 f}{\partial x_n \partial x_1} & \frac{\partial^2 f}{\partial x_n \partial x_2} & \cdots & \frac{\partial^2 f}{\partial x_n \partial x_n} \end{bmatrix} \begin{bmatrix} \frac{d\lambda}{d\,w_1}\frac{1}{\lambda} \\ \frac{d\,x_1}{d\,w_1} \\ \frac{d\,x_2}{d\,w_1} \\ \vdots \\ \frac{d\,x_n}{d\,w_1} \end{bmatrix} = \begin{bmatrix} 0 \\ \frac{1}{\lambda} \\ 0 \\ \vdots \\ 0 \end{bmatrix}. \tag{5.55}$$

Using Cramer's Rule, we can solve for dx_1/dw_1 by

$$\frac{dx_1}{dw_1} = \frac{\begin{vmatrix} 0 & 0 & \frac{\partial f}{\partial x_2} & \cdots & \frac{\partial f}{\partial x_n} \\ \frac{\partial f}{\partial x_1} & \frac{1}{\lambda} & \frac{\partial^2 f}{\partial x_1 \partial x_2} & \cdots & \frac{\partial^2 f}{\partial x_1 \partial x_n} \\ \frac{\partial f}{\partial x_2} & 0 & \frac{\partial^2 f}{\partial x_2 \partial x_2} & \cdots & \frac{\partial^2 f}{\partial x_2 \partial x_n} \\ \vdots & \vdots & \vdots & \ddots & \vdots \\ \frac{\partial f}{\partial x_n} & 0 & \frac{\partial^2 f}{\partial x_n \partial x_2} & \cdots & \frac{\partial^2 f}{\partial x_n \partial x_n} \end{vmatrix}}{\begin{vmatrix} 0 & \frac{\partial f}{\partial x_1} & \frac{\partial f}{\partial x_2} & \cdots & \frac{\partial f}{\partial x_n} \\ \frac{\partial f}{\partial x_1} & \frac{\partial^2 f}{\partial x_1 \partial x_1} & \frac{\partial^2 f}{\partial x_1 \partial x_2} & \cdots & \frac{\partial^2 f}{\partial x_1 \partial x_n} \\ \frac{\partial f}{\partial x_2} & \frac{\partial^2 f}{\partial x_1 \partial x_2} & \frac{\partial^2 f}{\partial x_2 \partial x_2} & \cdots & \frac{\partial^2 f}{\partial x_2 \partial x_n} \\ \vdots & \vdots & \vdots & \ddots & \vdots \\ \frac{\partial f}{\partial x_n} & \frac{\partial^2 f}{\partial x_n \partial x_1} & \frac{\partial^2 f}{\partial x_n \partial x_2} & \cdots & \frac{\partial^2 f}{\partial x_n \partial x_n} \end{vmatrix}}. \tag{5.56}$$

Hence, following the formulation in Equation (1.139),

$$\frac{dx_1}{dw_1} = \frac{1}{\lambda} \frac{\begin{vmatrix} 0 & 0 & \frac{\partial f}{\partial x_2} & \cdots & \frac{\partial f}{\partial x_n} \\ \frac{\partial f}{\partial x_1} & 1 & \frac{\partial^2 f}{\partial x_1 \partial x_2} & \cdots & \frac{\partial^2 f}{\partial x_1 \partial x_n} \\ \frac{\partial f}{\partial x_2} & 0 & \frac{\partial^2 f}{\partial x_2 \partial x_2} & \cdots & \frac{\partial^2 f}{\partial x_2 \partial x_n} \\ \vdots & \vdots & \vdots & \ddots & \vdots \\ \frac{\partial f}{\partial x_n} & 0 & \frac{\partial^2 f}{\partial x_n \partial x_2} & \cdots & \frac{\partial^2 f}{\partial x_n \partial x_n} \end{vmatrix}}{\begin{vmatrix} 0 & \frac{\partial f}{\partial x_1} & \frac{\partial f}{\partial x_2} & \cdots & \frac{\partial f}{\partial x_n} \\ \frac{\partial f}{\partial x_1} & \frac{\partial^2 f}{\partial x_1 \partial x_1} & \frac{\partial^2 f}{\partial x_1 \partial x_2} & \cdots & \frac{\partial^2 f}{\partial x_1 \partial x_n} \\ \frac{\partial f}{\partial x_2} & \frac{\partial^2 f}{\partial x_1 \partial x_2} & \frac{\partial^2 f}{\partial x_2 \partial x_2} & \cdots & \frac{\partial^2 f}{\partial x_2 \partial x_n} \\ \vdots & \vdots & \vdots & \ddots & \vdots \\ \frac{\partial f}{\partial x_n} & \frac{\partial^2 f}{\partial x_n \partial x_1} & \frac{\partial^2 f}{\partial x_n \partial x_2} & \cdots & \frac{\partial^2 f}{\partial x_n \partial x_n} \end{vmatrix}} = \frac{1}{\lambda} \frac{|F_{ij}|}{|F|}. \tag{5.57}$$

From our discussion in Section 1.2.4, we defined the elasticity of substitution in Equation (1.140):

$$\sigma_{ij} = \frac{\sum_{i=1}^{n} x_i f_i}{x_i x_j} \frac{|F_{ij}|}{|F|} \text{ where } \frac{|F_{ij}|}{|F|} = \left.\frac{dx_i}{dx_j}\right|_{dY=0}.$$

From Equation (5.57),

$$\frac{d\,x_i}{d\,w_j} = \frac{1}{\lambda}\frac{|F_{ij}|}{|F|} \Rightarrow \frac{|F_{ij}|}{|F|} = \lambda \frac{d\,x_i}{d\,w_j}. \tag{5.58}$$

In addition, by the first-order conditions, $f_i = w_i/\lambda$. Putting these two pieces together,

$$\sigma_{ij} = \frac{\sum_{k=1}^{n} x_k \left(\frac{w_k}{\lambda}\right)}{x_i x_j}\left(\lambda \frac{d\,x_i}{d\,w_j}\right) = \frac{\sum_{k=1}^{n} x_k w_k}{x_i x_j} \frac{\partial^2 c\,(w,y)}{\partial w_i \partial w_j}. \tag{5.59}$$

Cleaning up the notation in Equation (5.59) a little bit,

$$\sigma_{ij} = \frac{c\,(w,y)}{\dfrac{\partial c\,(w,y)}{\partial w_i}\dfrac{\partial c\,(w,y)}{\partial w_j}} \frac{\partial^2 c\,(w,y)}{\partial w_i \partial w_j}. \tag{5.60}$$

5.4 Empirical Examples of Cost Specifications

5.4.1 *Quadratic Cost Function*

As a starting point, let us consider the estimation of the original formulation of the cost function (i.e., without normalization by one input price). The dataset Quad-11-10-16.csv[1] was generated from

[1]This dataset is available at http://www.charlesbmoss.com:8080/Book.Production.Economics/Chapter-5/Quad-11-10-16.csv.

quadratic production function:

$$y = -54.2868 + \begin{bmatrix} -0.04821 \\ 0.1003 \\ 3.4294 \end{bmatrix}' \begin{bmatrix} x_1 \\ x_2 \\ x_3 \end{bmatrix}$$
$$+\frac{1}{2}\begin{bmatrix} x_1 \\ x_2 \\ x_3 \end{bmatrix}' \begin{bmatrix} -0.005625 & 0.01172 & 0.006094 \\ -0.01172 & -0.06250 & 0.2844 \\ 0.006094 & 0.02844 & -0.1056 \end{bmatrix} \begin{bmatrix} x_1 \\ x_2 \\ x_3 \end{bmatrix} + \varsigma \tag{5.61}$$

where ς is a random variable which is distributed $\Gamma(0.05, 1.25)$. The input levels were derived from profit-maximizing behavior for a randomly drawn vector of input and output prices. The simulated yield is then the optimal yield minus the randomly generated ς. The first 25 observations of this dataset are presented in Table 5.1.

Here, we want to demonstrate how we can use R to estimate the $N = 3$, $M = 1$, a quadratic cost system using maximum likelihood. As a first step, consider estimating a simple quadratic model for cost:

$$C_i = \alpha_0 + \alpha_1 y_i + \alpha_2 y_i^2 + \epsilon_i \tag{5.62}$$

using maximum likelihood. For this example, we will use the first 50 values of C and Y for Quad-11-10-16.csv presented in Table 5.2.

The first step is to assume a likelihood function. The typical assumption of convenience is the normal distribution. In addition, instead of maximizing the likelihood, most researchers choose to maximize the natural logarithm of the normal likelihood function:

$$\ln\left(L\left(\{\, C_i, y_i\}\,_{i=1}^{N} \left|\alpha_0, \alpha_1, \alpha_2, \sigma^2\right.\right)\right) = -\frac{N}{2}\ln\left(\sigma^2\right)$$
$$-\frac{1}{2\sigma^2}\sum_{i=1}^{N}\left[C_i - \alpha_0 - \alpha_1 y_i - \alpha_2 y_i^2\right]^2 \tag{5.63}$$

(see (Moss, 2014, pp. 271–278)). Typically, we concentrate the variance parameter (σ^2) by choosing its optimal value

$$\sigma_{ML}^2 = \frac{1}{N}\sum_{i=1}^{N}\left(C_i - \alpha_0 - \alpha_1 y_i - \alpha_2 y_i^2\right)^2. \tag{5.64}$$

Table 5.1 First 25 Observations of Quad-11-10-16.csv

p_y	w_1	w_2	w_3	Profit	Cost	y	x_1	x_2	x_3
3.0161	0.8229	0.2664	0.5491	59.9424	78.0628	45.7557	61.0998	28.5724	36.7318
3.5656	0.7137	0.1173	0.5198	98.2465	75.5441	48.7413	69.8637	32.8573	41.9887
3.4179	0.8611	0.2056	0.5603	75.7794	80.7443	45.7958	62.3338	29.3629	37.5382
3.6807	1.0623	0.3335	0.3781	79.9530	89.6165	46.0698	61.9472	29.0866	37.3182
2.7158	0.7564	0.1339	0.4441	57.8408	63.2158	44.5746	58.0660	27.6945	35.0892
3.8321	0.2847	0.2989	0.4903	137.5163	54.3928	50.0796	76.1364	34.9055	45.4373
3.6957	0.5203	0.2534	0.3540	118.9190	63.1090	49.2538	74.2718	34.4205	44.4837
3.1267	0.6941	0.1577	0.3913	82.2352	67.6718	47.9434	67.4077	31.7370	40.5714
3.6448	0.8824	0.3085	0.4843	86.3074	83.5219	46.5955	63.3681	29.6570	38.1125
3.8240	0.3104	0.0685	0.4239	146.0600	47.9203	50.7276	80.3978	37.4223	48.1350
3.8467	0.5458	0.2283	0.4948	121.2805	68.2694	49.2757	72.0160	33.3925	43.1336
2.8133	1.0386	0.3356	0.3995	42.6354	73.1076	41.1420	50.7571	24.1409	30.7640
3.6894	0.6672	0.1659	0.5228	102.1799	77.1104	48.5964	72.8851	34.0077	43.6934
2.8195	0.7928	0.2981	0.2708	61.8339	67.6518	45.9251	61.7488	28.9225	37.1960
3.3898	0.8106	0.1213	0.5005	82.4376	73.2841	45.9384	62.6443	29.6795	37.7743
4.0850	0.5189	0.2823	0.7059	122.7813	78.0750	49.1695	72.8756	33.6452	43.5779
3.5866	0.6570	0.3751	0.3059	102.0148	71.4096	48.3531	70.4536	32.5230	42.2319
3.6459	0.4966	0.3742	0.2932	117.7060	62.5407	49.4387	74.1149	34.0516	44.3284
3.5404	0.8495	0.3323	0.5786	79.4505	84.1332	46.2055	62.2143	29.0529	37.3792
3.4874	0.9397	0.2301	0.6527	71.6483	88.4163	45.8977	61.3321	28.9574	36.9485
3.6128	0.5539	0.1632	0.6489	104.5366	70.7105	48.5068	69.3962	32.3413	41.5998
3.7098	1.0357	0.3564	0.1817	82.3569	82.0802	44.3253	62.5030	29.4368	37.7365
3.2135	0.9870	0.2829	0.2404	67.2787	75.2762	44.3608	59.4445	28.1571	35.9433
3.5706	0.5235	0.2141	0.6316	101.8379	69.0499	47.8592	68.9787	32.0015	41.3035
4.3651	0.5832	0.1370	0.5522	139.6425	70.3120	48.0982	71.8322	33.6250	43.1198

Table 5.2 First 50 Observations of Cost and Output Levels

Cost	Output	Cost	Output
78.0628	45.7557	69.9756	46.6451
75.5441	48.7413	83.2198	41.3470
80.7443	45.7958	67.2822	48.0087
89.6165	46.0698	69.3915	38.8549
63.2158	44.5746	81.2308	46.8841
54.3928	50.0796	83.9510	44.8450
63.1090	49.2538	67.1763	49.6810
67.6718	47.9434	78.0296	45.0663
83.5219	46.5955	72.3940	49.3069
47.9203	50.7276	73.8403	43.0680
68.2694	49.2757	92.2462	45.3225
73.1076	41.1420	88.1850	43.5719
77.1104	48.5964	93.7272	44.7304
67.6518	45.9251	96.1181	47.2842
73.2841	45.9384	84.4306	46.4602
78.0750	49.1695	75.4786	48.4936
71.4096	48.3531	83.1851	46.0323
62.5407	49.4387	94.0239	42.9721
84.1332	46.2055	75.2241	48.0364
88.4163	45.8977	77.4479	44.8782
70.7105	48.5068	63.5159	46.8231
82.0802	44.3253	79.1255	47.3623
75.2762	44.3608	80.3350	48.3132
69.0499	47.8592	83.9782	47.2459
70.3120	48.0982	92.9421	46.2081

Substituting the result of Equation (5.64) into the log-likelihood function in Equation (5.64) yields

$$\ln\left(L\left(\{\ C_i, y_i\}\ _{i=1}^{N} |\alpha_0, \alpha_1, \alpha_2\right)\right)$$
$$= -\frac{N}{2}\ln\left(\frac{1}{N}\sum_{i=1}^{N}\left(C_i - \alpha_0 - \alpha_1 y_i - \alpha_2 y_i^2\right)^2\right) \qquad (5.65)$$

(see (Moss, 2014, pp. 176–177)). Up until this point, most students are used to solving the maximization problem in Equation (5.65) analytically (e.g., taking the derivatives by hand and numerically solving the first-order conditions). In fact, the maximization problem in Equation (5.65) is simple enough for this approach — the derivatives of the likelihood functions yield the "normal equations" from regression theory. However, given that the system likelihood formulations do not allow this approach, consider solving this problem using numerical methods. Most computer programs have procedures for optimization, but consider the implementation of the Equation (5.65) in R.

R Code — Simple Maximum Likelihood

```
 library(Rsolnp)

dta <- read.csv(file="Quad-11-10-16.csv")

simpleML <- function(a) {
  err <- dta[,"cst"]-(a[1]+a[2]*dta[,"y"]+a[3]*dta[,"y"]^2)
  sig <- t(err)%*%err/nrow(dta)
  return(as.numeric((nrow(dta)/2)*log(sig)))
}

a0 <- c(0.01,0.01,0.01)

res1 <- solnp(a0,simpleML)

print(res1$pars)

$
```

The first line of the R Code loads the procedure solnp (in the Rsolnp library Ghalanos and Theussl (2015)), which will be used to find the numeric maximum likelihood. The second line loads the dataset from a comma-separated values file (SmallQuad-11-10-16.csv). The next five lines of the code specifies the likelihood function (simpleML) which is a function of an unknown set of parameters (a). The second line in the routine specifies the errors based on the three parameters:

```
 err <- dta[,"cst"] - (a[1]+a[2]*dta[,"y"]+a[3]*dta[,"y"}^2)
```

The data vector of observed cost values are denoted dta[,"cst"] while the data for output level is dta[,"y"]. The unknown parameters are a[1] — α_0, a[2] — α_1, and a[3] — α_2. The third line of the code estimates the variance (denoted sig) as a function of estimated errors. Finally, the fourth line returns the negative of the log-likelihood function computed from the estimated variance. We use the negative of the likelihood function because **Rsolnp** minimizes the function's value. The eighth line of the code sets our initial guess at what is the optimal value. The ninth line calls the optimx procedure using a_0 as the initial guess, minimizing simpleML. The term method="BFGS" instructs optimx to use the Broyden–Fletcher–Goldfarm–Shanno algorithm which uses a numeric approximation of the Hessian matrix. The optimal values will be stored in a variable called res1. Finally, the last line of the program prints the values that optimize the likelihood.

Executing this code yields the result

```
[1] -268.0388462  13.7920001  -0.1422832
```

Hence, these are the estimated values of the parameters that maximize the likelihood function for the sample. To test this solution, consider the ordinary least squares estimates of these parameters from R in Table 5.3.

Next, we extend the cost function specification to the general quadratic form for $N = 3$ and $M = 1$. Based on Equation (5.10),

Table 5.3 Ordinary Least Squares Estimates of Cost–Output Model

Variable	Estimate
Constant	-268.0813^{**}
	(122.3654)[a]
y	13.7940^{**}
	(5.7864)
y^2	-0.1423^{**}
	(0.0679)

Notes: [a]Numbers in parenthesis denote standard errors.
**Denotes statistical significance at the 0.05 level of confidence.

this cost system becomes

$$c(w,y) = a_0 + \begin{bmatrix} a_1 \\ a_2 \\ a_3 \end{bmatrix}' \begin{bmatrix} w_1 \\ w_2 \\ w_3 \end{bmatrix} + \frac{1}{2} \begin{bmatrix} w_1 \\ w_2 \\ w_3 \end{bmatrix}' \begin{bmatrix} A_{11} & A_{12} & A_{13} \\ A_{12} & A_{22} & A_{23} \\ A_{13} & A_{23} & A_{33} \end{bmatrix} \begin{bmatrix} w_1 \\ w_2 \\ w_3 \end{bmatrix}$$
$$+ b_1 y + \frac{1}{2} b_2 y^2 + \begin{bmatrix} w_1 \\ w_2 \\ w_3 \end{bmatrix}' \begin{bmatrix} g_1 \\ g_2 \\ g_3 \end{bmatrix} y + \varsigma_1$$
$$x_1 = a_1 + A_{11} w_1 + A_{12} w_2 + A_{13} w_3 + g_1 y + \varsigma_2$$
$$x_2 = a_2 + A_{12} w_1 + A_{22} w_2 + A_{23} w_3 + g_2 y + \varsigma_3 \qquad (5.66)$$

where ς_i are errors. Note that we have imposed symmetry. In addition, while there are three demand functions, we can only estimate two of them with the cost function due to summing-up restrictions.

Assuming multivariate normality, the concentrated logarithmic likelihood function can be written, as specified in Equation (5.26):

$$L = -\frac{N}{2} \ln |\Omega_{ML}(\theta)|$$
$$\Omega_{ML} = \frac{1}{N} \sum_{i=1}^{N} \begin{bmatrix} \varsigma_{1i} \\ \varsigma_{2i} \\ \varsigma_{3i} \end{bmatrix} \begin{bmatrix} \varsigma_{1i} & \varsigma_{2i} & \varsigma_{3i} \end{bmatrix}.$$

Following the simple maximum likelihood example, we can write the likelihood function for the cost specification in Equation (5.66) as

R Code — General Quadratic Cost Function

```
quadlike <- function(a) {
  err <- matrix(0,nrow(dta),3)
  err[,1] <- dta[,"cst"]-(a[1]+a[2]*dta[,"w1"]+a[3]*dta[,"w2"]+a[4]*dta[,"w3"]+
                         a[5]*dta[,"w1"]*dta[,"w1"]/2+a[6]*dta[,"w1"]*dta[,"w2"]+
                         a[7]*dta[,"w1"]*dta[,"w3"]+a[8]*dta[,"w2"]*dta[,"w2"]/2+
                         a[9]*dta[,"w2"]*dta[,"w3"]+a[10]*dta[,"w3"]*dta[,"w3"]/2+
                         a[11]*dta[,"y"]+a[12]*dta[,"y"]*dta[,"y"]/2+
                         a[13]*dta[,"y"]*dta[,"w1"]+a[14]*dta[,"y"]*dta[,"w2"]+
                         a[15]*dta[,"y"]*dta[,"w3"])
  err[,2] <- dta[,"x1"] -(a[2]+a[5]*dta[,"w1"]+a[6]*dta[,"w2"]+a[7]*dta[,"w3"]+a[13]
  *dta[,"y"])
  err[,3] <- dta[,"x2"] -(a[3]+a[6]*dta[,"w1"]+a[8]*dta[,"w2"]+a[9]*dta[,"w3"]+a[14]
  *dta[,"y"])
  return(nrow(err)*log(det(t(err)%*%err/2)))
}
```

Table 5.4 List of Theoretical Parameters and R Code Parameters

Theoretical	Estimation	Theoretical	Estimation
a_0	a[1]	A_{23}	a[9]
a_1	a[2]	A_{33}	a[10]
a_2	a[3]	b_1	a[11]
a_3	a[4]	b_2	a[12]
A_{11}	a[5]	g_1	a[13]
A_{12}	a[6]	g_2	a[14]
A_{13}	a[7]	g_3	a[15]
A_{22}	a[8]		

In order to make the code a little more accessible, Table 5.4 provides the parameters in Equation (5.66) associated with each of the parameters in the R Code. Another change in the current code involves the selection of the initial conditions. Specifically, we will use the results of a regression form of the linear cost function in order to reduce the search time.

R Code — Setting the Initial Guess Using Ordinary Least Squares Estimates

```
bols <- lm(cst ~ w1 + w2 + w3,data=dta)

a0     <- matrix(0.005,15,1)
a0[1] <- bols$coefficients[4]
a0[2] <- bols$coefficients[1]
a0[3] <- bols$coefficients[2]
a0[4] <- bols$coefficients[3]
```

Further, we are going to use a different procedure for numerical optimization (**solnp** from the R-Project package (Ghalanos and Theussl (2015))

```
res1 <- solnp(a0,quadlike)
```

Table 5.5 Parameters that Maximize the Likelihood of the General Quadratic Cost

Theoretical	Estimation	Value	Theoretical	Estimation	Value
a_0	a[1]	38.3874	A_{23}	a[9]	−24.3400
a_1	a[2]	−127.4069	A_{33}	a[10]	−15.9473
a_2	a[3]	115.8392	b_1	a[11]	−2.2171
a_3	a[4]	39.1441	b_2	a[12]	0.0120
A_{11}	a[5]	−27.2510	g_1	a[13]	4.1888
A_{12}	a[6]	34.1728	g_2	a[14]	−1.9131
A_{13}	a[7]	14.4881	g_3	a[15]	−0.0001
A_{22}	a[8]	−59.9422			

The results of the estimation are presented in Table 5.5. For the moment, we ignore how the variance estimates can be derived from the likelihood function.

Returning to some of the question raised in Chapter 4, we have estimated a mathematical model that has cost on the left-hand side of the equation, but can we demonstrate that the estimated function is a dual cost function, that is, does it have the characteristics that are consistent with optimizing behavior from either Diewert or Shephard?

At this point, let us focus on five characteristics: (1) the demand curves are downward sloping in input prices, (2) the input demand system is concave in input, (3) the cost function is homogeneous in input prices, (4) the cost system is upward sloping in output level, and (5) the cost function is concave in output levels.

Consider whether the demand for x_1 is downward sloping (and hopefully positive). Given the estimates in Table 5.5, we can write the estimated demand for x_1 as

$$x_1 = -127.4069 - 27.2510w_1 + 34.1728w_2 + 14.4881w_3 + 4.1888y. \tag{5.67}$$

From Equation (5.67), the demand function is downward sloping in w_1. The real question is whether the value of the demand curve is positive in some relevant range. To address this question, we examine the characteristics of the demand functions around the sample mean

Table 5.6 Sample Averages for Input Levels and Prices

Variable	Mean	Variable	Mean
x_1	57.3450	w_1	0.7558
x_2	29.4271	w_2	0.2540
x_3	35.9952	w_3	0.4509
y	45.2783		

(with the mean values presented in Table 5.6). Substituting in these average values for w_2, w_3, and y, the demand equation for x_1 becomes

$$x_1 = 77.4674 - 27.2510 w_1. \tag{5.68}$$

So, the demand for x_1 at the mean of w_1 is 56.8718. Similarly, the demand curve for x_2 and x_3 is downward slopping in the area around the mean and the estimated value of x_2 at mean input prices and output levels is 29.6069 and that for x_3 is 36.7167. Hence, the function is consistent with the first characteristic of the cost function.

Next, we turn to the question of concavity in the input price space, or the Hessian of the cost function with respect to input prices. Given the quadratic specification in Equation (5.66), the Hessian matrix is constant:

$$A = \begin{bmatrix} A_{11} & A_{12} & A_{13} \\ A_{12} & A_{22} & A_{23} \\ A_{13} & A_{23} & A_{33} \end{bmatrix} = \begin{bmatrix} -27.2510 & 34.1728 & 14.4881 \\ 34.1728 & -56.9422 & -24.3400 \\ 14.4881 & -24.3400 & -15.9473 \end{bmatrix}. \tag{5.69}$$

To determine whether the Hessian is negative definite, we can examine its eigenvalues. Specifically, if a matrix is real-valued and symmetric, all of its eigenvalues are real. Further, if the maximum eigenvalue is negative (e.g., all the eigenvalues are negative), then the matrix is negative definite. Alternatively, if the minimum eigenvalue is positive, the matrix is positive definite. Given the results in Equation (5.69), the eigenvalues of A are as follows: 3.8317, −6.1592, and −90.1497 — so, the matrix is negative definite and the cost system is concave in input prices.

Turning to homogeneity, it is not as much the product of optimizing behavior, but it is imposed by the linear nature of the cost function:

$$c(w, y) = w_1 x_1 (w, y) + w_2 x_2 (w, y) + w_3 x_3 (w, y). \tag{5.70}$$

By its very structure in Equation (5.70), the cost function should be homogeneous in input prices. To derive the mathematical form of the property, we turn to Euler's homogenous function theorem. Given the definition of homogeneity of degree n,

$$f(tw_1, tw_2, tw_3) = t^n f(w_1, w_2, w_3). \tag{5.71}$$

Taking the derivative of the left-hand side of Equation (5.71) with respect to t yields

$$\begin{aligned} \frac{\partial f(tw_1, tw_2, tw_3)}{\partial t} &= \frac{\partial f}{\partial tw_1}\frac{\partial tw_1}{\partial t} + \frac{\partial f}{\partial tw_2}\frac{\partial tw_2}{\partial t} + \frac{\partial f}{\partial tw_3}\frac{\partial tw_3}{\partial t} \\ &= \frac{\partial f}{\partial tw_1} w_1 + \frac{\partial f}{\partial tw_2} w_2 + \frac{\partial f}{\partial tw_3} w_3. \end{aligned} \tag{5.72}$$

Taking the derivative of the right-hand side of Equation (5.71) with respect to t yields

$$\frac{\partial t^n f(w_1, w_2, w_3)}{\partial t} = n t^{n-1} f(w_1, w_2, w_3). \tag{5.73}$$

Equating Equations (5.72) and (5.73) and letting $t \to 1$ yield

$$\frac{\partial f}{\partial w_1} w_1 + \frac{\partial f}{\partial w_2} w_2 + \frac{\partial f}{\partial w_3} w_3 = n f(w_1, w_2, w_3). \tag{5.74}$$

Given that we are interested in showing that the cost function is homogeneous of degree one ($n = 1$), $nf(w_1, w_2, w_3) = f(w_1, w_2, w_3)$.

To examine whether the estimated cost function is homogeneous of degree one, we replace $f(w_1, w_2, w_3)$ with the cost function $c(w_1, w_2, w_3, y)$. Applying Shephard's lemma to this cost function and substituting the results into Equation (5.74) yields

$$\frac{\partial c}{\partial w_1} w_1 + \frac{\partial c}{\partial w_2} w_2 + \frac{\partial c}{\partial w_3} w_3$$
$$= x_1(w,y)\, w_1 + x_2(w,y)\, w_2 + x_3(w,y)\, w_3 = c(w,y)$$
$$\Rightarrow \frac{x_1(w,y)\, w_1}{c(w,y)} + \frac{x_2(w,y)\, w_2}{c(w,y)} + \frac{x_3(w,y)\, w_3}{c(w,y)} = 1. \qquad (5.75)$$

Substituting the derived demand curves into Equation (5.75) yields

$$1 = \frac{(a_1 + A_{11}w_1 + A_{12}w_2 + A_{13}w_3 + g_1 y)\, w_1}{\hat{c}} + \frac{(a_2 + A_{12}w_1 + A_{22}w_2 + A_{23}w_3 + g_2 y)\, w_2}{\hat{c}} + \frac{(a_3 + A_{13}w_1 + A_{23}w_2 + A_{33}w_3 + g_3 y)\, w_3}{\hat{c}}. \qquad (5.76)$$

Given the estimated parameters in Table 5.5 and the mean values of the input prices and the level of output in Table 5.6, the estimated value of the right-hand side of Equation (5.76) is 1.0215. Hence, the estimate system appears to be homogeneous of degree one.

Next, we turn to the conditions involving output. Again, the marginal cost of output can be derived from the quadratic cost function specification as

$$\frac{\partial c(w,y)}{\partial y} = -2.2171 + 0.0566y + 4.1888w_1 - 1.9131w_2 - 0.0001w_3. \qquad (5.77)$$

Hence, the marginal cost function is increasing in the level of output — the cost function is convex in output level. Again, we need to check to be sure that the estimated value of marginal cost is positive around the sample mean. Again, substituting in the values of the average input prices, Equation (5.77) becomes

$$\frac{\partial c(w,y)}{\partial y} = 0.4628 + 0.0566y. \qquad (5.78)$$

Hence, results of the cost function are consistent with optimizing behavior.

Table 5.7 Price Elasticity of Inputs Demanded

Input Level	Input Price 1	2	3
1	−0.3621	0.8724	0.2982
2	0.1526	−0.4886	−0.1684
3	0.1149	−0.3708	−0.1959

So, the cost function appears to be consistent with optimization behavior — is our analysis complete? No, given the cost function is consistent, we can shift to economic analysis. Why did you estimate the cost function in the first place? For example, we may be interested in the effect of a policy on producers that would increase the price they would pay for one of the inputs. In this case, we may be interested in computing the price elasticity of the derived demand for the inputs. For example, suppose that some policy would increase the price paid for input 1. We can compute the effect on the amount of input 1 used by the producer through the price elasticity of demand for each input. Starting with input 1,

$$\zeta_{11} = \frac{\%\Delta x_1}{\%\Delta w_1} = \frac{\partial x_1(w,y)}{\partial w_1}\frac{w_1}{x_1(w,y)}. \tag{5.79}$$

Substituting the parameters of the general quadratic function into Equation (5.79) yields

$$\zeta_{11} = A_{11}\frac{w_1}{a_1 + A_{11}w_1 + A_{12}w_2 + A_{13}w_3}. \tag{5.80}$$

For completeness, consider the response of quantity of input 2 used to a change in the price of input 1:

$$\zeta_{21} = A_{12}\frac{w_1}{a_2 + A_{12}w_1 + A_{22}w_2 + A_{23}w_3}. \tag{5.81}$$

Table 5.7 presents the estimated price elasticity of each input with respect to changes in each input price.

In addition, we may be interested in the elasticity of substitution between inputs, as developed in Section 5.3. Following Equation 5.61,

Table 5.8 Computed Elasticities of Input Substitution

	1	2	3
1	−0.5531	1.3324	0.4555
2	1.3324	−4.2653	−1.4700
3	0.4555	−1.4700	−0.7766

we can compute

$$\sigma_{ij} = \frac{\hat{c}\left(w, y\right)}{\left(a_i + A_{i1}w_1 + A_{i2}w_2 + A_{i3}w_3\right)} A_{ij}. \tag{5.82}$$

The estimated values for these elasticities are presented in Table 5.8.

Finally, let us take up the estimation of the variance of the parameter estimates. To provide some context, let us return to the simple least squares formulation in Equation (5.62). Under typical assumptions, the values of this model can be estimated using ordinary least squares:

$$\begin{bmatrix} \hat{\alpha}_0 \\ \hat{\alpha}_1 \\ \hat{\alpha}_2 \end{bmatrix} = \left[X'X\right]^{-1}\left(X'c\right) \tag{5.83}$$

where X is a matrix with $x_i = \left(1 \; y_i \; y_i^2\right)$ for $i = 1, \ldots, n$ and c is a vector of observed cost levels. Given this formulation and assuming that the residuals are normally distributed, we typically compute the variance matrix of the estimated coefficients as

$$V\begin{pmatrix} \hat{\alpha}_0 \\ \hat{\alpha}_1 \\ \hat{\alpha}_2 \end{pmatrix} = \hat{s}^2\left[X'X\right]$$

$$\hat{s}^2 = \frac{1}{n-1}\left(c - x\begin{bmatrix} \hat{\alpha}_0 \\ \hat{\alpha}_1 \\ \hat{\alpha}_2 \end{bmatrix}\right)'\left(c - x\begin{bmatrix} \hat{\alpha}_0 \\ \hat{\alpha}_1 \\ \hat{\alpha}_2 \end{bmatrix}\right). \tag{5.84}$$

Alternatively, under maximum likelihood, we assume that the variance of the parameters obtains the Cramer–Rao lower bound:

Table 5.9 Comparing Maximum Likelihood with Ordinary Least Squares Variance

Parameter	Maximum Likelihood	OLS	V_{ML}/V_{OLS}
$N = 50$			
α_0	95.6761	122.3654	0.7819
α_1	4.5313	5.7864	0.7831
α_2	0.05336	0.06786	0.7864
$N = 100$			
α_0	77.6947	82.0558	0.9467
α_1	3.6377	3.8395	0.9474
α_2	0.04232	0.04460	0.9491
$N = 150$			
α_0	56.8524	63.5571	0.8945
α_1	2.6601	2.9732	0.8947
α_2	0.03093	0.03453	0.8957
$N = 200$			
α_0	53.8858	53.3669	1.0097
α_1	2.5331	2.5097	0.1.0093
α_2	0.02954	0.02929	1.0087

$$Var\left(\beta\right) = \left[-E\left(\frac{\partial^2 L\left(\theta\right)}{\partial\theta\partial\theta'}\right)\right]^{-1}. \tag{5.85}$$

Remember that $L\left(\theta\right)$ is defined as the log-likelihood function. Hence, we compute the variance of the parameters as the inverse of the Hessian matrix from the likelihood function. Next question: Does this really work? Table 5.9 presents the estimated parameter standard deviations (e.g., the square root of own variances) using Equation (5.85) (e.g., maximum likelihood) and Equation (5.84) (e.g., or typical least squares estimator). In general, the estimates of the standard deviation for the parameters are of the same order, but the estimated standard deviations for Equation (5.85) are somewhat smaller.

A third way to estimate the variance matrix for the estimated coefficients is by bootstrapping, originally introduced by Efron (1981). To explain the approach, assume that we have estimated the function

$$c_i = \alpha_0 + \alpha_1 y_i + \alpha_2 y_i^2 + \varepsilon_i. \tag{5.86}$$

After estimating the model, we can generate the expected (or estimated value) dependent variable ($\hat{c}_i$) and the estimated value of the residual (ε_i) for each observation. For the first 20 values of our dataset, these values are presented in columns 3 and 4 of Table 5.10. Next, assume that we randomly draw from the estimated residuals and add their value to the estimated cost values. For example, suppose that we randomly draw $k = 20$. We can construct a new first observation by

$$\tilde{c}_1 = \hat{c}_1 + \varepsilon_{20}. \tag{5.87}$$

We can proceed and construct a new dataset (i.e., see columns 6 and 7 of Table 5.10 for one possible set of draws for the first 10 values). Given this new set of data, we can estimate a new set of coefficients using maximum likelihood which we will call $\tilde{\alpha}_k$. Suppose we repeated this procedure K times, we could then use this information to construct an estimate of the variance of the parameter vector

$$V(\alpha) = \sum_{k=1}^{K} (\alpha_k - \hat{\alpha})(\alpha_k - \hat{\alpha})'. \tag{5.88}$$

The bootstrapping approach is robust (e.g., it is independent of some of the distributional assumptions inherent in the other two approaches). However, the estimated standard deviations are typically much larger than those from maximum likelihood or ordinary least squares.

Table 5.11 presents the estimated coefficients and the standard deviations for those coefficients (in parenthesis) for the general quadratic cost function computed using the Cramer–Rao lower bound. Table 5.12 presents the estimated coefficients and the standard deviations computed using Efron's bootstrapping.

Regardless of the procedure used to estimate the variance matrix, several of the hypotheses that we are interested in testing involve more than one parameter. Taking a simple example, consider our hypothesis that the amount of x_i demanded must be greater than or equal to zero from Equation (5.67):

$$x_1 = a_1 + A_{11}\bar{w}_1 + A_{12}\bar{w}_2 + A_{13}\bar{w}_3 + g_1\bar{y}. \tag{5.89}$$

Applying the estimated coefficients and the means for the exogenous variables (i.e., in Equation (5.68)), we know that the expected value

Table 5.10 Bootstrapping Simple Linear Model

Obs.	c	y	$\hat{c}$	$\hat{\varepsilon}$	$\tilde{\varepsilon}_1$	$\tilde{c}_1$	$\tilde{\varepsilon}_2$	$\tilde{c}_2$	$\tilde{\varepsilon}_3$	$\tilde{c}_3$
1	53.0426	47.4454	66.0392	−12.9966	−4.6162	61.4230	8.9853	75.0246	−8.7314	57.3079
2	51.1910	39.0271	53.5094	−2.3183	−1.2151	52.2943	−12.2480	41.2614	17.3427	70.8521
3	50.7295	37.1746	48.0448	2.6847	−7.3010	40.7439	−13.6668	34.3781	−3.1290	44.9159
4	71.9088	49.3398	66.0792	5.8296	4.2848	70.3640	−17.9564	48.1229	9.0146	75.0939
5	60.3624	43.1755	62.2041	−1.8418	−6.7351	55.4691	17.3427	79.5469	5.8296	68.0337
6	61.4705	48.2093	66.1782	−4.7077	3.3822	69.5604	2.6847	68.8629	−9.7099	56.4684
7	62.0766	48.4281	66.1874	−4.1108	−17.1851	49.0023	−5.7083	60.4792	−17.9564	48.2311
8	55.4715	39.9400	55.8430	−0.3715	−12.2480	43.5950	−2.2231	53.6200	16.7223	72.5653
9	59.4486	48.6345	66.1837	−6.7351	−4.7077	61.4759	9.4566	75.6402	−4.1108	62.0728
10	44.6342	36.8109	46.8573	−2.2231	−8.2688	38.5884	−3.1818	43.6755	4.6435	51.5008
11	58.6529	47.1848	65.9538	−7.3010	14.2693	80.2231	−1.8418	64.1120	3.3822	69.3360
12	88.1669	46.1629	65.4325	22.7344	−2.2231	63.2094	−8.7314	56.7011	4.2848	69.7173
13	73.3238	43.3396	62.4475	10.8764	8.9349	71.3823	−4.7077	57.7397	8.7589	71.2063
14	43.8038	41.1087	58.4844	−14.6806	−8.7314	49.7530	5.8296	64.3140	−12.2480	46.2364
15	58.6969	37.6962	49.6822	9.0146	−0.3715	49.3107	9.0146	58.6969	8.9349	58.6171
16	62.9277	49.4261	66.0567	−3.1290	−1.8418	64.2149	−2.5378	63.5189	4.2626	70.3193
17	78.7115	43.0346	61.9892	16.7223	4.2626	66.2518	8.9349	70.9241	−4.7077	57.2815
18	75.4713	47.3644	66.0148	9.4566	−14.6806	51.3342	−0.3715	65.6433	−1.8418	64.1730
19	44.9101	38.4039	51.7801	−6.8701	−2.3183	49.4618	8.8428	60.6229	8.8651	60.6453
20	82.2486	45.4653	64.9059	17.3427	8.8428	73.7487	8.0096	72.9154	10.4027	75.3086

Table 5.11 Estimated Parameters of the Quadratic Cost Function with Standard Errors using the Cramer–Rao Lower Bound

Parameter	Estimate	Parameter	Estimate
a_0	38.3874 (116.5467)[a]	A_{23}	−24.3400 (19.6704)
a_1	−127.4069 (81.4292)	A_{33}	−15.9473 (86.7732)
a_2	115.8392* (66.5606)	b_1	−2.2171 (4.924)
a_3	39.1441 (79.1444)	b_2	0.0566 (0.1115)
A_{11}	−27.2510 (30.8323)	g_1	4.1888** (1.7316)
A_{12}	34.1728 (29.0267)	g_2	−1.9131 (1.3324)
A_{13}	14.4881 (29.6187)	g_3	−0.0001 (2.1369)
A_{22}	−56.9422* (34.2184)		

Notes: [a]Numbers in parenthesis denote standard errors.
**,*Denote statistical significance at the 0.05, 0.10 levels of confidence respectively.

Table 5.12 Estimated Parameters of the Quadratic Cost Function with Standard Errors Using Efron's Bootstrapping

Parameter	Estimate	Parameter	Estimate
a_0	38.3874 (51.5684)[a]	A_{23}	−24.3400 (56.3113)
a_1	−127.4069 (117.9468)	A_{33}	−15.9473 (60.1105)
a_2	115.8392 (146.1148)	b_1	−2.2171 (50.9826)
a_3	39.1441 (62.8613)	b_2	0.0566 (50.7192)
A_{11}	−27.2510 (59.5025)	g_1	4.1888 (51.2436)
A_{12}	34.1728 (59.3153)	g_2	−1.9131 (51.0148)
A_{13}	14.4881 (53.0577)	g_3	−0.0001 (50.7231)
A_{22}	−56.9422 (79.0489)		

Note: [a]Numbers in parenthesis denote standard errors.

of Equation (5.89) is 56.8738. To test whether or not this value is statistically different from zero, we need to derive the variance for Equation (5.89). Obviously, if the restriction is linear, this is relatively straightforward. In this case,

$$\sigma_R^2 = \begin{bmatrix} 0 \\ 1 \\ 0 \\ 0 \\ \bar{w}_1 \\ \bar{w}_2 \\ \bar{w}_3 \\ 0 \\ 0 \\ 0 \\ 0 \\ 0 \\ \bar{y} \\ 0 \\ 0 \end{bmatrix}' \hat{\Sigma}_{aa} \begin{bmatrix} 0 \\ 1 \\ 0 \\ 0 \\ \bar{w}_1 \\ \bar{w}_2 \\ \bar{w}_3 \\ 0 \\ 0 \\ 0 \\ 0 \\ 0 \\ \bar{y} \\ 0 \\ 0 \end{bmatrix} = 10.03602 \tag{5.90}$$

where $\hat{\Sigma}_{aa}$ is the estimated parameter variance matrix. The estimated value of the variance for this constraint implies a z of 18.5163, which can be rejected at any traditional level of statistical significance.

Of course, not all the results that we are interested in are linear which complicates the derivation of such test significantly. For example, we may be interested in whether our homogeneity result in Equation (5.76) is statistically different from 1.0. Rewriting Equation (5.76) and combining terms yield

$$\hat{T}(\theta) = \frac{\hat{K}(\theta)}{\hat{c}(\theta)} = 1$$

$$\begin{aligned} \hat{K}(\theta) = {} & \hat{a}_1\bar{w}_1 + \hat{a}_2\bar{w}_2 + \hat{a}_3\bar{w}_3 + \hat{A}_{11}\bar{w}_1\bar{w}_1 + 2\hat{A}_{12}\bar{w}_1\bar{w}_2 \\ & + 2\hat{A}_{13}\bar{w}_1\bar{w}_3 + \hat{A}_{22}\bar{w}_2\bar{w}_2 + 2\hat{A}_{23}\bar{w}_2\bar{w}_3 \\ & + \hat{A}_{33}\bar{w}_3\bar{w}_3 + \hat{g}_1\bar{y} + \hat{g}_2\bar{y} + \hat{g}_3\bar{y} \end{aligned}$$

$$\begin{aligned}\hat{c}(\theta) &= \hat{a}_0 + \hat{a}_1\bar{w}_1 + \hat{a}_2\bar{w}_2 + \hat{a}_3\bar{w}_3 + \frac{1}{2}\hat{A}_{11}\bar{w}_1\bar{w}_1 + \hat{A}_{12}\bar{w}_1\bar{w}_2 \\ &\quad + \hat{A}_{13}\bar{w}_1\bar{w}_3 + \frac{1}{2}\hat{A}_{22}\bar{w}_2\bar{w}_2 + \hat{A}_{23}\bar{w}_2\bar{w}_3 \\ &\quad + \frac{1}{2}\hat{A}_{33}\bar{w}_3\bar{w}_3 + \hat{b}_1\bar{y} + \frac{1}{2}b_2\bar{y}^2 + \hat{g}_1\bar{y}\bar{w}_1 + \hat{g}_2\bar{y}\bar{w}_2 + \hat{g}_3\bar{y}\bar{w}_3 \end{aligned} \tag{5.91}$$

where $\hat{c}(\theta)$ emphasizes the fact that the denominator is a function of estimated parameters; hence, we have to recognize their variability in deriving the variance of the homogeneity statistic. Hence, we are interested in deriving a normal statistic based on

$$z_{T(\theta)} = T(\theta) - 1. \tag{5.92}$$

If $z_{T(\theta)}$ is not statistically different from zero, we would fail to reject the hypothesis that the cost function is homogenous of degree one. The question is: How do we do this given the complexity of Equation (5.91)?

The answer is referred to as the "delta" approach. To derive this approach, we start with a first-order Taylor series expansion of $T(\theta)$:

$$\begin{aligned} T(\theta) &= T(\theta_0) + \nabla_\theta T(\theta_0)'(\theta - \theta_0) \\ T(\theta) - T(\theta_0) &= \nabla_\theta T(\theta_0)'(\theta - \theta_0) \\ (T(\theta) - T(\theta_0))^2 &= \nabla_\theta T(\theta_0)'[\theta - \theta_0][\theta - \theta_0]'\nabla_\theta T(\theta_0). \end{aligned} \tag{5.93}$$

where $\nabla_\theta T(\theta_0)$ is the vector of derivatives with respect to the estimated parameters θ at their estimated values (i.e., θ_0). Taking the expectation of Equation (5.93) yields

$$\mathrm{E}\left[\left(\hat{T}(\theta) - (\theta_0)\right)^2\right] = \nabla_\theta \hat{T}(\theta_0)'\Sigma_{aa}\nabla_\theta \hat{T}(\theta_0). \tag{5.94}$$

The simulated values for $\hat{c}(\theta)$, $\hat{K}(\theta)$, and $\hat{T}(\theta)$ are presented in Table 5.13.

Table 5.13 Simulated θ from the General Quadratic Cost Function

Draw	$\hat{c}(\theta)$	$\hat{K}(\theta)$	$\hat{T}(\theta)$	a_0	a_1	$\cdots$	g_3
1	−186.1678	7.8428	−0.0421	−75.4753	−193.4486	$\cdots$	0.0342
2	66.7358	16.6857	0.2500	31.8187	−181.6175	$\cdots$	−0.0297
3	95.3418	75.8788	0.7959	94.4611	−129.1316	$\cdots$	0.0124
4	250.9581	26.0509	0.1038	174.5314	−154.1352	$\cdots$	−0.0324
5	52.1726	56.9761	1.0921	136.8009	−148.9824	$\cdots$	0.0421
6	196.6943	87.9158	0.4470	201.1085	−147.3333	$\cdots$	0.0293
7	−65.4432	86.1905	−1.3170	−107.8341	−100.2757	$\cdots$	0.0024
8	251.7793	−27.1508	−0.1078	274.0893	−249.7551	$\cdots$	−0.0195
9	155.0408	91.0504	0.5873	47.8787	−135.5633	$\cdots$	−0.0304
10	−133.4810	−2.0902	0.0157	−16.8358	−222.5331	$\cdots$	0.0237
11	160.8550	39.0208	0.2426	302.9876	−147.9811	$\cdots$	0.0618
12	−70.2829	98.8354	−1.4063	−83.9889	−76.2572	$\cdots$	0.0231
13	−222.2886	14.4444	−0.0650	−105.1283	−182.1751	$\cdots$	0.0418
14	−50.9928	52.5754	−1.0310	0.4418	−168.0085	$\cdots$	0.0240
15	−211.3940	7.8576	−0.0372	−41.8907	−195.7174	$\cdots$	0.0755
16	234.6550	72.9995	0.3111	239.3950	−124.8822	$\cdots$	0.0241
17	−29.7228	60.4941	−2.0353	−110.6646	−205.1650	$\cdots$	−0.0206
18	219.1682	−0.3993	−0.0018	−12.3198	−227.5110	$\cdots$	−0.1250
19	219.8399	154.3673	0.7022	153.9636	−44.6138	$\cdots$	0.0206
20	42.1045	23.9269	0.5683	32.9137	−204.3698	$\cdots$	−0.0013

Using the formulation of $T(\theta)$ defined in Equation (5.91),

$$\frac{\partial \hat{T}(\theta)}{\partial \theta_j} = \frac{\partial \hat{K}(\theta)}{\partial \theta_j}\frac{1}{\hat{c}(\theta)} - \frac{\partial \hat{c}(\theta)}{\partial \theta_j}\frac{\hat{K}(\theta)}{[\hat{c}(\theta)]^2}. \tag{5.95}$$

Consider the derivative with respect to $\hat{a}_0$ (e.g., a parameter that affects $\hat{c}(\theta)$, but does not affect $\hat{K}(\theta)$):

$$\frac{\partial \hat{T}(\theta)}{\partial \hat{a}_0} = -\frac{\partial \hat{c}(\theta)}{\partial a_0}\frac{\hat{K}(\theta)}{[\hat{c}(\theta)]^2} = -\frac{\hat{K}(\theta)}{[\hat{c}(\theta)]^2}. \tag{5.96}$$

Next, consider the derivative with respect to $\hat{a}_1$ (e.g., a parameter that affects both $\hat{c}(\theta)$ and $\hat{K}(\theta)$):

$$\frac{\partial \hat{T}(\theta)}{\partial \hat{a}_1} = \bar{w}_1\frac{1}{\hat{c}(\theta)} - w_1\frac{\hat{K}(\theta)}{\hat{c}(\theta)^2}. \tag{5.97}$$

The variance for the homogeneity test then becomes

$$\nabla_\theta T(\theta) = \begin{bmatrix} -\dfrac{\hat{K}(\theta)}{\hat{c}(\theta)} \\ \dfrac{w_1}{\hat{c}(\theta)} - \dfrac{w_1\hat{K}(\theta)}{\hat{c}(\theta)^2} \\ \dfrac{w_2}{\hat{c}(\theta)} - \dfrac{w_2\hat{K}(\theta)}{\hat{c}(\theta)^2} \\ \dfrac{w_3}{\hat{c}(\theta)} - \dfrac{w_3\hat{K}(\theta)}{\hat{c}(\theta)^2} \\ \dfrac{w_1w_1}{\hat{c}(\theta)} - \dfrac{w_1w_1\hat{K}(\theta)}{2\hat{c}(\theta)^2} \\ \dfrac{2w_1w_2}{\hat{c}(\theta)} - \dfrac{w_1w_2\hat{K}(\theta)}{\hat{c}(\theta)^2} \\ \dfrac{2w_1w_3}{\hat{c}(\theta)} - \dfrac{w_1w_3\hat{K}(\theta)}{\hat{c}(\theta)^2} \\ \dfrac{w_2w_2}{\hat{c}(\theta)} - \dfrac{w_2w_2\hat{K}(\theta)}{2\hat{c}(\theta)^2} \\ \dfrac{2w_2w_3}{\hat{c}(\theta)} - \dfrac{w_2w_3\hat{K}(\theta)}{\hat{c}(\theta)^2} \\ \dfrac{w_3w_3}{\hat{c}(\theta)} - \dfrac{w_3w_3\hat{K}(\theta)}{2\hat{c}(\theta)^2} \\ 0 \\ 0 \\ \dfrac{yw_1}{\hat{c}(\theta)} - \dfrac{yw_1\hat{K}(\theta)}{\hat{c}(\theta)^2} \\ \dfrac{yw_2}{\hat{c}(\theta)} - \dfrac{yw_2\hat{K}(\theta)}{\hat{c}(\theta)^2} \\ \dfrac{yw_3}{\hat{c}(\theta)} - \dfrac{yw_3\hat{K}(\theta)}{\hat{c}(\theta)^2} \end{bmatrix}. \tag{5.98}$$

$$\sigma_T^2 = \nabla_\theta T(\theta)' \, \Sigma_{\theta\theta} \nabla_\theta T(\theta)$$

The variance by delta method is 12,225.89 which implies a standard deviation of 110.5707. Hence, the test for whether or not the estimated cost system is homogeneous is

$$z = \frac{1.0215 - 1.0}{110.5707} \sim N(0,1) \tag{5.99}$$

which can be rejected at any conventional confidence level. Hence, we conclude that the cost function is homogeneous of degree 1.

Apart from the delta method, there are two other techniques to estimate the variance of the homogeneity equation, both are based on simulation. The first involves using simulated parameters from the maximum likelihood estimation to estimate the variance of the linear restriction. Specifically, we assume that the estimated parameter vector from maximum likelihood is $\hat{\theta}_{ML}$ and the variance of those parameters computed using the Cramer–Rao lower bound is $\hat{\Sigma}_{\theta\theta'}$. Given these values, we can draw a random vector of parameters θ_k:

$$\theta_k = \hat{\theta}_{ML} + \text{Chol}\left(\hat{\Sigma}_{\theta\theta'}\right) \varsigma_k \tag{5.100}$$

where Chol(A) denotes the Cholesky decomposition of a matrix A. The simulated values of $T(\theta)$ can then be used to compute the variance:

$$\sigma_T^2 = \sum_{k=1}^{K} \left(T(\theta_k) - T(\theta_{ML})\right)^2. \tag{5.101}$$

The variance by simulation is 5,142.54 and standard deviation is 71.7115.

Finally, following Equation (5.87), we can estimate the variance of the homogeneity condition using Efron's bootstrapping. Specifically, we can compute $T(\theta_k)$ for each set of estimates (i.e., each outcome in Table 5.10). The variance by bootstrapping is 0.002647 and standard deviation is 0.05145.

5.4.2 *Normalized Quadratic Cost Function*

Most of the preceding scenarios involved whether or not the general quadratic cost function satisfied the homogeneity condition.

In general, we demonstrated that the estimated parameters satisfied this property. However, what do we do if the estimated parameters do not conform to the conditions developed in Equation (5.32)? As a starting point for this discussion, let us start from a very general form of the quadratic cost function:

$$
\begin{aligned}
c(w,y) = a_0 &+ \begin{bmatrix} a_1 \\ a_2 \\ \vdots \\ a_N \end{bmatrix}' \begin{bmatrix} w_1 \\ w_2 \\ \vdots \\ w_N \end{bmatrix} \\
&+ \frac{1}{2} \begin{bmatrix} w_1 \\ w_2 \\ \vdots \\ w_N \end{bmatrix}' \begin{bmatrix} A_{11} & A_{12} & \cdots & A_{1N} \\ A_{12} & A_{22} & \cdots & A_{2N} \\ \vdots & \vdots & \ddots & \vdots \\ A_{N1} & A_{N2} & \cdots & A_{NN} \end{bmatrix} \begin{bmatrix} w_1 \\ w_2 \\ \vdots \\ w_N \end{bmatrix} \\
&+ \begin{bmatrix} b_1 \\ b_2 \\ \vdots \\ b_m \end{bmatrix}' \begin{bmatrix} y_1 \\ y_2 \\ \vdots \\ y_M \end{bmatrix} + \frac{1}{2} \begin{bmatrix} y_1 \\ y_2 \\ \vdots \\ y_M \end{bmatrix}' \begin{bmatrix} B_{11} & B_{12} & \cdots & B_{1M} \\ B_{21} & B_{22} & \cdots & B_{2M} \\ \vdots & \vdots & \ddots & \vdots \\ B_{M1} & B_{M2} & \cdots & B_{MM} \end{bmatrix} \begin{bmatrix} y_1 \\ y_2 \\ \vdots \\ y_M \end{bmatrix} \\
&+ \begin{bmatrix} y_1 \\ y_2 \\ \vdots \\ y_M \end{bmatrix}' \begin{bmatrix} G_{11} & G_{12} & \cdots & G_{1N} \\ G_{21} & G_{22} & \vdots & G_{2N} \\ \vdots & \vdots & \ddots & \vdots \\ G_{M1} & G_{M2} & \cdots & G_{MN} \end{bmatrix} \begin{bmatrix} w_1 \\ w_2 \\ \vdots \\ w_N \end{bmatrix}
\end{aligned}
$$

$$
\begin{aligned}
\sum_{i=1}^{N} a_i &= 1 \\
\sum_{i=1}^{N} A_{ij} &= 0 \, \forall j \\
\sum_{i=1}^{N} G_{ik} &= 0 \, \forall k. \qquad (5.102)
\end{aligned}
$$

Using the estimated coefficients from the general quadratic cost function,

$$\sum_{i=1}^{3}\frac{w_i a_i}{\hat{c}(w,y)} = \frac{0.7627\times -41.6417}{81.2894}+\frac{0.2537\times 4.8022}{81.2894}$$
$$+\frac{0.4399\times 31.8071}{81.2894} = -2.48602$$

$$\sum_{i=1}^{3} A_{i1} = -6.0315 + 0.6205 + 0.1674 = 21.4099$$

$$\sum_{i=1}^{3} A_{i2} = 0.6205 - 4.6381 - 1.0874 = -50.1094$$

$$\sum_{i=1}^{3} A_{i3} = 0.1674 - 1.0874 - 8.5981 = -25.7992$$

$$\sum_{i=1}^{3} g_i = 3.6091 + 0.9370 + 0.5040 = 2.2758. \qquad (5.103)$$

Hence, while the system approaches homogeneity, the system does not meet the standard conditions. Implicitly, the foregoing estimates trade summing up in the linear terms for summing up in a quadratic term. For example, the linear terms may add up to a small positive while the quadratic terms sum to a small negative.

Several possible functional forms have been suggested to impose homogeneity on dual functions. One popular form is the normalized dual function developed by Lau (1976). While Lau develops his results for the dual profit function, consider the three-input one-output cost function introduced in Equation (5.66). Specifically, we equate the empirical value of the cost function with our dual approximation:

$$c(w,y) = w_1x_1 + w_2x_2 + w_3x_3$$
$$= a_0 + \begin{bmatrix} a_1\\ a_2\\ a_3\end{bmatrix}'\begin{bmatrix} w_1\\ w_2\\ w_3\end{bmatrix} + \frac{1}{2}\begin{bmatrix} w_1\\ w_2\\ w_3\end{bmatrix}'\begin{bmatrix} A_{11} & A_{12} & A_{13}\\ A_{12} & A_{22} & A_{23}\\ A_{13} & A_{23} & A_{33}\end{bmatrix}\begin{bmatrix} w_1\\ w_2\\ w_3\end{bmatrix}$$
$$+ b_1 y + \frac{1}{2}b_2 y^2 + \begin{bmatrix} w_1\\ w_2\\ w_3\end{bmatrix}'\begin{bmatrix} g_1\\ g_2\\ g_3\end{bmatrix} y. \qquad (5.104)$$

Next, assume that we normalize the representation by each of the input prices by a numeraire price — in this case, w_3:

$$\begin{aligned} c\left(w^*, y\right) &= \frac{c\left(w, y\right)}{w_3} = \frac{w_1}{w_3}x_1 + \frac{w_2}{w_3}x_2 + x_3 \\ &= a_0 + \begin{bmatrix} a_1 \\ a_2 \\ a_3 \end{bmatrix}' \begin{bmatrix} \frac{w_1}{w_3} \\ \frac{w_2}{w_3} \\ 1 \end{bmatrix} + \frac{1}{2} \begin{bmatrix} \frac{w_1}{w_3} \\ \frac{w_2}{w_3} \\ 1 \end{bmatrix}' \begin{bmatrix} A_{11} & A_{12} & A_{13} \\ A_{12} & A_{22} & A_{23} \\ A_{13} & A_{23} & A_{33} \end{bmatrix} \begin{bmatrix} \frac{w_1}{w_3} \\ \frac{w_2}{w_3} \\ 1 \end{bmatrix} \\ &\quad + b_1 y + \frac{1}{2} b_2 y^2 + \begin{bmatrix} \frac{w_1}{w_3} \\ \frac{w_2}{w_3} \\ 1 \end{bmatrix}' \begin{bmatrix} g_1 \\ g_2 \\ g_3 \end{bmatrix} y. \end{aligned} \tag{5.105}$$

Rewriting Equation (5.106) slightly,

$$\begin{aligned} c\left(w^*, y\right) &= a_0 + \begin{bmatrix} a_1 \\ a_2 \end{bmatrix}' \begin{bmatrix} w_1^* \\ w_2^* \end{bmatrix} \\ &\quad + \frac{1}{2} \begin{bmatrix} w_1^* \\ w_2^* \end{bmatrix}' \begin{bmatrix} A_{11} & A_{12} \\ A_{12} & A_{22} \end{bmatrix} \begin{bmatrix} w_1^* \\ w_2^* \end{bmatrix} \\ &\quad + b_1 y + \frac{1}{2} b_2 y^2 + \begin{bmatrix} w_1^* \\ w_2^* \end{bmatrix}' \begin{bmatrix} g_1 \\ g_2 \end{bmatrix} \\ &\quad + a_3 + 2A_{13} w_1^* + 2A_{23} w_2^* + A_{33} + g_3 y \end{aligned} \tag{5.106}$$

where $w_1^* = w_1/w_3$ and $w_2^* = w_2/w_3$. Collecting terms in Equation (5.107),

$$\begin{aligned} c\left(w^*, y\right) &= \left(a_0 + a_3 + A_{33}\right) + \begin{bmatrix} a_1 + 2A_{13} \\ a_2 + 2A_{23} \end{bmatrix}' \begin{bmatrix} w_1^* \\ w_2^* \end{bmatrix} \\ &\quad + \frac{1}{2} \begin{bmatrix} w_1^* \\ w_2^* \end{bmatrix}' \begin{bmatrix} A_{11} & A_{12} \\ A_{12} & A_{22} \end{bmatrix} \begin{bmatrix} w_1^* \\ w_2^* \end{bmatrix} \\ &\quad + \left(b_1 + g_3\right) y + \frac{1}{2} b_2 y^2 + \begin{bmatrix} w_1^* \\ w_2^* \end{bmatrix}' \begin{bmatrix} g_1 \\ g_2 \end{bmatrix}. \end{aligned} \tag{5.107}$$

Simplifying the notation slightly, we have

$$\begin{aligned} c\left(w^{*},y\right) = a_0^{*} &+ \begin{bmatrix} a_1^{*} \\ a_2^{*} \end{bmatrix}' \begin{bmatrix} w_1^{*} \\ w_2^{*} \end{bmatrix} \\ &+ \frac{1}{2} \begin{bmatrix} w_1^{*} \\ w_2^{*} \end{bmatrix}' \begin{bmatrix} A_{11} & A_{12} \\ A_{12} & A_{22} \end{bmatrix} \begin{bmatrix} w_1^{*} \\ w_2^{*} \end{bmatrix} \\ &+ b_1^{*} y + \frac{1}{2} b_2 y^2 + \begin{bmatrix} w_1^{*} \\ w_2^{*} \end{bmatrix}' \begin{bmatrix} g_1 \\ g_2 \end{bmatrix} \end{aligned} \tag{5.108}$$

where the * parameters denote parameters whose values are different from the general quadratic.

Following Lau (1976), the normalized cost function obeys Shephard's lemma; hence,

$$\begin{aligned} x_1^{*}\left(w^{*},y\right) &= a_1^{*} + A_{11}w_1^{*} + A_{12}w_2^{*} + g_1 y \\ x_2^{*}\left(w^{*},y\right) &= a_2^{*} + A_{12}w_1^{*} + A_{22}w_2^{*} + g_2 y. \end{aligned} \tag{5.109}$$

Note that we lose one of the demand equations because summing up now occurs over a smaller set of demand equations.

The parameter estimates for the normalized quadratic cost function are presented in Table 5.14.

5.4.3 *McFadden Cost Function*

Diewert and Wales (1987) proposed the McFadden cost system to impose concavity conditions globally. Specifically, their cost function can be written as

$$\begin{aligned} c\left(w,y\right) &= g\left(w\right)y + \sum_{i=1}^{N} b_{ii} w_i y + \sum_{i=1}^{N} b_i w_i + b_{yy}\left(\sum_{i=1}^{N} \theta_i w_i\right)^2 \\ g\left(w\right) &= \frac{1}{2w_1} \sum_{i=2}^{N}\sum_{j=2}^{N} c_{ij} w_i w_j \text{ s.t. } c_{ij} = c_{ji} \end{aligned} \tag{5.110}$$

where c is negative definite. Diewert and Wales assume that b_i, b_{ii}, and θ_i are pre-selected by the researcher. However, they also note that additional flexibility may be accomplished when these parameters can be identified (Diewert and Wales, 1987, p. 58). To apply

Table 5.14 Estimates of the Normalized Quadratic Cost Function

Parameter	Estimate	Parameter	Estimate
a_0^*	253.8439	A_{22}	−6.7244
	(429.1960)[a]		(22.6675)
a_1^*	−154.8710	b_1^*	−10.716
	(51.0088)		(19.8038)
a_2^*	157.2930***	b_2	0.2289
	(161.3609)		(0.4583)
A_{11}	−1.4875	g_1	4.7024***
	(2.6294)		(1.1098)
A_{12}	3.4402	g_2	−2.9078
	(7.9650)		(3.5539)

Notes: [a]Numbers in parenthesis denote standard errors. ***Denotes statistical significance at the 0.01 level of confidence.

Shephard's lemma to Equation (5.110), we start by deriving the general form:

$$\frac{\partial c\left(w,y\right)}{\partial w_i}=\frac{\partial g\left(w\right)}{\partial w_i}y+b_{ii}y+b_i+2b_{yy}\theta_i\left(\sum_{i=1}^{N}\theta_i w_i\right). \tag{5.111}$$

Taking two cases — first, $i = 1$ yields

$$\frac{\partial g\left(w\right)}{\partial w_1}=-\frac{1}{2w_1^2}\sum_{i=2}^{N}\sum_{j=2}^{N}c_{ij}w_i w_j. \tag{5.112}$$

When $i = 2, \ldots, N$,

$$\frac{\partial g\left(w\right)}{\partial w_i}=\frac{1}{w_1}\sum_{j=1}^{N}c_{ij}w_j. \tag{5.113}$$

Table 5.15 presents the estimated parameters and the standard deviations for the McFadden applied to the PseudoData-2016.csv[2] data. The likelihood function used to estimate this formulation in R is as follows:

[2]This data is available at http://www.charlesbmoss.com:8080/Book.Production.Economics/Chapter-5/PsuedoData-2016.csv.

Table 5.15 Estimates of the McFadden Cost System

Parameter	Estimate	Parameter	Estimate
c_{11}	-0.1091 (0.3065)[a]	b_2	118.4978*** (19.9856)
c_{12}	0.033 (0.1197)	b_3	30.8927 (25.6377)
c_{13}	-0.0144 (0.0488)	b_{yy}	-3.5112*** (0.9241)
b_{11}	4.2266*** (0.6395)	θ_1	-1.5294*** (0.4733)
b_{22}	-1.9123*** (0.3809)	θ_2	2.4837*** (0.5349)
b_{33}	0.1241 (0.5431)	θ_3	1.2228** (0.5286)
b_1	-135.9337*** (28.9348)		

Notes: [a]Numbers in parenthesis denote standard errors. ***,**Denote statistical significance at the 0.01, 0.05 levels of confidence respectively.

R Code – Unrestricted McFadden Likelihood Function

```
mcfaddenlike <- function(a) {
  ghat  <- (a[1]*dta[,"w2"]*dta[,"w2"]+2*a[2]*dta[,"w2"]*dta[,"w3"]+
            a[3]*dta[,"w3"]*dta[,"w3"])/(2*dta[,"w1"])
  chat  <- ghat*dta[,"y"]+a[4]*dta[,"w1"]*dta[,"y"]+a[5]*dta[,"w2"]
           *dta[,"y"]+
           a[6]*dta[,"w3"]*dta[,"y"]+a[7]*dta[,"w1"]+a[8]*dta[,"w2"]+
           a[9]*dta[,"w3"]+a[10]*(a[11]*dta[,"w1"]+a[12]*dta[,"w2"]+
           a[13]*dta[,"w3"])^2
  x1hat <- -ghat/(2*dta[,"w1"]^2)*dta[,"y"]+a[4]*dta[,"y"]+a[7]+2
           *a[10]*a[11]*
           (a[11]*dta[,"w1"]+a[12]*dta[,"w2"]+a[13]*dta[,"w3"])
  x2hat <- (a[1]*dta[,"w2"]+a[2]*dta[,"w3"])/dta[,"w1"]+a[5]*dta
           [,"y"]+a[8]+
           2*a[10]*a[12]*(a[11]*dta[,"w1"]+a[12]*dta[,"w2"]+a[13]*dta
           [,"w3"])
  err <- cbind(dta[,"cst"]-chat,dta[,"x1"]-x1hat,dta[,"x2"]-x2hat)
  return(log(nrow(err)*det(t(err)%*%err/2)))
}
```

Note that c

$$c = \begin{bmatrix} -0.1091 & 0.0033 \\ 0.0033 & -0.0144 \end{bmatrix} \tag{5.114}$$

is negative definite.

Returning to our previous discussion on concavity, there are two ways to impose the proper concavity on the McFadden cost function if your results are not negative definite. The first as described in Equation (5.38) is

$$c^* = \begin{bmatrix} c_{11}^* & 0 \\ c_{12}^* & c_{22}^* \end{bmatrix} \begin{bmatrix} c_{11}^* & c_{12}^* \\ 0 & c_{22}^* \end{bmatrix} = \begin{bmatrix} c_{11}^* c_{11}^* & c_{11}^* c_{12}^* \\ c_{11}^* c_{12}^* & c_{12}^* c_{12}^* + c_{22}^* c_{22}^* \end{bmatrix}. \tag{5.115}$$

The likelihood to implement the constrained McFadden cost system in R is as follows:

R Code — Constrained McFadden Likelihood Function

```
constlike <- function(a) {
  ghat  <- (-a[1]*a[1]*dta[,"w2"]*dta[,"w2"]-2*a[1]*a[2]*dta[,"w2"]
           *dta[,"w3"]+
           -(a[2]*a[2]+a[3]*a[3])*dta[,"w3"]*dta[,"w3"])/(2*dta
           [,"w1"])
  chat  <- ghat*dta[,"y"]+a[4]*dta[,"w1"]*dta[,"y"]+a[5]*dta[,"w2"]
    *dta[,"y"]+
    a[6]*dta[,"w3"]*dta[,"y"]+a[7]*dta[,"w1"]+a[8]*dta[,"w2"]+
    a[9]*dta[,"w3"]+a[10]*(a[11]*dta[,"w1"]+a[12]*dta[,"w2"]+
                          a[13]*dta[,"w3"])^2
  x1hat <- -ghat/(2*dta[,"w1"]^2)*dta[,"y"]+a[4]*dta[,"y"]+a[7]+2*a
    [10]*a[11]*
    (a[11]*dta[,"w1"]+a[12]*dta[,"w2"]+a[13]*dta[,"w3"])
  x2hat <- (-a[1]*a[1]*dta[,"w2"]-a[1]*a[2]*dta[,"w1"])/dta[,"w1"]
    +a[5]*dta[,"y"]+a[8]+
    2*a[10]*a[12]*(a[11]*dta[,"w1"]+a[12]*dta[,"w2"]+a[13]
    *dta[,"w3"])
  err <- cbind(dta[,"cst"]-chat,dta[,"x1"]-x1hat,dta[,"x2"]-x2hat)
  return(log(nrow(err)*det(t(err)%*%err/2)))
}
```

The second approach to imposing concavity on the McFadden cost system is to constrain the maximum eigenvalue. Specifically, we use the original likelihood function and specify a nonlinear constraint.

R Code — Nonlinear Constraint

```
concave <- function(a) {
  aa <- cbind(rbind(a[1],a[2]),rbind(a[2],a[3]))
  ll <- max(eigen(aa)$values)
  return(ll)
}

lb <- c(-1.0e+08)
ub <- c(0.0)

res3 <- solnp(a0,mcfaddenlike,ineqfun = concave,ineqLB =
lb,ineqUB = ub)
```

$

From our preceding discussion, this approach follows Talpaz *et al.* (1989).

To examine the concavity of the overall cost function, we take the Hessian of the cost function:

$$\nabla^2_{ww} C(w, y) = \nabla^2_{ww} g(w) = \begin{bmatrix} \frac{1}{w_1^3} w' c w & -\frac{1}{w_1^2} w' c \\ -\frac{1}{w_1^2} c w & \frac{1}{w_1} c \end{bmatrix}. \tag{5.116}$$

Applying this expression to the estimates in Table 5.15 yields

$$\nabla^2_{ww} C(w, y) = \begin{bmatrix} -0.0213 & 0.0459 & 0.0099 \\ 0.0459 & -0.1443 & 0.0044 \\ 0.0099 & 0.0044 & -0.0191 \end{bmatrix} \tag{5.117}$$

which is negative semi-definite.

5.4.4 *Concepts of Subadditivity*

The issue addressed in Evans and Heckman (1984) involves the emergence of natural monopolies. Specifically, is it possible that a single firm is the most cost-efficient way to generate the product? In the specific application, the researchers are interested in the Bell System (the phone company before it was split up).

Up until this point, we have focused on cost functions of single outputs. However, the cost frontier is easily extended to consider multiple outputs:

$$\begin{aligned}C\left(w_1,w_2,y_1,y_2\right) = {} & \alpha_0+\alpha_1w_1+\alpha_2w_2\\ & +\frac{1}{2}\alpha_{11}w_1w_1+\alpha_{12}w_1w_2+\alpha_{22}w_2w_2+\beta_1y_1+\beta_2y_2\\ & +\frac{1}{2}\beta_{11}y_1y_1+\beta_{12}y_1y_2+\frac{1}{2}\beta_{22}y_2y_2\\ & \gamma_{11}w_1y_1+\gamma_{12}w_1y_2+\gamma_{21}w_2y_1+\gamma_{22}w_2y_2. \quad (5.118)\end{aligned}$$

The cost function $C\left(y\right)$ is subadditive at some output level if and only if

$$\begin{aligned}C\left(y\right) &< \sum_{i=1}^{n} C\left(y_i\right)\\ \sum_{i=1}^{n} y_i &= y. \end{aligned} \quad (5.119)$$

which states that the cost function is subadditive if a single firm could produce the same output for less cost. As a mathematical nicety, the point must have at least two non-zero firms. Otherwise, the cost function is by definition the same.

To develop a formal test, Evans and Heckman assume a cost function based on two inputs:

$$\begin{aligned}&\sum_i C\left(a_iy_1,b_iy_2\right) > C\left(y_1,y_2\right)\ i=1,\ldots,n\\ &\sum_i a_i,\ \sum_i b_i = 1,\ a_i \geq 0,\ b_i \geq 0.\end{aligned} \quad (5.120)$$

Thus, each of i firms produces a_i percent of output y_1 and b_i percent of the output y_2.

A primary focus of the article is the region over which subadditivity is tested. The cost function is subadditive, and the technology implies a natural monopoly.

$$\sum_i C(a_i y_1, b_i y_2) > C(y_1, y_2). \tag{5.121}$$

The cost function is superadditive, and the firm could save money by breaking itself up into two or more divisions:

$$\sum_i C(a_i y_1, b_i y_2) < C(y_1, y_2). \tag{5.122}$$

The cost function is additive if

$$\sum_i C(a_i y_1, b_i y_2) = C(y_1, y_2). \tag{5.123}$$

The notion of additivity combines two concepts from the cost function: economies of scope and economies of scale. Under economies of scope, it is cheaper to produce two goods together. For example, it is typically cheaper to produce stocker cattle in Western Oklahoma if you grow winter wheat at the same time. However, we also recognize following the concepts of Coase (1937), Grossman and Hart (1986), and Williamson (1975, 1985) that there may be diseconomies of scope. The second concept is the economies of scale argument that we have discussed before.

5.4.4.1 *Measuring scope and scale economies in agricultural banking*

Featherstone and Moss (1994) use the subadditivity approach to analyze the economies of scope and scale in agricultural banking. Specifically, the 1990s saw a significant consolidation of agricultural banks. Some suggested that this consolidation made the remaining banks more competitive. Either they would be able to deliver some services at a lower cost or the consolidated banks could be more solvent and, hence, less susceptible to financial variations. However, others suggested that consolidations would increase market power, resulting in an increase in the cost of capital to agriculture. Featherstone and Moss address some of these questions by examining the economies of scope and scale in agricultural banks.

As a starting point, Featherstone and Moss define the *incremental cost* for activity i as the difference between producing that output as a part of a bundle of outputs ($C(y)$) and the cost of producing the remaining outputs in the bundle without that output ($C(y_{N-i})$):

$$\begin{aligned} IC_i &= C(y) - C(y_{N-i}) \\ \text{where}\, y_{N-i} &= \{y_1, y_2, \ldots, y_{i-1}, 0, y_{i+1}, \ldots, y_N\}. \end{aligned} \tag{5.124}$$

The *product-specific economies of scale* (S_i) can then be computed as the economies of scale average incremental cost of producing the output (IC_i/y_i) divided by the marginal incremental cost of producing the *i*th output:

$$S_i = \frac{IC_i/y_i}{\partial C/\partial y_i}. \tag{5.125}$$

Hence, if S_i is greater than one, product-specific economies of scale exist. The concept is that economies of scope exist if the cost function is subadditive (e.g., follows the concept in Equation (5.120)).

$$C(y_1) + C(y_2) > C(y). \tag{5.126}$$

They then define the *economies of scope* ($SC_N(y)$) as

$$SC_N = \frac{C(y_1) + C(y_2) - C(y)}{C(y)}. \tag{5.127}$$

Combining the product-specific economies of scope and the product-specific economies yields the overall *economies of scale*:

$$S_N(y) = \frac{\alpha_1 S_1(y) + (1 - \alpha_1) S_2(y)}{1 - SC_N(y)} \tag{5.128}$$

where α_1 is the firm's output times the marginal cost divided by the sum of all outputs multiplied by their respective marginal costs.

To implement these measures, Featherstone and Moss estimate a normalized quadratic cost function for 7,108 banks from the 1990 Federal Reserve Call Report. The outputs were the quarterly average of agricultural loans, non-agricultural real estate loans, other non-agricultural loans, transaction deposits, non-transaction deposits, and other bank outputs. The inputs were total assets, total deposits, number of employees, and fixed assets. As a first step, they estimated the normalized quadratic without restrictions, but concluded that the unrestricted function was not concave in input prices. Hence,

Table 5.16 Marginal Cost and Product-Specific Economies of Scale for Agricultural Banking

Output	Marginal Cost	Product-Specific Economies of Scale	Economies of Scope
Agricultural Loans	−0.702	1.0035	0.0008
Nonagricultural Real Estate Loans	1.717	0.9955	0.0015
Other Nonagricultural Loans	1.221	0.9942	0.0013
Transaction Deposits	14.773	0.9995	0.0010
Non-transaction Deposits	6.570	0.9978	0.0030
Other Bank Output	−1.467	1.0008	0.0009

Featherstone and Moss imposed concavity using Lau's decomposition (see Equation (5.38)). The marginal cost of each activity, product-specific economies of scale and economies of scope for the concavity constrained model are presented in Table 5.16. Overall, they find that the economies of scale for agricultural banking is 0.986, which is slightly less than one. Hence, constant returns to scale for agricultural banking cannot be rejected.

5.4.4.2 *General formulation for the economies of scope and scale*

Given the estimates for a cost function with n outputs, we can then measure economies of scope in two ways. The first measure, is a traditional measure:

$$\text{Scope} = \frac{\begin{array}{c} C\left(q_1, 0, \ldots, 0, r\right) + \cdots C\left(0, 0, \ldots, q_n, r\right) \\ -C\left(q_1, q_2, \ldots, q_n, r\right) \end{array}}{C\left(q_1, q_2, \ldots, q_n, r\right)}. \tag{5.129}$$

Another measure suggested by the article is "quasi" economies of scope

$$\text{Qscope} = \frac{\begin{array}{c} C\left(\{\, 1-(m-1)\,\epsilon\}\ q_1, q_2\epsilon, \ldots, r\right)\cdots \\ -C\left(q_1, q_2, \ldots, q_n, r\right) \end{array}}{C\left(q_1, q_2, \ldots, r\right)}. \tag{5.130}$$

The economies of scale for the general cost function are then defined as

$$\text{Scale} = \frac{C(q,r)}{\sum_i q_i \dfrac{\partial C(q,r)}{\partial q_i}}. \tag{5.131}$$

5.4.4.3 *Quadratic example with pseudo-data*

In order to flush out these concepts, consider the Pseudo-Dataset "JointProduct.csv,"[3] which has four inputs and two outputs. As a starting point, we estimate a quadratic cost function similar to the one estimated by Featherstone and Moss (1994):

$$\begin{aligned} c(w,y) = a_0 &+ \begin{bmatrix} a_1 \\ a_2 \\ a_3 \\ a_4 \end{bmatrix}' \begin{bmatrix} w_1 \\ w_2 \\ w_3 \\ w_4 \end{bmatrix} \\ &+ \frac{1}{2} \begin{bmatrix} w_1 \\ w_2 \\ w_3 \\ w_4 \end{bmatrix}' \begin{bmatrix} A_{11} & A_{12} & A_{13} & A_{14} \\ A_{12} & A_{22} & A_{23} & A_{24} \\ A_{13} & A_{23} & A_{33} & A_{34} \\ A_{14} & A_{24} & A_{34} & A_{44} \end{bmatrix} \begin{bmatrix} w_1 \\ w_2 \\ w_3 \\ w_4 \end{bmatrix} \\ &+ \begin{bmatrix} b_1 \\ b_2 \end{bmatrix}' \begin{bmatrix} y_1 \\ y_2 \end{bmatrix} + \frac{1}{2} \begin{bmatrix} y_1 \\ y_2 \end{bmatrix}' \begin{bmatrix} B_{11} & B_{12} \\ B_{12} & B_{22} \end{bmatrix} \begin{bmatrix} y_1 \\ y_2 \end{bmatrix} \\ &+ \begin{bmatrix} y_1 \\ y_2 \end{bmatrix}' \begin{bmatrix} G_{11} & G_{12} \\ G_{21} & G_{22} \\ G_{31} & G_{32} \\ G_{41} & G_{42} \end{bmatrix} \begin{bmatrix} w_1 \\ w_2 \\ w_3 \\ w_4 \end{bmatrix}. \end{aligned} \tag{5.132}$$

The estimated values for these parameters are presented in Table 5.17. As in Featherstone and Moss, the initial estimates were not concave in price space. However, instead of estimating the Lau decomposition, we impose concavity by constraining the eigenvalues

[3]This data is available at http://www.charlesbmoss.com:8080/Book.Production.Economics/Chapter-5/JointProduct.csv.

Table 5.17 Results for Two-Output Pseudo-Data

Parameter	Estimate	Parameter	Estimate
a_0	187.88320*** (1.47425)[a]	A_{44}	−56.97846*** (0.87454)
a_1	23.28581*** (1.34791)	b_1	−2.92653*** (0.94671)
a_2	53.24648*** (2.26989)	b_2	−2.36060 (4.30738)
a_3	23.74070*** (1.66318)	B_{11}	0.03363 (3.42409)
a_4	24.07961*** (9.17107)	B_{12}	−0.00039 (4.54960)
A_{11}	−26.89429*** (1.75782)	B_{22}	0.02400 (0.01981)
A_{12}	3.93272* (2.01562)	G_{11}	−0.12506*** (0.00320)
A_{13}	−10.15832*** (1.95042)	G_{12}	0.42369*** (0.02186)
A_{14}	29.36211*** (0.86915)	G_{21}	−0.07994 (0.75172)
A_{22}	−12.76261*** (1.12125)	G_{22}	0.67190* (0.40516)
A_{23}	−0.62450 (1.35797)	G_{31}	2.70168*** (0.48109)
A_{24}	10.96894** (4.98869)	G_{32}	0.97396 (3.12232)
A_{33}	−8.15251 (1.22150)	G_{41}	1.73415 (1.37927)
A_{34}	18.50573*** (3.66552)	G_{42}	−0.33443 (0.74781)

Notes: [a]Numbers in parenthesis denote standard errors. ***,**,*Denote statistical significance at the 0.01, 0.05, 0.10 levels of confidence respectively.

of the A matrix to be negative and the B matrix to be positive (following Talpaz *et al.* (1989)). The estimated A matrix is

$$A = \begin{bmatrix} -26.8943 & 3.9327 & -10.1583 & 29.3621 \\ 3.9327 & -12.7626 & -0.6245 & 10.9689 \\ -10.1583 & -0.6245 & -8.1525 & 18.5057 \\ 29.3621 & 10.9689 & 18.5057 & -56.9785 \end{bmatrix}$$

$$\lambda(A) = \{-0.0100 \quad -3.3669 \quad -19.6113 \quad -81.7996\} \tag{5.133}$$

where $\lambda(A)$ is the vector of eigenvalues. The constraint implemented in the code requires $\max[\lambda(A)] \leq 0.0100$; hence, the concavity constraint for the input price matrix is binding. However, given that the eigenvalue constraint for the output coefficients

$$B = \begin{bmatrix} 0.0336 & -0.0004 \\ -0.0004 & 0.0240 \end{bmatrix}$$
$$\lambda(B) = \{\ 0.03365 \quad 0.02398\} \tag{5.134}$$

the convexity constraint in output space is not constraining.

As depicted in Figure 5.1, the cost changes rapidly as output 1 (y_1) increases, but slowly as output 2 (y_2) increases. Starting from the average output level $\{y_1, y_2\} = \{151.78, 83.03\}$, we compute $c(\bar{w}, y_1 = 151.78, y_2 = 83.03) = 497.709$. The economies of scope can then be computed at the sample mean as

$$\begin{aligned} S_2(y) &= \frac{c(\bar{w}, y_1, 0) + c(\bar{w}, 0, y_2) - c(\bar{w}, y_1, y_2)}{c(\bar{w}, y)} \\ &= \frac{571.28 + 166.11 - 497.709}{497.709} \\ &= 0.4816. \end{aligned} \tag{5.135}$$

Next, we derive the product-specific economics of scale:

$$S_1 = \frac{IC_1/y_1}{\partial c/\partial y_1}$$
$$= \frac{\dfrac{497.71 - 166.11}{151.78}}{\begin{array}{c}-2.9266 - 0.1251w_1 - 0.0800w_2 + 2.7017w_3 + 1.7342w_4 \\ +\,0.03353y_1 - 0.0004y_2\end{array}} = 0.4612. \tag{5.136}$$

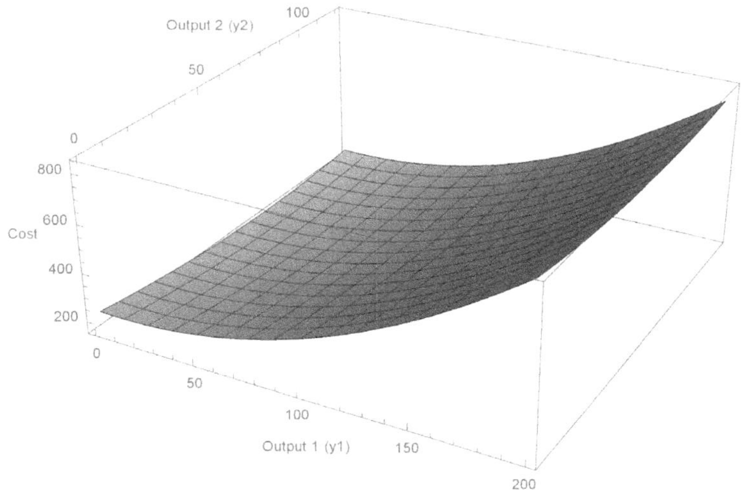

Fig. 5.1 Cost of Two Outputs

However, $S_2 = -8.0447$ since $c(\bar{w}, y_2, 0) = 571.279$, the increment cost is -73.57. Dividing by y_2 gives -0.8861 and then dividing by the marginal cost (of 0.1101) yields -8.0477.

5.4.4.4 *Subadditivity and the translog*

As stated previously, a primary focus of this article is the region of subadditivity. In our discussion of cost functions, I have mentioned the concepts of global versus local. To make the discussion more concrete, let us return to our analysis of concavity. From the properties of the cost function, we know that the cost function is concave in input price space. Thus, using the translog form,

$$\begin{aligned} \ln(C) &= \alpha_0 + \alpha' \ln(w) + \frac{1}{2}\ln(w)' \ln(w) \\ &\beta' \ln(y) + \frac{1}{2}\ln(y)' B \ln(y) + \ln(w)' \Gamma \ln(y). \end{aligned} \tag{5.137}$$

The gradient vector for the translog cost function is then

$$\nabla_w C(w, y) = \exp[\ln(C)] \begin{bmatrix} \dfrac{\alpha_1 + A_{\cdot 1} \ln(w) + \Gamma'_{1\cdot} \ln(y)}{w_1} \\ \vdots \\ \dfrac{\alpha_n + A_{\cdot n} \ln(w) + \Gamma'_{n\cdot} \ln(y)}{w_n} \end{bmatrix}. \tag{5.138}$$

Denoting the vector of share equations as $\phi(w,y)$

$$\phi(w,y) = \begin{bmatrix} \alpha_1 + A_{\cdot q}\ln(w) + \Gamma_{1\cdot}\ln(y) \\ \vdots \\ \alpha_n + A_{\cdot n}\ln(w) + \Gamma'_{n\cdot}\ln(y) \end{bmatrix}. \tag{5.139}$$

The Hessian of the translog can then be derived as

$$\begin{aligned} \nabla^2_{xx}C(w,y) &= \exp[\ln(C)] \begin{bmatrix} \frac{\phi_1(x,y)}{w_1} \\ \vdots \\ \frac{\phi_n(w,y)}{w_n} \end{bmatrix} \begin{bmatrix} \frac{\phi_1(w,y)}{w_1} \\ \vdots \\ \frac{\phi_n(w,y)}{w_n} \end{bmatrix}' \\ &\quad + \exp[\ln(C)] \begin{bmatrix} \frac{\phi_1(w,y)}{w_1^2} & \cdots & 0 \\ \vdots & \ddots & \vdots \\ 0 & \cdots & \frac{\phi_n(w,y)}{w_n^2} \end{bmatrix} \\ &\quad + \exp[\ln(C)] \begin{bmatrix} \frac{A_{11}}{w_1 w_1} & \cdots & \frac{A_{1n}}{w_1 w_n} \\ \vdots & \ddots & \vdots \\ \frac{A_{1n}}{w_1 w_n} & \cdots & \frac{A_{nn}}{w_n w_n} \end{bmatrix} \\ &= C(w,y) \begin{bmatrix} \frac{\phi_1(w,y)(\phi_1(w,y)-1)+A_{11}}{w_1 w_1} & \cdots & \frac{\phi_1\phi_n + A_{1n}}{w_1 w_n} \\ \vdots & \ddots & \vdots \\ \frac{\phi_1(w,y)\phi_n(w,y)+A_{1n}}{w_1 w_n} & \cdots & \frac{\phi_n(w,y)(\phi_n(w,y)-1)+A_{nn}}{w_n w_n} \end{bmatrix}. \end{aligned} \tag{5.140}$$

Given that cost is always positive, the concavity of the cost function can be determined by the eigenvalues of

$$A(w,y) = \begin{bmatrix} \frac{\phi_1(w,y)(\phi_1(w,y)-1) + A_{11}}{w_1 w_1} & \cdots & \frac{\phi_1\phi_n + A_{1n}}{w_1 w_n} \\ \vdots & \ddots & \vdots \\ \frac{\phi_1(w,y)\phi_n(w,y)+A_{1n}}{w_1 w_n} & \cdots & \frac{\phi_n(w,y)(\phi_n(w,y)-1) + A_{nn}}{w_n w_n} \end{bmatrix}. \tag{5.141}$$

Comparing this result with the result for the quadratic function, we see that

$$\nabla^2_{ww} C(w, y) = A. \tag{5.142}$$

Thus, the Hessian of the translog varies over input prices and output levels while the Hessian matrix for the quadratic does not. The literature sometimes develops concavity of the cost function by developing the concavity of the transformed cost function:

$$\tilde{A}(w, y) = A + \phi(w, y)\,\phi(w, y)'. \tag{5.143}$$

Unfortunately, Equation (5.120) ignores the actual question: Is the cost function concave in input price space? Specifically, the transformation into cost space (i.e., $C(w, y) = \exp(ln(C(w, y)))$ is a convex transformation.

In addition to the concavity with respect to input prices, we need to guarantee that the cost function is convex in output space. Like the formulation of the concavity results, we start by taking the gradient of the cost function with respect to output levels:

$$\nabla_y C(w, y) = \exp[C] \begin{bmatrix} \dfrac{\beta_1 + B_{\dot{1}} \ln(y) + \Gamma_{\dot{1}} \ln(w)}{y_1} \\ \vdots \\ \dfrac{\beta_n + B_{\dot{n}} \ln(y) + \Gamma_{\dot{n}} \ln(w)}{y} \end{bmatrix}. \tag{5.144}$$

Like Equation (5.139), we define $\psi(w, y)$ as

$$\psi(w, y) = \begin{bmatrix} \psi_1(w, y) = \beta_1 + B_{\dot{1}} \ln(y) + \Gamma_{\dot{1}} \ln(w) \\ \vdots \\ \beta_n + B_{\dot{n}} \ln(y) + \Gamma_{\dot{n}} \ln(w) \end{bmatrix}. \tag{5.145}$$

The Hessian with respect to outputs can then be defined as

$$B(w, y) = C(w, y) \begin{bmatrix} \dfrac{\begin{matrix}\psi_1(w, y)(\psi_1(w, y) - 1) \\ +B_{11}\end{matrix}}{y_1 y_1} & \cdots & \dfrac{\begin{matrix}\psi_1(w, y)\,\psi_1(w, y) \\ \psi_n(w, y) + B_{1n}\end{matrix}}{y_1 y_n} \\ \vdots & \ddots & \vdots \\ \dfrac{\begin{matrix}\psi_1(w, y)\,\psi_n(w, y) \\ +B_{1n}\end{matrix}}{y_1 y_n} & \cdots & \dfrac{\begin{matrix}\psi_n(w, y)(\psi_n(w, y) - 1) \\ +B_{nn}\end{matrix}}{y_n y_n} \end{bmatrix}. \tag{5.146}$$

Any discussion of subadditivity, especially if a translog cost function is used (or any cost function other than a quadratic), needs to consider the region over which the cost function is to be tested.

5.4.4.5 *Admissible region*

Thus, much of the discussion in Evans and Heckman (1984) involve the choice of the region for the test. Specifically, the test region is restricted to a region of the observed point (see Figure 5.2). Defining y_{1m}^* as the minimum amount of y_1 produced by any firm and y_{2m}^* as the minimum amount of y_2 produced, we can define alternative production bundles:

$$\begin{aligned} y_t^A &= \left(\phi y_{1t}^* + y_{1m}, (1-\omega)\, y_{2t}^* + y_{2m}\right) \\ y_t^B &= \left((1-\phi)\, y_{1t}^* + y_{1m}, \omega y_{2t}^* + y_{2m}\right) \\ & 0 \leq \phi \leq 1, 0 \leq \omega \leq 1. \end{aligned} \tag{5.147}$$

Thus, the production for any firm can be divided into two components within the observed range of output. Thus, subadditivity can be defined as

$$\begin{aligned} C_t^A(\phi,\omega) &= C\left(y_t^A\right) \\ C_t^B(\phi,\omega) &= C\left(y_t^B\right) \\ C_t = C\left(y_t^A + y_t^B\right) &= C\left(y_t\right) \\ \text{Sub}_t(\phi,\omega)\, & \frac{\left[C_t^A(\phi,\omega) + C_t^B(\phi\omega) - C_t(\phi,\omega)\right]}{C_t}. \end{aligned} \tag{5.148}$$

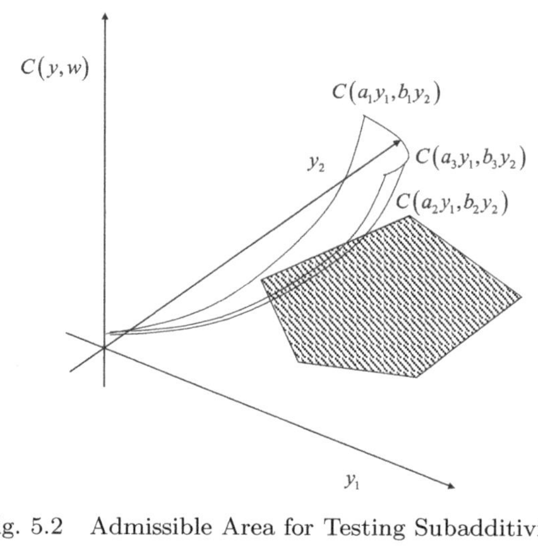

Fig. 5.2 Admissible Area for Testing Subadditivity

If $\text{Sub}_t(\phi, \omega)$ is greater than zero, the cost function is subadditive, if it is equal to zero, the cost function is additive, and if it is greater than zero, the cost function is superadditive. Consistent with their concept of the region of the test, Evans and Heckman calculate the maximum and minimum $\text{Sub}_t(\phi, \omega)$ for the region.

5.4.4.6 *Application with agricultural productivity data*

In order to demonstrate the issues involved in using a translog cost specification to estimate the economies of scope and scale, we estimate the translog cost function for three outputs (e.g., livestock, crops, and farm by related outputs) and three inputs (e.g., capital, labor, and intermediate goods) using annual data from the United States Department of Agriculture (Wang *et al.*, 2020) for 1948–2017. Given that these data are used to examine changes in technology, the standard translog specification will be modified to include a time component:

$$
\begin{aligned}
\ln(C) &= a_0 + \begin{bmatrix} a_1 \\ a_2 \end{bmatrix}' \begin{bmatrix} \ln(w_1^*) \\ \ln(w_2^*) \end{bmatrix} \\
&+ \frac{1}{2} \begin{bmatrix} \ln(w_1^*) \\ \ln(w_2^*) \end{bmatrix}' \begin{bmatrix} A_{11} & A_{12} \\ A_{12} & A_{22} \end{bmatrix} \begin{bmatrix} \ln(w_1^*) \\ \ln(w_2^*) \end{bmatrix} + \begin{bmatrix} b_1 \\ b_2 \\ b_3 \end{bmatrix}' \begin{bmatrix} \ln(y_1) \\ \ln(y_2) \\ \ln(y_3) \end{bmatrix} \\
&+ \frac{1}{2} \begin{bmatrix} \ln(y_1) \\ \ln(y_2) \\ \ln(y_3) \end{bmatrix}' \begin{bmatrix} B_{11} & B_{12} & B_{13} \\ B_{12} & B_{22} & B_{23} \\ B_{13} & B_{23} & B_{33} \end{bmatrix} \begin{bmatrix} \ln(y_1) \\ \ln(y_2) \\ \ln(y_3) \end{bmatrix} \\
&+ \begin{bmatrix} \ln(w_1^*) \\ \ln(w_2^*) \end{bmatrix}' \begin{bmatrix} G_{11} & G_{12} & G_{13} \\ G_{21} & G_{22} & G_{23} \end{bmatrix} \begin{bmatrix} \ln(y_1) \\ \ln(y_2) \\ \ln(y_3) \end{bmatrix} \\
&+ d_0 (t - 1947) + \begin{bmatrix} d_{11} \\ d_{12} \end{bmatrix}' \begin{bmatrix} \ln(w_1^*) \\ \ln(w_2^*) \end{bmatrix} (t - 1947) \\
&+ \begin{bmatrix} d_{21} \\ d_{22} \\ d_{23} \end{bmatrix}' \begin{bmatrix} \ln(y_1) \\ \ln(y_2) \\ \ln(y_3) \end{bmatrix} (t - 1947) + d_{00} (t - 1947)^2 . \qquad (5.149)
\end{aligned}
$$

In Equation (5.149), $\ln(w_i^*), i = 1, 2$ denotes the fact that the input prices have been normalized by subtracting the third price (e.g., the

Table 5.18 Translog Cost Results

Parameter	Estimate	Parameter	Estimate
a_0	21.53095 (14.99301)[a]	G_{11}	−0.08009 (0.33964)
a_1	0.40963 (0.62458)	G_{12}	0.06298 (0.30476)
a_2	0.76731 (1.03510)	G_{21}	−0.01605 (0.20703)
A_{11}	0.17554 (3.65913)	G_{22}	−0.07811 (1.98811)
A_{12}	−0.06906 (0.55213)	G_{31}	−0.02356 (2.17220)
A_{22}	0.10254 (0.17698)	G_{32}	0.01034 (1.22554)
b_1	−4.93946 (8.12036)	d_0	0.01781 (0.57984)
b_2	−1.49045 (3.42121)	d_{11}	−0.00054 (2.15076)
b_3	−0.82642 (2.39341)	d_{12}	−0.00166 (15.81095)
B_{11}	1.10638 (1.89823)	d_{21}	−0.00034 (8.30406)
B_{12}	−0.12810 (1.33094)	d_{22}	−0.00327 (5.10554)
B_{13}	0.19970 (1.11054)	d_{23}	−0.00133 (5.39868)
B_{22}	0.49057 (1.62525)	d_{00}	−0.00001 (5.11559)
B_{23}	−0.03607 (1.45919)	ρ	−0.55086*** (0.11957)
B_{33}	0.02472 (0.65663)		

Notes: [a]Numbers in parenthesis denote standard errors.
***Denotes statistical significance at the 0.01 level of confidence.

cost of intermediate materials). This normalizes the translog and imposes the homogeneity condition. In addition, the δ_0 and $\delta_{ij}(i = 1, 2,\ j = 1, 2, 3)$ terms are intended to remove the effect of changes

Table 5.19 Sample Distribution for Agricultural Production Quantities (1000)

	Arithmetic			Geometric		
	Livestock	Crops	Farm-Related	Livestock	Crops	Farm-Related
Sample Statistics						
Minimum	72.12	65.14	4.94	72.10	65.17	4.94
Q1	97.58	89.36	7.76	97.61	89.39	7.76
Median	113.17	142.12	14.36	113.18	142.17	14.35
Mean	117.89	136.25	16.62	114.66	127.23	13.69
Q3	144.80	179.60	25.90	144.75	179.65	25.89
Maximum	174.43	224.20	43.99	174.51	224.30	43.99
Output Levels						
	Y_a	Y_b	Y_c	Y_a	Y_b	Y_c
Livestock	64.84	26.53	26.53	63.04	28.63	28.63
Crop	30.66	74.94	30.66	28.63	69.98	28.63
Farm Related	3.74	3.74	9.14	3.08	3.08	7.83

in technology over time. In this specific formulation, we have set the base year to 1948 (i.e., $t = 1$ for 1948). In addition, we estimate a first-order autoregressive parameter ρ, which is constant across equations. The estimates for this specification are presented in Table 5.18.

We use maximum likelihood to estimate the cost function in Equation (5.149); however, we find that the second derivative with respect to input prices (e.g., Equation 5.141) is negative definite Hessian with respect to output levels.

In order to estimate the economics of scope using the translog, we need to define an admissible region along the lines developed by Evans and Heckman (1984). To construct this feasible region, consider the sample statistics for the livestock, crops, and farm-related products presented in Table 5.19. First, we define y_t as the geometric sample means for the output levels:

$$y_t = \left\{ 114.66 \; 127.23 \; 13.69 \right\}. \tag{5.150}$$

Next, we take a variation around the geometric mean that preserves the condition that the sum of amount each output produced sums to the geometric mean:

$$\begin{aligned} y_A &= \left\{ \phi y_{m,1} \ \frac{(1-\phi)}{2} y_{m,2} \ \frac{(1-\phi)}{2} y_{m,3} \right\} \\ y_B &= \left\{ \frac{(1-\phi)}{2} y_{m,1} \ \phi\phi_2 y_{m,2} \ \frac{(1-\phi)}{2} y_{m,3} \right\} \\ y_C &= \left\{ \frac{(1-\phi)}{2} y_{m,1} \ \frac{(1-\phi)}{2} y_{m,2} \ \phi y_{m,3} \right\}. \end{aligned} \tag{5.151}$$

Note that if we set $\phi = 1$, the result will be consistent with the subadditivity for the normalized quadratic cost function applied by Featherstone and Moss (1994). In general, we would not impose $\phi = 1$ for the translog cost specifications because it would imply taking the natural logarithm of zero, thus, we could consider $\phi = 0.95$. In this case, the convexity of the cost function with respect to output levels raises additional difficulties and we set $\phi = 0.55$. The resulting combinations we use to evaluate subadditivity are presented in Table 5.19. Hence, the values for the translog cost function become

$$\begin{aligned} c(\bar{w}, y_t) &= 334.48 \\ c(\bar{w}, y_A) &= 584.85 \\ c(\bar{w}, y_B) &= 1{,}220.92^{\cdot} \\ c(\bar{w}, y_C) &= 1{,}101.11 \end{aligned} \tag{5.152}$$

Given these results, the translog cost function is clearly subadditive:

$$\text{Sub}_t(\phi) = \frac{584.85 + 1{,}220.92 + 1{,}101.11 - 334.48}{334.48} = 7.69. \tag{5.153}$$

However, we could be cynical regarding this result. The scale of the subadditivity is largely a function of the imposition of concavity on the translog cost function. We should probably either consider imposing concavity and convexity at a different point in time (say from 2007–2017) or using another function form, such as composite cost function.

5.4.4.7 *Composite cost functions and subadditivity*

Pulley and Braunstein (1992) build on the concept of subadditivity and the global nature of the flexible function form, it is apparent that the estimation of subadditivity is dependent on functional form. They allow for a more general form of the cost function by allowing the Box–Cox transformation to be different for the inputs and outputs:

$$\begin{aligned} z^{(\phi)} &= \frac{\left(z^{\phi}-1\right)}{\phi} \ni : \phi \neq 0 \\ &= \ln(z) \ni : \phi = 0. \end{aligned} \tag{5.154}$$

The composite cost function form

$$\begin{aligned} C^{(\phi)} = \Bigg\{ &\exp\left[\alpha_0 + \alpha' y^{(\pi)} + \frac{1}{2} y^{(\pi)\prime} A y^{(\pi)} + y^{(\pi)} \Psi w\right]^{(\tau)} \\ &\exp\left[\beta_0 + \beta' w + \frac{1}{2} w' B w + y^{(\pi)} \Upsilon w\right]\Bigg\}^{(\phi)} \\ &f^{(\phi)}(q, \ln(w)). \end{aligned} \tag{5.155}$$

- If $\phi = 0$, $\pi = 0$, and $\tau = 1$, the form yields a standard translog with normal share equations.
- If $\phi = 0$ and $\tau = 1$, the form yields a generalized translog:

$$\begin{aligned} \ln(C) = \alpha_0 &+ \alpha' y^{(\pi)} + \frac{1}{2} y^{(\phi)\prime} A y^{(\pi)} + y^{(\pi)} \Psi \ln(w) \\ &+ \beta' \ln(w) + \frac{1}{2} \ln(w)' B \ln(w) \\ s &= \Psi y^{(\pi)} + \beta + B \ln(w). \end{aligned} \tag{5.156}$$

If $\pi = 1$, $\tau = 0$, and $\Psi = 0$, the specification becomes a separable quadratic specification:

$$\begin{aligned} C^{(\phi)} &= \Bigg\{ \left[\alpha_0 + \alpha' y + \frac{1}{2} y' A y\right] \\ &\quad \times \exp\left[\beta_0 + \beta' \ln(w) + \frac{1}{2} \ln(w)' B \ln(w)\right]\Bigg\}^{(\phi)} \\ s &= \beta + B \ln(w). \end{aligned} \tag{5.157}$$

The demand equations for the composite function is

$$\begin{aligned} s = &\left[\alpha_0 + \alpha' y + \frac{1}{2} y' A y + y \Psi \ln(r)\right]^{-1} \Psi y \\ &+ B \ln(r) + \Upsilon' y. \end{aligned} \tag{5.158}$$

5.4.5 *Estimating Revenue and Profit Functions*

5.4.5.1 *Univariate revenue function*

As a starting point, consider the simple univariate revenue function:

$$R(p,x) = pf(x_1, x_2, x_3, x_4, x_5). \tag{5.159}$$

Formulating this as a translog,

$$\ln(R(p,x)) = \alpha_0 + \alpha_1 \ln(p) + A_{11}\frac{\ln(p)^2}{2} + \begin{bmatrix}\beta_1\\ \beta_2\\ \beta_3\\ \beta_4\\ \beta_5\end{bmatrix}' \begin{bmatrix}\ln(x_1)\\ \ln(x_2)\\ \ln(x_3)\\ \ln(x_4)\\ \ln(x_5)\end{bmatrix}$$

$$+\frac{1}{2}\begin{bmatrix}\ln(x_1)\\ \ln(x_2)\\ \ln(x_2)\\ \ln(x_3)\\ \ln(x_4)\\ \ln(x_5)\end{bmatrix}' \begin{bmatrix}B_{11} & B_{12} & B_{13} & B_{14} & B_{15}\\ B_{12} & B_{22} & B_{23} & B_{24} & B_{25}\\ B_{13} & B_{23} & B_{33} & B_{34} & B_{35}\\ B_{14} & B_{24} & B_{34} & B_{44} & B_{45}\\ B_{15} & B_{25} & B_{35} & B_{34} & B_{44}\end{bmatrix} \begin{bmatrix}\ln(x_1)\\ \ln(x_2)\\ \ln(x_3)\\ \ln(x_4)\\ \ln(x_5)\end{bmatrix}$$

$$+\ln(p)\begin{pmatrix}\Gamma_{11}\\ \Gamma_{12}\\ \Gamma_{13}\\ \Gamma_{14}\\ \Gamma_{15}\end{pmatrix}' \begin{pmatrix}\ln(x_1)\\ \ln(x_2)\\ \ln(x_3)\\ \ln(x_4)\\ \ln(x_5)\end{pmatrix}. \tag{5.160}$$

Equation (5.160) can be viewed as a second-order Taylor series expansion of

Table 5.20 Translog Revenue Function Estimates for Food and Kindred Products

Parameter	Estimate	Parameter	Estimate
α_0	5421.98 (4380.60)[a]	B_{15}	−21.88 (170.65)
α_1	−120.81*** (27.83)	B_{22}	−38.38 (137.05)
A_{11}	10.79*** (2.30)	B_{23}	−69.25 (44.06)
β_1	892.37 (1060.43)	B_{24}	85.78 (108.24)
β_2	662.16 (850.75)	B_{25}	−17.42 (195.99)
β_3	862.39*** (286.51)	B_{33}	−123.10*** (35.48)
β_4	−1272.26 (1243.55)	B_{34}	12.29 (35.96)
β_5	−1275.69 (1130.78)	B_{35}	81.09** (41.36)
B_{11}	38.93 (131.75)	B_{44}	53.50 (208.90)
B_{12}	−42.35 (109.98)	B_{45}	−1.35 (167.91)
B_{13}	−10.25 (28.07)	B_{55}	86.64 (299.91)
B_{14}	−39.48 (158.68)		

Notes: [a]Numbers in parenthesis denote standard errors.
***,**Denote statistical significance at the 0.01, 0.05 levels of confidence respectively.

$$R(p,x) = p\left[\alpha_0 \prod_{i=1}^{5} \left(1 - \exp\left(\alpha_i x_i\right)\right)\right] \tag{5.161}$$

basically a Mitscherlich–Buale production function. In fact, we could estimate this relationship for the Food and Kindred product dataset from the online session. The estimated coefficients for this revenue function are presented in Table 5.20.

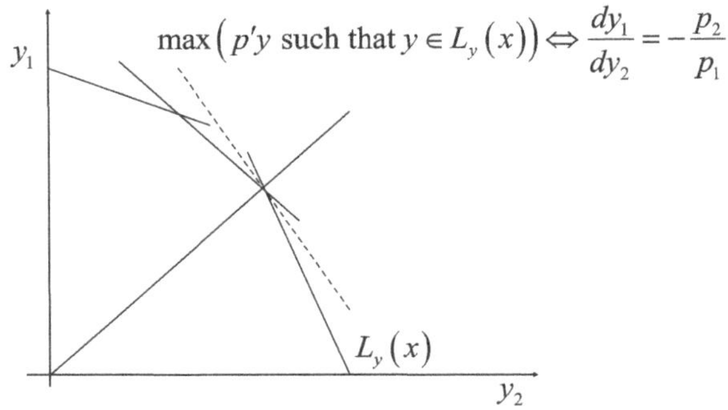

Fig. 5.3 Product–Product Problem

5.4.5.2 *Multioutput revenue function*

Given this general formula, all of our standard results from duality hold:

$$R(p,x) = \max_{y} \left(p'y : y \in L_y(x)\right). \tag{5.162}$$

Figure 5.3 depicts the revenue function in output space. Even the more esoteric distance function formulations

$$\begin{aligned} D_o(y,x) &= \max\left(\lambda : \lambda y \in L_y(x)\right) \\ R(p,x) &= \max_{y} \left(p'y : D_o(y,x) = 1\right). \end{aligned} \tag{5.163}$$

However, as in the cost function, the most useful results from the revenue function results from applying envelope theory to the indirect function:

$$\frac{\partial R(p,x)}{\partial p_i} = y_i(p,x). \tag{5.164}$$

Specifically, using the profit function specification,

$$\begin{aligned} \pi(p,w) &= \max_{x} \left[R(p,x) - w'x\right] \\ \nabla_p \pi(p,w) &= p = \nabla_p R(p,x) \ni: \nabla_x R(p,x) - w = 0. \end{aligned} \tag{5.165}$$

Consider a simple revenue function

$$R(p,x) = \alpha_0 + \begin{bmatrix} \alpha_1 \\ \alpha_2 \end{bmatrix}' \begin{bmatrix} p_1 \\ p_2 \end{bmatrix}$$

$$+ \frac{1}{2} \begin{bmatrix} p_1 \\ p_2 \end{bmatrix}' \begin{bmatrix} A_{11} & A_{12} \\ A_{12} & A_{22} \end{bmatrix} \begin{bmatrix} p_1 \\ p_2 \end{bmatrix} + \begin{bmatrix} \beta_1 \\ \beta_2 \\ \beta_3 \\ \beta_4 \end{bmatrix}' \begin{bmatrix} x_1 \\ x_2 \\ x_3 \\ x_4 \end{bmatrix}$$

$$+ \frac{1}{2} \begin{bmatrix} x_1 \\ x_2 \\ x_3 \\ x_3 \end{bmatrix}' \begin{bmatrix} B_{11} & B_{12} & B_{13} & B_{14} \\ B_{12} & B_{22} & B_{23} & B_{24} \\ B_{13} & B_{23} & B_{33} & B_{34} \\ B_{14} & B_{24} & B_{34} & B_{44} \end{bmatrix} \begin{pmatrix} x_1 \\ x_2 \end{pmatrix}$$

$$+ \begin{bmatrix} p_1 \\ p_2 \end{bmatrix}' \begin{bmatrix} \Gamma_{11} & \Gamma_{12} & \Gamma_{13} & \Gamma_{14} \\ \Gamma_{21} & \Gamma_{22} & \Gamma_{23} & \Gamma_{24} \end{bmatrix} \begin{bmatrix} x_1 \\ x_2 \\ x_3 \\ x_4 \end{bmatrix}$$

$$y(p,x) = \begin{bmatrix} y_1(p,x) \\ y_2(p,x) \end{bmatrix} = \begin{bmatrix} \alpha_1 \\ \alpha_2 \end{bmatrix} + \begin{bmatrix} A_{11} & A_{12} \\ A_{12} & A_{22} \end{bmatrix} \begin{bmatrix} p_1 \\ p_2 \end{bmatrix}$$

$$+ \begin{bmatrix} \Gamma_{11} & \Gamma_{12} & \Gamma_{13} & \Gamma_{14} \\ \Gamma_{21} & \Gamma_{22} & \Gamma_{23} & \Gamma_{24} \end{bmatrix} \begin{bmatrix} x_1 \\ x_2 \\ x_3 \\ x_4 \end{bmatrix}. \quad (5.166)$$

Applying the model in Equation (5.166) to the "JointProd.csv" data (e.g., from Section 5.4.4.3) yields the estimates in Table 5.21.

5.4.5.3 *Empirical profit function*

The empirical profit function can be developed from a variety of frameworks. The most general framework involves a direct specification of the profit maximization problem using a production function:

$$\begin{aligned} \pi(p,w) &= p'y - w'x \\ \text{s.t. } \{y,x\} &\in T \end{aligned} \quad (5.167)$$

Table 5.21 Two Product Revenue Function Estimates — Pseudo-Data

Parameter	Estimate	Parameter	Estimate
a_0	48.7739*** (1.7993)[a]	B_{22}	−7.6642*** (2.5434)
a_1	−12.6843*** (1.0192)	B_{23}	−2.9986 (1.8443)
a_2	67.9217*** (2.3669)	B_{24}	9.0882*** (2.1975)
A_{11}	0.0564 (5.4964)	B_{33}	−26.9929*** (2.7181)
A_{12}	0.4915 (1.4215)	B_{34}	48.7827*** (2.4961)
A_{22}	4.2855*** (1.2177)	B_{44}	−90.0000 (3.8393)
b_1	49.4732*** (1.0276)	G_{11}	0.5512 (4.6750)
b_2	−35.4079*** (7.6521)	G_{12}	29.2871*** (6.4470)
b_3	−78.5727*** (1.5685)	G_{13}	2.4843*** (0.3088)
b_4	81.1128*** (3.0411)	G_{14}	−61.1836*** (3.5224)
B_{11}	−2.7660* (1.4347)	G_{21}	0.9019* (0.5324)
B_{12}	4.2996*** (1.0764)	G_{22}	23.5524*** (5.5485)
B_{13}	3.0296 (3.2225)	G_{23}	−5.7092*** (0.7951)
B_{14}	−7.4790** (3.1046)	G_{24}	24.5158*** (3.0689)

Notes: [a]Numbers in parenthesis denote standard errors.
***,**,*Denote statistical significance at the 0.01, 0.05, 0.10 levels of confidence respectively

where $\{y, x\} \in T$ denotes a feasible technology set (which allows for multiple outputs — $y \in M_{r\times 1}$ for r outputs). We can derive the properties of the profit function directly based on this technology. However, an alternative approach is to use the dual results that we have already generated from other dual relationships. For example, we can re-express the profit function in Equation (5.167) as a function of the cost function:

$$\pi\left(p, w\right) = \max_{y}\left(p'y - c\left(w, y\right)\right). \tag{5.168}$$

Taking the derivative with respect to the output level yields

$$\nabla_y \pi\left(p, w\right) = p - \nabla_y c\left(w, y\right). \tag{5.169}$$

Alternatively, we can derive the profit function from the revenue function:

$$\pi\left(p, w\right) = \max_{x}\left(R\left(p, x\right) - w'x\right). \tag{5.170}$$

Again, the first-order conditions yield the relationship between

$$\nabla_x \pi\left(p, w\right) = \nabla_x R\left(p, x\right) - w. \tag{5.171}$$

Consider a simple quadratic specification of the dual profit function for the "JointProduct.csv" data used in Table 5.21:

$$\pi\left(p, w\right) = \alpha_0 + \begin{bmatrix}\alpha_1 \\ \alpha_2\end{bmatrix}' \begin{bmatrix}p_1 \\ p_2\end{bmatrix} + \frac{1}{2}\begin{bmatrix}p_1 \\ p_2\end{bmatrix}' \begin{bmatrix}A_{11} & A_{12} \\ A_{12} & A_{22}\end{bmatrix} \begin{bmatrix}p_1 \\ p_2\end{bmatrix}$$
$$+ \begin{bmatrix}\beta_1 \\ \beta_2 \\ \beta_3 \\ \beta_4\end{bmatrix}' \begin{bmatrix}w_1 \\ w_2 \\ w_3 \\ w_4\end{bmatrix} + \frac{1}{2}\begin{bmatrix}w_1 \\ w_2 \\ w_3 \\ w_4\end{bmatrix}' \begin{bmatrix}B_{11} & B_{12} & B_{13} & B_{14} \\ B_{12} & B_{22} & B_{23} & B_{24} \\ B_{13} & B_{23} & B_{33} & B_{34} \\ B_{14} & B_{24} & B_{34} & B_{44}\end{bmatrix} \begin{bmatrix}w_1 \\ w_2 \\ w_3 \\ w_4\end{bmatrix}$$
$$+ \begin{bmatrix}p_1 \\ p_2\end{bmatrix}' \begin{bmatrix}\Gamma_{11} & \Gamma_{12} & \Gamma_{13} & \Gamma_{14} \\ \Gamma_{21} & \Gamma_{22} & \Gamma_{23} & \Gamma_{24}\end{bmatrix} \begin{bmatrix}w_1 \\ w_2 \\ w_3 \\ w_4\end{bmatrix}$$

$$y(p,w)=\begin{bmatrix}y_1(p,w)\\ y_2(p,w)\end{bmatrix}=\begin{bmatrix}\alpha_1\\ \alpha_2\end{bmatrix}+\begin{bmatrix}A_{11} & A_{12}\\ A_{12} & A_{22}\end{bmatrix}\begin{bmatrix}p_1\\ p_2\end{bmatrix}$$
$$+\begin{bmatrix}\Gamma_{11} & \Gamma_{12} & \Gamma_{13} & \Gamma_{14}\\ \Gamma_{21} & \Gamma_{22} & \Gamma_{23} & \Gamma_{24}\end{bmatrix}\begin{bmatrix}w_1\\ w_2\\ w_3\\ w_4\end{bmatrix}$$
$$x(p,w)=\begin{bmatrix}x_1(p,w)\\ x_2(p,w)\\ x_3(p,w)\\ x_4(p,w)\end{bmatrix}=\begin{bmatrix}\beta_1\\ \beta_2\\ \beta_3\\ \beta_4\end{bmatrix}+\begin{bmatrix}B_{11} & B_{12} & B_{13} & B_{14}\\ B_{12} & B_{22} & B_{23} & B_{24}\\ B_{13} & B_{23} & B_{33} & B_{34}\\ B_{14} & B_{24} & B_{34} & B_{44}\end{bmatrix}\begin{bmatrix}w_1\\ w_2\\ w_3\\ w_4\end{bmatrix}$$
$$+\begin{bmatrix}\Gamma_{11} & \Gamma_{21}\\ \Gamma_{12} & \Gamma_{22}\\ \Gamma_{13} & \Gamma_{23}\\ \Gamma_{14} & \Gamma_{24}\end{bmatrix}\begin{bmatrix}p_1\\ p_2\end{bmatrix}. \tag{5.172}$$

5.4.6 *Quasi-Fixed Inputs and Dual Cost Functions*

As a starting point, we derive the implications of quasi-fixed variables for revenue and profit functions with a single output. This restriction allows us to concentrate on linkage without the complication of multiple inputs. Once we have established the implications of quasi-fixity for the revenue and profit functions, we can then extend the implications of quasi-fixity for cost functions for both single output and multiple output scenarios.

5.4.6.1 *Empirical revenue function with quasi-fixed variable*

Suppose we start off with a Mitscherliche–Baule production function:

$$\begin{aligned}y_1&=\beta_{10}\left(1-\exp\left(-\beta_{12}x_1\right)\right)\left(1-\exp\left(-\beta_{13}x_2\right)\right)\left(1-\exp\left(-\beta_{14}x_3\right)\right)\\&\quad\times\left(1-\exp\left(-\beta_{15}x_4\right)\right)\\ y_2&=\beta_{20}\left(1-\exp\left(-\beta_{21}\tilde{y}_1\right)\right)\left(1-\exp\left(\beta_{22}x_1\right)\right)\left(1-\exp\left(\beta_{23}x_2\right)\right)\\&\quad\times\left(1-\exp\left(-\beta_{24}x_3\right)\right)\left(1-\exp\left(-\beta_{25}x_4\right)\right)\end{aligned} \tag{5.173}$$

where $x_1, \ldots, x_4$ are standard inputs and $\tilde{y}_1$ is some quantity of output 1 used to produce output 2 (i.e., corn fed to cattle). Given this formulation, we maximize profit defined as

$$\max_{y,x} p_1 \times (y_1 - \tilde{y}_1) + p_2 y_2 - w'x$$
$$y_1 - \tilde{y}_1 \geq 0. \tag{5.174}$$

Adding this last constraint to the standard technology notation,

$$\left.\begin{array}{l} \max\limits_{y,x} p'y - w'x \\ \text{s.t. } \{\ y, x\}\ \in T \end{array}\right\} \Rightarrow \bar{y}, \bar{x} \tag{5.175}$$

where $\bar{y}$ denotes the optimal level of observed sales (i.e., we do not observe the amount of corn transferred to livestock feed) and $\bar{x}$ denotes the optimal level of input used.

Next, consider drawing a sample assuming the amount of x_4 is quasi-fixed:

$$\begin{array}{c} \tilde{x}_4 = \bar{x}_4 \ni : \bar{x}_4 \leq x_4^* \\ \tilde{x}_4 = \phi\left(\bar{x}_4 - x_4^*\right) \ni : \bar{x}_4 > x_4^* \quad \text{and} \quad 0 \leq \phi < 1 \end{array} \tag{5.176}$$

for some fixed x_4^*. Thus, Equation (5.175) is resolved as

$$\left.\begin{array}{c} \max_{y,x} p'y - w'x \\ \text{s.t. } \{\ y, x\}\ \in T\ ,\ x_4 = \tilde{x}_4 \end{array}\right\} \Rightarrow \bar{y}, \bar{x}. \tag{5.177}$$

Next, we estimate the revenue function:

$$\begin{aligned} R\left(p, x\right) &= \alpha_0 + \alpha_1 p^* + A_{11} p^{*2} + \beta' x + \frac{1}{2} x' B x + p^* \Gamma x \\ y\left(p, x\right) &= \alpha_1 + A_{11} p^* + \Gamma x \\ p^* &= \frac{p_1}{p_2}. \end{aligned} \tag{5.178}$$

The results for this estimation are presented in Table 5.22. Given these results, we can define the marginal value product of each input:

Table 5.22 Revenue Function with Quasi-Fixed Input

Parameter	Estimate	Parameter	Estimate
α_0	872.303** (442.867)[a]	B_{14}	−0.209 (0.178)
α_1	3.239 (3.601)	B_{22}	−0.213 (0.236)
A_{11}	−3.925*** (0.166)	B_{23}	0.122 (0.146)
β_1	−0.001 (0.096)	B_{24}	0.527** (0.263)
β_2	−31.882*** (12.020)	B_{33}	−0.377*** (0.100)
β_3	22.139** (9.421)	B_{34}	−0.146 (0.126)
β_4	−42.410** (19.062)	B_{44}	1.176** (0.464)
B_{11}	−0.220 (0.143)	Γ_{11}	0.181*** (0.050)
B_{12}	0.578*** (0.170)	Γ_{12}	0.171*** (0.053)
B_{13}	−0.045 (0.113)	Γ_{13}	0.240*** (0.033)
Γ_{14}	0.719*** (0.072)		

Notes: [a]Numbers in parenthesis denote standard errors. ***,**Denote statistical significance at the 0.01 and 0.05 levels of confidence, respectively.

$$\nabla_x R(p,x) \Rightarrow \begin{cases} \beta_1 + B_{11}x_1 + B_{12}x_2 + B_{13}x_3 + B_{14}x_4 + \Gamma_{11}p^* \Rightarrow \hat{w}_1 \\ \beta_2 + B_{12}x_1 + B_{22}x_2 + B_{23}x_3 + B_{24}x_4 + \Gamma_{12}p^* \Rightarrow \hat{w}_2 \\ \beta_3 + B_{13}x_1 + B_{23}x_2 + B_{33}x_3 + B_{34}x_4 + \Gamma_{13}p^* \Rightarrow \hat{w}_3 \\ \beta_4 + B_{14}x_1 + B_{24}x_2 + B_{34}x_3 + B_{44}x_4 + \Gamma_{14}p^* \Rightarrow \hat{w}_4 \end{cases}. \tag{5.179}$$

Next, we use the results in Equation (5.179) to test whether the choice of input levels maximized profit:

$$\epsilon = w - \hat{w} \Rightarrow \begin{cases} \dfrac{\hat{\mu}_{\epsilon i}}{\hat{\sigma}_{\epsilon i}} \\ \hat{\mu}_\epsilon \Leftarrow \mathrm{E}\left[\epsilon_i\right] \\ \hat{\sigma}_{\epsilon i} \Leftarrow \mathrm{E}\left[(\epsilon - \mu_\epsilon)'(\epsilon - \mu_\epsilon)\right] \end{cases}. \tag{5.180}$$

Table 5.23 Test for Marginal Value Equal to Market Price

Input	Test Statistic
w_1	0.669
w_2	0.762
w_3	0.835
w_4	3.702

These results are presented in Table 5.23 — profit maximization cannot be rejected except in the case of input 4.

5.4.6.2 *Quasi-fixed inputs and the profit function*

Given our results in Tables 5.22 and 5.23, the estimation of the profit function

$$\begin{aligned}
\pi(p,w) &= \alpha_0 + \alpha' \begin{bmatrix} p_1^* \\ w_1^* \\ w_2^* \\ w_3^* \\ w_4^* \end{bmatrix} + \frac{1}{2} \begin{bmatrix} p_1^* \\ w_1^* \\ w_2^* \\ w_3^* \\ w_4^* \end{bmatrix}' A \begin{bmatrix} p_1^* \\ w_1^* \\ w_2^* \\ w_3^* \\ w_4^* \end{bmatrix} \\
y(p,w) &= \alpha_1 + A_{11}p_1^* + A_{12}w_1^* + A_{13}w_2^* + A_{14}w_3^* + A_{15}w_4^* \\
-x(p,w) &= \alpha_2 + A_{12}p_1^* + A_{22}w_1^* + A_{23}w_3^* + A_{24}w_4^* + A_{25}w_4^* \\
-x(p,w) &= \alpha_3 + A_{13}p_1^* + A_{23}w_1^* + A_{33}w_3^* + A_{34}w_4^* + A_{35}w_4^* \\
-x(p,w) &= \alpha_4 + A_{14}p_1^* + A_{24}w_1^* + A_{34}w_3^* + A_{44}w_4^* + A_{45}w_4^* \\
-x(p,w) &= \alpha_5 + A_{15}p_1^* + A_{25}w_1^* + A_{35}w_3^* + A_{45}w_4^* + A_{55}w_4^* \\
p_1^* &= \frac{p_1}{p_2},\ w_1^* = \frac{w_1}{p_2},\ \ldots,\ w_4^* = \frac{w_4}{p_2}
\end{aligned} \tag{5.181}$$

would appear to be incorrect:

$$\frac{\partial \pi(p,w)}{\partial w_4} \neq -x(p,w). \tag{5.182}$$

As an alternative, we formulate the problem as

$$\begin{aligned} \pi(p,w,z) &= p'y - w'x \\ \text{s.t. } \{y,\tilde{x},z\} &\in T \\ \tilde{x} &= \begin{pmatrix} x_1 \\ x_2 \\ x_3 \end{pmatrix} \quad z = x_4. \end{aligned} \tag{5.183}$$

As a starting point, consider the segmentation of inputs from Equation (5.183) on the revenue function:

$$\begin{aligned} &\max_y p'y \\ &\text{s.t. } \{y,\tilde{x},z\} \in T \\ R(p,\tilde{x},z) &= \alpha_0 + \alpha_1 p_1^* + \frac{1}{2}A_{11}p_1^{*2} + \begin{bmatrix} \beta_1 \\ \beta_2 \\ \beta_3 \end{bmatrix}' \begin{bmatrix} \tilde{x}_1 \\ \tilde{x}_2 \\ \tilde{x}_3 \end{bmatrix} \\ &+ \frac{1}{2}\begin{bmatrix} \tilde{x}_1 \\ \tilde{x}_2 \\ \tilde{x}_3 \end{bmatrix}' \begin{bmatrix} B_{11} & B_{12} & B_{13} \\ B_{12} & B_{22} & B_{23} \\ B_{13} & B_{23} & B_{33} \end{bmatrix} \begin{bmatrix} \tilde{x}_1 \\ \tilde{x}_2 \\ \tilde{x}_3 \end{bmatrix} \\ &+ p_1^* \begin{bmatrix} \Gamma_{11} & \Gamma_{12} & \Gamma_{13} \end{bmatrix} \begin{bmatrix} \tilde{x}_1 \\ \tilde{x}_2 \\ \tilde{x}_3 \end{bmatrix} \\ &+ \phi_1 z + z \begin{bmatrix} \Phi_{11} & \Phi_{12} & \Phi_{13} \end{bmatrix} \begin{bmatrix} \tilde{x}_1 \\ \tilde{x}_2 \\ \tilde{x}_3 \end{bmatrix} + \frac{1}{2}\Phi_{44} z^2 + \gamma_1 p_1^* z \\ y(p,\tilde{x},z) &= \alpha_1 + A_{11}p_1^* + \Gamma_{11}\tilde{x}_1 + \Gamma_{12}\tilde{x}_2 + \Gamma_{13}\tilde{x}_3 + \gamma_1 z. \end{aligned} \tag{5.184}$$

Constructing the profit function from the revenue function,

$$
\begin{aligned}
\pi\left(p,w\right) &= \max_{\tilde{x}} R\left(p,\tilde{x},z\right) - w'\tilde{x} \\
&\Rightarrow \beta + B\begin{bmatrix}\tilde{x}_1\\ \tilde{x}_2\\ \tilde{x}_2\end{bmatrix} = \begin{bmatrix}w_1\\ w_2\\ w_3\end{bmatrix} \\
&\Rightarrow \tilde{x}^* = \begin{bmatrix}\tilde{x}_1^*\\ \tilde{x}_2^8\\ \tilde{x}_3^*\end{bmatrix} = B^{-1}\left[\begin{bmatrix}w_1\\ w_2\\ w_3\end{bmatrix} - \beta\right].
\end{aligned} \tag{5.185}
$$

Substituting the optimal values for inputs into the objective function then yields

$$
\begin{aligned}
\pi\left(p,w,z\right) &= R\left(p,\tilde{x}^*\left(p,w,z\right),z\right) - w'\tilde{x}^*\left(p,w,z\right) \\
y\left(p,w,z\right) &= \nabla_p \pi\left(p,w,z\right) \\
-x\left(p,w,z\right) &= \nabla_w \pi\left(p,w,z\right).
\end{aligned} \tag{5.186}
$$

The empirical quasi-fixed profit function then becomes

$$
\begin{aligned}
\pi\left(p,w,z\right) = \alpha_0 &+ \begin{bmatrix}\alpha_1\\ \alpha_2\\ \alpha_3\\ \alpha_4\end{bmatrix}' \begin{bmatrix}p_1^*\\ w_1^*\\ w_2^*\\ w_3^*\end{bmatrix} \\
&+ \frac{1}{2}\begin{bmatrix}p_1^*\\ w_1^*\\ w_2^*\\ w_3^*\end{bmatrix}' \begin{bmatrix}A_{11} & A_{12} & A_{13} & A_{14}\\ A_{12} & A_{22} & A_{23} & A_{24}\\ A_{13} & A_{23} & A_{33} & A_{34}\\ A_{14} & A_{24} & A_{34} & A_{44}\end{bmatrix} \begin{bmatrix}p_1^*\\ w_1^*\\ w_2^*\\ w_3^*\end{bmatrix} + \beta z + \frac{1}{2}Bz^2 \\
&+ z\begin{bmatrix}\Gamma_{11} & \Gamma_{12} & \Gamma_{13} & \Gamma_{14}\end{bmatrix} \begin{bmatrix}p_1^*\\ w_1^*\\ w_2^*\\ w_3^*\end{bmatrix}.
\end{aligned} \tag{5.187}
$$

Note that the marginal value of the quasi-fixed input can be estimated by taking the derivative of profit function in Equation (5.187) with respect to the quasi-fixed variable z.

5.4.6.3 *Quasi-fixed variables and the cost function*

The equivalent cost function with quasi-fixed assets can be derived using the formulation

$$\pi(p,w,z) = \max_y \left[p'y - c(y,w,z)\right]. \tag{5.188}$$

Specifically, equating the profit function from Equation (5.188) with the profit function based on the revenue function,

$$\begin{aligned} K &= \max_y \left[p'y - c(y,w,z)\right] - \max_x \left[R(p,x) - w'x\right] = 0 \\ \nabla_w K &= -\nabla_w c(y,w,z) + x = 0 \Rightarrow x(y,w,z) = \nabla_w c(y,w,z). \end{aligned} \tag{5.189}$$

Hence, the dual result is that the cost function conditional on a quasi-fixed input obeys the standard dual results from the simple cost function specification (i.e., Shephard duality).

5.5 Chapter Summary

- Like the discussion of Chapter 3, the dual formulation is important to agricultural and applied economics because it provides a mechanism for addressing empirical questions. For example, we can use a cost function to estimate the elasticity of demand for an agricultural input such as seed or fertilizer.
- Dual specifications include the cost function, the profit function, and the revenue function. In the case of the cost function, the cost of producing a set of outputs is determined by the observed input prices assuming optimizing behavior. The derived demands are specified as a secondary set of equations where the level of each input used is a function of output levels and input prices. The profit function models firm profit as a function of output and input prices. The secondary equations used in the specification include the quantity supplied as a function of output and input prices and the quantity of input demanded as functions of the output and input prices. Finally, the revenue function models the revenue

of the firm as a function of output prices and input levels. The secondary equations involve the quantity supplied as a function of output prices and input levels.

- A critical point is that an estimated cost function is only a cost function if it obeys the properties in Section 4.2. For example, if the cost function is not concave in input prices, it cannot represent optimization behavior. This raises an epistemological issue: If our estimates do not possess the required characteristics, do we impose them and proceed with our analysis? Alternatively, we could take the rejection of the required properties as a sign of misspecification.

5.6 Review Questions

1. Using a general quadratic cost function with two outputs and three inputs, derive the demand curve for input 1.
2. Starting with the general quadratic cost function with two outputs and four inputs, impose homogeneity to derive the normalized quadratic cost function.
3. Derive the Lau formulation to impose convexity in output for a normalized quadratic with three outputs and four inputs.
4. Derive the Leontief cost function as a second-order expansion of an unknown function.

5.7 Exercises

1. Derive the cost and conditional input demand functions for the Cobb–Douglas production function with three inputs. Using the data in Assignment05-01.csv, estimate the production function and cost function for the Cobb–Douglas function. Do the results of the production function and cost function conform with the restrictions from Diewert? Are the estimates of the production function and the cost function consistent?
2. Using the data in PsuedoPanelData.csv,[4] estimate normalized quadratic cost function. Are these results consistent with the properties of the cost function?

[4]This data is available at http://www.charlesbmoss.com:8080/Book.Production.Economics/Chapter-2/PsuedoPanelData.csv.

3. Using the data in PsuedoPanelData.csv,[5] estimate the translog cost function with homogeneity imposed. Are these results consistent with the properties of the cost function?
4. Using the data in TwoOutputCost.csv, estimate the translog cost function with homogeneity imposed. Are these results consistent with the properties of the cost function?
5. Estimate the translog profit function for TwoOutputCost.csv. Check the regularity conditions. Derive the elasticity of supply for this cost function along with the associated standard errors.
6. Estimate the revenue function using the data in TwoOutput-Cost.csv. Check to see if x_3 is quasi-fixed.
7. Estimate the normalized quadratic cost function using TwoOutput Cost.csv and test for subadditivity.

[5]This data is available at http://www.charlesbmoss.com:8080/Book.Production.Economics/Chapter-5/TwoOutputDual.csv.

Chapter 6

Technical Change and Efficiency

6.1 The Economics of Technical Change

The most basic concept of changes in productivity is that for a given level of inputs, we now get more output. This basic notion is presented in Figure 6.1. In this figure, we assume that the inputs are constant at x, but the total level of outputs shifts from (y_1, y_2) to (y_1', y_2'). Alternatively, as depicted in Figure 6.2 in input space, it now takes fewer inputs to produce the same level of outputs. In both cases, most would agree that a technical change has taken place. Further, most would agree that the technical change has increased the economic well-being of the society. We now have more stuff for the same level of inputs. However, there are some issues that need to be addressed.

First, one could raise the question about embodied versus disembodied technical change. This debate regards whether there has been an increase in knowledge or whether there has been an increase in the quality of inputs. If the increase in output is associated with an increase in the quality of inputs, the question is whether it represents technical change in agriculture or in the input sector? For example, a large portion of the gains to research literature can be traced to the Griliches (1957) discussion of hybrid corn. In this case, the increase in technology was associated with the improvement in the input — seed. More recently, some of the increased productivity may be traced to genetically modified organisms (GMOs). Under most concepts of productivity, these increases do not represent changes in the productivity of agriculture, but can be traced to changes in the input bundle.

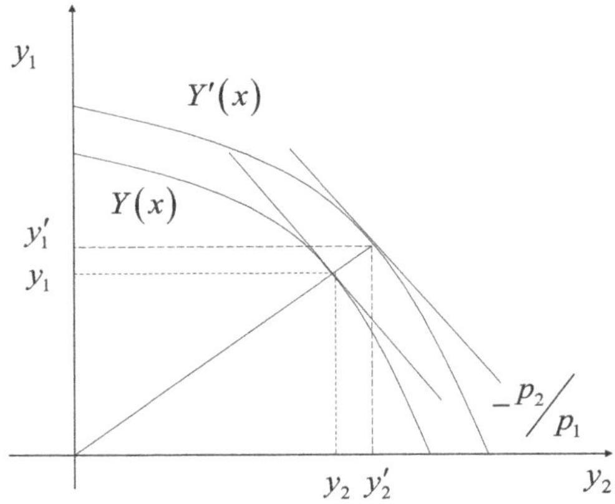

Fig. 6.1 Iso-Output Surface

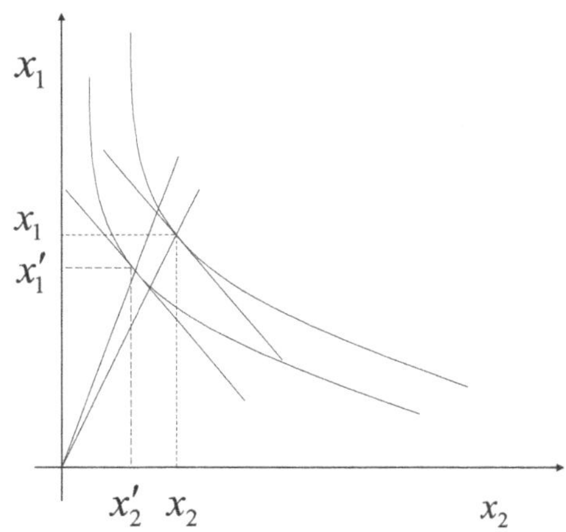

Fig. 6.2 Iso-Input Surface

A second area of concern is whether the changes in technology are neutral with regard to the input bundle. In Figure 6.2, the change in technology implies that relatively more x_1 is used after the change — the technology is biased toward x_1. In the hybrid corn example, additional fertilizer complemented the use of hybrid corn. In the classical discussion, Hicks developed the notion of labor or capital augmenting technical development.

6.1.1 Measuring Technical Change with Cost or Profit Functions

In the single input–single output analysis, one could directly measure technical change:

$$y = f(x,t) \Rightarrow \theta(t) = \frac{y}{x} \Rightarrow t = \theta^{-1}\left(\frac{y}{x}\right). \tag{6.1}$$

Several factors should be considered. We know that profit-maximizing behavior changes the point of production even in the univariate case. Specifically, we know that the decision maker chooses to produce where the marginal value product equals the price of the input. Thus, if either the price of the input or the price of the output changes, the ratio of outputs to inputs will change. Even in the single variable case, we would wonder about excluded factors (e.g., things beyond the decision maker's control).

Extending the analysis to the multivariate world, we begin by examining the product–product relationship in Figure 6.1. First, the value ratio

$$\theta(t) = \frac{Y'(x)}{Y(x)} = \frac{p_1 y_1' + p_2 y_2'}{p_1 y_1 + p_2 y_2} \tag{6.2}$$

could be used as one measure of technical change. Similarly, in the input–input relationship,

$$\theta(t) = \frac{V'(y)}{V(y)} = \frac{w_1 x_1' + w_2 x_2'}{w_1 x_1 + w_2 x_2} \tag{6.3}$$

could be hypothesized as a measure of technical change. Equation (6.2) asks how much more output are we getting from the same level of input while Equation (6.3) asks how much less input are we using to produce the same level of output? Each formulation can be justified from the profit-maximizing behavior. Specifically, the dual results suggest that

$$\theta(t) = \frac{Y'(x)}{Y(x)} = \frac{p_1 y_1(p,w,t=1) + p_2 y_2(p,w,t=1)}{p_1 y_1(p,w,t=0) + p_2 y_2(p,w,t=0)} \tag{6.4}$$

or the ratio can be viewed as the outcome of the optimal choice of output levels. Similarly, in the case of the inputs,

$$\theta(t) = \frac{V'(y)}{V(y)} = \frac{w_1 x_1(w, y, t = 1) + w_2 x_2(w, y, t = 1)}{w_1 x_1(w, y, t = 0) + w_2 x_2(w, y, t = 0)} \tag{6.5}$$

where the ratio depicts the difference in input choices. Implicitly, each ratio changes because of a change in technology — t (e.g., the shift from $t = 0$ to $t = 1$).

More formally, from duality, we know that

$$\begin{aligned} C\left(w, y, t\right) &= \min_{x>0} \left[w \cdot x : x \in V\left(y, t\right)\right] \Leftrightarrow \\ V^*\left(y, t\right) &= \left[x : w \cdot x \geq C\left(w, y, t\right), w > 0\right]. \end{aligned} \tag{6.6}$$

Thus, by gross simplification, we could envision a cost function:

$$\begin{aligned} C(w, y, t) &= \alpha_0 + \alpha' w + \frac{1}{2} w' A w + \beta' y + \frac{1}{2} \beta' y \\ &\quad + w' \Gamma y + \theta(w, y, t) \\ x(w, y, t) &= \alpha + A w + \Gamma y + \nabla_w \theta(w, y, t) \end{aligned} \tag{6.7}$$

where $\theta(w, y, t)$ is a measure of technical change.

This formulation allows us to discuss several key features of technology measurement. First, in the grossest sense, technological change tends to be a measurement of factors that we do not understand. From the preceding equation, what is the difference between technology and a residual? One approach is to proxy technical change with a simple time trend. Alternatively, several studies have used other proxy variables such as spending on agricultural research.

This formulation allows the research to examine the neutrality of technical change:

$$\frac{\frac{\partial C(w, y, t)}{\partial w_i}}{\frac{\partial C(w, y, t)}{\partial w_j}} = \frac{x_i(w, y, t)}{x_j(w, y, t)} = \frac{x_i(w, y)}{x_j(w, y)} \tag{6.8}$$

implies that the technical innovation does not change the relative input use — there is no factor bias.

Finally, it is possible to envision adjusting this measure for differences in input quality. For example, if one of the inputs increases in equality over time, we could adjust the price of that input upward to account for this increase in quality.

6.1.2 *Total Factor Productivity and Index Number Theory*

The index number approach can be looked at as an extension of the single input–single product scenario in Equation (6.1):

$$y = f(x,t) \Rightarrow \frac{dy}{dt} = \frac{\partial f(x,t)}{\partial x}\frac{dx}{dt} + \frac{\partial f(x,t)}{\partial t}. \tag{6.9}$$

In a multivariate context,

$$\frac{dy}{dt} = \sum_i \frac{\partial f(x,t)}{\partial x_i}\frac{dx_i}{dt} + \frac{\partial f(x,t)}{\partial t}. \tag{6.10}$$

Replacing the differentiation in Equation (6.10) with logarithmic differences,

$$\frac{d\ln(y)}{d\,t} = \sum_i \frac{\partial \ln(y)}{\partial \ln(x_i)}\frac{d\ln(x_i)}{d\,t} + T(x,t). \tag{6.11}$$

First, we replace the $\partial \ln(y)/\partial \ln(x_i)$ term in Equation (6.11) and then substitute the first-order condition $\partial y/\partial x_i = w_i$ to yield

$$\begin{aligned} \frac{\partial \ln(y)}{\partial \ln(x_i)} &= \frac{x_i}{y}\frac{\partial y}{\partial x_i} \\ &= \frac{x_i w_i}{y}. \end{aligned} \tag{6.12}$$

Extending the formulation slightly, we recognize that y may be a vector of outputs; hence, we replace the denominator in Equation (6.12) with $p'y$ to yield

$$\Rightarrow T(x,t) = \frac{d\ln(y)}{d\,t} - \sum_i \frac{w_i x_i}{p'y}\frac{d\ln(x_i)}{d\,t}. \tag{6.13}$$

This formulation is sometimes approximated as

$$\begin{aligned} T(x,t) &= \ln(y_t) - \ln(y_{t-1}) \\ &\quad - \sum_i \left(\frac{1}{2}\left[f_{it} + f_{i,t-1}\right]\right)\left[\ln(x_{it}) - \ln(x_{i,t-1})\right] \end{aligned} \tag{6.14}$$

where $f_i = w_i x_i/C$. This approximation is referred to as the Tornqvist–Theil measure.

Working backward from Equation (6.10),

$$\begin{aligned} d\ln(y) &= d\ln(x) + T(x,t) \\ \Rightarrow d\ln(y) - d\ln(x) &= T(x) \\ \Rightarrow d\ln\left(\frac{y}{x}\right) &= T(x,y) \\ \Rightarrow d\ln\left(\frac{Q_y}{Q_x}\right) &= T(x,y) \end{aligned} \tag{6.15}$$

where Q_y and Q_x are index numbers representing the total quantity of inputs and outputs. In the Tornqvist–Theil index, the indices were implicitly Divisia output and input indices.

To demonstrate the construction of productivity measures using indices, consider the pseudo-data in Table 6.1. First, we construct the change in the Tornqvist–Theil measure of the change in output. Defining the output equivalent to Equation (6.14),

$$T(y,t) = \sum_r \left(\frac{1}{2}\left[g_{rt} + g_{r,t-1}\right]\right)\left[\ln\left(y_{rt}\right) - \left(y_{r,t-1}\right)\right] \tag{6.16}$$

where g_{rt} is the revenue share for output r. Using data from observation 2 in Table 6.1,

$$\begin{aligned} T(y,2) = {} & \frac{1}{2}(0.2416 + 0.2110)(\ln(6.5943) - \ln(6.2087)) \\ & + \frac{1}{2}(0.7890 + 0.7584)(\ln(8.2542) - \ln(7.5093)) = 0.0868. \end{aligned} \tag{6.17}$$

The result in Equation (6.17) indicates that total output grew at an annual rate of 8.68% between observation 1 and observation 2. Following a similar process for inputs, we see that total input use grew at an annual rate of 4.25% over this time period.

To derive the overall change in productivity, we assign year 1 as the base period. The total output and input levels can then be computed as

$$\begin{aligned} Q_{O,2} = 1.0 \times \exp(0.0868) = 1.0907 \quad Q_{I,2} = 1.0 \times \exp(0.0425) \\ = 1.0433. \end{aligned} \tag{6.18}$$

Table 6.1 Pseudo-Data for Productivity Numbers

Obs.	P_1	P_2	Y_1	Y_2	W_1	W_2	W_3	W_4	X_1	X_2	X_3	X_4
1	4.8651	12.6280	6.2087	7.5093	0.8290	1.6317	0.4637	1.5876	19.2236	29.0506	26.7150	58.3115
2	4.1317	12.3392	6.5943	8.2542	0.7912	1.3875	0.5072	1.2729	21.3079	31.9155	32.9362	56.6725
3	5.1091	12.2345	10.9512	12.4249	1.1123	1.3125	0.2648	1.5517	27.7925	32.3141	45.1186	121.4830
4	5.4730	12.1324	15.0423	14.9603	1.1880	1.0187	0.4048	1.4982	37.3774	34.8442	68.2242	105.7197
5	5.4270	13.2377	19.3225	19.0186	1.1417	1.0369	0.4228	1.3243	49.2134	49.6437	86.4361	120.8777
6	5.3563	13.1265	7.2714	8.2599	1.2055	1.4531	0.5894	1.5906	13.8618	19.6120	27.9133	43.1010
7	5.5331	12.8955	10.5272	10.8114	0.9227	1.3395	0.5051	1.8560	16.8556	31.4352	36.0842	59.3978
8	5.5023	12.1974	6.2739	6.9911	1.2259	1.4893	0.5839	1.7475	10.0520	14.2549	19.2941	32.2826
9	5.4446	12.5119	7.7622	8.0762	1.0746	1.4028	0.6774	1.7001	11.7757	18.6948	23.5999	31.5483
10	6.2098	12.4120	9.1291	9.4767	0.9454	1.6943	0.7317	1.7158	13.3646	22.4804	19.5049	30.5815
11	6.8144	12.2336	17.7108	16.7633	0.4474	2.2228	0.5753	2.0270	23.1693	87.3674	24.1643	65.6856
12	6.4542	11.0890	10.2832	11.2014	0.4328	2.4727	0.7240	1.8530	14.9212	49.6407	11.6043	29.3499
13	6.5929	11.2353	10.6753	11.5371	0.3676	2.7537	0.7842	1.8977	14.8384	58.5246	10.3063	26.6134
14	6.7255	11.4802	14.1237	14.5122	0.3870	2.4992	0.6961	1.9655	19.7161	72.8032	14.4682	37.6510
15	6.5639	10.8120	17.7730	18.7824	0.0973	2.3567	0.9451	1.7868	23.8362	136.3101	16.9838	31.5538
16	6.5989	11.4516	20.6246	22.1114	0.0451	2.3533	1.0718	1.4551	31.1124	136.3180	20.4843	32.5473
17	6.0488	10.0773	20.5192	21.7896	0.0528	2.1523	1.1694	1.2659	32.0014	132.6965	17.7628	25.6037
18	6.6053	10.4464	26.0615	29.0823	0.1378	2.1954	1.1072	1.0649	55.7562	134.2954	23.8359	38.0089
19	6.1591	10.0125	22.0799	22.0950	0.6215	2.0553	1.0532	0.8346	57.3373	58.0985	19.0430	31.6528
20	6.1966	9.8453	22.9041	22.4572	0.5023	2.1692	0.9797	0.9606	47.7608	68.5136	16.8258	32.7178
21	5.4192	10.4917	22.2817	22.8747	0.2850	2.3364	1.1129	0.9526	33.6712	98.9769	13.8395	24.3601
22	4.2185	11.1648	8.6205	10.7753	0.2410	2.7170	1.0554	1.1516	8.3304	46.3112	5.9140	12.2092
23	3.3210	12.3220	4.2334	6.7255	0.4655	2.6687	0.9263	1.1642	5.3497	19.3176	5.0682	11.5527
24	3.9269	13.1274	12.9610	16.3477	0.3155	2.3533	0.9448	1.0204	12.4905	61.4290	11.7486	21.8587
25	4.2035	13.5667	10.8238	14.0328	0.6616	2.1425	1.1403	0.8424	11.0532	25.4525	10.8921	16.2264
26	4.4515	13.2130	11.0278	13.5748	0.8420	1.9843	1.2481	0.7927	10.7697	18.0154	10.4439	13.4404
27	4.6755	12.7143	6.0028	7.8099	0.9182	2.1410	1.2039	1.2109	4.5643	9.6765	5.2714	8.5594
28	6.1959	15.0560	21.7100	22.3120	0.9181	1.9515	1.2351	1.1395	16.5395	28.4854	16.1861	21.5361
29	6.4094	15.7319	22.8215	21.9588	1.2959	1.6641	1.2009	1.2264	15.5676	20.7195	19.0829	22.8150
30	7.3834	15.3362	45.7300	37.6650	0.9113	1.4984	1.1298	1.4820	28.9985	53.1289	34.4187	39.8929

Table 6.2 Tornqvist–Theil Total Factor Productivity Computation

Obs.	$d\ln(y)/dt$	Output	$d\ln(x)/dt$	Input	Total Factor Productivity
1		1.0000		1.0000	1.0000
2	0.0868	1.0907	0.0425	1.0434	1.0454
3	0.4326	1.6810	0.5030	1.7254	0.9743
4	0.2240	2.1030	−0.0064	1.7143	1.2267
5	0.2432	2.6819	0.2036	2.1014	1.2762
6	−0.8740	1.1191	−1.0605	0.7277	1.5378
7	0.2974	1.5066	0.3339	1.0162	1.4826
8	−0.4597	0.9513	−0.6414	0.5351	1.7779
9	0.1643	1.1212	0.0940	0.5878	1.9073
10	0.1606	1.3166	0.0261	0.6034	2.1820
11	0.6025	2.4049	0.9654	1.5844	1.5179
12	−0.4536	1.5279	−0.6479	0.8289	1.8433
13	0.0323	1.5780	0.0818	0.8995	1.7542
14	0.2475	2.0211	0.2562	1.1622	1.7389
15	0.2477	2.5891	0.4358	1.7971	1.4407
16	0.1580	3.0324	0.0144	1.8232	1.6632
17	−0.0113	2.9985	−0.0565	1.7231	1.7401
18	0.2708	3.9309	0.0769	1.8608	2.1124
19	−0.2343	3.1098	−0.6211	0.9999	3.1100
20	0.0241	3.1857	0.0721	1.0746	2.9644
21	0.0017	3.1912	0.2052	1.3194	2.4187
22	−0.8086	1.4217	−0.7731	0.6090	2.3343
23	−0.5166	0.8481	−0.7102	0.2994	2.8332
24	0.9270	2.1432	1.0481	0.8538	2.5102
25	−0.1580	1.8300	−0.6788	0.4331	4.2256
26	−0.0226	1.7891	−0.2364	0.3419	5.2328
27	−0.5649	1.0170	−0.6254	0.1829	5.5591
28	1.1094	3.0842	1.0745	0.5357	5.7569
29	0.0033	3.0942	−0.0926	0.4884	6.3359
30	0.5914	5.5896	0.7125	0.9958	5.6132

The Total Factor Productivity (TFP) for observation 2 is $1.0907/1.0433 = 1.0454$, as presented in Table 6.2. Given the data in Table 6.1, we can compute $T(y,2) = 0.4326$ and $T(x,3) = 0.5030$. This allows for the calculation of the output and input indices for period 3 as

$$Q_{O,3} = 1.0907 \times \exp(0.4326) = 1.6810 \quad Q_{I,3} = 1.0433 \times \exp(0.5030) = 1.7254. \tag{6.19}$$

These calculations imply a TFP in period 3 of 0.9742. While it is somewhat unusual for TFP to decline, the Tornqvist–Theil results presented in Table 6.2 indicate a general growth in productivity over time. Again, it is important to note that the data is pseudo-data.

While the Tornqvist–Theil index is typically a superior index number, it does have disadvantages. Specifically, the logarithmic formulation does not allow for zero output or input levels. Another index number formulation that does not have this disadvantage is the Fisher index which is the geometric average of two indices — the Laspeyres and the Paasche indices. The difference between the two formulations involves the assumption of the base price. The Laspeyres index uses the $t-1$ price as its base while the Paasche index uses the t price as its base when computing changes in quantity. As an example, suppose that we want to compute $dQ^L_{O,2}$ (the rough equivalence of $T(y,2)$ developed in Equation (6.17) for the Laspeyres index). Again, using the data in Table 6.1,

$$\begin{aligned} dQ^L_{O,2} &= \frac{y_{1,2}p_{1,1} + y_{2,2}p_{2,1}}{y_{1,1}p_{1,1} + y_{2,1}p_{1,1}} \\ &= \frac{6.5943 \times 4.8651 + 8.2542 \times 12.6280}{6.2087 \times 4.8651 + 7.5093 \times 12.6280} = 1.0902 \end{aligned} \tag{6.20}$$

which means that the output grew at 9.02% between periods 1 and 2. The results for the Laspeyres indices are presented in Table 6.3. The Paasche formulation is similar, but uses the prices from the second observation:

$$\begin{aligned} dQ^P_{0,2} &= \frac{y_{1,2}p_{1,2} + y_{2,2}p_{2,2}}{y_{1,1}p_{1,2} + y_{2,1}p_{1,2}} \\ &= \frac{6.5943 \times 4.1317 + 8.2542 \times 12.3392}{6.2087 \times 4.1317 + 7.5093 \times 12.3392} = 1.0912. \end{aligned} \tag{6.21}$$

The Fisher index is the geometric average of the Laspeyres and Paasche indices ($\sqrt{1.0902 \times 1.0912} = 1.0907$). These Fisher indices for both outputs and inputs are presented in Table 6.3. Like the Tornqvist–Theil formulation, these computations depict the change in productivity between two observations; hence, we have to specify a base period. Again, if we choose observation 1 as the base period,

Table 6.3 Fisher Index Total Factor Productivity

Obs.	Laspeyres	Paasche	Fischer	Output	Laspeyres	Paasche	Fischer	Output	TFP
1				1.0000	0.0000	0.0000	0.0000	1.0000	1.0000
2	1.0902	1.0912	1.0907	1.0907	1.0397	1.0467	1.0432	1.0432	1.0455
3	1.5381	1.5442	1.5411	1.6809	1.6291	1.6874	1.6580	1.7296	0.9718
4	1.2497	1.2523	1.2510	2.1028	0.9841	0.9989	0.9915	1.7149	1.2262
5	1.2754	1.2751	1.2753	2.6816	1.2227	1.2287	1.2257	2.1019	1.2758
6	0.4173	0.4173	0.4173	1.1190	0.3452	0.3475	0.3464	0.7280	1.5370
7	1.3456	1.3470	1.3463	1.5065	1.3957	1.3978	1.3968	1.0169	1.4814
8	0.6317	0.6312	0.6314	0.9513	0.5267	0.5263	0.5265	0.5354	1.7767
9	1.1788	1.1782	1.1785	1.1211	1.0984	1.0987	1.0985	0.5881	1.9062
10	1.1742	1.1743	1.1742	1.3164	1.0240	1.0286	1.0263	0.6036	2.1810
11	1.8246	1.8287	1.8266	2.4046	2.5566	2.7223	2.6382	1.5924	1.5101
12	0.6358	0.6349	0.6353	1.5277	0.5210	0.5256	0.5233	0.8333	1.8333
13	1.0328	1.0328	1.0328	1.5778	1.0829	1.0880	1.0855	0.9045	1.7444
14	1.2808	1.2808	1.2808	2.0208	1.2901	1.2939	1.2920	1.1686	1.7293
15	1.2812	1.2809	1.2811	2.5888	1.5484	1.5563	1.5524	1.8141	1.4271
16	1.1711	1.1713	1.1712	3.0321	1.0147	1.0144	1.0145	1.8404	1.6475
17	0.9888	0.9888	0.9888	2.9981	0.9451	0.9453	0.9452	1.7395	1.7235
18	1.3114	1.3106	1.3110	3.9304	1.0808	1.0780	1.0794	1.8776	2.0933
19	0.7914	0.7908	0.7911	3.1094	0.5150	0.5484	0.5314	0.9978	3.1162
20	1.0244	1.0245	1.0244	3.1853	1.0695	1.0816	1.0755	1.0732	2.9681
21	1.0007	1.0028	1.0017	3.1909	1.2179	1.2499	1.2338	1.3241	2.4099
22	0.4429	0.4484	0.4456	1.4220	0.4609	0.4634	0.4621	0.6119	2.3240
23	0.5933	0.6006	0.5969	0.8488	0.4889	0.4905	0.4897	0.2996	2.8326
24	2.5222	2.5307	2.5264	2.1444	2.8548	2.8546	2.8547	0.8554	2.5069
25	0.8539	0.8538	0.8539	1.8310	0.4960	0.5122	0.5040	0.4312	4.2468
26	0.9773	0.9780	0.9776	1.7901	0.7842	0.7941	0.7891	0.3402	5.2614
27	0.5687	0.5682	0.5684	1.0175	0.5315	0.5384	0.5349	0.1820	5.5912
28	3.0243	3.0395	3.0319	3.0851	2.9251	2.9311	2.9281	0.5329	5.7893
29	1.0033	1.0032	1.0033	3.0951	0.9045	0.9203	0.9124	0.4862	6.3660
30	1.8011	1.8115	1.8063	5.5907	2.0488	2.0282	2.0384	0.9911	5.6410

Table 6.4 Comparing the Tornqvist–Theil and Fisher Total Factor Productivities

Obs.	Tornqvist–Theil	Fisher
1	1.0000	1.0000
2	1.0454	1.0455
3	0.9743	0.9718
4	1.2267	1.2262
5	1.2762	1.2758
6	1.5378	1.5370
7	1.4826	1.4814
8	1.7779	1.7767
9	1.9073	1.9062
10	2.1820	2.1810
11	1.5179	1.5101
12	1.8433	1.8333
13	1.7542	1.7444
14	1.7389	1.7293
15	1.4407	1.4271
16	1.6632	1.6475
17	1.7401	1.7235
18	2.1124	2.0933
19	3.1100	3.1162
20	2.9644	2.9681
21	2.4187	2.4099
22	2.3343	2.3240
23	2.8332	2.8326
24	2.5102	2.5069
25	4.2256	4.2468
26	5.2328	5.2614
27	5.5591	5.5912
28	5.7569	5.7893
29	6.3359	6.3660
30	5.6132	5.6410

$Q_{O,2} = 1.0 \times 1.0907 = 1.0907$ and $Q_{O,3} = 1.0907 \times 1.5411 = 1.6809$. The TFP for period 2 is then $Q_{O,2}/Q_{I,2} = 1.0907/1.0432 = 1.0455$. Note as depicted in Table 6.4 that the TFPs computed using the Tornqvist–Theil and Fisher approaches are quite similar.

6.1.3 *Valuing State-Level Research*

Building on the derivation of TFP, we can examine whether investments in agricultural research and development drives agricultural

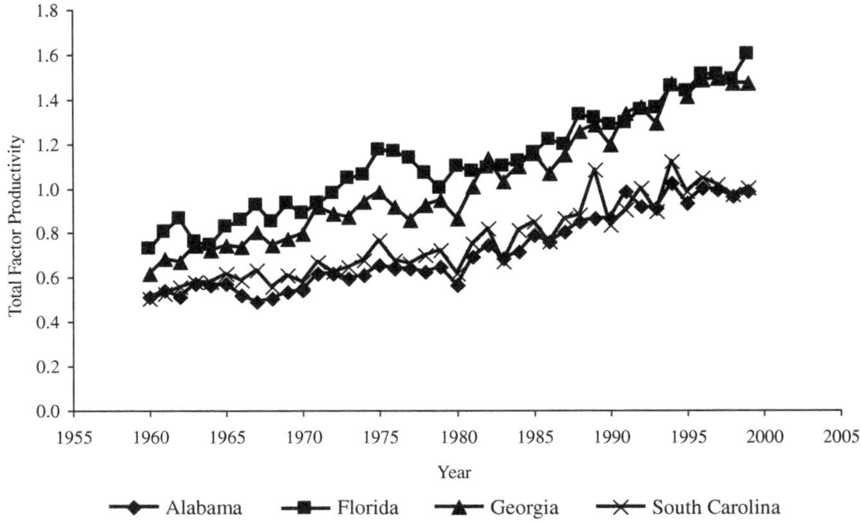

Fig. 6.3 TFP Growth in the Southeast

productivity. Moss (2006) examines whether investments in agricultural research in Florida are associated with increases in TFP using the cointegration analysis. As depicted in Figure 6.3, Florida's productivity has been above that of other southeastern states. In addition, the growth in productivity is correlated with the stock of expenditures on agricultural research in Florida. Note that both TFP and the R&D stock in Figure 6.4 appear non-stationary (e.g., there are no multiple crossing for any fixed point in the data). This non-stationarity means that any simple regression results may be spurious. As a result, Moss uses Johansen's (1996) cointegration specification.

6.1.3.1 *Cointegration estimator*

The Johansen (1988) approach involves estimating a vector error-correction mechanism expressed as

$$\Delta x_t = \Pi x_{t-1} + \sum_{i=1}^{k} \Gamma_i \Delta x_{t-i} + \Phi D_t + \epsilon_t \tag{6.22}$$

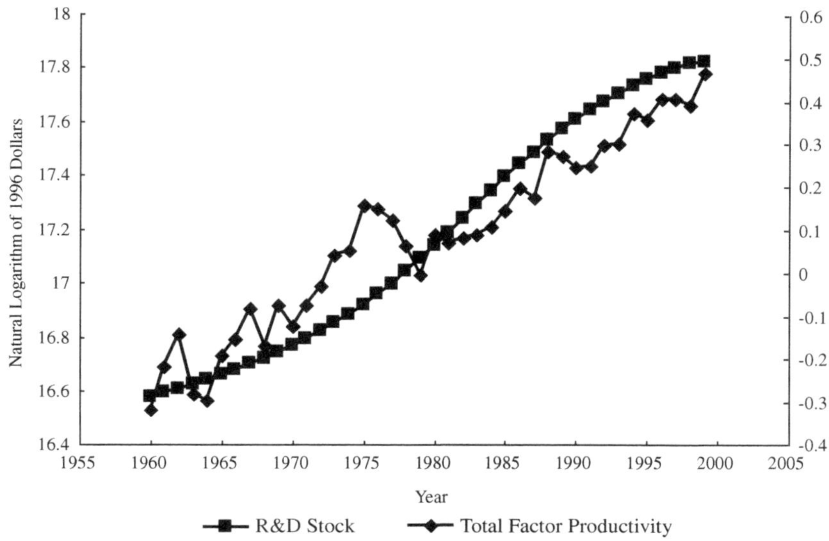

Fig. 6.4 TFP Growth Versus R&D Stock

where x_t is a vector of endogenous variables, Δx_t denotes the time difference of that vector, D_t is a vector of exogenous variables, ϵ_t is a vector of residuals, and Π, Γ_i, and Φ are estimated parameters. If a long-run relationship (e.g., cointegrating vector) exists, the Π matrix is singular ($\Pi = \alpha'\beta$). The β vector is the cointegrating vector or the long-run equilibrium. The statistical properties of the cointegrating vector are determined by the eigenvalues of the estimated Π matrix.

Denoting λ_i as the ith eigenvalue (in descending order of significance), the test for significance of the cointegrating vector can be written as

$$2\ln\left[Q(H_1(r)|H_1(p))\right] = -T\sum_{i=r+1}^{p}\ln(1-\hat{\lambda}_i) \tag{6.23}$$

which tests the hypothesis that r cointegrating vectors are present, $H_1(r)$, against the hypothesis that p cointegrating vectors are present, $H_1(p)$.

The existence of a cointegrating vector in this framework implies that the linear combination (z_t) of the natural logarithm of TFP and research and the natural logarithm of research and development stocks (RD_t) is stationary, or a long-run equilibrium between these two series exists. While this cointegrating vector is not uniquely identified, the long-run relationship can be expressed as

$$z_t = \begin{bmatrix} 1.000 \\ -0.794 \end{bmatrix}' \begin{bmatrix} \ln(\mathrm{TFP}_t) \\ \ln(\mathrm{RD}_t) \end{bmatrix} + 13.433. \quad (6.24)$$

Building on this expression, the long-run relationship can be expressed as

$$\ln(\mathrm{TFP}_t) - 0.794 \ln(\mathrm{RD}_t) + 13.433 = z_t. \quad (6.25)$$

Manipulating this result further yields

$$\frac{d\mathrm{TFP}_t}{d\mathrm{RD}_t} = 0.794 \frac{\mathrm{TFP}_t}{\mathrm{RD}_t}. \quad (6.26)$$

Using the geometric mean of both TFP and research and development stocks, TFP increases 0.0302 with a one million dollar increase in the research and development stock. This number appears small, but it represents 113% of the average annual increase in the productivity observed in the state. While the results indicate that productivity growth is associated with increased investment in agricultural research, Moss finds that TFP is not associated with either net cash income or farmland values. This implies that the gains to productivity do not affect agricultural wealth or income. Moss hypothesizes that most of the gains to productivity accrues to consumers.

6.1.4 *Technological Change and Factor Bias*

One possibility, as mentioned earlier in this chapter, is that changes in technology are biased toward a particular input. The scenario discussed earlier in this chapter is the possibility that hybrid seeds required the use of additional fertilizer. To develop this possibility, we start with the quadratic production function:

$$f(x_1, x_2) = a_0 + a_1 x_1 + a_2 x_2 + \frac{1}{2}(A_{11} x_1^2 + 2A_{12} x_1 x_2 + A_{22} x_2^2). \quad (6.27)$$

Assuming an output price of p and input prices of w_1 and w_2 for inputs x_1 and x_2, respectively, the derived demands for each input can be expressed as

$$\begin{aligned} x_1^*(p, w_1, w_2) &= \frac{A_{12}a_2p - A_{22}a_1p + A_{22}w_1 - A_{12}w_2}{p(A_{11}A_{22} - A_{12}^2)} \\ x_2^*(p, w_1, w_2) &= \frac{A_{12}a_1p - A_{11}a_2p - A_{12}w_1 + A_{11}w_2}{p(A_{11}A_{22} - A_{12}^2)}. \end{aligned} \tag{6.28}$$

In order to analyze the possible effect of technological change, we hypothesize an input augmenting technical change similar to the general form of technological innovation introduced by Hayami and Ruttan.

We introduce two functions:

$$\begin{aligned} x_1^* &= \gamma_1(\psi)x_1 \\ x_2^* &= \gamma_2(\psi)x_2 \end{aligned} \tag{6.29}$$

where $\gamma_1(\psi)$ and $\gamma_2(\psi)$ are augmentation factors and ψ is a technological change. Hence, $\gamma_1(\psi),\ \gamma_2(\psi) \geq 1$ for any $\psi > 0$.

Thus, technological change increases the output created by each unit of input. Integrating these increases into the foregoing production framework, the derived demands for each input becomes

$$\begin{aligned} x_1^*(p, w_1, w_2, \psi) &= \frac{\begin{matrix} A_{12}a_2\gamma_1(\psi)\gamma_2(\psi)p - A_{22}a_1\gamma_1(\psi)\gamma_2(\psi)p \\ +A_{22}\gamma_2(\psi)w_1 - A_{12}\gamma_1(\psi)w_2 \end{matrix}}{p(A_{11}A_{22} - A_{12}^2)\gamma_1^2(\psi)\gamma_2(\psi)} \\ x_2^*(p, w_1, w_2, \psi) &= \frac{\begin{matrix} A_{12}a_1\gamma_1(\psi)\gamma_2(\psi)p - A_{11}a_2\gamma_1(\psi)\gamma_2(\psi)p \\ -A_{12}\gamma_2(\psi)w_1 + A_{11}\gamma_1(\psi)w_2 \end{matrix}}{p(A_{11}A_{22} - A_{12}^2)\gamma_1(\psi)\gamma_2^2(\psi)}. \end{aligned} \tag{6.30}$$

In order to simplify our discussion, we assume that the new technology does not affect the effectiveness of x_1, or $\gamma_1(\psi) \to 1$.

Under this assumption, the derived demand for each input becomes

$$x_1^*(p, w_1, w_2, \psi) = \frac{\begin{array}{c} A_{12}a_2\gamma_2(\psi)p - A_{22}a_1\gamma_2(\psi)p - A_{12}w_2 \\ +A_{22}\gamma_2(\psi)w_1 \end{array}}{p(A_{11}A_{22} - A_{12}^2)\gamma_2(\psi)}$$

$$x_2^*(p, w_1, w_2, \psi) = \frac{\begin{array}{c} A_{12}a_1\gamma_2(\psi)p - A_{11}a_2\gamma_2(\psi)p - A_{12}\gamma_2(\psi)w_1 \\ +A_{11}w_2 \end{array}}{p(A_{11}A_{22} - A_{12}^2)\gamma_2^2(\psi)}. \tag{6.31}$$

Finally, we track the derivative of each derived demand curve with $\gamma_2(\psi) \to 1$ (or the instantaneous change in technology) yielding

$$\left.\frac{\partial x_1^*(p, w_1, w_2, \psi)}{\partial \psi}\right|_{\gamma_2(\psi)\to 1} = \frac{(A_{12}a_2p - A_{22}a_1p + A_{22}w_1)\,\gamma_1'(\psi)}{\left(A_{11}A_{22} - A_{12}^2\right)p} - \frac{(A_{12}a_2p - A_{22}a_1p - A_{12}w_2 + A_{22}w_1)\,\gamma_1'(\psi)}{\left(A_{11}A_{22} - A_{12}^2\right)p}$$

$$\left.\frac{\partial x_2^*(p, w_1, w_2, \psi)}{\partial \psi}\right|_{\gamma_2(\psi)\to 1} = \frac{(A_{12}a_1p - A_{11}a_2p - A_{12}w_1)\,\gamma_1'(\psi)}{\left(A_{11}A_{22} - A_{12}^2\right)p} - \frac{(A_{12}a_1p - A_{11}a_2p - A_{12}w_1 + A_{11}w_2)\,\gamma_1'(\psi)}{\left(A_{11}A_{22} - A_{12}^2\right)p}. \tag{6.32}$$

In order to demonstrate how this formulation works, we estimate at slightly modified quadratic production function using the aggregate productivity data from the United States Department of Agriculture, Economic Research Service.[1] Specifically, the quadratic production is

$$\gamma(t) = \exp(\beta_1 + \beta_2 t + \beta_3\cos(2\pi t) + \beta_4\sin(2\pi t) + \beta_5\cos(4\pi t) + \beta_6\sin(4\pi t))$$

[1]These data are available at www.charlesbmoss.com:8080/Book.Production.Economics/AggregateUSDA.csv.

$$
\begin{aligned}
f\left(x_1, x_2, x_3\right) = & \alpha_{00} + \alpha_{01} t + \alpha_1 x_1 + \alpha_2 x_2 + \left(\alpha_3 \gamma\left(t\right)\right) \\
& + \frac{1}{2} A_{11} x_1 x_1 + A_{12} x_1 x_2 \\
& + \left(A_{13} \gamma(t)\right) x_1 x_3 + \frac{1}{2} A_{22} x_2 x_2 \\
& + \left(A_{23} \gamma(t)\right) x_2 x_3 + \frac{1}{2}\left(A_{33} \gamma(t)^2\right) x_3 x_3 \qquad (6.33)
\end{aligned}
$$

where $f(x_1, x_2, x_3) = Y$ is total agricultural output, x_1 is capital, x_2 is labor, and x_3 is intermediate input. The time variable t is normalized by dividing by 70 to scale the sinusoids. Hence, in this formulation, we examine whether changes in technology affect the relative use of intermediate inputs. We estimate the production function in Equation (6.33) along with the first-order conditions for profit maximization. In addition, we restrict $\gamma\left(t\right) = 1.0$ for $t = 35$ or 1982. In addition, we restrict the Hessian matrix to be negative semi-definite and the marginal products at the mean to be greater than or equal to zero. The estimated coefficients for this specification are presented in Table 6.5.

The estimated parameters in Table 6.5 implies a significant increase in $\gamma(t)$ over time, as presented in Figure 6.5. In order to apply the concepts in Equations (6.31) and (6.32), we collapse the production function into a two-dimensional function. We also increase the diagonal of the A matrix since the concavity constraint essentially makes this matrix singular. The resulting production function can be written as

$$
\begin{aligned}
f(x_1, x_3) = & 0.5480 + 6.0923 x_1 + 5.0053 x_3 - 1.3302 x_1 x_1 \\
& + 0.1028 x_1 x_3 - 1.3072 x_2 x_2. \qquad (6.34)
\end{aligned}
$$

Substituting this result into Equation (6.32) yields

$$
\begin{aligned}
\frac{\partial x_1}{\partial t} = & \frac{0.1439\left(2.6105 p - 2.6143 w_1\right)}{p} \frac{\partial \gamma(t)}{\partial t} \\
& - \frac{0.1439(16.4416 p - 2.6143 - 0.1028 w_2)}{p} \frac{\partial \gamma(t)}{\partial t} \\
= & - 1.9795 \frac{\partial \gamma(t)}{\partial t} \qquad (6.35)
\end{aligned}
$$

Table 6.5 Model of Factor Bias

Parameter	Estimate	Parameter	Estimate
β_0	-0.6835^{***} (0.1970)[a]	α_2	0.6359^{***} (0.0842)
β_1	1.3065^{***} (0.3100)	α_3	0.6404^{***} (0.0243)
β_2	-0.0876 (0.0962)	A_{11}	-0.1381 (0.1566)
β_3	-0.0163 (0.0615)	A_{12}	-0.1393 (0.1494)
β_4	-0.0573 (0.0520)	A_{13}	0.1028^{*} (0.0552)
β_5	-0.0180 (0.0206)	A_{22}	-0.2180^{***} (0.0604)
α_{00}	-0.6668^{***} (0.1527)	A_{23}	0.1383 (0.0885)
α_{01}	1.0358^{***} (0.2313)	A_{33}	-0.0920 (0.0663)
α_1	0.8395^{***} (0.0989)		

Notes: [a]Numbers in parenthesis denote standard errors.
***,*Denote statistical significance at the 0.01, 0.10 levels of confidence respectively.

$$\begin{aligned}\frac{\partial x_2}{\partial t} &= \frac{0.1439(13.9429p - 0.1028w_1)}{p}\frac{\partial \gamma(t)}{\partial t} \\ &\quad - \frac{0.1439(13.9429p - 0.1028w_1 - 2.6605w_2)}{p}\frac{\partial \gamma(t)}{\partial t} \\ &= 0.3125\frac{\partial \gamma(t)}{\partial t}.\end{aligned}$$

Hence, the results suggest that the change in technology has increased the use of intermediate inputs relative to capital; however, the magnitude of these changes are determined by $\partial\gamma(t)/\partial t$. Taking the change in $\gamma(t)$ for 2001–2010 as 0.0626 (based on the estimated $\gamma(t)$ function), the change in the demand for capital is –0.1240 while the change in the demand for intermediate inputs becomes 0.0196.

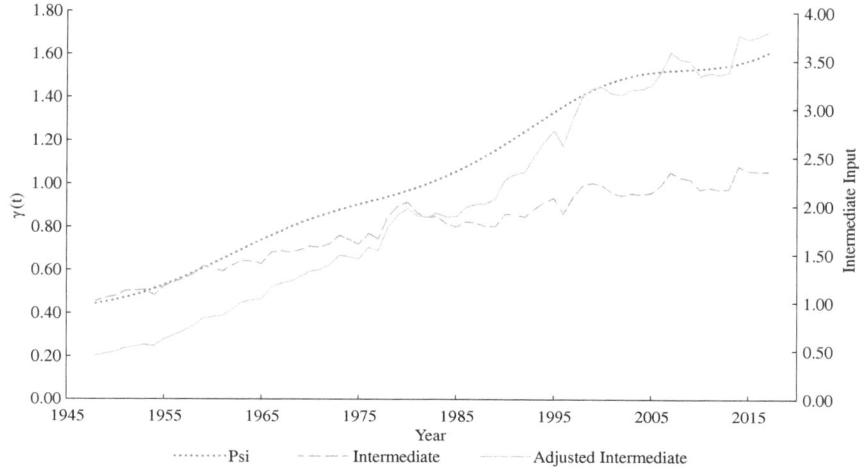

Fig. 6.5 Measurement of Change in Effectiveness of Intermediate Inputs over Time

6.2 Measuring Economic Efficiency

6.2.1 *An Overview of Economic Efficiency*

The most basic concept of the production function is that they represent some kind of frontier. For example, in our discussion of Diewert, we defined the production function as

$$f\,(x) = \max\left[\mu : x \text{ belongs to } L(\mu)\right]. \tag{6.36}$$

Thus, $y = f(x)$ was the largest output possible for a given set of inputs. This concept of "maximum possible yield" is depicted graphically in Figure 6.6. Specifically, the output for individual firms is somewhat below this outer or *efficient* envelope. This gap between the production frontier and the firm's output is an *inefficiency*. There are two ways to view the shortfall. Specifically, consider point A where the firm uses input x^* and produces y^*. One way to think about the inefficiency is that the firm should be able to produce output $\tilde{y}$ from input x^*. Alternatively, the firm could reduce its input level to $\tilde{x}$ and still produce y^*. Either way, the firm could increase its returns from reducing the inefficiency. For example, the firm could increase output, yielding a profit of

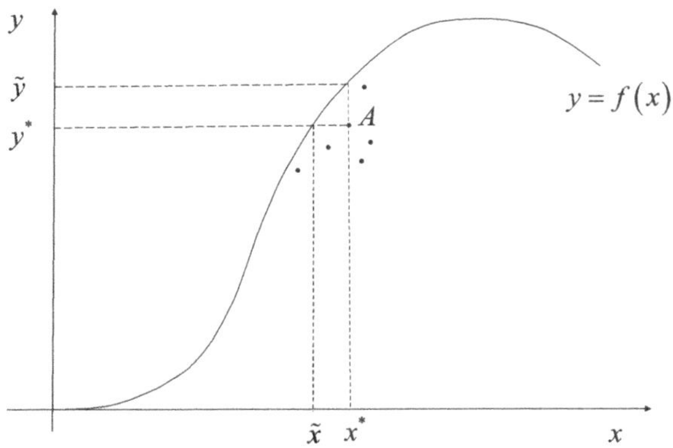

Fig. 6.6 Univariate Output Case

$$\pi_1 = p\tilde{y} - wx^* \gg py^* - wx^* \tag{6.37}$$

or the firm could reduce the level of input used, resulting in

$$\pi_2 = py^* - w\tilde{x} \gg py^* - wx^*. \tag{6.38}$$

Hence, from an economic perspective, the firm is not as profitable as it could be — essentially, the firm is not getting all the outputs possible from its inputs.

The two different moves toward the frontier (e.g., Equations (6.37) and (6.38) do not tell the whole story. Specifically, consider the profit maximization problem:

$$\hat{\pi} = \max_x [pf(x) - wx] \Rightarrow \frac{\partial f(x)}{\partial x} = \frac{w}{p}. \tag{6.39}$$

The solution to Equation (6.39) is denoted by point B in Figure 6.6. By definition of the optimal value $\hat{x}$ in Equation (6.39), $\hat{\pi} \geq \pi_1$ and $\hat{\pi} \geq \pi_2$ from Equations (6.37) and (6.38). Hence, the difference between the point of production and the feasible production function alone does not tell the whole inefficiency story. In the vernacular of economics, our goal is to decompose overall inefficiency into technical inefficiency — not getting all the possible output from your inputs — and allocative inefficiency — not using the appropriate levels of inputs.

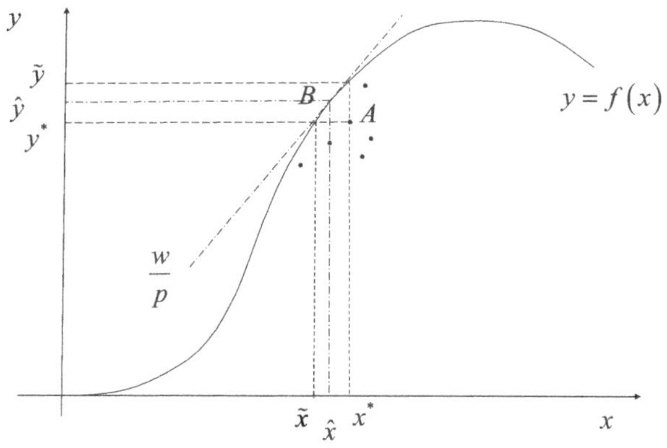

Fig. 6.7 Univariate Output — Profit Maximization

6.2.1.1 *Technical inefficiency*

As a starting point, consider the implications of Equations (6.37), (6.38) and (6.39) constructed from the implications of Figures 6.6 and 6.7. First, using these results, we could envision a total measure of economic inefficiency (ξ_T):

$$\xi_T = [pf(\hat{x}) - w\hat{x}] - [py^* - wx^*] \tag{6.40}$$

however, we could decompose this inequality in two ways:

$$\begin{aligned}\xi_T &= ([pf(\hat{x}) - w\hat{x}] - [p\tilde{y} - wx^*]) - ([p\tilde{y} - wx^*] - [py^* - wx^*]) \text{ or}\\ \xi_T &= ([pf(\hat{x}) - w\hat{x}] - [py^* - w\tilde{x}]) - ([py^* - w\tilde{x}] - [py^* - wx^*]).\end{aligned} \tag{6.41}$$

An alternative approach to constructing measures of technical and allocative efficiency is to reformulate the problem in factor–factor space.

Figure 6.8 depicts the scenario where the firms are using too much input to produce a given level of output y. To develop the measure of technical inefficiency that we typically apply, consider the firm producing at point A. It is clear that the firm operating at point A is inefficient — it is using too much of both inputs to produce y. Again, we could either compute the amount of input that could be reduced by producing the same level of output or the additional level of output that could be produced for the same level of inputs.

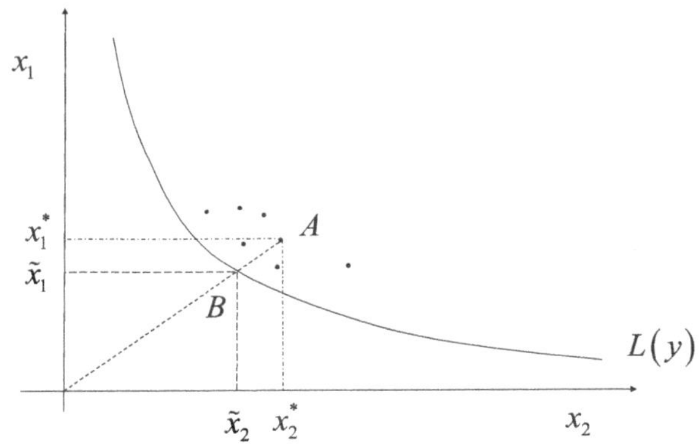

Fig. 6.8 Technical Inefficiency Defined on the Input Level Set

For the current discussion, let us focus on the former (e.g., the amount that the inputs could be reduced maintaining the level of output).

As a first step, let us assume that we are going to use a radial measure of inefficiency (e.g., a measure based on the ray from the origin to the observed point of production $\{x_1^*, x_2^*\}$. Given this radial concept, the "technically efficient" point of comparison is point B (e.g., using $\{\tilde{x}_1, \tilde{x}_2\}$ to produce output y). The question then becomes: How do we define the difference between point $\{x_1^*, x_2^*\}$ and point $\{\tilde{x}_1, \tilde{x}_2\}$? In general, we are interested in two measures of this technical inefficiency. The first is based on the relative distance between the origin and each point:

$$\lambda = \frac{\sqrt{\tilde{x}_1^2 + \tilde{x}_2^2}}{\sqrt{x_1^{*2} + x_2^{*2}}} \tag{6.42}$$

which is our standard distance function measure from Chapter 4. However, given that we actually have input prices, an alternative measure of the technical inefficiency is the excess dollars spent (TE):

$$\text{TE} = [w_1 x_1^* + w_2 x_2^*] - [w_1 \tilde{x}_1 + w_2 \tilde{x}_2]. \tag{6.43}$$

Note that the point $\{\tilde{x}_1, \tilde{x}_2\}$ is not economically optimal.

For completeness, it is also possible to develop technical efficiency in output space. For example, consider the product–product graph in Figure 6.9. Again, we start from an observed output combination

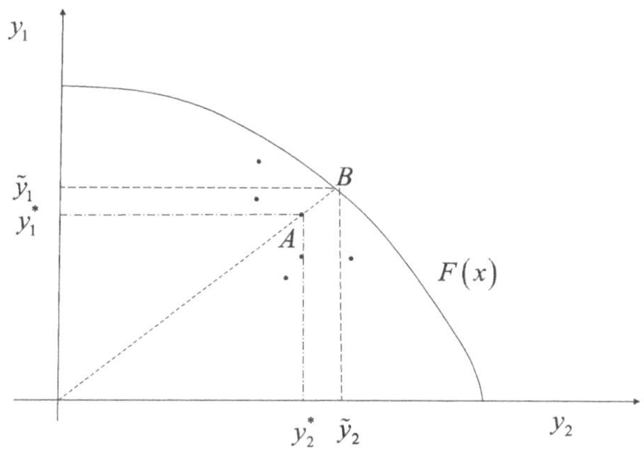

Fig. 6.9 Technical Inefficiency Defined on the Output Level Set

A where the bundle of outputs $\{y_1^*, y_2^*\}$ is produced from a given set of inputs x. This set of outputs is inefficient in that more output can be produced from the inputs. Again, adopting the radial measure for technical inefficiency, we can measure the overall technical inefficiency using a radial distance measure:

$$\theta = \frac{\sqrt{y_1^{*2} + y_2^{*2}}}{\sqrt{\tilde{y}_1^2 + \tilde{y}_2^2}} \tag{6.44}$$

or as a dollar measure based on output prices (TE):

$$\mathrm{TE} = [p_1\tilde{y}_1 + p_2\tilde{y}_2] - [p_1y_1^* + p_2y_2^*]. \tag{6.45}$$

6.2.1.2 *Allocative inefficiency*

Given that we can define the technical inefficiency (e.g., we have a couple of measures that quantify the difference between what could possibly be produced and what is produced), the next question is how economically inefficient the decision of the firm is. Specifically, in Figure 6.7, how does point B differ from the technically efficient possibilities?

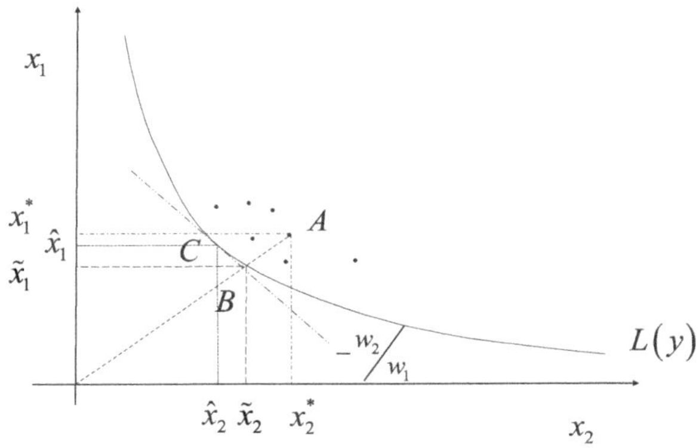

Fig. 6.10 Technical and Allocative Inefficiency Defined on the Level Set

Focusing first on the input–input dimensions, our optimal combination of inputs used in production is defined by

$$\frac{MPP_2}{MPP_1} = \frac{\dfrac{\partial f(x)}{\partial x_2}}{\dfrac{\partial f(x)}{\partial x_1}} = \frac{dx_1}{dx_2} = -\frac{w_2}{w_1}. \tag{6.46}$$

If inputs do not correspond to this allocation, then the firms could trade one input for another and reduce cost. For example, consider the factor–factor graph depicted in Figure 6.10. The technically efficient point of production developed above (e.g., B) is not the cost-minimizing point of production ($C - \{\hat{x}_1, \hat{x}_2\}$). We can quantify this inefficiency as the allocative inefficiency (AE):

$$\text{AE} = [w_1\tilde{x}_1 + w_2\tilde{x}_2] - [w_1\hat{x}_1 + w_2\hat{x}_2] \tag{6.47}$$

which yields a dollar measure of the inefficiency.

Using our definitions of cost to increase the rigor of our measure, we use the definition of the cost function from Diewert:

$$c(w, y) = \min_x [w'x : x \text{ belongs to } L(y)]. \tag{6.48}$$

The measure of allocative inefficiency can then be defined as

$$\text{AE} = w'x_0 - c(w, y)$$

where

$$c(w, y) \equiv \min_x [w'x : x \in L(y)]. \tag{6.49}$$

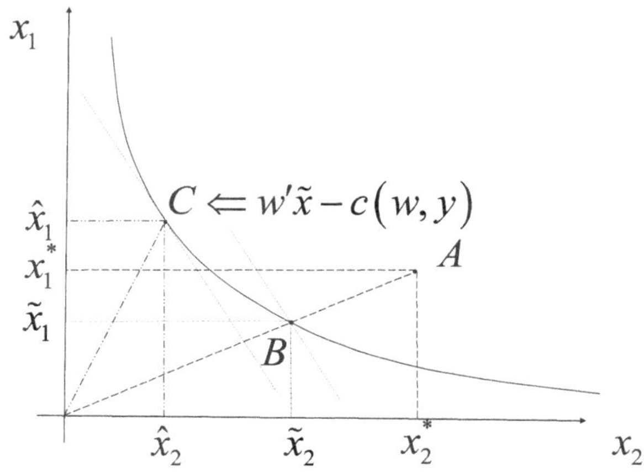

Fig. 6.11 Allocative Inefficiency

Thus, we can provide a graphical depiction of the allocative inefficiency in Figure 6.11. In Figure 6.11, point B is a point that is technically efficient, but not economically efficient. Analytically, we have derived point B using a radial distance function from the origin. Next, we can derive the cost-minimizing vector of inputs sufficient to produce y (e.g., $c(w, y)$ – point C). Taking the difference between the cost of production at B and C gives a measure of allocative inefficiency.

6.2.1.3 *Total inefficiency*

Putting the two halves together, we can measure total inefficiency. From Figure 6.11, the observed point of production A together with the point on the isoquant derived from the radial distance function can be used to measure technical efficiency (TE):

$$\text{TE} = [w_1 x_1^* + w_2 x_2^*] - [w_1 \tilde{x}_1 + w_2 \tilde{x}_2]. \tag{6.50}$$

Taking the allocative inefficiency as defined in Equation (6.50), we can define the total economic inefficiency T^* as the technical inefficiency plus the allocative inefficiency:

$$\begin{aligned} T^* &= [w_1 x_1^* + w_2 x_2^*] - [w_1 \hat{x}_1 + \hat{x}_2] \\ &= ([w_1 x_1^* + w_2 x_2^*] - [w_1 \tilde{x}_1 + w_2 \tilde{x}_2]) \\ &\quad + ([w_1 \tilde{x}_1 + w_2 \tilde{x}_2] - [w_1 \hat{x}_1 + w_2 \hat{x}_2]) = \text{TE} + \text{AE}. \end{aligned} \tag{6.51}$$

6.2.2 *Distance Function Formulations of Technical and Allocative Inefficiency*

To develop a mathematical statement of efficiency, we return to concepts used to develop Shephard's proof of duality in Chapter 4. Restating the level set from Chapter 4 slightly, we can define a production technology as

$$L_{\Phi}(u) = \{x : \{u, x\} \text{ is feasible}\} \tag{6.52}$$

where x is the level of inputs and u is an output level. In this definition, we define $T = \{u, x\}$ as the set of feasible points or combinations of inputs and outputs that can be produced. This is the basic production possibility set in Diewert:

$$L(u) = [x : f(x) \geq u,\ x \text{ non-negative}] \tag{6.53}$$

where $f(x)$ is our traditional production function.

Next, we revisit the construction of the distance function in input space starting with the definition of the radial distance:

$$\lambda = \min_{\lambda}\{\lambda : \lambda x \in L_{\Phi}(u)\}. \tag{6.54}$$

The standard definition of the radial distance function in Shephard was then

$$\Psi(u, x) = \frac{||x||}{||\xi||} = \frac{1}{\lambda} \tag{6.55}$$

where ξ is the original input vector (e.g., the vector that is possibly inefficient). Economically, we expect $\lambda \leq 1$, or at most the firm is technically efficient. We define a point as technically efficient if $\lambda = 1$ which implies that $\Psi(x, u) = 1$. Using this distance function, we can define the isoquant (e.g., any reduction in x will not produce the output level u) as

$$E(u) = \{x : \Psi(u, x) = 1\}. \tag{6.56}$$

This definition rules out the interior points to the level set. Based on this definition, the *input distance function* is written as

$$D_I(u, x) = \max\{\lambda : \left(\frac{x}{\lambda}\right) \in L(u)\} \tag{6.57}$$

where the isoquant is defined as

$$E(u) = \{x : D_I(u, x) = 1\}. \tag{6.58}$$

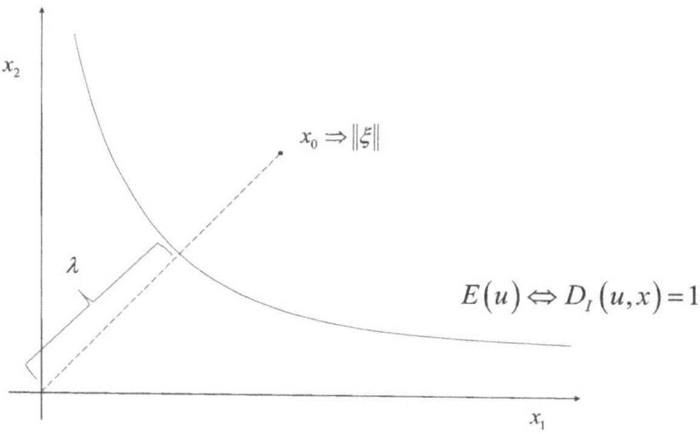

Fig. 6.12 Distance Function as a Measure of Inefficiency

The definitions of the isoquant in Equations (6.56) and (6.58) are identical. However, the definition of the isoquant in Equation (6.58) highlights the fact that the isoquant is defined by the input-distance measure (i.e., $D_I(u, x)$).

The Debreu–Farrell input-oriented measure of technical efficiency can then be expressed as

$$\begin{aligned} DF_I(u,x) &= \min\{\lambda : \lambda x \in L_\Phi(u)\} \\ DF_I(u,x) &\leq 1 \\ DF_I(u,x) &= \frac{1}{D_I(u,x)}. \end{aligned} \tag{6.59}$$

As depicted in Figure 6.12, $\lambda \leq 1$. If $\lambda = 1$, the observation is technically efficient. However, if $\lambda \ll 1$, the observation implies some level of technical inefficiency. Either the firm could reduce the level of inputs without reducing output or increase output without changing input use. Note that this deviation is purely technical — the only economic principle we are imposing is that we do not want to throw away inputs.

6.2.2.1 *Fare and Primont's approach to distance functions*

A slightly different development is given by Fare and Primont (1995). In the univariate case,

$$\begin{aligned} F &: R_+^N \to R_+ \\ F(x) &= \max_u\{u : (x,u) \in T\} \end{aligned} \tag{6.60}$$

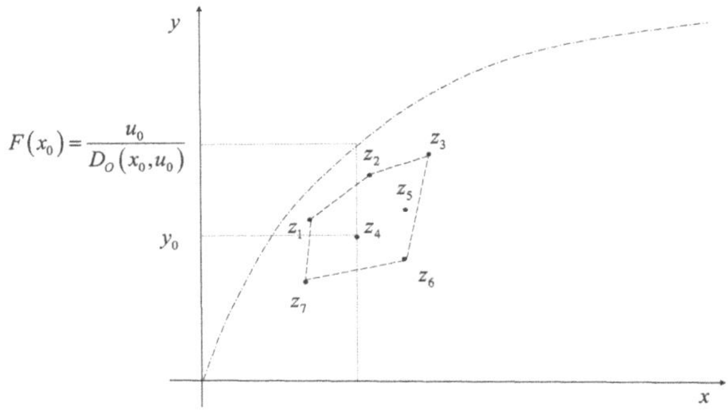

Fig. 6.13 Fare and Primont Depiction of a Production Technology

where T is the technology set. Or

$$T = \{(x, u) : F(x) \geq u, u \subset R_+\}. \tag{6.61}$$

This depiction of the production technology is presented graphically in Figure 6.13. The points $z_1, z_2, \ldots, z_7$ are observed production points (i.e., $z_i = \{x_{1i}, x_{2i}, \ldots, x_{Ni}, u_i, u_i, \ldots, u_i\}$ such that $u \geq u^*$ for some target u^*. Note that these points form a convex space (i.e., we can draw a line from any point of production to another point of departure without leaving the production possibilities defined by the dotted line).

Assuming that as we collect more information, the concave production set in Figure 6.13 approaches some smooth frontier, the output distance function is then given by

$$D_O(x, u) = \min_\theta \left\{\theta : F(x) \geq \frac{u}{\theta}\right\}. \tag{6.62}$$

Alternatively, the distance function can be written in terms of the technology set:

$$D_O(x, u) = \min_\theta \left\{\theta : (x, \frac{u}{\theta}) \in T\right\}. \tag{6.63}$$

The last representation is then expandable into multivariate space:

$$\begin{gathered} F : R_+^N \to R_+^M \;\; D_O : R_+^N \times R_+^M \to R_+ \cup \{+\infty\} \\ D_O(x, u) = \inf_\theta\{\theta > 0 : (x, \tfrac{u}{\theta}) \in T\}. \end{gathered} \tag{6.64}$$

Specifically, one example of the multioutput technology is presented graphically in Figure 6.14. Again, the points $z_1, z_2, \ldots, z_7$

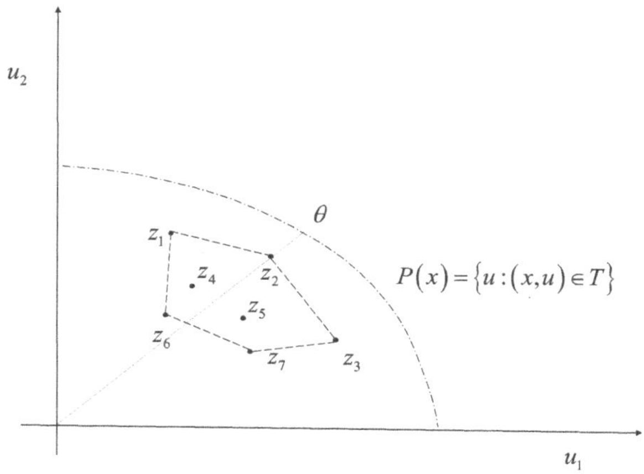

Fig. 6.14 Definition of Technology in Output Space — T

are observed production points (i.e., $z_i = \{x_{1i}, x_{2i}, \ldots, x_{Ni}, u_{1i}, u_{2i}, \ldots, u_{Mi}\}$. As in our discussion of Figure 6.13, we assume that as the number of observed production points becomes large, the set of possible outputs approaches the smooth frontier $P(x)$ defined as

$$P(x) = \{u : (x, u) \in T\} \tag{6.65}$$

as depicted in Figure 6.14. Taking the point z_2 as an example, we can graphically define the value $\theta \gg 1$ consistent with Equation (6.64).

Following Equation (6.61), the definition of the *production possibilities frontier* in Equation (6.65) allows us to define feasible technologies in a multioutput space:

$$T = \{(x, u) : u \in P(x), x \in R_+^N\}. \tag{6.66}$$

In addition, in a fashion similar to Equation (6.63), we can define the multioutput distance function as

$$D_O(x, u) = \inf_\theta \{\theta > 0 : \left(\frac{u}{\theta}\right) \in P(x)\}. \tag{6.67}$$

This formulation gives us the same consistency between the input and output sets for the multioutput production system we developed for the univariate production function in our discussion of Shephard in Chapter 4. Specifically, if we start with any input vector x_0, we can map out the combinations of outputs that are technically feasible using $u \in P(x_0)$. We can define this set of outputs using the output distance function $D_O(x, u) \leq 1$. By similar construction, we can show that if $x_1 \leqq x_1$, then $P(x_1) \subset P(x_0)$.

6.2.2.2 *Properties of Debreu–Farrell measures of technical efficiency*

The Fare–Primont, distance function formulation has direct consequences for the measurement of technical inefficiency:

- $DF_I(y, x)$ is homogeneous of degree -1 in inputs and $DF_O(y, x)$ is homogeneous of degree -1 in outputs.
- $DF_I(y, x)$ is weakly monotonically decreasing in inputs and $DF_O(y, x)$ is weakly monotonically decreasing in outputs.
- $DF_I(y, x)$ and $DF_O(y, x)$ are invariant with respect to changes in units of measurement.

In addition to the theoretical implications, the Fare–Primont formulation leads directly to an empirical specification for technical efficiency. Specifically, let us return to the empirical formulation in Figure 6.14. Let us assume that the observed points in Figure 6.14 are the outcomes of choices for three inputs (e.g., in Equation (6.64), $N = 3$ and $M = 2$). Given these five points, we can form a "synthetic" production point as a linear combination of the observed production combinations:

$$\begin{aligned} \tilde{z} &= \lambda_1 z_1 + \lambda_2 z_2 + \lambda_3 z_3 + \lambda_4 z_4 + \lambda_5 z_5 \\ \lambda_i &\geq 0 \quad \text{and} \quad \sum_{i=1}^{5} \lambda_i \leq 1. \end{aligned} \tag{6.68}$$

If each of the individual points is technologically feasible, then a linear combination of these points must also be technologically feasible. To create a measure of technical inefficiency, we want to ask whether a linear combination of observed input–output points will produce at least the same level of outputs for no more input. Mathematically,

$$\begin{aligned} &\min_{\lambda_i} \sum_{i=1}^{N} \lambda_i \\ \text{s.t. } &\sum_{i=1}^{N} \lambda_i u_{ij} \geq u_k,\ j = 1, 2 \\ &\sum_{i=1}^{N} \lambda_i x_{ij} \leq x_k,\ j = 1, 2, 3 \\ &\lambda_i \geq 0 \end{aligned} \tag{6.69}$$

for some set of outputs u_k and inputs x_k. Table 6.6 presents a subsample of this formulation. Observation 1 from Table 6.6 indicates that a linear combination of other observed output–input combinations could produce the same set of outputs for 52.3% of the inputs. However, such a reduction is not available for Observation 2.

Following the formulation in Equation (6.69), we can transform the minimization problem to derive the cost inefficiency. Specifically, we start with the cost function

$$c(y, w, \beta) = \min_{x}\{w'x : D_I(y, x; \beta) \geq 1\}. \tag{6.70}$$

The cost function representation of Equation (6.69) can be expressed as

$$\begin{aligned} &\min_{\lambda_i} \sum_{i=1}^{N} \lambda_i c_i \\ \text{s.t. } &\sum_{i=1}^{N} \lambda_i u_{ij} \geq u_j\, j = 1, 2 \\ &\sum_{i=1}^{N} \lambda_i x_{ij} \leq x_j\, j = 1, 2, 3 \\ &\lambda_i \geq 0. \end{aligned} \tag{6.71}$$

Table 6.6 Distance Results for Two Output–Three Input Formulation

Obs.	Profit	y_1	y_2	Cost	x_1	x_2	x_3	p_1	p_2	w_1	w_2	w_3	λ
1	10,184.57	803.52	25,966.79	71,572.66	28,053.60	55,113.90	14,747.34	3.176	3.050	1.052	0.747	0.060	0.5232
2	18,434.81	29.86	27,448.34	38,937.19	11,785.51	25,676.65	501.88	1.664	2.088	1.134	0.963	1.679	1.0000
3	8,985.03	70.52	22,777.65	64,187.37	18,477.95	23,925.72	642.12	2.898	3.203	1.143	1.742	2.176	0.6285
4	2,815.26	29.19	7,816.99	14,392.34	1,864.62	5,400.28	959.64	2.016	2.194	2.431	1.777	0.276	1.0000
5	26,950.69	89.97	14,849.91	22,782.68	4,912.33	13,479.00	813.34	2.838	3.332	2.399	0.630	3.080	0.9003
6	3,827.56	76.43	17,830.89	27,190.02	28,515.94	10,305.66	341.12	1.557	1.733	0.272	1.830	1.675	1.0000
7	23,920.60	123.41	28,953.70	92,183.84	24,904.79	39,162.18	1,116.33	3.710	3.994	1.325	1.454	2.007	0.6486
8	3,731.07	4,070.97	89.99	10,765.11	1,854.36	7,160.16	2,531.27	3.546	0.653	2.730	0.493	0.859	1.0000
9	40,801.93	165.36	31,073.32	35,001.91	11,066.73	94,077.97	660.59	2.206	2.428	2.068	0.113	2.210	0.9831
10	5,020.63	5,830.26	251.76	15,959.40	5,566.09	6,030.56	3,957.17	3.553	1.055	1.321	0.894	0.811	1.0000
11	120,577.36	967.27	54,092.05	48,012.89	122,363.56	81,520.64	2,104.89	3.053	3.062	0.101	0.402	1.393	0.9719
12	1,060.05	46.33	5,508.05	12,332.77	2,072.19	3,321.39	134.84	3.450	2.402	1.854	2.480	1.877	0.8611
13	630.90	169.36	22,319.71	39,585.58	26,132.18	28,994.75	520.16	2.116	1.786	0.499	0.883	1.828	0.4655
14	292.33	1,878.75	58.30	4,267.32	3,730.07	983.36	343.21	2.404	0.752	0.526	1.473	2.502	1.0000
15	4,398.79	90.38	18,814.72	48,820.67	6,335.70	35,696.32	469.02	3.919	2.810	2.912	0.818	2.482	0.6153
16	953.02	1,798.53	22.33	3,265.62	912.18	823.17	2,272.32	2.335	0.860	1.666	1.335	0.285	1.0000
17	1,777.49	60.23	19,625.29	39,749.11	8,657.50	49,129.44	840.49	2.039	2.110	1.911	0.452	1.198	0.5325
18	4,936.22	6.34	11,834.88	20,312.64	3,040.13	9,631.20	281.20	1.618	2.133	2.144	1.391	1.397	1.0000
19	14.28	89.53	7,124.10	11,853.65	2,294.05	6,227.91	233.58	3.247	1.625	1.647	1.252	1.185	0.5008
20	102,961.92	516.59	41,240.37	50,825.49	33,733.84	110,181.75	1,752.73	3.119	3.690	1.153	0.082	1.649	0.8329
21	1,155.77	37.07	4,132.37	4,937.28	2,456.51	1,419.21	68.80	1.882	1.458	0.619	2.335	1.497	1.0000
22	11,806.52	52.53	20,000.89	45,577.60	7,317.61	21,082.59	460.07	3.521	2.860	2.115	1.381	2.119	0.7861
23	1,841.99	2,046.32	27.48	8,043.31	1,998.79	1,428.84	499.58	4.815	1.211	1.866	1.889	3.233	1.0000
24	3,842.53	145.65	18,824.29	29,647.58	8,017.02	24,490.16	252.37	3.332	1.753	1.285	0.761	2.824	0.7331
25	41,425.06	568.04	40,968.39	59,337.14	36,967.49	45,820.67	992.78	4.560	2.396	0.575	0.788	1.987	1.0000

6.2.3 *Parametric Estimation of Inefficiency — Econometrics*

In Section 2.7.1, we introduced the concept of technical inefficiency in the form of the stochastic production function. Specifically, in Equation (2.170), we formulated observed production as a function of technical efficiency (TE_i)

$$y_i = f(x_i, \beta)\text{TE}_i \tag{2.170}$$

where $\text{TE}_i \leq 1$. However, since we could not observe TE_i, we inferred it from the production function — from Equation (2.171),

$$\text{TE}_i = \frac{y_i}{f(x_i, \beta)}. \tag{2.171}$$

Conceptually, if we could estimate the production function, we could compute the technical inefficiency given the estimated parameters.

As a starting point for our discussion, consider the cotton production data for Mississippi presented in Table 6.7. To facilitate our discussion, consider a basic quadratic formulation:

$$y_t = \alpha_0 + \alpha_1 x_t + \alpha_2 x_t^2 + \alpha_3 t + \alpha_4 t^2 + \alpha_5 t^3 + v_t. \tag{6.72}$$

The maximum likelihood estimates for this production function coupled with the profit-maximizing constraint (assuming that ϵ_t is normally distributed) are presented in Table 6.8. Note that these estimates are not very good (i.e., they are not statistically significant), but we will use the estimated production function to develop our econometric model of technical efficiency.

The defining nature of estimating technical efficiency involves the specification of the error term. Specifically, dropping the time effects from Equation (6.72), we can specify the production function for cotton in Mississippi as

$$y = \alpha_0 + \alpha_1 x + \alpha_2 x^2 + \nu. \tag{6.73}$$

The typical assumption is that v is distributed normal with zero mean and an unknown variance. However, this assumption is somewhat inconsistent with the estimation of technical inefficiency. Specifically, under the assumption of normality, the possible outcomes of v are

Table 6.7 Cotton Yield and Fertilizer Use for Mississippi, Selected Years 1964–2010

Year	Nitrogen Applied (lbs/acre)	Cotton Yield (lbs/acre)	Cotton Price ($/lb)	Nitrogen Price ($/lbs)	Year	Nitrogen Applied (lbs/acre)	Cotton Yield (lbs/acre)	Cotton Price ($/lb)	Nitrogen Price ($/lbs)
1964	77	732	0.319	0.0399	1985	104	764	0.559	0.0960
1965	104	678	0.305	0.0394	1986	102	571	0.509	0.0855
1966	98	653	0.227	0.0383	1987	106	829	0.636	0.0785
1967	98	567	0.297	0.0371	1988	110	736	0.537	0.0830
1968	91	660	0.239	0.0340	1989	103	731	0.629	0.0945
1969	93	534	0.232	0.0309	1990	109	728	0.654	0.0900
1970	96	658	0.219	0.0300	1991	109	888	0.552	0.0920
1971	93	613	0.276	0.0317	1992	112	760	0.526	0.0890
1972	92	599	0.292	0.0324	1993	111	572	0.575	0.0930
1973	90	651	0.379	0.0357	1994	122	806	0.717	0.0980
1974	103	448	0.465	0.0695	1995	112	622	0.734	0.1115
1975	92	454	0.525	0.0930	1996	100	819	0.680	0.1165
1976	90	376	0.615	0.0675	1997	109	901	0.649	0.1135
1977	98	581	0.525	0.0705	1998	107	737	0.604	0.0965
1978	92	561	0.600	0.0700	1999	111	704	0.451	0.0905
1979	87	657	0.635	0.0690	2000	114	642	0.505	0.0970
1980	92	488	0.764	0.0825	2001	112	719	0.265	0.1300
1981	91	626	0.584	0.0925	2003	109	934	0.604	0.1215
1982	94	853	0.600	0.0975	2007	117	966	0.576	0.1910
1983	98	640	0.662	0.0925	2010	100	993	0.791	0.1990
1984	103	767	0.560	0.0990					

Table 6.8 Estimated Coefficients for Quadratic Production for Cotton

Parameter	Estimate
α_0	−0.645
	(4.454)[a]
α_1	13.374
	(39.066)
α_2	−0.066
	(0.200)
α_3	−20.309
	(358.453)
α_4	1.141
	(18.977)
α_5	−0.013
	(0.271)

Notes: [a]Numbers in parenthesis denote standard errors.

symmetric and potentially very large (e.g., the upper bound of v is ∞ — even though we typically assume that most of the values will be less than 2.5) or very small (again, the lower bound is $-\infty$ even though we typically assume that most of the values will be greater than -2.5). However, following Figure 6.6, we expect that ϵ is bounded by the efficient frontier (e.g., our production function). Hence,

$$\begin{aligned} f(x) &= \alpha_0 + \alpha_1 x + \alpha_2 x^2 \geq y \\ &\Rightarrow f(x) + v = y \ni: v \leq 0. \end{aligned} \tag{6.74}$$

Hence, we conceptualize the error function in a model with technical inefficiency as one-sided.

Implicitly, the formulation in Equation (6.74) assumes that the errors in the model are primarily the result of technical inefficiency. This assumption appears extreme. To develop the broader model, assume that there is a second input in our cotton model:

$$f(x) = \alpha_0 + \alpha_1 x + \alpha_2 x^2 + \beta_1 z + \beta_2 z^2 + \beta_3 xz + v \tag{6.75}$$

where z is uncontrollable and unobservable. Since we cannot observe or control this input, we could reformulate Equation (6.75) as

$$f(x) = \alpha_0 + \alpha_1 x + \alpha_2 x^2 + u(x) - v \tag{6.76}$$

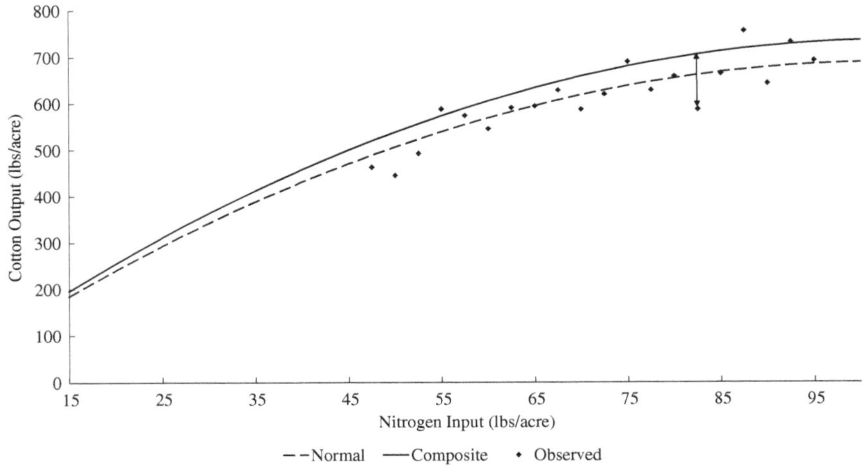

Fig. 6.15 Cotton Production Functions with Normal and Composed Errors

where $u(x)$ denotes the fact that u will depend on x because of the interaction term (e.g., β_3). However, for simplicity, let us assume that $u(x) \rightarrow u$ (e.g., $\beta_3 = 0$ or there is no heteroscedasticty). Note that the quadratic formulation in Equation (6.76) follows the general formulation in Equation (2.184):

$$\tilde{y} = \tilde{x}\beta + u - v. \tag{2.184}$$

The econometric problem involves disentangling the two effects. For example, consider two versions of the cotton production function for Mississippi presented in Figure 6.15. Focusing on the output at $N = 77.5$, we have two predictions. Assuming that the residuals to the production function are only normal, the estimated residual is -17.62. However, if we allow for a composed error term which includes the possibility of non-normal component in the residuals, the estimated residual is -60.19. The question is then. How do we know the difference? The answer, as discussed in Section 2.7.1, is the possible skewness of the estimated residuals. If the residuals are negatively skewed, technical inefficiency is possible and we can fit the stochastic frontier model.

While the original residuals exhibit a slight degree of skewness, we will construct data with various degrees of skewness for pedagogic purposes. For our purposes, we would like to define a set of cotton production levels such that

$$y = -0.645 + 13.374x - 0.066x^2 + \sigma \left[u\left(\delta\right) - v\left(\delta\right)\right] \tag{6.77}$$

where σ is related to the standard error from the original cotton production function (i.e., 10% of the original standard deviation of 104.41), $u(\delta)$ is normally distributed and $v(\delta)$ is distributed gamma and $0 \leq \delta \leq 1$ such that $\mathrm{E}\left[u\left(\delta\right) - v\left(\delta\right)\right] = 0$ and $\mathrm{V}\left[u\left(\delta\right) - v\left(\delta\right)\right] = 1$. In this formulation, δ would be correlated with the relative level of technical inefficiency in the sample — as δ increases, the relative importance of technical inefficiency increases.

Before we develop the stochastic frontier model with a gamma distribution for our measure of technical inefficient, let us review the assumptions of the stochastic frontier model with the half-normal distribution. In Equation (2.191), we specified the half-normal as

$$g(z) = \begin{cases} \dfrac{f(z/\sigma)}{\sigma[1 - \Phi(-a/\sigma)]}, & z \geq -a \\ 0 \; z < -1 \end{cases}. \tag{2.191}$$

Technically, this distribution is a left-truncated normal with a truncation point of a. To make the distribution a half-normal distribution, we would set $a = 0$. Given that $\Phi(0) = 0.5$ (e.g., the zero point is the center of the normal distribution), Equation (2.191) can be rewritten as

$$g(z) = \frac{2f(z/\sigma)}{\sigma}, \quad z \geq 0 \tag{6.78}$$

where $f(z/\sigma)$ is the standard normal distribution function. For our purposes here, we will use a slight reformulation of Equation (6.78):

$$g(z, \sigma) = \frac{\sqrt{2}}{\sigma\sqrt{\pi}} \exp\left(-\frac{x^2}{2\sigma^2}\right), \quad x \geq 0. \tag{6.79}$$

Here, we want to develop the assumption of the distribution of technical inefficiency across firms for the half-normal distribution versus the implications of the gamma distribution implemented by Greene (1990). Like the half-normal distribution, there are several ways to write the gamma distribution. To be consistent with Greene's derivation here, we write the gamma distribution as

$$h(x,\Theta,P)=\frac{\Theta^{P}}{\Gamma(P)}x^{P-1}\exp(-\Theta x),\quad x\geq 0,\Theta,P>0. \tag{6.80}$$

As stated above, we want to start by assuming that the total variance for the cotton production scenario is 10% of the standard error from the empirical estimator or 10.44. In our initial comparisons, we further assume that 50% of this variance is attributable to inefficiency, or $\sigma^2=5.22$. Given this assumption,

$$\begin{aligned}\sigma^2&=\frac{5.22}{\left(1-\dfrac{2}{\pi}\right)}=14.3651\\ \mathrm{E}[x]&=\frac{\sqrt{14.3651}\sqrt{2}}{\sqrt{\pi}}=3.0241.\end{aligned} \tag{6.81}$$

To derive the gamma distribution with the same mean and variance, we solve

$$\left.\begin{aligned}\frac{\alpha}{\beta}&=3.0241\\ \frac{\alpha}{\beta^2}&=14.3651\end{aligned}\right\}\Rightarrow\alpha=0.8776,\quad\beta=0.2052. \tag{6.82}$$

The half-normal and gamma distribution functions given these parameters are presented in Figure 6.16. In this figure, the half-normal distribution and the gamma (original) distribution have the same mean and variance. Given this parameterization for the gamma distribution, both the gamma and the half-normal distribution imply that there are many firms that are almost technically efficient (e.g., the probability density function around zero is higher than any other probability density function value for these distributions). However, if we scale the gamma distribution by keeping the same mean, but reducing the variance,

$$\frac{4\alpha}{4\beta}=\frac{\alpha}{\beta},\quad\frac{4\alpha}{(4\beta)^2}=\frac{\alpha}{4\beta}. \tag{6.83}$$

After these changes, the mode (e.g., point with the maximum value of the probability density function) of the gamma distribution is

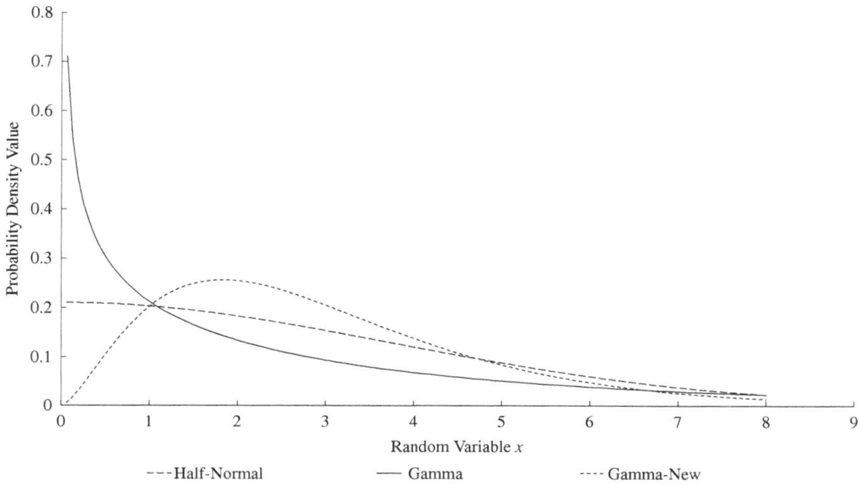

Fig. 6.16 Comparison of Half-Normal and Gamma Distributions

1.8366.[2] Hence, in the gamma-new distribution, very few firms are "almost technically efficient."

To the degree that the gamma distribution allows both scenarios (e.g., the scenario where a large number of firms are almost technically efficient and the scenario where a small number of firms are almost technically efficient), the gamma specification of the stochastic frontier model is preferred to the half-normal specification.

In order to derive Greene's (1990) Gamma specification of the stochastic frontier function, we return to the basic composite error function specification:

$$y = f(x, \beta) + v - u. \tag{6.84}$$

Note that β is now the parameters of the production function (e.g., the quadratic production function parameters). In addition, u enters as a negative because positive values imply a technical inefficiency (e.g., the quantity actually produced y is less than the frontier value

[2]The mode of the gamma distribution is

$$\frac{\alpha - 1}{\beta} \forall \alpha \geq 1.$$

at that set of inputs x). To construct the probability density function of the composite error term, Greene assumes that

$$f(\epsilon, u) = f_\epsilon(\epsilon + u) f_u(u) \tag{6.85}$$

where $f_\epsilon()$ is a normal density function and $f_u()$ is a gamma distribution function. This approach is similar to that used in Equation (2.187) in the derivation of the half-normal system. Given this assumption,

$$f(\epsilon, u) = \frac{1}{\sqrt{2\pi\sigma^2}} \exp\left[-\frac{(\epsilon+u)^2}{2\sigma^2}\right] \frac{\Theta^P}{\Gamma(P)} u^{P-1} \exp(-\Theta u). \tag{6.86}$$

Expanding the quadratic term in the normal density function yields

$$\begin{aligned} f(\epsilon, u) = {} & \frac{1}{\sqrt{2\pi\sigma^2}} \exp\left[-\frac{\epsilon^2}{2\sigma^2}\right] \exp\left[-\frac{u^2}{2\sigma^2}\right] \exp\left[-\frac{\epsilon u}{\sigma^2}\right] \\ & \times \frac{\Theta^P}{\Gamma(P)} u^{P-1} \exp(-\Theta u). \end{aligned} \tag{6.87}$$

Next, we need to collect the terms involving u:

$$\begin{aligned} f(\epsilon, u) &= \frac{\Theta^P}{\Gamma(P)\sqrt{2\pi\sigma^2}} \exp\left(-\frac{\epsilon^2}{2\sigma^2}\right) \exp\left(-\frac{u^2}{2\sigma^2} - \frac{\epsilon u}{\sigma^2} - \Theta u\right) u^{P-1} \\ &= K \exp\left[-\frac{\epsilon^2}{2\sigma^2}\right] \exp\left[-\frac{u^2}{2\sigma^2} - \frac{\epsilon u}{\sigma^2} - \Theta u\right] \\ K &= \frac{\Theta^P}{\Gamma(P)\sqrt{2\pi\sigma^2}}. \end{aligned} \tag{6.88}$$

Next, we need to work with the second exponential term in Equation (6.88):

$$\begin{aligned} -\frac{u^2}{2\sigma^2} - \frac{\epsilon u}{\sigma^2} - \Theta u &= -\frac{u^2}{2\sigma^2} - u\left[\frac{\epsilon}{\sigma^2} + \Theta\right] \\ &= -\frac{1}{2}\left[u^2 + 2u\sigma^2\left(\frac{\epsilon}{\sigma^2} + \Theta\right)\right]\frac{1}{\sigma^2} \\ &= -\frac{1}{2}[u^2 + 2u(\epsilon + \Theta\sigma^2)]\frac{1}{\sigma^2}. \end{aligned} \tag{6.89}$$

Given the results of Equation (6.89), we can complete the square. Letting $u = u$ and $z = (\epsilon + \Theta\sigma^2)$, the square term we have to add and subtract is $(\epsilon + \Theta\sigma^2)^2$. Hence, the result is

$$f(\epsilon, u) = K \exp\left[-\frac{\epsilon^2}{2\sigma^2}\right] \times \exp\left[-\frac{1}{2}\left(u^2 + 2u\left(\epsilon + \Theta\sigma^2\right) + \left(\epsilon + \Theta\sigma^2\right)^2 - \left(\epsilon + \Theta\sigma^2\right)^2\right)\frac{1}{\sigma^2}\right] u^{P-1}. \quad (6.90)$$

The first portion of the exponential term in the second line becomes

$$u^2 + 2u(\epsilon + \Theta\sigma^2) + (\epsilon + \Theta\sigma^2)^2 = (u + (\epsilon + \Theta\sigma^2))^2. \quad (6.91)$$

The second part of the exponential term in the second line of Equation (6.90) is merged with the exponential term on the first line of Equation (6.90):

$$\exp\left(-\frac{\epsilon^2}{2\sigma^2}\right)\exp\left(-\frac{1}{2}\left(\epsilon + \Theta\sigma^2\right)^2\frac{1}{\sigma^2}\right) = \exp\left(-\frac{\epsilon^2}{2\sigma^2} + \frac{\left(\epsilon + \Theta\sigma^2\right)^2}{2\sigma^2}\right). \quad (6.92)$$

Given these substitutions, Equation (6.90) becomes

$$f(\epsilon, u) = K \exp\left[-\frac{\epsilon^2}{2\sigma^2} + \frac{\left(\epsilon\Theta\sigma^2\right)}{2\sigma^2}\right] \times \exp\left[-\frac{1}{2}\left[u + \left(\epsilon + \Theta\sigma^2\right)\right]^2\frac{1}{\sigma^2}\right] u^{P-1}. \quad (6.93)$$

In order to derive the distribution of ϵ, we must integrate the terms involving u out of Equation (6.93). Specifically, we need to integrate

$$h = \frac{1}{\sqrt{2\pi\sigma^2}}\int_0^\infty \exp\left[-\frac{1}{2}\frac{\left(u + \left(\epsilon + \Theta\sigma^2\right)^2\right)^2}{\sigma^2}\right] u^{P-1}du. \quad (6.94)$$

As is the case in several of these distributions, Equation (6.94) is a normal distribution for the random variable u with a mean of $-\left(\epsilon+\Theta\sigma^2\right)^2$ and a variance of σ^2. Following Greene (1990, p. 146), substituting Q for u yields

$$\frac{1}{2\pi\sigma^2}\int_0^{\infty}\exp\left[-\frac{\left[Q+\left(\epsilon+\Theta\sigma^2\right)\right]^2}{2\sigma^2}\right]dQ=\text{Prob}\left[Q>0|\epsilon\right] \quad (6.95)$$

which defines the probability of $Q>0$ for any value ϵ.

Next, we define the density function for Q:

$$\frac{\exp\left[-\frac{\left(Q+\left(\epsilon+\Theta\sigma^2\right)\right)^2}{2\sigma^2}\right]}{\int_0^{\infty}\exp\left[-\frac{\left(Q+\left(\epsilon+\Theta\sigma^2\right)\right)^2}{2\sigma^2}\right]dQ}=f\left(Q|Q>0,\epsilon\right). \quad (6.96)$$

Hence, the integral in Equation (6.94) can be written as

$$\begin{aligned}\text{Prob}\left[Q>0|\epsilon\right]&\int_0^{\infty}Q^{P-1}f\left(Q|Q>0,\epsilon\right)dQ\\&=\text{P}\left[Q>0|\epsilon\right]\text{E}\left[Q^{P-1}|Q>0,\epsilon\right].\end{aligned} \quad (6.97)$$

The distribution function for ϵ can now be written as

$$f(\epsilon)=\frac{\Theta^P}{\Gamma\left(P\right)}\exp\left[\Theta\epsilon+\frac{\sigma^2\Theta^2}{2}\right]\text{Prob}\left[Q>0|\epsilon\right]\text{E}\left[Q^{P-1}|Q>0,\epsilon\right] \quad (6.98)$$

where both $\text{Prob}\left[Q>0|\epsilon\right]$ and $\text{E}\left[Q^{P-1}|Q>0,\epsilon\right]$ are defined by the normal distribution with mean $-\left(\epsilon+\Theta\sigma^2\right)$ and variance σ^2. Greene (1990, p. 148) gives the log-likelihood function for estimation as

$$\begin{aligned}\ln\left(L\right)=\sum_{i=1}^{N}&\left[P\ln(\Theta)-\ln(\Gamma(\Theta))+\frac{\Theta^2\sigma^2}{2}+\Theta\epsilon_i\right.\\&\left.+\ln\left(\text{Prob}[Q>0|\epsilon_i]\right)+\ln\left(E\left[Q^{P-1}|Q>0,\epsilon_i\right]\right)\right].\end{aligned} \quad (6.99)$$

From an implementation point of view, the toughest components of Equation (6.99) are the numeric integrals. Both integrals are based on the probability density function

$$f\left(Q|\epsilon,\Theta,\sigma^2\right) = \frac{1}{\sqrt{2\pi\sigma^2}} \exp\left[-\frac{\left(Q+\left(\epsilon+\Theta\sigma^2\right)\right)^2}{2\sigma^2}\right]. \tag{6.100}$$

As a first step, let us consider a transformation of random variables into the standard normal density function:

$$z = \frac{Q+\left(\epsilon+\Theta\sigma^2\right)}{\sigma}. \tag{6.101}$$

Solving for Q in terms of z,

$$\begin{aligned} z\sigma &= Q+\left(\epsilon+\Theta\sigma^2\right) \\ Q &= z\sigma - \left(\epsilon+\Theta\sigma^2\right). \end{aligned} \tag{6.102}$$

The lower bound of the integrals is then defined as $Q = 0$ which using the results of (6.102) yields

$$\begin{aligned} z\sigma &= \epsilon+\Theta\sigma^2 = 0 \\ \Rightarrow z &= \frac{\epsilon+\Theta\sigma^2}{\sigma}. \end{aligned} \tag{6.103}$$

Hence, we can rewrite the integrals as

$$\begin{aligned} &\frac{1}{\sqrt{2\pi\sigma^2}} \int_0^\infty \exp\left[-\frac{\left(Q+\left(\epsilon+\Theta\sigma^2\right)\right)^2}{2\sigma^2}\right] dQ \\ &= \frac{1}{\sqrt{2\pi}} \int_{z_L}^\infty \exp\left[-\frac{z^2}{2}\right] dz \end{aligned}$$

where

$$z_L = \frac{\epsilon+\Theta\sigma^2}{\sigma} \tag{6.104}$$

and

$$\begin{aligned} &\frac{1}{\sqrt{2\pi\sigma^2}} \int_0^\infty Q \exp\left[-\frac{\left(Q+\left(\epsilon+\Theta\sigma^2\right)\right)^2}{2\sigma^2}\right] dQ \\ &= \frac{1}{\sqrt{2\pi}} \int_{z_L}^\infty \left(z\sigma - \left(\epsilon+\Theta\sigma^2\right)\right) \exp\left[-\frac{z^2}{2}\right] dz. \end{aligned} \tag{6.105}$$

These transformations make the integral easier to solve within the likelihood function in R.

R Code — Gamma Stochastic Frontier Model

```
gmmaLike <- function(b) {
  li <- matrix(0,nrow(xdta),3)
  err <- f - (b[1]+b[2]*xdta[,2]+b[3]*xdta[,2]^2)
  for (i in 1:nrow(xdta)) {
    li[i,3] <- err[i]
    zLow <- (err[i]+b[4]*b[6])/sqrt(b[6])
    if (zLow <= 2.5) {
      li[i,1] <- integrate(dnorm,zLow,2.5)$value
      integrand2 <- function(z) {dnorm(z)*(z*sqrt(b[6])-
        (err[i]+b[4]*b[6]))}
      li[i,2] <- integrate(integrand2,0,2.5)$value }
  else {
      li[i,1] <- 0
      li[i,2] <- 0}
    like <- b[5]*log(b[4]) - lgamma(b[4])
         + b[4]^2*b[6]/2 + b[4]*li[i,3] + log(li[i,1])
         + log(li[i,2])
  }
  return(sum(like))
}

b0 <- c(12.50,13.374,-0.066,0.8776,0.2052,20.0)

a0 <- startpars(b0,gmmaLike,fixed=NULL,
                UB = c(1.0e+02,1.0e+02,1.0e+02,1.0e+01,
                       1.0e+01,1.0e+03),
                LB = c(-1.0e+02,-1.0e+02,-1.0e+02,
                        1.0e-03,1.0e-03,1.0e-03))

res <- solnp(a0[3,1:6],gmmaLike,
             UB = c(1.0e+02,1.0e+02,1.0e+02,1.0e+01,
                    1.0e+01,1.0e+03),
             LB = c(-1.0e+02,-1.0e+02,-1.0e+02,1.0e-03,
                     1.0e-03,1.0e-03))
```

The empirical estimates of this code are presented in Table 6.9. As a final point, we can estimate the technical inefficiency for the

Table 6.9 Estimates for the Gamma Stochastic Frontier Model

Parameter	Estimate
b_0	-75.367^{***}
	(1.000)[a]
b_1	35.947^{***}
	(3.713)
b_2	58.770
	(624.048)
Θ	9.859^{***}
	(0.888)
P	5.862^{***}
	(1.043)
σ^2	983.645^{***}
	(3.576)

Notes: [a]Numbers in parenthesis denote standard errors.
***Denotes significance at the 0.01 level of confidence.

sample by taking the expectation of the gamma component of the distribution. This yields an estimate of 0.5945 with a variance of 0.0603.

6.3 Chapter Summary

- This chapter addresses two topics that have grown in importance in the policy arena:
  - The first question is whether agricultural productivity has increased over time. The importance of increasing productivity is two-fold. First, as the population grows, more output will be required with a relatively fixed land mass. The question is basically whether technical change is sufficient to stave off the Malthusian catastrophe. A second point of contention is that productivity growth could help save environmentally sensitive land.
  - The importance of economic efficiency is then in part related to meeting the world's food needs, but it also raises questions of educational opportunities. In the United States, each state's

extension service was historically charged with disseminating information to make farmers more competitive. Hence, one question is whether participation in extension increases farm efficiency.

- Several different techniques have been used to measure changes in technology, including the introduction of different measures into the cost function. For example, several studies have appended a time trend to measure changes in productivity. This change in productivity would be evidenced by a reduction in cost over time. Other possibilities include a stock measure of a state's investment in agricultural research.
- Another approach is the construction of index numbers to measure the total quantity of output produced and inputs used in that production. The ratio of outputs to inputs then creates a measure referred to as Total Factor Productivity that provides a measure of technical change.

6.4 Review Questions

1. Staring with the Cobb–Douglas production function from Chapter 1, derive the optimal level of inputs and outputs for the sample mean output and input prices. Suppose that the constant increases from 3.1610 to 3.3610. Compute optimal levels of outputs and inputs at the sample mean. Discuss the implications of the two solutions. What is the change in productivity?

- A significant question in the discussion of technical change is: Who is better off? Following the results of Moss (2006), it appears that consumers benefited from agricultural research in Florida. This result calls into question the notion that farmers are typically the ones that support spending on agricultural research in state legislatures.
- What is an embodied technical change?
- One hypothesis is that the development of hybrid seeds increased the demand for fertilizers. What is factor bias?
- Draw a graph which demonstrates the difference between technical and allocative efficiency.

6.5 Exercises

1. Use the data in AggregateUSDA.csv [3] to compute Tornqvist–Theil and Fisher measures of Total Factor Productivity. [*Hint*: Use the three outputs, livestock, crops, and farm-related outputs, and the inputs, capital, labor, and intermediate inputs]. Are the measures similar?
2. Use the output variable in AggregateUSDA.csv along with the capital, labor, and intermediate inputs to estimate a stochastic frontier model. [*Hint*: You can choose between Cobb–Douglas, Mitscherlich–Baule or quadratic, but each choice has implications for measurement of technical inefficiency.]
3. The mathematical specification in Equation (6.71) is typically known as Data Envelope Analysis (DEA). The measure $c_i - \sum_{i=1}^{N} \lambda_i c_i$ is a measure of technical inefficiency. Adding the condition $\sum_{i=1}^{N} \lambda_i = 1$ to the formulation, solve for technical inefficiency of each firm in the dataset DEA-Data.csv.[4]

[3] This dataset is available at: www.charlesbmoss.com:8080/Book.Production.Economics/Chapter-1/AggregateUSDA.csv''.

[4] DEA-Data.csv is available at: www.charlesbmoss.com:8080/Book.Produciton.Economics/Chapter-6/DEA-Data.csv.

Chapter 7

Differential Models of Production

Before turning to the detail of the differential models of production, consider a scenario where we want to estimate the elasticity of demand for a good. One approach would be to start by estimating a parametric specification of the derivative of the demand instead of the demand itself:

$$Q_D(p) \Leftrightarrow \frac{\partial Q_D(p)}{\partial p} \approx \Delta q = a_0 + a_1 p. \tag{7.1}$$

We could estimate the parameters a_0 and a_1 using ordinary least squares. The estimated price elasticity of demand could then be expressed as

$$\epsilon_D(p) = [a_0 + a_1 p] \frac{p}{Q_D(p)} \tag{7.2}$$

such that p and $Q_D(p)$ is observed in the dataset.

The formulation in Equation (7.1) raises several difficulties. First, we could ask what p is associated with Δq. This scenario is easily rectified by approximating

$$\left.\begin{aligned} \Delta q_t &= q_t - q_{t-1} \\ \bar{p}_t &= \tfrac{1}{2}(p_t + p_{t-1}) \end{aligned}\right\} \Rightarrow \Delta q_t = a_0 + a_1 \bar{p}_t. \tag{7.3}$$

A more substantial question is whether this simple differential approach improves the mathematical flexibility of the model. Essentially, the specification in Equation (7.1) is a quadratic specification of demand. One way to increase the flexibility of the system is to consider logarithmic changes:

$$\frac{\partial \ln(q)}{\partial \ln(p)} \Rightarrow \frac{p}{q}\frac{\partial q}{\partial p}. \tag{7.4}$$

Thus, we replace the simple difference approximation in Equation (7.1) with

$$d\ln(q) = a_0 + a_1 d\ln(p). \tag{7.5}$$

We could estimate this specification by replacing $d\ln(q_t)$ with $\ln(q_t) - \ln(q_{t-1})$ and $d\ln(p_t)$ with $\ln(p_t) - \ln(p_{t-1})$.

The differential approaches developed in this chapter involve developing a structural approach to these differential specifications. That is, we want to develop differential formulations that include theoretical restrictions consistent with firm-level optimizing behavior.

7.1 Overview of the Differential Approach

Until this point, we have mostly been concerned with envelopes or variations of deviations from envelopes in the case of stochastic frontier models. The production function was defined as an envelope of the maximum output level that could be obtained from a given quantity of inputs. The cost function was the minimum cost of generating a fixed bundle of outputs based on a vector of input costs. The differential approach departs from this basic formulation by examining changes in optimizing behavior.

7.1.1 *Consumer Demand*

Given the similarity between the consumption and production models, it is convenient to start our development of the differential model of production by developing the differential model of consumer behavior. Specifically, the differential model of consumer behavior is somewhat simpler because it holds the total expenditures of the household constant. The starting point for the development of the differential model of consumption behavior is the consumer's utility maximization problem:

$$\left.\begin{array}{r}\max U(q)\\ \text{s.t. } p'q \leq Y\end{array}\right\} \Rightarrow \frac{\partial U\left(q\right)}{\partial q_i} = \lambda p_i \tag{7.6}$$

where $U\left(q\right)$ is the consumer's utility or preference function, q is the level of goods chosen by the household, p is the conformable vector of input prices, Y is the level of consumer income, and λ is the Lagrange multiplier for the income constraint. If we assume that consumers choose the levels of consumption so that these first-order conditions are satisfied, the question is then. What can we learn by observing changes in these first-order conditions or changes in the optimizing behavior? Put a little differently, how do the observed variables (i.e., levels of consumption goods) change given potential changes in the level of exogenous variables (e.g., changes in prices and income).

7.1.2 *Setting Up the Differential Formulation of Consumer Behavior*

Following the general conceptual approach outlined in Equations (7.1)–(7.5), we examine the implications of these changes in prices and income. We start by writing the first-order conditions out in matrix form:

$$\begin{bmatrix}\dfrac{\partial U\left(q\right)}{\partial q_1}\\ \vdots\\ \dfrac{\partial U\left(q\right)}{\partial q_n}\end{bmatrix} = \begin{bmatrix}\lambda p_1\\ \vdots\\ \lambda p_n\end{bmatrix}. \tag{7.7}$$

Given n goods, we are working with a system of $n + 1$ first-order conditions (i.e., the n first-order conditions in Equation (7.7) plus the income constraint). Specifically, we could rewrite Equation (7.7) as

$$\begin{bmatrix} \frac{\partial U(q)}{\partial q_1} \\ \vdots \\ \frac{\partial U(q)}{\partial q_n} \\ p'q \end{bmatrix} = \begin{bmatrix} \lambda p_1 \\ \vdots \\ \lambda p_n \\ Y \end{bmatrix}. \tag{7.8}$$

Next, taking a little liberty with the calculus, imagine differentiating Equation (7.8) with respect to p_1:

$$\begin{bmatrix} \frac{d\frac{\partial U(q)}{\partial q_1}}{dp_1} \\ \vdots \\ \frac{d\frac{\partial U(q)}{\partial q_n}}{dp_1} \\ \frac{dp'q}{dp_1} \end{bmatrix} = \begin{bmatrix} \frac{d\lambda p_1}{dp_1} \\ \vdots \\ \frac{d\lambda p_n}{dp_1} \\ \frac{dY}{dp_1} \end{bmatrix}. \tag{7.9}$$

Implicit in this formulation are $n+1$ conditions:

$$\begin{aligned} \frac{d\frac{\partial U(q)}{\partial q_1}}{dp_1} &= \frac{d\lambda p_1}{dp_1} \\ &\vdots \\ \frac{d\frac{\partial U(q)}{\partial q_n}}{dp_1} &= \frac{d\lambda p_n}{dp_1} \\ \frac{dp'q}{dp_1} &= \frac{dY}{dp_1}. \end{aligned} \tag{7.10}$$

If we consider all the potential price changes, Equation (7.9) becomes

$$\begin{bmatrix} \dfrac{d\dfrac{\partial U(q)}{\partial q_1}}{dp_1} & \cdots & \dfrac{d\dfrac{\partial U(q)}{\partial q_1}}{dp_n} \\ \vdots & \ddots & \vdots \\ \dfrac{d\dfrac{\partial U(q)}{\partial q_n}}{dp_1} & \cdots & \dfrac{d\dfrac{\partial U(q)}{\partial q_n}}{dp_n} \\ \dfrac{dp'q}{dp_1} & \cdots & \dfrac{d\,p'q}{dp_n} \end{bmatrix} = \begin{bmatrix} \dfrac{d\lambda p_1}{dp_1} & \cdots & \dfrac{d\lambda p_1}{dp_n} \\ \vdots & \ddots & \vdots \\ \dfrac{d\lambda p_n}{dp_1} & \cdots & \dfrac{d\lambda p_n}{dp_n} \\ \dfrac{dY}{dp_1} & \cdots & \dfrac{dY}{dp_n} \end{bmatrix}. \tag{7.11}$$

The formulation in Equation (7.11) yields $(n+1) \times n$ conditions.

To complete the formulation, we differentiate Equation (7.8) with respect to income:

$$\begin{bmatrix} \dfrac{d\dfrac{\partial U(q)}{q_1}}{dY} \\ \vdots \\ \dfrac{d\dfrac{\partial U(q)}{q_n}}{dY} \\ \dfrac{dp'q}{dY} \end{bmatrix} = \begin{bmatrix} \dfrac{d\lambda p_1}{dY} \\ \vdots \\ \dfrac{d\lambda p_n}{dY} \\ \dfrac{dY}{dY} \end{bmatrix}. \tag{7.12}$$

Merging the results from Equation (7.11) with those from Equation (7.12), we have

$$\begin{bmatrix} \dfrac{d\dfrac{\partial U(q)}{\partial q_1}}{dp_1} & \cdots & \dfrac{d\dfrac{\partial U(q)}{\partial q_1}}{dp_n} & \dfrac{d\dfrac{\partial U(q)}{q_1}}{dY} \\ \vdots & \ddots & \vdots & \vdots \\ \dfrac{d\dfrac{\partial U(q)}{\partial q_n}}{dp_1} & \cdots & \dfrac{d\dfrac{\partial U(q)}{\partial q_n}}{dp_n} & \dfrac{d\dfrac{\partial U(q)}{q_n}}{dY} \\ \dfrac{dp'x}{dp_1} & \cdots & \dfrac{dp'q}{dp_n} & \dfrac{dp'q}{dY} \end{bmatrix}$$

$$= \begin{bmatrix} \frac{d\lambda p_1}{dp_1} & \cdots & \frac{d\lambda p_1}{dp_n} & \frac{d\lambda p_1}{dY} \\ \vdots & \ddots & \vdots & \vdots \\ \frac{d\lambda p_n}{dp_1} & \cdots & \frac{d\lambda p_n}{dp_n} & \frac{d\lambda p_n}{dY} \\ \frac{dY}{dp_1} & \cdots & \frac{dY}{dp_n} & \frac{dY}{dY} \end{bmatrix}. \tag{7.13}$$

To develop the differential formulation of consumer demand, it is useful to partition the matrix in (7.13) into four parts:

$$\begin{bmatrix} \begin{pmatrix} \frac{d\frac{\partial U(q)}{q_1}}{dp_1} & \cdots & \frac{d\frac{\partial U(q)}{\partial q_1}}{dp_n} \\ \vdots & \ddots & \vdots \\ \frac{d\frac{\partial U(q)}{\partial q_n}}{dp_1} & \cdots & \frac{d\frac{\partial U(q)}{\partial q_n}}{dp_n} \end{pmatrix} & \begin{pmatrix} \frac{d\frac{\partial U(q)}{\partial q_1}}{dY} \\ \vdots \\ \frac{d\frac{\partial U(q)}{\partial q_n}}{dY} \end{pmatrix} \\ \begin{pmatrix} \frac{dp'q}{dp_1} & \cdots & \frac{dp'q}{dp_n} \end{pmatrix} & \frac{dp'q}{dY} \end{bmatrix}$$

$$= \begin{bmatrix} \begin{pmatrix} \frac{d\lambda p_1}{dp_1} & \cdots & \frac{d\lambda p_1}{p_n} \\ \vdots & \cdots & \vdots \\ \frac{d\lambda p_n}{p_1} & \cdots & \frac{d\lambda p_n}{dp_n} \end{pmatrix} & \begin{pmatrix} \frac{d\lambda p_1}{dY} \\ \vdots \\ \frac{d\lambda p_n}{dY} \end{pmatrix} \\ \begin{pmatrix} \frac{dY}{dp_1} & \cdots & \frac{dY}{dp_n} \end{pmatrix} & \frac{dY}{dY} \end{bmatrix} \tag{7.14}$$

which yields a 4×4 partition of $(n+1) \times (n+1)$ equations.

Focusing on the matrix of first-order conditions and first on the potential changes in the levels of the vector of prices (e.g., the first

$n \times n$ matrix of equations),

$$\begin{bmatrix} \frac{\partial^2 U(q)}{\partial q_1 \partial q_1}\frac{\partial q_1}{\partial p_1} + \cdots \frac{\partial^2 U(q)}{\partial q_1 \partial q_n}\frac{\partial q_n}{\partial p_1} & \cdots & \frac{\partial^2 U(q)}{\partial q_1 \partial q_1}\frac{\partial q_1}{\partial p_n} + \cdots \frac{\partial^2 U(q)}{\partial q_1 \partial q_n}\frac{\partial q_n}{\partial p_n} \\ \vdots & \ddots & \vdots \\ \frac{\partial^2 U(q)}{\partial q_n \partial q_1}\frac{\partial q_1}{\partial p_1} + \cdots \frac{\partial^2 U(q)}{\partial q_n \partial q_n}\frac{\partial q_n}{\partial p_1} & \cdots & \frac{\partial^2 U(q)}{\partial q_n \partial q_1}\frac{\partial q_1}{\partial p_n} + \cdots \frac{\partial^2 U(q)}{\partial q_n \partial q_n}\frac{\partial q_n}{\partial p_n} \end{bmatrix}$$

$$\times \begin{bmatrix} dp_1 \\ \vdots \\ dp_n \end{bmatrix} = \begin{bmatrix} \lambda_1 & \cdots & 0 \\ \vdots & \ddots & \vdots \\ 0 & \cdots & \lambda \end{bmatrix} \begin{bmatrix} dp_1 \\ \vdots \\ dp_n \end{bmatrix}$$

$$+ \begin{bmatrix} p_1 \frac{\partial \lambda}{\partial p_1} & \cdots & p_1 \frac{\partial \lambda}{\partial p_n} \\ \vdots & \ddots & \vdots \\ p_n \frac{\partial \lambda}{\partial p_1} & \cdots & p_n \frac{\partial \lambda}{\partial p_n} \end{bmatrix} \begin{bmatrix} dp_1 \\ \vdots \\ dp_2 \end{bmatrix}. \tag{7.15}$$

To develop Equation (7.15), we first note that for the left-hand side elements, $d[\partial U/\partial q_i] = \partial^2 U/\partial q_i \partial q_j \times \partial q_j/\partial p_k \times dp_k$. The right-hand side of Equation (7.15) is somewhat more complicated. In general, $d[\lambda p_i] = \lambda \times \partial p_i/\partial p_k + p_i \times \partial\lambda/\partial p_k$. Thus, we have two results: if $i = k$, then $d[\lambda p_i] = \lambda + p_i \times \partial\lambda/\partial p_i$; however, if $i \neq k$, then the differential simplifies to $d[\lambda p_i] = p_i \times \partial\lambda/\partial p_k$.

To simplify derivations, we denote the matrices in Equation (7.15) as

$$U = \begin{bmatrix} \frac{\partial^2 U}{\partial q_1 \partial q_1} & \cdots & \frac{\partial^2 U}{\partial q_1 \partial q_n} \\ \vdots & \ddots & \vdots \\ \frac{\partial^2 U}{\partial q_n \partial q_1} & \cdots & \frac{\partial^2 U}{\partial q_n \partial q_n} \end{bmatrix}, \quad \frac{\partial q}{\partial p'} = \begin{bmatrix} \frac{\partial q_1}{\partial p_1} & \cdots & \frac{\partial q_1}{\partial p_n} \\ \vdots & \ddots & \vdots \\ \frac{\partial q_n}{\partial p_1} & \cdots & \frac{\partial q_n}{\partial p_n} \end{bmatrix} \tag{7.16}$$

$$U \frac{\partial q}{\partial p'} dp = \left(\lambda I + p \frac{\partial \lambda}{\partial p'} \right) dp$$

where U is the Hessian of the consumer's utility function, $\partial q/\partial p'$ is the matrix of changes in consumption levels due to changes in the price of consumption goods.

Note that changes in the price of consumption goods also has implications for the income constraint. Specifically, differentiating the income constraint with respect to consumption prices using the $\partial q/\partial p'$ result from Equation (7.16) yields

$$\begin{bmatrix} p_1 \cdots p_n \end{bmatrix} \begin{bmatrix} \frac{\partial q_1}{\partial p_1} & \cdots & \frac{\partial q_1}{p_n} \\ \vdots & \ddots & \vdots \\ \frac{\partial q_n}{\partial p_1} & \cdots & \frac{\partial q_n}{\partial p_n} \end{bmatrix} \begin{bmatrix} dp_1 \\ \vdots \\ dp_n \end{bmatrix}$$

$$+ \begin{bmatrix} q_1 \cdots q_n \end{bmatrix} \begin{bmatrix} dp_1 \\ \vdots \\ dp_2 \end{bmatrix} = 0$$

$$\Rightarrow p' \frac{\partial q}{\partial p'} dp = -q' dp. \tag{7.17}$$

This result has implications for the "bottom" $1 \times n$ conditions in Equation (7.14). Specifically, the last row in Equation (7.14), can be rewritten as

$$\begin{bmatrix} \frac{dp'q}{dp_1} & \cdots & \frac{dp'q}{dp_n} \end{bmatrix} \begin{bmatrix} dp_1 \\ \vdots \\ dp_n \end{bmatrix}$$

$$= \begin{bmatrix} p_1 \frac{\partial x_1}{\partial p_k} & \cdots & p_n \frac{\partial q_n}{\partial p_n} \end{bmatrix} \begin{bmatrix} dp_1 \\ \vdots \\ d\,p_n \end{bmatrix} + \begin{bmatrix} q_1 & \cdots & q_n \end{bmatrix} \begin{bmatrix} d\,p_1 \\ \vdots \\ dp_n \end{bmatrix}. \tag{7.18}$$

Next, we examine the effect of changes in income on the first-order conditions by differentiating these conditions with respect to income — the "right" $n \times 1$ partition of Equation (7.14). First, we differentiate the first-order conditions with respect to input prices (in Equation (7.7) with respect to income), yielding

$$\begin{bmatrix} \frac{\partial^2 U}{\partial q_1 \partial q_1}\frac{\partial q_1}{\partial Y} + \cdots \frac{\partial^2 U}{\partial q_1 \partial q_n}\frac{\partial q_n}{\partial Y} \\ \vdots \\ \frac{\partial^2 U}{\partial q_n \partial q_1}\frac{\partial q_1}{\partial Y} + \cdots \frac{\partial^2 U}{\partial q_n \partial q_n}\frac{\partial q_n}{\partial Y} \end{bmatrix} dY = \begin{bmatrix} p_1 \\ \vdots \\ p_2 \end{bmatrix} \frac{\partial \lambda}{\partial Y} dY \tag{7.19}$$

$$\Rightarrow U\frac{\partial q}{\partial Y}dY = \frac{\partial \lambda}{\partial Y} p dY.$$

The last set of differentials are then the change of the income constraint with respect to changes in income:

$$\begin{bmatrix} p_1 & \ldots & p_n \end{bmatrix} \begin{bmatrix} \frac{\partial q_1}{\partial Y} \\ \vdots \\ \frac{\partial q_n}{\partial Y} \end{bmatrix} = 1 \Rightarrow p' \frac{\partial q}{\partial Y} = 1. \tag{7.20}$$

7.1.3 *Barten's Fundamental Matrix*

Given the foregoing derivations, we can derive Barten's fundamental matrix. Putting the results of these Equations (7.16), (7.17), and (7.18) into the matrix in Equation (7.14),

$$\begin{bmatrix} U\frac{\partial q}{\partial p'} & U\frac{\partial q}{\partial Y} \\ p\frac{\partial q}{\partial p'} & p'\frac{\partial q}{\partial Y} \end{bmatrix} \begin{bmatrix} dp \\ dY \end{bmatrix} = \begin{bmatrix} \lambda I + p\frac{\partial \lambda}{\partial p'} & \frac{\partial \lambda}{\partial Y} p \\ -q & 1 \end{bmatrix} \begin{bmatrix} dp \\ dY \end{bmatrix}. \tag{7.21}$$

Given that we want this equality to hold for any change in price or income,

$$\begin{bmatrix} U\frac{\partial q}{\partial p'} & U\frac{\partial q}{\partial Y} \\ p\frac{\partial q}{\partial p'} & p'\frac{\partial q}{\partial Y} \end{bmatrix} = \begin{bmatrix} \lambda I + p\frac{\partial \lambda}{\partial p'} & \frac{\partial \lambda}{\partial Y} p \\ -q & 1 \end{bmatrix}. \tag{7.22}$$

Solving for the zero matrix (e.g., solving for the general form of the system of differential equations),

$$\begin{bmatrix} U\frac{\partial q}{\partial p'} - \lambda I - p\frac{\partial \lambda}{\partial q'} & U\frac{\partial q}{\partial Y} - \frac{\partial \lambda}{\partial Y}p \\ p\frac{\partial q}{\partial p'} + q & p'\frac{\partial q}{\partial Y} - 1 \end{bmatrix} = \begin{bmatrix} 0\,0 \\ 0\,0 \end{bmatrix}. \tag{7.23}$$

Next, let us move the fixed variables back to the right-hand side of the expression:

$$\begin{bmatrix} U\frac{\partial q}{\partial p'} - p\frac{\partial \lambda}{\partial p'} & U\frac{\partial q}{\partial Y} - \frac{\partial \lambda}{\partial Y}p \\ p\frac{\partial q}{\partial p'} & p'\frac{\partial q}{\partial Y} \end{bmatrix} = \begin{bmatrix} \lambda I & 0 \\ -q & 1 \end{bmatrix}. \tag{7.24}$$

While it seems a little counter-intuitive, the level of the goods consumed (q) is technically exogenous from the standpoint of the derivatives in this formulation. Finally, consider rewriting the left-hand side of Equation (7.24) as a matrix:

$$\begin{bmatrix} U & p' \\ p & 0 \end{bmatrix} \begin{bmatrix} \frac{\partial q}{\partial p'} & \frac{\partial q}{\partial Y} \\ -\frac{\partial \lambda}{\partial p'} & -\frac{\partial \lambda}{\partial Y} \end{bmatrix} = \begin{bmatrix} \lambda I & 0 \\ -q & 1 \end{bmatrix}. \tag{7.25}$$

Inverting the leftmost matrix using an explicit row-reduction approach, the first matrix on the left-hand side of Equation (7.25) yields a solution for the consumer's demand curve (i.e., $\partial x / \partial p'$):

$$\begin{bmatrix} \frac{\partial q}{\partial p'} & \frac{\partial q}{\partial Y} \\ -\frac{\partial \lambda}{\partial p'} & -\frac{\partial \lambda}{\partial Y} \end{bmatrix} = \begin{bmatrix} U\; p' \\ p\; 0 \end{bmatrix}^{-1} \begin{bmatrix} \lambda I\; 0 \\ -q\; 1 \end{bmatrix}. \tag{7.26}$$

Inverting the first matrix on the right-hand side of the equality yields

$$\left[\begin{array}{cc|cc} U & p' & I & 0 \\ p & 0 & 0 & 1 \end{array}\right] U^{-1}R_1$$

$$\left[\begin{array}{cc|cc} I & U^{-1}p' & U^{-1} & 0 \\ p & 0 & 0 & 1 \end{array}\right] R_2 - pR_1$$

$$\left[\begin{array}{cc|cc} I & U^{-1}p' & U^{-1} & 0 \\ 0 & -pU^{-1}p' & -pU^{-1} & 1 \end{array}\right] R_1 - U^{-1}p'R_2$$

$$\left[\begin{array}{cc|cc} I & 0 & U^{-1} - \frac{1}{pU^{-1}p'}\left(U^{-1}p'\right)\left(pU^{-1}\right) & \frac{1}{pU^{-1}p'}U^{-1}p' \\ 0 & 1 & \frac{1}{pU^{-1}p'}pU^{-1} & -\frac{1}{pU^{-1}p} \end{array}\right]$$

$$\therefore \begin{bmatrix} U & p' \\ p & 0 \end{bmatrix}^{-1}$$

$$= \frac{1}{pU^{-1}p'}\begin{bmatrix} \left(pU^{-1}p'\right)U^{-1} - \left(U^{-1}p'\right)\left(pU^{-1}\right)' & -U^{-1}p' \\ pU^{-1} & 1 \end{bmatrix}. \tag{7.27}$$

Multiplying the first row and column of Equation (7.26) using the inverse in Equation (7.27) yields

$$\begin{aligned} \frac{\partial q}{\partial p'} &= \frac{1}{pU^{-1}p'}\left[\left(pU^{-1}p'\right)U^{-1} - \left(U^{-1}p'\right)\left(pU^{-1}\right) \quad -U^{-1}p'\right]\begin{bmatrix} \lambda I \\ -q \end{bmatrix} \\ &= \lambda U^{-1} - \frac{\lambda}{pU^{-1}p'}\left(U^{-1}p'\right)\left(pU^{-1}\right) + \frac{1}{pU^{-1}p'}U^{-1}p'q. \end{aligned} \tag{7.28}$$

Note that this matrix is $n \times n$. Next, multiplying the second row by the second column yields

$$\begin{aligned} -\frac{\partial \lambda}{\partial Y} &= \frac{1}{pU^{-1}p'}\left[pU^{-1}\ 1\right]\begin{bmatrix} 0 \\ 1 \end{bmatrix} \\ &= \frac{1}{pU^{-1}p'} \Rightarrow \frac{\partial \lambda}{\partial Y} = -\frac{1}{pU^{-1}p'} \end{aligned} \tag{7.29}$$

which is a scalar. Multiplying the first row by the second column yields

$$\begin{aligned}\frac{\partial q}{\partial Y} &= \frac{1}{pU^{-1}p'}\left[(pU^{-1}p')U^{-1} - (U^{-1}p')(pU^{1}) - U^{-1}p'\right]\begin{bmatrix}0\\1\end{bmatrix}\\ &= -\frac{1}{p'U^{-1}p}U^{-1}p \end{aligned} \quad (7.30)$$

which is a $1 \times n$ vector.

The above equations will give us the parts required to finish the derivation. First, consider the "center term" in Equation (7.28):

$$\frac{\lambda}{pU^{-1}p'}(U^{-1}p')(pU^{-1}) = \lambda(pU^{-1}p')\left(\frac{U^{-1}p'}{pU^{-1}p'}\right)\left(\frac{pU^{-1}}{pU^{-1}p'}\right). \quad (7.31)$$

That is, we multiply by $1 = (pU^{-1}p')/(pU^{-1}p')$ to make two similar terms. Given the result from Equation (7.30), Equation (7.31) can be rewritten as

$$\lambda(pU^{-1}p')\frac{d\,q'}{dY}\frac{dq}{d\,Y}. \quad (7.32)$$

Further, defining the income flexibility (ϕ) as

$$\frac{1}{\phi} = \frac{d\,\lambda}{d\,Y}\frac{Y}{\lambda}. \quad (7.33)$$

and substituting Equation (7.32) into Equation (7.31) yields

$$\frac{\partial q}{\partial p'} = \lambda U^{-1} - \phi Y\frac{d\,q'}{d\,Y}\frac{d\,q}{d\,Y} - \frac{d\,q'}{d\,Y}q. \quad (7.34)$$

Note that we substituted the result from Equation (7.30) into the last term in Equation (7.29).

To bring everything together, consider totally differentiating the Divisia quantity index:

$$s_i d(\log q_i) = \frac{\partial(p_i q_i)}{\partial Y}d(\log Y) + \sum_{i=1}^{n}\frac{p_i p_j}{Y}\frac{\partial q_i}{\partial p_j}d(\log p_j). \quad (7.35)$$

Letting $\partial(p_iq_i)/\partial E = \theta_i$,

$$s_i d(\log q_i) = \theta_i d(\log Y) + \sum_{i=1}^{n} \frac{p_i p_j}{Y} \frac{\partial q_i}{\partial p_j} d(\log p_j). \tag{7.36}$$

Next, focusing on the $d\,q_i/dY$ term in Equation (7.34) (e.g., one element from the matrix partial derivative),

$$\frac{\partial q_i}{\partial p_j} = \lambda u^{ij} - \phi Y \frac{dq_i}{dY} \frac{d\,q_j}{d\,Y} - \frac{\partial q_i}{\partial Y} q_j \tag{7.37}$$

where we denote the $\{i, j\}$-th element of the inverse of the Hessian of the utility function as u^{ij}. Next, we multiply this result by $(p_i p_j)/Y$ to yield

$$\frac{\partial q_i}{\partial p_j} = \frac{p_i p_j}{Y} \lambda u^{ij} - \phi \frac{d\,(p_i q_i)}{d\,Y} \frac{d\,(p_j q_j)}{d\,Y} - \frac{\partial (p_i q_i)}{\partial Y} q_j \tag{7.38}$$

noting that the prices are constant; hence, $p_i \partial q_i/\partial Y = \partial(p_i q_i)/\partial Y$.

Substituting Equation (7.38) into Equation (7.36) yields

$$\begin{aligned} s_i d(\log q_i) &= \theta_i d(\log Y) \\ &\quad + \sum_{j=1}^{n} \left(\frac{p_i p_j}{Y} \lambda u^{ij} - \phi \frac{d\,(p_i q_i)}{d\,Y} \frac{d\,(p_j q_j)}{d\,Y} \right. \\ &\quad \left. - \frac{\partial (p_i q_i)}{\partial Y} q_j \right) d(\log p_j). \end{aligned} \tag{7.39}$$

Finally, letting $\theta_{ij} = \lambda p_i p_j u^{ij}/\phi E$ and again using the result that $\partial\,(p_i q_i)\,/\partial E = \theta_i$ yields

$$s_i d(\log q_i) = \theta_i d(\log Y) + \sum_{j=1}^{n} (\phi \theta_{ij} - \phi \theta_i \theta_j - \theta_i s_j) d(\log p_j). \tag{7.40}$$

Pulling the share term $\theta_i \sum_{j=1}^{n} s_j d\,(\log p_j)$ out of the summation and grouping it with the income change yields

$$\begin{aligned} s_i d(\log q_i) &= \theta_i \left(d(\log Y) - \sum_{j=1}^{n} s_j d(\log p_j) \right) + \phi \sum_{j=1}^{n} \\ &\quad \times (\theta_{ij} - \theta_i \theta_j) d(\log p_j). \end{aligned} \tag{7.41}$$

Note that

$$d(\log Y) - \sum_{j=1}^{n} s_j d(\log p_j) \equiv d(\log Q) \tag{7.42}$$

(e.g., substituting the Divisia quantity index) yields

$$s_i d(\ln(q_i)) = \theta_i d(\ln(Q)) + \phi \sum_{j=1}^{n} (\theta_{ij} - \theta_i\theta_j)\, d(\log p_j). \tag{7.43}$$

Typically, the specification is simplified by restricting $\phi(\theta_{ij} - \theta_i\theta_j) = \pi_{ij}$. Equation (7.44) with the assumption defining π_{ij} is typically referred to as the Rotterdam model of consumer demand.

7.2 Differential Model of Production

A similar approach yields the system of input demand equations for a firm that produces a single product. Following Theil (1980), we use a logarithmic specification for a general production function:

$$\ln(y) = h(x) \tag{7.44}$$

where y is the level of the output and x is a vector of inputs. For example, the Cobb–Douglas function can be specified as

$$\ln(y) = a + \sum_{i=1}^{n} b_i \ln(x_i). \tag{7.45}$$

7.2.1 *Derivation of the Single Product Input Demand Model*

Following the demand example in the preceding section, we formulate the firm's constrained optimization problem and take the first-order conditions:

$$L(x, \rho) = \sum_{i=1}^{n} w_i x_i + \rho[\ln(y) - h(x)]$$
$$\Rightarrow \frac{\partial L(x, \rho)}{\partial \ln(x_j)} = w_j \frac{\partial x_j}{\partial \ln(x_j)} - \rho \frac{\partial h(y)}{\partial \ln(x_j)} = 0 \tag{7.46}$$

where w_i denotes the input price for input i and ρ is the Lagrange multiplier that represents the change in cost with respect to a change in the level of output. Transforming the first term on the right-hand side of the result in Equation (7.46) from a natural logarithm to a level:

$$\begin{aligned} \frac{\partial x_j}{\partial \ln(x_j)} &\Rightarrow \frac{1}{\frac{\partial \ln(x_j)}{\partial x_j}} = \frac{1}{\frac{1}{x_j}} = x_j \\ \frac{\partial L(x, \rho)}{\partial \ln(x_j)} &= w_j x_j - \rho \frac{\partial h(x)}{\partial \ln(x_j)} = 0. \end{aligned} \tag{7.47}$$

Following the setup from the consumer's model, we can transform the results of the differential production model into a formulation involving the expenditure shares for each input. As a starting point, consider multiplying each side of the last result in Equation (7.47) by $1/C$ where C is the total cost of production (i.e., $C = \sum_{i=1}^{n} w_i x_i$):

$$\frac{w_i x_i}{C} - \frac{\rho}{C} \frac{\partial h(y)}{\partial \ln(x_i)} = 0. \tag{7.48}$$

Given the result in Equation (7.48), we substitute $f_i = w_i x_i / C$ as the factor share, yielding

$$f_i - \frac{\rho}{C} \frac{\partial h(y)}{\partial \ln(x_i)}. \tag{7.49}$$

Then we transform the expression ρ/C (e.g., the change in the cost of production resulting from a change in the logarithm of the output level $\rho = \partial C/\partial \ln(y)$ where y is the level of output):

$$\rho \equiv \frac{\partial C}{\partial \ln(y)} \Rightarrow \frac{1}{C}\frac{\partial C}{\partial \ln(y)} = \frac{\frac{\partial C}{C}}{\partial \ln(y)} = \frac{\partial \ln(C)}{\partial \ln(y)} = \gamma. \tag{7.50}$$

Substituting this result into Equation (7.49) yields

$$\begin{aligned} f_i - \frac{\rho}{C}\frac{\partial h(x)}{\partial \ln(x_i)} &= f_i - \gamma\frac{\partial h(x)}{\partial \ln(x_i)} = 0 \\ \Rightarrow \frac{\partial h(x)}{\partial \ln(x_j)} &= \frac{f_j}{\gamma}. \end{aligned} \tag{7.51}$$

Moss *et al.* (2010) provide a detailed development of the differential demand system for the single product firm. Following the discussion, the next step in this development is to differentiate Equation (7.51) with respect to the natural logarithm of input j:

$$\frac{\partial^2 L(x,\rho)}{\partial \ln(x_i)\partial \ln(x_j)} = \frac{\partial f_i}{\partial \ln(x_j)} - \gamma\frac{\partial^2 h(x)}{\partial \ln(x_i)\partial \ln(x_j)}. \tag{7.52}$$

Focusing on the derivative of the input share,

$$\frac{\partial f_i}{\partial \ln(x_j)} = \frac{\partial\left(\frac{w_i x_i}{C}\right)}{\partial \ln(x_j)} = \begin{cases} \frac{w_i x_i}{C} \; i = j \\ 0 \; i \neq j \end{cases}. \tag{7.53}$$

Again, to explain the result in Equation (7.53), we note that

$$\frac{\partial g(x)}{\partial \ln(x)} = \frac{\partial g(x)}{\partial x}\frac{\partial x}{\partial \ln(x)} \tag{7.54}$$

where by Greene's theorem,

$$\frac{\partial x}{\partial \ln(x)} = \frac{1}{\frac{\partial \ln(x)}{\partial x}} = x. \tag{7.55}$$

Therefore,

$$\frac{\partial\left(\frac{w_i x_i}{C}\right)}{\partial \ln(x_i)} = \frac{1}{C}\frac{\partial w_i x_i}{\partial x_i}x_i = \frac{w_i x_i}{C} \tag{7.56}$$

where we are interested in the partial derivative instead of the total derivative (i.e., we hold the level of C constant).

Extending our formulation slightly, we conceptualize the results of Equation (7.53) in matrix form:

$$\left[\frac{\partial f_i}{\partial \ln(x_j)}\right]_{i,j=1,\cdots n} = \begin{bmatrix} \frac{w_1 x_1}{C} & \cdots & 0 \\ \vdots & \ddots & \vdots \\ 0 & \cdots & \frac{w_n x_n}{C} \end{bmatrix} = \begin{bmatrix} f_1 & \cdots & 0 \\ \vdots & \ddots & \vdots \\ 0 & \cdots & f_n \end{bmatrix} = F. \tag{7.57}$$

Similarly, we can define the Hessian matrix of the production function with respect to the logarithm of inputs (H) as

$$H = \left[\frac{\partial^2 h(y)}{\partial \ln(x_i)\partial \ln(x_j)}\right]_{i,j=1,\ldots n}. \tag{7.58}$$

Combining the results from Equations (7.57) and (7.58) with Equation (7.52) yields

$$\frac{\partial^2 L(x,\rho)}{\partial \ln(x_i)\partial \ln(x_j)} = F - \gamma H. \tag{7.59}$$

Given the general form of the derivative of Lagrange problem in Equation (7.59), we can then develop differential model of the single product firm, specifically differentiating the first-order condition in Equation (7.47) with respect to the logarithm of output levels and the logarithm of input prices. Starting with the derivative with respect to the logarithm of output levels,

$$\begin{aligned} \frac{\partial^2 L(x,\rho)}{\partial \ln(x_i)\partial \ln(y)} &= w_i x_i \frac{\partial \ln(x_i)}{\partial \ln(y)} - \rho \frac{\partial h(x)}{\partial \ln(x_i)} \frac{\partial \ln(\rho)}{\partial \ln(y)} \\ &\quad - \rho \sum_{i=1}^{n} \frac{\partial^2 h(x)}{\partial \ln(x_i)\partial \ln(x_j)} \frac{\partial \ln(x_j)}{\partial \ln(y)} \\ &\quad - \rho \frac{\partial^2 h(x)}{\partial \ln(x_i) \ln(y)} = 0. \end{aligned} \tag{7.60}$$

To simplify Equation (7.60), we impose the first-order condition to the second term on the right-hand side. Specifically, from Equation (7.47),

$$w_i x_i - \rho \frac{\partial h(x)}{\partial \ln(x_i)} = 0 \Rightarrow \frac{\partial h(x)}{\partial \ln(x_i)} = \frac{w_i x_i}{\rho}. \tag{7.61}$$

Therefore, Equation (7.60) becomes

$$\begin{aligned} \frac{\partial^2 L(x,\rho)}{\partial \ln(x_i) \partial \ln(y)} &= w_i x_i \frac{\partial \ln(x_i)}{\partial \ln(y)} - w_i x_i \frac{\partial \ln(\rho)}{\partial \ln(y)} \\ &\quad -\rho \sum_{i=1}^{n} \frac{\partial^2 h(x)}{\partial \ln(x_i) \partial \ln(x_j)} \frac{\partial \ln(x_j)}{\partial \ln(y)} \\ &\quad -\rho \frac{\partial^2 h(x)}{\partial \ln(x_i) \ln(y)} = 0. \end{aligned} \tag{7.62}$$

Regrouping the expressions in Equation (7.62) slightly,

$$\begin{aligned} &\left[w_i x_i \frac{\partial \ln(x_i)}{\partial \ln(y)} - \rho \textstyle\sum_{i=1}^{n} \frac{\partial^2 h(x)}{\partial \ln(x_i) \partial \ln(x_j)} \frac{\partial \ln(x_j)}{\partial \ln(y)} \right] \\ &\quad - w_i x_i \frac{\partial \ln(\rho)}{\partial \ln(y)} = \rho \sum_{i=1}^{n} \frac{\partial^2 h(x)}{\partial \ln(x_i) \partial \ln(x_j)} \frac{\partial \ln(x_j)}{\partial \ln(y)} \\ &\Rightarrow \left[w_i x_i - \rho \sum_{i=1}^{n} \frac{\partial^2 h(x)}{\partial \ln(x_i) \partial \ln(x_j)} \right] \frac{\partial \ln(x_i)}{\partial \ln(y)} - w_i x_i \frac{\partial \ln(\rho)}{\partial \ln(y)} \\ &\quad = \rho \sum_{i=1}^{n} \frac{\partial^2 h(x)}{\partial \ln(x_i) \partial \ln(x_j)} \frac{\partial \ln(x_j)}{\partial \ln(y)}. \end{aligned} \tag{7.63}$$

Using the result of Equation (7.50), we divide the result of Equation (7.63) by C to yield

$$\begin{aligned} (F - \gamma H) \frac{\partial \ln(y)}{\partial \ln(x)} - F\iota \frac{\partial \ln(\rho)}{\partial \ln(y)} &= \gamma H^* \\ H^* &= \left[\frac{\partial^2 h(x)}{\partial \ln(x_i) \partial \ln(y)} \right]_{i=1,\ldots,n} \end{aligned} \tag{7.64}$$

and ι is a vector of ones. Note that $\iota\partial\ln(\rho)/\partial\ln(y)$ gives a column vector of $\partial\ln(\rho)/\partial\ln(y)$ (i.e., unlike the other derivatives in Equation (7.64), $\partial\ln(\rho)/\partial\ln(y)$ is a scalar).

Next, we differentiate Equation (7.47) with respect to the natural logarithm of input prices to yield

$$\begin{aligned}\frac{\partial^2 L(x,\rho)}{\partial\ln(x_i)\partial\ln(w_j)} &= \delta_{ij}w_i x_j\frac{\partial\ln(x_i)}{\partial\ln(w_i)} + \delta_{ij}w_i x_j\frac{\partial\ln(w_i)}{\partial\ln(w_j)}\\ &\quad -w_i x_j\frac{\partial\ln(\rho)}{\partial\ln(w_j)} - \rho\sum_{k=1}^{n}\frac{\partial^2 h(y)}{\partial\ln(x_i)\partial\ln(x_k)}\\ &\quad \times\frac{\partial\ln(x_k)}{\partial\ln(w_j)} = 0 \end{aligned} \tag{7.65}$$

where δ_{ij} is the Kronecker δ (i.e., $\delta_{ij} = 1$ if $i = j$ and 0 if $i \neq j$). Equation (7.65), can then be written in matrix form (e.g., along the same lines as Equation (7.64) as

$$(F-\gamma H)\frac{\partial\ln(x)}{\partial\ln(w')} - F\iota\frac{\partial\ln(\rho)}{\partial\ln(w')} = -F. \tag{7.66}$$

Recall in our development of the differential model for consumer demand we had $n+1$ conditions (e.g., the first-order conditions with respect to the price of each good plus the income constraint — implicitly the derivative with respect to the Lagrange multiplier). In the production model, our additional condition (or our Lagrange multiplier condition) comes from the production function. We start by differentiating the production function with respect to the natural logarithm of output:

$$\sum_{i=1}^{n}\frac{\partial h(x)}{\partial\ln(x_i)}\frac{\partial\ln(x_i)}{\partial\ln(y)} = 0 \Rightarrow \iota' F\frac{\partial\ln(x)}{\partial\ln(y)} = \gamma \tag{7.67}$$

and then we differentiate the production function with respect to the vector of input prices, yielding

$$\sum_{j=1}^{n}\frac{\partial h(x)}{\partial\ln(x_i)}\frac{\partial\ln(x_i)}{\partial\ln(w_j)} = 0 \Rightarrow \iota' F\frac{\partial\ln(x)}{\partial\ln(w')}. \tag{7.68}$$

Combining Equations (7.64), (7.66), (7.67), and (7.68) into a system of differential equations (i.e., along the line of Equation (7.22) in our development of the consumer's problem), we have

$$\begin{bmatrix} F-\gamma H & \iota \\ \iota' & 0 \end{bmatrix} \begin{bmatrix} \dfrac{\partial \ln(x)}{\partial \ln(y)} & \dfrac{\partial \ln(x)}{\partial \ln(w')} \\ -\dfrac{\partial \ln(\rho)}{\partial \ln(y)} & \dfrac{\partial \ln(\rho)}{\partial \ln(w')} \end{bmatrix} = \begin{bmatrix} \gamma H^* & -F \\ \gamma & 0 \end{bmatrix}. \tag{7.69}$$

Unlike the consumer model, it is useful to adjust the first row of the second matrix in Equation (7.69) slightly. Modifying the first row and second column element of (7.69),

$$\begin{aligned} & F^{-1}\left[(F-\gamma H)\frac{\partial \ln(x)}{\partial \ln(w')} - F\iota\frac{\partial \ln(\rho)}{\partial \ln(w')}\right] \\ & = F^{-1}(F-\gamma H)[FF^{-1}]\frac{\partial \ln(x)}{\partial \ln(w')} - FF^{-1}\iota\frac{\partial \ln(\rho)}{\partial \ln(w')} = -I \\ & \Rightarrow F^{-1}(F-\gamma H)F^{-1}F\frac{\partial \ln(x)}{\partial \ln(w')} - \iota\frac{\partial \ln(\rho)}{\partial \ln(w')} = -I. \end{aligned} \tag{7.70}$$

Specifically, Equation (7.70) involves multiplying the first term by a special form of one (or the identity matrix in this case: $F^{-1}F$).

Given these modifications, the differential matrix in Equation (7.69) can be rewritten as

$$\begin{bmatrix} F^{-1}(F-\gamma H)F^{-1} & \iota \\ \iota' & 0 \end{bmatrix} \begin{bmatrix} F\dfrac{\partial \ln(x)}{\partial \ln(y)} & F\dfrac{\partial \ln(x)}{\partial \ln(w')} \\ -\dfrac{\partial \ln(\rho)}{\partial \ln(y)} & \dfrac{\partial \ln(\rho)}{\partial \ln(w')} \end{bmatrix} = \begin{bmatrix} \gamma F^{-1}H^* & -I \\ \gamma & 0 \end{bmatrix}. \tag{7.71}$$

Following the general approach from the differential demand model, we solve Equation (7.71) for the matrix of partial derivatives:

$$\begin{aligned} \begin{bmatrix} F\dfrac{\partial \ln(x)}{\partial \ln(y)} & F\dfrac{\partial \ln(x)}{\partial \ln(w')} \\ -\dfrac{\partial \ln(\rho)}{\partial \ln(y)} & \dfrac{\partial \ln(\rho)}{\partial \ln(w')} \end{bmatrix} &= \begin{bmatrix} F^{-1}(F-\gamma H)F^{-1} & \iota \\ \iota' & 0 \end{bmatrix}^{-1} \\ &\quad \times \begin{bmatrix} \gamma F^{-1}H^* & -I \\ \gamma & 0 \end{bmatrix}. \end{aligned} \tag{7.72}$$

While the details may seem tedious, it is informative to derive the inverse of Barten's fundamental matrix. We invert Barten's fundamental matrix from Equation (7.72) by applying row operations to the fundamental matrix augmented by the identity matrix:

$$\left[\begin{matrix} F^{-1}(F-\gamma H)F^{-1} & \iota \\ \iota' & 0 \end{matrix}\middle|\begin{matrix} I & 0 \\ 0 & 1 \end{matrix}\right]. \tag{7.73}$$

Multiplying the first row of the matrix in Equation (7.73) by $\left(F^{-1}\left[F-\gamma H\right]F^{-1}\right)^{-1}$ yields

$$\left[\begin{matrix} I\ \left(F^{-1}\left[F-\gamma H\right]F^{-1}\right)^{-1}\iota \\ \iota' \qquad\qquad 0 \end{matrix}\middle|\begin{matrix} \left(F^{-1}\left[F-\gamma H\right]F^{-1}\right)^{-1} & 0 \\ 0 & 1 \end{matrix}\right]. \tag{7.74}$$

Next, we subtract ι times row 1 from row 2, yielding

$$\left[\begin{matrix} I & (F^{-1}[F-\gamma H]F^{-1})^{-1}\iota \\ 0 & -\iota'\left(F^{-1}\left[F-\gamma H\right]F^{-1}\right)^{-1}\iota \end{matrix}\middle|\begin{matrix} (F^{-1}[F-\gamma H]F^{-1})^{-1} & 0 \\ -\iota'\left(F^{-1}\left[F-\gamma H\right]F^{-1}\right)^{-1} & 1 \end{matrix}\right]. \tag{7.75}$$

Note that in Equation (7.75), $\iota'\left(F^{-1}[F-\gamma H]F^{-1}\right)^{-1}\iota$ is a scalar, thus we can divide the last row by this scalar, yielding

$$\left[\begin{matrix} I & \left(F^{-1}\left[F-\gamma H\right]F^{-1}\right)^{-1}\iota \\ 0 & 1 \end{matrix}\middle|\begin{matrix} \left(F^{-1}\left[F-\gamma H\right]F^{-1}\right)^{-1} & 0 \\ \dfrac{\iota'\left(F^{-1}\left[F-\gamma H\right]F^{-1}\right)^{-1}}{\iota'\left(F^{-1}\left[F-\gamma H\right]F^{-1}\right)^{-1}\iota} & -\dfrac{1}{\iota'\left(F^{-1}\left[F-\gamma H\right]F^{-1}\right)^{-1}\iota} \end{matrix}\right]. \tag{7.76}$$

To complete the derivation, we subtract $\left(F^{-1}\left[F-\gamma h\right]F^{-1}\right)^{-1}\iota$ times row 2 from row 1 to yield an identity on the left-hand side matrix and the inverse:

$$\begin{bmatrix} \left(F^{-1}\left[F-\gamma H\right]F^{-1}\right)^{-1} - \dfrac{\left[\left(F^{-1}\left[F-\gamma H\right]F^{-1}\right)^{-1}\iota\right]\left[\iota'\left(F^{-1}\left[F-\gamma H\right]F^{-1}\right)^{-1}\right]}{\iota'\left(F^{-1}\left[F-\gamma H\right]F^{-1}\right)^{-1}\iota} & \dfrac{\left(F^{-1}\left[F-\gamma H\right]F^{-1}\right)^{-1}\iota}{\iota'\left(F^{-1}\left[F-\gamma H\right]F^{-1}\right)^{-1}\iota} \\ \dfrac{\iota'\left(F^{-1}\left[F-\gamma H\right]F^{-1}\right)^{-1}}{\iota'\left(F^{-1}\left[F-\gamma H\right]F^{-1}\right)^{-1}\iota} & -\dfrac{1}{\iota'\left(F^{-1}\left[F-\gamma H\right]F^{-1}\right)^{-1}\iota} \end{bmatrix}. \tag{7.77}$$

To clean up the formulation, we note that

$$(F^{-1}[F-\gamma H]F^{-1})^{-1} = F[F-\gamma H]^{-1}F. \tag{7.78}$$

Next, we define

$$\psi = \iota' F[F-\gamma H]^{-1}F\iota. \tag{7.79}$$

Dealing with the first row and column element, we substitute the results of Equations (7.78) and (7.79) to yield

$$\begin{aligned} F\left[F-\gamma H\right]^{-1}F &- \frac{\left(F\left[F-\gamma H\right]^{-1}F\iota\right)\left(\iota' F\left[F-\gamma H\right]^{-1}F\right)}{\psi} \\ &= \psi\left(\frac{1}{\psi}F[F-\gamma H]^{-1}F - \left(\frac{F[F-\gamma H]^{-1}F\iota}{\psi}\right)\right. \\ &\quad \times \left.\left(\frac{\iota' F\left[F-\gamma H\right]^{-1}F}{\psi}\right)\right). \end{aligned} \tag{7.80}$$

First, note the structure of the last portion of Equation (7.80). If we let $z = F[F-\gamma H]^{-1}F\iota$ (which is an $n \times 1$ matrix), then $\iota' F[F-\gamma H]F = z'$ (which is an $1 \times n$ matrix). Multiplying $z \times z'$ yields an $n \times n$ matrix conformable with the $F[F-\gamma H]^{-1}F$. Further note that these vectors are linear combinations of the first matrix. Hence, if we define

$$\Theta = \frac{1}{\psi} F[F - \gamma H]^{-1} F \tag{7.81}$$

we can define

$$\theta = \Theta \iota. \tag{7.82}$$

Thus, we can write the inverse of Barten's fundamental equation as

$$\begin{bmatrix} F^{-1}(F - \gamma H)F^{-1} & \iota \\ \iota' & 0 \end{bmatrix}^{-1} = \begin{bmatrix} \psi(\Theta - \theta\theta') & \theta \\ \theta' & -\frac{1}{\psi} \end{bmatrix}. \tag{7.83}$$

The matrix expression in Equation (7.72) can then be rewritten using the results in Equation (7.83) as

$$\begin{bmatrix} F\dfrac{\partial \ln(x)}{\partial \ln(y)} & F\dfrac{\partial \ln(x)}{\partial \ln(w')} \\ -\dfrac{\partial \ln(\rho)}{\partial \ln(y)} & \dfrac{\partial \ln(\rho)}{\partial \ln(w')} \end{bmatrix} = \begin{bmatrix} \psi(\Theta - \theta\theta') & \theta \\ \theta' & -\frac{1}{\psi} \end{bmatrix} \begin{bmatrix} \gamma F^{-1} H^* & -I \\ \gamma & 0 \end{bmatrix}. \tag{7.84}$$

Given the results in Equation (7.84), we have

$$F\frac{\partial \ln(x)}{\partial \ln(w')} = -\psi(\Theta - \theta\theta') \tag{7.85}$$

which yields the basic differential demand model for production inputs. Specifically, defining the logarithmic change in input demand for input i,

$$d\ln(x_i) = \frac{\partial \ln(x_i)}{\partial \ln(y)} d\ln(y) + \frac{\partial \ln(x)}{\partial \ln(w')} d\ln(w'). \tag{7.86}$$

Substituting $\partial \ln(x_j)/\partial \ln(y)$ from the first row times the first column in Equation (7.72) and $\partial \ln(x)/\partial \ln(w')$ from the first row times the second column of the same equation yields

$$f_i d\ln(x_i) = \theta_i d\ln(y) - \psi \sum_{j=1}^{n} \theta_{ij} d\ln\left(\frac{w_i}{W}\right) \tag{7.87}$$

where W is the Frisch price index.

7.2.2 Change in Marginal Cost of Production

While it is easy to see the implications for the differential model of single product firm for factor demand, the implications for the cost and choice of output level are lost in the shuffle (or matrix calculus). In order to bring the results from the differential model for output decisions into focus, consider the most basic results from the output choice model in terms of the differential model developed in the preceding section:

$$\max_{x} \pi = py - C(y, w) \tag{7.88}$$

where $C(y, w)$ is the cost function (in the case of the differential model $C(y, w) = \sum_{i=1}^{n} w_i x_i(y, w)$ where $x_i(y, w)$ follows from Equation (7.87) and p is the price of the output, and following our previous discussion, y is the level of output and w is the price vector for the input prices. Given this profit specification, the maximum profit is determined by

$$\frac{\partial \pi}{\partial y} = p - \frac{\partial C(y, w)}{\partial y} = 0. \tag{7.89}$$

This equilibrium is depicted in Figure 7.1.

To estimate the increase in the quantity produced by the firm given that the output price increases from p to p', we would

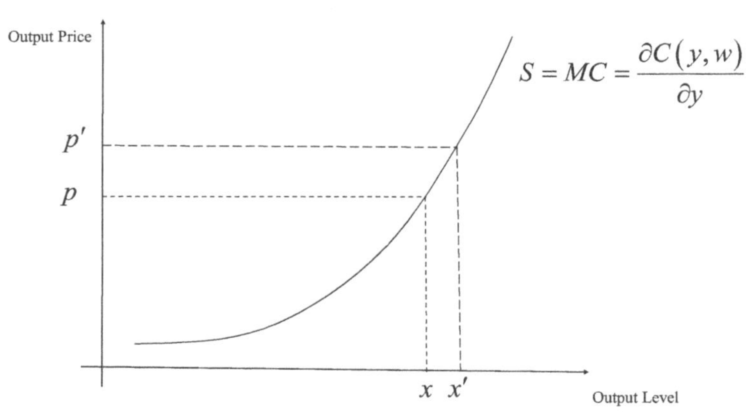

Fig. 7.1 Simple Production Equilibrium for Output

solve

$$(p' - p) = \frac{\Delta \dfrac{\partial C(y,w)}{\partial y}}{\Delta y}(x' - x)$$
$$\Rightarrow x' = x + \left[\frac{\Delta \dfrac{\partial C(y,w)}{\partial y}}{\Delta y}\right]^{-1}(p' - p). \tag{7.90}$$

Essentially, this involves estimating the change in the marginal cost function associated with a change in the level of output.

Returning to the differential cost approach,

$$\frac{\partial C(y,w)}{\partial y} = \sum_{i=1}^{n} \frac{\partial(w_i x_i(y,w))}{\partial y}. \tag{7.91}$$

To derive the change in the marginal cost with respect to the level of output, we start by considering the marginal share of each input price (θ_i — defined in Equation (7.84):

$$\theta_i = \frac{\dfrac{\partial(w_i x_i)}{\partial y}}{\dfrac{\partial C}{\partial y}}\; i = 1, \ldots n. \tag{7.92}$$

Breaking this result down a little bit, we know that a change in the desired output level affects all inputs, hence the change in the output level changes total cost. This effect is represented in the denominator of Equation (7.92) ($\partial C/\partial z$). However, we are interested here in the effect of the cost spent on a particular input (i.e., input $i - \partial(w_i x_i(y,w))/\partial y$). These individual effects are implicitly derived in Equation (7.84).

Based on this definition of the change in input share due to a change in the level of output, we define a Frisch price index for inputs as

$$d\left(\ln\left(W'\right)\right) = \sum_{i=1}^{n} \theta_i d\left(\ln\left(w_i\right)\right). \tag{7.93}$$

Note that Frisch price index is the change in the input prices weighted by the marginal input share defined in Equation (7.92) instead of the average share:

$$d\ln(W) = \sum_{i=1}^{n} s_i d\left(\ln\left(w_i\right)\right) \ni: \; s_i = \frac{w_i x_i}{C}. \tag{7.94}$$

Using (in part) Equation (7.94), the change in the natural logarithm of the marginal cost can be derived to be

$$\begin{aligned} d\left[\ln\left(\frac{\partial C}{\partial y}\right)\right] &= \left(\frac{\gamma}{\psi} - 1\right) d\ln\left(y\right) + d\ln(W') \\ \frac{1}{\psi} &= 1 + \frac{1}{\gamma^2}\frac{\partial^2 \ln(C)}{\partial \ln(y)\partial \ln(y)}. \end{aligned} \tag{7.95}$$

To develop these expressions, note that the left-hand side variables in Barten's fundamental matrix includes $\partial\ln(\rho)/\partial\ln(y)$ and not $\partial\ln(\gamma)/\partial\ln(y)$. To get from one expression to the other, we used the expression

$$\gamma = \frac{\rho}{C} = \frac{\dfrac{\partial C}{C}}{\partial \ln\left(y\right)} = \frac{\partial \ln\left(C\right)}{\partial \ln(y)} \tag{7.96}$$

(see Equation (7.50). Hence, as a starting point, we recognize that

$$\frac{\partial \ln\left(\rho\right)}{\partial \ln\left(y\right)} = \frac{\partial \ln\left(\dfrac{\partial C}{\partial \ln\left(y\right)}\right)}{\partial \ln(y)}. \tag{7.97}$$

To explain the derivation, allow me to take a little liberty with calculus notation

$$\partial \ln\left(\frac{\partial C}{\partial \ln\left(y\right)}\right) = \frac{1}{\dfrac{\partial C}{\partial \ln\left(y\right)}}\partial\left[\frac{\partial C}{\partial \ln\left(y\right)}\right]. \tag{7.98}$$

Taking the denominator in Equation (7.98) first, we have

$$\frac{\partial C}{\partial \ln\left(y\right)} = C\frac{\dfrac{\partial C}{C}}{\partial \ln\left(y\right)} = C\frac{\partial \ln\left(C\right)}{\partial \ln\left(y\right)} = C\gamma. \tag{7.99}$$

Following the same general approach in the second term in Equation (7.98),

$$\partial\left[\frac{\partial C}{\partial\ln(y)}\right]=\partial\left[C\frac{\frac{\partial C}{C}}{\partial\ln(y)}\right]=\partial\left[C\frac{\partial\ln(C)}{\partial\ln(y)}\right]. \tag{7.100}$$

Hence,

$$\begin{aligned}\frac{\partial\frac{\partial C}{\partial\ln(y)}}{\partial\ln(y)}&=\frac{\partial C}{\partial\ln(y)}\frac{\partial\ln(C)}{\partial\ln(y)}+C\frac{\partial^2\ln(C)}{\partial\ln(y)^2}\\&=C\gamma+C\frac{\partial^2\ln(C)}{\partial\ln(y)^2}.\end{aligned} \tag{7.101}$$

Putting the two parts together (i.e., Equations (7.99) and (7.101),

$$\begin{aligned}\frac{\partial\ln\left(\frac{\partial C}{\partial\ln(y)}\right)}{\partial\ln(y)}&=\frac{1}{C\gamma}\left[C\gamma+C\frac{\partial^2\ln(C)}{\partial\ln(y)^2}\right]\\&=1+\frac{1}{\gamma}\frac{\partial^2\ln(C)}{\partial\ln(y)^2}\\&=\gamma\left[1+\frac{1}{\gamma^2}\frac{\partial^2\ln(C)}{\partial\ln(y)^2}\right].\end{aligned} \tag{7.102}$$

Combining the result in Equation (7.102) with the appropriate multiplication from Equation (7.84),

$$\begin{aligned}-\gamma\left[1+\frac{1}{\gamma^2}\frac{\partial^2\ln(C)}{\partial\ln(y)^2}\right]&=\left[\theta'-\frac{1}{\psi}\right]\left[\begin{matrix}\gamma F^{-1}H^*\\\gamma\end{matrix}\right]\\\Rightarrow-\gamma\left[1+\frac{1}{\gamma^2}\frac{\partial^2\ln(C)}{\partial\ln(y)^2}\right]&=\theta'F^{-1}H^*-\frac{\gamma}{\psi}.\end{aligned} \tag{7.103}$$

Taking $\lim\theta'F^{-1}H^*\to 0$,

$$1+\frac{1}{\gamma^2}\frac{\partial^2\ln(C)}{\partial\ln(y)^2}=\frac{1}{\psi}. \tag{7.104}$$

Finally, to justify the first equation in Equation (7.95), we begin with

$$d\ln\left[\frac{\partial C}{\partial y}\right] = d\ln\left[\frac{1}{y}\frac{\partial C}{\partial \ln(y)}\right]$$
$$= \frac{1}{\frac{1}{y}\frac{\partial C}{\partial \ln(y)}}\left[-\frac{1}{y^2}dy\frac{\partial C}{\partial \ln(y)} + \frac{1}{y}d\left[\frac{\partial C}{\partial \ln(y)}\right]\right]. \tag{7.105}$$

Taking Equation (7.105) a piece at a time,

$$\frac{1}{y}\frac{\partial C}{\partial \ln(y)} = \frac{1}{y}C\gamma \tag{7.106}$$

(see Equation (7.99). Next,

$$-\frac{1}{y^2}dy\frac{\partial C}{\partial \ln(y)} = -\frac{1}{y}d\ln(y)\,C\gamma. \tag{7.107}$$

Finally,

$$\frac{1}{y}d\left[\frac{\partial C}{\partial \ln(y)}\right] = \frac{1}{y}d\left[C\frac{\partial \ln(C)}{\partial \ln(y)}\right]$$
$$= \frac{1}{y}\left[dC\frac{\partial \ln(C)}{\partial \ln(y)} + C\frac{\partial^2 \ln(C)}{\partial \ln(y)^2}d\ln(y)\right] \tag{7.108}$$
$$= \frac{1}{y}\left[dC\gamma + C\frac{\partial^2 \ln(C)}{\partial \ln(y)^2}\right].$$

Putting the pieces together,

$$d\ln\left[\frac{\partial C}{\partial y}\right] = \left(\frac{y}{C\gamma}\right)\left[-\frac{1}{y}d\ln(y)C\gamma + \frac{1}{y}\left(dC\gamma + C\frac{\partial^2 \ln(C)}{\partial \ln(y)^2}d\ln(y)\right)\right]$$
$$= \left(-1 + \frac{1}{\gamma}\frac{\partial^2 \ln(C)}{\partial \ln(y)^2}\right)d\ln(y) + \frac{dC}{C}. \tag{7.109}$$

We are almost there. The rest of the development focuses on dC/C. First, note that

$$\frac{dC}{C} = \frac{1}{C}\sum_{i=1}^{n} w_i x_i \frac{\partial \ln(x_i)}{\partial \ln(y)} d\ln(y) + \frac{1}{C}\sum_{i=1}^{n} w_i x_i \frac{\partial \ln(x_i)}{\partial \ln(w_i)} d\ln(w_i). \tag{7.110}$$

The first part of Equation (7.110) goes to $d\ln(y)$ while the second part of Equation (7.110) becomes the Frisch index, completing the proof.

7.2.3 *Multiproduct Firm*

Next, we expand the differential approach to include the possibility of more than one output. The multiproduct production function can be written in implicit form as

$$h(x, y) = 0$$
$$\sum_{r=1}^{m} \frac{\partial h(x, y)}{\partial \ln(y_r)} = -1. \tag{7.111}$$

Like the previous scenario, we start with the Lagrange formulation

$$L(y, \rho) = \sum_{i=1}^{n} w_i x_i - \rho h(x, y). \tag{7.112}$$

Following our standard approach, we assume that decision makers choose the level of inputs that minimize cost consistent with the first-order conditions:

$$\frac{\partial L(x, \rho)}{\partial \ln(x_i)} = w_i x_i - \rho \frac{\partial h(x, y)}{\partial \ln(x_i)} = 0 \tag{7.113}$$

yielding an $n \times 1$ matrix of conditions. Also note that there is a single production constraint $h(x, y) = 0$. In the development of the differential, we will follow the general approach of differentiating these $n + 1$ conditions first with respect to the level of outputs and then with respect to the price of inputs. Like the single product firm, this process will yield a system of $(n + 1) \times (n + 1)$ differential equations which provide the parameterization for estimation which incorporates cost minimization.

As a first step, consider taking the derivative of equation i with respect to $\ln(y_r)$ (the natural logarithm of output y_r):

$$w_i x_i \frac{\partial \ln(x_i)}{\partial \ln(y_r)} - \rho \frac{\partial h(x,y)}{\partial \ln(x_i)} \frac{\partial \ln(\rho)}{\partial \ln(y_r)}$$

$$-\rho \sum_{j=1}^{n} \frac{\partial^2 h(x,y)}{\partial \ln(x_i) \partial \ln(x_j)} \frac{\partial \ln(x_j)}{\partial \ln(y_r)} - \rho \frac{\partial^2 h(x,y)}{\partial \ln(x_i) \partial \ln(y_r)} = 0. \tag{7.114}$$

Next, we return to note that Equation (7.113) implies

$$w_i x_i = \rho \frac{\partial h(x,y)}{\partial \ln(x_i)}. \tag{7.115}$$

Given the result in Equation (7.115), we can rewrite Equation (7.114) as

$$w_i x_i \frac{\partial \ln(x_i)}{\partial \ln(y_r)} - w_i x_i \frac{\partial \ln(\rho)}{\partial \ln(y_r)}$$

$$-\rho \sum_{j=1}^{n} \frac{\partial^2 h(x,y)}{\partial \ln(x_i) \partial \ln(x_j)} \frac{\partial \ln(x_j)}{\partial \ln(y_r)} - \rho \frac{\partial^2 h(x,y)}{\partial \ln(x_i) \partial \ln(y_r)} = 0. \tag{7.116}$$

Next, we substitute $f_i = w_i x_i / C$ into Equation (7.116) to yield

$$f_i \frac{\partial \ln(x_i)}{\partial \ln(y_r)} - f_i \frac{\partial \ln(\rho)}{\partial \ln(y_r)}$$

$$-\frac{\rho}{C} \sum_{j=1}^{n} \frac{\partial^2 h(x,y)}{\partial \ln(x_i) \partial \ln(x_j)} \frac{\partial \ln(x_j)}{\partial \ln(y_r)} - \frac{\rho}{C} \frac{\partial^2 h(x,y)}{\partial \ln(x_i) \ln(y_r)} = 0. \tag{7.117}$$

Given that $\gamma = \rho / C$ (using the result from the single output firm), this result can be restated in matrix form as

$$(F - \gamma H) \frac{\partial \ln(x)}{\partial \ln(y')} - F\iota \frac{\partial \ln(\rho)}{\partial \ln(y')} = \gamma H^*. \tag{7.118}$$

Note that $(F - \gamma H)$ is the same as the single output case. Specifically, $(F - \gamma H)$ is an $n \times n$ matrix that captures the trade-offs between inputs. Similarly, $F\iota$ is the same as the single output case (e.g., it is an $n \times 1$ matrix). However, H^* is now an $n \times r$ matrix which captures the effect of changes in the various levels of outputs:

$$H^* = \begin{bmatrix} \frac{\partial \ln(x_1)}{\partial \ln(y_1)} & \cdots & \frac{\partial \ln(x_1)}{\partial \ln(y_r)} \\ \vdots & \ddots & \vdots \\ \frac{\partial \ln(x_n)}{\partial \ln(y_1)} & \cdots & \frac{\partial \ln(x_n)}{\partial \ln(y_r)} \end{bmatrix}. \tag{7.119}$$

Next, we want to construct the changes in input and output levels in such a way that makes the production choice feasible. Mathematically, this restriction implies

$$\sum_{i=1}^{n} \frac{\partial h(x,y)}{\partial \ln(x_i)} \frac{\partial \ln(x_i)}{\partial \ln(y_r)} + \frac{\partial h(x,y)}{\partial \ln(y_r)} = 0. \tag{7.120}$$

To understand this restriction, assume that we want to increase the level of $\ln(y_r)$ by one unit. To maintain feasibility, we must increase the level of inputs by an amount related to the marginal product of each input.

Returning momentarily to Equation (7.113),

$$w_i x_i - \rho \frac{\partial h(x,y)}{\partial \ln(x_i)} = 0 \Rightarrow \frac{w_i x_i}{\rho} = \frac{\partial h(x,y)}{\partial \ln(x_i)}. \tag{7.121}$$

Substituting this result into Equation (7.120) yields

$$\frac{1}{\rho} \sum_{i=1}^{n} w_i x_i \frac{\partial \ln(x_i)}{\partial \ln(y_r)} + \frac{\partial h(x,y)}{\partial \ln(y_r)} = 0. \tag{7.122}$$

Next, multiplying the first term of Equation (7.122) by $C/C = 1$ yields

$$\frac{C}{\rho} \sum_{i=1}^{n} f_i \frac{\partial \ln(x_i)}{\partial \ln(y_r)} + \frac{h(x,y)}{\partial \ln(y_r)} = 0. \tag{7.123}$$

While Equation (7.123) is derived from the first-order conditions, let us develop an economic interpretation for the result. We start by taking the derivative of cost with respect to the output level:

$$\frac{\partial C}{\partial y_r} = \sum_{i=1}^{n} w_i \frac{\partial x_i}{\partial y_r}. \tag{7.124}$$

Substituting for the logarithmic derivative,

$$\begin{aligned}\frac{\partial C}{\partial y_r} &= \frac{C}{y_r} \sum_{i=1}^{n} \frac{w_i x_i}{C} \frac{\partial \ln(x_i)}{\partial \ln(y_r)} \\ &= \frac{C}{y_r} \sum_{i=1}^{n} f_i \frac{\partial \ln(x_i)}{\partial \ln(y_r)}.\end{aligned} \tag{7.125}$$

Thus,

$$\sum_{i=1}^{n} f_i \frac{\partial \ln(x_i)}{\partial \ln(y_r)} = \frac{\partial C}{\partial y_r} \times \frac{y_r}{C}. \tag{7.126}$$

Substituting the result in Equation (7.126) into Equation (7.123) yields

$$\frac{y_r}{\rho} \frac{\partial C}{\partial y_r} + \frac{\partial h(x, y)}{\partial \ln(y_r)} = 0. \tag{7.127}$$

Using Equation (7.127), we can define g_r as

$$g_r \equiv \frac{y_r}{\rho} \frac{\partial C}{\partial y_r} = -\frac{\partial h(x, y)}{\partial \ln(y_r)}. \tag{7.128}$$

Intuitively, we can define the result of Equation (7.123) as

$$\frac{C}{\rho} \sum_{i=1}^{n} f_i \frac{\partial \ln(x_i)}{\partial \ln(y_r)} = -\frac{\partial h(x, y)}{\partial \ln(y_r)} \tag{7.129}$$

in two ways. As written in Equation (7.123), it follows from the condition that the change in the output y_r must balance the change in the inputs. Equation (7.128) relates to the result to a change in the cost. Note that Equation (7.129) is independent of Equation (7.128).

Thus, we will use the conditions together. Modifying Equation (7.129) by multiplying by γ (equal to ρ/C by definition),

$$\sum_{i=1}^{n} f_i \frac{\partial \ln(x_i)}{\partial \ln(y_r)} = -\gamma \frac{\partial h(x,y)}{\partial \ln(y_r)}. \tag{7.130}$$

Next, we substitute the result from Equation (7.128) into Equation (7.130) to yield

$$\sum_{i=1}^{n} f_i \frac{\partial \ln(x_i)}{\partial \ln(y_r)} = \gamma g_r. \tag{7.131}$$

In matrix form, Equation (7.131) can be written as

$$\iota' F \frac{\partial \ln(x)}{\partial \ln(y_r)} = \gamma g_r \tag{7.132}$$

where ι is an n element vector of ones.

The change in the first-order conditions for the input prices are identical to the formulation for the single output model:

$$(F - \gamma H)\frac{\partial \ln(x)}{\partial \ln(w')} - F\iota \frac{\partial \ln(\rho)}{\partial \ln(w')} = -F. \tag{7.133}$$

In addition, the change in the derivatives of the production function with respect to input levels (e.g., the derivatives of the differential of the constraint with respect to the logarithm of quantities) with respect to a change in the input prices is the same as single output model:

$$\sum_{i=1}^{n} \frac{\partial h(x,y)}{\partial \ln(x_i)} \frac{\partial \ln(x_i)}{\partial \ln(w_j)} = 0 \Rightarrow \iota' F \frac{\partial \ln(x)}{\partial \ln(w')}. \tag{7.134}$$

The system of differential equations can then be written as

$$\begin{bmatrix} F - \gamma H & \iota F \\ \iota' F & 0 \end{bmatrix} \begin{bmatrix} \dfrac{\partial \ln(x)}{\partial \ln(y')} & \dfrac{\partial \ln(x)}{\partial \ln(w')} \\ -\dfrac{\partial \ln(\rho)}{\partial \ln(y')} & -\dfrac{\partial \ln(\rho)}{\partial \ln(w')} \end{bmatrix} = \begin{bmatrix} \gamma H^* & -F \\ \gamma g' & 0 \end{bmatrix}. \tag{7.135}$$

In order to understand this formulation, it is useful to work through the multiplication in Equation (7.135). In this development, we will start with the second row of the first matrix times the first column of the second matrix — those elements related to changes in the level of output:

$$\left[\iota' F \; 0\right] \begin{bmatrix} \dfrac{\partial \ln(x)}{\partial \ln(y')} \\ -\dfrac{\partial \ln(\rho)}{\partial \ln(y')} \end{bmatrix} = \gamma g'$$

$$\iota' F \frac{\partial \ln(x)}{\ln(y')} = \gamma g' \tag{7.136}$$

which is a vector form of Equation (7.132). To understand this formulation more fully, consider the matrix operations on the left-hand side of Equation (7.136) one step at a time. Starting with

$$F\frac{\partial \ln(x)}{\partial \ln(y')} = \begin{bmatrix} f_1 & 0 & \cdots & 0 \\ 0 & f_2 & \cdots & 0 \\ \vdots & \vdots & \ddots & \vdots \\ 0 & 0 & \cdots & f_n \end{bmatrix} \begin{bmatrix} \dfrac{\partial \ln(x_1)}{\partial \ln(y_1)} & \dfrac{\partial \ln(x_1)}{\partial \ln(y_2)} & \cdots & \dfrac{\partial \ln(x_1)}{\partial \ln(y_r)} \\ \dfrac{\partial \ln(x_2)}{\partial \ln(y_1)} & \dfrac{\partial \ln(x_2)}{\partial \ln(y_2)} & \cdots & \dfrac{\partial \ln(x_2)}{\partial \ln(y_r)} \\ \vdots & \vdots & \ddots & \vdots \\ \dfrac{\partial \ln(x_n)}{\partial \ln(y_1)} & \dfrac{\partial \ln(x_n)}{\partial \ln(y_2)} & \cdots & \dfrac{\partial \ln(x_n)}{\partial \ln(y_r)} \end{bmatrix}$$

$$= \begin{bmatrix} f_1\dfrac{\ln(x_1)}{\partial \ln(y_1)} & f_1\dfrac{\partial \ln(x_1)}{\partial \ln(y_2)} & \cdots & f_1\dfrac{\partial \ln(x_1)}{\partial \ln(y_r)} \\ f_2\dfrac{\partial \ln(x_2)}{\partial \ln(y_1)} & f_2\dfrac{\partial \ln(x_2)}{\partial \ln(y_2)} & \cdots & f_2\dfrac{\partial \ln(x_2)}{\partial \ln(y_r)} \\ \vdots & \vdots & \ddots & \vdots \\ f_n\dfrac{\partial \ln(x_n)}{\partial \ln(y_1)} & f_n\dfrac{\partial \ln(x_n)}{\partial \ln(y_2)} & \cdots & f_n\dfrac{\partial \ln(x_n)}{\partial \ln(y_r)} \end{bmatrix}. \tag{7.137}$$

Complete the multiplication

$$\left[1 \; 1 \cdots 1\right] \begin{bmatrix} f_1\dfrac{\ln(x_1)}{\partial \ln(y_1)} & f_1\dfrac{\partial \ln(x_1)}{\partial \ln(y_2)} & \cdots & f_1\dfrac{\partial \ln(x_1)}{\partial \ln(y_r)} \\ f_2\dfrac{\partial \ln(x_2)}{\partial \ln(y_1)} & f_2\dfrac{\partial \ln(x_2)}{\partial \ln(y_2)} & \cdots & f_2\dfrac{\partial \ln(x_2)}{\partial \ln(y_r)} \\ \vdots & \vdots & \ddots & \vdots \\ f_n\dfrac{\partial \ln(x_n)}{\partial \ln(y_1)} & f_n\dfrac{\partial \ln(x_n)}{\partial \ln(y_2)} & \cdots & f_n\dfrac{\partial \ln(x_n)}{\partial \ln(y_r)} \end{bmatrix}$$

$$= \begin{bmatrix} f_1 \dfrac{\partial \ln(x_1)}{\partial \ln(y_1)} + f_2 \dfrac{\partial \ln(x_2)}{\partial \ln(y_1)} + \cdots f_n \dfrac{\partial \ln(x_n)}{\partial \ln(y_1)} \\ f_1 \dfrac{\partial \ln(x_1)}{\partial \ln(y_2)} + f_2 \dfrac{\partial \ln(x_2)}{\partial \ln(y_2)} + \cdots f_n \dfrac{\partial \ln(x_n)}{\partial \ln(y_2)} \\ \vdots \\ f_1 \dfrac{\partial \ln(x_1)}{\partial \ln(y_r)} + f_2 \dfrac{\partial \ln(x_2)}{\partial \ln(y_r)} + \cdots f_n \dfrac{\partial \ln(x_n)}{\partial \ln(y_r)} \end{bmatrix}' . \quad (7.138)$$

Thus, the result in Equation (7.138) is equal to the row vector $\gamma g'$.

Shifting to the result of the first row times the first column of Equation (7.135),

$$\begin{bmatrix} F - \gamma H & F \end{bmatrix} \begin{bmatrix} \dfrac{\partial \ln(x)}{\partial \ln(y')} \\ -\dfrac{\partial \ln(\rho)}{\partial \ln(y')} \end{bmatrix} = \gamma H^*$$

$$\Rightarrow (F - \gamma H) \frac{\partial \ln(x)}{\partial \ln(y')} - \iota F \frac{\partial \ln(\rho)}{\partial \ln(y')} = \gamma H^*. \quad (7.139)$$

Note first that $F - \gamma H$ is an $n \times n$ matrix while $\partial \ln(x)/\partial \ln(y')$ is an $n \times r$ matrix (see Equation (7.137): hence, the result is an $n \times r$ matrix. In the second term of Equation (7.139), ι is an $n \times 1$ multiplied by $\partial \ln(\rho)/\partial \ln(y')$ which is a $1 \times r$ yielding an $n \times r$ matrix. Following our definition of H^* in Equation (7.119), we know that γH^* is an $n \times r$ matrix.

Hence, we define Equation (7.135) as Barten's fundamental matrix for the multiproduct firm. Noting the similarity between Equation (7.135) in the case of the multivariate firm and Equation (7.69) for the single output firm, we redefine the differential formulation in a similar way (i.e., premultiplying and postmultiplying the first row by $F^{-1}F = I$), yielding

$$\begin{bmatrix} F^{-1}(F - \gamma H) F^{-1} & \iota \\ \iota' & 0 \end{bmatrix} \begin{bmatrix} F \dfrac{\partial \ln(x)}{\partial \ln(y')} & F \dfrac{\partial \ln(x)}{\partial \ln(w')} \\ -\dfrac{\partial \ln(\rho)}{\partial \ln(y')} & -\dfrac{\partial \ln(\rho)}{\partial \ln(w')} \end{bmatrix}$$

$$= \begin{bmatrix} \gamma F^{-1} H^* & -I \\ \gamma g' & 0 \end{bmatrix}. \quad (7.140)$$

Also noting that the first matrix on the left-hand side for the multivariate firm is identical to the first matrix on the left-hand side for the single product firm, we conclude that they have the same matrix inverse. Hence, we conclude that

$$\begin{bmatrix} F^{-1}(F-\gamma H)F^{-1} & \iota \\ \iota' & 0 \end{bmatrix}^{-1} = \begin{bmatrix} \psi\left(\Theta-\theta\theta'\right) & \theta \\ \theta' & -\frac{1}{\psi} \end{bmatrix} \tag{7.141}$$

where ψ is defined in Equation (7.79), Θ is defined in Equation (7.81), and θ is defined in Equation (7.82). The solution for the multioutput firm can be expressed as

$$\begin{aligned} &\begin{bmatrix} F\dfrac{\partial\ln(x)}{\partial\ln\left(y'\right)} & F\dfrac{\partial\ln(x)}{\partial\ln\left(w'\right)} \\ -\dfrac{\partial\ln\left(\rho\right)}{\partial\ln\left(y'\right)} & -\dfrac{\partial\ln\left(\rho\right)}{\partial\ln\left(w'\right)} \end{bmatrix} \\ &= \begin{bmatrix} \psi\left(\Theta-\theta\theta'\right) & \theta \\ \theta' & -\frac{1}{\psi} \end{bmatrix} \begin{bmatrix} \gamma F^{-1}H^* & -I \\ \gamma g' & 0 \end{bmatrix} \\ &= \begin{bmatrix} \gamma\psi\left(\Theta-\theta\theta'\right)F^{-1}H^* + \gamma\theta g' & -\psi\left(\Theta-\theta\theta'\right) \\ \gamma\theta' F^{-1}H^* - \frac{\gamma}{\psi}g' & \theta' \end{bmatrix}. \end{aligned} \tag{7.142}$$

Separating the solution into parts,

$$\begin{aligned} F\frac{\partial\ln(x)}{\partial\ln\left(w'\right)} &= -\psi\left(\Theta-\theta\theta'\right) \\ F\frac{\partial\ln(x)}{\partial\ln\left(y'\right)} &= \gamma\theta g' + \gamma\psi\left(\Theta-\theta\theta'\right)F^{-1}H^* \\ \frac{\partial\ln\left(\rho\right)}{\partial\ln\left(w'\right)} &= \theta' \\ \frac{\partial\ln\left(\rho\right)}{\partial\ln\left(y'\right)} &= \frac{\gamma}{\psi}g' - \gamma\theta' F^{-1}H^*. \end{aligned} \tag{7.143}$$

The extended form of the differential supply system is then, starting with the derivative of $\ln(q)$,

$$d\ln(x)=\frac{\partial\ln(x)}{\partial\ln\left(y'\right)}d\ln\left(y\right)+\frac{\partial\ln(x)}{\partial\ln\left(w'\right)}d\ln(w). \tag{7.144}$$

Premultiplying Equation (7.144) by F,

$$Fd\ln(x)=F\frac{\partial\ln(x)}{\partial\ln(y')}d\ln(y)+F\frac{\partial\ln(x)}{\partial\ln\left(w'\right)}d\ln(w) \tag{7.145}$$

by the results in Equation (7.143)

$$F\frac{\partial\ln(x)}{\partial\ln\left(w'\right)}=-\psi(\Theta-\theta\theta') \tag{7.146}$$

and

$$\begin{aligned}Fd\ln(x)&=F\frac{\partial\ln(x)}{\partial\ln(y')}d\ln(y)+F\frac{\partial\ln(x)}{\partial\ln(w')}d\ln(w)\\ \Rightarrow Fd\ln(x)&=F\frac{\partial\ln(x)}{\partial}\ln(y')d\ln(y)-\psi(\Theta-\theta\theta')d\ln(w).\end{aligned} \tag{7.147}$$

Defining θ_i^r as the share of the ith input in the marginal cost of the rth product,

$$\theta_i^r=\frac{\dfrac{\partial(w_ix_i)}{\partial y_r}}{\dfrac{\partial C}{\partial y_r}}. \tag{7.148}$$

We can sum the marginal cost over all inputs:

$$\theta_i=\sum_{r=1}^{m}g_r\theta_i^r=\frac{1}{\rho}\sum_{r=1}^{m}\frac{\partial\left(w_ix_i\right)}{\partial\ln\left(y_r\right)}. \tag{7.149}$$

Using the definition in Equation (7.149) and defining $K = [\theta_i^r]$ (an $n \times r$ matrix of parameters), we have the result

$$F\frac{\partial \ln(x)}{\partial \ln(y')} = \gamma K G$$

where

$$G = \begin{bmatrix} g_1 = \frac{y_1}{\rho}\frac{\partial C}{\partial y_1} & \cdots & 0 \\ \vdots & \ddots & \vdots \\ 0 & \cdots & g_m = \frac{y_m}{\rho}\frac{\partial C}{\partial y_m} \end{bmatrix}. \tag{7.150}$$

Therefore, the differential specification for the multiproduct firm becomes

$$\begin{aligned} F d\ln(x) &= \gamma K G d\ln(y) - \psi\left(\Theta - \theta\theta'\right) d\ln(w) \\ f_i d\ln(x_i) &= \gamma \sum_{r=1}^{m} \theta_i^r g_r d\ln(y_r) - \psi \sum_{j=1}^{n} \theta_{ij} d\ln\left(\frac{w_j}{W'}\right). \end{aligned} \tag{7.151}$$

To complete our formulation of the multiproduct firm, it is useful to construct the empirical specification typically derived from each model. As a point of reference, the empirical form of the input demand for the single product firm depicted in Equation (7.87) is typically written as

$$\bar{f}_{it}\Delta\ln(x_{it}) = \theta_i \Delta\ln(y_t) + \sum_{ij} \pi_{ij}\Delta\ln(w_{jt}) + \epsilon_{it} \tag{7.152}$$

where $\bar{f}_{it} = \frac{1}{2}(f_{it} + f_{i,t-1})$, and $\Delta x_{it} = \ln(x_{it}) - \ln(x_{i,t-1})$ for x_{it}, y_t, and w_{it}. The largest parameterization assumption is then $\pi_{ij} = \psi(\Theta_{ij} - \theta_i\theta_j)$ and the assumption that both π_{ij} and θ_i are constants. Following from Equation (7.151), one empirical specification of the multiproduct formulation is

$$\bar{f}_{it}\Delta\ln(x_{it}) = \bar{\gamma}_t \sum_{r=1}^{m} \theta_i^r \bar{g}_{rt}\Delta\ln(y_{rt}) + \sum_{j=1}^{n} \pi_{ij}\ln(w_{jt}) + \epsilon_{it} \tag{7.153}$$

where $\bar{g}_{rt} = \frac{1}{2}\left(g_{rt} + g_{r,t-1}\right)$ is defined as the average share of output r in total revenue. Comparing Equation (7.152) with Equation (7.153), it is clear that the effect of the change in output level has become much more complex.

To develop the change in the output side of Equation (7.153) (or more generally Equation (7.151), we introduce the revenue side of the firm's profit. Specifically, letting $p = [p_1\ p_2\ \ldots\ p_m]'$ be the vector of output prices, the firm's revenue can be defined as

$$R = p'y. \tag{7.154}$$

The profit function can then be written as

$$\pi = p'y - w'x \tag{7.155}$$

where the cost ($C = w'x$) is determined by the cost-minimizing behavior developed above. To link the models (i.e., the profit-maximizing and cost-minimizing models) together, it is sufficient to determine the optimal levels of

$$d\ln(y) = \left[d\ln(y_1)\ d\ln(y_2)\ \ldots\ d\ln(y_m)\right]. \tag{7.156}$$

From the typical optimality conditions (i.e., the derivative of Equation (7.155) with respect to y_r), we know that

$$\frac{\partial C}{\partial y_r} = p_r \tag{7.157}$$

for $r = 1, \ldots, r$. Returning to our definition of g_r in Equation (7.128), we know that

$$\rho g_r = \frac{\partial C}{\partial y_r}\frac{y_r}{\rho} = p_r y_r \tag{7.158}$$

(e.g., imposing profit maximization), which implies that

$$R = \rho \sum_{r=1}^{m} g_r. \tag{7.159}$$

Recalling the condition from Equation (7.111) and the definition of g_r in Equation (7.128).

$$\frac{\partial h\left(x,y\right)}{\partial \ln\left(y_r\right)} = -1 \Rightarrow \rho\sum_{r=1}^{m} g_r = -\sum_{r=1}^{m}\frac{\partial h\left(x,y\right)}{\partial \ln\left(y_r\right)} = \rho. \tag{7.160}$$

Therefore, by Equations (7.159) and (7.160), $\rho = R$. Hence,

$$g_r = \frac{p_r y_r}{R} \tag{7.161}$$

or g_r becomes the share of revenue from output r, explaining this term in Equation (7.153).

Recalling from Equation (7.148),

$$\theta_i^r = \frac{\dfrac{\partial(w_i x_i)}{\partial y_r}}{\dfrac{\partial C}{\partial y_r}} \Rightarrow \theta_i^r = \frac{\partial w_i x_i}{\partial p_r y_r} \tag{7.162}$$

since from the profit maximization condition in Equation (7.157), $\partial C/\partial y_r = p_r$ — the change in cost on the ith input per dollar of return for the rth product (Laitinen and Theil, 1978, p. 120). As a final substitution, Laitinen and Theil conclude that

$$\gamma = \frac{R}{C} \tag{7.163}$$

or since marginal revenue equals marginal cost

$$\gamma = \frac{1}{C}\frac{R}{1}\frac{\dfrac{\partial \ln(C)}{\partial \ln(y_r)}}{\dfrac{\partial \ln(R)}{\partial \ln(y_r)}} = \frac{R}{C} \tag{7.164}$$

when $\partial \ln(C)/\partial \ln(y_r) = \partial \ln(R)/\partial \ln(y_r)$.

The Final piece of puzzle is the estimation of the firm's supply response

$$g_r d \ln(y_r) = \psi^* \sum_{s=1}^{m} \theta_{rs}^* d \ln\left(\frac{p_s}{P'}\right) \tag{7.165}$$

where P' is the Frisch index for output prices. Equation (7.165) is the counterpart to the input demand in Equation (7.153) (basically Equation (7.165) defines the $\bar{g}_r \Delta \ln(y_r)$ term in Equation (7.153). Note that ψ^* is different from ψ in the foregoing development and θ_{rs}^* is different form θ_i^r.

To develop this formulation, we start by noting that y_r is now a choice variable. Given the fact that the producer now chooses the level of each output we can logarithmic differentiate Equation (7.157) with respect to changes in output prices

$$d\frac{\partial C}{\partial y_r} = \sum_{t=1}^{m} \frac{\partial^2 C}{\partial y_r \partial y_t} y_t d\ln(y_t). \tag{7.166}$$

Focusing on the change of cost with respect to a change in output prices yields

$$\sum_{t=1}^{m} \frac{\partial^2 C}{\partial y_r \partial y_t} y_t \frac{\partial \ln(y_t)}{\partial \ln(p_s)} = \delta_{rs} p_s \tag{7.167}$$

where we have substituted $\partial p_s / \partial \ln(p_s)$ on the right-hand side of Equation (7.167). Substituting $y_t = Rg_t/p_t$ by Equation (7.161), Equation (7.167) becomes

$$R\sum_{t=1}^{m} \frac{\partial^2 C}{\partial y_r \partial y_t} \frac{g_t}{p_t} \frac{\partial \ln(y_t)}{\partial \ln(p_s)} = \delta_{rs} p_s. \tag{7.168}$$

Using the matrix specification of G in Equation (7.150) and defining P as a diagonal matrix of output prices, Equation (7.168) can be written as

$$R\frac{\partial^2 C}{\partial y \partial y'} P^{-1} G \frac{\partial \ln(y)}{\partial \ln(p')} = P. \tag{7.169}$$

Solving Equation (7.169) by premultiplying it by $1/R(Y[\partial^2 C/\partial y \partial y']^{-1})$ yields

$$G\frac{\partial \ln(y)}{\partial \ln(p')} = \frac{1}{R} Y \left(\frac{\partial^2 C}{\partial y \partial y'}\right)^{-1} Y. \tag{7.170}$$

Note that the left-hand side of Equation (7.170) is a matrix form of Equation (7.165). Specifically, if we substitute

$$\psi^* = \frac{1}{R} p' \left(\frac{\partial^2 C}{\partial y \partial y'}\right)^{-1} y \quad \text{and} \quad \Theta^* = \frac{1}{\psi^* R} Y \left(\frac{\partial^2 C}{\partial y \partial y'}\right)^{-1} Y \tag{7.171}$$

we would have

$$G\frac{\partial \ln(y)}{\partial \ln(p')} = \psi^* \Theta^*. \tag{7.172}$$

To finish the derivation, we differentiate the first-order condition for profit maximization in Equation (7.157) with respect to input price i to yield

$$\frac{\partial^2 C}{\partial y_r \partial w_i} + \sum_{s=1}^{m} \frac{\partial^2 C}{\partial y_r \partial y_s}\frac{\partial y_s}{\partial w_i} = 0. \tag{7.173}$$

Solving Equation (7.173) yields

$$\frac{\partial y}{w'} = -\left(\frac{\partial^2 C}{\partial y \partial y'}\right)^{-1}\frac{\partial^2 C}{\partial y \partial w'} = -\left(\frac{\partial^2 C}{\partial y \partial y'}\right)^{-1} PK'W^{-1} \tag{7.174}$$

where $K = [\theta_i^r]$ as in Equation (7.150). Premultiplying Equation (7.174) by $(1/R)P$ and postmultiplying by W yield

$$G\frac{\partial \ln(y)}{\partial \ln(w')} = -\psi^* \Theta^* K'. \tag{7.175}$$

Putting the two parts together, we have

$$d\ln(y) = \frac{\partial \ln(y)}{\ln(p')}d\ln(p) + \frac{\partial \ln(y)}{\partial \ln(w')}d\ln(w) \tag{7.176}$$

or

$$g_r d\ln(y_r) = \sum_{r=1}^{m} \psi^* \theta_{rs}^* \left(d\ln(p_s) - \sum_{i=1}^{n} \theta_i^s d\ln(w_i)\right). \tag{7.177}$$

7.2.4 *Introduction of Quasi-Fixed Variables*

Expanding the differential model further, we introduce quasi-fixed variables into the production set following the approach introduced by Livanis and Moss (2006). Livanis and Moss introduce the technological frontier using the general set notation similar to the set theory notation used in Chapter 4:

$$T(x, y, z) = 0 \tag{7.178}$$

where x is a vector of inputs, y is a vector of outputs, and z is a vector of quasi-fixed variables. We will use the implicit production function $h(x, y, z) = 0$ following the preceding formulations in this chapter. Given this implicit formulation of production function, we define the differential demand based on the decision maker's choice to minimize short run (or variable cost)

$$\begin{gathered} \tilde{C}(w, y, z^*) \\ \text{s.t. } h(x, y, z) = 0 \\ z = z^* \end{gathered} \tag{7.179}$$

where $z = z^*$ denotes that the level of quasi-fixed inputs is subject to a constraint. $\tilde{C}\,(w, y, z^*)$ is defined as a short-run cost function.

Following the general differential formulation, we derive the first-order conditions for optimality as

$$w_i x_i = \lambda \frac{\partial h\,(x, y, z)}{\partial x_i} = 0. \tag{7.180}$$

Based in part on our derivation of the multiproduct firm, we define

$$\begin{aligned} g_r &= -\frac{\partial h(x, y, z)}{\partial \ln(y_r)} \quad \mu_k - \frac{\partial h(x, y, z)}{\partial \ln(z_k)} \\ \gamma_1 &= \frac{\lambda}{\tilde{C}\,(w, y, z^*)}. \end{aligned} \tag{7.181}$$

In addition, we modify the second derivative matrices slightly from their definitions in the derivation of the multiproduct firm:

$$\begin{aligned} H &= \left[\frac{\partial^2 h(x, y, z)}{\partial \ln(x_i) \partial \ln(x_j)}\right]_{n\times n} \qquad H_1 = \left[\frac{\partial^2 h(x, y, z)}{\partial \ln(x_i) \partial \ln(y_r)}\right]_{n\times m} \\ H_3 &= \left[\frac{\partial^w h\,(x, y, z)}{\partial \ln\,(x_i)\,\partial \ln\,(z_k)}\right]_{n\times l}. \end{aligned} \tag{7.182}$$

Given these definitions, Barten's fundamental matrix for the quasi-fixed form of the differential supply model can be written as

$$\begin{bmatrix} F^{-1}(F - \gamma_1 H)F^{-1} & \iota_n \\ \iota_n & 0 \end{bmatrix} \begin{bmatrix} F\dfrac{\partial \ln(x)}{\partial \ln(y')} & F\dfrac{\partial \ln(x)}{\partial \ln(w')} & F\dfrac{\partial \ln(x)}{\partial \ln(z')} \\ -\dfrac{\partial \ln(\lambda)}{\partial \ln(y')} & -\dfrac{\partial \ln(\lambda)}{\ln(w')} & \dfrac{\partial \ln(\lambda)}{\partial \ln(z')} \end{bmatrix}$$
$$= \begin{bmatrix} \gamma_1 F^{-1} H_1 & -I & \gamma_1 F^{-1} H_3 \\ \gamma_1 g' & 0 & \gamma_1 \mu' \end{bmatrix}. \tag{7.183}$$

While more complicated, Equation (7.183) is very similar to Equation (7.140). In fact, the "solutions" of both systems are equal to the inverse of the first matrix on the left-hand side:

$$\begin{bmatrix} F^{-1}(F-\gamma_1 H)F^{-1} & \iota_n \\ \iota_n & 0 \end{bmatrix} = \begin{bmatrix} \psi(\Theta - \theta\theta') & \theta \\ \theta' & -\frac{1}{\psi} \end{bmatrix}. \tag{7.184}$$

Based on these results, Livanis and Moss's differential supply function for this specification becomes

$$\begin{aligned} f_i d\ln(x_i) &= \gamma_2 \sum_{r=1}^{m} \theta_i^r \tilde{g}_r d\ln(y_r) + \gamma_3 \sum_{k=1}^{l} \xi_i^k \tilde{\mu}_k d\ln(z_k) \\ &\quad - \psi \sum_{j=1}^{n} (\phi_{ij} - \phi_i\phi_j) d\ln(w_j) \end{aligned} \tag{7.185}$$

where $\gamma_2 = \gamma_1 \sum_r g_r = \epsilon_{C,y}$ denotes the elasticity of cost with respect to a proportional change in output and $\gamma_3 = \gamma_1 \sum_k \mu_k = \epsilon_{Cz}$ denotes the elasticity of cost with respect to a change in the level of quasi-fixed variables.

7.3 Empirical Examples

Section 7.2 focused on the theoretical development of the firm's differential cost function. Admittedly, these developments have been exceedingly complex. The basic concept is for students and practitioners to understand how the differential model is developed and how this development differs from the development and implied assumptions of the indirect or dual approach. Given this theoretical development, we turn to the more important question: How are specifications applied and do they have an advantage over the dual approach? This section presents three applications of the differential model for the firm. First, we develop the differential application for a single output. Next, we consider the multiproduct firm. Finally, we consider the existence of quasi-fixed variables.

7.3.1 *Empirical Estimates Using Single Product Formulation*

Starting with the simplest application of the differential model of the firm, Moss *et al.* (2010) apply the single product model to aggregate data using Jorgenson's KLEM (capital (K), labor (L), energy (E), and materials (M)) data. The KLEM dataset contains a single composite measure of agricultural output. The input and output prices in the KLEM data are generated using Divisia price indices.[1] In this approach, an index of the real change in individual input price categories and the output price are computed as the weighted logarithmic change in prices within each category. A sequential price index is then created by defining a base year (in the KLEM data 1996). The quantity is then computed as the value of output divided by the price index level.

Moss, Livanis, and Schmitz are interested in the effect of increases in energy prices on input usage in agriculture. This interest grew in part from the factors contributing to the significant increase in corn prices from 2007 to 2013. Specifically, the Energy Independence and Security Act of 2007 created mandates for the share of biofuels used in the United States.[2] However, since most of the biofuel produced from 2008 to 2015 was ethanol (primarily produced from corn), the act put upward pressure on corn prices. Thus, the benefit of the Energy Independence and Security Act from higher energy prices was partially offset by the effect of higher energy prices for farmers. The goal of Moss, Livanis, and Schmitz was to estimate the elasticity of demand for agricultural inputs to provide an empirical estimate for the magnitude of this effect.

Moss, Livanis, and Schmitz estimate the single product form of the differential demand model:

$$\bar{f}_{it}\Delta \ln (x_{it}) = \theta_i \Delta \ln (y_t) + \sum_{i=1}^{4} \pi_{ij} \Delta \ln (w_{it}) + \epsilon_{it} \tag{7.186}$$

where $\bar{f}_{it}$ is the share of capital, labor, energy and material expenditures on agriculture where $\bar{f}_{it} = \frac{1}{2}(f_{it} + f_{i,t-1})$, $\Delta \ln (x_{it}) =$

[1]Add linkage to Chapter 6 — index number theory.

[2]Explanation of the Renewable Fuel Standard.

$\ln(x_{it}) - \ln(x_{i,t-1})$ for each input, $\Delta \ln(w_{it})$ is the logarithmic change in each input price, and $\Delta \ln(y_{it})$ is the logarithmic change in agricultural output level. While we derived this differential demand specification in Section 7.2.1, we need to discuss some empirical restrictions implicit in the formulation. First, the input share (θ_i) is assumed to be greater than or equal to zero and sums to one by definition (i.e., $\sum_{i=1}^{n} \theta_i = 1$). In addition, the π_{ij} matrix is symmetric by Young's theorem and sums to zero for all i and the overall matrix is negative semi-definite to be consistent with cost minimization. The result is that we typically estimate $n-1$ input demand equations in Equation (7.187), imposing the summing up restriction by subtracting one of the input prices:

$$\bar{f}_{it} \Delta \ln(x_{it}) = \theta \Delta \ln(y_t) + \sum_{i=1}^{3} \pi_{ij} [\Delta \ln(w_{it}) - \Delta \ln(w_{4t})] + \epsilon_{it} \quad i = 1, 2, 3 \tag{7.187}$$

where $\pi_{ij} = \pi_{ji}$. These steps are similar to the procedures for imposing symmetry and homogeneity on dual cost and profit functions, as described in Section 5.2.4. In addition, Moss, Livanis, and Schmitz imposed concavity on the π_{ij}s following Terrell's (1998) resampling approach.

Table 7.1 presents the Moss, Livanis, and Schmitz's estimated coefficients with and without concavity. Of course, the coefficients are not extremely useful for economic analysis. One alternative is to express the results in terms of the elasticity of substitution:

$$\zeta_{ij} = \frac{\dfrac{\Delta x_i}{x_i}}{\dfrac{\Delta w_j}{w_j}} = \frac{\psi\left(\Theta_{ij} - \theta_i \theta_j\right)}{f_i f_j} = \frac{\pi_{ij}}{f_i f_j} \tag{7.188}$$

see Theil (1980, p. 91). The elasticities for the energy demand specification are presented in Table 7.2. In elasticities, it is important to remember that they are constructed with random variables (i.e., they have a distribution). Hence, we could rewrite the elasticity in

Table 7.1 Estimated Derived Demand for Parameters for Aggregate U.S. Agriculture, 1958–2005 ($\times 100$)

Parameter	Without Concavity	Concavity Imposed
θ_1 (Capital)	1.284	3.243***
	(1.142)[a]	(0.903)
θ_2 (Labor)	−6.316*	−3.943
	(4.735)	(4.040)
θ_3 (Energy)	1.601*	2.303***
	(1.034)	(0.905)
π_{11}	0.289	−0.256**
	(0.320)	(0.127)
π_{12}	1.023*	0.806*
	(0.682)	(0.283)
π_{13}	0.427**	0.190
	(0.247)	(0.172)
π_{22}	−6.806**	−7.992***
	(3.113)	(2.646)
π_{23}	−0.191	−0.507
	(0.637)	(0.487)
π_{33}	−0.540*	−0.863**
	(0.408)	(0.401)

Notes: [a]Numbers in parenthesis denote standard errors.
***,**,*Denote statistical significance at the 0.01, 0.05, 0.10 levels of confidence respectively.

Equation (7.188) as

$$\zeta_{ij}(\theta) = \frac{\hat{\pi}_{ij}(\theta)}{\hat{f}_i(\theta)\hat{f}_j(\theta)} \tag{7.189}$$

where θ is the vector of random variables from the estimation procedure to emphasize their random nature. To complicate factors, while typically hypothesizing that each of the estimated random variables (i.e., $\hat{\pi}_{ij}(\theta)$, $\hat{f}_i(\theta)$, and $\hat{f}_j(\theta)$) are normally distributed, the complex function of random variables in Equation (7.189) may be only asymptotically normal according to the central limit theorem

Table 7.2 Compensated Input Elasticities

		Elasticity with Respect to			
Change in Demand for	Output Level	Capital Prices	Labor Prices	Energy Prices	Materials Prices
Capital	0.1589**	−0.0126*	−0.0394*	0.0093	−0.0362
	(0.0542)[a]	(0.0067)	(0.0228)	(0.0087)	(0.0220)
Labor	−0.1968	0.0402	−0.3989**	−0.0253	−0.3840**
	(0.2108)	(0.0241)	(0.1640)	(0.0255)	(0.1571)
Energy	0.9078*	0.0748	−0.1999	−0.3403*	0.4654*
	(0.4501)	(0.0732)	(0.2061)	(0.1896)	(0.2687)
Materials	1.7971***	−0.0135*	0.1405***	0.0216*	−0.1486***
	(0.1759)	(0.0078)	(0.0473)	(0.0069)	0.0471)

Notes: [a]Numbers in parenthesis denote standard errors.
***,**,*Denote statistical significance at significance at the 0.01, 0.05, 0.10 levels of confidence respectively.

(see Moss, 2014, pp. 145–148). An additional complexity involves the fact that we have not estimated the parameters of the differential demand function for materials.

Taking the points in inverse order, we address the lack of material parameters. Quite simply, the missing parameters are defined by the summing-up conditions that were imposed on the function:

$$\sum_{i=1}^{4}\theta_i \Rightarrow \theta_4 = 1-\theta_1-\theta_2-\theta_3$$

$$\sum_{i=1}^{4}\pi_{ij} = 0 \Rightarrow \pi_{i4} = -\pi_{i1}-\pi_{i2}-\pi_{i3} \quad i=1,2,3$$

$$\sum_{i=1}^{4}\pi_{44} = 0 \Rightarrow \pi_{44} = -\pi_{41}-\pi_{42}-\pi_{43}. \tag{7.190}$$

Note that these conditions can be used to define the variance for each of the imputed coefficients. Specifically, as a part of the estimation procedure that yielded the coefficients in Table 7.1, we have also have a variance matrix:

$$V\left[\begin{pmatrix}\theta_1\\ \theta_2\\ \theta_2\\ \pi_{11}\\ \pi_{12}\\ \pi_{13}\\ \pi_{22}\\ \pi_{23}\\ \pi_{33}\end{pmatrix}\right]=\Omega \tag{7.191}$$

where Ω is a 9×9 matrix. The variance of θ_4 can then be computed as

$$\omega_{\theta_4}=\begin{bmatrix}-1\\-1\\-1\\0\\0\\0\\0\\0\\0\end{bmatrix}'\Omega\begin{bmatrix}-1\\-1\\-1\\0\\0\\0\\0\\0\\0\end{bmatrix}. \tag{7.192}$$

Thus, it is relatively straightforward to populate full variance matrix for the coefficients using summing conditions.

The next question is how to compute the variance of the nonlinear definition of the elasticity in Equation (7.188) using the variance matrix defined above. Again, we are faced with two choices. The first possibility is to use a first-order Taylor series expansion:

$$V\left(\eta_{ij}\left(\theta\right)\right)=\begin{bmatrix}\dfrac{\partial\zeta_{ij}\left(\theta\right)}{\partial\theta_1}\\ \dfrac{\partial\zeta_{ij}\left(\theta\right)}{\partial\theta_2}\\ \vdots\\ \dfrac{\partial\zeta_{ij}\left(\theta\right)}{\partial\pi_{33}}\end{bmatrix}'\Omega\begin{bmatrix}\dfrac{\partial\zeta_{ij}\left(\theta\right)}{\partial\theta_1}\\ \dfrac{\partial\zeta_{ij}\left(\theta\right)}{\partial\theta_2}\\ \vdots\\ \dfrac{\partial\zeta_{ij}\left(\theta\right)}{\partial\pi_{33}}\end{bmatrix} \tag{7.193}$$

(see Moss, 2014, pp. 211–212). An alternative approach is to draw parameters based on the estimated distribution and then compute the value of the elasticities for each draw. This sample of elasticities can then be used to compute the variance of the elasticities. A slight variation is to use the bootstrapped estimates from the concavity-estimator to compute the sample of "concavity-consistent" parameters to compute the variance of the elasticities.

7.3.2 *Empirical Estimates Using Multiple Product Formulation*

Another possible impact of the Renewable Fuel Standard implemented in the Energy Independence and Security Act of 2007 was an increase in the cost of feeding livestock. Suh and Moss (2017) analyze the implications of increased feed grain prices on the demand for feed grain by the livestock sector and the composition of the supply of livestock (i.e., the aggregate choice of beef, pork, and chicken supplied to consumers). In general, feed costs account for over 60% of the overall cost of livestock production (Lawrence *et al.*, 2008). The dominance of feed costs in the production of livestock has raised concerns about the effect of biofuel policy on the price and availability of meat in the United States. Specifically, while corn accounts for more than 90% of total feed grain production and use, it has been the most dramatically affected by the Renewable Fuel Standard. The biofuel requirements have largely been met by blending ethanol with gasoline — the second generation biofuels have been slow to emerge. Further, the supply of ethanol has largely been produced from corn. Again, the promise of cellulosic ethanol at an economically viable cost of production has been elusive. Thus, the demand for corn for the production of ethanol to meet the Renewable Fuel Standard has directly reduced the amount of corn available for the production of livestock. This increased demand for corn has increased the feeding cost for livestock producers.

Suh and Moss estimate the interaction between the increase in corn prices and livestock supplied using the multiple product formulation. They extend the elasticities beyond the standard differential formulation to include "output effects." Specifically, most of the input elasticities assume that the overall output level is held constant. Suh and Moss follow Chambers (1982) by examining the effect of changes in output prices on input demand. Chambers demonstrates that the response in input level from the profit-maximizing behavior is similar to response in the consumer demand depicted in the Slutksy decomposition. Specifically, the firm has two responses to a change in the input price. The first response is the traditional

$$\left.\frac{\partial x_i\,(w,y)}{\partial w_j}\right|_{y=y_0} \tag{7.194}$$

which represents the rotation around the isoquant. The second response involves the change in the level of outputs:

$$\sum_{k=1}^{m}\frac{\partial x_i(w,y)}{\partial y_k}\frac{\partial y_k}{\partial w_j}. \tag{7.195}$$

To implement this concept, Suh and Moss estimate the system of differential demand equations:

$$\tilde{x}_{it}=\bar{\gamma}_t\sum_{r=1}^{m}\theta_i^r\bar{g}_r\Delta\ln\left(y_{rt}\right)+\sum_{j=1}^{n}\pi_{ij}\Delta\ln\left(w_{jt}\right)+\epsilon_{it} \tag{7.196}$$

where $\tilde{x}_{it}=\bar{f}_{it}\Delta\ln(x_{it})$ given that $\bar{f}_{it}=1/2(f_{it}+f_{i,t-1})$ and $\Delta\ln(x_{it})=\ln(x_{it})-\ln(x_{i,t-1})$, $\bar{\gamma}_t$ is defined as

$$\bar{\gamma}_t=\sqrt{\frac{R_t\times R_{t-1}}{C_t\times C_{t-1}}} \tag{7.197}$$

(i.e., the average revenue/cost ratio), $\bar{g}_r=1/2(g_{rt}+g_{r,t=1})$ represents the average revenue share for output r, and $\Delta\ln(y_{rt})$ and $\Delta\ln(w_{jt})$ are the finite logarithmic changes in output levels and input prices (e.g., similar to their definition of $\Delta\ln(x_{it})$). For identification purposes, θ_i^r is assumed to be a fixed constant and $\pi_{ij}=\psi(\Theta_{ij}-\theta_i\theta_j)$ is held constant. The output supply equations are then specified as

$$\tilde{y}_{rt}=\sum_{s=1}^{m}\alpha_{rs}\left(\Delta\ln\left(p_{st}\right)-\sum_{i=1}^{n}\theta_i^s\Delta\ln\left(w_{it}\right)\right)+\epsilon_{rt} \tag{7.198}$$

where $\tilde{y}_{rt}=\bar{\gamma}_t\bar{g}_{rt}\Delta\ln\left(y_{rt}\right)$. For identification purposes, $\alpha_{rs}=\bar{\gamma}_t\psi^*\theta_{rs}^*$ is treated as a constant.

Based on this formulation, Suh and Moss define

$$\zeta_{ir} = \frac{\theta_i^r \bar{\gamma}_t \bar{g}_{rt}}{\bar{f}_{it}} \tag{7.199}$$

as the elasticity of the input demand for input i with respect to a change in output price r. Similarly,

$$\zeta_{ij} = \frac{\pi_{ij}}{\bar{f}_{it}} \tag{7.200}$$

is defined as the elasticity of input demand for input i with respect to a change in input price j. To develop these estimates in a little more detail, assume that $\tilde{y}_{rt} = 1/T \sum_{t=1}^{T} \Delta \bar{g}_r \ln(y_{it})$ and $\tilde{w}_{ij} = 1/T \sum_{t=1}^{T} \Delta \ln(w_{it})$. Given these values, we can compute the expected left-hand side of Equation (7.196) as

$$\bar{x}_{it} = \left(\frac{\sum_{t=1}^{T} \bar{\gamma}_t}{T} \right) \sum_{r=1}^{m} \hat{\theta}_i^r \tilde{y}_{rt} + \sum_{j=1}^{n} \hat{\pi}_{ij} \tilde{w}_{ij} \tag{7.201}$$

or the predicted value of the dependent variable at the mean value of the independent variables. The estimated input share can then be defined as

$$\hat{f}_{it} = \frac{\bar{x}_{it}}{\frac{1}{T} \sum_{t=1}^{T} \ln(x_{it})}. \tag{7.202}$$

Note that, following our discussion of the single product scenario, $\hat{f}_{it}$ has a distribution depending on the distribution of the estimated parameters. The elasticity for output r with respect to output price s is then defined as

$$\xi_{rs} = \frac{\alpha_{rs}}{\bar{\gamma}_t \bar{g}_{rt}}. \tag{7.203}$$

Returning to the concept presented in Equation (7.195), we are interested in formulating the elasticity based on the change in input

i from a change in input price j defined as

$$\frac{\partial x_i(p,w)}{\partial w_j} = \frac{\partial x_i(w,y^*)}{\partial w_j} + \sum_{s=1}^{m} \frac{\partial x_i(w,y^*)}{\partial y_s} \frac{\partial y_s(p,w)}{\partial w_j} \tag{7.204}$$

where $y^s = y(p,w)$. The elasticity which depicts this change is computed as

$$\zeta_{ij} = \zeta_{ij}^* + \sum_{s=1}^{m} \zeta_{is}\eta_{sj} \tag{7.205}$$

where ζ_{ij}^* is the cost-minimizing demand elasticity for input i with respect to a change in input price j and η_{sj} is the elasticity of output supply. The elasticity of output supply with respect to a change in input price can be defined as

$$\eta_{ri} = -\frac{w_i x_i}{p_r y_r} \sum_{s=1}^{n} \zeta_{is}\xi_{sr} \tag{7.206}$$

where ξ_{sr} is elasticity of the output supply for output s with respect to a change in the output price for output r (see Equation (7.203).

Suh and Moss depart from Moss *et al.* (2010) by estimating the differential model with a two-step generalized method of moments approach. In the first step, they estimate input demand function from Equation (7.196), using an *ex ante* approximation to estimate the values of θ_i^s. Given these estimated values, the output Equations (7.198) are then estimated conditional on the input demand equations. This approach is justified by Laitinen (1980) and Theil (1980), who suggest a hierarchy of production decisions.

The estimated values for this specification are presented in Table 7.3. Individual parameters are often hard to interpret, but it is worth noting that the diagonal matrix of second-order input prices (π_{ij}) is negative and statistically significant while the diagonal matrix of second-order output-level terms (α_{rs}) is positive and statistically significant. In general, terms these are consistent with the concavity and convexity results for the differential demand system.

Turning to the elasticity results, the elasticity of demand for feedstocks are presented in Table 7.4. These results indicate that an increase in each livestock output results in an increase in the demand for each feedstock with the exception of the effect of an increase in the

Table 7.3 Estimated Parameters of the Multiproduct Differential Model of Feed Demand

Parameter	Estimate	Parameter	Estimate
θ_1^a	0.7567***	π_{11}	−0.1465**
	(0.0702)[a]		(0.0648)
θ_2^a	0.0783*	π_{12}	0.0568
	(0.0403)		(0.0417)
θ_3^a	0.1000	π_{13}	0.0295
	(0.0956)		(0.0238)
θ_1^b	0.5540***	π_{22}	−0.0558*
	(0.1382)		(0.0293)
θ_2^b	−0.1074	π_{23}	0.0096
	(0.0739)		(0.0145)
θ_3^b	0.5310***	π_{33}	−0.0405*
	(0.1817)		(0.0241)
θ_1^c	0.5801***	α_{aa}	0.1042***
	(0.1241)		(0.0308)
θ_2^c	0.1254*	α_{ab}	−0.0351**
	(0.0674)		(0.0160)
θ_3^C	0.2188	α_{bb}	0.0259**
	(0.1531)		(0.0117)

Notes: [a]Numbers in parenthesis denote standard errors.
***,**,*Denote statistical significance at the 0.01, 0.05, 0.10 levels of confidence respectively.

Table 7.4 Output Elasticities of Demand for Feed Grains

Feed	Cattle Output	Chicken Output	Pork Output
Corn demand	1.0362Z***	0.3763***	0.3492***
	(0.0950)[a]	(0.0938)	(0.0747)
Sorghum demand	1.6427*	−1.1308	1.1699*
	(0.8455)	(0.7785)	(0.6288)
Soybean demand	0.3102	0.8267***	0.3019
	(0.2966)	(0.2829)	(0.2112)
DDGS demand	1.8885	0.3799	1.1345
	(1.7705)	(1.7126)	(1.2518)

Notes: [a]Numbers in parenthesis denote standard errors.
***,*Denote statistical significance at the 0.01 and 0.10 levels of confidence, respectively.

output of poultry on sorghum. This result may reflect the high feed conversion rate required in the poultry industry. Typically switching form corn which is 88% totally digestible matter to sorghum which is 78% digestible matter does not affect the feed conversion for beef cattle or pork; however, the shift may have a dramatic effect on chickens which have a smaller digestive system. Whether or not this concept is significant is questionable since the estimate coefficient is not statistically significant at any conventional confidence level. The statistically significant elasticity involve all the corn demand elasticities. The largest impact appears to be the effect of an increase in cattle production on corn (1.04). However, the increase in corn demand resulting from an increase in the level of poultry (0.38) and pork (0.35) are also significant. Another interesting result is that the elasticities of the demand for distillers grain is not statistically significant for any livestock output.

The elasticities of demand for each feedstock with respect to a change in the price of feedstocks presented in Table 7.5 are also consistent with our expectations. In general, the diagonal elasticities are negative and statistically significant. Note that the elasticity matrix is not symmetric. While the estimated π_{ij} coefficients are symmetric, as denoted in Equation (7.200), the estimated π_{ij} coefficient is divided by the average budget share for each input. Hence, π_{12} is divided by the average share of expenditure on corn in Equation (1) and the average share of expenditure on sorghum in Equation (2). An interesting result in Table 7.5 is the elasticity of demand for corn with respect to an increase in the price of distillers grain and the elasticity of the demand for distillers grain with respect to an increase in the price of corn. Both are positive, indicating that as the price of corn increases, the demand for distillers grain increases. This ends up being the result of an indirect causality. As the demand for corn for the production of ethanol increases, the price of corn increases. On the "back side" of the relationship, as the amount of corn used to produce ethanol increases, the supply of distillers grain increases. Suh and Moss use an ancillary regression to remove this endogeneity.

Table 7.6 presents the elasticity of supply with respect to changes in output prices. Like the price elasticities of demand with respect to input prices, the output elasticities have the "correct signs" (i.e., the diagonal elasticities are positive and statistically significant). All of these elasticities are relatively inelastic — less than 1.0. This result

Table 7.5 Output Elasticities of Demand for Feed Grains

Feed	Corn Price	Sorghum Price	Soybean Price	DDGS Price
Corn demand	−0.2257**	0.0876	0.0455	0.0926***
	(0.0999)	(0.0642)	(0.0368)	(0.0279)
Sorghum demand	1.3577	−1.3330*	0.2295	−0.2541
	(1.3778)	(0.7015)	(0.3483)	(0.2905)
Soybean demand	0.1043	0.0339	−0.1430*	0.0047
	(0.0843)	(0.0515)	(0.0853)	(0.0534)
DDGS demand	2.3127***	−0.4098	0.0516	−1.9546***
	(0.6988)	(0.4684)	(0.5827)	(0.5412)

Notes: [a]Numbers in parenthesis denote standard errors.
***,**,*Denote statistical significance at the 0.01, 0.05, 0.10 levels of confidence respectively.

Table 7.6 Price Elasticities of Livestock Supply

Livestock	Cattle Price	Chicken Price	Pork Price
Cattle supply	0.1187***	−0.0400**	−0.0786***
	(0.0350)[a]	(0.0182)	(0.0296)
Chicken supply	−0.0797**	0.0588**	0.0209
	(0.0363)	(0.0266)	(0.0243)
Pork supply	−0.1768***	0.0235	0.1532**
	(0.0666)	(0.0275)	(0.0691)

Notes: [a]Numbers in parenthesis denote standard errors.
***,**Denote statistical significance at the 0.01 and 0.05 level of confidence, respectively.

would be consistent with a short-run supply response. Examining the off-diagonal elements, an increase in either the chicken or pork prices reduces the supply of cattle. However, while an increase in the cattle price reduces the supply of pork, the supply of chicken is not affected by changes in the pork price.

Finally, we turn to the differential specification with quasi-fixed inputs. To demonstrate this scenario, we turn to Suh and Moss (2021)

Table 7.7 Estimated Coefficients With Quasi-fixed Variables

Parameter	Estimate	Parameter	Estimate
θ_1^1	-0.011 (0.083)[a]	π_{23}	0.000* (0.000)
θ_2^1	0.004 (0.011)	ξ_1	2.340*** (0.650)
θ_1^2	0.256 (0.177)	ξ_2	-0.022 (0.084)
θ_2^2	0.051** (0.025)	α_{11}	0.016* (0.010)
θ_1^3	0.271*** (0.023)	α_{12}	0.005 (0.006)
θ_2^3	0.020*** (0.002)	α_{22}	0.009 (0.007)
π_{11}	-0.067*** (0.014)	μ_1	-0.694*** (0.197)
π_{12}	0.003** (0.104)	μ_2	-0.101 (0.104)

Notes: [a]Numbers in parenthesis denote standard errors.
***,**,*Denote statistical significance at the 0.01, 0.05, 0.10 levels of confidence respectively.

who extend the differential specification by including land as a quasi-fixed input and estimating Equation (7.185) combined with the output equations:

$$\bar{\gamma}_t \bar{g}_{rt} \Delta \ln(y_{rt}) = \sum_{s=1}^{m} \alpha_{rs} \left(\Delta \ln(p_{st}) - \sum_{i=1}^{n} \theta_i^s \Delta \ln(w_{it}) \right) + \mu_r \ln(z_t). \tag{7.207}$$

Econometrically, Suh and Moss use a similar two-step approach to estimation, but this time they use a maximum likelihood estimator instead of a generalized method of moments estimator. The parameter estimates for this specification are presented in Table 7.7. Again, the point of this estimation is that the level of the quasi-fixed variable (in this case land) affects the demand for variable inputs and output levels. Table 7.8 presents the variable input elasticities for changes in input prices and the level of the quasi-fixed input.

Table 7.8 Input Elasticity with Respect to Input Prices with Quasi-fixed Variables

Input	Labor Price	Capital Price	Intermediate Price	Land Quantity
Labor Demand	-0.250^{***}	0.010^{**}	0.239^{***}	1.971^{***}
	(0.052)[a]	(0.005)	(0.052)	(0.547)
Capital Demand	0.163^{**}	-0.020^{*}	-0.143^{*}	-0.295
	(0.079)	(0.011)	(0.075)	(1.101)
Intermediates Demand	0.090^{***}	-0.003^{*}	-0.087^{***}	-0.418^{**}
	(0.019)	(0.002)	(0.019)	(0.212)

Notes: [a]Numbers in parenthesis denote standard errors.
***,**,*Denote statistical significance at the 0.01, 0.05, 0.10 levels of confidence respectively.

7.4 Chapter Summary

- The difference between the dual specification developed in this chapter and the methodologies developed in the previous chapters is that the differential models change in optimal decisions. In the consumer model, we ask how does the amount of good q_i change as either the price of that good (p_i) changes or as income changes. In the production model, we ask how does the demand for an input (x_i) change with a change in input price (w_i) or the level of output (y).
- The differential demand for the consumer and the differential demand for the firm that produces a single output are quite similar.

7.5 Review Questions

1. Use the parameters of the estimated production function from Table 1.1 along with the average level of input use from Table 1.2 to define $F^{-1}(F - \gamma H) F^{-1}$. Use these results to compute a numerical version of the inverse of Barten's fundamental matrix in Equation (7.77).
2. Differentiate the first-order conditions for the multiproduct formulation. Use the first-order condition to derive Equation (7.117).

7.6 Exercises

1. Using the data PsuedoData-2016.csv,[3] estimate the differential model for a firm with a single output.
2. Using the data AggregateUSDA.csv,[4] estimate the multiproduct differential model. Here, use three outputs, livestock, crops, and farm-related, and three inputs, capital, labor, and intermediate inputs.
3. Extending Question 3, use the same three outputs, but use the non-land capital as a variable input and divide labor into own and hired labor. Treat land as a quasi-fixed input.

[3]This data is available at www.charlesbmoss.com:8080/Book.Production.Economics/Chapter-5/PsuedoData-2016.csv.

[4]This data is available at www.charlesbmoss.com:8080/Book.Production/Economics/Chapter-1/AggregateUSDA.csv.

Chapter 8

Topics and Applications

8.1 An Economist's Lament — A State-Space Approach to Production Functions

This chapter examines an extension to the standard production function formulation that explicitly recognizes some of the significant interactions of an artificial fertilizer with the characteristics of the soil. This extension is then used to model the stochastic structure of production within a state-space structure. After some years of playing the academic game — chasing the next journal article — I have started to ask myself a basic question: Why am I interested in this issue, or if I get it right who cares? Undoubtedly, journals are full of papers that claim to make significant advancements that no one ever reads let alone cites. So, let us start our basic discussion by asking the question: Do economists worry about production functions and, if so, why? While Austrian economists have become less studied over time, one Ludwig von Mises proposed a definition of economics as the study of human action. This definition may be a little pretentious, but it provides an interesting insight — I am interested in the production decisions in that they are economic actions based on input and output prices that signal values in economy. Hence, I am interested in production functions because these functions "map out" the basis and consequences of these decisions. In addition to the positive notion inherent in agricultural policy analysis, a secondary reason agricultural economists may have is to make production recommendations through each state's extension service. The use of production functions to analyze farmer decisions has largely vanished as the economics profession has moved to dual specifications that estimate farmer choices of inputs such as fertilizers as functions of input and output prices. However, given that the dual approach largely neglects the implications of risk and uncertainty, I hope that the production function approach developed in this section will shed light on emerging questions such as the effect of agricultural policies such as the subsidization of crop insurance.

8.1.1 *Deriving the State-Space Production Function*

As a starting point in my development of the production function, let us consider the economic decision that we want to model. Typically, the economic decision is framed in one of two problems — we could be interested in the choice of inputs that maximize profit:

$$\pi(w,p) = \max pf(x) - w'x \tag{8.1}$$

where w is a vector of input prices, p is a scalar output price, and $f(x)$ is a production function (implicitly, $y = f(x)$ is the level of output chosen by the decision maker). A second, but related, problem is to choose the combination of inputs that minimizes the cost of producing a given level of output:

$$\begin{aligned} c(w,y) &= \min w'x \\ \text{s.t.}\, y &= f(x). \end{aligned} \tag{8.2}$$

In the parlance of the economist, the production function in either case is an envelope function that traces out the maximum output that can be produced from any set of inputs. One example of this function based on soybean production in Illinois is presented in Figure 8.1. Note that this yield is a maximum potential yield for a given amount of potash per acre. We anticipate that the observed yields fall below this frontier, as depicted in Figure 8.2. The concept is that the frontier depicts the highest output that can be obtained from a given level of fertilizer, but this highest level is not obtained due to production inefficiencies. For example, the farmer may not apply the fertilizer at the "right time." However, Figures 8.1 and 8.2 hide many of the complexities involved in modeling the production process. For example, several fertilizers may contribute to the

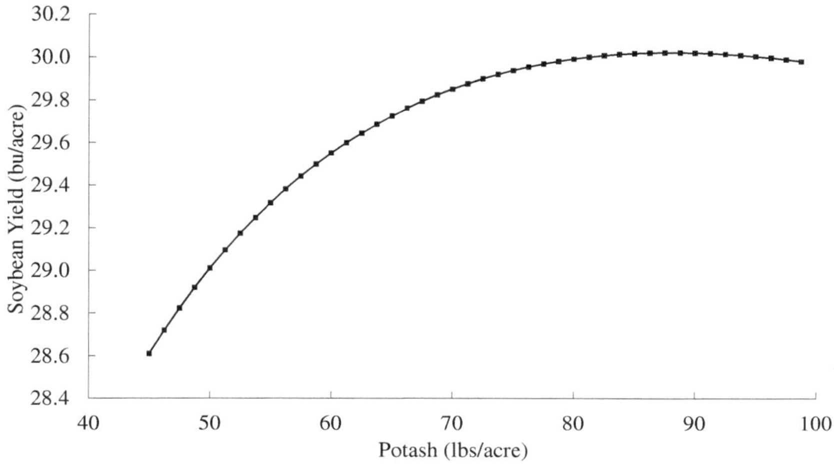

Fig. 8.1 Soybean Production Function for Potash (Phosphorous: 51.875 lbs/acre)

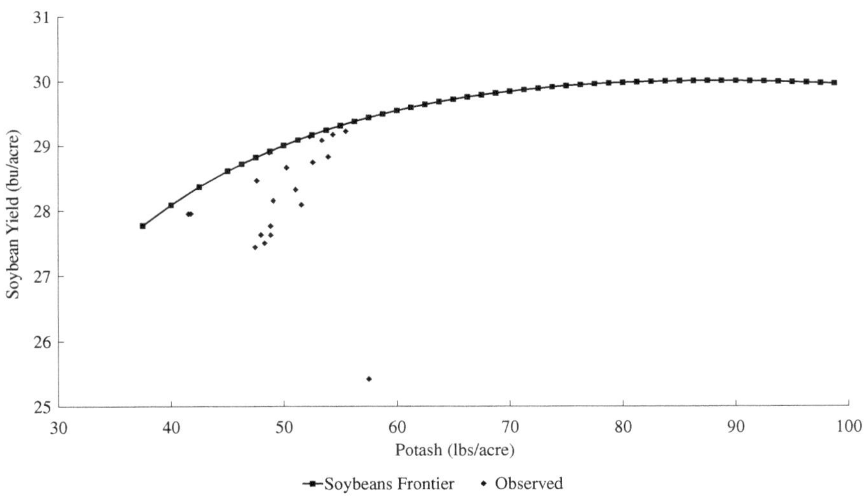

Fig. 8.2 Observed Soybean Production using Potash (Phosphorous: 51.875 lbs/acre)

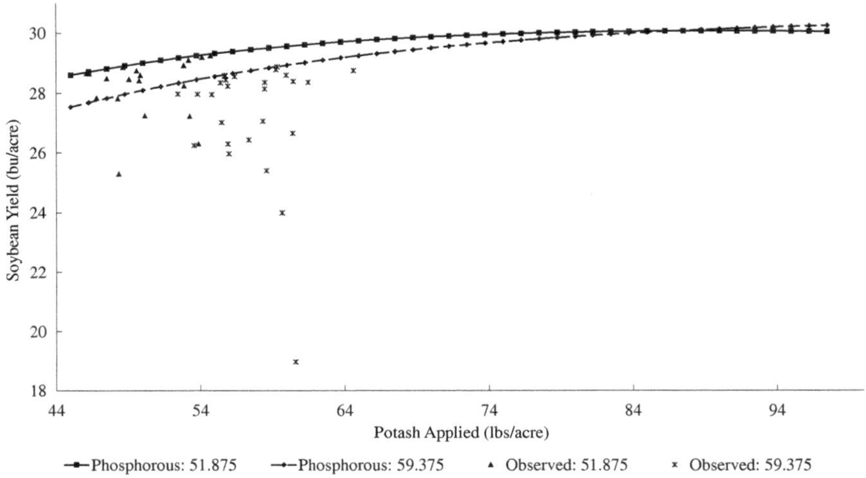

Fig. 8.3 Observed Soybean Production using Potash (Varying Phosphorous Levels)

production of soybeans. Figure 8.3 depicts soybean production as a function of phosphorous and potash. In this scenario, the production function rotates — soybean yields are higher for lower levels of potash when the phosphorous is held to 51.875 lbs/acre, but the yield of soybeans is higher for higher levels of potash when phosphorous expands to 59.375 lbs/acre. In economic terms, potash and phosphorous are compliments over this region of the production function.

The results in Figures 8.2 and 8.3 raise an important question: What causes the randomness below the production function? To develop this random component, we start by expanding our production function to include several controllable and uncontrollable factors of production. Specifically, we assume that

$$f(x, \epsilon) = f(x_1, x_2, x_3, z_1, z_2, \epsilon) \tag{8.3}$$

where x_1 is the amount of phosphorous, x_2 is the level of potash, x_3 is the level of some other controllable input like labor, z_1 and z_2 are the levels of inputs which are beyond the control of the decision maker (i.e., soil moisture and growing degree days), and ϵ is a random factor that measures the inefficiency of the farm firm. In this formulation, the third controllable input adds an additional dimension to the controllable surface. Similar to the comparison between the production function with different levels of phosphorous in Figure 8.3, there is another source of variation due to the amount of labor (hours/acre) used by the farmer. However, it is the possibility of different levels of non-controllable variables that really changes the problem. Specifically, we could rewrite the profit-maximizing model such that the decision maker chooses the level of the controllable input to maximize expected profit:

$$\pi_e(w,p) = \max p \int_{a_1}^{b_1} \int_{a_2}^{b_2} f(x_1, x_2, x_3, z_1, z_2) \times g(z_1, z_2) dz_1 dz_2 - w_1 x_1 - w_2 x_2 - w_3 x_3 \qquad (8.4)$$

where $\pi_e(w,p)$ denotes maximum expected profit and $g(z_1, z_2)$ denotes the probability density function for the uncontrollable inputs. In this formulation, we have dropped the random variable for technical inefficiency because nobody plans on being technically inefficient.

The stochastic specification in Equation (8.4) is fairly general. In this study, we propose a state-space formulation of the stochastic process:

$$\tilde{\pi}_e(w,p) = \max p \sum_{j=1}^{J} f(x_1, x_2, x_3, \tilde{z}_{1j}, \tilde{z}_{2j}) g_j - w_1 x_1 - w_2 x_2 - w_3 x_3 \qquad (8.5)$$

where the set $\{\tilde{z}_{1j}, \tilde{z}_{2j}, g_j\}$ is a probabilistic state-space. For example, suppose that z_1 is the soil moisture level measured as Palmer Dought Severity Index and z_2 is the number of heat days — the state-space can be represented using two sets of numbers:

$$Z = \begin{bmatrix} -0.79 & 162 \\ -1.82 & 239 \\ -0.37 & 198 \\ -2.24 & 108 \\ 1.41 & 157 \end{bmatrix}, \quad g = \begin{bmatrix} 0.20 \\ 0.20 \\ 0.20 \\ 0.20 \\ 0.20 \end{bmatrix} \qquad (8.6)$$

where Z is the possible set of values for the uncontrollable input and g is the probability of each outcome. The advantage to this formulation can be demonstrated by considering a second-order Taylor series expansion of the production function:

$$\tilde{f}(x_1, x_2, x_3, z_1, z_2) = \alpha_0 + \begin{bmatrix} \alpha_1 \\ \alpha_2 \\ \alpha_3 \\ \alpha_4 \\ \alpha_5 \end{bmatrix}' \begin{bmatrix} x_1 \\ x_2 \\ x_3 \\ z_1 \\ z_2 \end{bmatrix} + \frac{1}{2} \begin{bmatrix} x_1 \\ x_2 \\ x_3 \\ z_1 \\ z_2 \end{bmatrix}' \begin{bmatrix} A_{11} & A_{12} & A_{13} & A_{14} & A_{15} \\ A_{12} & A_{22} & A_{23} & A_{24} & A_{25} \\ A_{13} & A_{23} & A_{33} & A_{34} & A_{35} \\ A_{14} & A_{24} & A_{34} & A_{44} & A_{45} \\ A_{15} & A_{25} & A_{35} & A_{45} & A_{55} \end{bmatrix} \begin{bmatrix} x_1 \\ x_2 \\ x_3 \\ z_1 \\ z_2 \end{bmatrix} \tag{8.7}$$

where the α and A variables are parameters that are valid for a small change around some point. The advantage of the state-space formulation is the ability of modeling interaction between the levels of controllable inputs and uncontrollable inputs:

$$\nu_1(x_1, x_2, x_3, z_1, z_2) = \begin{bmatrix} z_1 \\ z_2 \end{bmatrix} \begin{bmatrix} A_{14} & A_{15} \\ A_{24} & A_{25} \\ A_{34} & A_{35} \end{bmatrix} \begin{bmatrix} x_1 \\ x_2 \\ x_3 \end{bmatrix}. \tag{8.8}$$

In addition to the interaction, we can write a "pure random term":

$$\nu_2(z_1, z_2) = \frac{1}{2} \begin{bmatrix} z_1 \\ z_2 \end{bmatrix}' \begin{bmatrix} A_{44} & A_{45} \\ A_{45} & A_{55} \end{bmatrix} \begin{bmatrix} z_1 \\ z_2 \end{bmatrix} \tag{8.9}$$

putting these factors back into the original production function specification:

$$f(x_1, x_2, x_3, z_1, z_2) = f_1(x_1, x_2, x_3) + \nu_1(x_1, x_2, x_3, z_1, z_2) + \nu_2(z_1, z_2). \tag{8.10}$$

To depict the effect of state-space formulation on production decisions, consider the derivative of the production function in

Equation (8.10):

$$\begin{aligned}\frac{\partial f()}{\partial x_1} &= \alpha_1 + A_{11}x_1 + A_{12}x_2 + A_{13}x_3 + \frac{\partial \nu_1()}{\partial x_1}\\ &= \alpha_1 + A_{11}x_1 + A_{12}x_2 + A_{13}x_3 + [A_{14}z_1 + A_{15}z_2]. \qquad (8.11)\end{aligned}$$

Thus, the choice of x_1 influences how the uncontrollable variables affect production. Turning to the general formulation in Equation (8.5),

$$\frac{\partial f()}{\partial x_1} = \alpha_1 + A_{11}x_1 + A_{12}x_2 + A_{13}x_3 + \sum_{j=1}^{J} g_j[A_{14}z_{1j} + A_{15}z_{2j}]. \qquad (8.12)$$

This change has two general sets of implications. First, from an econometric vantage point, error has two components: one related to the set of observable inputs (e.g., $\nu_1(x_1, x_2, x_3, z_1, z_2)$) and one unrelated to the observable inputs (e.g., $\nu_2(z_1, z_2)$). Second, from an economic point of view, decisions concerning the controllable inputs affect the distribution of outcomes in state-space.

8.1.2 *Beyond Economic Abstraction*

8.1.2.1 *Variations in soil types*

In addition to the concept of state-space, I would like to take a step toward a better agronomic form of the production function. Economist like a simple formulation of the production process. As depicted above, the concept is that an observed change in a control variable (i.e., phosphorous) is associated with an observable change in the output (i.e., soybeans per acre). We like assumptions that hold the parameters of the production function (i.e., αs and As in Equation (8.7)) constant. However, this assumption (constant parameters) may be largely unacceptable.

As a starting point, I will assume that the actual production function in Equation (8.7) is dependent on the level of each nutrient (phosphorous and potash) available to the plant. Further, I will assume that the level of nutrient available to the plant is a function of the nature of the soil and the amount of nutrient applied.

Explicitly, I will replace the level of phosphorous and potash with soil objects ($\delta_1(x_1, z_1, z_2, s_1)$, $\delta_2(x_2, z_1, z_2, s_2)$ where s_1 and s_2 are vectors of soil characteristics). Again, relying on a second-order Taylor series expansion, we could derive two expressions for the level of nutrients available to the plant:

$$\tilde{x}_1 = \delta_1(x_1, z_1, z_2, s_1) = \gamma_{01} + \gamma_1 \begin{bmatrix} x_1 \\ z_1 \\ z_2 \\ s_1 \end{bmatrix} + \frac{1}{2} \begin{bmatrix} x_1 \\ z_1 \\ z_2 \\ s_1 \end{bmatrix}' \Gamma_1 \begin{bmatrix} x_1 \\ z_1 \\ z_2 \\ s_1 \end{bmatrix}$$

$$\tilde{x}_2 = \delta_2(x_2, z_1, z_2, s_2) = \gamma_{02} + \gamma_1 \begin{bmatrix} x_2 \\ z_1 \\ z_2 \\ s_2 \end{bmatrix} + \frac{1}{2} \begin{bmatrix} x_2 \\ z_1 \\ z_2 \\ s_2 \end{bmatrix}' \Gamma_2 \begin{bmatrix} x_2 \\ z_1 \\ z_2 \\ s_2 \end{bmatrix}. \quad (8.13)$$

The mathematically adventurous can substitute the approximations in Equation (8.13) into Equation (8.7) for a complete model of the production function.

To demonstrate the implications of this specification, consider the data that an economist uses to estimate a production function. Table 8.1 presents a stylized dataset: there are four farms in Illinois, three farms in Indiana, and five farms in Iowa. These farms can either choose to produce soybeans in a given year (i.e., 2000, 2001, and 2002). If the firm chooses to produce soybeans, it then chooses to the level of phosphorous, potash, and labor to use. Whether or not the farm chooses to produce soybeans, we can observe the level of uncontrolled input (e.g., firm moisture in the PDSI and the heat degree days in May). Hence, when the farmer chooses not to produce soybeans in a given year, Table 8.1 shows a "zero value" for the controllable inputs and the output level. Hence, farmer 4 in Illinois chooses not to grow soybeans in 2000. In addition to observations on the observed inputs, Table 8.1 highlights the fact that we do not observe the latent soil factors (i.e., $\tilde{s}^{IL}_{11,2000}$ is the first latent soil factor for farmer 1 in 2000). The question is then: When does the typical empirical estimation of a production function make sense? As a starting point, consider a "typical" specification of the production

Table 8.1 Stylized Dataset for Estimation

Year	State	Individual	x_1	x_2	x_3	z_1	z_2	s_1	s_2	Y
2000	IL	1	61.05	114.16	1.83	0.11	78.36	$\tilde{s}^{IL}_{11,2000}$	$\tilde{s}^{IL}_{21,2000}$	47.11
2000	IL	2	47.75	94.78	1.94	1.48	119.17	$\tilde{s}^{IL}_{12,2000}$	$\tilde{s}^{IL}_{22,2000}$	43.41
2000	IL	3	47.66	115.02	1.84	0.74	147.36	$\tilde{s}^{IL}_{13,2000}$	$\tilde{s}^{IL}_{23,2000}$	44.01
2000	IL	4	0	0	0	1.40	124.85	$\tilde{s}^{IL}_{14,2000}$	$\tilde{s}^{IL}_{24,2000}$	0
2000	IL	Mean	52.15	107.99	1.87	0.78	114.96	NA	NA	44.84
2001	IL	1	91.23	134.55	1.56	−1.53	199.14	$\tilde{s}^{IL}_{11,2001}$	$\tilde{s}^{IL}_{21,2001}$	44.31
2001	IL	2	79.87	122.41	1.90	−0.29	274.28	$\tilde{s}^{IL}_{12,2001}$	$\tilde{s}^{IL}_{22,2001}$	44.02
2001	IL	3	0	0	0	−0.53	218.07	$\tilde{s}^{IL}_{13,2001}$	$\tilde{s}^{IL}_{23,2001}$	0
2001	IL	4	77.40	116.43	1.73	0.41	233.92	$\tilde{s}^{IL}_{14,2001}$	$\tilde{s}^{IL}_{24,2001}$	44.14
2001	IL	Mean	82.83	124.46	1.73	−0.47	235.78	NA	NA	44.16
2002	IL	1	55.90	109.45	1.64	1.41	150.89	$\tilde{s}^{IL}_{11,2002}$	$\tilde{s}^{IL}_{21,2002}$	42.81
2002	IL	2	59.15	97.10	1.99	1.60	186.79	$\tilde{s}^{IL}_{12,2002}$	$\tilde{s}^{IL}_{22,2002}$	43.79
2002	IL	3	35.89	76.93	2.00	0.90	242.46	$\tilde{s}^{IL}_{13,2002}$	$\tilde{s}^{IL}_{23,2002}$	39.43
2002	IL	4	77.85	153.80	1.34	−0.18	261.26	$\tilde{s}^{IL}_{14,2002}$	$\tilde{s}^{IL}_{24,2002}$	46.83
2002	IL	Mean	57.20	109.32	1.74	0.93	210.35	NA	NA	43.22
2000	IN	1	0	0	0	2.55	247.17	$\tilde{s}^{IN}_{11,2000}$	$\tilde{s}^{IN}_{21,2000}$	0
2000	IN	2	67.25	118.48	2.66	2.38	168.46	$\tilde{s}^{IN}_{12,2000}$	$\tilde{s}^{IN}_{22,2000}$	47.72
2000	IN	3	57.61	113.89	2.67	0.00	154.84	$\tilde{s}^{IN}_{13,2000}$	$\tilde{s}^{IN}_{23,2000}$	45.66
2000	IN	Mean	62.43	116.19	2.67	1.19	161.65	NA	NA	46.69
2001	IN	1	42.93	98.46	2.75	0.61	170.04	$\tilde{s}^{IN}_{11,2001}$	$\tilde{s}^{IN}_{21,2001}$	44.03
2001	IN	2	0	0	0	2.71	80.26	$\tilde{s}^{IN}_{12,2001}$	$\tilde{s}^{IN}_{22,2001}$	0
2001	IN	3	60.25	106.20	2.67	3.15	60.81	$\tilde{s}^{IN}_{13,2001}$	$\tilde{s}^{IN}_{23,2001}$	48.59
2001	IN	Mean	51.59	102.33	2.71	1.88	115.43	NA	NA	46.31
2002	IN	1	0	0	0	−0.74	121.90	$\tilde{s}^{IN}_{11,2002}$	$\tilde{s}^{IN}_{21,2002}$	0
2002	IN	2	51.77	102.50	2.73	2.30	80.39	$\tilde{s}^{IN}_{12,2002}$	$\tilde{s}^{IN}_{22,2002}$	45.36
2002	IN	3	53.39	102.90	2.88	2.56	165.59	$\tilde{s}^{IN}_{13,2002}$	$\tilde{s}^{IN}_{23,2002}$	46.27
2002	IN	Mean	52.58	102.7	2.81	2.43	122.99	NA	NA	45.82
2000	IA	1	47.52	58.50	2.77	2.21	163.13	$\tilde{s}^{IA}_{11,2000}$	$\tilde{s}^{IA}_{21,2000}$	43.38
2000	IA	2	59.62	73.13	2.36	2.58	62.99	$\tilde{s}^{IA}_{12,2000}$	$\tilde{s}^{IA}_{22,2000}$	44.04
2000	IA	3	57.73	77.28	2.65	3.28	151.91	$\tilde{s}^{IA}_{13,2000}$	$\tilde{s}^{IA}_{23,2000}$	44.14
2000	IA	4	57.26	84.43	2.88	1.39	247.82	$\tilde{s}^{IA}_{14,2000}$	$\tilde{s}^{IA}_{24,2000}$	48.56
2000	IA	5	66.23	101.35	2.68	1.00	266.32	$\tilde{s}^{IA}_{15,2000}$	$\tilde{s}^{IA}_{25,2000}$	49.66
2000	IA	Mean	57.67	78.94	2.67	2.09	178.43	NA	NA	45.96
2001	IA	1	0	0	0	0.50	247.76	$\tilde{s}^{IA}_{11,2001}$	$\tilde{s}^{IA}_{21,2001}$	0
2001	IA	2	74.12	104.71	2.15	2.42	196.04	$\tilde{s}^{IA}_{12,2001}$	$\tilde{s}^{IA}_{22,2001}$	48.81
2001	IA	3	62.70	94.60	2.58	−0.66	265.41	$\tilde{s}^{IA}_{13,2001}$	$\tilde{s}^{IA}_{23,2001}$	44.23
2001	IA	4	22.28	29.67	3.26	−1.36	231.77	$\tilde{s}^{IA}_{14,2001}$	$\tilde{s}^{IA}_{24,2001}$	43.89
2001	IA	5	60.76	100.99	2.54	−0.94	221.14	$\tilde{s}^{IA}_{15,2001}$	$\tilde{s}^{IA}_{25,2001}$	47.02
2001	IA	Mean	54.97	82.49	2.63	−0.14	228.59	NA	NA	45.99
2002	IA	1	66.77	71.51	2.35	3.82	121.08	$\tilde{s}^{IA}_{11,2002}$	$\tilde{s}^{IA}_{21,2002}$	46.11
2002	IA	2	47.22	62.65	2.82	2.48	173.85	$\tilde{s}^{IA}_{12,2002}$	$\tilde{s}^{IA}_{22,2002}$	43.58
2002	IA	3	43.62	41.68	2.62	0.17	135.32	$\tilde{s}^{IA}_{13,2002}$	$\tilde{s}^{IA}_{23,2002}$	44.49
2002	IA	4	28.94	39.40	3.15	2.75	177.53	$\tilde{s}^{IA}_{14,2002}$	$\tilde{s}^{IA}_{24,2002}$	43.24
2002	IA	5	0	0	0	2.27	271.51	$\tilde{s}^{IA}_{15,2001}$	$\tilde{s}^{IA}_{25,2001}$	0
2002	IA	Mean	46.64	53.81	2.74	2.31	151.95	NA	NA	44.36

function:

$$\ln(y) = \alpha_0 + \begin{bmatrix} \alpha_1 \\ \alpha_2 \\ \alpha_3 \\ \alpha_4 \\ \alpha_5 \end{bmatrix}' \begin{bmatrix} \ln(x_1) \\ \ln(x_2) \\ \ln(x_3) \\ \ln(z_1) \\ \ln(z_2) \end{bmatrix}$$

$$+ \frac{1}{2} \begin{bmatrix} \ln(x_1) \\ \ln(x_2) \\ \ln(x_3) \\ \ln(z_1) \\ \ln(z_2) \end{bmatrix}' \begin{bmatrix} A_{11} & A_{12} & A_{13} & A_{14} & A_{15} \\ A_{12} & A_{22} & A_{23} & A_{24} & A_{25} \\ A_{13} & A_{23} & A_{33} & A_{34} & A_{35} \\ A_{14} & A_{24} & A_{34} & A_{44} & A_{45} \\ A_{15} & A_{25} & A_{35} & A_{45} & A_{55} \end{bmatrix} \begin{bmatrix} \ln(x_1) \\ \ln(x_2) \\ \ln(x_3) \\ \ln(z_1) \\ \ln(z_2) \end{bmatrix} \tag{8.14}$$

which is typically referred to as the translog production function. The basic question is whether estimating the translog production function to state-level data (e.g., using the means for each state as the observation for each state) yields an adequate representation of the production relationship — it depends on the assumptions.

First, if we were to assume that the level of the unobserved variables is the same across all farms and states, a standard ordinary least squares analysis will yield an acceptable representation of the production relationship regardless of the levels of the unobserved variables which depict the characteristics of the soils. This adequacy is maintained if we introduce a small variation in the unobservable factors if this variation is random and uncorrelated with the controllable and uncontrollable factors of production. Of course as the size of this random component increases, the noise or standard errors of the estimated parameters increase.

A second variation is to assume that the unobserved factors vary by state. For example, suppose that $s^{\mathrm{IL}}_{1j,k}$ for $j = 1, 2, 3, 4$ and $k = 2000, 2001, 2002$ is higher than the similar figures for Indiana and Iowa. This systematic variation will introduce difficulties in estimation. The question is whether we can systematically correct for these difficulties. The answer is — sometimes. A typical approach is to use panel techniques which essentially add a dummy variable for Illinois (e.g., a variable that takes on the value of 1 if the observation is for Illinois and 0 otherwise). Again, this adjustment will still be valid if the individual variation is random — either because the value of the variation for the individual farm is random or if the variation for the farm is fixed, but the farm does or does not produce soybeans in a given year. In this case (the random variation in unobserved factors), we move toward random effects models in panel analysis.

8.2 Non-Normality and the Cost Function

An important question in the empirical estimation of the dual is the distributional assumption of the errors. Akridge (1989) examines the efficiency of agribusiness firms assuming that the residual of the cost function is distributed gamma. However, little attention is given to the effect of this assumption on correlation between the residual for the cost function and the residuals for the derived demand equations. In this section, we follow the formulation for non-normal correlated random variables developed by Ramirez *et al.* (1994).

As a starting point, consider the standard normalized quadratic cost function discussed in detail in Chapter 5. In Chapter 5, we estimated this system of equations by assuming that $\xi \sim N(\mu, \Sigma)$. The implicit construction in Akridge assumes that the non-normal error for the cost function is independent of the residuals of the derived demand equations. Ramirez *et al.* (1994) extend the formulation of Moss and Shonkwiler (1993) as

$$\begin{aligned}
\max_{\alpha_0,\alpha_0,\theta,\mu,\Omega} L &= -\frac{T}{2}\ln|\Omega| - \frac{1}{2}\sum_{t=1}^{T}(z_t-\mu)\Omega^{-1}(z_t-\mu)' \\
&\quad -\frac{1}{2}\sum_{t=1}^{T}\sum_{i=1}^{m}\ln(1+v_{it}^2\theta_i^2) \\
v_{it} &= y_{it} - \alpha_{i0} - \alpha_{i1}t,\ i=1,\ldots,m\ t=1,\ldots,T \\
z_{it} &= \frac{\ln\left(v_{it}\theta_i + \sqrt{1+v_{it}^2\theta_i^2}\right)}{\theta_i} \\
\Omega &= \frac{1}{T}\sum_{t=1}^{T} z_{it}z_{it}'.
\end{aligned} \tag{8.15}$$

To demonstrate the formulation where the residuals of a cost function are potentially correlated non-normal, we start with a normalized quadratic cost function for aggregate production in the United States using the Agricultural Productivity data from the United States Department of Agriculture, Economic Research Service (Ball *et al.*, 2016). Mathematically, we define the cost of agricultural production as a function of the aggregate input of capital, labor, and intermediate inputs. We then normalize by dividing through by the price of intermediate inputs yielding the cost function:

$$\begin{aligned} C^* &= \beta_1 + \beta_2 w_C^* + \beta_3 w_L^* + \frac{1}{2}\beta_4 w_C^* w_C^* + \beta_5 w_C^* w_L^* + \frac{1}{2}\beta_6 w_L^* w_L^* \\ &\quad + \beta_7 Y + \beta_8 Y^2 + \beta_9 w_C^* Y + \beta_{10} w_L^* Y + \xi_1 \\ x_C^* &= \beta_2 + \beta_4 w_C^* + \beta_5 w_L^* + \beta_9 Y + \xi_2 \\ x_L^* &= \beta_3 + \beta_5 w_C^* + \beta_6 w_L^* + \beta_{10} Y + \xi_3 \end{aligned} \tag{8.16}$$

where C^* denotes the cost divided by the price of intermediate inputs, w_C^* denotes the price of capital divided by the price of intermediate inputs, and w_L^* denotes the price of labor divided by the price of intermediate inputs.

We use two different likelihood functions based on this specification. The first likelihood function is the standard multivariate normal likelihood function:

$$\begin{aligned} \ln(L) &= -\frac{T}{2}\ln|\Omega(\theta)| \\ \Omega &= \sum_t^T \begin{bmatrix} \xi_{1t} \\ \xi_{2t} \\ \xi_{3t} \end{bmatrix} \begin{bmatrix} \xi_{2t}\ \xi_{3t}\ \xi_{4t} \end{bmatrix} \end{aligned} \tag{8.17}$$

where the residuals (ξ_{1t}, ξ_{2t}, and ξ_{3t}) are defined in Equation (8.16). The likelihood function for the transformation to normality is then defined as

$$\begin{aligned} \ln(L^*) &= \frac{T}{2}\ln|\Omega(\theta)| - \frac{1}{2}\sum_{t=1}^{T}\ln(\xi_{1t}^2\theta_1^2 + 1) \\ &\quad - \frac{1}{2}\sum_{t=1}^{T}\ln(\xi_{2t}^2\theta_2^2 + 1) - \frac{1}{2}\sum_{t=1}^{T}\ln(\xi_{3t}^2\theta_3^2 + 1) \end{aligned}$$

$$\nu_{1t} = \frac{\ln\left(\xi_{1t}\theta_1 + \sqrt{\xi_{1t}^2\theta_1^2 + 1}\right)}{\theta_1} - \delta_1$$

$$\nu_{2t} = \frac{\ln\left(\xi_{2t}\theta_2 + \sqrt{\xi_{2t}^2\theta_2^2 + 1}\right)}{\theta_2} - \delta_2$$

$$\nu_{3t} = \frac{\ln\left(\xi_{3t}\theta_3 + \sqrt{\xi_{3t}^2\theta_3^2 + 1}\right)}{\theta_3} - \delta_3$$

$$\Omega = \sum_t^T \begin{bmatrix} \nu_{1t} \\ \nu_{2t} \\ \nu_{3t} \end{bmatrix} \begin{bmatrix} \nu_{2t} \; \nu_{3t} \; \nu_{4t} \end{bmatrix} \tag{8.18}$$

where again residuals (ξ_{1t}, ξ_{2t}, and ξ_{3t}) are defined in Equation (8.16).

As a first step, we estimate the cost function under the assumption of normality (i.e., using Equation (8.16)) and compute the skewness, kurtosis, and Jarque–Bera statistics. These estimates are presented in Table 8.2. The residuals for the cost function and capital demand using the normal specification (Equation (8.17)) depart significantly from normality. The cost function appears to be positively skewed, which is consistent with some structural inefficiencies in the data. In addition, the residuals for capital demand appear to be positively skewed. In addition, both the cost function and the capital demand both appear to be leptokurtotic (e.g., the distributions have fatter tails than the normal distribution, which has a kurtosis of 3). Moving to the Jarque–Bera statistics, normality is rejected at any conventional level of confidence. Given these results, we will assume that the residual for the labor demand curve is normally distributed (i.e., $\theta_3 = \delta_3 - 0$).

Table 8.2 Test for Normality of Cost Function Residuals

			Jarque–Bera	
Equation	Skewness	Kurtosis	Statistic	Probability
Cost	1.7623	7.8297	104.2659	0.0000
Capital Demand	1.5624	6.0713	55.9936	0.0000
Labor Demand	0.2917	2.5051	1.7072	0.4259

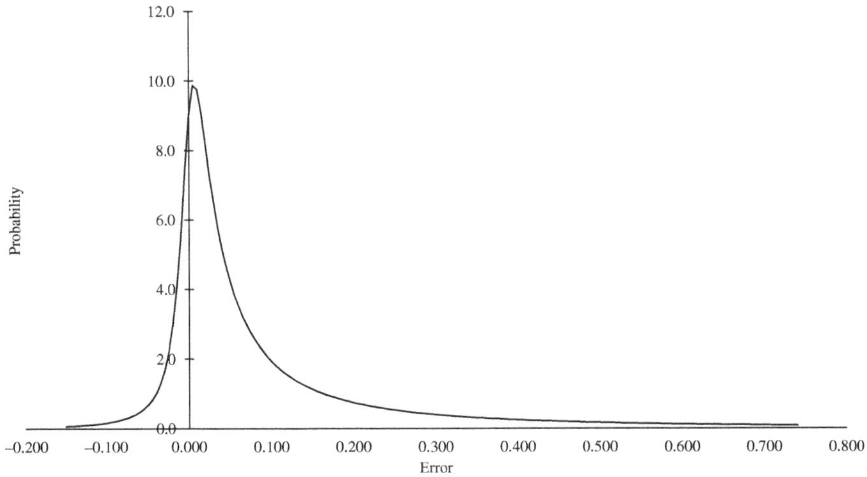

Fig. 8.4 Probability Density Function for Residuals of Cost Function

The estimates for both the normal and non-normal specifications are presented in Table 8.3. The transformation approach allows us to test for non-normality since the likelihood functions are nested (i.e., imposing $\theta_1 = \theta_2 = \delta_1 = \delta_2 = 0$ on Equation (8.18) yields Equation (8.17)). Taking two times the difference in the logarithmic likelihood functions yields a likelihood ratio statistic of 2038.37, which is distributed χ^2_6. Hence, the inverse hyperbolic sine parameters are significant at any conventional confidence level.

The effect of the transformation on the distribution can be seen in the probability density function for the cost function presented in Figure 8.4 and the demand for capital in Figure 8.5.

8.3 Derived Demand for Corn in the Production of Ethanol

Several factors affected the relationship between the corn and ethanol markets in 2020. First, in 2012, the Volumetric Ethanol Excise Tax Credit was replaced with second Renewable Fuel Standard implemented through the Renewable Identification Number system. Second, COVID dramatically affected the demand for gasoline as

Table 8.3 Normalized Quadratic Cost Function for U.S. Agriculture, 1948–2017

α_0	1.133413***	1.551593***
	(0.251311)	(0.444852)
α_1	1.376875***	1.266792***
	(0.022879)	(0.099877)
α_2	2.807216***	2.620314***
	(0.154411)	(0.210004)
A_{11}	−0.033855*	−0.133155***
	(0.019939)	(0.037284)
A_{12}	−0.141232***	−0.168295***
	(0.036575)	(0.055414)
A_{22}	−0.589171***	−0.888724***
	(0.131841)	(0.335471)
β_1	−0.045158	−0.314229
	0.208483	0.312655
B_{11}	0.061847	0.082062**
	(0.037703)	(0.040964)
γ_{11}	−0.056738***	−0.038971
	(0.016278)	(0.025375)
γ_{12}	−0.375379	−0.200384
	(0.063772)	0.155796
θ_1		59.754090
		(51.722930)
δ_1		0.026438
		(0.057515)
θ_2		124.510000***
		(1.409571)
δ_2		0.029516***
		(0.003747)

Notes: [a]Numbers in parenthesis denote standard errors. ***,**,*Denote statistical significance at the 0.01, 0.05, and 0.10 levels of confidence, respectively.

social distancing mandates confined significant numbers of individuals to their homes. Andrew Schmitz and Schmitz (2020) examine several facets of these changes including the derived demand for ethanol in the creation of motor fuel. To this end, Schmitz, Moss, and Schmitz

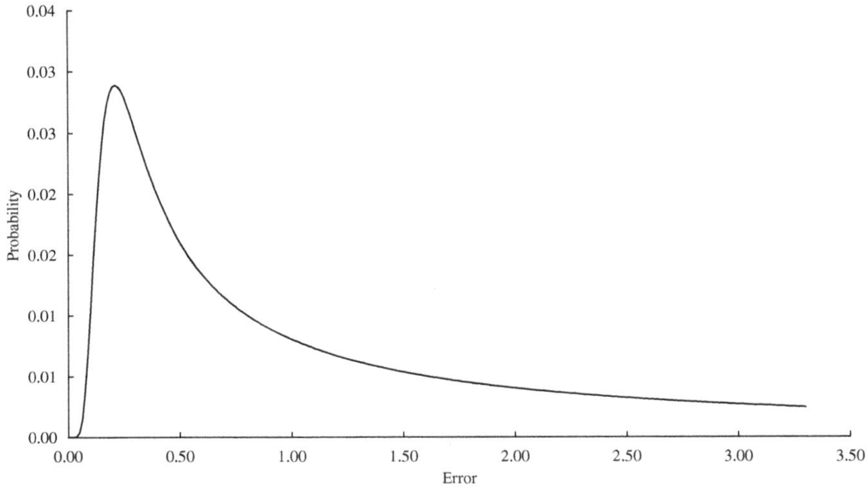

Fig. 8.5 Probability Density Function for Residuals of the Demand for Capital

estimate the derived demand for ethanol using the multiproduct form of the differential supply system.

To estimate the effect of changes in policy on the combination choice between crude oil and ethanol, we start with the general differential multiproduct model formulated by Laitinen (1980) and Laitinen and Theil (1978), as estimated by Suh and Moss (2017) and Moss and Suh (2020). This formulation is based on changes in the first-order conditions of the firm as

$$\begin{aligned}\bar{\gamma}_t \bar{g}_{rt} \Delta \ln(y_{rt}) &= \sum_{s=1}^{n} \alpha_{rs} \left(\Delta \ln(p_s t) - \sum_{i=1}^{m} \theta_i^s \Delta \ln(w_{it}) \right) \\ &\quad + \phi_r \Delta \ln(z_t) + \delta_r D_t \\ \bar{f}_{it} \Delta \ln(x_{it}) &= \bar{\gamma}_t \sum_{r=1}^{n} \theta_i^r \Delta \ln(y_{rt}) + \sum_{i=1}^{m} \pi_{ij} \Delta \ln(w_{jt}) \\ &\quad + \delta_i \ln(z_t) + \delta_i D_t \end{aligned} \tag{8.19}$$

where $\bar{\gamma}_t = \sqrt{R_t R_{t-1}/C_t C_{t-1}}$, R_t is the firm's revenue, C_t is the cost, $\bar{g}_{rt}$ is the average output revenue share (between periods t and $t-1$) for output r, y_{rt} is the output level for output r, p_{rt} is the output price for output r at time t, w_{it} is the input price for input i at time

t, z_t is the level of a quasi-fixed variable at time t, D_t is a dummy variable that is one after the Volumetric Ethanol Excise Tax Credit was allowed to expire, $\bar{f}_{it}$ is the average input share (between periods t and $t-1$) for input i, and x_{it} is the input level for input i at time t.

8.3.1 *Data and Econometric Methods*

To estimate this model, we constructed a dataset of motor fuel, jet fuel, distillates, and residual oil from the Department of Energy. Each of these figures are in thousands of barrels per month. The data on the blended gasoline price, the price of jet fuel, and the price of distillate (largely diesel) are available from the Department of Energy in dollars per gallon. The level of crude oil and ethanol used by the refiners and blenders is taken from the Department of Energy in thousand barrels. In addition, the price of crude oil is taken as the West Texas spot price (in dollars per barrel) while the price of ethanol is taken from the Nebraska Department of Energy in dollars per gallon. The labor quantities and prices are taken from the Bureau of Labor Statistics. The labor prices are the wages per hour for all workers in the refinery sector (34110). The quantity of labor is derived by multiplying hours worked per week into the number of workers in the sector. In addition, we use the refining capacity as a quasi-fixed variable. All prices are deflated using the Personal Consumption Expenditures component of the Implicit Gross Domestic Product deflator from the economic data at the Federal Reserve Bank of St. Louis.

The system of equations in Equation (8.19) are estimated using maximum likelihood, but similar to Moss and Suh, we suspect that the unconstrained estimation may violate concavity. Hence, we impose concavity by constraining the matrix of $[\alpha_{rs}]$ to be convex by restricting the minimum eigenvalue of the matrix to be positive. Similarly, we constrain the maximum of the $[\pi_{ij}]$ matrix to be negative.

8.3.2 *Results*

The estimated parameters for the multiproduct differential model are presented in Table 8.4. The results indicate that the demand for crude oil increases significantly as the production of blended gasoline increases ($\theta^M_{CO}F$). In addition, while the quantity of ethanol

Table 8.4 Estimated Parameters for Multiproduct Formulation for Refineries

Parameter	Estimate	Parameter	Estimate
θ_{CO}^{MF}	0.21698*** (0.04989)[a]	$\alpha_{JF,DF}$	−0.02445 (0.0196)
θ_{CO}^{JF}	−0.12456 (0.08425)	$\alpha_{DF,DF}$	0.08611** (0.03851)
θ_{CO}^{DF}	0.15546 (0.16201)	ϕ_{CO}	−0.31811 (0.54143)
θ_{ET}^{MF}	0.00064 (0.00025)	ϕ_{ET}	−0.00352 (0.00455)
θ_{MF}^{JF}	−0.00039 0.00067	ϕ_{MF}	0.10684 (0.14387)
θ_{ET}^{DF}	0.00028 0.00076	ϕ_{JF}	−0.05487 (0.09291)
$\pi_{CO,CO}$	−0.00046 (0.00187)	ϕ_{DF}	−0.38328 (0.42513)
$\pi_{CO,ET}$	0.00012 (0.0001)	δ_{CO}	−0.00024 (0.00526)
$\pi_{ET,ET}$	−0.00003 (0.00008)	δ_{ET}	0.00000 (0.00002)
$\alpha_{MF,MF}$	0.00765 (0.00664)	δ_{MF}	−0.00039 (0.00058)
$\alpha_{MF,JF}$	0.00943 (0.00719)	δ_{JF}	−0.00005 (0.00082)
$\alpha_{MF,DF}$	0.00701 (0.01161)	δ_{DF}	−0.00025 (0.00268)
$\alpha_{JF,JF}$	0.02537 (0.01977)		

Notes: [a]Numbers in parenthesis denote standard errors. ***,**Denote statistical significance at the 0.01 and 0.05 level of confidence, respectively.

demanded increases with an increase in blended gasoline (θ_{ET}^{MF}), this effect is not statistically significant at any traditional confidence interval. From the output choice parameters, the amount of blended motor fuel increases with an increase in the price of blended motor fuel ($\alpha_{MF,MF}$). However, there appears to be only one substitution

Table 8.5 Estimated Elasticities for Multiproduct Formulation for Refineries

Parameter	Estimate	Parameter	Estimate
$\xi_{MF,MF}$	0.03654 (0.03099)[a]	$\zeta_{CO,JF}$	−0.01637 (0.01106)
$\xi_{MF,JF}$	0.08407 (0.06414)	$\zeta_{CO,DF}$	0.06459 (0.06734)
$\xi_{MF,DF}$	0.01980 (0.03281)	$\zeta_{ET,MF}$	0.05712** (0.02221)
$\xi_{JF,MF}$	0.04505 (0.0343)	$zeta_{ET,JF}$	−0.01889 (0.03185)
$\xi_{JF,JF}$	0.2263 (0.17659)	$\zeta_{ET,DF}$	0.04307 (0.11528)
$\xi_{JF,DF}$	−0.0690 (0.05551)	$\eta_{CO,CO}$	−0.00054 (0.00219)
$\xi_{DF,MF}$	0.03352 (0.05527)	$\eta_{CO,ET}$	0.00014 (0.00012)
$\xi_{DF,JF}$	0.21809 (0.1751)	$\eta_{ET,CO}$	0.05115 (0.04215)
$\xi_{DF,DF}$	0.25053*** (0.10214)	$\eta_{ET,ET}$	−0.01315 (0.03239)
$\zeta_{CO,MF}$	0.05324*** (0.01235)		

Notes: [a]Numbers in parenthesis denote standard errors. ***,**Denote statistical significance at the 0.01 and 0.05 level of confidence, respectively.

relationship (i.e., only one of α_{rs} is negative). This may be the result of a fixed-proportion output structure. For example, there may be little that a refinery can do to change the proportion of products produced from a barrel of crude. The exception is for the negative coefficient for the choice between jet fuel and distillate fuel (e.g., diesel). The results also indicate that changes in the capacity of refineries in the United States has little effect on the production of output or the input demands. Further, the expiration of the Volumetric Ethanol Excise Tax Credit is not significant at any conventional confidence level.

Turning to the estimated elasticities in Table 8.5, the two elasticities most relevant in our discussion are statistically significant. Specifically, the elasticity of crude oil production with respect to an increase in the price of blended motor fuel is 0.05324 while the elasticity of ethanol demand with respect to an increase in the price of blended motor fuel is 0.05712. However, the estimated demand elasticity of the quantity of crude oil demand is negative, but not statistically significant at any conventional confidence level. Similarly, the elasticity of demand for ethanol is negative, but not statistically significant. Further, the cross-price elasticity indicates that the quantity of crude oil demanded is rather inelastic with respect a change in ethanol prices while the price of ethanol is inelastic, but somewhat more responsive, with respect to changes in crude oil prices.

8.4 Chapter Summary

- This chapter presents three working topics that I am interested in. The first working topic involves the nature of soils in production. Specifically, the observed production is a function of observable variables such as seeding rate and fertilizer applied. These variables are under the control of the farmer. However, other factors such as rainfall are not under the control of the decision maker. Finally, there is a set of variables that are not "chosen" in the classical sense of the word. In this case, I am thinking about the fertility of the soil which is determined by past farming practices and the parent material of the soil. My question is how to appropriately adjust for these characteristics.
- The second topic involves the potential non-normality of residuals in a dual cost system. Many of the classic adjustments for this possibility involve using a non-normal specification for the cost function and then assuming that this random variable is uncorrelated with the other errors (i.e., the errors in the demand equations). My solution is to use a general transformation to normality called the inverse hyperbolic sine function. This allows the residuals of the cost function to be non-normal while remaining correlated with the residuals in the derived demand equations.

- The last topic involves the extension of the multivariate differential system to fuel refineries. In this case, we consider a refinery producing three outputs: motor fuel (consumer gasoline), jet fuel, and diesel. These refineries use three major inputs: crude oil, ethanol, and labor. The parameters estimated in this model are then used to compute producer surplus in Andrew Schmitz and Schmitz (2020). The complicating fact in this analysis is that the demand for motor fuel experienced a significant change as COVID spread through the U.S. population.

Chapter 9

Conclusions and Suggestions for Further Research

This book has focused on the economics of the decision-making process. Specifically, we developed a variety of models of producer's decision-making problem. In Chapter 1, we developed the primal approach where the decision maker's problem is analyzed based on the technological envelope or production function. In Chapter 4, we developed the dual model where the decision maker's choices are directly observed. The primary concept was that under certain conditions, a model of economic behavior consistent with an underlying technology and the optimal decisions of the producer can be estimated. Chapter 6 demonstrates how these representations (e.g., primal and dual) are affected by changes in technology and efficiency. Chapter 7 presents the estimation of economic behavior within the differential framework. Other chapters showed how empirical analysis based on these theoretical models could be used to estimate producer behavior. In each case, the issue at hand was economic behavior.

To complete our discussion, this chapter reviews several current modes of examining production decisions. First, we review literature that basically subsumes much of the behavior that we examined in the book into a time trend. Most of these efforts are primarily interested in the valuation of insurance products and the possible effect of climate change. Next, we look at some research that explicitly uses production functions to address several issues, including the shape of the production function around the maximum output. Finally, we conclude with recent literature into potential failures of some of the models we have developed.

9.1 Reduction of the Production Decisions to Time

In the past 20 years, there has been a significant growth in research that examines the effect of weather and climate on production. Much of this literature resulted from the growth in insurance programs in the United States and other countries. Schmitz *et al.* (2010, pp. 222–227) develops the history of crop insurance in Canada and the United States. From one perspective, the growth in crop insurance can be seen as an effort to replace *ad hoc* disaster payments with market-based insurance products. Specifically, the *ad hoc* disaster payments represented free insurance which were basically transfers to the farm sector. This transfer subsidized farmers, encouraging risky behavior (possibly by crop selection). A second possibility is a general move from implicit price insurance policies (in the guise of loan rates and deficiency payments) to programs that are clearly insurance programs with a different name (such as Agricultural Risk Coverage). These changes occurred in other program areas such as the dairy sector were traditional market supports were replaced with the Dairy Margin Protection program.

Moving to market-based crop insurance programs then led to an endogenization of these costs, several issues were raised with this development, including moral hazard. One of the most vexing problems, however, involved the estimation of the yield distributions. Stepping back to Chapter 2, consider a slight modification to the Just and Pope production function in Equation (2.73):

$$y_t = f(x_t, z_t, \alpha) + h(x_t, z_t, \beta)\epsilon_t \tag{9.1}$$

where y_t is the level of output, x_t are controlled inputs, x_t are the set of controlled inputs, and z_t is a set of inputs beyond the control of the decision maker. Suppose that we normalize the input prices by dividing by the output price. Under these assumptions, the firm's profit maximization problem becomes

$$\max_x((f(x_t, z_t, \alpha) + h(x_t, z_t, \beta)\epsilon_t) - w'x_t. \tag{9.2}$$

In this formulation, the level of variable inputs x_t is conditional on the level of uncontrollable variables z_t. Assuming that the expected value of ϵ_t is zero, the derived demand for the variable or controllable inputs is a function of the expected value of the uncontrollable inputs:

$$x_t^* = x(w_t^*, \mathrm{E}[z_t]). \tag{9.3}$$

The observed level of production is a function of the observed values of z_t conditional on these decisions:

$$y_t^* = f(x_t^*(w_t^*, \mathrm{E}[z_t]), z_t, \alpha) + h(x_t^*(w_t^*, \mathrm{E}[z_t]), z_t, \beta)\epsilon_t. \tag{9.4}$$

The specification in Equation (9.4) raises several difficulties. One of the biggest problems is that input and output prices are not observed in the data. Specifically, many of these papers estimate output at the county or individual level.

Given these difficulties, these articles replace the optimal choice of inputs with a time variable:

$$y_{it} = \gamma_{1t} + \gamma_{2i} + h\left(\gamma_{3it}, z_t, \beta\right)\epsilon_t \tag{9.5}$$

where γ_{1t} is a time component and $gamma_{2i}$ is an individual component. These research efforts are interested in the characteristics of $h\left(\gamma_{3it}, z_t, \beta\right)$. Some of my early works follow this concept. Specifically, Moss and Shonkwiler (1993) uses a stochastic trend model in place of γ_{1t} and estimates $h(\gamma_{3it}, z_t, \beta)$ using an inverse hyperbolic sine transformation.

To provide a brief review of some of this research, we start with the formulation in Ker and Coble (2003), where yield is modeled as a one-knot spline:

$$\begin{aligned} y_t = \alpha &+ \beta_1[tI_{(0,\delta)}(t) + \delta(1 - I_{(0,\delta)}(t))] \\ &+ \beta_2[1 - I_{(0,\delta)}(t)][t - \delta I_{(0,\delta)}(t)] + \epsilon \end{aligned} \tag{9.6}$$

where δ is a knot point in time. Ker and Coble estimate this formulation using ordinary least squares to derive the residuals (i.e., $h(\gamma_{3it}, z_t, \beta)$ in Equation (9.5). They then use a variety of methodologies to estimate the distribution of the residual. These distributions are then used to estimate differences in insurance prices. Ker and Tolhurst (2019) use a similar specification to estimate changes in heteroscedasticity over time.

Apart from the emphasis on crop insurance, similar models have been estimated to examine the effect of climate change or temperatures on yields. Ruiqing Miao and Huang (2015) develop a model that includes output prices and lagged fertilizer prices to estimate the effect of temperature deviations in yields. Most recently, Metaxoglou and Smith (2020) estimates the effect of NOx on corn and soybean yields. This formulation uses a county-level constant (α_c). Finally, Ramsey (2020) uses a more Bayesian quantile regression formulation to estimate crop distributions. In this application, the author uses a normalized time trend variable with precipitation variables to estimate the distribution of corn and soybean distributions.

9.2 Estimating the Production Function

Most of the production functions developed in Chapter 1 are continuous in the second moments. However, several studies have adopted a linear response plateau model. Gleson Tembo and Tostao (2008) formulate production as a function of a single input:

$$y_{it} = \min\left(\beta_0 + \beta b_1 x_{it} + \kappa_{it}, \mu_m + \omega_{it}\right). \tag{9.7}$$

In this formulation, there is a linear response $y_{it} = \beta_0 + \beta_1 x_{it}$ up to a stochastic point (i.e., κ_{it}) after which the level of input does not affect the output level. This specification leads to two optimal levels of input $x^* = 0$ or (if $\beta_1 \geq w^*$) $x^* = x_{it}$. What are the gains to this formulation? The greatest advantage is robustness of fertilizer recommendations. For example, if the goal of estimating the production function is to make fertilizer recommendations, the fertilizer recommendation under this specification does not change unless the price of the crop drops dramatically.

In a somewhat more general specification, Moeltner *et al.* (2021) start with the specification

$$y_t = \min\left(x'_{1t}\beta_1, x'_{2t}\beta_2 + \cdots x'_{Gi}\beta_G, P\right) \tag{9.8}$$

where x_{jt} is a specific input. This specification addresses a question raised by formulation in Equation (9.7); specifically, if x_{it} is fertilizer, is it nitrogen, phosphorous, or potash? Maybe it is a blended fertilizer. In any case, the specification in Equation (9.8) implies no substitution between inputs.

The basic question with either specification is whether it represents the production technology. We can obtain many of these properties — a plateau production function with no substitution between inputs can be found in Mitscherlich–Baule specification.

A second change in a specification covered in this textbook involves an innovation in the estimation of stochastic frontier models. The innovation involves the application of simulated maximum likelihood. Bravo-Ureta *et al.* (2020) formulate a standard stochastic production function

$$y_{it} = \beta' x_{it} + v_{it} - u_{it} \tag{9.9}$$

where v_{it} is a normal distribution and v_{it} is a half-normal distribution. Additional complications involving a selection formulation are then layered on the formulation. Not to complicate the formulation excessively, but consider the formulation

$$\begin{aligned}\ln(L) = d_i &\left[\exp\left(-\frac{1}{2}\left(y_it - \beta' x_{it} + U_{it}\right)^2 / \sigma_v^2\right)\right.\\ &\left.\times \Phi\left(\frac{\rho\left(y_{it} - \beta' x_{it} + U_{it}\right)/\sigma_\epsilon + a_i}{\sqrt{1-\rho^2}}\right)\right] + (1 - d_i)\,\Phi(-a_i).\end{aligned} \tag{9.10}$$

I recognize the complexity of the formulation in Equation (9.10). Focusing on the general form, $\exp((y - f(x))^2/sigma) \times \Phi(\rho(y - f(x))/sqrt1 - \rho^2)$ is a fairly standard selection specification. The real complication comes in the integration of the U_{it} term (the composite error). The innovation in this approach is the result of integration by simulation instead of the tortured integration approaches applied in the text. In this case, Bravo-Ureta *et al.* specify

$$\begin{aligned}\hat{f}_U = \exp&\left(-\frac{1}{2}\frac{\left(y_{it} - \beta' x_{it} + U_{it}\right)^2 / \sigma_v^2}{\sigma_v\sqrt{2\pi}}\right)\\ &\times \Phi\left(\rho\left(\frac{(y_{it} - \beta' x_{it} + U_{it})/\sigma_v + a_i}{\sqrt{1-\rho^2}}\right)\right).\end{aligned} \tag{9.11}$$

The concept is once the values of the parameters have been chosen (i.e., the β and the parameters inside U_{it}), the integral of the U_{it} function can be accomplished by drawing from the implied distribution function for U_{it}. This draw yields the value of the likelihood function $\hat{f}(U)$. The expected value of the likelihood function is then $\hat{B}_U = \sum_{k=1}^{K} \hat{f}(U)/K$. The simulated maximum likelihood result is the one that maximizes $\hat{B}_U$. Another interesting point is that the data for Bravo-Ureta *et al.* (2020) are from a randomized control trial.

9.3 Misspecification of the Dual

A final set of literature that I would like to draw the student's attention to is an emerging set of literature involving difficulties with the dual. Starting with Rosas and Lence (2019), the question is how well the dual estimation process returns the underlying production relationship. Rosa and Lence begin their discussion with a quotation from Shumway:

> According to Shumway (1995), attractive features of the dual approach include the facts that (a) no system of first-order equations has to be solved to obtain input (output) demands (supplies); (b) more functional forms can be used; (c) it is less prone to computational errors; (d) it requires data that are usually easier to obtain; and (e) it is more accurate and tractable for multi-output technologies (Rosas and Lence, 2019, p. 825).

After this somewhat glowing recommendation, they cite the classical difficulties with concavity and the multicollinearity of prices. Base on this framework, Rosa and Lence lay out a strategy for testing the reliability of the dual function.

To test the reliability of the dual, Rosa and Lence start by modeling the producer's choice of inputs and outputs based on expected utility (i.e., $\max_y \mathrm{E}[U(W_0 + p'y + G(y, K; \alpha))]$) where $G(y, K; \alpha)$ is a pre-specified production function. Under duality, there is a relationship between the production function $G(y, K; \alpha)$ and the profit function $\pi_k\,(p, K; \beta)$. Rosa and Lence then generate datasets using among other things the USDA/ERS's productivity data (Wang *et al.*, 2020). The concept is to start without additional noise and then add shocks to expected prices and quantity variables, omitting variables and aggregating across input and output variables.

Rosa and Lence's results indicate that the "noiseless" simulations do a good job recovering the elasticities with respect to input and output prices. However, adding additional complications such as aggregation of inputs and outputs and/or the omission of variables yield dramatic difference in the estimated elasticities "difference ranges between 6% and 690%, and is less than 18% in only once entry (Rosas and Lence, 2019, p. 835)." The take-home message appears to be that the adequacy of the specification of the dual is very sensitive to a variety of factors. Most troublesome is the fact that when we estimate the dual, we have few empirical cues that the specification is inadequate. One of the most obvious errors is probably the difficulties with the concavity restrictions. This raises the question whether you should impose concavity or search for a better specification. One clue as to the appropriate approach may be the difficulty in imposing concavity. Specifically, if concavity is rejected (e.g., the Lagrange multiplier of the concavity equation is statistically significant), the data may be suggesting that the specification is inadequate.

Plastina and Lence (2019) examine whether a production function estimated from the state-level productivity data obeys the classical regularity conditions. They are particularly focused on monotonicity and concavity. To examine this possibility, they estimate a quadratic production including a time trend and autoregressive parameter. To increase the power of their estimation, they estimate a logarithmic form of a derived demand function for each input. Their unconstrained results (i.e., without monotonicity or concavity restrictions) yield an estimated quadratic parameter for land greater than zero (i.e., $\beta_{LL} \gg 0$ at a 95% confidence level). This is noted as evidence that estimated relationship fails classical regularity conditions — the function is not concave in land. Granted that their results indicate that this implies that the aggregate production function does not obey regularity conditions, I would like to suggest that in the case of farmland, there may be a reason to suspect these regularity conditions. Specifically, we all agree that the production function itself is devoid of economic content. There is no reason for a production function to be concave. We impose concavity because it is required for economic decisions. If the production function is not concave, we cannot derive an optimal level of inputs. My problem with the conclusion that the lack of concavity in price invalidates the production function is that land may be constrained — it may not be part of the profit problem *per se*.

9.4 Final Thoughts

It is my experience that students spend a lot of time taking classes like production economics. In these classes, they learn about theoretical and empirical innovations. With this experience, they think that the goal of economic analysis is to achieve a similar advancement. However, significant advancements are few and far between. The only novel applications that I will claim are the inverse hyperbolic sine mapping to normality (Moss and Shonkwiler, 1993) and the introduction of quasi-fixed variables into the multiproduct differential model of the firm (Livanis and Moss, 2006). In each of these cases, I benefited from brilliant collaborators. While it is a great feeling to produce a new or novel approach, I believe that the real goal is to use the techniques in this book to answer policy-relevant questions. For example, Moss and Suh (2020) use the differential model to examine whether agricultural banks were adversely affected by Dodd–Frank (legislation that intended to make the banking system more secure, but imposed additional compliance cost). Hence, I believe that the goal in most cases is to identify an important or at least interesting economic problem. In the case of production economics, the problem should involve some degree of producer choice. Given this problem, the next step is to identify the appropriate technique. It is somewhat incongruous to select the technique first and then try to identify a problem which fits it. In the past, this has led me to various degrees of frustration. The choice of technique will take the potential data sources into account. Given the selection of a problem, technique and potential data, the defined problem may require a novel approach. If it does, do the novel. The goal is to answer an economic question. In the 1990s, I was honored to work with Henri Theil (an internationally known econometrician). Henri is the only person I have worked with, who would choose an economic question to prove an econometric point.

Appendix A

Closed-Form Solutions

Most students have been introduced to the concept of a closed-form solution at the very outset of first algebra course. For example, an early problem may have been specified as

$$x = 5 + 3y \tag{A.1}$$

where the student is asked to give the value of y where $x = 5$. Using almost trivial mechanics,

$$y = \frac{x-5}{3} \Rightarrow y = 0. \tag{A.2}$$

Slightly later that month, the student is probably asked to solve the general form of the problem

$$x = a + by \Rightarrow y = \frac{x-a}{b} \ni: b \neq 0. \tag{A.3}$$

Hence, Equation (A.3) implies that a series of simple algebraic steps (i.e., addition, subtraction, division and multiplication) yields a simple *generalizable* solution to the original problem. A related concept is the idea of *tractable* — problems are tractable if they can be solved for closed-form solutions.

A.1 Polynomials

To extend the concept a little further, consider the basic algebraic question that most students solve before high school — find the values of x that solves

$$ax^2 + bx + c = 0 \tag{A.4}$$

(or solve the quadratic equation). The path is easily trodden. First, we solve c to the other side of the zero and divide through by a to yield

$$x^2 + \frac{b}{a}x = -\frac{c}{a}. \tag{A.5}$$

From the solution in Equation (A.5), it is easy to conceptualize a perfect square

$$x^2 + \frac{b}{a}x + \frac{b^2}{4a^2}. \tag{A.6}$$

Thus, we add $b^2/4a^2$ to both sides of Equation (A.5) to yield

$$x^2 + \frac{b}{a}x + \frac{b^2}{4a^2} = \frac{b^2}{4a^2} - \frac{c}{a}. \tag{A.7}$$

Solving for a common denominator on the left-hand side of Equation (A.7),

$$\left(a + \frac{b}{2a}\right)^2 = \frac{b^2 - 4ac}{4a^2}. \tag{A.8}$$

Taking the square root of both sides of Equation (A.9),

$$x + \frac{b}{2a} = \pm\frac{\sqrt{b^2 - 4ac}}{2a} \tag{A.9}$$

which yields the standard quadratic equation that we have all come to know and love:

$$x = \frac{-b^2 \pm \sqrt{b^2 - 4ac}}{2a}. \tag{A.10}$$

This solution has a certain simple certitude about it. For any set of a, b, and c, the equation will either give a real result or an imaginary result (i.e., if the number under the radical is negative). Another way to look at the concept is that Equation (A.10) provides a finite list of basic algebraic operations that yields an answer (either real or imaginary).

The simplicity of the quadratic and basic straightforward nature of the solution might lead the student to think that higher order solutions are possible. In fact, the cubic equation

$$x^3 + ax^2 + bx + c = 0 \tag{A.11}$$

has a solution typically attributed to Gerolamo Cardono (1501–1576) (Weisstein, 2015). A similar solution exists for a fourth-order polynomial, but the Abel–Ruffini theorem states that no algebraic solutions exist for polynomial equations of five degrees or higher. Stated slightly differently, an algebraic solution for a fifth or higher order polynomial with arbitrary coefficients does not exist by the Abel–Ruffini theorem. Special cases may exist, or certain sets of restrictions on parameters may produce algebraic solutions, but the general form akin to the quadratic formula in Equation (A.10) does not exist.

Does this fact limit our ability to work with these more general functions? The answer is somewhat complex. Appendix B presents a variety of numerical techniques that can be used to maximize highly nonlinear systems. These maximization approaches typically involve finding the zeros (i.e., solving for the zeros) of the derivatives of the objective function. Hence, the researcher's ability to solve an equation analytically does not necessarily limit his or her ability to use a particular function. Further, most of the time in production economics, we are interested in the derivative of a function at some value (i.e., we may be interested in the marginal product of a production function or the elasticity of a derived demand curve). Thus, the process is to solve for the profit-maximizing point numerically and then to take the derivative of the production function at that point (e.g., in the primal approach).

The downside is a matter of parameters as conventions. One of the most common approaches to production has been to estimate a closed-form production function (e.g., a production surface that can be written as a Cobb–Douglas or quadratic) and then to use these parameters to test an economic assumption such as concavity or develop a policy model such as a supply function. In this scenario, the academic discussion typically focuses on the characteristics of the parameters (i.e., are all the parameters of the Cobb–Douglas specification positive and do they sum to one?). If instead of a traditional parameterization (or closed-form formulation), a more general functional mapping was used, the academic acceptability may be less general.

Appendix B

Numerical Approximations and Methods

B.1 Approximating a Production Function with a Quadratic

By this point in an economist's training, the Taylor series approximation has become second nature. From a univariate perspective, the general form of the Taylor series expansion can be written as

$$f(x) = f(x_0) + \left.\frac{\partial f(x)}{\partial x}\right|_{x=x_0}(x - x_0) + \frac{1}{2!}\left.\frac{\partial^2 f(x)}{\partial x^2}\right|_{x=x_0}(x - x_0)^2$$
$$+\frac{1}{k!}\left.\frac{\partial^k f(x)}{\partial x^k}\right|_{x=x_0}(x - x_0)^k + \frac{1}{(k+1)!}\left.\frac{\partial^{k+1} f(x)}{\partial x^{k+1}}\right|_{x=x_0}$$
$$\times (x - x^*)^{k+1} \tag{B.1}$$

for some $x^* \in [x, x_0]$. Thus, in its most general form, the Taylor series is not an approximation, but an equality for some x^* which is unknown. The use of the Taylor series as an approximation result is due to the assumption that all the derivatives higher than order k are equal to zero (i.e., truncating the approximation). The error in the approximation is then

$$\varepsilon(x, x_0) = \frac{1}{(k+1)!}\left.\frac{\partial^k + 1 f(x)}{\partial x^{k+1}}\right|_{x=x_0} = 0. \tag{B.2}$$

The implicit assumption is that the higher order derivatives are "small" or that x^* is relatively close to the point of approximation.

In most econometric applications, we limit our focus to the second-order Taylor series expansion (or approximation), as depicted in matrix form in Equation (1.19). There are two primary reasons for this restriction. First, the second-order approximation in Equation (1.19) is consistent with the simple matrix form for the multivariate production function. Second, the quadratic formulation is consistent with the derivation of classical optimization conditions (Gill *et al.*, 1981).

Apart from other applications, one useful application of the Taylor series expansion is to create a quadratic approximation of a more general function form. Specifically, we can derive a quadratic approximation for the Transcendental production function. Specifically, using the Transcendental production function estimated by Mohaddes and Mazhari (2008)

$$f(x) = e^{6.94} x_1^{0.55} e^{-0.00000143 x_1} x_2^{0.43} e^{0.00000705 x_2} \tag{B.3}$$

which is depicted graphically in Figure B.1. To derive a second-order approximation to this function, we first take the first and second derivatives around some point of approximation (say $x_1 = 50$ and

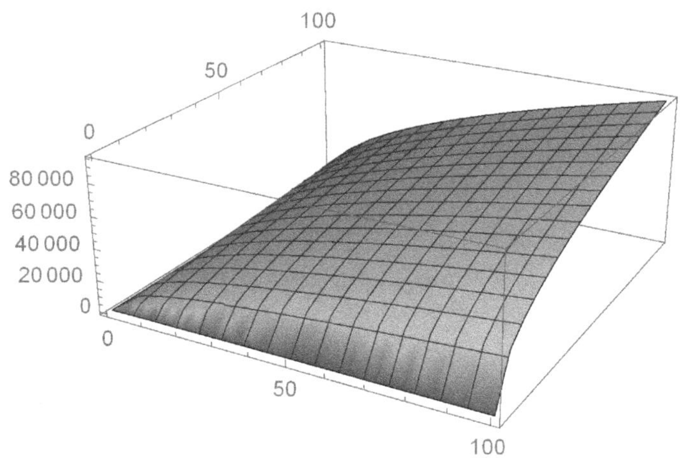

Fig. B.1 Transcendental Production Function with Two Inputs

$x_2 = 50$). Starting with the first-order derivatives,

$$
\begin{aligned}
f_1 = \frac{\partial f(x_1, x_2)}{\partial x_1} &= \frac{568.024 e^{-0.00000143 x_1 + 0.00000705 x_2} x_2^{0.43}}{x_1^{0.45}} \\
&\quad - 0.00147686 e^{-0.00000143 x_1 + 0.00000705 x_2} x_1^{0.55} x_2^{0.43} = 525.355 \\
f_2 = \frac{\partial f(x_1, x_2)}{\partial x_2} &= \frac{444.091 e^{-0.00000143 x_1 + 0.00000705 x_2} x_1^{0.55}}{x_2^{0.57}} \\
&\quad + 0.00728103 e^{-0.00000143 x_1 + 0.00000705 x_2} x_1^{0.55} x_2^{0.43} = 411.122.
\end{aligned}
\tag{B.4}
$$

The analytical solutions of the second derivatives are cumbersome, but the matrix of second derivatives can be expressed as

$$
\begin{bmatrix} f_{11} & f_{12} \\ f_{21} & f_{22} \end{bmatrix} = \begin{bmatrix} -4.73031 & 4.52175 \\ 4.52175 & -4.67716 \end{bmatrix}. \tag{B.5}
$$

B.2 A Quick Primer on Numeric Optimization

The real workhorse in our development of applied optimality is the Taylor series expansion. First, some terminology. Let us begin by assuming that there exists a univariate function $f(x)$ defined over a given range $x \in [x_0, x_1]$. x^* is defined as a strong local minimum if $f(x^*) < f(x)$ for all $x \in N(x^*, \delta)$, $x \neq x^*$. x^* is a weak local minimum if $f(x^*) \leq f(x)$ for all $x \in N(x^*, \delta)$, $x \neq x^*$. However, local optimals are not sufficient, i.e., additional assumptions are required to guarantee that local optimal are also global.

Next, we derive the conditions for optimality from Taylor series. First, note that the value of the function $f(x)$ can be derived for any point $x \in N(x^*, \delta)$ using the Taylor series expansion of that function from the point x^* ($f(x^*)$):

$$
f(x) = f(x^*) + f'(x^*)(x - x^*) + \frac{1}{2} f''(x^*)(x - x^*)^2 + R_3. \tag{B.6}
$$

Assuming that $R_3 \to 0$ as $\delta \to 0$ and rearranging, we have

$$
f(x) - f(x^*) = f'(x^*)(x - x^*) + \frac{1}{2} f''(x^*)(x - x^*)^2 \tag{B.7}
$$

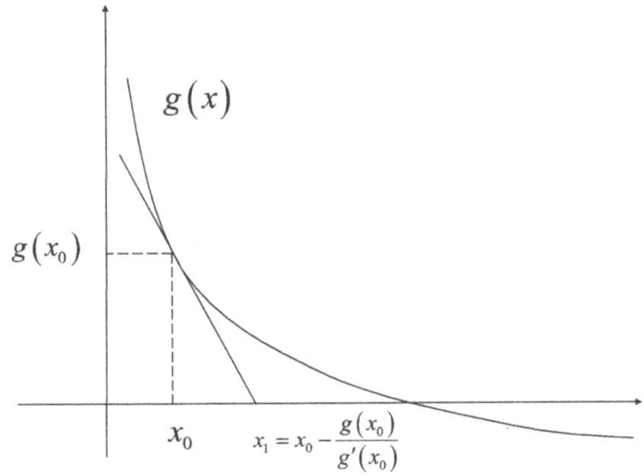

Fig. B.2 Inscribed Triangles in Newton Algorithm

If $f(x^*) < f(x)$ for all $x \in N(x^*)$, then $f(x) - f(x^*) > 0$ for $x \in N(x^*)$. Thus, if x^* is a strong local minimum, then

$$f'(x^*)(x - x^*) + \frac{1}{2}f''(x^*)(x - x^*)^2 > 0. \tag{B.8}$$

Given that $x \in N(x^*)$ is a two-sided concept $(x - x^*) \gtrless 0$. Thus, as $x \to x^*$ from the left, $f'(x) \leq 0$. Similarly, if $x \to x^*$ from the right, $f'(x) \geq 0$. If the first derivative is smooth, these conditions imply that $f'(x^*) = 0$ in order for the derivative to switch from negative to positive at x^*. In addition, if the first derivative is smooth so that the derivative switches from negative to positive, $f''(x^*) > 0$ for $x \in N(x^*)$.

Based on these general concepts, numerical optimization routines are typically developed to search for the point where the gradient of the objective function is zero ($f'(x) = 0$). The most common search algorithm used for this search is the Newton process. Specifically, a Newton algorithm is designed to search for a solution to an equation. In the case of optimality, we are designing an algorithm to search for the value of the variable that makes the gradient zero. As a starting point, consider the first-order expansion of a general function $g(x)$:

$$g(x) \approx g(x_0) + g'(x_0)(x - x_0). \tag{B.9}$$

Next, we set $g(x) = 0$ and solve for the value of x:

$$x - x_0 = -\frac{g(x_0)}{g'(x_0)}$$

$$x = x_0 - \frac{g(x_0)}{g'(x_0)}. \tag{B.10}$$

The process implicitly solves a series of inscribed triangles, as depicted in Figure B.2.

Returning to the original maximization problem, suppose we want to maximize the function $f(x)$. We would define the gradient matrix $\nabla_x f(x)$. The numeric approach would be to find the zeros of this gradient matrix using the Newton algorithm:

$$x = x_0 - \left[\nabla^2_{xx} f(x)\right]^{-1} \nabla_x f(x). \tag{B.11}$$

Empirical implementation has largely focused on the replacement of the Hessian matrix with a conjugate value — a value that is built up based on the changes in the gradient.

Glossary

Average physical product: The total physical product divided by the number of units used — the output per unit of input.

Corner solutions: A corner solution refers to a solution on the bounds of a set. In production economics, the corner solution is a solution at one of the axes — a zero level for one of the inputs.

Diminishing rate of technical substitution: The concept that as more input is added, more input is required to keep output on the same level set.

Dual: Dual or duality in mathematical programming typically refers to the fact that the Lagrange multipliers in one formulation can be used as variables in an equivalent formulation. The resource constraints in a minimization problem infer values in an equivalent maximization problem. In economics, duality typically refers to the concept that the frontier in a primal formulation can be derived from a formulation that directly models economic behavior.

Elasticity of substitution: The percent change in one input that is required to keep output constant as another input level is changed.

Free disposal: The assumption that excess input can be disposed of without cost. This assumption is suspect in agricultural production functions. If too much fertilizer is added, it could negatively impact production.

Gradient: A stacked vector of first derivatives.

Input requirement sets: The set of input combinations that produce at least a fixed level of output $V(y)$.

Isoclines: The set of points that have the same rate of technical substitution.

Isoquant: The locus of inputs that yield the same level of output.

Law of variable proportions The concept that if one input is increased at a constant rate with all the other factors of production held constant, the incremental increase in output will decline.

Marginal physical product: The change in physical associated with the change in the level of input.

Microeconomics: The economic study of decisions of individuals — households and firms.

Primal: The production approach where the researcher starts by estimating a technical relationship and then using an economic formulation to infer economic behavior.

Production function: The technical relationship between inputs and outputs.

Rate of technical substitution: The rate at which one input must be traded for another such that the level of output remains unchanged.

Ray average product: The output level divided by the level of input for each input — essentially the average product for a ray originating at the origin.

Ray marginal product: The change in the production surface along the ray originating at the origin.

Ridgelines: The locus of points that bound the feasible region of production — the points where the rate of technical substitution is zero or infinity.

Sigmoid-shaped: sigmoid refers to an "s-shaped" curve where the function starts by increasing at an increasing rate up until an infection point where it increases at a decreasing rate. Finally, the curve reaches a maximum after which it starts to decline.

Total physical product: The total output result from the use of a given level of input.

Young's theorem: The theory that states that the second cross-derivatives are the same for continuous functions — $\partial^2 f(x_1, x_2)/\partial x_1 \partial x_2 = \partial^2 f(x_1, x_2)/\partial x_2 \partial x_1$.

References

Afriat, S. (1972). Efficiency estimation and production functions, *International Economic Review* **13**, 3, pp. 568–598, doi:10.2307/2525845, http://www.jstor.org/stable/252584.

Aigner, D., Lovell, C., and Schmidt, P. (1977). Formulation and estimating of stochastic frontier production function models, *Journal of Econometrics* **6**, pp. 21–37.

Akridge, J. T. (1989). Measuring productive efficiency in multiple product agribusiness firms: A dual approach, *American Journal of Agricultural Economics* **71**, 1, pp. 116–125.

Allen, R. (1938). *Mathematical Analysis for Economists* (MacMillan and Co., Limited).

Alston, J. M. (1986). An analysis of growth of U.S. farmland prices, 1963-82, *American Journal of Agricultural Economics* **68**, 1, pp. 1–9.

Andrew Schmitz, C. B. M. and Schmitz, T. G. (2020). The economic effects of covid-19 on the producers of ethanol, corn, gasoline, and oil, *Journal of Agricultural & Food Industrial Organization* **18**, 2.

Anselin, L., Bongiovanni, R., and Lowenberg-DeBoer, J. (2004). A spatial econometric approach to the economics of site-specific nitrogen management in corn production, *American Journal of Agricultural Economics* **86**, 3, pp. 675–687.

Arrow, K. J., Chenery, H., Minhas, B., and Solow, R. M. (1961). Capital–labor substitution and economic efficiency, *Review of Economics and Statistics* **43**, 3, pp. 225–250.

Ball, V., Wang, S., Nehring, R., and Mosheim, R. (2016). Agricultural productivity in the U.S. https://www.ers.usda.gov/data-products/agricultural-productivity-in-the-us/.

Bawerk, E. B. (2007). *Capital and Interest - A Critical History of Economic Theory*, kindle edition edn. (Evergreen Review, Inc.).

Becker, G. S. (1965). A theory of the allocation of time, *Economic Journal* **75**, 299, pp. 493–517, http://www.jstor.org/stable/2228949.

Berndt, E. and Christensen, L. (1973). The internal structure of functional relationships: Separability, substitution, and aggregation, *Review of Economic Studies* **40**, 3, pp. 403–410.

Black, J. (1929). *Agricultural Reform in the United States* (McGraw-Hill Book Company).

Black, J. (1962). *Production Economics* (George C. Harrap).

Blackorby, C., Primont, D., and Russell, R. (1977). On testing separability restrictions with flexible functional forms, *Journal of Econometrics* **5**, pp. 195–209.

Blackorby, C. and Russell, R. (1981). The Morishima elasticity of substitution; symmetry, constancy, separability, and its relationship to the Hicks and Allen elasticities, *Review of Economic Studies* **48**, pp. 147–158.

Blackorby, C. and Russell, R. (1989). Will the real elasticity of substitution please stand up? (A comparison of the Allen/Uzawa and Morishima elasticities, *American Economic Review* **79**, pp. 882–888.

Bowden, R. and Turkington, D. (1984). *Instrumental Variables* (Cambridge University Press).

Bravo-Ureta, B. E., Gonzalez-Flores, M., Greene, W., and Solis, D. (2020). Technology and technical efficiency change: Evidence from a difference in differences selection corrected stochastic production frontier, *American Journal of Agricultural Economics* **103**, 1, pp. 352–385.

Capalbo, S. and Denny, M. (1986). Testing long-run productivity models for the Canadian and U.S. agricultural sectors, *American Journal of Agricultural Economics* **68**, 3, pp. 615–625.

Chalfant, J. A. and Gallant, A. R. (1985). Estimating substitution elasticities with the Fourier cost function, *Journal of Econometrics* **28**, pp. 205–222.

Chambers, R. and Vasavada, U. (1983). Testing asset fixity for U.S. agriculture, *American Journal of Agricultural Economics* **65**, 4, pp. 761–769.

Chambers, R. G. (1988). *Applied Production Analysis* (Cambridge University Press).

Chavas, J. P. and Thomas, A. (1999). A dynamic model of land prices, *American Journal of Agricultural Economics* **81**, pp. 772–784.

Christensen, L., Jorgenson, D., and Lau, L. (1973). Transcendental logarithmic production frontiers, *Review of Economics and Statistics* **55**, 1, pp. 28–45, doi:10.2307/1927992, http://www.jstor.org/stable/1927992.

Clark, J. (1923). *Studies in the Economics of Overhead Costs* (University of Chicago Press).

Coase, R. (1937). The nature of the firm, *Economica* **4**, pp. 386–405.

Cobb, C. and Douglas, P. (1928). A theory of production, *American Economic Review* **18**, 1, pp. 139–165, www.jstor.org/stable/1811556.

Diewert, W. (1971). An application of the Shephard duality theorem: A generalized Leontief production function, *Journal of Political Economy* **79**, 3, pp. 481–507, http://www.jstor.org/stable/1830768.

Diewert, W. and Wales, T. (1987). Flexible functional forms and global curvature conditions, *Econometrica* **55**, 1, pp. 43–68, doi:10.2307/1911156.

Douglas, P. (1934). *The Theory of Wages* (MacMillan Company).

Douglas, P. H. (1969). A plea for further work on the production function, *Nebraska Journal of Economics and Business* **8**, 4, pp. 3–13.

Efron, B. (1981). Nonparametric standard errors and confidence intervals, *The Canadian Journal of Statistics (La revue canadienne de statistque)* **9**, pp. 139–158, doi:10.2307/3314608.

Evans, D. and Heckman, J. (1984). A test for subadditivity of the cost function with an application to the bell system, *American Economic Review* **74**, 4, pp. 615–623.

Fare, R. and Primont, D. (1995). *Multi-Output Production and Duality Theory: Theory and Applications* (Kluwer Academic Publishers, 101 Philip Drive Assinippi Park Norwell, Massachusetts).

Farrell, M. (1957). The measurement of productive efficiency, *Journal of the Royal Statistical Society — Series A*, pp. 253–281.

Featherstone, A. M. and Baker, T. G. (1987). An examination of farm sector real asset dynamics, *American Journal of Agricultural Economics* **69**, pp. 532–546.

Featherstone, A. M. and Moss, C. B. (1994). Measuring economies of scale and scope in agricultural banking, *American Journal of Agricultural Economics* **76**, 3, pp. 655–661.

Frisch, R. (1965). *Theory of Production* (Rand McNally & Company).

G., C. R. (1982). Duality, the output effect, and applied comparative statics, *American Journal of Agricultural Economics* **64**, 1, pp. 152–156.

Ghalanos, A. and Theussl, S. (2015). Package 'rsolnp', https://cran.r-project.org/web/packages/Rsolnp/Rsolnp.pdf.

Gill, P. E., Murray, W., and Wright, M. H. (1981). *Practical Optimization* (Academic Press, New York).

Gleson Tembo, F. M. E., B. Wade Brorsen and Tostao, E. (2008). Crop input response functions with stochastic plateaus, **90**, 2, pp. 424–434.

Gorman, W. (1976). *Essays in Economic Analysis*, chap. Tricks with Utility Functions (Cambridge University Press), pp. 211–243.

Greene, W. (1990). A gamma distributed stochastic frontier model, *Journal of Econometrics* **46**, 1–2, pp. 141–163.

Greene, W. (2008). *The Econometric Approach to Efficiency Analysis* (Oxford University Press), pp. 92–250.

Griliches, Z. (1957). Hybrid corn: An exploration in the economics of technological change, *Econometrica* **25**, 4, pp. 501–522.

Grossman, S. and Hart, O. (1986). The costs and benefits of ownership: A theory of vertical and lateral integration, *Journal of Political Economy* **94**, pp. 691–719.

Halcrow, H. (1953). *Agricultural Policy of the United States* (Prentice-Hall, New York).

Heady, E. O., Jacobson, N. L., Freeman, A. E., and Madden, J. P. (1964). Milk production functions incorporating variables for cow characteristics and environment, *Journal of Farm Economics* **46**, 1, pp. 1–19.

Halter, A. N., Carter, H. O., and Hocking, J. (1957). A note on the transcendental production function cx1 a1 eb1x1 x2 a2 eb2x2, *Journal of Farm Economics* **39**, 4, pp. 966–974.

Hardle, W. (1990). *Applied Nonparametric Regression* (Cambridge University Press), https://www.amazon.com/Applied-Nonparametric-Regression-Econometric-Monographs/dp/0521382483%3FSubscriptionId%3D0JYN1NVW651KCA56C102%26tag%3Dtechkie-20%26linkCode%3Dxm2%26camp%3D2025%26creative%3D165953%26creativeASIN%3D0521382483.

Heady, E. (1946). Production functions from a random sample of farms, *Journal of Farm Economics* **28**, 4, pp. 989–1004, http://www.jstor.org/stable/1232361.

Heady, E. O. (1952). *Economics of Agricultural Production and Resource Use* (Prentice-Hall, Inc.).

Heady, E. O. and Dillon, J. L. (1961). *Agricultural Production Functions* (Iowa State University Press).

Henderson, J. and Quandt, R. (1980). *Microeconomic Theory: A Mathematical Approach*, 3rd edn. (McGraw-Hill).

Hildreth, C. and Houck, J. (1968). Some estimators for a linear model with random coefficients, *Journal of the American Statistical Association* **63**, 322, pp. 584–595.

Hoch, I. (1958). Simultaneous equations bias in the context of the Cobb–Douglas production function, *Econometrica* **36**, 4, pp. 566–578.

Hsiao, C. (1986). *Analysis of Panel Data* (Cambridge University Press).

Humphrey, T. (1997). Algebraic production functions and the uses before Cobb–Douglas, *Federal Reserve Bank of Richmond — Economic Quarterly* **83**, 1, pp. 51–83.

Isik, M. and Khanna, M. (2002). Variable-rate nitrogen application under uncertainty: Implications for profitability and nitrogen use, *Journal of Agricultural and Resource Economics* **27**, 1, pp. 61–76.

Jarque, C. and Bera, A. (1987). A test for normality of observations and regression residuals, *International Journal of Statistics* **55**, 2, pp. 163–172.

Johansen, S. (1996). *Likelihood Based Inference on Cointegration in the Vector Autoregressive Model*, 2nd edn. (Oxford University Press).

Johnson, D. (1948a). Allocation of agricultural income, *Journal of Farm Economics* **30**, 4, pp. 724–749, http://www.jstor.org/stable/1232788.

Johnson, D. (1948b). The use of econometric models in the study of agricultural policy, *Journal of Farm Economics* **30**, 1, pp. 117–130, http://www.jstor.org/stable/1232685.

Just, R. and Pope, R. (1978). Stochastic specification of production functions and economic implications, *Journal of Econometrics* **7**, pp. 67–86.

Just, R., Zilberman, D., and Hochman, E. (1983). Estimation of multicrop production functions, *American Journal of Agricultural Economics* **65**, pp. 770–780.

Ker, A. P. and Coble, K. (2003). Modeling conditional yield densities, *American Journal of Agricultural Economics* **85**, 2, pp. 291–304.

Ker, A. P. and Tolhurst, T. N. (2019). On the treatment of heteroscedasticity in crop yield data, *American Journal of Agricultural Economics* **101**, 4, pp. 1247–1261.

Klein, L. (1946). Macroeconomics and the theory of rational behavior, *Econometrica* **14**, 2, pp. 93–108.

Kumbhakar, S. and Lovell, C. (2000). *Stochastic Frontier Analysis* (Cambridge University Press)

Laitinen, K. (1980). *A Theory of the Multiproduct Firm* (North-Holland Publishing Company).

Laitinen, K. and Theil, H. (1978). Supply and demand of the multiproduct firm, *European Economic Review* **11**, pp. 107–154.

Lau, L. J. (1976). A characterization of the normalized restricted profit function, *Journal of Economic Theory* **12**, pp. 131–163.

Lawrence, J., Mintert, J., Anderson, J., and Anderson, D. (2008). Feed grain and livestock: Impacts on meat supplies and prices, *Choices* **23**, 2, pp. 11–15.

Lence, S. and Miller, D. (1999). Transaction costs and the present value model of farmland: Iowa, 1900–1994, *American Journal of Agricultural Economics* **8**, 2, pp. 257–272.

Leontief, W. (1947a). Introduction to a theory of the internal structure of functional relationships, *Econometrica* **15**, 4, pp. 361–373.

Leontief, W. (1947b). A note on the interrelationship of subsets of independent variables of a continuous function with continuous first derivatives, *Bulletin of the American Mathematical Society* **53**, 4, pp. 343–350.

Livanis, G. and Moss, C. B. (2006). Quasi-fixity and multiproduct firms, *Economics Letters* **93**, 2, pp. 228–234.

Metaxoglou, K. and Smith, A. (2020). Productivity spillovers from pollution reduction: Reducing coal use increases crop yields, *American Journal of Agricultural Economics* **102**, 1021, pp. 259–280.

Mishra, A. K., Moss, C. B. and Erickson, K. (2004). Valuing farmland with multiple quasi-fixed inputs, *Applied Economics* **36**, pp. 1669–1675.

Moeltner, K., Ramesey, A. F., and Neill, C. L. (2021). Bayesian kinked regression with unobserved thresholds: An application to the von Liebig hypothesis, *American Journal of Agricultural Economics* (In Press).

Mohaddes, S. and Mazhari, M. (2008). Total and input factor productivity analysis of poultry production in Khorasan province, Iran, *American-Eurasian Journal Agricultural and Environmental Science* **2**, pp. 151–154.

Moss, C. (2014). *Mathematical Statistics for Applied Econometrics* (CRC/Chapman Hall).

Moss, C. and Schmitz, T. (2001). Investing in precision agriculture.

Moss, C. and Schmitz, T. (2006). A semiparametric estimator of the Zellner production function for corn: Fitting the univariate primal, *Applied Economics*, pp. 863–867.

Moss, C., Livanis, G., and Schmitz, A. (2010). The effect of increased energy prices on agriculture: A differential supply approach, *Journal of Agricultural and Applied Economics* **42**, 4, pp. 711–718.

Moss, C. B. (1997). Returns, interest rates, and inflation: How they explain changes in farmland values, *American Journal of Agricultural Economics* **79**, 3, pp. 1311–1318.

Moss, C. B. (2000). Estimation of the Cobb–Douglas with zero input levels: Bootstrapping and substitution, *Applied Economics Letters* **7**, pp. 677–679.

Moss, C. B. (2006). Valuing state level funding for research: Results for Florida, *Journal of Agricultural and Applied Economics* **38**, 1, pp. 169–183.

Moss, C. B. (2010). *Risk, Uncertainty, and the Agricultural Firm* (World Scientific, Hackensack, NJ).

Moss, C. B. and Shonkwiler, J. S. (1993). Estimating yield distributions with a stochastic trend and nonnormal errors, *American Journal of Agricultural Economics* **75**, 4, pp. 1056–1062, http://www.jstor.org/stable/1243993.

Moss, C. B. and Suh, D. H. (2020). Effect of compliance cost on the supply of bank credit to agriculture: A differential approach, *American Journal of Agricultural Economics* **102**, 2, pp. 713–726.

Mundlak, Y. (1964). Transcendental multiproduct production functions, *International Economic Review* **5**, 3, pp. 273–284.

Murota, T. (1977). On the symmetry of Robinson elasticities of substitution: A three-factor case, *Review of Economic Studies* **44**, 1, pp. 173–176, http://www.jstor.org/stable/2296981.

United States Department of Agriculture (1995). Crop crop practices; 1990–95 data, Archived Dataset - http://webarchives.cdlib.org/sw1vh5dg3r/http://ers.usda.gov/data/archive/93018/, http://webarchives.cdlib.org/sw1vh5dg3r/http://ers.usda.gov/data/archive/93018/.

Paris, Q., Malossini, F., Pilla, A., and Romita, A. (1970). A note on milk production functions, *American Journal of Agricultural Economics* **52**, 4, pp. 594–598, www.jstor.org/stable/1237269.

Plastina, A. and Lence, S. H. (2019). Theoretical production restrictions and agricultural technology in the United States, *American Journal of Agricultural Economics* **101**, 3, pp. 849–869.

Powell, A. A. and Gruen, F. (1968). The constant elasticity of transformation production frontier and linear supply system, *International Economic Review* **9**, 3, pp. 315–328.

Pulley, L. and Braunstein, Y. (1992). A composite cost function for multiproduct firms with an application to economies of scope in banking, *Review of Economics and Statistics* **74**, 2, pp. 221–230.

Ramirez, O. A., Moss, C. B., and Boggess, W. G. (1994). Estimation and use of the inverse hyperbolic sine transformation to model nonnormal correlated random variables, *Journal of Applied Statistics* **21**, pp. 289–304, http://www.tandfonline.com/doi/abs/10.1080/757583872.

Ramsey, A. F. (2020). Probability distributions of crop yields: A Bayesian spatial quantile regression approach, *American Journal of Agricultural Economics* **102**, 1, pp. 220–239.

Roberts, R., English, B., and Mahajanashetti, S. (2000). Evaluating the returns to variable rate nitrogen applications, *Journal of Agricultural and Applied Economics* **32**, 1, pp. 133–143.

Robinson, J. (159). Some problems of definition and measurement of capital, *Oxford Economic Papers* **11**, 2, pp. 157–166.

Rosas, F. and Lence, S. H. (2019). How reliable is duality theory in empirical work? *American Journal of Agricultural Economics* **101**, 3, pp. 825–848.

Rossi, P. and Zellner, A. (1989). The et interview: Professor Arnold Zellner, *Econometric Theory* **5**, 2, pp. 287–317.

Ruiqing Miao, M. K. and Huang, H. (2015). Responsiveness of crop yield to acreage to prices and climate, *American Journal of Agricultural Economics* **98**, 1, pp. 191–211.

Ruttan, V. and Stout, T. (1960). Regional differences in factors shares in American agriculture: 1925–1957, *Journal of Farm Economics* **42**, 1, pp. 52–68, http://www.jstor.org/stable/1235321.

Samuelson, P. A. (1947). *Foundations of Economic Analysis* (Harvard University Press).

Sandmo, A. (1971). On the theory of the competitive firm under price uncertainty, *American Economic Review* **61**, 1, pp. 65–73, http://www.jstor.org/stable/1910541.

Schmitz, A. (1995). Boom/bust cycles and Ricardian rent, *American Journal of Agricultural Economics* **77**, 5, pp. 1110–1125, http://www.jstor.org/stable/1243332.

Schmitz, A., Moss, C. B., Schmitz, T. G., Furtan, H. W., and Schmitz, H. C. (2010). *Agricultural Policy, Agribusiness, and Rent-Seeking Behaviour* (University of Toronto Press).

Schumpeter, J. (1994). *History of Economic Analysis* (Oxford University Press).

Scott, D. (1992). *Multivariate Density Estimation: Theory, Practice, and Visualization* (John wiley Interscience), doi:10.1002/9780470316849.

Shephard, R. W. (1970). *Theory of Cost and Production Functions* (Princeton University Press).

Shumway, R. C. (1995). Recent duality contributions in production economics, *Journal of Agricultural and Resource Economics* **20**, 1, pp. 178–194.

Suh, D. H. and Moss, C. B. (2017). Decompositions of corn price effects: Implications for feed grain demand and livestock supply, *Agricultural Economics* **48**, 4, pp. 491–500, doi:10.1111/agec.12350, University of Florida, Food and Resource Economics Department Working Paper.

Suh, D. H. and Moss, C. B. (2021). Examining the input and output linkages in the agricultural production systems, *agriculture* (In Press).

Talpaz, H., Alexander, W. P., and Shumway, C. R. (1989). Estimation of systems of equations subject to curvature constraints, *Journal of Statistical Computation and Simulation* **32**, pp. 201–214.

Taylor, T. and Kalaitzandonakes, N. (1990). A test for fixity in southeastern U.S. agriculture, *Southern Journal of Agricultural Economics* **22**, 1, pp. 105–112.

Terrell, D. (1998). Incorporating monotonicity and concavity in flexible functional forms, *Journal of Applied Econometrics* **11**, 2, pp. 179–194, http://www.jstor.org/stable/2285203.

Theil, H. (1953). Repeated Least-squares Applied to Complete Equation Systems, Central Planning Bureau (The Hague, Mimeo).

Theil, H. (1954). Econometric models and welfare maximization, *Weltwirtschaftliches Archiv* **72**, pp. 60–83.

Theil, H. (1980). *The System Wide Approach to Microeconomics* (University of California Press).

Tintner, G. (1944). A note on the derivation of production functions from farm records, *Econometrica* **12**, 1, pp. 26–34, http://www.jstor.org/stable/1905565.

Tintner, G. and Brownlee, O. (1944). Production functions derived from farm records, *Journal of Farm Economics* **26**, 3, pp. 566–571.

von Hayek, F. (2009). *The Pure Theory of Capital* (Ludwig von Mises Institute).

Wang, S. L., Mosheim, R., Nehring, R., and Njuki, E. (2020). Agricultural productivity in the U.S. https://www.ers.usda.gov/data-products/agricultural-productivity-in-the-us/.

Weisstein, E. W. (2015). Cubic Formula, From MathWorld — A Wolfram Web Resource, http://mathworld.wolfram.com/CubicFormula.html.

Wicksteed, P. (1933). *The Common Sense of Political Economy* (Routledge).

Wicksteed, P. H. (1894). *The Co-ordination of the Laws of Distribution* (MacMillan & Co.).

Williamson, O. (1975). *Markets and Hierarchies: Analysis and Antitrust Implications* (The Free Press).

Williamson, O. E. (1985). *The Economic Institutions of Capitalism* (The Free Press).

Winsten, C. (1957). Discussion on Mr. Farrell's paper, *Journal of the Royal Statistical Society — Series A*, pp. 282–284.

Wolfson, R. (1958). An econometric investigation of regional differences in American agricultural wages, *Econometrica* **26**, 2, pp. 225–257, http://www.jstor.org/stable/1907588.

Zellner, A. (1951). An interesting general form for a production function, *Econometrica* **19**, 2, pp. 188–189.

Index

O

P

Q

R

S

www.ingramcontent.com/pod-product-compliance
Lightning Source LLC
LaVergne TN
LVHW010339220926
848484LV00004BB/937
9789811238864